# ⇜CATO⇝
# SUPREME COURT
# REVIEW
## 2003—2004

# ⁓ CATO ⁓
# SUPREME COURT
# REVIEW
## 2 0 0 3 — 2 0 0 4

ROGER PILON
Publisher

MARK K. MOLLER
Editor in Chief

ROBERT A. LEVY
Associate Editor

TIMOTHY LYNCH
Associate Editor

## Editorial Board

## CENTER FOR CONSTITUTIONAL STUDIES
### CATO
#### INSTITUTE
Washington, D.C.

ISBN I-930865-58-9

Printed in the United States of America.

Cover design by Elise B. Rivera.

Cato Institute
1000 Massachusetts Ave., N.W.
Washington, D.C. 20001
www.cato.org

# Contents

FOREWORD
*Roger Pilon*                                                                    vii

INTRODUCTION
*Mark K. Moller*                                                                    1

ANNUAL B. KENNETH SIMON LECTURE

The Indivisibility of Economic Rights and Personal Liberty
*Walter Dellinger*                                                                  9

SYMPOSIUM: THE CONSTITUTION AT WAR

Power and Liberty in Wartime
*Timothy Lynch*                                                                    23

Executive and Judicial Overreaction in the Guantanamo Cases
*Neal K. Katyal*                                                                    49

Art and the Constitution: The Supreme Court and the Rise
of the Impressionist School of Constitutional Interpretation
*Jonathan Turley*                                                                   69

ARTICLES

FEDERALISM

Making a Federal Case Out of It: *Sabri v. United States*
and the Constitution of Leviathan
*Gary Lawson*                                                                      119

*Tennessee v. Lane*: How Illegitimate Power Negated
Non-Existent Immunity
*Robert A. Levy*                                                                    161

v

**SEPARATION OF POWERS**

The *Cheney* Decision—A Missed Chance to Straighten Out
Some Muddled Issues
   *Vikram David Amar*      185

Old Puzzles, Puzzling Answers: The Alien Tort Statute and
Federal Common Law in *Sosa v. Alvarez Machain*
   *Mark K. Moller*      209

**FREEDOM OF SPEECH**
*McConnell v. FEC*: Rationing Speech to Prevent "Undue"
Influence
   *Erik S. Jaffe*      245

*Ashcroft v. ACLU II*: The Beat Goes On
   *Robert Corn-Revere*      299

**RELIGIOUS LIBERTY AND THE STATE**

Function Follows Form: *Locke v. Davey*'s Unnecessary Parsing
   *Susanna Dokupil*      327

**CRIMINAL LAW**

A Bird Called Hiibel: The Criminalization of Silence
   *M. Christine Klein*      357

The *Pringle* Case's New Notion of Probable Cause: An Assault
on *Di Re* and the Fourth Amendment
   *Tracey Maclin*      395

The Confrontation Clause Re-Rooted and Transformed
   *Richard D. Friedman*      439

**MISSED OPPORTUNITIES**

A Fistful of Denial: The Supreme Court Takes a Pass on
Commerce Clause Challenges to Environmental Laws
   *John C. Eastman*      469

**COMING UP**

The Upcoming 2004-2005 Term
   *Thomas C. Goldstein*      493

**CONTRIBUTORS**      509

# FOREWORD

# Can Law This Uncertain Be Called Law?

*Roger Pilon*

The Cato Institute's Center for Constitutional Studies is pleased to publish this third volume of the *Cato Supreme Court Review*, an annual critique of the Court's most important decisions from the term just ended, plus a look at the cases ahead—all from a classical Madisonian perspective, grounded in the nation's first principles, liberty and limited government. As in previous years, we will release this volume on September 17, at the Center's annual Constitution Day conference. And again this year, the annual B. Kenneth Simon Lecture in Constitutional Thought will follow the conference. Last year's Simon Lecture by Duke University's Walter Dellinger, "The Indivisibility of Economic Rights and Personal Liberty," is the lead essay in the present volume. This year's lecture by the University of Chicago's Richard A. Epstein, "The Progressive Vision of the Constitution," will lead next year's volume.

Our Simon Lecture series was instituted to encourage leading figures in the law to address fundamental issues in constitutional thought. Two years ago, Judge Douglas Ginsburg did that with his inaugural lecture, "On Constitutionalism." Pointing to the virtues of a written constitution, among the most important of which is the assurance it gives citizens that they can plan and live their lives under a fairly clear rule of law, Judge Ginsburg went on to show what happens when those charged with securing that law—primarily judges, in our system—fail to abide by the authority granted them. Whether ignoring the restraints the Constitution places on the political branches, as during the New Deal, or ignoring the restraints it places on their own branch, as later judges would do, the result is the same—the triumph of policy over principle, politics over law.

But in his own Simon Lecture a year later, appearing below, Professor Dellinger, in the spirit of continuing dialogue, took some small exception to Judge Ginsburg's thesis—not that it did not raise fundamental issues, and raise them well, but that it, too, ignored crucial elements in our constitutional structure, namely, the unwritten, yet implicit aspects of our Constitution. There are, in particular, certain principles that should structure our thought about the document, and a substantive vision that flows from those principles, which the text captures only in broad language. Thus, it falls to the judge not so much to *create* those principles and that vision as to *discover* and be guided by them. Central to that effort, as Dellinger writes, is the idea that "before the state deprives a citizen of liberty, it must have a reason—and a good one, too." Under a Constitution written to secure liberty through limited government, that idea should guide a judge and inform his understanding of the rights implicit in the document's broad language.

Yet down that path is peril, as both Ginsburg and Dellinger are aware; for the line between discovering and creating law is fine, and judges do not always discern it clearly. At the same time, responsible judges, sworn to uphold the Constitution, cannot ignore written text simply because it is broad. On the contrary, they must grapple with it, in the knowledge that the Framers could not have committed every detail to writing; yet neither did the Framers mean to leave most matters to political determination. In fact, they wrote a constitution designed to leave most of life *free* from political determination—most of life, in a word, free. Their broad strokes, whether in the enumeration of powers or in the articulation of the Ninth, Tenth, and Fourteenth Amendments, were meant to frame that vision and afford judges general guidance toward securing it. That guidance will lead to sound opinions, however, only if judges bring to their craft a sure grasp of the underlying principles of our constitutional order—the theory of political legitimacy that underpins the Constitution, the theory of moral rights that underpins that.

A term ago, we had a wonderful example of how the Court might undertake its responsibilities with that understanding in mind. In *Lawrence v. Texas,* Justice Anthony Kennedy cut through the methodological distractions that have arisen since the notorious *Carolene Products* case of 1938 to ask a refreshingly simple question—not where in the Constitution Mr. Lawrence found the right he claimed, but what justification the state had for interfering with Mr. Lawrence's liberty. It was not Mr. Lawrence's burden to justify his liberty, that is; under our Constitution, he was presumed to be free. Rather, it was the state of Texas that had to justify its restrictions. The best it could do, in that regard, was to speak of that subset of morality, morals. Since "defending morals" could be said of virtually any legislation, Kennedy noted, it was not good enough; and so Mr. Lawrence's moral right to do as he pleased, even if it offended some in the community, was secured.

One would like to have seen the same approach taken in the other case that term that drew so much attention, *Grutter v. Bollinger.* Instead, paying lip service to *Carolene Products* methodology, Justice Sandra Day O'Connor turned "strict scrutiny" on its head by accepting, uncritically, the state of Michigan's assertion that having a racially diverse student body is a "compelling state interest" and that racial discrimination is necessary to achieve that end. Thus, instead of taking the Fourteenth Amendment's broad Equal Protection Clause at face value, and presuming that Ms. Grutter had a right to be free from state discrimination, O'Connor reversed the presumptions, in essence, by reducing the state's burden to a virtual nullity. The opinion is a textbook example of policy trumping principle—an opinion devoid of discipline, leaving us altogether unclear about when a state may and may not discriminate (witness the companion case, *Gratz v. Bollinger,* which went the other way). If a cardinal purpose of law is to give notice about what is permitted and prohibited, we are without law on this matter.

That is the theme for the term just ended. And where better to illustrate it than with the term's first decision (technically, a carry-over from the previous term), after a special oral argument last September, *McConnell v. FEC.* Perhaps the best thing that can be said of the opinion is that it came down in only 298 pages, compared with the lower court's 1,638 pages. With three majority opinions and five other opinions concurring in part and dissenting in part—numbers that hardly capture the complexity of the cross-references—the "decision" drives one to Latin: *res ipsa loquitur.* If ever a decision spoke for itself, albeit in the negative, and illustrated a court without a compass, this is it. After this decision, can anyone credibly claim to understand our campaign finance law? It was unclear enough under the *Buckley v. Valeo* decision of 1976, which opened the door to broad restrictions on campaign contributions. Today, on the campaign trail, this "law" is an endless source of charges, countercharges, and calls for still more "reform." Yet the core principle, to which the Court's majority seemed oblivious, could not be simpler: Campaign contributions are political speech; political speech is protected by the First Amendment. The government's claim that restrictions were needed to prevent corruption was incredible on its face, given the absence of evidence. But once the principle of the matter was abandoned in *Buckley*, it was all tinkering, trying to "get it right." The result is a body of "law" that looks like the IRS code. For those with the patience, Erik Jaffe plows through the details below.

Fortunately, in the three national security cases that drew so much attention late in the term, the Court did stand for principle, at least on first impression. But the impression is doubtless as much a function of the president's overreaching, as Professor Neal Katyal argues, as it is of the Court's having articulated the kind of principled approach to the issues that our Timothy Lynch sets forth. In fact, Professor Jonathan Turley's clever perspective piece treating all three of the cases draws out several uncertainties with which the Court has left us and many of the confusions that beset "the O'Connor Court" generally—confusions that are better understood, perhaps, through the analogies he draws with the world of modern art. Ambiguity in art is often a virtue. In law it seldom is.

The Rehnquist Court's "new federalism" may still be alive, barely, but it is no clearer than it ever was. Back in 1995, when *United States v. Lopez* returned us at last to "first principles," Justice Clarence Thomas cautioned the Court that its reading of the Commerce Clause, however welcome after nearly sixty years of misreading, was still wide of the mark. If the Framers had wanted to empower Congress to regulate anything that substantially affects interstate commerce, he said, they could have written that. They did not. And so the Court's reading to that effect was still mistaken. The Court had a chance this term to begin correcting its misreading of another of the Constitution's most important provisions, the Necessary and Proper Clause. It ducked the opportunity, as Professor Gary Lawson shows in his searching treatment of *Sabri v. United States*, and so we are left with uncertainty about the reach of federal criminal law. Given the ubiquity of the federal funding federal criminal law follows, the reach could be vast.

Not surprisingly, the Court continues to struggle with federalism in those complex cases that implicate both the Eleventh and the

Fourteenth Amendments. Two years ago in these pages our Robert Levy straightened out the mess the Court left us in *Federal Maritime Commission v. South Carolina State Ports Authority*. We call on him to do the same again this year with *Tennessee v. Lane*. If ever there were a need to return to first principles to get clear about an issue, it is here. Yet the Court seems content to "wing it," unable to shed the errors of the past.

And it does the same with a relatively simpler issue, property rights. Fourteen years ago, in *Lucas v. South Carolina Coastal Council*, Justice Antonin Scalia spoke of the Court's seventy odd years of ad hoc regulatory takings jurisprudence, even as he was adding yet another year to the string. As Professor John Eastman demonstrates below, in an essay about the dog that didn't bark, things are little better today, since the Court is declining to hear a string of cases that cry out for its attention—circuit splits involving property rights cases replete with unresolved federalism issues. This is an area in which the Court could relatively easily bring order out of chaos, but it would require the Court's grasping the principle of the matter, and that it seems unprepared to do.

A final example from a disquieting year is a case so simple that one wonders why it was even before the Court. When Dudley Hiibel, standing beside his pick-up truck on the shoulder of a rural Nevada road, was asked by a local sheriff for identification, he declined to provide any. In Nevada, as in many other states, that is a crime. In fact, many state laws require individuals to provide police officers with their names, their addresses, and their business about. Both the Fourth and Fifth Amendments are implicated here, of course— the right to be free from "arrest" (being stopped) on less than proba- ble cause; and the right to remain silent so as to avoid the possibility of self-incrimination. As Christine Klein details below, the Court allowed an inroad on the first right in 1968 when it sanctioned the so-called *Terry*-stop—a stop based on mere suspicion. This term it went further when it upheld the Nevada statue. We have a situation, then, in which an officer may demand identification; and if that proves incriminating, the officer must then say, "You have a right to remain silent." Where we go from here, whether state statutes that require divulging considerably more information are legal, is anyone's guess.

Unlike mere legislation, which is rooted in will, law is supposed to be rooted in reason. That is an ancient distinction, drawn to serve legitimacy. Under our system, legislators pursue policy—when the Constitution authorizes them to do so. Judges check that effort to ensure that it is authorized and that it is done in a way that respects our rights, enumerated and unenumerated alike. Judges ensure, in a word, the rule of law. When they are overwhelmed with a surfeit of legislation, however, as ours have been since they opened the floodgates during the New Deal, it is all too easy for them to start thinking like legislators, to abandon principle, as they did then, and to think only of policy. We see too much of that on this Court. We need a Court of judges, not policymakers.

# Introduction

This is the third volume of the *Cato Supreme Court Review*, an annual review of the most significant opinions of the Supreme Court of the United States. This volume includes cases from the term beginning in October 2003 and ending in late-June 2004.

For readers new to our pages, the *Cato Supreme Court Review* has three principal aims: First, it provides the earliest in-depth review of each Court term. The *Review* appears on Constitution Day—September 17—soon after the Court completes its work, and shortly before the next term begins on the first Monday in October.

Second, the editors believe that the Constitution is not a technical document of interest only to lawyers and judges. Rather, we aim to bring together top-flight contributors to analyze the term in a manner that will make the Court's work accessible, insofar as possible, to a diverse audience. Although the *Review* is a "law" book, in the sense that it is about the Court and the Constitution, it is written for all citizens interested in the Constitution and the Court's interpretation of it.

Third, and most important, the *Cato Supreme Court Review* has a distinctive point of view, which we happily confess: The *Review* analyzes the Court and its decisions from a classical Madisonian perspective, emphasizing the Constitution's first principles: individual liberty; secure property rights; federalism; and a government of delegated, enumerated, and thus limited powers.

Fundamental constitutional questions about Madisonian first principles were not in short supply this term, as the trilogy of much-watched "national security" cases amply demonstrated. Each of the cases presented disturbingly broad presidential claims to power—claims that went to the heart of what it means to live under a system of checks-and-balances. In *Hamdi v. Rumsfeld* and *Rumsfeld v. Padilla*, the president claimed the unilateral authority to declare an American citizen an enemy combatant and strip him of constitutional rights, including access to courts or counsel. And in *Rasul v. Bush*, the president contended that his powers as commander-in-chief permitted him to create his own prison system, with its own standards, just beyond our borders, without any meaningful judicial oversight.

Timothy Lynch begins analysis of these cases by articulating a framework, grounded in the Constitution, for balancing civil liberty and national security. Lynch starts with the premise that the Constitution limits the government in *both* peacetime *and* wartime, and then articulates a series of fundamental rules to protect civil liberties. Those rules, he explains, turn on three fundamental questions: What is the citizenship of the individual arrested? Where was he arrested, on American soil or on the battlefield? And, what punishment does the government seek to impose? Those questions, says Lynch, lead us back to the text of the Constitution, which underscores that during wartime, the Constitution is *not* silent and the president is *not* a power unto himself.

Neal Katyal takes up *Rasul v. Bush*, which asked whether accused enemy aliens, captured on foreign battlefields and detained in Guantanamo Bay, have any right to test the legality of their detention in U.S. courts. In an opinion that will no doubt be fodder for litigation for years to come, Justice John Paul Stevens ruled that the Guantanamo detainees do have such a right. Just why the Court believed so is less clear. Based on a close reading of Justice Stevens' opinion, Katyal concludes that *Rasul* is a potentially revolutionary case, one that has taken us from a constitutional regime in which no alien outside of the United States could challenge detention to one in which virtually anyone held by American forces beyond our shores may do so—and in which the president faces far more restraints on his powers as commander-in-chief than ever before. Katyal concludes that much blame lies with the administration, which pushed for extreme powers—and provoked a judicial backlash.

Finally, Jonathan Turley rounds out the analysis of the national security trilogy with a creative article that examines the Court's methods of constitutional interpretation by likening them to artistic styles. Turley finds much reason for concern. While the outcomes of these cases could have been worse, he says, *Hamdi, Padilla,* and *Rasul* collectively demonstrate that the Court, led by Justice Sandra Day O'Connor, has embraced what he calls "judicial impressionism": a style of judging that treats constitutional text and history as something that can be creatively altered to fit the needs of the moment. As Turley notes, this is hardly a new style of judicial analysis in the realm of national security. And, if the past is prologue, its resurgence this term bodes ill for the Court's commitment to safeguarding our rights.

While the national security cases raised unusually important questions, this was a term replete with cases that illuminate first principles. Indeed, the next case addressed by this year's *Review* may well have dealt the most *under*-reported blow to constitutional structure. The facts of *Sabri v. United States* seem humdrum: The Court upheld the federal power to prosecute a private developer accused of bribing a Minnesota state municipal official. The case is important, argues Gary Lawson—the author of Cato's friend-of-the-court brief in *Sabri*—because it presented the Court with an opportunity to reinvigorate the Necessary and Proper Clause, and with it the Founders' conception of our government as one of limited, enumerated powers. The Court missed that opportunity—underscoring the limits of the supposedly "revolutionary" federalism jurisprudence of the Rehnquist Court. As Lawson details, *Sabri* is a microcosm of how far the Court's understanding of the Constitution has traveled from the Founders' original design.

In *Tennessee v. Lane*, the Court once again confronts the dubious claim that states are "immune" from suit under federal law, this time in a suit alleging the state of Tennessee discriminated against disabled persons and so violated Title II of the Americans with Disabilities Act. Cato scholar Robert Levy argues that the case is a study in constitutional confusion: On the immunity question, says Levy, the Court got it right, recognizing that Tennessee was not entitled to immunity. But the Court reached that result for the wrong reason, by ruling Congress validly "abrogated" Tennessee's immunity under section 5 of the Fourteenth Amendment. In fact, according to Levy, there was no need to abrogate state immunity, because the Eleventh Amendment does not grant states "immunity" from suits under federal law. Levy concludes by confronting the important unasked question in *Lane*: whether the Commerce Clause provides a constitutional pedigree for Title II of the Americans with Disabilities Act.

Vikram Amar writes that the Court's decision in *Cheney v. U.S. District Court for the District of Columbia* provides a window on a key theme this term: the Court's repeated decision not to decide tough questions. In *Cheney*, public interest groups sued the vice president in an attempt to obtain the names of private lobbyists and oil company officials who allegedly participated in an energy policy working group headed by Cheney. The vice president argued that the doctrine of "executive privilege"—under which the president is protected from disclosing certain confidential communications— also protected him from making any disclosures. As Amar analyzes the case, the *Cheney* Court refused to answer a number of important and unsettled questions about the contours of executive privilege, leaving the constitutional limits on executive secrecy in a continued state of disarray.

Too often the Court ignores the robust role that our system of separation of powers has designed for it. Less often, the Court assumes powers inconsistent with constitutional structure. That, I argue in my essay, is what happened in *Sosa v. Alvarez-Machain*. In *Sosa*, the immediate question seems rather technical: The plaintiff argued that an obscure 1789 statute, the so-called Alien Tort Statute, authorizes foreign persons to vindicate violations of "customary international law" in U.S. federal courts. *Sosa*, however, raises important questions about which branch has primary responsibility for incorporating international law into our legal framework. As I argue in my essay, our constitutional structure places limits on the role of courts in this area—limits weakened by the Court in *Sosa*.

From constitutional structure, we move to individual rights. Political speech is at the core of the First Amendment: That makes modern campaign finance laws, and their regulation of financial support for political speech, difficult to justify. Nonetheless, at the very beginning of the October 2003 term, the Court upheld one of the most sweeping expansions of campaign finance restrictions in decades: the McCain-Feingold Act. The Supreme Court's decision in *McConnell* v. *FEC*, argues Erik Jaffe—the author of Cato's friend-of-the-court brief in the case—strikes at the heart of the First Amendment's "jealous protection for core political speech." Jaffe concludes that the Court in *McConnell* has handed Congress a powerful weapon against speech, and that "both freedom and the First Amendment will be the victims."

This year's internet free speech case, *Ashcroft v. ACLU II*, presented the Court with its latest opportunity to clarify the confused application of the First Amendment to the internet. In particular, *Ashcroft* asked whether the Child Online Protection Act (COPA), which broadly regulates online speech in the interest of children, passes constitutional muster. The Court had long avoided resolution of COPA's constitutionality. But in *Ashcroft II*, the Court gave us the clearest sign yet that it believes COPA to be constitutionally infirm. First Amendment lawyer and Cato adjunct scholar Robert Corn-Revere argues that the case, even though it did not finally settle the constitutionality of COPA, is highly important, for two reasons. First, the case set a high bar for future regulatory efforts. Second, it highlights a significant doctrinal division between what he identifies as "collectivist" and "individualist" accounts of the First Amendment's protections.

As schoolchildren know, or should know, the American experiment began when persecuted Europeans fled to the New World seeking religious liberty and freedom of conscience. In *Locke v. Davey*, a case closely watched by school choice advocates, the Court considered whether a Washington State constitutional provision, with nativist roots, justifies exclusion of theology majors from a state scholarship program. As Susanna Dokupil argues, *Locke* presented the Court with an important opportunity to uphold the principle that the state cannot single out and penalize persons based on their choice to pursue educational ends dictated by religious belief. Unfortunately, in *Locke*, the Court missed that opportunity, upholding the challenged discrimination. Dokupil discusses the implications of the case for the First Amendment, the future of educational choice, and religious liberty.

In the wake of the September 11 terrorist attacks, federal and state governments have flexed their power to search and arrest citizens—and not just in cases involving "enemy combatants." In *Hiibel v. Sixth Judicial District Court of Nevada*, Nevada police arrested Nevada cowboy Dudley Hiibel. The charge? Hiibel's refusal to answer police questions—a "crime" under a Nevada law penalizing "noncooperation" with police investigations. The Nevada Supreme Court—citing the need to protect citizens against terrorism—upheld the arrest. So, unfortunately, did the U.S. Supreme Court. Christine Klein served as co-counsel on Cato's friend-of-the court brief in *Hiibel*. In her article, she argues that the decision represents a new low in the Court's willingness to police the police; further blurs the content of the "right to remain silent"; and erodes constitutional protection against police coercion and intimidation.

*Hiibel* is not the only blow to civil rights: The Fourth Amendment had its roots in American colonists' hatred of general search warrants, which permitted agents of the Crown to search houses and other property without individualized suspicion. *Maryland v. Pringle* therefore would have come as a shock to the Founders. In that case, the Court upheld the power of police to arrest persons who are not individually suspected of wrongdoing in certain cases where they are "guilty by association." Criminal law expert Tracey Maclin, who authored the ACLU's friend-of-the-court brief in *Pringle*, offers a comprehensive analysis of the case, which underscores that the Court effectively has abandoned fidelity to an individualized conception of "probable cause." *Pringle*, much like *Hiibel*, is likely to bolster police use of the arrest power to coerce the cooperation of innocent citizens.

The Court's criminal docket has at least one bright spot: *Crawford v. Washington*, a landmark decision in which the Court rediscovered the principle that an accused has a right to confront his accuser. Richard Friedman, a Confrontation Clause expert who has long advocated a sea change in the Court's understanding of the confrontation right, dissects *Crawford* and its implications. As Friedman emphasizes, *Crawford* is an important victory for constitutional text, original intent, and the rights of the accused, and promises to curb a longstanding prosecutorial abuse: The use of testimony made to police behind closed doors, and out of the presence of the accused, to obtain convictions.

Sometimes, the appeals that the Court doesn't take are as important as those it does consider. In the October 2003 term, says John Eastman, the Court's refusal to consider a series of Commerce Clause challenges to environmental land use regulations raises questions about the Court's commitment to *Lopez v. United States* and *United States v. Morrison*, cases in which the Court finally put some restraints on Congress's power to regulate interstate commerce. As Eastman analyzes the matter, the environmental land use cases before the Court in 2003 showcased an exercise of federal power directly at odds with *Lopez* and *Morrison*, and so cried out for review. The Court's failure to take these cases on appeal, says Eastman, lends credence to the claim that property rights are low on the Court's list of priorities.

Finally, in a look ahead to the October 2004 term, Supreme Court litigator Thomas C. Goldstein identifies the cases thus far of greatest interest—and the principles at stake. The next term will feature important questions concerning the scope of the Commerce Clause, state power to interfere with freedom of interstate trade, and First Amendment protections for commercial speech. The 2004 term will also bring to a head questions about the constitutionality of the Federal Sentencing Guidelines, as the Court squarely confronts the application of *Blakely v. Washington* to our federal sentencing system. Goldstein outlines the issues at stake, and ventures some predictions.

I thank our contributors for their generous participation: There would be no *Cato Supreme Court Review* without them. I thank my colleagues at the Cato Institute's Center for Constitutional Studies, Roger Pilon, Timothy Lynch, Robert A. Levy—as well as Cato friend Jerry Brito—for valuable editorial contributions; David Lampo for producing and Parker Wallman and Elise Rivera for designing the *Review*; research assistants Elizabeth Kreul-Starr, Madison Kitchens, Tim Lee, and Thomas Pearson for valuable work in preparing the manuscripts for publication; and interns Jacinda Lanum and Henry Thompson for key all-around assistance.

Again, we reiterate our hope that this volume will deepen understanding of our too often forgotten Madisonian first principles, and give voice to the Framers' belief that ours is a government of laws and not of men. In so doing we hope also to do justice to a rich legal tradition—now eclipsed by the rise of the modern regulatory state—in which jurists understood that the Constitution reflects, and protects, natural rights of liberty and property, and serves as a bulwark against the abuse of state power.

We hope that you enjoy the third volume of the *Cato Supreme Court Review*.

*Mark K. Moller*
Editor in Chief

# The Indivisibility of Economic Rights and Personal Liberty

*Walter Dellinger*

## I. Introduction

It is an honor to have been asked to give this lecture in memory of the man for whom this series of lectures has been named, Ken Simon, whose generosity has made possible today's annual Cato Constitution Day Conference. With much of what I have to say, I believe that Mr. Simon would have found himself in congenial agreement. From some other parts of my remarks, he would perhaps have dissented. But what he has shown by his life and by this lecture series is that he was committed both to libertarian values and to lively, engaged debate. If at times this evening I fall short of advancing all the goals of libertarian thought, I hope at least to advance the goal of engaged debate.

It is a further honor to be the second speaker in a lecture series inaugurated by one of our nation's most respected jurists, Chief Judge Douglas H. Ginsburg. In the spirit of making this series a continuing dialogue, I will note points of disagreement with Judge Ginsburg's remarks of a year ago. But I know you all will benefit as much as I have from a careful reading of his essay, which is sweeping in its scope and sharp in its critique of much of American judicial review.[1]

Here is my thesis, simply put:

> The disparagement by some liberal scholars and jurists of the constitutional protection of economic rights weakens the constitutional foundations of personal liberty.

*Douglas B. Maggs Professor of Law, Duke University Law School; Head of Appellate Practice, O'Melveny & Myers LLP; Acting Solicitor General of the United States, 1996–97. These remarks, the second annual B. Kenneth Simon Lecture in Constitutional Thought, were delivered at the Cato Institute on September 17, 2003.

[1]Douglas H. Ginsburg, On Constitutionalism, 2002–2003 Cato Sup. Ct. Rev. 7 (2003).

> *And conversely*: The disparagement by some conservative jurists and scholars of unenumerated personal liberties weakens the constitutional foundation for rights of property, contract, and occupational freedom.

> The Constitution—written and unwritten—protects both economic and non-economic liberty. Both are essential, and each supports the other.

## II. Is Constitutional Text Exclusive?

Let me begin, as Judge Ginsburg did, with the question of whether the text of the Constitution contains all the liberties—economic and personal—that are rightfully accorded constitutional protection. Here I both endorse some of what he said a year ago, and join issue with him as well.

First, let me say that I agree with Judge Ginsburg about the centrality of the written Constitution and the binding authority of the text as it was generally understood at the time it was written and ratified. As his colleague, Judge Steven Williams, put it correctly and succinctly a few years ago, "The search for original understanding is for the meaning that a reasonable person in the relevant setting would have assigned the language."[2] Divorced from adopters' understanding of what they were adopting, the text is simply a set of words without legal authority.

The constitutional text, however, cannot contain all of the constitutionally binding fundamental law. There is at least one point of constitutional law, for example, both obvious and profound, that cannot be found within the text of the Constitution. And that is the principle that recognizes the Constitution I hold in my hand—the Federal Constitution of 1787, as amended—as "The" Constitution, the one that is binding law. You may object that the text of the Constitution does indeed address and resolve the question of whether this Constitution is "The" Constitution. And you could point to the Article VI Supremacy Clause which states explicitly that "This Constitution . . . shall be the supreme Law of the Land, . . . any Thing in the Constitution or Laws of any State to the Contrary notwithstanding . . . ."[3] Now, I have no doubt that this is one of the

---

[2]Stephen F. Williams, Restoring Context, Distorting Text: Legislative History and the Problem of Age, 66 Geo. Wash. L. Rev. 1366, 1368 (1998).

[3]U.S. Const. art. VI, § 1 cl. 2.

most powerful phrases in the Constitution. It resolves once and for all the question of federal supremacy over the states, and in a masterstroke it speaks directly to state court judges, saying that "Judges in every State shall be bound thereby."[4]

But neither the Supremacy Clause nor any other provision *within* the Constitution can make the document the supreme, binding law. That principle of constitutional law must come from *outside* the document. There is no doubt that our larger "constitutional law" establishes the federal Constitution of 1787, as amended, as supreme, binding law. Its immediate acceptance, even by opponents of ratification, and the inescapable fact that virtually every interest in every succeeding generation has invoked the document repeatedly as supreme, binding law, are among the powerful indications of this most fundamental of constitutional propositions. But it remains an "unwritten" constitutional principle.

If a principle external to the written Constitution is necessary to make the Constitution binding, some similar external principle must be invoked to establish either the proposition that "This [written] Constitution" is the exclusive source of enforceable constitutional rights, or the contrary proposition that it is not the exclusive source. Neither of those propositions can be justified merely by looking inside the document itself.

### III. The Assumption of Rights Beyond Text

But that is abstract theory. The more convincing proof of the existence of binding norms outside the text is to be found in the debates surrounding the drafting of the Constitution itself, and in the Framers' understanding that there were rights—binding rights— before there was a written constitution. During all the years that I taught law students about the debates at the Constitutional Convention, nothing surprised them more than the Framers' clear recognition that there were norms—binding "constitutional" norms, in the larger sense of that word—that preceded the drafting of "the Constitution," norms that would be binding whether or not included in the document.

One example, discussed at the convention, is the principle of double jeopardy as a limit on the government's right to appeal,

---

[4]*Id.*

which found its way into the Constitution only after the Bill of Rights was ratified in 1791.[5] Another is the assumption of at least some Framers that ex post facto principles would preclude retroactive criminal legislation, whether or not such a prohibition was placed in constitutional text. The exchange at the convention between Oliver Ellsworth and Hugh Williamson illustrates this assumption. According to Madison's notes, Ellsworth "contended that there was no lawyer, no civilian who would not say that ex post facto laws were void of themselves," and he concluded that "It can not then be necessary to prohibit them."[6] Hugh Williamson responded not by denying that such a principle existed prior to and outside of any written constitution, but by arguing that placement in text had independent value, observing that "Such a prohibitionary clause is in the Constitution of N. Carolina, and tho it has been violated, it has done good there & may do good here, because the Judges can take hold of it."[7] Moreover, and particularly important here, the text of the Constitution itself refers to rights not named in the document: The Ninth Amendment does not list rights; but it does presume the existence of rights outside the corners of the document.[8]

Similarly, the Fourteenth Amendment, written by the 39th Congress, employs broad language guaranteeing "life, liberty, and property," "due process," "equal protection," and, most important, "privileges or immunities" against state interference.[9] Those who

---

[5]Indeed, are we to suppose that we had no rights against the federal government, except those few that were in the original document, until *after* the Bill of Rights was added? See Roger Pilon, Restoring Constitutional Government, 2001–2002 Cato Sup. Ct. Rev. vii, xx (2002).

[6]James Madison, Notes of Debates in the Federal Convention of 1787 510 (1966).

[7]*Id.* at 511.

[8]U.S. Const. amend. IX. The Ninth Amendment was written to address a practical problem discussed at the Convention. Because we have in principle an infinite number of rights, thanks to the creativity language allows in describing them, it would be impossible to list all of our rights in a bill of rights. Therefore, since the standard canon of legal construction—*expressio unius exclusio alterius*—implies that the enumeration of some rights for protection should be read as excluding other, unenumerated rights from protection, the Ninth Amendment had to be written: "The enumeration in the Constitution, of certain rights, shall not be construed to deny or disparage others retained by the people." See The Rights Retained by the People: The History and Meaning of the Ninth Amendment, Vol. I and II (Randy Barnett ed., 1989, 1993).

[9]U.S. Const. amend. XIV. See Kimberly C. Shankman and Roger Pilon, Reviving the Privileges or Immunities Clause to Redress the Balance Among States, Individuals, and the Federal Government (Cato Policy Analysis No. 326, 1998).

argue against the existence of rights not specifically enumerated in the text have a formidable problem with the text and with its delegation of significant interpretative authority to future courts. One can criticize the delegation on grounds of institutional policy—that is, it was unwise to confer such authority—but the rights and the authority to secure them cannot be ignored as constitutional text. Moreover, those who wrote and ratified the Fourteenth Amendment were fully aware that judicial review was an established feature of the Constitution and that broad constitutional phrases were to be given "latitudinarian" construction: see, for example, *Marbury v. Madison*,[10] *McCulloch v. Maryland*,[11] *Gibbons v. Ogden*,[12] *Fletcher v. Peck*,[13] and *Swift v. Tyson*.[14] Thus, even the text of the Constitution contemplates the enforcement of rights not specified in the text.

## IV. The Excessive Rejection of Economic Rights

Assuming, then, that the "liberty" protected against state interference includes rights not specifically named in the text, should it be read to include judicially enforceable economic and commercial rights? Throughout much of American history, especially recent history, that has been one of the federal judiciary's most contentious issues. In the last major shift, the New Deal Court abandoned judicial protection of economic rights. But in its zeal to curb what some saw as the Court's excessive invalidation of state and federal legislation during the so-called *Lochner* era,[15] the New Deal Court swept far too broadly in repudiating the protection of economic liberties. For in so doing, the Court also weakened the basis for protecting personal liberties.

No justice was more influential in weakening the protection of both economic rights and unenumerated personal liberties than William O. Douglas. In 1941, writing for a unanimous Court in *Olsen v. Nebraska*,[16] Douglas sustained a legislative limit on the amount of

---

[10] 5 U.S. 137 (1803).
[11] 17 U.S. 316 (1819).
[12] 22 U.S. 1 (1824).
[13] 10 U.S. 87 (1810).
[14] 41 U.S. 1 (1842).
[15] *Lochner v. New York*, 198 U.S. 45 (1905).
[16] 313 U.S. 236 (1941).

compensation an employment agency could collect for its services. What is striking about the opinion is not its rejection of the challenge to the law but its virtual rejection of judicial review itself in the field of economic regulation. The agency had argued that the law advanced no legitimate goal, since excessive charges—the presumed evil to be remedied—did not exist due to the vigorous and open competition among employment agencies. Douglas's response was abrupt and startling: *"There is no necessity for the state to demonstrate before us that evils persist despite the competition which attends bargaining in this field."*[17] That blunt contention that the state owes no explanation for its restraint on liberty casts aside what ought to be a fundamental principle of constitutional jurisprudence: Before the state deprives a citizen of liberty, it must have a reason—and a good one, too. Unlike the overwrought parent, the state cannot say simply: "Because I say so, that's why." Here the challenger claims the state's asserted reason is without foundation. Instead of determining whether the state's reason is in fact plausible, however, the Court says simply that "it is not necessary" for the state to give a reason.

The right approach was demonstrated a few years later by a state court judge—Sam Ervin of North Carolina, who was later to win fame as the senator chairing the Watergate hearings. Ervin would not have struck down regulatory legislation that plausibly advanced workplace safety or clean air and water, but he did demand that the state have an actual justification for any restrictions it imposed. Raw preferences were not enough to sustain a statute. A leading example of Ervin's approach is found in his opinion in 1949 in *State v. Ballance.*[18]

Owen Ballance was convicted of the misdemeanor crime of being a photographer for hire without first having been licensed by the Board of Photographic Examiners of North Carolina, a group appointed by the governor, each of whom must have been a professional photographer for not fewer than five years. Needless to say, as is so often the case with occupational licensing schemes, the members of the board were not anxious to license competitors. Ervin understood that and more. In overturning Ballance's conviction, he wrote that the framers of the North Carolina Constitution "loved

---

[17] *Id.* at 246 (emphasis added).
[18] 51 S.E.2d 731 (N.C. 1949).

liberty and loathed tyranny, and were convinced that government itself must be compelled to respect the inherent rights of the individual if freedom is to be preserved and oppression is to be prevented."[19]

Yet a month before Ervin wrote that, the U.S. Supreme Court had expressly stated in the *Lincoln Federal* case[20] that the federal Constitution placed no limits on the power to legislate in the area of business and commercial affairs "so long as [the] laws do not run afoul of some *specific* federal constitutional prohibition . . . ."[21] Applying a provision of the North Carolina Constitution,[22] but making clear that he disagreed with the U.S. Supreme Court's constricted view of "liberty," Ervin wrote that the liberty of the individual "does not consist simply of the right to be free of arbitrary physical restraint or servitude, but . . . 'includes the right of the citizen to be free to use his faculties in all lawful ways; to live and work where he will; to earn his livelihood by any lawful calling; to pursue any livelihood or vocation . . . .'"[23]

Ervin noted that these liberties can be limited by the exercise of the police powers, but went on to make the essential point that "in exercising these powers the legislature must have in view the good of the citizens as a whole rather than the interests of a particular class."[24] In a succinct formulation of the proper judicial standard, he concluded that his exercise of the power to curb liberty by legislation must be "reasonably necessary to promote the accomplishment of a public good, or to prevent the infliction of a public harm."[25]

Rather than follow the U.S. Supreme Court's wholesale abandonment of judicial scrutiny of economic legislation, Ervin put the state

---

[19] *Id.* at 734.

[20] Lincoln Federal Labor Union v. Northwestern Iron & Metal Co., 335 U.S. 525 (1949).

[21] *Id.* at 536 (emphasis added).

[22] Article I, section 1 of the North Carolina Constitution, adopted after the Civil War, provides that among the "inalienable rights" of individuals are "life, liberty and the enjoyment of the fruits of their own labor, and the pursuit of happiness," and section 17 provides that no person shall be "in any manner deprived of his life, liberty, or property, but by the law of the land." That last phrase, Erwin wrote, "is synonymous with 'due process of law'. . . .," 51 S.E.2d at 734

[23] *Id.* (quoting Am. Jur. Constitutional Law § 329).

[24] 51 S.E.2d at 735.

[25] *Id.*

to its proof, and found that proof lacking in *Ballance*. "It is undoubtedly true that the photographer must possess skill. But so must the actor, the baker, the bookbinder, the bookkeeper, the carpenter, the cook, the editor, the farmer, the goldsmith, the horseshoer . . ." and on and on through the alphabet until he concluded by asking "[w]ho would maintain that the legislature would promote the general welfare by requiring a mental and moral examination preliminary to permitting individuals to engage in these vocations merely because they involve knowledge and skill?"[26]

In an eloquent passage that refutes the notion that economic liberties are unworthy of protection, Ervin wrote that "In the economy of nature, toil is necessary to support human life, and essential to develop the human spirit."[27] Photography, he observed, "is an honored calling which contributes much satisfaction to living. Like all honest work, it is ennobling."[28]

Ervin was not an advocate of returning to the *Lochner* era in which justices freely set aside state and local legislation.[29] Indeed, he had recently joined the opinion of the North Carolina Supreme Court[30] that was one of the two decisions upheld in *Lincoln Federal*.[31] But neither would he abandon wholesale the protection of economic liberty.

## V. The Weakened Foundation for Personal Liberty

The New Deal Court's elimination of any effective protection of economic rights seriously weakened the bases for protecting personal liberty as well. This was dramatically illustrated by Justice Douglas's inept opinion in *Griswold v. Connecticut*.[32] Because he and his New Deal colleagues, as part of their project of abandoning protection of economic rights, had rejected any meaningful judicial protection of liberties not specifically mentioned in the constitutional

---

[26] *Id.* at 735–36.

[27] *Id.* at 735.

[28] *Id.*

[29] But see David E. Bernstein, Lochner Era Revisionism, Revised: Lochner and the Origins of Fundamental Rights Constitutionalism, 82 Geo. L.J. 1 (2003).

[30] State v. Whitaker, 45 S.E.2d 860 (N.C. 1947).

[31] 335 U.S. 521, 530–37 (1949).

[32] 381 U.S. 479 (1965).

text, he was forced to write a disingenuous opinion in *Griswold* in order to strike down a state law that prohibited couples in Connecticut from buying contraceptives, a right not specifically mentioned in the text.

*Griswold*—profoundly right in its result—is one of the modern era's most important constitutional decisions. But it should never have rested on such an inadequate foundation as Douglas erected. Given the Court's repudiation of economic liberty, however, he must have felt that he had to distort otherwise important supporting decisions like *Pierce v. Society of Sisters*,[33] *Pierce v. Hill Military Academy*,[34] and *Meyer v. Nebraska*[35] to avoid acknowledging that those decisions had recognized and protected economic liberties. As Douglas's *Griswold* opinion shows, a jurisprudence indifferent to whether there is any public purpose served by depriving Owen Ballance of his right to his chosen occupation is hard-pressed to articulate a theory for protecting access to contraceptives against a state's flimsy arguments restricting access.[36]

In the inaugural Simon Lecture, Judge Ginsburg is properly dismissive of the Douglas opinion in *Griswold* and its reliance on "penumbras" and "emanations" from tangentially relevant clauses.[37] But while right in critiquing Douglas's opinion in *Griswold*, Ginsburg fails to recognize the proper basis that *does* exist for protecting personal liberties. Thus, his critique could serve also to undercut the case for the judicial protection of economic rights.

Judge Ginsburg believes that "a jurist devoted to the Constitution as written might conclude that the document says nothing about the privacy of 'intimate relation[s] of husband and wife,' and thereby remits the citizenry to the political processes of their respective states . . . "[38] While true—such a jurist might so conclude—the view expressed there does not resolve the issue. For nowhere does the text confirm that state legislatures have such extraordinary regulatory

---

[33] 268 U.S. 510 (1925).

[34] *Id.*

[35] 262 U.S. 390 (1923).

[36] See also Randy E. Barnett, Justice Kennedy's Libertarian Revolution: Lawrence v. Texas, 2002–2003 Cato Sup. Ct. Rev. 21, 29–31 (2003).

[37] Douglas H. Ginsburg, On Constitutionalism, 2002–2003 Cato Sup. Ct. Rev. 7, 19 (2003).

[38] *Id.* (quoting Griswold v. Connecticut, 381 U.S. 479, 482 (1965)).

power in the first instance. For reasons I have set forth at greater length elsewhere,[39] there is a sound historical basis for assuming that fundamental personal liberties can be invaded only by a government with a compelling interest in doing so, and the text itself in the Ninth and Fourteenth Amendments recognizes the existence of such rights and privileges.

## VI. The Weakened Foundation of Economic Rights

The failure to protect either economic or personal liberty inevitably weakens both. Subjecting the Connecticut birth control ordinance to the kind of judicial scrutiny that Justice Ervin gave the North Carolina occupational licensing law would properly have brought about its demise. But the Supreme Court's economic decisions had taken that argument away from those who challenged the Connecticut ban. Conversely, a version of constitutional law that so defers to legislative fiat that it would leave the birth control law standing surely weakens the case for protecting economic rights. If the state, on such flimsy grounds as were put forward to justify the birth control ban, could intrude to such an extraordinary degree in the intimate lives of individuals and couples, it would be difficult to justify judicial intervention in the state's economic choices, however poorly grounded.

Consider, for example, the Court's decisions last term involving punitive damages and homosexual sodomy. In *State Farm Mutual Automobile Insurance Co. v. Campbell*[40] the Court sharply limited state awards of punitive damages. In *Lawrence v. Texas*[41] the Court struck down the state's law criminalizing homosexual sodomy. Neither opinion cited a textual provision in the Constitution that addressed, specifically, sexual intimacy or punitive damages. Both decisions imposed constitutional limits on what "sovereign" states could do with their civil and criminal enforcement machinery. In both cases the opinion of the Court was written by Justice Anthony Kennedy.

---

[39] Walter Dellinger & Gene Sperling, Abortion and the Supreme Court: The Retreat from Roe v. Wade, 138 U. Pa. L. Rev. 83 (1989).

[40] 538 U.S. 408 (2003). See Robert A. Levy, The Conservative Split on Punitive Damages: State Farm Mutual Automobile Insurance Co. v. Campbell, 2002–2003 Cato Sup. Ct. Rev. 159 (2003).

[41] 539 U.S. 558 (2003). See Barnett, Justice Kennedy's Libertarian Revolution, *supra* note 36.

Both seem to me to be correctly decided, and each rests on a judicial determination that property and liberty, respectively, were being compromised by governmental actions that had no sufficient public justification. Read the two opinions by Justice Kennedy back to back. They seem like one case, with two applications. Each is strengthened by the other.

Indeed, it is hard to imagine either *State Farm* or *Lawrence* without the other, or without their precursors beginning with *Griswold*. In an alternative constitutional universe in which the Court had found that Connecticut was free to criminalize the use of birth control by married couples and Texas was free to criminalize homosexual relations, it is difficult to imagine that same Court would override Utah's determination to utilize very high punitive damages.[42] Yet if one accepts Judge Ginsburg's critique of *Griswold*, and his rejection of any efforts to enforce personal liberties not specifically set out in text, one searches in vain for a convincing ground for intervening in the punitive damage determinations of Utah and other states.

Economic rights, property rights, and personal rights have been joined, appropriately, since the time of the founding. In *Federalist* No. 10, for example, when Madison spoke of the rights that will be more secure in a national republic, he intermingled protection against "paper money" with protection against repressive "religious sects."[43] He echoed and elaborated on those thoughts a few years later in his famous essay, "Property," in the *National Gazette*: "[A]s a man is said to have a right to his property, he may be equally said to have a property in his rights,"[44] after which he gave several examples of both "economic" and "personal" rights. In a passage from a nineteenth century case that eerily echoes today's debates on personal and economic liberty, a nearly unanimous Supreme Court in *Loan Association v. Topeka* wrote:

> There are limitations on . . . [the] power of [our governments, state and national] which grow out of the essential nature of all free governments. [These are] implied reservations of individual rights, without which the social compact could not exist, and which are respected by all governments entitled

[42]538 U.S. 408 (2003).

[43]The Federalist No. 10, at 79 (James Madison) (C. Kesler & C. Rossiter eds., 1961).

[44]James Madison, Property, 1 National Gazette 174, Mar. 29, 1792.

> to the name. No court, for instance, would hesitate to declare
> void a statute which . . . should enact that the homestead
> now owned by A. should no longer be his, but should hence-
> forth be the property of B. The court also says: Nor would
> any court "hesitate to declare void a statute which enacted
> that A. and B. who were husband and wife to each other
> should be so no longer, but that A. should thereafter be the
> husband of C., and B. the wife of D."[45]

The intertwined nature of economic liberty and personal freedom has never been better explicated than by the author whose name this auditorium bears, F.A. Hayek. In his most famous critique of centralized planning, *The Road to Serfdom*, Hayek speaks of economic freedom as the "prerequisite of all other freedoms."[46]

As a practical matter, however, the pressing question is not whether economic liberties are protected by the Constitution but how aggressive or restrained unelected judges should be in securing liberty—whether economic or personal. Of particular importance in that regard is the question of how much deference judges should give to elected representatives pursuing public policy. When should libertarian principles give way? A truer libertarian than I would invalidate far more legislation than I would think appropriate. For me, at least, the outcomes of democratic processes have great claim to legitimacy, and a lack of certainty about whether one's own read-ing of the Constitution is correct counsels caution and restraint.

Yet reading Hayek is instructive. In *The Road to Serfdom*, at least, he was not as doctrinaire as some have believed. He recognized a significant role for government, for example, especially in establish-ing the rule of law. Hayek believed that it is possible to deliberately create "a system within which competition will work as beneficially as possible," but he also criticized "the wooden insistence of some [classical] liberals on some certain rough rules of thumb, above all the principle of laissez faire. Yet, in a sense, this was necessary and unavoidable,"[47] he notes.

Thus, Hayek believed that some controls on the methods of pro-duction—as long as they affect all potential producers equally—may not be anti-competitive:

---

[45] 87 U.S. 655, 663 (1875).

[46] F.A. Hayek, The Road to Serfdom 110 (50th anniv. edition, 1994).

[47] *Id.* at 21.

> To prohibit the use of certain poisonous substances or to require special precautions in their use, to limit working hours or to require certain sanitary arrangements, is fully compatible with the preservation of competition. The only question here is whether in the particular instance the advantages gained are greater than the social costs which they impose.[48]

Nor, for Hayek, was the preservation of competition incompatible with an extensive system of social services—"so long as the organization of these services is not designed in such a way as to make competition ineffective over wide fields."[49] Consistent with his respect for the rule of law, Hayek also believed, of course, that preventing fraud and deception, including exploitation of ignorance, was a legitimate governmental function.

"There is nothing in the basic principles of [classical] liberalism," Hayek believed, "that make it a stationary creed; there are no hard and fast rules fixed once and for all."[50] But there is a fundamental principle, "a principle capable of an infinite variety of applications." That principle is that "in the ordering of our affairs we should make as much use as possible of the spontaneous forces of society, and resort as little as possible . . . to coercion."[51] What a wonderful phrase that is—"the spontaneous forces of society." How perfectly it captures Hayek's vision. And how nicely it ties together the economic and personal liberties that in every century seek refuge from coercion and oppression.

---

[48] *Id.* at 43.

[49] *Id.* Hayek was not making a normative judgment about such services, of course; he was simply making a point about their compatibility with preserving competition. In fact, in the preface to the 1976 edition, he said: "When I wrote [*The Road to Serfdom*], I had by no means sufficiently freed myself from all the prejudices and superstitions dominating general opinion." F.A. Hayek, The Road to Serfdom xxii (1976).

[50] Hayek, *supra* note 46, at 21.

[51] *Id.* at 9.

# Power and Liberty in Wartime

*Timothy Lynch*

## I. Introduction

*Inter arma silent leges* is a legal maxim that says when a country is at war, the laws must be silent. It is a controversial legal concept because it basically means that individual liberty must be subordinated to state power in wartime. America's political and legal institutions have grappled with this doctrine in previous wars and are grappling with it once again in the aftermath of the catastrophic terrorist attacks of September 11, 2001. To protect the country from additional attacks, President Bush made it clear that he wanted to wield extraordinary powers. Many of the constitutional protections that had been designed to safeguard individual liberty would have to yield to those powers. To be sure, President Bush did not make a dramatic announcement to that effect before a joint session of Congress, but his position was clear enough from the official papers that his legal representatives filed in federal court in terrorism-related litigation. Although the president did not explicitly invoke the *inter arma silent leges* maxim, it was the essence of his plan to combat terrorists.

In three landmark arguments before the Supreme Court—*Hamdi v. Rumsfeld*,[1] *Rumsfeld v. Padilla*,[2] and *Rasul v. Bush*[3]—Bush administration lawyers maintained that the president could, in his discretion as commander-in-chief, arrest any person in the world and confine that person incommunicado in a prison cell indefinitely. No access had to be granted to family members and no access had to be granted to a lawyer. According to President Bush, it did not matter if the prisoner was an American citizen, and it did not matter if the person was seized on a battlefield overseas or off the streets of an American

---

[1] 124 S. Ct. 2633 (2004).
[2] 124 S. Ct. 2711 (2004).
[3] 124 S. Ct. 2686 (2004).

city. So long as the president designated the prisoner as an "enemy combatant," the secretary of defense could treat the prisoner as if he essentially had no legal rights. Through his legal representatives, the president informed the Supreme Court that it could not "second-guess" his decision to imprison such individuals.[4] Even though there were only two American citizens imprisoned on the basis of this legal rationale, the constitutional stakes were enormous. If the president could secure a legal precedent from the Supreme Court that validated his interpretation of the Constitution, there would be no limit on the number of citizens who might be arrested and imprisoned in years to come. Fortunately, in a triumph for liberty, the Supreme Court decisively rejected the president's reading of the law. By a margin of 8–1, the Court declared President Bush's "enemy combatant" detention policy to be unconstitutional in *Hamdi*.[5] The Supreme Court did not reach the merits of the *Padilla* case because it found a fatal jurisdictional problem in the litigation.[6] And in *Rasul*, the Court held that federal courts had jurisdiction to entertain habeas corpus petitions from foreign nationals held abroad.[7]

The war against al-Qaeda is unlike any war that America has ever fought. Al-Qaeda terrorists are much more dangerous than a band of criminals. Simply to file a murder indictment against Osama bin Laden and his top lieutenants for the mass murder of September 11, 2001, would have been woefully inadequate. This is a real war—and yet, this enemy cannot be pinpointed on a map because it is not a nation-state. Further, al-Qaeda operatives do not wear uniforms—they impersonate civilians and, worse, their objective is to commit war crimes by murdering as many Americans as they possibly can. Given the unusual character of this war, the rationale of some of the Supreme Court's wartime precedents may be inapplicable. Other precedents were wrongheaded when they were initially decided. To sort through the complexities of this new conflict, this article will present a legal paradigm that can properly resolve the tension between power and liberty in wartime under the American Constitution.

---

[4] Brief for Respondent at 34, Hamdi v. Rumsfeld, 124 S. Ct. 2633 (2004) (No. 03-6696).
[5] Hamdi, 124 S. Ct. at 2651.
[6] *Id.* at 2715.
[7] *Id.* at 2699.

Unlike the simple and sweeping "rules-of-war-paradigm" advanced by the Bush administration, the paradigm set out below begins with three threshold questions, each of which has constitutional implications: (1) What is the status of the individual in question—is he a citizen, illegal immigrant, or nonresident alien? (2) Where was the individual seized—on American soil or an overseas battlefield? (3) What punishment does the government seek to impose—deportation, detention, or execution? Such factors can be pivotal in resolving a constitutional controversy involving arrest, imprisonment, and trial.

The primary objective of this article is not to analyze the Supreme Court's decisions in *Hamdi, Padilla,* and *Rasul.* Rather, the goal is to outline a normative model that describes how the Court should have tackled those cases, as well as similar cases that are likely to arise as the war on terror unfolds. In that context, the Court's three opinions provide a starting point to establish principles that can guide the justices in balancing civil liberties and national security. Naturally, the ground rules that control that tradeoff cannot be finalized in this brief article. But crucial issues are at stake, and a timely examination of those issues—if only to settle on a framework that might lead to ultimate solutions—is urgently needed.

The baseline, insists Justice Antonin Scalia, must be the U.S. Constitution. He reminds us that the doctrine of *inter arma silent leges* "has no place in the interpretation and application of [our] Constitution."[8] That is because our founding document fully anticipates the necessity of wartime measures. It is a legal charter that empowers and limits government in both peacetime and wartime. Our commitment to liberty, the Constitution, and the rule of law is put to the ultimate test when government officials seek to "silence" those limits during wartime.

## II. The Enemy Combatant Cases

Before delving into many of the complex constitutional issues that have arisen in recent years, it will be useful to briefly review the facts of the landmark "enemy combatant" cases that were handed down by the Supreme Court at the conclusion of its 2003–2004 term. It will also be useful to review an enemy combatant case that has

---

[8]Hamdi, 124 S. Ct. at 2674 (Scalia, J., dissenting).

not yet reached the Supreme Court, or received much notoriety, namely, the imprisonment of Ali Saleh Kahlah al-Marri.

## A. Yaser Hamdi: American Citizen Seized Abroad

After the vicious attacks of September 11, 2001, President Bush dispatched U.S. military forces to Afghanistan "with a mission to subdue al-Qaeda and quell the Taliban regime that was known to support it."[9] Yaser Hamdi was taken prisoner by soldiers of the Northern Alliance, which is a coalition of military groups opposed to the Taliban government. The U.S. military, in turn, transferred Hamdi to the U.S. Naval Base at Guantanamo Bay, Cuba, in January 2002.[10] A few months later, the prison authorities at Guantanamo discovered that Hamdi was an American citizen by virtue of his having been born in Louisiana in 1980.[11] After that revelation, the Department of Defense transferred Hamdi to a naval brig in Norfolk, Virginia. President Bush declared Hamdi an "enemy combatant," which meant that Hamdi was not going to be charged with a crime and that he was not entitled to "prisoner of war" protections under international law.[12]

In June 2002, Hamdi's father, Esam Foulid Hamdi, filed a petition for a writ of habeas corpus on his son's behalf. President Bush's lawyers urged the federal courts to summarily dismiss the petition because the courts could not "second-guess" the president once he designated any person to be an "enemy combatant."[13] Hamdi's lawyers argued that a summary procedure would be unconstitutional. Before a habeas petition could be dismissed, they maintained, Hamdi had to have an opportunity to present his side of the case and to rebut the government's allegations.

The issue fractured the Supreme Court.[14] Although only a plurality of the Court could agree on the proper way to handle such habeas

---

[9]*Id.* at 2635.

[10]*Id.* at 2636.

[11]*Id.* at 2635–36.

[12]*Id.* at 2636.

[13]See Brief for Respondents-Appellants at 12, Hamdi v. Rumsfeld, 296 F.3d 278 (4th Cir. 2002) (No. 02-6895).

[14]See Hamdi, 124 S. Ct. at 2652–60 (Souter, J., concurring in part, dissenting in part, and concurring in the judgment); *id* at 2660–74 (Scalia, J., dissenting); *id.* at 2674–85 (Thomas, J., dissenting).

petitions, fully eight members of the Court agreed with Hamdi that a summary procedure would violate the Constitution. Only one member of the Court, Justice Clarence Thomas, agreed with the sweeping proposition that the courts were "incapable" of resolving habeas petitions in wartime.[15]

### B. *Jose Padilla: American Citizen Seized in the United States*

Jose Padilla was arrested by federal law enforcement agents at Chicago's O'Hare International Airport in May 2002. Padilla, who is an American citizen, had just alighted from a flight that had originated in Pakistan.[16] Attorney General John Ashcroft announced the arrest and said Padilla was engaged in a plot to detonate a "dirty bomb" in the United States.[17]

President Bush declared Padilla an "enemy combatant" who had "close ties" to al-Qaeda.[18] The president then ordered Secretary of Defense Donald Rumsfeld to take Padilla into custody and to transfer him to a military brig.[19] Padilla was taken to the Consolidated Naval Brig in Charleston, South Carolina. Like Hamdi, Padilla was held incommunicado—no access to family members or an attorney.

A petition for a writ of habeas corpus was filed on Padilla's behalf and that petition alleged that his imprisonment was unlawful. The Bush administration responded to that petition by urging the federal district court to summarily dismiss the petition because it had been filed in the wrong jurisdiction and because, on the merits, the court could not "second-guess" President Bush's "enemy combatant" designation.[20] Padilla's attorneys argued that, at a bare minimum, they had to have their "day in court" to present a defense to the government's allegations.[21]

---

[15]*Id.* at 2674–75 (Thomas, J., dissenting).

[16]Rumsfeld v. Padilla, 124 S. Ct. 2711, 2715 (2004).

[17]See David Savage, Detention of a Citizen Questioned, Los Angeles Times, June 12, 2002, at A1.

[18]Padilla, 124 S. Ct. at 2715.

[19]*Id.*

[20]Respondents' Response to, And Motion to Dismiss, the Amended Petition for a Writ of Habeas Corpus at 11, Padilla v. Bush, 233 F. Supp. 2d 564 (S.D.N.Y. 2002) (No. 02-Civ-4445).

[21]Petitioners' Reply to Motion to Dismiss Petition for Writ of Habeas Corpus, Padilla v. Bush, 233 F. Supp. 2d. 564 (S.D.N.Y. 2002) (No. 02-Civ-4445).

In a 5–4 decision, the Supreme Court ruled that Padilla's habeas petition did suffer from a fatal jurisdictional defect.[22] The petition could be refiled in the appropriate jurisdiction, but the case would have to be reargued. Four members of the Court found no jurisdictional problem. On the merits, the four dissenters said there could be "only one possible answer to the question whether [Padilla] is entitled to a hearing on the justification for his detention."[23] Given that strong statement, it is abundantly clear that when the case is reargued, the Bush administration will not be able to prevent Padilla from having his day in court to present a defense to the allegations that have been leveled against him.[24]

## C. Fawzi Khalid Abdullah Fahad al-Odah: Foreign National Seized Abroad

Fawzi Khalid Abdullah Fahad al-Odah is a citizen of Kuwait.[25] He was seized in Afghanistan during the war between American military forces and the forces of the Taliban regime. Because the U.S. military considered al-Odah to be a member of the hostile forces, he was transferred to the Guantanamo Bay prison camp, where he has been imprisoned with approximately 600 other non-Americans who have been captured abroad.[26]

A petition for a writ of habeas corpus was subsequently filed on al-Odah's behalf and that petition alleged that his imprisonment was illegal because he had never been a combatant against the United States. President Bush had previously designated al-Odah and all of the other prisoners at Guantanamo Bay to be "enemy combatants." Thus, the president's lawyers urged the federal judiciary to summarily dismiss the petition because the federal judiciary could not "second-guess" the president's enemy combatant designation

---

[22]Padilla, 124 S. Ct. at 2727.

[23]Id. at 2735 (Stevens, J., dissenting).

[24]Indeed, a strong argument can be made that Padilla will not only get a hearing, he will likely go free if the Department of Justice does not file formal criminal charges. See Robert A. Levy, Will They Let Padilla Go?, Legal Times, August 2, 2004.

[25]Al-Odah's case was briefed and argued with Rasul. See Al-Odah v. United States, 124 S. Ct. 2686 (2004) (companion case) (No. 03-343). Shafiq Rasul, a British citizen who was one of the original petitioners, has since been released from custody.

[26]Rasul v. Bush, 124 S. Ct. 2686, 2690 (2004).

and because the federal judiciary lacked jurisdiction to hear habeas claims from noncitizens who are captured abroad and held abroad.[27]

The Supreme Court, in a 6–3 decision, held that U.S. courts do have jurisdiction to hear habeas corpus petitions that allege illegal imprisonment by foreign nationals that are captured and held abroad.[28] Three members of the Court concluded that the federal habeas statute simply did not extend to "aliens detained by the United States overseas, outside the sovereign borders of the United States and beyond the territorial jurisdictions of all its courts."[29]

### D. Ali Saleh Kahlah al-Marri: Foreign National Seized in the United States

Ali Saleh Kahlah al-Marri is a citizen of Qatar. Just a day before the September 11, 2001, terrorist attacks, al-Marri entered the United States with his wife and five children. Al-Marri was traveling on a student visa and he says that his plan was to earn a master's degree at Bradley University in Peoria, Illinois, where he had previously earned a bachelor's degree in 1991.[30]

Al-Marri was arrested on a material witness warrant by the Federal Bureau of Investigation in December 2001. He was subsequently charged with making false statements to the FBI and with identity and credit card fraud. Al-Marri denied the allegations and prepared for his trial on those charges. With his trial only four weeks away, President Bush declared al-Marri to be an "enemy combatant."[31] Acting on the president's orders, the U.S. military removed al-Marri from a civilian prison facility in Illinois and transferred him to a navy brig in South Carolina. Like Hamdi and Padilla, al-Marri was then held incommunicado—no access to family members and no access to legal counsel.

---

[27]Brief for the Respondents at 43, Rasul v. Bush, 124 S. Ct. 2686 (2004).

[28]Rasul, 124 S. Ct. at 2699. Justice Anthony Kennedy, concurring in the judgment, would have ruled more narrowly. Kennedy wrote: "In light of the status of Guantanamo Bay and the indefinite pretrial detention of the detainees, I would hold that federal-court jurisdiction is permitted in these cases. This approach would avoid creating automatic statutory authority to adjudicate the claims of persons located outside the United States." *Id.* at 2701.

[29]*Id.* at 2701 (Scalia, J., dissenting).

[30]Al-Marri v. Rumsfeld, 360 F.3d 707, 708 (7th Cir. 2004), petition for cert. filed, No. 03-1424 (U.S. Apr. 9, 2004).

[31]*Id.*

In July 2003, a petition for a writ of habeas corpus was filed on al-Marri's behalf and that petition alleged that his imprisonment was unlawful. President Bush's lawyers responded by urging the district court to summarily dismiss the petition because of jurisdictional errors.[32] Al-Marri's petition was dismissed by the district court and an appeal to the Supreme Court is presently pending.[33]

## III. The Power of Government to Seize and Imprison Citizens Within American Borders

### A. Seizure

Absent an invasion or rebellion on U.S. territory, the Fourth Amendment establishes the fundamental law regarding the parameters of the government's power to arrest an individual. The Fourth Amendment provides, "The right of the people to be secure in their persons, houses, papers, and effects, against unreasonable searches and seizures, shall not be violated, and no Warrants shall issue, but upon probable cause, supported by Oath or affirmation, and particularly describing the place to be searched, and the persons or things to be seized."[34]

The arrest of a person is the quintessential "seizure" under the Fourth Amendment.[35] That amendment shields the citizenry from overzealous government agents by placing limits on the powers of the police. The primary "check" is the warrant application process. That process requires the police to apply for arrest warrants, allowing impartial judges to exercise independent judgment regarding whether sufficient evidence has been gathered to meet the probable cause standard of the Fourth Amendment.[36] When government agents seize a person without an arrest warrant, the prisoner must be brought before a judicial magistrate within forty-eight hours so that an impartial judicial officer can examine the government's conduct and discharge anyone illegally seized.[37]

---

[32]Motion to Dismiss or Transfer Petition for Writ of Habeas Corpus, Al-Marri v. Bush, 274 F. Supp. 2d 1003 (2003) (No. 03-1220).

[33]*Supra* note 30.

[34]U.S. Const. amend. IV.

[35]See Payton v. New York, 445 U.S. 573 (1980).

[36]See McDonald v. United States, 335 U.S. 451 (1948).

[37]See County of Riverside v. McLaughlin, 500 U.S. 44 (1991).

There are indications that the Bush administration has a much more expansive view of the government's power to seize individuals. In one of its briefs to the Supreme Court, for example, the president's lawyers wrote, "The Commander in Chief . . . has authority to seize and detain enemy combatants wherever found, including within the borders of the United States."[38] Former Deputy Assistant Attorney General John Yoo has also advanced the idea of a military arrest authority by drawing a sharp distinction between criminal law investigations and terrorism investigations that implicate national security. According to Yoo, the president is not constrained by Fourth Amendment procedures when he is seeking to apprehend enemy combatants.[39]

Thus far, there has not been any enemy combatant-related litigation involving Fourth Amendment issues. Padilla and al-Marri were both arrested on material witness warrants. Still, it is worth exploring the issue here, even if only briefly, because it will likely arise sometime soon. The unstated premise of President Bush's invocation of his commander-in-chief authority seems to be that every single American jurisdiction—from Daytona Beach, Florida, to Fort Wayne, Indiana, to Reno, Nevada, to Fairbanks, Alaska—is a war zone. Indeed, this is one of the startling legal consequences of President Bush's wartime paradigm. That is, on the president's view, the homes in sleepy American neighborhoods are no different from neighborhoods in Baghdad, Iraq, or Kabul, Afghanistan. Military commanders can search and arrest at will. Of course, the fact that this power has been exercised infrequently (or perhaps even not at all) does not alter the legal proposition that has been asserted.

Al-Qaeda operatives may well be on U.S. soil plotting additional attacks against innocent civilians, but to say the president can search any American home or arrest any American citizen without having to bother with the Fourth Amendment's warrant application process—so long as his objective is to find an enemy combatant—is

---

[38]Brief for the United States at 38, Rumsfeld v. Padilla, 124 S. Ct. 2711 (2004) (No. 03-1027).

[39]See, e.g., Testimony of John Yoo before the U.S. House Permanent Select Committee on Intelligence (October 30, 2003) ("The federal government and the executive branch have broader sources of constitutional authority to protect the national security that do not require a warrant."), available at http://www.aei.org/news/filter.newsID.19374/news_detail.asp.

absurd. Such a bold assertion was not advanced even during the Korean and Vietnam wars when there were communist spies on U.S. territory and the Soviet Union had a nuclear arsenal that targeted the American homeland.

The Fourth Amendment does not bar arrests or searches—but it does regulate them. Law enforcement agents must first gather evidence of wrongdoing before they can obtain and execute arrest warrants. Although the Fourth Amendment doctrine of exigent circumstances permits government agents to act without warrants in emergencies, the war on terrorism does not give the police a roving, general warrant to arrest any person, anytime on suspicion of terrorism. The Constitution never would have been ratified by the American revolutionaries if the president could wield such power over citizens—even in wartime.[40]

## B. Imprisonment

The Constitution places several limitations on the power of the government to deprive an American citizen of his liberty on American soil. As noted, the Fourth Amendment prohibits unreasonable seizures. The Fifth Amendment guarantees due process. The Sixth Amendment guarantees a speedy and public trial. The Bush administration has sidestepped those provisions by declining to file formal criminal charges against its enemy combatant prisoners. Since there is no criminal proceeding under way, it is argued, the ordinary rules of criminal procedure do not apply.

Given the noncriminal nature of the imprisonment, defense counsel for the prisoners have turned to the law of habeas corpus. The Constitution provides that "[t]he Privilege of the Writ of Habeas Corpus shall not be suspended, unless when in Cases of Rebellion or Invasion the public safety may require it."[41] The right to habeas corpus is, in essence, a right to judicial protection against lawless incarceration by executive authorities. It is a legal writ that was lauded by American and English jurists as a great bulwark for individual liberty. Here is how Joseph Story defined the writ in his treatise on constitutional law:

---

[40]If America can no longer "afford the luxury" of the Fourth Amendment, proponents of that view must try to persuade their fellow citizens to amend the Constitution.

[41]U.S. Const. art. 1, § 9, cl. 2.

*Habeas corpus,* literally, Have you the Body. The phrase designates the most emphatic words of the writ, issued by a Judge or Court, commanding a person, who has another in custody, or in imprisonment, to have his body (Habeas Corpus) before the Judge or Court, at a particular time and place, and to state the cause of his imprisonment. The person, whether a sheriff, gaoler, or other person, is bound to produce the body of the prisoner at the time and place appointed: and, if the prisoner is illegally or improperly in custody, the Judge or Court will discharge him. Hence it is deemed the great security of the personal liberty of the citizen against oppression and illegal confinement.[42]

William Blackstone said the writ of habeas corpus was "the most celebrated writ in English law."[43] Indeed, its esteemed reputation is such that it is typically referred to as the "Great Writ."[44]

President Bush's expansive assertion of his commander-in-chief authority strikes at the heart of habeas corpus. According to President Bush and his lawyers, Article III courts may not "second-guess" the president's decision to designate a person as an enemy combatant.[45] That may be the case if the writ of habeas corpus has been suspended; but otherwise, the courts must review the legality of the imprisonment. If the citizen has been unlawfully deprived of his liberty, the court should see to it that his liberty is promptly restored. That is what habeas corpus is all about.[46]

A habeas proceeding that involves an American citizen on American soil should not even require an evidentiary hearing.[47] Citizens

[42]Joseph Story, A Familiar Exposition of the Constitution of the United States 396 (1840).

[43]3 Blackstone Commentaries 129.

[44]39 Am. Jur. 2d Habeas Corpus and Postconviction Remedies § 1 (1999).

[45]*Supra* note 13.

[46]See Harris v. Nelson, 394 U.S. 286, 292 (1969) ("[T]he power of inquiry on federal habeas corpus is plenary.") (citation and internal quotation marks omitted).

[47]Jose Padilla's seizure might not have been "on American soil." Because law enforcement agents seized Padilla immediately after he alighted from an international flight from Pakistan, it is far from clear that his particular case ought to be treated any differently than if he had been arrested as he was boarding the plane in Pakistan. This point is discussed more fully in Brief of the Cato Institute, Rumsfeld v. Padilla, 124 S. Ct. 2711 (2004) (No. 03-1027). For purposes of this article, however, that issue will be set aside in order to analyze the parameters of the government's power to seize and imprison an American citizen within America's borders. See, e.g., Padilla v. Rumsfeld, 352 F.3d 695, 722 (2d Cir. 2003).

at home enjoy the broadest constitutional protections against the power of the government. In such circumstances, the government must either file formal criminal charges or release the prisoner.[48]

A president who is conscientious about his responsibility to defend the lives of the innocent while respecting the rights of those who seem to be collaborating with the enemy is not without options. First, when the evidence is insufficient for prosecution, the suspect can be placed under surveillance. Second, if the exigencies of war are apparent, the president can seek to persuade the Congress to suspend the writ of habeas corpus. When the writ is suspended, the police can move quickly against suspected persons without having to present evidence to a judge. Suspending the writ is an extraordinary step that leaves the liberty of every citizen resting on the judgment or even whim of any law enforcement agent. That is why the suspension procedure is vested in the legislature—it was too drastic a measure to leave in the hands of a single official.

After the catastrophic attacks of September 11, 2001, the Bush administration initially planned to ask the Congress to suspend the writ.[49] For whatever reason, the plan was abandoned, but President Bush then tried to bypass the Constitution's checks and balances with his "enemy combatant" legal theory. He asserted, on one hand, that habeas corpus petitions can be filed with the courts; but he insisted, on the other hand, that the courts must throw the petitions out because the judges may not "second-guess" the president's decision.[50] President Bush cannot avoid habeas review by simply employing the "enemy combatant" designation against citizens. The law of habeas corpus cannot be so easily evaded.

Over and above the constitutional safeguard afforded by habeas review, Congress has enacted a federal law that pertains to the imprisonment of American citizens on American soil. The Non-Detention Act, 18 U.S.C. § 4001(a), states that "[n]o citizen shall be imprisoned or otherwise detained by the United States except

[48]See generally Hamdi v. Rumsfeld, 124 S. Ct. 2633, 2660 (2004) (Scalia, J., dissenting).

[49]Jonathan Alter, Justice vs. Terror, Newsweek, December 10, 2001 ("When Attorney General John Ashcroft sent the secret first draft of the antiterrorism bill to Capitol Hill in October, it contained a section explicitly titled: 'Suspension of the Writ of Habeas Corpus.'").

[50]See, e.g., Brief for the Petitioner at 43, Rumsfeld v. Padilla, 124 S. Ct. 2711 (2004) (No. 03-1027).

pursuant to an Act of Congress." That law was designed to prevent a future president from issuing an executive order that would set up prison camps (or "detention centers") for citizens who are perceived to be a threat to national security. On the government's view, however, the law means that if such a prison system is contemplated, the president need only place the system under military rather than civilian control. On the government's reading of the law, it is illegal for the attorney general to set up prison facilities for people who are accused of being enemy combatants, but it is legal for the secretary of defense to administer such facilities: "Section 4001(a) pertains solely to the detention of American citizens by *civilian* authorities. It has no bearing on the settled authority of the *military* to detain enemy combatants in a time of war."[51] That is a fanciful interpretation of Section 4001(a).

The Non-Detention Act prohibits unilateral executive incarceration in circumstances where the president might be tempted to imprison citizens without formal criminal charges. Of course, one could argue that the act is impractical in a war against al-Qaeda terrorists, but that is an argument for repealing the law, not evading it. The civilian-military distinction that has been advanced by the Bush administration is specious.

In sum, the liberty of citizens on American soil has the strongest protections of American law. Unless the writ of habeas corpus has been suspended, the president can only imprison a citizen by prosecution in federal court on a formal criminal charge, where the full panoply of constitutional rights must be accorded to the accused.

## IV. The Power of Government to Seize and Imprison Citizens Outside American Borders

### A. Seizure

Given the unusual character of America's war with al-Qaeda, it is appropriate for the judiciary to afford the president a measure of deference in the exercise of his executive authority as commander-in-chief. When the U.S. military is sent abroad to vanquish terrorist training camps, soldiers have the authority to capture and detain both enemy personnel and their collaborators. The Supreme Court

---

* [51]Brief for the Petitioner at 45, Rumsfeld v. Padilla, 124 S. Ct. 2711 (2004) (No. 03-1027) (emphasis in original).

has never held that arrest warrants are required on the battlefield. Although the Bush administration and others have repeatedly argued that the rules of the criminal justice system are ill-suited for war, they fail to mention that there has been no legal challenge to the *capture of enemy forces outside of America's borders*. Counsel for Hamdi challenged the legality of his indefinite detention, but Hamdi's initial capture was *not* challenged in the Supreme Court or the lower courts. Similarly, when the "American Taliban," John Walker Lindh, was captured in a combat zone in Afghanistan, there was no serious contention that the U.S. military had perpetrated an "illegal arrest." The strenuous pleas to give the military latitude to *seize* enemy combatants, including combatants who turn out to have been born in America, amount to sound and fury that signifies little. The objection turns out to be a classic straw man.

*B. Imprisonment*

While it is sensible to afford military authorities some deference with respect to the capture and brief detention of enemy personnel on the battlefield, it is another matter when the president has made a determination to imprison an American citizen without formal criminal charges. As the U.S. Court of Appeals for the Second Circuit observed, once a person has been confined to a jail cell, any immediate threat that he may have posed has been effectively neutralized.[52] If the government determines that an American citizen must be deprived of his liberty because he poses a threat to public safety, it must be prepared to defend that assessment in a court of law.

In *Hamdi*, the Supreme Court acknowledged that American citizenship entitles a prisoner to file a petition for a writ of habeas corpus to challenge his detention.[53] As noted, the right to petition for a writ of habeas corpus is, in essence, a right to seek judicial protection against lawless incarceration by executive authorities. If an independent body could not review and reject the president's decision to incarcerate a citizen, the writ never would have acquired its longstanding reputation in the law as the "Great Writ." If habeas corpus has not been suspended, the writ retains its full legal force— no matter where the seizure of a citizen takes place.

[52]See Padilla, 352 F.3d at 700.
[53]See Hamdi v. Rumsfeld, 124 S. Ct. 2633, 2644 (2004).

Thus, citizens who are captured abroad cannot be imprisoned on the basis of an allegation leveled by the president. Citizens must have access to counsel and an opportunity to rebut the government's allegation before an impartial judge. If the government can persuade the judge that the citizen is an enemy combatant, continued incarceration in a military brig would be legitimized.

## V. The Power of Government to Seize and Imprison Foreign Nationals Within American Borders

### A. Seizure

One argument that has been ubiquitous since the war with al-Qaeda began has been that "noncitizens do not have the same rights as citizens." Does that mean the police have plenary authority to stop, question, and arrest foreign nationals on U.S. soil? The proposition has some surface appeal, but it cannot withstand close scrutiny.

The notion that noncitizens do not have the same rights as citizens can be true or false depending upon the circumstances. Such a notion is too sweeping for universal application to the Fourth Amendment or other constitutional provisions. First, it should be noted that while some provisions of the Constitution employ the term "citizens," other provisions employ the term "persons" or "the people" or "the accused."[54] Thus, it is safe to say that when the Framers of the Constitution wanted to use a narrow or broad classification, they did so. The Fourth Amendment, for example, establishes standards and procedures with respect to searches, arrests, probable cause, and warrants. It applies to the people.[55] There are no exceptions for noncitizens.

Second, the Supreme Court has repeatedly held that constitutional guarantees generally apply to aliens as well as to citizens.[56] The

---

[54]See, e.g. U.S. Const. amend. XV ("The right of citizens of the United States to vote shall not be denied or abridged . . ."); U.S. Const. amend. V ("No person shall be held to answer for a capital, or otherwise infamous crime, unless on a presentment or indictment of a grand jury . . .").

[55]U.S. Const. amend. IV ("The right of the people to be secure in their persons, houses, papers, and effects, against unreasonable searches and seizures, shall not be violated, and no Warrants shall issue, but upon probable cause . . .").

[56]See generally Wong Wing v. United States, 163 U.S. 228 (1896); Yick Wo v. Hopkins, 118 U.S. 356 (1886). See also Au Yi Lau v. INS, 445 F.2d 217 (D.C. Cir. 1971). Indeed, under the Equal Protection Clause, classifications based on alienage are inherently suspect and subject to heightened judicial scrutiny. See, e.g., Graham v. Richardson, 403 U.S. 365, 371–72 (1971).

police, for example, are not permitted to conduct raids on the homes of lawful immigrants or on the hotel rooms of European tourists simply because they are "not Americans."[57] Whatever the territorial limitations of the Fourth Amendment may be, it shields the liberty of individuals in the homeland—citizen and noncitizen alike.[58]

### B. Imprisonment

President Bush shocked the American legal community by asserting what was essentially a "new day of executive detentions."[59] But absent an invasion or rebellion on American soil, it is farfetched to suggest that any person in America can be imprisoned on the mere say-so of the president.

However, it is not unreasonable or implausible to suggest that wartime circumstances can mean a change in the rules, methods, and procedures by which the government can deal with the problem of illegal aliens. American law generally denies the benefit of a transaction to one who procures the transaction with fraud. Thus, why should an individual who has entered the United States surreptitiously or through false pretenses benefit from that wrong by acquiring the full panoply of constitutional rights that are accorded to citizens and long-term permanent residents?

Before a nonresident alien can acquire standing to assert constitutional protections against detention and imprisonment, the first order of business ought to be an examination of the prisoner's immigration status. "If that status was obtained by fraud, misrepresentation or other unlawful means, then it should be deemed void ab initio. Such an alien should be treated under the law as if he never was lawfully admitted to the United States—because in a very real sense he was not."[60]

---

[57]Circumstances do matter, however. When the police know in advance that a particular person is an illegal immigrant, they have more leeway to stop and arrest that person. See Aguirre v. INS, 553 F.2d 501, 501–02 (1977).

[58]The controlling precedent concerning the Fourth Amendment's application to aliens abroad is United States v. Verdugo-Urquidez, 494 U.S. 259, 275 (1990) (Fourth Amendment does not apply to property owned by a nonresident alien and located in a foreign country).

[59]Hamdi v. Rumsfeld, 316 F.3d 450, 476 (2003) (Wilkinson, J., op.).

[60]George Terwilliger, et al., The War on Terrorism: Law Enforcement or National Security?, Federalist Society National Security White Paper, available at http://www.fed-soc.org/Publications/Terrorism/militarytribunals.htm (last checked Aug. 17, 2004).

The danger of government overreaching in this context can be "checked" with habeas actions and judicial review by impartial Article III judges. That is, if the president can persuade an independent federal judge that the prisoner's presence on U.S. soil was accomplished by fraud (or other illegal means) and that the prisoner is an enemy combatant, the prisoner can be incarcerated in a military brig. Such a person need not be charged with a criminal offense.

These are the legal principles that come to the fore in the al-Marri case. Al-Marri is the foreign national who claims that he came to the United States to pursue a graduate degree. President Bush, on the other hand, claims that al-Marri is an al-Qaeda operative who entered the United States under false pretenses. Many civil liberties advocates argue that al-Marri must be "charged or released." President Bush maintains that al-Marri can be imprisoned indefinitely. Both claims are overstated.

If the writ of habeas corpus has not been suspended, the president cannot prevent meaningful judicial review. But al-Marri's insistence upon a full-blown trial where the government must introduce enough evidence to convince a jury beyond a reasonable doubt is also overblown. To resolve the competing claims of liberty and security, an impartial federal judge ought to hear both sides. If the president can convince a judge that al-Marri is not a bona fide student, he should be deported. If the president can present evidence that al-Marri has associations with al-Qaeda, he ought to be detained in a military brig.

## VI. The Power of Government to Seize and Imprison Foreign Nationals Outside American Borders

### A. Seizure

President Bush and his legal representatives have urged the federal judiciary to set aside the ordinary rules of criminal procedure and recognize a sweeping rule-of-war-paradigm.[61] This legal theory is dangerously misguided with respect to the homeland, but makes perfect sense with respect to military and intelligence operations

---

[61]Others have propounded this wartime paradigm as well. See William P. Barr and Andrew G. McBride, Military Justice for al Qaeda, Washington Post, November 18, 2001, at B7; Brad Berenson, Earth to Second Circuit: We're at War, Wall Street Journal, December 29, 2003, at A15.

abroad. As previously noted, however, there has been no serious legal challenge to the idea that the U.S. military has broad discretion to capture enemy personnel abroad. The Supreme Court has never held that the Fourth Amendment's requirements apply in the battlefield, and rightly so.

## B. Imprisonment

In *Rasul v. Bush*,[62] the Supreme Court confronted the question of whether the federal judiciary has jurisdiction to consider a challenge to the legality of the detention of foreign nationals captured abroad in connection with the ongoing war with the al-Qaeda terrorist network. By a 6–3 vote, the Court concluded that the federal courts do have jurisdiction to hear such cases.

Although *Rasul* turned upon an interpretation of the terms of the federal habeas statute,[63] all of the justices acknowledged that the Constitution itself could confer habeas jurisdiction in certain situations. It will be useful to examine the constitutional bases for jurisdiction here, even if only briefly.

Habeas actions most certainly involve the prisoner, but only indirectly. The real legal action is between the court and the party responsible for the prisoner's incarceration, that is, the custodian. Thus, when the writ of habeas corpus has not been suspended, a prisoner such as al-Odah should have an opportunity to present a petition to a federal judicial forum that his incarceration is mistaken or unlawful. Since the president and the secretary of defense are al-Odah's custodians, the issue is whether *they* are within the jurisdiction of a federal judicial forum, which, of course, they are.

This idea is hardly a novel innovation in the law of habeas corpus. Indeed, Judge Cooley emphasized the jurisdictional component of the custodian in 1867. Here is an excerpt from Judge Cooley's opinion:

> The important fact to be observed in regard to the mode of procedure upon this [habeas] writ is, that it is directed to, and served upon, not the person confined, but his jailor. It does not reach the former except through the latter. The officer or person who serves it does not unbar the prison doors, and set the prisoner free, but the court relieves him

[62] *Supra* note 3.
[63] 28 U.S.C. § 2241.

by compelling the oppressor to release his constraint . . . . This is the ordinary mode of affording relief, and if other means are resorted to, they are only auxiliary to those which are usual. *The place of confinement is, therefore, not important to the relief, if the guilty party is within reach of process, so that by the power of the court he can be compelled to release his grasp.* The difficulty of affording redress is not increased by the confinement being beyond the limits of the state [of Michigan], except as greater distance may affect it. The important question is, where is the power of control exercised?[64]

The "power of control" for prisoners held by the U.S. military is in Washington, D.C.

There are, to be sure, legitimate *practical* issues that will arise in habeas litigation. In all of America's previous wars, there were strong incentives for enemy personnel to remain in uniform even if there was a strong likelihood of imminent capture. Staying in uniform meant qualification for "prisoner of war" status under the terms of the Geneva Convention. Getting caught out-of-uniform might put one into the category of spy and war criminal (a status that is punishable by death). That legal framework kept the vast majority of cases outside of the American court system.[65] The war with the al-Qaeda network will entail a steady influx of cases in which the government will accuse a "civilian" of actually being an enemy combatant. The *practical* legal problems—forum shopping by prisoners, rules of evidence that may require disclosure of intelligence information—are not inconsiderable. But nearly all of those problems can be addressed by modifying the federal habeas statutes. And such modifications can be accomplished without violating the core principles of habeas review.

## VII. The Power of Government to Prosecute and Execute Citizens and Foreign Nationals

### A. Military Trials Within American Borders

Article III, section 2 of the Constitution provides, "The Trial of all Crimes, except in Cases of Impeachment; shall be by Jury." The Sixth Amendment to the Constitution provides, "In all criminal

---

[64]In re Jackson, 15 Mich. 417, 439–440 (1867) (emphasis added).

[65]Few, of course, crept in. See In re Territo, 156 F.2d 142 (9th Cir. 1946).

prosecutions, the accused shall enjoy the right to a speedy and public trial, by an impartial jury." To limit the awesome powers of government, the Framers designed a system where juries would stand between the apparatus of the state and the accused. If the government can convince a citizen jury that the accused has committed a crime and belongs in prison, the accused will lose his liberty and perhaps his life. If the government cannot convince the jury with its evidence, the prisoner will go free. In America, an acquittal by a jury is final and may not be reviewed by state functionaries.

Unfortunately, during the Civil War, the government set up military tribunals and denied many people their rights to trial by jury. To facilitate that process, the government also suspended the writ of habeas corpus—so that prisoners could not challenge the legality of their arrests or convictions.[66] The one case that did reach the Supreme Court, *Ex parte Milligan*,[67] deserves careful attention.

In *Ex parte Milligan*, the attorney general of the United States, James Speed, argued that the legal guarantees set forth in the Bill of Rights were "peace provisions."[68] During wartime, he argued, the government can suspend the Bill of Rights and impose martial law. If the government chooses to exercise that option, the commanding military officer becomes "the supreme legislator, supreme judge, and supreme executive."[69] That was not simply an abstract legal theory published in a legal periodical. That was the official policy of the government—and it had real-world consequences. Some men and women were arrested, imprisoned, prosecuted, and executed without the benefit of the legal mode of procedure set forth in the Constitution—trial by jury.[70]

The Supreme Court ultimately rejected the legal position advanced by Attorney General Speed. Here is one passage from the ruling:

> The great minds of the country have differed on the correct interpretation to be given to various provisions of the Federal

---

[66]William H. Rehnquist, All the Laws but One: Civil Liberties in Wartime 11–25 (1998).

[67]71 U.S. (4 Wall.) 2 (1866).

[68]*Id.* at 20 (argument for the United States).

[69]*Id.* at 14 (argument for the United States).

[70]Mary Surratt, for example, was prosecuted for conspiring to kill President Abraham Lincoln. Surratt was executed after her conviction by a military commission. See Rehnquist, *supra* note 66, at 162–66.

Constitution; and judicial decision has often been invoked to settle their true meaning; but until recently no one ever doubted that the right to trial by jury was fortified in the organic law against the power of attack. It is *now* assailed; but if ideas can be expressed in words, and language has any meaning, *this right*—one of the most valuable in a free country—is preserved to every one accused of crime who is not attached to the army, or navy, or militia in actual service. The sixth amendment affirms that "in all criminal prosecutions the accused shall enjoy the right to a speedy and public trial by an impartial jury," language broad enough to embrace all persons and cases.[71]

The *Milligan* ruling is sound. The Constitution does permit the suspension of habeas corpus in certain circumstances and Congress does have the power "To make Rules for the Government and Regulation of the land and naval Forces," and "To provide for organizing, arming, and disciplining, the Militia."[72] To reconcile those provisions with the provisions pertaining to trial by jury, the Supreme Court ruled that the jurisdiction of the military could not extend beyond those people who were actually serving in the army, navy, and militia. That is an eminently sensible reading of the constitutional text.

There is only one case in which the Supreme Court has explicitly upheld the constitutionality of using military tribunals in America to try individuals who were not in the military—*Ex parte Quirin*.[73] Because the *Quirin* ruling carved out an exception to the *Milligan* holding, it must be scrutinized carefully.

The facts in *Quirin* were fairly straightforward. In June 1942 German submarines surfaced off the American coast and two teams of saboteurs landed ashore—one team in New York, the other team in Florida. Both teams initially wore German uniforms, but the uniforms were discarded after they landed on the beach. Wearing civilian clothes, they proceeded inland to meet American accomplices and to make plans for sabotage. Within a matter of weeks, however,

[71]Milligan, 71 U.S. (4 Wall.) at 122–123 (emphasis in original).
[72]U.S. Const. art. 1, § 8, cl. 14 & 16.
[73]317 U.S. 1 (1942).

all of the German saboteurs were apprehended by the Federal Bureau of Investigation.[74]

President Franklin Roosevelt wanted these German prisoners to be tried before a military commission so he ordered that the men be turned over to the military authorities. President Roosevelt then set up a military commission and decreed that the prisoners would not have access to the civilian court system. A secret trial was held and all of the prisoners were convicted of war crimes. The military lawyers that had been assigned to defend the saboteurs challenged the legality of the proceedings and appealed the case to the Supreme Court. Although Attorney General Francis Biddle strenuously argued that the Supreme Court had no jurisdiction over the case, the Court agreed to hear arguments in the matter.

The defense team for the saboteurs argued that the trial before the military commission was inconsistent with the *Milligan* precedent and that the Supreme Court ought to order a new trial in a civilian court. The Supreme Court rejected that argument and sought to distinguish the *Milligan* ruling from the circumstances found in *Quirin*. The Court ruled that the jurisdiction of military commissions could extend to persons accused of "unlawful belligerency."[75] The Court characterized the *Milligan* case as one involving a nonbelligerent. And since *Quirin* involved prisoners who *admitted* that they were unlawful belligerents, the *Milligan* precedent did not apply.[76] Under the rationale of *Quirin*, then, anyone who is accused of and admits to being an unlawful belligerent can be deprived of trial by jury. Even an American citizen arrested on American soil could be tried and presumably executed by U.S. military authorities as long as he is charged and convicted of "unlawful belligerency."

The *Quirin* ruling is unpersuasive for two reasons. First, the attempt to distinguish *Milligan* is unconvincing. The charges that were leveled against Milligan were quite serious. He was accused of treasonous acts—spying and essentially levying war against the U.S. military. The Supreme Court did not elaborate on the nature of the charges against Milligan because it held that the accused would get a jury trial regardless. It was disingenuous of the *Quirin* Court to distinguish *Milligan* on the ground that the *Milligan* Court

---

[74]See Louis Fisher, Nazi Saboteurs on Trial 46 (2003).

[75]Quirin, 317 U.S. at 36–38, 48.

[76]*Id.* at 45.

had not been confronted with crimes that were subject to the laws of war. That claim is unsupported by the record and is plainly wrong.

Second, and more fundamentally, the *Quirin* ruling cannot be reconciled with the constitutional guarantee of trial by jury. The Court's reasoning in *Quirin* is defective because it is circular: The government informs the prisoner that he is not entitled to a trial by jury because he is an unlawful combatant. The prisoner denies the charge and demands his constitutional rights so that he can establish his innocence. The government responds by diverting the case to a military tribunal because the charges subject the accused to the laws of war. A subsequent conviction by the tribunal supposedly confirms the fact that the case was properly diverted outside of the civilian court system in the first place. Of course, that is like saying that a convicted rapist should not be allowed to conduct an independent DNA test on the evidence in his case by virtue of his conviction. As Justice Scalia has noted, the *Quirin* ruling was not the Supreme Court's "finest hour."[77]

In sum, the issue is not whether war crimes can be perpetrated on U.S. soil. They most certainly can be. Rather, the issue is what are the constitutional procedures governing the investigation and prosecution of such events. The constitutional text is clear: If the government is going to level charges, prosecute, and possibly execute a person, it must proceed according to the mode of trial set forth in the Bill of Rights—trial by jury.

## B. Military Trials Outside American Borders

There is no easy answer to the question of whether the government can use military commissions to prosecute and execute foreign nationals who are accused of war crimes. There is historical support for military commissions in such circumstances. After World War II, for example, some German and Japanese military officials were tried for war crimes before military tribunals.[78] History, however, is no substitute for constitutionality.

Historical precedents aside, there is some force to the argument that foreigners that have never set foot on American soil have no standing to demand the constitutional safeguards that are set forth

---

[77]Hamdi v. Rumsfeld, 124 S. Ct. 2633, 2669 (2004) (Scalia, J., dissenting).
[78]Johnson v. Eisentrager, 339 U.S. 763 (1950); see In re Yamashita 327 U.S. 1 (1946).

in the American Constitution.[79] But that argument suffers from a questionable premise. A proper inquiry would begin with an examination of the source of whatever power the president is claiming and only then determine the implications for the rights of individual persons. Justice Hugo Black expressed this point well in *Reid v. Covert*[80]: "The United States [government] is entirely a creature of the Constitution. Its power and authority have no other source. It can act only in accordance with all of the limitations imposed by the Constitution."[81] If there are any exceptions to that proposition, then surely the proponents of military commissions must bear the burden of persuasion on the matter. What is their source of authority to prosecute and execute persons with procedures that are nowhere mentioned in the Constitution? If the safeguards that are set forth in the Bill of Rights do not apply, what limits on presidential power exist—and what is their source? Can the president set up a system of summary trials to be followed by firing squads? Can Congress establish such procedures? If such procedures would be illegal, *why* would they be illegal?

Given the nature of the American Constitution and the clear language of the jury trial provisions, the most sensible interpretation would seem to be that the government does not have the power to create an alternative system of justice by which it can try and execute individuals. The Constitution does reference a military court system, but that system only applies to members of the U.S. military. If Congress could, in its discretion, expand the jurisdiction of those courts to others, the jury trial guarantee would be worth very little.

It does not necessarily follow that every single rule of procedure pertaining to civilian jury trials must be extended to a foreign national who is accused of war crimes. Indeed, Congress would be well-advised to consider the enactment of relaxed rules that would apply in special circumstances. An extended discussion of such rules is beyond the scope of this article, but once the most basic guarantees—the right to an indictment, right to a public jury trial, right to confront witnesses and so forth—are honored by the government, the burden of persuasion could fairly be shifted to the accused to demonstrate that a statutory or judge-made rule is illegal or unjust.

---

[79]See Eisentrager, 339 U.S. at 777.

[80]354 U.S. 1 (1957).

[81]*Id.* at 6.

## VIII. Conclusion

At this juncture, no one knows how long America's war on the al-Qaeda terrorist network will last. It may well turn into America's longest war. Whatever the ultimate timeline turns out to be, there can be little doubt that an important phase of the conflict has just concluded. President Bush sought sweeping powers pursuant to his commander-in-chief authority, but that move was decisively rebuffed by the Supreme Court in the "enemy combatant" cases.

As new controversies arise, it will be crucially important for the judiciary not to conflate separate and distinct legal issues. To properly resolve the tension between power and liberty in wartime, the courts must begin with three threshold questions: (1) What is the status of the individual—is he a citizen, illegal immigrant, or nonresident alien? (2) Where did capture or seizure take place—on American soil or an overseas battlefield? (3) What punishment does the government seek to impose—deportation, detention, or execution? The parameters of the government's power can vary depending upon the answers to those questions.

The modern threat to the Constitution and individual liberty comes not only from terrorists, but also from well-meaning policymakers and intellectuals who opt for expediency and subterfuge over candor and accountability. Almost no one seeks a formal modification of the Constitution, but there is no shortage of people who seem to think it is necessary to improvise constitutional procedures during wartime. The legal maxim, *inter arma silent leges*, is invoked to rationalize the improvisation. As Justice Scalia noted in his *Hamdi* dissent, the American Constitution anticipates the exigencies of war and accommodates them *consistent with certain safeguards and democratic principles*.[82] If wartime can be used as an excuse to weaken those safeguards and principles, which are the "supreme law of the land," they are likely to be frittered away.[83] Thus, anyone who prizes ordered liberty must be vigilant against those who threaten it—some are foreign; some are domestic.

---

[82]See Hamdi, 124 S. Ct. at 2674 (Scalia, J., dissenting).

[83]History does not support the notion that America will "swing back toward liberty once the war is over." The state may surrender some of its wartime powers at the conclusion of the conflict, but it typically retains more power than when the war began. That "ratchet effect" means that our liberties will steadily diminish over the long term. See James Bovard, Terrorism and Tyranny (2003); Paul Craig Roberts and Lawrence Stratton, The Tyranny of Good Intentions (2000); Robert Higgs, Crisis and Leviathan: Critical Episodes in the Growth of American Government (1989).

# Executive and Judicial Overreaction in the Guantanamo Cases

*Neal K. Katyal*

## I. Introduction

The U.S. Supreme Court in *Rasul v. Bush*[1] and *Al-Odah v. United States*[2] held that detainees at Guantanamo Bay may challenge their detentions via writs of habeas corpus. Justice Stevens' majority opinion held that "the federal courts have jurisdiction to determine the legality of the Executive's potentially indefinite detention of individuals who claim to be wholly innocent of wrongdoing."[3] This holding is potentially unbounded, perhaps enabling someone detained at Kandahar or even Diego Garcia to challenge his detention via the great writ. It appears to be a striking break from the 1950 *Johnson v. Eisentrager*[4] decision, which strongly intimated that no such lawsuits were possible. How did we go from a constitutional regime where no alien outside of the United States could challenge his detention to one in which virtually anyone may be able to do so?

One answer may be that the executive branch overplayed its hand in these cases. By asserting that it had the ability to build an offshore facility to evade judicial review, do what it wanted at that facility to detainees under the auspices of the commander-in-chief power, and keep the entire process (including its legal opinions) secret, the executive branch appears to have provoked a judicial backlash. The president is far more fettered now than he has ever been. The country, according to the administration's own argument, is now weaker than before June 28, 2004, because generalist courts will be interjecting themselves into military operations.

[1] Rasul v. Bush, 124 S. Ct. 2686 (2004).
[2] Al-Odah v. United States, 124 S. Ct. 2686 (2004).
[3] Rasul, 124 S. Ct. at 2699.
[4] 339 U.S. 763 (1950).

This jurisprudential backlash is not something unknown to recent presidencies. In the most dramatic contemporary example, President Clinton's ungrounded claims of executive privilege in the Lewinsky investigation had a similar effect, spurring the creation of precedent that was hostile to the concept of executive privilege.[5] President Clinton's arguments about the solemnity of executive secrecy and the lofty principle at stake for all presidents boomeranged—leading future presidents to inherit a world with less executive privilege.[6]

The Bush administration took the sporadically undisciplined constitutional claims of President Clinton and elevated them into an entire legal strategy built on executive supremacy and relentless secrecy. In the process, the administration obscured some of the good arguments it actually had against the position taken by the detainees in the *Rasul* and *Al-Odah* cases. This essay will begin by outlining what those arguments were, and will then discuss implications of the Guantanamo decisions for the future.

## II. The Detention Cases

### A. The Astonishing Breadth of Rasul

*Rasul* and *Al-Odah* centered around the question of whether federal courts have jurisdiction to review challenges by "foreign nationals captured abroad in connection with hostilities and incarcerated at the Guantanamo Bay Naval Base, Cuba."[7] In finding that such jurisdiction exists, Justice Stevens' opinion for the Court distinguished away the leading case on the subject, *Johnson v. Eisentrager*.[8] In *Eisentrager*, the Court's rather confused holding suggested that federal courts lacked jurisdiction to review habeas petitions by "21 German citizens who had been captured by U.S. forces in China, tried and convicted of war crimes by an American military commission headquartered in Nanking, and incarcerated in the Landsberg Prison in occupied Germany."[9] *Rasul* eviscerates that holding, leading Justice

---

[5]See In re Grand Jury Proceedings, 5 F. Supp. 2d 21 (D.D.C. 1998), aff'd in part, rev'd in part sub nom. In Re Lindsey, 158 F.3d 1263 (D.C. Cir. 1998).

[6]Neal Katyal, The Public and Private Lives of Presidents, 8 Wm. & Mary Bill Rts. J. 677 (2000) (making this argument).

[7]Rasul, 124 S. Ct. at 2690.

[8]339 U.S. 763 (1950).

[9]Rasul, 124 S. Ct. at 2693 (discussing *Eisentrager*).

Scalia in his dissent to lament that "[t]oday's opinion, and today's opinion alone, overrules *Eisentrager*; today's opinion, and today's opinion alone, extends the habeas statute."[10]

To understand just how broad the *Rasul* holding is, it is worth reflecting back on the arguments made on behalf of the Guantanamo detainees. The detainees' lawyers did not emphasize that *Eisentrager* was overruled by subsequent cases, or contend that it should be overruled by this Supreme Court. Instead, they justified the *Eisentrager* result[11]: "[I]t is apparent that the Court *sensibly* concluded in *Johnson* [*v. Eisentrager* ] that war criminals tried, convicted, and sentenced by a lawful commission, whose procedural protections were not the subject of a complaint, were not 'due' any additional process in a civilian court; certainly they could not claim a fifth amendment right to be free from military trial."[12] In effect, they argued that *Eisentrager* only barred habeas relief of detainees who received process in a military tribunal, and that it did not bar such relief when asserted by a detainee who has had no process at all.

The detainees' lawyers also distinguished *Eisentrager* in a second way, arguing that the decision only applied outside of U. S. territory. The detainees told the Supreme Court that Guantanamo was different from other areas of the globe because it is U.S. soil: "As the United States Navy declares on its internet site, Guantanamo 'for all practical purposes, is American territory.' Although Cuba retains

---

[10] *Id.* at 2706 (Scalia, J., dissenting).

[11] See, e.g., Petition for Writ of Certiorari at 10, Rasul v. Bush, 124 S. Ct. 2686 (2004) (No. 03-334) ("It is one thing to hold that war criminals . . . cannot seek further review in a civilian court. It is quite another to extend that holding to people who have never been charged or afforded any process."); *id.* at 14 ("Unlike Petitioners, the prisoners seeking habeas relief in *Johnson* [*v. Eisentrager*] were convicted war criminals."); Petitioners' Brief on the Merits at 26, Al-Odah v. United States, 124 S. Ct. 2686 (2004) (No. 03-343) ("The Court in *Eisentrager* did not adjudicate—nor is there any reason to suppose it intended to pass upon—the rights of nonresident aliens who are nationals of countries friendly to the United States and who have never been charged, let alone convicted by a court or military tribunal."); Petitioners' Brief on the Merits at 40, Rasul v. Bush, 124 S. Ct. 2686 (2004) (No. 03-334) ("Just as the habeas statute gave the Court the power to act in *Johnson*, the statute provides the power to act in this case; but the very factors that called for restraint in *Johnson* are notable here for their absence, and now call for the opposite result.").

[12] Petition for Certiorari at 17, Rasul v. Bush, 124 S. Ct. 2686 (2004) (No. 03-334) (emphasis added).

'ultimate' sovereignty, it has no current sovereignty over Guantanamo. Its laws do not apply and its courts have no jurisdiction."[13]

But the Supreme Court pointedly refused to accept these two distinctions. It first declined to ground its holding in the arguments of Rasul and al-Odah that they were differently situated than the petitioners in *Eisentrager* because they had received no military process. The outset of the Court's opinion genuflected to the fact that petitioners "are not nationals of countries at war with the United States, and they deny that they have engaged in or plotted acts of aggression against the United States; they have never been afforded access to any tribunal, much less charged with and convicted of wrongdoing; and for more than two years they have been imprisoned in territory over which the United States exercises exclusive jurisdiction and control."[14] But, having made that factual observation, the Court carefully made sure that this was not the basis for its holding, finding instead that:

> Not only are petitioners differently situated from the *Eisentrager* detainees, but the Court in *Eisentrager* made quite clear that all six of the facts critical to its disposition were relevant only to the question of the prisoners' *constitutional* entitlement to habeas corpus. The Court had far less to say on the question of the petitioners' *statutory* entitlement to habeas review. . . .
>
> . . . .
>
> . . . Because subsequent decisions of this Court have filled the statutory gap that had occasioned *Eisentrager*'s resort to "fundamentals," persons detained outside the territorial jurisdiction of any federal court no longer need rely on the Constitution as the source of their right to federal habeas review.[15]

---

[13] Petitioners' Brief on the Merits at 34, Al-Odah v. United States, 124 S. Ct. 2686 (2004) (No. 03-343); see also Petitioners' Brief on the Merits at 45, Rasul v. Bush, 124 S. Ct. 2686 (2004) (No. 03-334) ("Cuba's laws are wholly ineffectual in Guantanamo. United States governance, now entering its second century, is potentially permanent and in no way dependent on the wishes or consent of the Cuban government.").

[14] Rasul, 124 S. Ct. at 2693.

[15] *Id.* at 2693, 2695 (citations omitted).

The Court went on to point out that *Braden v. 30th Judicial Circuit Court of Kentucky*[16] explicitly held that, as a statutory matter, habeas corpus writs can be issued even when there is no federal district court in the immediate area, as long as "the custodian can be reached by service of process."[17]

Justice Stevens' opinion for the Court also did not confine its holding by claiming that Guantanamo is U.S. soil. To the contrary, the holding of *Rasul*, as set out in the first paragraph of this essay, is not restricted by geography or specific to Guantanamo in some other way. Again, Part IV of the Court's opinion starts the discussion by looking like it will announce such restrictions (stating that Guantanamo is an area in which "the United States exercises 'complete jurisdiction and control'"),[18] but the Court then proceeds to do little with that point. (Indeed, that fact alone would not distinguish Guantanamo Bay from conquered Kandahar or other battlefield locales.) Once more, Justice Scalia is prompted to write:

> Part IV of the Court's opinion dealing with the status of Guantanamo Bay is a puzzlement. The Court might have made an effort (a vain one, as I shall discuss) to distinguish *Eisentrager* on the basis of a difference between the status of Landsberg Prison in Germany and Guantanamo Bay Naval Base. But Part III flatly rejected such an approach . . . . Once that has been said, the status of Guantanamo Bay is entirely irrelevant to the issue here.[19]

The breadth of the majority's opinion takes on additional meaning not only by its comparison to the relatively restrained arguments of the detainees, but also by assessing it alongside the opinion concurring in the judgment filed by Justice Kennedy. Speaking only for himself, Justice Kennedy stated that he would reach the same result as the majority by accepting the two distinctions of the petitioners, that Guantanamo is different from other areas around the globe and that the detainees, unlike those in *Eisentrager*, had no resort to military process:

---

[16] 410 U.S. 484 (1973).

[17] *Id.* at 495.

[18] Rasul, 124 S. Ct. at 2696.

[19] *Id.* at 2707 (Scalia, J., dissenting).

> [T]he Court's approach is not a plausible reading of *Braden* or *Johnson v. Eisentrager*. In my view, the correct course is to follow the framework of *Eisentrager*. . . . The facts here are distinguishable from those in *Eisentrager* in two critical ways, leading to the conclusion that a federal court may entertain the petitions. First, Guantanamo Bay is in every practical respect a United States territory, and it is one far removed from any hostilities . . . . The second critical set of facts is that the detainees at Guantanamo Bay are being held indefinitely, and without benefit of any legal proceeding to determine their status. In *Eisentrager*, the prisoners were tried and convicted by a military commission . . . .
>
> . . . .
>
> . . . In light of the status of Guantanamo Bay and the indefinite pretrial detention of the detainees, I would hold that federal-court jurisdiction is permitted in these cases. This approach would avoid creating automatic statutory authority to adjudicate the claims of persons located outside the United States, and remains true to the reasoning of *Eisentrager*.[20]

But the majority opinion never confined itself in any of these ways, despite being urged to do so not only by their colleagues, but also by the detainees themselves. For the coup de grâce is this remarkable footnote from the *Rasul* majority:

> Petitioners' allegations—that, although they have engaged neither in combat nor in acts of terrorism against the United States, they have been held in Executive detention for more than two years in territory subject to the long-term, exclusive jurisdiction and control of the United States, without access to counsel and without being charged with any wrongdoing—unquestionably describe "custody in violation of the Constitution or laws or treaties of the United States." 28 U.S.C. § 2241(c)(3). Cf. United States v. Verdugo-Urquidez, 494 U.S. 259, 277–78 (1990) (Kennedy, J., concurring), and cases cited therein.[21]

Without briefing or oral argument, the Court may have cut back on an argument the executive branch has held in its back pocket for

---

[20] *Id.* at 2699, 2700, 2701 (Kennedy, J., concurring).

[21] *Id.* at 2698 n.15.

many years: Even if someone has the power to ask for a writ of habeas corpus, they do not have a substantive claim because the Constitution does not apply extraterritorially.[22] The sharp reference to Justice Kennedy's *Verdugo* concurrence underscores the point— that certain fundamental rights may apply abroad. In recent days, the government has advanced a novel theory that this *Rasul* footnote is about "treaties" or "laws," but the problem with that interpretation is that the Court cited not an opinion about the extraterritoriality of statutes or treaties, but rather Justice Kennedy's seminal opinion on the extraterritoriality of the *Constitution*.

In sum, the Court issued an unconfined holding that extends the rights of habeas corpus far beyond even what the detainees had requested. The majority refused to cabin its holding to nonmilitary tribunal detainees or to those only at Guantanamo. And the justices may have tipped their hands about a pivotal issue, the extraterritorial application of the Constitution to the detainees. But is any of this surprising, when the administration stood before the Court asking for their blessing in turning Guantanamo Bay into a legal black hole, where no law applied and no court would review what they were doing to the detainees at any moment, even if the government decided to trump up capital offenses and summarily execute them? Against this backdrop, it is worth asking whether, had the administration pressed a more narrow claim, it would have left itself and future presidents in a far better position.

## B. The More Plausible Argument Against the Detainees

Instead of pushing forth its unbridled claim for executive supremacy, the administration could have made a far more plausible case by distinguishing between types of detainees. One can side with the administration's broad proposition, that the Commander-in-Chief Clause[23] gives it the power to detain people who are threats to the peace, but nevertheless believe that when the president takes the

---

[22] See, e.g., Brief for the Respondents in Opposition to Petition for Writ of Certiorari at 13, Rasul v. Bush, 124 S. Ct. 2686 (2004) (No. 03-334) ("This Court has repeatedly cited *Eisentrager* as a seminal decision defining the application of the Constitution to *all* aliens abroad, not simply *enemy* aliens .... In *Zadvydas*, the Court—again pointing to *Eisentrager*—stated that '[i]t is well established that certain constitutional protections available to persons inside the United States are unavailable to aliens outside of our geographic borders.' ").

[23] U.S. Const. art. II, § 2, cl. 1.

further step to actually try people for violations, civil process exists to review the circumstances under which those trials will take place. The case for civilian jurisdiction should be at its apogee once the president decides to cross the threshold from detention and seeks an adjudication of guilt and innocence in a calculated and deliberate fashion. Had the administration acknowledged that the case for jurisdiction for those facing tribunals stands on a different, and stronger, footing than the *Rasul* and *al-Odah* detainees, it may not have provoked the broad holding it got.

In the Declaration of Independence, our Founders penned, among their charges against King George, that "[h]e has affected to render the Military independent of and superior to the Civil Power"; "depriv[ed] us, in many Cases, of the benefits of trial by jury"; "made Judges dependent on his Will alone"; and "transport[ed] us beyond Seas to be tried for pretended Offences."[24]

There was a way to maintain fidelity to these bedrock constitutional principles without forcing all detentions to be managed by the federal courts. For in the theatre of war, the president does not need congressional permission to decide how and when, within the laws of war, to take custody of enemy combatants upon their capture or surrender for the purpose of detention until the war ends and repatriation is possible. That is implicit in the commander-in-chief function itself. The moment the president ventures beyond detaining enemy combatants as war prisoners to actually adjudicating their guilt and meting out punishment, however, he really has moved outside the perimeter of his role as commander-in-chief. The fact that the president wears military garb cannot obscure the fact that he is now pursuing a different goal—assessing guilt and meting out retrospective justice rather than waging war.

This type of limited argument also would have explained why the Supreme Court has required civilian courts to exercise jurisdiction over military commissions. There are any number of examples, drawn from cases involving American civilians, American servicemen, and enemy belligerents. In the case of American civilians, the Court has expansive jurisdiction not only to question the legal authority and power of military tribunals, but also to hear Bill of

[24] The Declaration of Independence para. 11, 20, 21 (U.S. 1776).

Rights challenges.[25] In the case of American servicemen, moreover, the Court has long held that, on habeas, the lawful power of tribunals can be challenged.[26] Habeas is permissible to examine whether the tribunal: (1) is legally constituted; (2) has personal jurisdiction over the accused; and (3) has subject-matter jurisdiction to hear the offense charged.[27]

In the case of enemy belligerents, *Ex parte Quirin*[28] held that "neither the Proclamation nor the fact that they are enemy aliens forecloses consideration by the courts of petitioners' contentions that the Constitution and laws of the United States constitutionally enacted forbid their trial by military commission."[29] *Quirin* in fact declined to hold that enemy aliens lacked the ability to file habeas petitions, even though Attorney General Biddle opened his argument with that claim.[30] Moreover, the *Quirin* Court never held, contrary to the administration's claims, that the basis for jurisdiction was that the saboteurs decided to directly threaten the United States by landing on its shores instead of remaining abroad. To do so would have meant *rewarding* with special rights those who had infiltrated American soil. As enemy belligerents, they were not entitled to Fifth and Sixth Amendment rights.[31] Rather, *Quirin* offered the saboteurs the same habeas rights that had been historically extended to American servicemen.[32]

Similarly, in *In re Yamashita*,[33] the Court permitted a convicted enemy belligerent, a Japanese army general, to file a habeas petition:

[25] See Ex parte Milligan, 71 U.S. 2 (1866).

[26] See In re Grimley, 137 U.S. 147, 150 (1890) ("It cannot be doubted that the civil courts may in any case inquire into the jurisdiction of a court-martial, and . . . may discharge him from the sentence."). *Hamdi* embraces a similar standard for review. See text accompanying footnote 57 *infra*.

[27] Hiatt v. Brown, 339 U.S. 103, 111 (1950).

[28] 317 U.S. 1 (1942).

[29] *Id.* at 25.

[30] See *id.* at 11 (reprinting argument).

[31] *Id.* at 45.

[32] See *id.* at 48 (concluding that the president's "Order convening the Commission was a lawful order and that the Commission was lawfully constituted" and that "Charge I . . . alleged an offense which the President is authorized to order tried by military commission.").

[33] 327 U.S. 1 (1946) (citations omitted).

> [W]e held in *Ex parte Quirin,* as we hold now, that Congress
> .... has not foreclosed their right to contend that the Consti-
> tution or laws of the United States withhold authority to
> proceed with the trial. It has not withdrawn, and the Execu-
> tive ... could not, unless there was suspension of the writ,
> withdraw from the courts the duty and power to make such
> inquiry into the authority of the commission as may be made
> by habeas corpus.[34]

Today, some of those who face military commissions at Guantanamo Bay may stand in the same procedural position as General
Yamashita, in that they may be labeled "enemy aliens" who contend
that the "Constitution or laws" "withhold authority to proceed"
with their trials. The Court's consideration of the petitioners' claims
in *Quirin* and *Yamashita* stemmed not from any right gained by
sneaking into America or from the fact that Yamashita was in territory that was subsequently regained by the United States. Rather,
jurisdiction stemmed from the fundamental principle recognized in
cases from *Grimley* to *Milligan* and *Yamashita* to *Quirin*: We are a
nation bound by law and claim no power to punish except that
permitted by law.

To be sure, there was language in the subsequent *Eisentrager* decision that appeared to cut back on these rights of habeas corpus for
enemy aliens. While *Quirin* and *Yamashita* recognized that belligerents had the same right to challenge the lawfulness of a tribunal as
American service members, *Eisentrager* appeared to decline to extend
the Bill of Rights to extraterritorial enemy aliens. As Part III of
*Eisentrager* explained, if the Fifth Amendment denied the military
tribunal personal jurisdiction over the petitioners, then the Sixth
Amendment would deny it to district courts, leaving the petitioners
completely unpunished.[35]

---

[34] *Id.* at 9. See also *id.* at 30 (Murphy, J., dissenting) ("This Court fortunately has
taken the first and most important step toward insuring the supremacy of law ....
Jurisdiction properly has been asserted to inquire 'into the cause of restraint of liberty'
of such a person. 28 U.S.C. § 452. Thus the obnoxious doctrine asserted by the
government in this case, to the effect that restraints of liberty resulting from military
trials of war criminals are political matters completely outside the arena of judicial
review, has been rejected fully and unquestionably.").

[35] Johnson v. Eisentrager, 339 U.S. 763, 782-83 (1950).

And so the U.S. government got seduced into over-reading *Eisentrager*. After all, *Eisentrager* did not end at Part III. In Part IV the Court reached the merits of the military commission's legality. In so doing, it quoted *Yamashita*'s key language, that "'[w]e consider here only the lawful power of the commission to try the petitioner for the offense charged.'"[36] This distinction between "lawful power" and Bill-of-Rights challenges undergirds the Court's heavy focus in Part II on the fact that Yamashita's case was brought from American territory.[37] In Parts II and III, the Court concerned itself with individual rights, in particular the Fifth and Sixth Amendments.[38] But the Court in Part IV at no point invoked this discussion to justify rejection of the structural and jurisdictional challenges to the tribunals themselves. To the contrary, it quoted the foundational language from *Yamashita* where the Court held that it must consider such claims on habeas.

*Eisentrager*'s approach in Part IV mirrored the system of military justice at the time, where despite the uncertainty about what Fifth and Sixth Amendment rights existed, habeas review was always present to examine whether the tribunals had "lawful power," meaning whether they were properly constituted and had personal and subject-matter jurisdiction.[39] Ever since *Milligan*'s warning,[40] those latter inquiries have been the foundational questions that every Court has reached. This reading of *Eisentrager* also accords with the way the Court treated other claims by enemy aliens at the time.[41]

---

[36]*Id.* at 787 (quoting In re Yamashita, 327 U.S. 1, 8 (1950)).

[37]Eisentrager, 339 U.S. at 780.

[38]See, e.g., *id.* at 782–85.

[39]See Hiatt v. Brown, 339 U.S. 103, 111 (1950); In re Grimley, 137 U.S. 147, 150 (1890); Reaves v. Ainsworth, 219 U.S. 296, 304 (1911).

[40]See Ex parte Milligan, 71 U.S. 2, 124–25 (1866) (criticizing the view that a military commander can "punish all persons, as he thinks right and proper, without fixed or certain rules" because "if true, republican government is a failure, and there is an end of liberty regulated by law" and because the principle "destroys every guarantee of the Constitution, and effectually renders the military independent of and superior to the civil power.") (internal quotation omitted).

[41]For example, in *Knauff v. Shaughnessy*, 338 U.S. 537 (1950), the Court exercised jurisdiction over a claim made by an alien enemy "war bride" whom the attorney general detained at Ellis Island without a hearing. Despite the fact that the detainee was born in Germany and labeled a security threat by the attorney general, and despite the fact that she had not been admitted into the United States, the Court found jurisdiction to examine, on the merits, her claim that the president lacked the constitutional power to summarily exclude her. *Id.* at 542–44.

It is by no means impossible to read *Eisentrager* to stand for more than this, but, as we pointed out in our amicus curiae (friend-of-the-court) brief,[42] such a reading would be in considerable tension with the Court's unbroken treatment of challenges to the jurisdiction and composition of military tribunals. A contrary interpretation of the decision, moreover, would also be in tension with *Eisentrager's* recognition that those claiming citizenship were entitled to habeas review to "assure fair hearing of [their] claims to citizenship."[43] If person A is entitled to habeas to decide whether she is a citizen (because being a citizen is so jurisdictionally important), then, so too, should person B receive a habeas hearing to decide whether she is an enemy belligerent (since that status is of equivalent jurisdictional importance.)

Such a reading of *Eisentrager* also squares with the unusual choice by Eisentrager's counsel—a choice that went unmentioned by the parties in *Rasul* and *Al-Odah*—to assert only one type of habeas jurisdiction, that for "'being a citizen of a foreign state and domiciled therein . . . in custody for an act done or omitted under any alleged . . . order or sanction of any foreign state, or under order thereof, the validity and effect of which depend upon the law of nations.'"[44] Lothar Eisentrager thus stood in a different position from Tomoyuki Yamashita, for Yamashita asserted that his trial violated the Constitution or laws of the United States under 28 U.S.C. § 2241(c)(3).[45]

As such, Eisentrager could not benefit from, and the Court did not confront the possible tension with, *Yamashita's* foundational claim. *Yamashita* built on the bedrock of *Ex parte McCardle*,[46] where the Supreme Court observed that the habeas corpus statute "is of the most comprehensive character. It brings within the habeas corpus

---

[42] Brief of Amicus Curiae Military Attorneys Assigned to the Defense in the Office of Military Commissions, Al-Odah v. United States, 124 S. Ct. 2686 (2004) (No. 03-343) available at http://www.law.georgetown.edu/faculty/nkk/publications.html# Chapters.

[43] Johnson v. Eisentrager, 339 U.S. 763, 769 (1950).

[44] 28 U.S.C. § 2241 (c)(4). See also Brief for Respondent at 2, Johnson v. Eisentrager, 339 U.S. 763 (1950) (No. 306) (reprinting statute involved and only reprinting subsections (a) and (c)(4)); *id.* at 24–26 (making argument based solely on subsection (c)(4)).

[45] See *supra* note 34 and accompanying text.

[46] 73 U.S. (6 Wall.) 318, 325–26 (1867).

jurisdiction of every court and of every judge every possible case of deprivation of liberty contrary to the National Constitution, treaties, or law. It is impossible to widen this jurisdiction."[47] Mr. Eisentrager's decision to assert only jurisdiction predicated on "the law of nations" led the Supreme Court to analogize his claim to the private-law disputes the New York courts rejected during the war of 1812.[48] But that jurisdictional mistake cannot preclude individuals who face military commissions from asserting the (c)(3) claim that Yamashita and others used based on the Constitution or laws of the United States.

The government in the detention cases also ignored other limitations in *Eisentrager*, such as the Court's emphasis on the fact that the petitioners had been "captured outside of our territory and there held in military custody as a prisoner of war."[49] Strong justification exists for this holding, as the president's hands should not be tied on the battlefield, particularly when the territory is under the control of many nations. It would have been entirely reasonable for the government to defend this position, pointing out, for example, that an international tribunal for former president Saddam Hussein in Iraq would not be a matter that the American courts could review. The administration could have defended this principle had they put it forth in a circumscribed way, acknowledging that the situation shifts when justice is administered off the battlefield, particularly in those places where no other nation offers legal remedies.[50] In those areas, the fear of interfering with battlefield operations is at its nadir. The likelihood that the decisions are being made on the spur of the moment in the midst of crisis drops precipitously, while the

---

[47] *Id.* at 326–27.

[48] See Johnson v. Eisentrager, 339 U.S. 763, 776–77 (1950) (citing authorities).

[49] *Id.* at 777.

[50] Unlike *Eisentrager*, where the government claimed "enemy aliens in enemy lands are not subject to duties under the American Constitution and laws, and . . . like Englishmen in England, or Frenchmen in France, they must look to the rights and remedies open to them under their country's present laws and government," Brief of United States at 67, Johnson v. Eisentrager, 339 U.S. 763 (1950) (No. 306), there appears to be no inclination whatsoever to let Cuban law apply to those facing military tribunals. Deference to local practices (as in Puerto Rico or the Philippines, see Balzac v. Porto Rico, 258 U.S. 298 (1922); Dorr v. United States, 195 U.S. 138 (1904)) is not compatible with American policy.

likelihood that the key decisions are being made in the continental United States increases.[51]

The government's argument in the detention cases, for all those held at Guantanamo, had no logical stopping point. If there were no right to civilian review, the government would be free to conduct sham trials and condemn to death those who do nothing more than pray to Allah.[52] The president's claim was for the absence of any legal restraint whatsoever on the actions of the executive branch at Guantanamo, commensurate with absolute duties and subjugation for those held there.

In this sense, the government's reading of *Eisentrager* was both under- and over-inclusive. Its reading would have extended habeas rights to those, such as the Nazi saboteurs in *Quirin*, who lacked any connection to this country beyond a surreptitious entrance, but denied habeas to those who have done far less (and perhaps no) damage to American interests. The upshot of *Rasul* is to say that the Constitution cannot be contorted into this senseless position without doing grave damage to the rule of law.

In sum, the executive branch in the detention cases missed an opportunity to craft a limited argument for review. Instead of emphasizing the legal black hole, they could have said that the law, and civilian review, apply to trials that take place at Guantanamo Bay. This claim conceivably may have been in tension with some loose language in *Eisentrager*, but it was a far more plausible reading of civil/military court relationships than the wallop the administration put forth. The result of the administration's legal extremism is a counter-wallop from the justices, and one that binds future presidents in precisely the one area where they should not be easily shackled—when they believe that detentions are necessary to keep the peace.

---

[51] See Brief of United States at 23, Johnson v. Eisentrager, 339 U.S. 763 (1950) (No. 306) (distinguishing cases where courts found habeas jurisdiction over extraterritorial prisons in Lorton and Occoquan, Virginia, by stating that "these institutions were controlled and staffed by District officials").

[52] Were *Eisentrager's* conception of "sovereignty" converted into the wholesale deprivation of liberty that the government asserted, it would directly conflict with U.S. Const. amend. XIII, which reaches not simply "the United States," but also "any place subject to their jurisdiction."

## III. The Future

*Rasul* and *al-Odah* will probably force the government to change a number of things about the way it has handled the treatment of individuals at Guantanamo Bay. But the changes may be resisted by the same forces that pushed for an extremist view of the president's commander-in-chief power. And that resistance will grow as it becomes clearer just how much the Court's decisions left unresolved. Consider, to take just a handful of examples, the timing of judicial review, the proper forum for bringing such lawsuits, the application of the Classified Information Procedures Act[53] and other rules governing sensitive information in the courtroom, the right to counsel, the extraterritorial application of the Constitution, and the applicability of the Geneva Conventions. If the administration continues its boldly aggressive constitutional and legal strategy to exploit every unresolved issue in a contorted way, one can predict with some confidence further defeats in the courtroom. This section will analyze two areas for reform, the annualized detainee review process and the military commissions.

### A. Detainee Review

The specter of judicial review has already forced a number of procedures to be altered, the first of which occurred even before the *Rasul* decision came down, namely, the Pentagon's decision to review detentions annually. This procedure was announced in early March of 2004 on the very day the government's brief in the detention cases was due at the Supreme Court.[54] Perhaps unwittingly, the government wound up making the best case for judicial review— the only process the detainees ever received was when the administration started to fear judicial review.

In the week before June 28, the date the detention cases were decided, the administration offered more details about the procedures for annualized detention review.[55] Having adopted the procedures to try to reassure the Court that some process existed on Guantanamo Bay, the administration then appeared ready to gut

---

[53] 18 U.S.C.A. App. 3 §§ 1–16 (West 2000 & Supp. 2003).

[54] See http://www.defenselink.mil/news/Mar2004/d20040303ar.pdf (draft review procedures).

[55] See Department of Defense Press Release, available at http://www.defenselink.mil/releases/2004/nr20040623-0932.html.

most of the substance from them. They were ramshackle creatures, with no rights to lawyers. Instead, the detainee was expected to plead his case in front of three military officers, with the only support being that of an assistant who was not a lawyer and not trained in the nuances of interrogation statements or the proper examination of such statements for reliability. There was no guarantee that the detainee would have access to complete statements, either the ones he made or those made by others. There was little in the way of specified procedures for these panels. Perhaps most damaging, the Pentagon rules never explained who bore the burden of proof, or for what. What standard would be used for a detainee to be released? Could the government simply say that anyone held in confinement at Guantanamo for two years was likely to be hostile to the United States and preclude everyone from release on that projected hostility? There was absolutely no guidance, making it impossible even for an experienced legal advocate to defend a detainee, let alone someone who lacks such training.

The list of problems extended far beyond even those grave matters. The Pentagon rules permitted the judges to be handpicked by the secretary of the navy, giving rise to the inference that political appointees would be exercising control over the quasi-judicial process. The rules not only permitted, but required, one member of the three-judge panel to be an intelligence officer, despite the pervasive belief that intelligence officers always prefer to keep people detained on the theory that they might one day have useful information. And there was no guarantee that the press could see the proceedings and exercise an independent check on the process. The strong impression left by the procedures was that they were crafted not to do justice, but to whitewash the lack of it.

As of this writing, the administration has not said whether it will alter the pre-June 28 annualized review process. They should. While such a regime might have been thinkable before Abu Ghraib's horrors were broadcast for the world to see (and after the Defense Department kept *that* problem hidden), it has no place in the United States of America today, regardless of whether judicial review exists. At a minimum, a new regime has to specify a set of procedures and burdens of proof. It must, in order to be meaningful at all, permit access to counsel who are trained to understand the problems with translated interrogation statements. If civilian counsel posed logistical and security difficulties, military counsel could be used. With

600 detainees, being staggered over a year, fifty cases would be heard each month, which would translate into a need for about ten judge advocate general officers. Without those ten individuals, or some other group of ten attorneys, the process will look suspect from the get-go.

Furthermore, the actual rules for the review process must be crafted more carefully. Prior statements of the detainee must be provided in full (the so-called "Rule of Completeness") instead of being given piecemeal to the detainee. The background of any detainee statement, including the name and contact information of the translator, must be given to the detainee as well. Cautionary instructions should be given to the panel in cases in which the only evidence offered by the government in favor of continued detention is the interrogation statement of the detainee himself. (It bears noting that the "Tipton Three"—three individuals held at Guantanamo— confessed to being in league with Mohamed Atta. They would still be confined today had it not been for an MI5 record showing that the individuals had never left the country to meet Atta.)[56]

In addition, the Pentagon should use standing court-martial panels to select members of the review boards. Without some sort of ran- domized process for appointing judges, the members of the board will look like a bunch of handpicked rubber-stampers. The require- ment that an intelligence officer be a voting member of the board should be scrapped, and replaced with an intelligence officer who is a nonvoting member. In addition, a psychologist or psychiatrist should be a nonvoting board member on every panel because so much of what these cases will turn on is the behavioral projections of the detainee. The model here is something like a "family advocacy panel," in the military justice system, whereby a security official

---

[56] See David Rose, Revealed: The Full Story of the Guantanamo Britons, The Observer (London), March 14, 2004:

> [The Tipton three] endured three months of solitary confinement in Camp Delta's isolation block last summer after they were wrongly identified by the Americans as having been pictured in a video tape of a meeting in Afghanistan between Osama bin Laden and the leader of the 11 September hijackers Mohamed Atta. Ignoring their protests that they were in Britain at the time, the Americans interrogated them so relentlessly that eventually all three falsely confessed. They were finally saved—at least on this occasion—by MI5, which came up with documentary evidence to show they had not left the UK.

*Id.* at 1.

and a psychiatrist are placed on a board when difficult family-law issues arise. The system I am suggesting would have a security officer (the intelligence official) and a mental health expert integrally involved in the process.

With these types of changes, the detainee review process would appear far more vibrant. Again, my view is that these procedures are not constitutionally compelled, but the Supreme Court appears to disagree. In any event, regardless of judicial oversight, these (or steps like them) are necessary if we want to create a meaningful review process.

### B. The Military Commissions

Military commissions differ from screening and annualized detainee review panels because they do not concern themselves with detention, but rather punishment (including the death penalty). Yet again, instead of adopting a balanced regime that was tailored to the post-September 11 world, the administration went overboard. Three factors explain why the current rules for the military commissions are so shoddy. First, the drafters of the commissions assumed the lack of judicial review: The government attempted to house the military commissions at Guantanamo in an attempt to evade civilian court oversight. Second, low visibility: By stationing the commission locale offshore, hoping to exclude the press, and only applying the commissions to aliens (unlike past commissions in World War II), the government also insulated itself from much political pressure about the commissions and their rules and procedures. And third, secrecy: The government has classified much of what it is doing at Guantanamo, as well as much about the commissions process itself. The mix of low visibility, secrecy, and the lack of judicial review is a recipe for poor decisionmaking, and that is exactly what has happened.

The Supreme Court has now made clear that judicial review applies at Guantanamo, and at least a plurality also appears to accept the proposition from our amicus brief that judicial review exists to ensure that a military tribunal is "appropriately authorized and properly constituted."[57] These developments should force a tremendous rethinking of the way the commissions will operate. In my

---

[57] Hamdi v. Rumsfeld, 124 S. Ct. 2633, 2651 (2004).

view, the entire process for the commissions is flawed from start to finish, from their procedure to their substance to their adjudication. Instead of belaboring the point, I will provide one example from each of these three categories.

Procedurally, consider the rules of evidence. American military law excludes evidence obtained through torture as a prophylactic measure designed to discourage the abuse of prisoners. But the rules for the military commissions offer no such guarantee. Indeed, they may even permit evidence obtained by torture to be introduced into a proceeding without informing the defense counsel or even the commission's judges of the dubious provenance of such evidence.[58] This is a marked departure from American military and civilian law, and one that is particularly troublesome in light of recent disclosures at Abu Ghraib and elsewhere.

Substantively, consider the offenses that are triable by a military commission. While Congress has specifically made available a list of crimes that are triable by a military commission, the Pentagon was not satisfied. Instead, the Pentagon took it upon itself to write a twenty-plus page list of offenses, and purported to define the elements of those offenses as well.[59] This spectacular usurpation of the legislative function is bound to have predictable consequences: offenses are consistently defined in ways that benefit the prosecution. Indeed, the offenses are all defined after the fact, raising the concern that the offenses are defined to fit particular offenders, rather than being demarcated in a sober and evenhanded way.

With respect to adjudication, consider the composition of the commission itself, which is the body that is to function as judge and jury. In an ordinary military court-martial, the members of the panel are selected randomly, like civilian juries. In the military commission process, however, the commission's members and the review board

[58] See Letter from Lieutenant Colonel Sharon A. Shaffer, Lieutenant Commander Charles Swift, Lieutenant Commander Philip Sundel, Major Mark A. Bridges, Major Michael D. Mori, and Neal Katyal to the Honorable John Warner, the Honorable Orrin Hatch, the Honorable Carl Levin, and the Honorable Patrick Leahy, June 1, 2004, available at http://www.law.georgetown.edu/faculty/nkk/publications.html#Chapters.

[59] General Counsel, U.S. Department of Defense, Military Commission Instruction No. 2, Crimes and Elements for Trial by Military Commission (April 30, 2003), available at http://www.dtic.mil/whs/directives/corres/mco/mci2.pdf.

appear to have been handpicked by the leadership of the Pentagon. This creates at least the appearance, if not the reality, of bias within the commission itself. If we are going to hold up the military commissions to the world as an example, not only for their own citizens, but also for our servicemen and servicewomen who may face such trials, it would be a tremendously dangerous step if the commissions were to go forward with handpicked judges.

These are three of many different problems—problems so rampant that they would take a book to be catalogued and detailed in full. But they give a sense of the magnitude of the problem, and suggest that a major overhaul is necessary. Without such changes, the commissions will flatly violate the Constitution as well as American military law, and the federal courts will be compelled to nullify their judgments.

## IV. Conclusion

The Guantanamo cases may be seen as a reaction, indeed an overreaction, to the broad claims the administration put forth in the name of executive power. By asking for complete insulation from judicial review, the administration missed an opportunity to distinguish between types of detainees and put forth a more modest argument. The result is that the federal courts are now going to interject themselves into many different aspects of the detention process. Some of those interjections will be good for the country, such as those involving military commissions, where judicial review will probably be needed to fix a constitutionally dubious plan that has little in common with commissions from past wars. Others might prove to be more destabilizing, such as the possibility of judicial review for ordinary detentions—perhaps even near battlefields.

The Guantanamo cases thus serve as a sober reminder that those who seek to defend the broadest conception of presidential power in the name of national security may do damage to our security as a result. By seeking middle ground, and working within our constitutional tradition, future defenders of the presidency can be more successful in promoting the values and vision of our Founders, including the protection of both life and liberty.

# Art and the Constitution: The Supreme Court and the Rise of the Impressionist School of Constitutional Interpretation

*Jonathan Turley*

## I. Introduction

Since the end of the last Supreme Court term, academic panels and conferences have developed the feel of a freshman art appreciation class as scholars debated the "nuance," "thrust," and "texture" of the recent trilogy of national security cases. *Hamdi v. Rumsfeld,*[1] *Rumsfeld v. Padilla,*[2] and *Rasul v. Bush*[3] were generally viewed as among the most significant national security cases in decades. Yet, well after their release, these opinions are still being examined from every angle. Academics speak of the trilogy as if they are viewing some abstract composition by Wassily Kandinsky, debating different meanings or images that are suggested from different vantage points. Not surprisingly, legal experts who contemplated the same opinions came away with wildly varying interpretations, from clear victories to embarrassing defeats for President Bush.[4] For David Rivkin and Lee Casey, the decisions were a victory and a "significant reaffirmation" of administration policies[5] while David Cole and Neal K. Katyal

---

[1]124 S. Ct. 2633 (2004).

[2]124 S. Ct. 2711 (2004).

[3]124 S. Ct. 2686 (2004).

[4]Editorial, Terror and the Court, Wall Street Journal, June 29, 2004, at A14 (noting that the Associated Press had concluded that the cases were "a setback" and clear defeat for the administration while the *Journal* found them to be "an important victory"); see also Supreme Court Grants Suspected Terrorists Access to US Courts, Frontrunner, June 29, 2004 (quoting diverse interpretations from academics and commentators).

[5]David B. Rivkin Jr. & Lee A. Casey, Bush's Good Day in Court, Washington Post, August 4, 2004, at A19.

viewed the cases as a clear "rejection" of those policies and a repudiation of the administration.[6]

This search for meaning has become an annual ritual for academics due to the Supreme Court's tendency toward increasingly vague and abstract rulings. The decreasing quality and clarity of decisions is in part due to the realities of a long-divided Court.[7] When struggling to maintain a plurality or slim majority, justices will often gloss over core issues to simply deliver a holding that is driven more by its result than its reasoning. But, the *Hamdi*, *Padilla*, and *Rasul* opinions reflect something more than the ambiguous product of compromise decisionmaking. They reveal a fundamental difference in how the Constitution is viewed as an object for judicial interpretation. In many ways, the endeavors of law and art seem to have converged in the interpretation of the Constitution as the Court has moved from more classic to more impressionistic interpretations of constitutional provisions, particularly in the area of national security law.

Like classic art, constitutional interpretation began with a long period of formalism and structure. The Supreme Court favored fairly static interpretations of the Constitution; the text was given determinative emphasis and any interpretative departures from that text were minimized in favor of plain meaning. As the legal profession developed, particularly the teaching academy, classic interpretations became increasingly passé. Academics began to favor more fluid interpretations that gave moral or political theories, rather than the text, greater influence. Where the art community moved toward French Impressionism and ultimately abstract art, the legal community adopted equally impressionistic or abstract approaches to legal interpretation. The text of the Constitution was now viewed as a necessary starting place, but the "true" meaning was now viewed

[6]Jeffrey Smith, Slim Legal Grounds for Torture Memos; Most Scholars Reject Broad View of Executive's Power, Washington Post, July 4, 2004, at A12 (quoting Cole as calling the cases a rejection of the extreme views of the president while Katyal is quoted as interpreting these recent events to mean that "the administration's legal war on terror is utterly repudiated").

[7]See generally Jonathan Turley, Unpacking the Court: The Expansion of the Supreme Court in the Twenty-First Century, 33 Persp. On Pol. Sci. 155 (2004) (discussing the effect of a closely divided court and proposing the expansion of the Supreme Court to nineteen members).

as evolutionary and dynamic. This new genre of legal reasoning released the pent-up creativity of law professors who sought to fashion new truths from old words. Conversely, those academics who favored more structured and clear interpretations were viewed as uncreative oafs, the way that classic painters were viewed after the modern art period began. A professor arguing for a textualist interpretation was tantamount to some paint-by-the-numbers hack filling hotel rooms with faux classics while "theorists" brought the "living" Constitution to life.

Abstract art and constitutional theory share a tendency toward the transcendent. Both often begin with an object but then transcend that object through a process of creative translation. In his famous work on surrealism, "The Surrealist Manifesto," Andre Breton explained that modern artists took from the rational world but then created "an absolute reality, a surreality."[8] In the same fashion, modern legal theory often takes an object—the Constitution or a statute—and then reconstructs that object according to a new preferred reality. Sometimes constitutional provisions remain largely intact but distorted like the limp watches of Salvador Dali's 1931 *Persistence of Memory*—the treatment of the Fourteenth Amendment in *Grutter v. Bollinger*[9] is one such example. Sometimes otherwise clear constitutional provisions are reproduced with a type of intentional blurring or ambiguity as in Edgar Degas' *Ballet Dancers*—the treatment of the First Amendment in *Virginia v. Black*[10] has such Degas elements. Other times, provisions are reconstructed from clear text into something different by severing or ignoring clauses as in a cubist piece by Pablo Picasso—the treatment of the Fourth

---

[8]Andre Breton, Manifestoes of Surrealism 14 (1969); see also Jennifer Mundy, Surrealism: Desire Unbound (2003); H.H. Arnason, History of Modern Art 271 (3d ed. 1986).

[9]539 U.S. 306, 342 (2003) (acknowledging the demands of the Fourteenth Amendment to "do away with all governmentally imposed discrimination based on race" but then allowing such race-conscious admissions for roughly twenty-five years more); see Roger Pilon, Principle and Policy in Public University Admissions: Grutter v. Bollinger and Gratz v. Bollinger, 2002–2003 Cato Sup. Ct. Rev. 43 (2003).

[10]538 U.S. 343 (2003); see also Steven J. Heyman, Nideological Conflict and the First Amendment, 78 Chi.-Kent L. Rev. 531, 599 (2003) (noting that the decision allowing state bans on cross burning was a "retreat[] from the rigid formalism of [the Court's decision in] R.A.V"); James L. Swanson, Unholy Fire: Cross-Burning, Symbolic Speech, and the First Amendment in Virginia v. Black, 2002–2003 Cato Sup. Ct. Rev. 81 (2003).

Amendment in *Terry v. Ohio*[11] or *Board of Education v. Earls*[12] reveal such cubist influences.[13] While the image changes, the impressionist and abstract legal artists all strive for a new constitutional reality, a constitutional surreality.

I confess to harboring a love for the classic in constitutional interpretation, favoring less interpretative treatments of the subject, and I still cling to the dated belief that text can have a discernible meaning. There are several artistic styles that appeal to such legal tastes. An analogy can be drawn to a Rockwell, but such a style is perhaps too literal to capture a classic form of intentionalism. Norman Rockwell painted in a highly narrative and univocal fashion. The Constitution must be interpreted, of course, and does not convey the instant narrative meaning of Rockwell's *Four Freedoms* or his more campy magazine covers. Likewise, it is not as sterile or severe as the work of Grant Woods. It is not *American Gothic*. The Constitution is meant to be interpreted, but a classic judicial artist does not view the interpretive element to be license for reconstruction of its meaning. A closer analogy could be drawn to the work of Andrew Wyeth, particularly his masterpiece *Winter 1946*. Admittedly my favorite painting, the picture shows a boy running down a barren hill in winter. It is both beautiful and haunting. It is a picture that calls for interpretation and an understanding of the purpose behind the images. It is legitimate to interpret the painting with a knowledge of its history and original conception. The painting was autobiographical and completed immediately after the death of Wyeth's father, the famous illustrator N.C. Wyeth. The boy's swinging arms seem to capture the sense of loss and untethered status of the fatherless Wyeth. For Wyeth, the hill was his father and, indeed, it was at the bottom of the hill that his father died in a car accident. The use of this information brings a deeper meaning to the images of the picture. Where there was clearly a sense of loneliness, the historical evidence defines the reason for the loneliness and deepens its affect and meaning. In the same way, the Constitution is often read with an effort to understand the intent or meaning given terms by its

---

[11]392 U.S. 1 (1968).

[12]536 U.S. 822 (2002).

[13]*Id.* at 829. See Roger Pilon, Tenants, Students, and Drugs: A Comment on the War on the Rule of Law, 2001–2002 Cato Sup. Ct. Rev. 227 (2002).

Framers. In both exercises, the object is not changed but the meaning is clarified and deepened by the act of interpretation. The figure of a boy remains a figure of a boy. We simply learn more about the boy.

Narrative artists are often shunned by the artistic elite. Despite the presence of interpretation in Wyeth paintings, it remains too fixed to a single meaning and confines the viewer and artist alike. Likewise, for many law professors, the Constitution (and law generally) is viewed as transcending such finite meaning. Students are taught that they must accept the indeterminacy of language. For these academics, textual or even intentionalist approaches seem more like Andy Warhol's *Campbell Soup* paintings—a parody of pre-packaged legal theory. Those who strive for fixed meaning are viewed as academically lowbrow; unimaginative intellectual eunuchs who fail to understand the complexities of legal theory. Modern legal theory transcends language. Indeed, once free of the restraints of the determinacy of language and restrictive rules of intentionalism, legal scholars found themselves in the same position as modern artists when they broke from classic styles. New scientific theories, particularly atomic physics, had freed artists of the hold of the objects they painted. As Wassily Kandinsky said, "[a]ll things become flimsy, with no strength or certainty."[14] In a similar fashion, constitutional theory at law schools has increasingly freed itself of the structural rigidity of text. The resulting theories are as abstract as Picasso's cubism and at times appear as random as a Jackson Pollack painting.

Such abstraction, while in vogue in law schools, is not as popular with the courts. Rather, many judges favor more impressionistic views of the Constitution. This view is certainly apparent among members of the current Supreme Court. For justices like Sandra Day O'Connor, the Constitution is often presented as a mosaic of nuance where subtle shadings offer alternative meanings. It remains largely impressionistic rather than overtly surreal. Otherwise clear provisions are reproduced in a limp, Daliesque fashion—as in *Hamdi v. Rumsfeld*,[15] where the Suspension Clause is recognized but presented al dente. It is a legal version of a Monet, more beautiful at a distance and less clear as one gets closer to the individual brushstrokes. It

[14]Sam Hunter & John Jacobus, Modern Art 10 (1985) (quoting Kandinsky).
[15]*Supra* note 1.

has indeed the makings of impressionism. Impressionists, Frederick Chevalier noted in 1877, emphasize the "contradictory qualities" and "conscious incoherence" of their subjects.[16] Impressionists strive "not to render a landscape but the sensation produced by a landscape."[17] In the same way, the judicial impressionist takes clear constitutional provisions and, rather than derive and apply clear lines of authority, strives to convey their thrust or function—often in balanced interplay with other constitutional values.

As will be shown, the three national security cases of this term favor more abstract judicial interpretations, particularly O'Connor's highly impressionistic opinion in *Hamdi*. Instinctively avoiding bright lines, both the *Hamdi* and *Rasul* decisions seem to consciously struggle to preserve abstractions and uncertainties in meaning. It would be comforting to view Monet-like opinions as the outgrowth of some deep-seated personal belief or artistic bent. But, this term offered further evidence that impressionistic interpretations are more a matter of convenience than conviction. Justices like O'Connor often adopt clear lines in areas like federalism or takings. For them, the use of a more fluid style appears simply a way to cut any number of compromises, excusing them from the need to hold to a difficult line on constitutional values. They are Rockwellians painting Monets. They are not alone. Many liberals and civil libertarians want to see a bold and clear Rockwell on civil liberties and other individual constitutional rights, yet they prefer a more impressionistic interpretation on issues like states rights and affirmative action. Many conservatives have the opposite preference. It is perhaps the ultimate expression of Mies Van der Roe's concept of "form follows function"—the Constitution is either firm or fluid depending on the needs of a given moment in time.

On close examination, the Impressionist School of Constitutional Interpretation has long dominated decisions in the national security area.[18] Whether due to conviction or convenience, justices often

---

[16]Hunter & Jacobus, *supra* note 14, at 10 (quoting Chevalier's review of the Third Impressionist Exhibition).

[17]*Id.* (quoting an 1874 critique of impressionism).

[18]I have previously written about the different and disparate treatment given legal interpretations in the national security field. See generally Jonathan Turley, The Military Pocket Republic, 97 Nw. U. L. Rev. 1 (2002); Jonathan Turley, Pax Militaris: The Feres Doctrine and the Retention of Sovereign Immunity in the Military System of Governance, 71 Geo. Wash. L. Rev. 1 (2003); Jonathan Turley, Tribunals and Tribulations: The Antithetical Elements of the Military Justice System in a Madisonian

embrace interpretations that avoid bright or, at times, even discernible lines in favor of a fluid style where the powers of the respective branches blend into indistinguishable hues. This interpretative school has long held influence with the Court in national security cases where the branches come into the sharpest conflict. Historically, the Supreme Court has avoided conflict in favor of compromise decisions. Classicists in every other area suddenly become Impressionists when the subject and audience change in wartime or national security cases. Indeed, the Court has developed ad hoc balancing and reasonableness tests to facilitate such impressionist opinions, as was evident in the *Hamdi* decision.

The dark side of judicial impressionism is found in national security cases in which the Court seeks to avoid an interbranch conflict by yielding to a president. Considered over its entire history, the Supreme Court has a mixed record in defending civil liberties and minorities. There have been moments of clarity, and even courage, in the protection of religious and political minorities. During periods of national crisis, however, the Court has repeatedly yielded to the demands of convenience over clarity. In the worst of times, the Court has even used its respected position to give prejudice and ignorance a patina of legitimacy, as in *Korematsu v. United States*.[19] This term's trilogy of national security cases can be best understood along that historical continuum. *Hamdi*, *Padilla*, and *Rasul* reflect the Court's tradition of highly political, often vague, and at times opportunistic decisions during periods of unrest. In these cases, the Court had an opportunity to rehabilitate its tattered reputation in the area of national security, but chose the path of least resistance. It is certainly not the Court at its worst, but we have yet to see the Court at its best in protecting rights during wars or national emergencies.[20]

Democracy, 70 Geo. Wash. L. Rev. 649 (2002); Jonathan Turley, Through a Looking Glass Darkly: National Security and Statutory Interpretation, 53 SMU L. Rev. 205 (2000).

[19]323 U.S. 214 (1944); see also Scott v. Sandford, 60 U.S. 393, 407 (1856) (observing that blacks "had for more than a century before [the founding] been regarded as beings of an inferior order, and altogether unfit to associate with the white race, either in social or political relations; and so far inferior, that they had no rights which the white man was bound to respect; and that the negro might justly and lawfully be reduced to slavery for his benefit").

[20]See, e.g., Reid v. Covert, 354 U.S. 1 (1957); Ex parte Milligan, 71 U.S. (4 Wall.) 2 (1866).

In the case of Yaser Esam Hamdi, the Supreme Court considered one of the president's most extreme assertions of power: his claim to have the unilateral and absolute authority to declare a citizen to be an enemy combatant and to strip him of his constitutional rights, including his right of access to court or counsel. In a plurality decision, Justice O'Connor found that a brief and ambiguous congressional resolution gave the president some such authority. While not ruling on the president's claim of inherent authority pursuant to his commander-in-chief power, the plurality ruled that Hamdi could be imprisoned indefinitely, but that he was entitled to some small modicum of due process to establish his status as an enemy combatant. This process, however, was left largely undefined.

For those frustrated by the blurred reasoning and holding in *Hamdi*, the *Padilla* decision was positively maddening. The Court sent the case back on the most technical of grounds, finding that Padilla had simply named the wrong official in his original lawsuit and should sue in a different district. Finally, in *Rasul*, the Court did make an important ruling that detainees were entitled to judicial review, but again, the reasoning and the holding proved less clear on close examination. Rather than offer a clear view on the constitutional issues raised by the Bush policy or on the continued reliance of the presumption against extraterritoriality, the Court first articulated a bold new view of jurisdiction but then largely confined that view (at least for the moment) to the unique characteristics of Guantanamo Bay.

This article will begin with a brief look at the Court's checkered history on civil liberties in times of war—with an emphasis on the issues of enemy combatant status and military tribunals. Section II will focus on the decision in *Ex parte Quirin*,[21] where the Court abandoned not just the Constitution, but basic principles of judicial ethics. In Section III, the article will closely examine the trilogy of cases and the divergent methodologies adopted within them.

Ultimately, there is less than meets the eye in the three cases. While civil libertarians were quick to capitalize on clear losses for the administration, a close review of the cases shows something of a constitutional bait and switch. The Court speaks of first principles and vital constitutional guarantees in cases like *Hamdi* and *Rasul*,

---

[21]317 U.S. 1 (1942).

but in reality it imposes little on the administration to protect those values and rights. To be sure, the Court clearly rejects the extremist views of the Bush administration and the president's claim of unilateral and absolute authority. Yet the Court avoids any clear rules in favor of signature vagueness and ambiguity. Indeed, almost immediately the government rushed into the gaps left by the Court to minimize the impact of the cases and maximize the authority of the president. This article, in short, takes a critical view of the Court and its continued failure to stand by first principles. The plain fact is that this term's impressionistic opinions leave fundamental constitutional principles undefined—and therefore unprotected—at a time when they are most in need of clear expression.

## II. Deference, Balance, and the Darker Side of Judicial Impressionism

In designing the broad contours of their new republic, the Framers were divided with respect to the office of the chief executive. Many were opposed to a single strong president, often citing the dangers of war-making and the abuses perpetrated by supreme leaders in other systems.[22] While the Framers would ultimately reject the idea of an executive committee in favor of a president, they accommodated those concerns by strictly limiting the president's authority in the area of war making and habeas corpus. The Framers refused to give a president unilateral war-making authority and instead gave the power to declare war to Congress in Article I, section 8.[23] Yet, the Supreme Court, particularly in the mid-twentieth century, has shown a powerful preference toward a more fluid relationship between the president and Congress, which left the Court as the arbiter between the two branches in conflicts over national security. Justice Jackson captured this preference in his famous concurrence in *Youngstown Sheet & Tube Co. v. Sawyer*[24] when he stated that "[p]residential powers are not fixed but fluctuate, depending on their disjunction or conjunction with those of Congress."[25] In laying

---

[22]See generally Turley, The Military Pocket Republic, *supra* note 18, at 1.

[23]U.S. Const. art. I, § 8; see also 1 The Records of the Federal Convention of 1781 66–67 (M. Farrand ed., 1911); 6 The Writings of James Madison 174 (G. Hunt ed., 1903).

[24]343 U.S. 579 (1952).

[25]*Id.* at 635 (Jackson, J., concurring).

out his famous three categories of executive branch authority, Jackson noted that, even when the president is acting "in the absence of either a congressional grant or a denial of authority," "there is *a zone of twilight* in which he and Congress may have concurrent authority, or in which its distribution is uncertain."[26] On one level, Jackson's concurrence stated the obvious. In a system of shared powers, there must be different levels of deference or presumption depending on the specific authority used for executive action. But the Court has readily embraced the notion of fluidity as an invitation for judicial impressionism.[27] Even the three categories, vague as they are, have been questioned as too rigid. In *Dames & Moore v. Regan*,[28] then-Justice William Rehnquist noted that "it is doubtless the case that executive action in any particular instance falls, not neatly in one of three pigeonholes, but rather at some point along a spectrum running from explicit congressional authorization to explicit congressional prohibition."[29] When the president acted under his express or implied powers under Article II in wartime, the Court quickly embraced a level of extreme deference that bordered on willful blindness. The case often cited for this "deference" is *Ex parte Quirin*.[30]

In both the *Hamdi* and *Rasul* opinion, *Quirin* is the foundation for references to deference and inherent presidential power. The determinative weight given *Quirin*, particularly in the plurality decision in *Hamdi*, is remarkable and alarming given its infamous record.

---

[26]*Id.*

[27]Jackson readily embraced the notion that the text and history of the Constitution were unavailing to any clear interpretation—a self-fulfilling prophesy that invited judicial invention:

> A judge, like an executive adviser, may be surprised at the poverty of really useful and unambiguous authority applicable to concrete problems of executive power as they actually present themselves. Just what our forefathers did envision, or would have envisioned had they foreseen modern conditions, must be divined from the materials almost as enigmatic as the dreams Joseph was called upon to interpret for Pharaoh.

Youngstown Sheet & Tube Co. v. Sawyer, 343 U.S. 579, 634–35 (1952) (Jackson, J., concurring).

[28]453 U.S. 654 (1981).

[29]*Id.* at 669.

[30]*Supra* note 21.

To fully understand the Court's tendency toward judicial impressionism, it is essential to understand the true facts of *Quirin*, a case that reveals a Court frantically searching for justifications for the premature judgment that led to the executions of all but two captured German prisoners.[31] It is the *Quirin* case, more than any other, that shows convenience rather than conviction guiding judicial styles of constitutional interpretation.

*A. The Supreme Court and the Saboteurs in* Quirin

The *Quirin* case actually began in 1941 when German military intelligence began Operation Pastorius,[32] which called for two teams of saboteurs to commit a series of attacks on America's industry and economy. The plan was to put the two teams ashore by submarine. The saboteurs included two who were naturalized Americans: Ernest Peter Burger and Herbert Hans Haupt.[33] What the Germans did not know is that two of the saboteurs, including the operation's leader, George John Dasch, did not intend to go through with the plan. But Dasch and his colleague Burger would prove as great an inconvenience to American leaders as to the German high command.

Dasch was a former waiter who had spent nineteen years in the United States.[34] He claimed that he was eager to leave Nazi Germany and used the operation as a ruse to get to the United States. Such a claim by a captured war criminal would normally be viewed with suspicion except for one thing: Dasch's immediate efforts to reveal the operation after he landed. Early in the operation, Dasch revealed to his colleague, Ernest Peter Burger, that he intended to reveal the operation to the FBI.[35] He chose his co-conspirator with care. Burger was once a committed Nazi who participated in the 1932 Beer Hall putsch with Hitler.[36] In a crackdown shortly before the war, however,

---

[31] The account below is taken from two prior publications dealing with *Quirin*. Turley, Tribunals and Tribulations, *supra* note 18; Jonathan Turley, Quirin Revisited: The Dark History of Military Tribunals, Nat'l L. J., Oct. 28, 2002, at A20. *Tribunals and Tribulations* contains references and citations to a broad set of academic pieces by other authors.

[32] David J. Danelski, The Saboteurs' Case, 1 J. Sup. Ct. Hist. 61 (1996); see also Turley, Tribunals and Tribulations, *supra* note 18, at 734–35.

[33] Danelski, *supra* note 32, at 63.

[34] Turley, Quirin Revisited, *supra* note 31, at A20.

[35] Francis Biddle, In Brief Authority 336 (1962); Danelski, *supra* note 32, at 64.

[36] Turley, Tribunals and Tribulations, *supra* note 18, at 735 n.537.

he and his wife were arrested. The Gestapo tortured his wife, causing her to miscarry and leaving Burger with a deeply held hatred of the regime.[37]

Dasch and Burger landed with the first boat on a beach at Amagansett, New York, just after midnight on June 13, 1942. A lone Coastguardsman almost immediately came upon them burying their supplies.[38] When the other men advocated killing the man, Dasch intervened and, in front of the others, gave the American guardsman money to forget about what he saw. However, he then quietly asked the guardsman to remember his identity.[39] The next day, Dasch called the FBI and revealed the operation, including the scheduled landing of the second boat in Florida.[40] Nothing happened and the report was apparently set aside on a pile. The following day, Dasch decided to take matters into his own hands and went to D.C. to get the FBI to act. When he showed up with $80,000, the agents finally believed him and Dasch proceeded to dictate a 254-page statement.[41] Dasch emphasized that Burger was not supporting the operation and was working with him to disclose the entire matter to the FBI.

Dasch's information unraveled the entire operation. This is when a critical decision was made by FBI Director J. Edgar Hoover. Eager to take credit for the arrests, Hoover released a false account to the public, claiming that he and his agents had uncovered the plot.[42] In a false account given to President Roosevelt, Hoover even changed the date of Dasch's arrest—making it appear as if he was captured after the FBI broke the case. Hoover was made the hero of the hour and Roosevelt asked Congress to award him a special medal. This false account threatened to backfire, however, if Dasch or Burger were allowed to testify publicly on their critical role in disclosing the operation, including Dasch's repeated efforts to get the FBI to act. Hoover wanted either summary executions or a secret trial.

---

[37]Id.

[38]Danelski, *supra* note 32, at 533.

[39]Id.

[40]Id. at 64; Turley, Tribunals and Tribulations, *supra* note 18, at 735.

[41]Danelski, *supra* note 32, at 65; Turley, Tribunals and Tribulations, *supra* note 18, at 735.

[42]Danelski, *supra* note 32, at 65; George Lardner, Jr., Nazi Saboteurs Captured! FDR Orders Secret Tribunal, Washington Post Magazine, Jan. 13, 2002, at 14.

He found a willing ear in Roosevelt, who wanted a guarantee of conviction and capital punishment.[43]

The effort to gag and dispatch the saboteurs, particularly Dasch, would require the cooperation of the Supreme Court. The greatest problem was the two American citizens, particularly Haupt.[44] To guarantee results in the case, the administration proceeded to arrange a series of highly improper meetings with justices like Felix Frankfurter on how to structure the tribunal in anticipation of a Supreme Court appeal.[45] The level of collusion, dishonesty, and prejudice that appeared in the Supreme Court may be unrivaled in its history. It proved to be an institution acutely vulnerable to influence and even coercion by a determined president.

President Roosevelt left no question that he would not tolerate an independent, adverse ruling from the Supreme Court. Roosevelt gave his attorney general, Francis Biddle, a warning that was conveyed to the justices: "I won't give them up . . . I won't hand them over to any United States marshal armed with a writ of habeas corpus. Understand?"[46] This message was conveyed by Biddle, who warned the Court that the president would not accept anything but its total support. It was Justice Roberts who agreed to convey this message to the full Court in private. On July 29, 1942, Roberts told his colleagues that FDR intended to have all eight men shot if the Court did not acknowledge his authority.[47] The justices were advised that Biddle "feared that F.D.R. would execute the petitioners despite any Court action." Stone responded that "that would be a dreadful thing."[48]

In a cascading failure of independent review—indeed, of the separation of powers—the Court now had a direct ultimatum from the president. At least three members—Frankfurter, Stone, and Roberts—had personal involvement in the development of the case,

---

[43]Biddle, *supra* note 35, at 330; Danelski, *supra* note 32, at 66–67.

[44]The Court only noted Haupt's claim to citizenship. Ex parte Quirin, 317 U.S. 1, 20 (1942).

[45]Turley, Tribunals and Tribulations, *supra* note 18, at 737–38.

[46]Biddle, *supra* note 35, at 331; Danelski, *supra* note 32, at 28.

[47]Danelski, *supra* note 32, at 69.

[48]*Id.*

including ex parte communications.[49] Justice Roberts had had ex parte conversations with the attorney general, and Justice Frankfurter had given an advisory opinion on the proper structure of the tribunal.[50] Justice Frank Murphy, a reserve army lieutenant colonel, brought this coalescing of conflicts and collusion into sharp relief by appearing in his military uniform.[51] Finally, Chief Justice Stone, the author of the *Quirin* opinion, informed his colleagues that his son, Major Lauson Stone, was a member of the defense team.[52]

But it was Justice James F. Byrnes Jr. who held perhaps the most glaring conflict. Byrnes had been working for the president for over seven months in an effectively full-time executive position while also sitting on the Court. Brynes' role is made all the more suspect by the fact that he waited until after the decision to resign to assume a full-time position as Director of Economic Stabilization and later Director of War Mobilization.[53] Despite these conflicts and unethical contacts, only Murphy would recuse himself from the decision after being confronted by a hypocritical objection from Frankfurter.[54]

Despite the secret meetings and messages, oral argument remained a danger for the administration in disclosing the true facts of the case. That danger seemed to be realized when Justice Jackson asked defense counsel sarcastically why some of the men did not go to the authorities if they were only using the operation as a subterfuge to leave Nazi Germany (as they claimed). Jackson adopted a mocking tone and noted that "They did not go to any agency and say, 'We got away from the Germans. Thank God we are free and we shall tell where we buried the [explosives].'"[55] In a

---

[49]Turley, Tribunals and Tribulations, *supra* note 18, at 739.

[50]*Id.*

[51]*Id.*

[52]*Id.* To his credit, Chief Justice Stone raised this possible conflict with the parties before sitting in the case.

[53]*Id.* (noting that Byrnes had spent so much time working with the administration that Biddle actually thought that he had resigned from the Court); Danelski, *supra* note 32, at 69.

[54]Ironically, in light of the range of conflicts and improper conduct of his colleagues, Murphy recused himself "lest a breath of criticism be leveled at the Court." Michael R. Belknap, The Supreme Court Goes to War: The Meaning and Implications of the Nazi Saboteur Case, 89 Mil. L. Rev. 59, 78 (1980). The only other justice to address a conflict was Stone who properly raised the issue and solicited the views of counsel.

[55]*Id.* at 70.

baffling response, defense counsel Royall publicly agreed that they did not take such an action and that "if they did that, there would not have been this litigation."[56] In reality, Dasch had done exactly what Jackson had stated, with the support of Burger. While it is true that Dasch was not part of the appeal, Royall should have corrected Jackson's statement, particularly since Burger had agreed to disclose the operation. Instead, the only public argument in the case reaffirmed a clearly false account by Hoover and the FBI.

With that opportunity missed, the Court was free to make fast work of the men. Knowing that Roosevelt did not want any further delay, the Court took the extraordinary step of issuing its conclusion without giving an opinion or detailed reason. Instead, it yielded to the president and promised to publish an opinion at some later date to explain why. What followed was a sham proceeding in which command influence was openly applied and rules of evidence discarded.[57] All eight men were convicted and sentenced to death on August 3, 1942. Six were executed by electric chair on August 8. For their part, Burger and Dasch were first sentenced to death and then given commutations. Burger's sentence was commuted to life imprisonment while Dasch was given thirty years' imprisonment.[58]

It was only after the execution of the six men that members of the Court began to seriously deliberate the constitutional basis for their decision. Chief Justice Stone assumed the task of writing a post-execution justification. He found the task so difficult that he referred to it as "a mortification of the flesh."[59] Some members were beginning to balk at the scope of executive authority claimed by Roosevelt and seemingly sanctioned by the ruling. Stone struggled with the justification, particularly in light of *Ex parte Milligan*.[60] His initial distinction of *Milligan* was transparent and unconvincing: "I distinguish *Milligan* on the ground that, whether or not Milligan violated the law of war, the petitioners clearly did."[61] His colleagues

---

[56]*Id.*

[57]Turley, Tribunals and Tribulations, *supra* note 18, at 739.

[58]*Id.*

[59]Alpheus T. Mason, Harlan Fiske Stone: Pillar of the Law 659 (1959).

[60]71 U.S. (4 Wall.) 2 (1866).

[61]Danelski, *supra* note 32, at 73.

objected to the draft, and Justice Hugo Black specifically criticized
the sweeping authority that the Court had given the president:

> While Congress doubtless could declare all violation of the
> laws of war to be crimes against the United States, I seriously
> question whether Congress could constitutionally confer
> jurisdiction to try all such violations before military tribunals.
> In this case I want to go no further than to declare that
> these particular defendants are subject to the jurisdiction of
> a military tribunal because of the circumstances and purposes
> of their entry into this country as part of the enemy's war
> forces.[62]

Black objected to the absence of any language stating that the president had exceeded his authority in seeking to bar access to the
courts.[63] Frankfurter voiced an extreme position, stating that he
believed that "the President has the power to suspend the writ [of
habeas corpus], and so believing, I conclude also that his determination whether an emergency calls for such suspension is not subject
to judicial review."[64] Frankfurter was not alone in taking an extreme
position. Justice Robert H. Jackson suggested that he might write a
concurrence that yielded entirely to the executive branch, and he
expressed his doubt that the courts had the authority to "review[]
the legality of the President's order [when] experience shows the
judicial system is ill-adapted to deal with matters in which we must
present a united front to a foreign foe."[65]

Jackson's memorandum reflects a common trend on the Court—
reaching conclusions on the preferred outcome and then desperately
searching for a methodology or theory to justify it. Whether a Rockwell or a Monet, the style is merely a matter of convenience. This
was evident in the work of Stone: He submitted alternative justifications for the earlier order with only the conclusion in common. Stone
circulated memoranda that resembled the alternative pleadings of
an attorney—openly discarding the notion that the question should
not be how but why the Court reaches a particular result. Instead,

[62]*Id.* at 76.

[63]*Id.* at 75.

[64]*Id.*

[65]*Id.* at 76; see also Carl Tobias, Terrorism and the Constitution: Civil Liberties in
a New America, 6 U. Pa. J. Const. L. 1116, 1139 (2004).

Stone wrote "[a]bout all I can say for what I have done is that I think [the draft] will present the Court all tenable and pseudo-tenable bases for decision."[66] The search for even "pseudo-tenable" rationales shows a Court untethered from the text of the Constitution or its institutional obligations.

Frankfurter was particularly irate at even the suggestion that constitutional principles should undermine the need to give total support to the president. He encouraged his colleagues to look beyond the terms of the Constitution and to adopt an intentionally vague, impressionistic opinion. This pitch was made in a memorandum that can only be described as bizarre. Only recently discovered, the confidential memorandum takes the form of a long hypothetical dialogue between Frankfurter and the now dead saboteurs. Entitled "F.F.'s Soliloquy," the dialogue begins with Frankfurter explaining how he would hold a hearing as a "judge" with the men he calls "saboteurs"—before any conviction:

> Saboteurs: Your Honor, we are here to get a writ of habeas corpus from you.
>
> F.F.: What entitles you to it?
>
> Saboteurs: [making a *Milligan* argument].
>
> F.F.: . . .You damned scoundrels have a helluva cheek to ask for a writ that would take you out of the hands of the Military Commission and give you the right to be tried, if at all, in a federal district court. You are just low-down, ordinary, enemy spies who, as enemy soldiers, have invaded our country and therefore could immediately have been shot by the military when caught in the act of invasion. Instead you were humanely ordered to be tried by a military tribunal convened by the Commander-in-Chief himself . . . . So I will deny your writ and leave you to the just deserts with the military.
>
> Saboteurs: But, Your Honor, since as you say the President himself professed to act under the Articles of War, we appeal to those Articles of War as the governing procedure, even bowing to your ruling that we are not entitled to be tried by civil courts and may have our lives declared forfeit by this Military Commission . . . .

---

[66]Danelski, *supra* note 32, at 75.

F.F.: . . . You've done enough mischief already without leaving the seeds of a bitter conflict involving the President, the courts and Congress after your bodies will be rotting in lime. It is a wise requirement of courts not to get into needless rows with the other branches of the government by talking about things that need not be talked about if a case can be disposed of with intellectual self-respect on grounds that do not raise such rows. I therefore do not propose to be seduced into inquiring what powers the President has or has not got, what limits the Congress may or may not put upon the Commander-in-Chief in time of war, when, as a matter of fact, the ground on which you claim to stand . . . exists only in your foolish fancy. That disposes of you scoundrels. Doubtless other judges may spell this out with appropriate documentation and learning . . . . But it all comes down to what I have told you . . . . the Articles of War[ ] don't apply to you. And so you will remain in your present custody and be damned.[67]

Frankfurter then addressed his colleagues directly:

Some of the very best lawyers I know are now in the Solomon Island battle, some are seeing service in Australia, some are sub-chasers in the Atlantic, and some are on the various air fronts . . . . And I [can] almost hear their voices were they to read more than a single opinion in this case. They would say something like this but in language hardly becoming a judge's tongue: "What in hell do you fellows think you are doing? Haven't we got enough of a job trying to lick the Japs and the Nazis without having you fellows on the Supreme Court dissipate the thoughts and feelings and energies of the folks at home by stirring up a nice row as to who has what power when all of you are agreed that the President had the power to establish this Commission and that the procedure under the Articles of War for courts-martial and military commissions doesn't apply to this case. [sic] Haven't you got any more sense than to get people by the ear on one of the favorite American pastimes—abstract constitutional discussions . . . . Just relax and don't be too engrossed in your own interest in verbalistic conflicts because the inroads on energy and national unity that such conflict inevitably

---

[67]Turley, Tribunals and Tribulations, *supra* note 18, at 740.

produce [sic], is a pastime we had better postpone until peacetime.[68]

One would expect that such a clearly unhinged and biased memorandum would yield at least one objection or, even better, a condemnation. To the contrary, it seemed to actually sway members like Jackson, who fell in line.[69] The members wanted a unanimous decision despite the fact that they could not agree on the actual basis. Stone simply announced that they had "agreed to disagree" and issued an opinion of maddening ambiguity.

The Court declined to address the question of whether the president had the inherent authority to establish military tribunals. It declined to delineate the respective lines of authority between Congress and the president.[70] It declined even to articulate "the ultimate boundaries of the jurisdiction of military tribunals to try persons according to the law of war."[71] As Professors Christopher Bryant and Carl Tobias have noted, the justices simply "could not articulate the reasoning for their conclusion."[72] The result was a unanimous opinion that used broad, vague strokes to justify the Court's earlier decision yielding to Roosevelt. The Court found congressional authority for the tribunals and rejected the habeas relief.[73] As for the true facts of the case, the Court merely dropped a footnote that observed, "a defense offered before the Military Commission was that petitioners had no intention to obey the orders given them by the officer of the German High Command."[74] There was no mention that two of the men not only possessed no intention but in fact disclosed the operation to the FBI.

The treatment of Haupt, who had a claim of citizenship, was one of the most disturbing aspects of the case. The Court held:

[68]*Id.* at 741–42.

[69]Danelski, *supra* note 32, at 78.

[70]Ex parte Quirin, 317 U.S. 1, 47 (1942).

[71]*Id.* at 45.

[72]A. Christopher Bryant & Carl Tobias, Quirin Revisited, 2003 Wis. L. Rev. 309, 330 (2003).

[73]Professors Bryant and Tobias have argued that the case reflected an earlier and narrower view of habeas corpus and should have been limited as precedent on that basis. *Id.* at 332–333.

[74]Ex parte Quirin, 317 U.S. at 25 n.4.

> Citizenship in the United States of an enemy belligerent does not relieve him from the consequences of a belligerency which is unlawful because in violation of the law of war. Citizens who associate themselves with the military arm of the enemy government, and with its aid, guidance and direction enter this country bent on hostile acts, are enemy belligerents within the meaning of the Hague Convention and the law of war. It is as an enemy belligerent that petitioner Haupt is charged with entering the United States, and unlawful belligerency is the gravamen of the offense of which he is accused.[75]

Missing is any attention to the interplay between the authority to try and execute unlawful combatants and the countervailing rights of citizens to due process and other basic guarantees. Obviously, the question of whether "citizens . . . associate themselves with the military arm of the enemy government" is the matter in dispute in such cases. Missing also is an answer to the question of why a citizen, due to the simple fact of citizenship, cannot demand greater legal rights than noncitizens. That question would not go unnoticed, sixty years later, by individuals in the Bush administration seeking to radically expand the inherent powers of the president.

B. *The Resurrection of* Quirin *and the Claim of Absolute Presidential Power in Times of National Crisis*

For decades after the *Quirin* decision (and long before the disclosure of the Court's shameful internal conduct), scholars questioned it, as well as the *Korematsu*[76] decision, on any number of grounds. Even Frankfurter would belatedly speak of the case as "not a happy precedent," and Justice Douglas singled it out, causing the entire Court to regret its actions.[77] Judicial clerks serving the Court during the *Quirin* decision were especially scathing, insisting that the decision was made without legal authority and adding that it constituted a mockery of justice.[78] In law school classrooms, professors would

---

[75]*Id.* at 38–39.

[76]*Supra* note 19.

[77]Turley, Tribunals and Tribulations, *supra* note 18, at 743 n.601.

[78]Justice Black's clerk, John Frank, would later accuse the Court of being "stampeded" by the president and added that "if judges are to run a court of law and not a butcher shop, the reasons for killing a man should be expressed before he is dead." John P. Frank, Marble Palace 249, 250 (1972).

routinely suggest that *Korematsu* and *Quirin* may be legal relics of the period with more historical than precedential value.

It was a considerable surprise, therefore, to find *Quirin* embraced almost immediately after September 11, 2001, as the very foundation for the administration's authority in the war on terror. President Bush, Attorney General John Ashcroft, White House Counsel Alberto Gonzales, and others repeatedly cited the case as a virtual blank check for both military tribunals and the enemy combatant policy. The impressionistic opinion lent itself to the most extreme interpretations. President Bush promulgated tribunal rules modeled on the Roosevelt orders, including his own outcome-determinative rules of evidence and standards of proof. In federal court, the Justice Department insisted that federal judges had no constitutional role beyond confirming that the government had declared an individual to be an enemy combatant.[79] It simply submitted declarations filled with conclusory statements that individuals like Padilla and Hamdi were enemy combatants—with no underlying support for the assertions.[80] And it barred those prisoners from access to counsel. When pressed in court, the government insisted that revealing details or allowing the individuals access to counsel would present grave dangers to the nation's security.

*Padilla* and *Hamdi* were perhaps the inevitable consequences of *Quirin*. Once a president was given such unbridled authority over a citizen and the Court exercised such limited review, it was all but certain that a future president would push his power to its limit. That point came when Jose Padilla, an American citizen arrested at O'Hare International Airport, was stripped of his constitutional rights, including access to counsel, on the basis of a conclusory declaration. The government's legal position was denounced widely in both the United States and abroad. Lower court judges rejected the authority claimed in both *Hamdi* and *Padilla*, although the Fourth Circuit Court of Appeals would later rule in favor of the government in the *Hamdi* case.[81]

---

[79]Hamdi v. Rumsfeld, 124 S. Ct. 2633, 2644 (2004) (noting the extreme view of both DOJ and the Fourth Circuit as "easily rejected").

[80]*Id.* at 2636 (discussing the "Mobbs Declaration").

[81]To its credit, the Supreme Court dismissed the extreme opinion of the Fourth Circuit with little serious attention. *Id.* at 2644.

Despite its earlier representations in lower courts, the government's position changed when facing final decisions from the Supreme Court. Shortly before the decisions came down, the government allowed Hamdi and Padilla to meet with counsel, though under tight restrictions.[82] Then, in a highly inappropriate move, the Justice Department held a press conference only weeks before the expected issuance of the opinions to announce incriminating facts about Padilla. Although the government had earlier refused to reveal these same facts as a matter of dire national security, it now released them along with statements of interrogations of Padilla. When reporters challenged the Department of Justice for appearing to influence the Supreme Court, its defense was that it was not trying to influence the Court but rather "the court of public opinion."[83] It was immediately clear that this was an effort to influence not just the Court but, specifically, Justice O'Connor—viewed by some as susceptible to such extrajudicial influence.[84] It was a thoroughly improper and hypocritical act by the Justice Department, showing its opportunistic use of "national security" in the past to refuse disclosures. The department's desire to influence "the court of public opinion" served only to illustrate the dangers of leaving an administration with the extreme powers sanctioned by the *Quirin* court.[85]

## III. "Discontent with . . . Destiny": The Court's Transcendence of Constitutional Text

> *Man, that inveterate dreamer, daily more discontent with his destiny, has trouble assessing the objects he has been led to use, objects that his nonchalance has brought his way.*[86]

[82]*Id.* at 2652.

[83]Scott Turow, Trial by News Conference: No Justice in That, Washinton Post, June 13, 2004, at B01 (stating as "as a former federal prosecutor and a criminal defense lawyer, [the department's] performance constituted one more legally and ethically dubious maneuver by our government in a case that I already regarded as one of the most troubling in memory").

[84]Jonathan Turley, You Have Rights—if Bush Says You Do, Los Angeles Times, June 3, 2004, at 11.

[85]With a vote of five to four (with O'Connor in the majority), the administration's "dog and Padilla" show may has achieved its purpose.

[86]Andre Breton, Surrealist Manifesto 10 (1924).

In the world of modern art, objects begin in clarity and become more abstract in interpretation. Judicial impressionists like Sandra Day O'Connor often approach the object of the Constitution in the same way. A provision like the Suspension Clause is abundantly, if not inescapably, clear. But, the judicial impressionist views the object through the lens of experience and contemporary realities, distorting and reproducing it in a new interpretative form. In this sense, O'Connor's plurality decision in *Hamdi* was a masterwork of judicial impressionism. Indeed, unlike less honest impressionists— the authors of *Quirin*, for example—O'Connor openly engages in reconstructing meaning from the text of the Constitution to meet her view of the preferred balance of individual rights and executive powers. She has long favored balancing and reasonableness tests in constitutional interpretation, precisely because they allow such reconstructive and impressionistic rulings. Under such tests (like the *Mathews* test that she applied in *Hamdi*), the Court becomes a sort of constitutional jury, applying its own community standards on reasonable policies and practices. The array of opinions in the national security trilogy this year reflects the ad hoc approach of the Court in dealing with most of the fundamental guarantees of the Constitution.

## A. The Faux-Impressionism of Hamdi v. Rumsfeld

Many modern artists have strived to escape the hold of the object and have sought to present their unique view of it through the act of artistic translation or interpretation. For a true impressionist, such translation is the very essence of its truth or meaning. For a faux-impressionist, the act of changing or manipulating the object is not a matter of truth but convenience. Justice O'Connor has repeatedly shown herself to be a faux-impressionist, adopting this style simply as a convenient vehicle to achieve her pre-conceived outcome. Thus, in one case she strikes a decidedly Rockwellian style in strictly reading federalism provisions, while in another she treats the Constitution as a mere object for extrapolation and reinvention. It is true that O'Connor is not alone in her embrace of faux judicial art; nonetheless, as the Court's consistent swing vote, her changes in artistic style have produced sweeping changes in national policies and practices.[87]

---

[87]See Jonathan Turley, *Justice O'Connor Wields A Mighty Vote*, Los Angeles Times, July 4, 2002, at A17.

From the very beginning of the *Hamdi* decision, O'Connor reveals her intent to reinvent the objects of the case. The case presented a pair of obvious and difficult threshold questions that she clearly wished to avoid. First, there was the question of a president's inherent authority to unilaterally declare a citizen to be an enemy combatant and thereby strip him of his constitutional rights. Second, there was the related question of whether the "war on terrorism" declared by the president could trigger such unilateral authority. From the outset of her decision, O'Connor establishes that she will not address either of those questions. The only way to avoid the knotty issue of the president's inherent authority and the issue of what is truly meant by a declared war would be to find that Congress actually gave the president the authority over such enemy combatants. After all, 18 U.S.C. § 4001(a) clearly states "no citizen shall be imprisoned or otherwise detained by the United States except pursuant to an Act of Congress."[88] The only problem is that no such congressional authorization can be found in the plain words or legislative history of the congressional resolution that followed the 9/11 attacks— an omission that was quickly corrected with some impressionistic judicial artistry.

In *Hamdi*, O'Connor was faced with two legal objects to interpret. The first was a clear constitutional provision that mandated that only Congress could suspend habeas corpus.[89] The second was a federal statute expressly denying the president the right to detain citizens except pursuant to congressional authorization.[90] O'Connor quickly set aside the restraints of the federal statute by adopting a radically impressionistic interpretation of a third legal object, the Authorization for Use of Military Force, or the "Force Resolution."[91] Congress passed the Force Resolution one week after the 9/11 attacks with the smoke still rising over the World Trade Center. It was a fairly predictable piece of legislation expressing national commitment to hunt down the culprits and affirming the president's authority to do so. The president is specifically authorized, under the Force

---

[88] 18 U.S.C. § 4001(a).

[89] U.S. Const. art I, § 9, cl. 2 ("The Privilege of the Writ of Habeas Corpus shall not be suspended, unless when in Cases of Rebellion or Invasion the public safety may require it.").

[90] 18 U.S.C. § 4001(a).

[91] Authorization for Use of Military Force, Pub. L. No. 107–40, 115 Stat. 224 (2001).

Resolution, to "use all necessary and appropriate force against those nations, organizations, or persons he determines planned, authorized, committed, or aided the terrorist attacks" or "harbored such organizations or persons, in order to prevent any future actions of international terrorism against the United States by such nations, organizations or persons."[92]

Normally, the generality of the Force Resolution should have produced little difficulty for a jurist faced with a claim of congressional authorization for extreme detention policies. The resolution says nothing about the detention of citizens or even hints at the type of sweeping enemy combatants policies that the administration would eventually advocate. More important, the countervailing language in § 4001(a) is quite clear on the need for specific authorization for such detentions. In enacting the law, Congress repealed a 1950 statute that expressly gave the attorney general the authority to detain individuals who were suspected of espionage or sabotage—the very justification of the Bush enemy combatant policy.[93] Congress repealed this law in 1971 in light of the infamous internment of Japanese-American citizens during World War II.[94] Rather than simply repeal the 1950 statute, however, Congress went further, requiring express congressional authority for any future detentions to protect the nation from "arbitrary executive action, with no clear demarcation of the limits of executive authority."[95]

Thus, Congress expressly enacted § 4001(a) to avoid the very arguments made in *Hamdi*: The idea that detentions could be based on vague justifications by a president. In light of such a clear and direct statute, the vagueness of the Force Resolution is placed into even sharper relief. This vagueness is further magnified by the fact that, after enacting the Force Resolution, Congress passed the Uniting and Strengthening America by Providing Appropriate Tools Required to Intercept and Obstruct Terrorism Act of 2001 (USA PATRIOT ACT),[96] which expressly limited the detention of aliens to

---

[92]*Id.*

[93]Emergency Detention Act of 1950 (formerly 50 U.S.C. § 811 et seq. (1970 ed.)).

[94]H.R. Rep. No. 92-116, at 2–5 (1971).

[95]H.R. Rep. No. 92-116, at 5; see also Hamdi v. Rumsfeld, 124 S. Ct. 2633, 2654–2657 (2004).

[96]USA PATRIOT ACT of 2001, Pub. L. No. 107–56, 115 Stat. 272 (2001) (codified in scattered sections of the United States Code).

no more than seven days without criminal charge or deportation proceedings.[97] It would be rather odd if Congress intended to allow aliens greater rights than U.S. citizens.[98]

Yet, even without § 4001(a), authority for detentions should have required an express statement in light of the countervailing constitutional values contained in provisions like the Due Process and Suspension Clauses. Such a stretch required not just impressionistic judicial art but extreme impressionism. Citing the phrase, "all necessary and appropriate force," O'Connor interpreted the Force Resolution as being perfectly clear on the use of detentions against citizens and non-citizens alike:

> There can be no doubt that individuals who fought against the United States in Afghanistan as part of the Taliban, an organization known to have supported the al Qaeda terrorist network responsible for the attacks, are individuals Congress sought to target in passing AUMF. We conclude that detention of individuals falling into the limited category we are considering, for the duration of the particular conflict in which they were captured, is so fundamental and accepted an incident to war as to be an exercise of the "necessary and appropriate force" Congress authorized the President to use.[99]

Relying on *Quirin*, O'Connor simply observes that such detentions are part of war-making.[100] Thus, she dismisses the notion that more is required: "[I]t is of no moment that the [Force Resolution] does not use specific language of detention."[101] By insisting that the resolution's meaning is clear, she gives the impression that she is actually still tracking the language. Yet, her interpretation is vintage impressionism, beginning with the object and then translating its appearance according to her own view of its essential meaning.[102]

---

[97]8 U.S.C. § 1226a(5) (2000 ed. Supp. I).

[98]This anomaly was addressed skillfully by Justices Souter and Ginsburg in their concurring and dissenting opinion. Hamdi v. Rumsfeld, 124 S. Ct. 2633, 2659 (2004).

[99]*Id.* at 2640.

[100]*Id.*

[101]*Id.* at 2641.

[102]It is the view espoused by another impressionist of language: "When I use a word," Humpty Dumpty said, in a rather scornful tone, "it means just what I choose it to mean—neither more nor less." Lewis Carroll, Through the Looking Glass, in The Complete Works of Lewis Carroll 196 (1939).

To achieve this result in the face of an express countervailing congressional statute, O'Connor not only embraces *Quirin* but reinforces its continuing authority. She notes that "nothing in *Quirin* suggests that [Hamdi's] citizenship would have precluded his mere detention for the duration of the relevant hostilities."[103] While cases like *Milligan* seem to contradict such sweeping deference to the president, O'Connor stresses that *Quirin* was "a unanimous opinion [that] both postdates and clarifies *Milligan*, providing us with the most apposite precedent that we have on the question of whether citizens may be detained in such circumstances."[104] It is telling that O'Connor would emphasize *Quirin*, the case that most reflects the type of political, impressionist decisionmaking that has characterized her own jurisprudence. Yet the resurrection of *Quirin* without even a hint of concern or correction is distressing. In the Court's checkered history on civil liberties in wartime, *Quirin* stands out as an institutional disgrace. Like the *Hamdi* plurality opinion, it was anything but an example of justices who revealed their "discontent . . . with destiny."[105]

In *Hamdi* the Court had an opportunity to expunge the stain of *Quirin*, to show that it could transcend transient fears to protect the Constitution's first principles. Instead, *Hamdi* showed that at least four members—O'Connor, Rehnquist, Kennedy and Breyer—remain willing to ignore both constitutional provisions and clear congressional statutory language to fashion their own preferred balance of individual rights, congressional authority, and presidential power. To this group must be added Justice Thomas, who wrote a dissent that virtually dismisses the Suspension Clause as an inconvenient relic in modern wartime. Indeed, he challenges the authority of courts to play any meaningful role in enemy combatant cases.[106]

---

[103]*Hamdi*, 124 S. Ct. at 2640.

[104]*Id.* at 2643.

[105]Andre Breton, Surrealist Manifesto 10 (1924).

[106]A jurist who had often defined himself as faithful to the Constitution and its text, Thomas sets aside both language and tradition to accommodate the administration's demands in *Hamdi*:

> Undeniably, Hamdi has been deprived of a serious interest, one actually protected by the Due Process Clause. Against this, however, is the Government's overriding interest in protecting the Nation. If a deprivation of liberty can be justified by the need to protect a town, the protection of the Nation, *a fortiori*, justifies it.

*Hamdi*, 124 S. Ct. at 2685.

95

In addition to his extreme view of inherent executive authority, Thomas expands on a long and questionable line of cases expressing institutional incompetence as a basis for extreme deference.[107] Yet even with such cases, Thomas' level of judicial deference to unilateral executive authority has not been seen since the 1627 *Case of the Five Knights*.[108] It is impossible to maintain a doctrine of separation of powers if the Court systemically yields by voluntary concession what was given by constitutional design.

Once the plurality broke from the clarity of the legal objects, the impressionist style freed them in the remainder of the opinion from any need for clarity or specificity. The first natural question concerns the meaning of the category "enemy combatants" for future cases. The plurality expressly refuses to grapple with that question, simply noting in a footnote that "[t]he legal category of enemy combatant has not been elaborated upon in great detail. The permissible bounds of the category will be defined by the lower courts as subsequent cases are presented to them."[109] And despite the fact that citizens have been detained without access to courts or counsel, the plurality feels no compulsion to define the scope of the detention authority, even as upholds the authority as a legal principle.

The second obvious question concerns the scope of the due process that must be given accused enemy combatants. The plurality, to its credit, rejects the absolute authority asserted by President Bush.[110]

---

[107]*Id.* at 2674 ("The plurality utterly fails to account for the Government's compelling interests and for our own institutional inability to weigh competing concerns correctly."); see generally Turley, Pax Militaris, *supra* note 18 (discussing the questionable foundation for institutional incompetence rationales).

[108]In that case, the King's Bench found that defendants were entitled to habeas review but deferred on the legality of detention—a ruling that led to reforms in Parliament. Darnel's Case, 3 How. St. Tr. 1 (K.B. 1627).

[109]Hamdi, 124 S. Ct. at 2642 n.1 (Thomas, J., dissenting).

[110]O'Connor addresses the separation-of-powers arguments raised by the president rather than the threat posed by yielding to the president on the scope of the due process entitled to a citizen accused of being an enemy combatant. On the government's separation of powers argument, she profoundly states:

> [W]e necessarily reject the Government's assertion that separation of powers principles mandate a heavily circumscribed role for the courts in such circumstances. Indeed, the position that the courts must forgo any examination of the individual case and focus exclusively on the legality of the broader detention scheme cannot be mandated by any reasonable view of separation of powers, as this approach serves only to *condense* power into a single branch of govern-

Specifically, it states that the approach of the Fourth Circuit (and the Justice Department) could be "easily rejected."[111] Thus, the Court insists that accused enemy combatants are entitled to judicial review and access to counsel. When the specific process is addressed, however, the plurality adopts a standard that is ready-made for judicial impressionism: *Mathews v. Eldridge.*[112] A case that dealt with disability benefits rather than core issues of separation of powers and individual rights, *Mathews* gave the Court a license to use its own translation of rights in light of other contemporary concerns and issues: "*Mathews* dictates that the process due in any given instance is determined by weighing 'the private interest that will be affected by the official action' against the Government's asserted interest, 'including the function involved' and the burdens the Government would face in providing greater process."[113] After adopting this broad "balancing test," the Court proceeds to issue a standard that is so general and prosaic that it is virtually unintelligible on a practical level. The Court holds that the Constitution protects the right of "a citizen-detainee . . . to challenge his classification, and a fair opportunity to rebut the Government's factual assertions before a neutral decisionmaker."[114] In case this standard were not vague enough, O'Connor adds presumptions and accommodations for the government:

> [T]he exigencies of the circumstances may demand that, aside from these core elements, enemy combatant proceedings may be tailored to alleviate their uncommon potential to burden the Executive at a time of ongoing military conflict. Hearsay, for example, may need to be accepted as the most reliable

---

ment. We have long since made clear that a state of war is not a blank check for the President when it comes to the rights of the Nation's citizens. Hamdi, 124 S. Ct. at 2650.

[111]*Id.* at 2644.

[112]424 U.S. 319 (1976). Justice Scalia correctly criticizes the use of this standard in his dissenting opinion: "Whatever the merits of this technique when newly recognized property rights are at issue (and even there they are questionable), it has no place where the Constitution and the common law already supply an answer." Hamdi, 124 S. Ct. at 2672.

[113]Hamdi, 124 S. Ct. at 2626 (quoting Mathews v. Eldridge, 424 U.S. at 33).

[114]124 S. Ct. at 2649.

> available evidence from the Government in such a proceeding. Likewise, the Constitution would not be offended by a presumption in favor of the Government's evidence, so long as that presumption remained a rebuttable one and fair opportunity for rebuttal were provided. Thus, once the Government puts forth credible evidence that the habeas petitioner meets the enemy-combatant criteria, the onus could shift to the petitioner to rebut that evidence with more persuasive evidence that he falls outside the criteria. A burden-shifting scheme of this sort would meet the goal of ensuring that the errant tourist, embedded journalist, or local aid worker has a chance to prove military error while giving due regard to the Executive once it has put forth meaningful support for its conclusion that the detainee is in fact an enemy combatant.[115]

Regarding the forum for such a hearing, O'Connor once again favors the broad-brush technique, stating simply that "[t]here remains the possibility that the standards we have articulated could be met by an appropriately authorized and properly constituted military tribunal."[116]

O'Connor's insistence that "the Constitution would not be offended" by such a proceeding is conceivable only if one has redefined that legal object into a new judicial form. The plurality succeeded in creating a procedure designed to (1) achieve minimal due process, (2) eliminate core evidentiary protections, and (3) shift the burden to the defendant to essentially "prove the negative" of not being an enemy combatant once a perfunctory showing is made. To say that such a process does not offend the Constitution requires the Court's own unique community standard of the constitutionally obscene.

Despite all of this, it must be said that *Hamdi* does show an institutional improvement since *Quirin*. This was a plurality decision, after all; there are members of this Court who are unwilling to adopt O'Connor's opportunistic and impressionistic methodology. Indeed, the honor of the Court as an institution was upheld in dissent by Justices Scalia and Stevens. In his dissent, Scalia takes as his legal object the Suspension Clause and, rather than reconstruct it, uses

---

[115]*Id.*

[116]*Id.* at 2651.

its clear meaning to structure his interpretation.[117] For Scalia and Stevens, the arrest of a citizen engaged as a member of an enemy force requires a charge under a criminal statute, such as treason, in the absence of a congressional suspension of habeas corpus.[118] The dissent is a model of classic judicial form: honoring the clear lines of the Constitution and allowing history to inform us of the reasons for those lines. To use the earlier Wyeth example of *Winter 1946*, we learn about the reason the boy is running without changing the image of the boy.

Where Scalia and Stevens fail is not in their methodology or conclusion, but in their effort to accommodate rather than repudiate *Quirin*. Scalia notes that "the case was not this Court's finest hour," a unique (albeit fleeting) recognition of *Quirin*'s problems.[119] Scalia

---

[117]Scalia also takes a justified, trademark swipe at the plurality:

There is a certain harmony of approach in the plurality's making up for Congress's failure to invoke the *Suspension Clause* and its making up for the Executive's failure to apply what it says are needed protections—an approach that reflects what might be called a Mr. Fix-it Mentality. The plurality seems to view it as its mission to Make Everything Come Out Right, rather than merely to decree the consequences, as far as individual rights are concerned, of the other two branches' actions and omissions . . . . The problem with this approach is not only that it steps out of the courts' modest and limited role in a democratic society; but that by repeatedly doing what it thinks the political branches ought to do it encourages their lassitude and saps the vitality of government by the people.

*Id.* at 2673.

[118]Among the sources supporting this obvious reading of the Constitution is an interesting exchange between Jefferson and Madison on the meaning of and need for a Suspension Clause. Jefferson wrote:

Why suspend the Hab. Corp in insurrections and rebellions? The parties who may be arrested may be charged instantly with a well-defined crime. Of course, the judge will remand them. If the publick safety requires that the government should have a man imprisoned on less probable testimony in those than in other emergencies; let him be taken and tried, retaken and retried, while the necessity continues, only giving him redress against the government for damages.

13 Papers of Thomas Jefferson 442 (July 31, 1788) (J. Boyd ed., 1956). As noted by Scalia and Stevens, such sources reflect a clear understanding supporting the clear text that the government has two and only two options in cases like *Hamdi*: a criminal charge in federal court or a request for suspension from Congress. Hamdi, 124 S. Ct. at 2667 (Scalia, J., dissenting).

[119]Hamdi, 124 S. Ct. at 2669.

then stumbles when he tries to distinguish the case on the ground that "it was uncontested that the petitioners were members of enemy forces. They were '*admitted* enemy invaders.'"[120] O'Connor correctly chastises the dissent on the relevance of such a concession in a system "in which the only options are congressional suspension of the writ of habeas corpus or prosecution of treason or some other crime."[121] Moreover, the statement is factually wrong. While the record before the Court in *Quirin* did indicate such concessions by all of the accused (and, as previously noted, this was curiously affirmed by defense counsel), that was not the case. Again, two of the men never intended to engage in sabotage and were responsible for revealing the operation. The fact that the record was false was relevant to the need for a true hearing on the status of the men—a fact that Scalia could have included as a matter of judicial notice. Notwithstanding their failure to repudiate *Quirin*, however, Scalia and Stevens remained the most faithful to the legal object and can be credited with refusing to untether their decision from the text.

Justices Souter and Ginsburg also showed greater attention to the Constitution and the other legal sources in their concurring and dissenting opinion, lashing the plurality for its failure to give force to the express statement of Congress in § 4001(a) and masterfully rebutting the plurality's reinvention of the language of the Force Resolution.[122] And they challenge the plurality's presumption in favor of the government in such cases by returning to first principles and the separation of powers:

> In a government of separated powers, deciding finally on what is a reasonable degree of guaranteed liberty whether in peace or war (or some condition in between) is not well entrusted to the Executive Branch of Government, whose particular responsibility is to maintain security. For reasons of inescapable human nature, the branch of the Government asked to counter a serious threat is not the branch on which to rest the Nation's entire reliance in striking the balance between the will to win and the cost in liberty on the way to victory; the responsibility for security will naturally

[120]*Id.* at 2670 (quoting Ex parte Quirin , 317 U.S. 1, 47 (1942) (emphasis in original)).
[121]124 S. Ct. at 2643.
[122]*Id.* at 2654–56.

amplify the claim that security legitimately raises. A reasonable balance is more likely to be reached on the judgment of a different branch, just as Madison said in remarking that "the constant aim is to divide and arrange the several offices in such a manner as that each may be a check on the other— that the private interest of every individual may be a sentinel over the public rights."[123]

Given such clear and powerful language, it is doubly distressing to see Souter and Ginsburg stumble in the specific standards and their ultimate conclusion. First, they partially embrace *Quirin* and vaguely hint at possible support for its extreme application: "[T]he United States may detain captured enemies, and *Ex parte Quirin* . . . *may perhaps be* claimed for the proposition that the American citizenship of such a captive does not as such limit the Government's power to deal with him under the usages of war."[124] Whatever this "may perhaps be claimed" language means, it is clear that Souter and Ginsburg are not repudiating but, rather, reconciling their opinion with *Quirin*. More important, Souter accepts the ad hoc due process measures outlined by the plurality on the basis that it "will allow Hamdi to offer evidence that he is not an enemy combatant, and he should at the least have the benefit of that opportunity."[125] But, Souter then proceeds to say, "I do not mean to imply agreement that the Government could claim an evidentiary presumption casting the burden of rebuttal on Hamdi . . . or that an opportunity to litigate before a military tribunal might obviate or truncate enquiry by a court on habeas."[126] This ending is both confusing and unworthy of Souter and Ginsburg. It will remain a matter of debate just why they agreed to concur with the plurality rather than simply dissent. Their opinion remains a freakishly divided piece, part classic and part impressionistic. It would be best-captioned an "unfinished work" of Souter except that he allowed it to be published.

*Hamdi* should become a textbook example of the opportunistic styles of the Supreme Court and, in the case of Justices Scalia and Stevens, the lingering potential of members of the Court to fulfill

---

[123]*Id.* (quoting the Federalist No. 51, at 349 (James Madison) (J. Cooke ed., 1961)).
[124]124 S. Ct. at 2657 (emphasis added).
[125]*Id.* at 2660.
[126]*Id.*

the vaunted purposes of that institution as a guarantor of individual liberty. Unfortunately, as the *Rasul* opinion shows, at least four or five members have continued a long history of concessions to presidents in the national security context.[127] With the adoption of the *Mathews* test, the *Hamdi* Court has produced the potential for even greater concessions. In the play, *A Man for All Seasons*, an associate of Sir Thomas More criticized his tendency to yield to the demands of friends:

> My master Thomas More would give anything to anyone. Some say that good and some that that's bad, but I say he can't help it—and that's bad—because some day someone's going to ask him for something that he wants to keep; and he'll be out of practice.[128]

When it comes to civil liberties and due process, the Supreme Court has proven an easy touch for the executive branch and, while sharing More's giving personality, has lacked his allegiance to core principles. While declining to give the president his claim of absolute authority, *Hamdi* reflected this predisposition to give rather than to withhold from the chief executive. As such cases mount, one fears that when the Court majority finally decides that there is something it wants to keep in wartime, it will discover it is "out of practice," with no precedent to easily withhold what is demanded.

## B. Padilla *and Pointillism*

In *Hamdi* and *Padilla* the administration was advancing some of its most extreme interpretations of inherent presidential powers in the area of national security. President Bush asserted the right to unilaterally designate a citizen to be an enemy combatant and then strip him of his constitutional rights, including his access to courts and counsel. As noted earlier, Jose Padilla presented the most difficult case for the administration—a citizen arrested not on a "hot" battlefield like Hamdi but at O'Hare International Airport. Even if the accounts of the administration are correct and Padilla was pursuing potential terrorist targets, he was indistinguishable from a host of criminal defendants indicted and tried under the criminal code for terrorist activities. He claimed innocence, but the president

---

[127]Rasul v. Bush, 124 S. Ct. 2686, 2701 (2004) (Scalia, J., dissenting).

[128]Robert Bolt, A Man for All Seasons, act 1, sc. 2 (Metheun Drama 1995).

declared him an enemy combatant and refused to give him access to courts or counsel to prove his innocence. If there were ever an opportunity for a clear and classic interpretation of the Constitution, *Rumsfeld v. Padilla*[129] was the case for it.

The Great Writ remains the touchstone of a free society, the quintessential protection of a society committed to the rule of law.[130] In recognition of its importance, the Supreme Court has traditionally strived to resist its denial on technical grounds. Indeed, the Court has "consistently rejected interpretations that would suffocate the writ in stifling formalisms or hobble its effectiveness with the manacles of arcane and scholastic procedural requirements."[131] The result is a litany of past cases in which the Court granted exceptions to hear flawed habeas actions.[132] Although there was disagreement over the likely outcome of a decision on the merits, it was widely assumed that, given the gravity of the case, the Court would look beyond the jurisdictional and venue errors of the original Padilla filing—which sued Secretary of Defense Rumsfeld in New York. Instead, five justices ordered Padilla's case dismissed without prejudice because he sued Rumsfeld rather than Commander Melanie Marr, the commander of the brig in which Padilla is being held.[133] Likewise, the Court found that the Southern District of New York was not the proper federal district in which to bring the action. Obviously, those objections are technically correct, and the defense clearly blundered in the early fashioning of the case. The longer question, however,

---

[129]*Supra* note 2.

[130]Justice Story wrote of the Great Writ in such terms:

It is . . . justly esteemed the great bulwark of personal liberty; since it is the appropriate remedy to ascertain, whether any person is rightfully in confinement or not, and the cause of his confinement; and if no sufficient ground of detention appears, the party is entitled to his immediate discharge. This writ is most beneficially construed; and is applied to every case of illegal restraint, whatever it may; for every restraint on a man's liberty is, in the eye of the law, an imprisonment, wherever may be the place or whatever may be the manner, in which the restraint is effect.

3 Joseph Story, Commentaries on the Constitution 1333–1336 (1883).

[131]Hensley v. Municipal Court, 411 U.S. 345, 350 (1973); see also Rumsfeld v. Padilla, 124 S. Ct. 2711, 2729 (2004) (Stevens, J., dissenting).

[132]See, e.g., Braden v. 30th Judicial Circuit Court, 410 U.S. 484, 495 (1973); Ex parte Endo, 323 U.S. 283 (1944); see also Padilla, 124 S. Ct. at 2727 (Kennedy, J., concurring).

[133]Padilla, 124 S. Ct. at 2724.

is whether such errors justified the dismissal of the action under these circumstances. Chief Justice Rehnquist insisted that Padilla's case is "not unique in any way" and the government "did not attempt to hide from Padilla's lawyer where it had taken him."[134]

That portrayal of Padilla's case was overtly evasive and artificial. The Court seemed to go out of its way to focus on the most insular procedural facts while ignoring the larger picture. To extend the earlier artistic analogy, the Rehnquist opinion read like a type of judicial pointillism. Georges Seurat made the pointillist style famous with his masterpiece *A Sunday in the Park on the Island of La Grande Jatte*, a massive picture composed of an estimated 3,346,000 individual dots. In some ways, pointillism is a highly deceptive style of painting. A precursor to more abstract art, pointillism retains a narrative object, depicting the true image in a slightly idealized fashion. Yet, as one draws closer, the picture is lost and one finds a series of individual dots. Thus, one requires distance to achieve the effect of "optical mixing" in which the colors and objects are fully apparent. Rehnquist takes the style in reverse. He reduces a case of sweeping importance to individual legal dots and then forces the attention of the Court to the smallest possible dot. The larger picture is apparent only when one stands back and contemplates the authoritarian character of the powers claimed by President Bush, or the deprivation of the citizen's basic liberties for almost two years. Rehnquist focuses instead on the caption of the case, the smallest dot.

By focusing on the smallest dot, Rehnquist avoids the broader pictures of separation-of-powers issues.[135] In holding a citizen for almost two years without charge or trial, President Bush was asserting supremacy over both legislative and judicial authority. Moreover, this usurpation of authority was done for the worst of possible

---

[134]*Id.* at 2721.

[135]Chief Justice Rehnquist has long been thought to hold the most extreme view of inherent presidential power of anyone on the Court—at least before Justice Thomas' dissent in *Hamdi*. Rehnquist had previously stated that aspects of *Korematsu* were rightly decided and had criticized the inclination of civil libertarians to resolve disputes by favoring liberty interests over governmental interests:

> In any civilized society the most important task is achieving a proper balance between freedom and order. In wartime, reason and history both suggest that this balance shifts to some degree in favor of order—in favor of the government's ability to deal with conditions that threaten the national well-being. It simply cannot be said, therefore, that in every conflict between individual liberty and governmental authority the former should prevail. And if we feel

reasons under the Constitution: to elicit information from a suspect.[136] Contrary to Rehnquist's account, the government did not tell Padilla's lawyer where he was held. It is unclear what constitutes the hiding of a prisoner, but Padilla was clearly being held incommunicado, and his location was discovered only through the media.[137] The government claimed the right to move Padilla secretly and unilaterally. As an enemy combatant under the Bush policy, Padilla's location was virtually arbitrary since he was held and interrogated at the whim of the chief executive. Thus, the Court's refusal to see a basis for an exception in such a case appears more an act of willful blindness than admirable restraint, particularly given the Court's past willingness to grant exceptions in less significant cases—not to mention its willingness this term to blissfully set aside a host of

---

free to criticize court decisions that curtail civil liberty, we must also feel free to look critically at decisions favorable to civil liberty.

William H. Rehnquist, All the Laws But One: Civil Liberties in Wartime 222–23 (1998). While few would argue that civil liberties should always trump national security claims, there are solid constitutional arguments for a presumption in favor of civil liberties. See generally Randy Barnett, Restoring the Lost Constitution: The Presumption of Liberty (2004). Moreover, this quote does suggest that Rehnquist, like O'Connor, is inclined toward a fluid balancing test that leaves the Court as the arbiter of such conflicts.

[136]There was surprisingly little discussion, except in Justice Stevens' dissent, of the open motivation of the government to use such long-term, isolated detention as a method of interrogation. The flagrant use of unconstitutional measures for interrogation clearly reflects an ends-justifies-the-means approach in the Bush administration that seems to have contributed to such abuses as the torture scandal at Abu Ghraib prison and allegations of homicides in interrogation. It is remarkable that the administration's repeated references to the benefits of such interrogations (including in its public press conference on *Padilla* before the ruling) did not warrant greater attention from the Court. Instead, there remains an appearance that, at least for some of the members, such abuses are less reprehensible when done for the "right reason." It is precisely what Justice Louis Brandeis cautioned against in his famous warning on the inherent dangers to liberty:

> Experience should teach us to be most on our guard to protect liberty when the Government's purposes are beneficent. Men born to freedom are naturally alert to repel invasion of their liberty by evil-minded rulers. The greatest dangers to liberty lurk in insidious encroachment by men of zeal, well-meaning but without understanding.

Olmstead v. United States, 277 U.S. 438, 479 (1928) (Brandeis, J., dissenting). It is a warning that seems prophetic for both the policies of the current administration and the unguarded attitude of a majority of the current Supreme Court.

[137]Padilla, 124 S. Ct. at 2732 (Stevens, J., dissenting).

procedural barriers in the case of Vice President Dick Cheney.[138] In *Cheney v. United States District Court*[139] the majority had little difficulty facing the separation of powers issue; it didn't focus on the insular procedural dots, as it did in *Padilla*. To the contrary, Kennedy (with Rehnquist joining) repeatedly brought the focus back from the dots to the broader picture:

> These separation-of-powers considerations should inform a court of appeals' evaluation of a mandamus petition involving the President or the Vice President. Accepted mandamus standards are broad enough to allow a court of appeals to prevent a lower court from interfering with a coequal branch's ability to discharge its constitutional responsibilities . . . .
>
> . . . A party's need for information is only one facet of the problem. An important factor weighing in the opposite direction is the burden imposed by the discovery orders. This is not a routine discovery dispute. The discovery requests are directed to the Vice President and other senior Government officials . . . to give advice and make recommendations to the President . . . . This Court has held, on more than one occasion, that "[t]he high respect that is owed to the office of the Chief Executive . . . is a matter that should inform the conduct of the entire proceeding, including the timing and scope of discovery," . . . and that the Executive's "constitutional responsibilities and status [are] factors counseling judicial deference and restraint" in the conduct of litigation against it.[140]

That broader picture was omitted when the interest at stake was that of an individual—and, by extension, all citizens subject to a unilateral enemy combatant determination. Whereas a discovery case against the vice president is clearly "not a routine discovery dispute," Padilla's case was "not unique in any way." Whereas mandamus rules were "broad enough" to hear the merits of Cheney's claims, there was no special reason to grant an exception to a simple citizen languishing for nearly two years in a Navy brig. Rather than address those issues, Rehnquist raised the spectre of

---

[138]Cheney v. U.S. Dist. Court for the Dist. of Columbia, 124 S. Ct. 2576 (2004).

[139]*Id.*

[140]*Id.* at 2589–2590.

"rampant forum shopping" by habeas prisoners[141] if an exception were granted—despite the fact that the Court could easily craft this exception so narrowly as to avoid any such floodgate of litigation. While the Court in *Padilla* and *Hamdi* repeatedly refers to the need to offer deference and support to a president in wartime, it does not see the countervailing exigency in protecting the rights of citizens during wartime. History has shown that citizens are at greatest risk of abuse during wartime, but there is no countervailing urgency to support their interests in cases like *Padilla*.

In his dissenting opinion, Justice Stevens excoriates the majority for its refusal to hear the merits of a case of such "profound importance."[142] To refuse on such technical grounds begs the question of why, when the Court can grant an exception, it chose not to do so. Stevens notes that it is rather hard to maintain a "bright line rule" rationale in an area riddled with exceptions.[143] Even without a single past exception, however, the *Padilla* case would justify such a measure of discretion—particularly when, as Stevens points out, the government was preventing access to courts and counsel to assist in unlawful interrogations.

> [Executive detention] may not . . . be justified by the naked interest in using unlawful procedures to extract information. Incommunicado detention for months on end is such a procedure. Whether the information so procured is more or less reliable than that acquired by more extreme forms of torture is of no consequence. For if this Nation is to remain true to the ideals symbolized by its flag, it must not wield the tools of tyrants even to resist an assault by the forces of tyranny.[144]

Stevens correctly labels the policies used against Padilla for what they are: tools of tyranny. Clearly, many Framers would have viewed such measures in the same terms—regardless of the motivation or promises of self-restraint in the use of unchecked authority.

---

[141]Ironically, while the Justice Department emphasized this danger, it was silent on its own record of blatant forum shopping, of moving defendants like John Walker Lindh, Yaser Hamdi, and Zacarias Moussoui to the U.S. Court of Appeals for the Fourth Circuit because of its reputation for extreme deference to the government and political conservatism.

[142]Padilla, 124 S. Ct. at 2729 (Stevens, J., dissenting).

[143]*Id.* at 2732.

[144]*Id.* at 2735.

Blackstone once observed that if "the preservation of . . . personal liberty . . . were left in the power of any, the highest magistrate to imprison arbitrarily whoever he or his officers thought proper, . . . there would soon be an end of all other rights and immunities."[145] Blackstone's admonition could not have been more relevant and compelling than in the case of Jose Padilla. The majority's effort to downplay the importance of the case, or its sweeping implications, is nevertheless impressive. It takes remarkable concentration to stare at this single pointillist dot and not allow the overall picture to enter one's peripheral vision. After all, these same justices were willing to circumvent clear federal statutes and the Suspension Clause in *Hamdi* to adopt a more flexible accommodation of the president. Likewise, in the *Cheney* case, these same justices overcame procedural barriers to accommodate the interests of the vice president.[146] In such cases, these justices proudly highlighted their constitutional *realpolitik* in balancing interests and creating ad hoc procedures. But, when a citizen has been imprisoned for nearly two years in flagrant violation of the Constitution, the Court can find no basis to grant a procedural exception to protect not just his liberty but the integrity of the tripartite system itself. In *Padilla*, the Court came face to face with the raw use of autocratic power and walked past it, without comment, to rule on an insular procedural point. It was a failure of the highest order for a court designed as the final line of defense against governmental abuse.

## C. A Question of Control: Rasul and the Near Extraterritorial Application of U.S. Constitutional Law

The final case of the trilogy, *Rasul v. Bush*,[147] presented a different claim of authority on the part of the president. Like *Hamdi* and *Padilla*, *Rasul* involves a claim of unilateral and absolute authority—a claim so extreme that it threatened the balance of power in our tripartite system. In *Rasul*, however, the president was in a far stronger position because the individuals were neither U.S. citizens nor held in the United States. In establishing the prison camp at Guantanamo Bay, Cuba, the government clearly sought not just

---

[145]1 W. Blackstone, Commentaries on the Laws of England 132.

[146]Cheney v. U.S. Dist. Court for the Dist. of Columbia, 124 S. Ct. 2576, 2593 (2004).

[147]See *supra* note 3.

added security from foreign terrorists but also added protection from federal jurists. President Bush sought to create his own prison system, with its own standards, just beyond our borders. As such, this action represented one of the greatest threats to the independent judicial system since *Marbury v. Madison*.[148] If the president could operate such an alternative legal system, he would have a kind of "railroad switch" with which to control which cases went to the federal courts and which went to his own court system.

Indeed, President Bush had already displayed a taste for such plenary power. Zacarias Moussaoui is a foreign national who was arrested in the United States as an alleged al-Qaeda terrorist.[149] He was sent to federal court for trial. Jose Padilla is a U.S. citizen arrested in the United States as an alleged al-Qaeda terrorist. He was denied access to counsel or the courts. Richard Reid is a foreign citizen arrested in the United States as an admitted al-Qaeda member.[150] He was given access to counsel and the courts. Hundreds of other suspected terrorists were sent to Guantanamo Bay and denied access to federal court. Yaser Hamdi is a citizen who was sent to Guantanamo Bay, but was then sent to the United States. He was denied access to counsel or the courts. John Walker Lindh is a citizen arrested, like Hamdi, on a battlefield, but then was given access to counsel and the courts.[151] These cases reflect a Caesar-like power in the president in which fundamental rights under the Constitution become a matter of pure discretion.[152] Central to this power is the maintenance of a parallel alternative judicial system that can be utilized at the will or whim of the president.

Because of the location of the prison and the nationality of the detainees, *Rasul* was admittedly a more difficult case than either *Padilla* or *Hamdi*. Although I have called for greater extraterritorial

---

[148]5 U.S. 137 (1803).

[149]Jerry Markin, Terror Case Is Cleared For Trial, Washington Post, April 23, 2004, at A1.

[150]Bomb Suspect Offers Guilty Plea, Washington Post, October 3, 2002, at A1.

[151]See Katherine Q. Seelye, The American in the Taliban; Regretful Lindh Gets 20 Years in the Taliban Case, New York Times, Oct. 5, 2002, at A1.

[152]Jonathan Turley, Naked Power, Arbitrary Rule, Los Angeles Times, July 21, 2003, at 14.

application of U.S. laws in statutory[153] and constitutional cases[154] and criticized the presumption against extraterritorial application, there are compelling arguments that can be made against such extraterritoriality. Moreover, a president's inherent authority is at its apex in the case of actions taken abroad in the name of foreign policy or national security. If a president has authority to order the assassination of a foreign national abroad, a detention or trial before execution could be viewed simply as a lesser power included in the greater.[155] *Rasul* seemed to pit the authority of all three branches in a zero-sum struggle on the question of authority over noncitizen detainees held abroad.

The two Australian and twelve Kuwaiti citizens who were plaintiffs in *Rasul* forced the Court to confront whether the president has the right to bar access to counsel and the courts for foreign nationals indefinitely detained. The Supreme Court was not prepared to answer such questions, however. Instead, Justice Stevens structured

---

[153]See generally Jonathan Turley, "When in Rome": Multinational Misconduct and the Presumption Against Extraterritoriality, 84 Nw. U. L. Rev. 598 (1990); Jonathan Turley, Transnational Discrimination and the Economics of Extraterritorial Regulation, 70 B.U. L. Rev. 339 (1990).

[154]Turley, Tribunals and Tribulations, *supra* note 18.

[155]The answer to such questions may be found in the very fact of long-term detention. A president is sometimes required to issue special orders to kill a foreign national as a matter of urgency and immediate threat to the United States. President Bush would and could not execute such orders for the hundreds of prisoners being detained, particularly given the relative paucity of evidence that some of these detainees are actually unlawful combatants. Once detained, the claim of exigency, while not eliminated entirely, is certainly reduced. This point was raised by Justice Kennedy in his concurring opinion:

> Indefinite detention without trial or other proceeding presents altogether different considerations. It allows friends and foes alike to remain in detention. It suggests a weaker case of military necessity and much greater alignment with the traditional function of habeas corpus. Perhaps, where detainees are taken from a zone of hostilities, detention without proceedings or trial would be justified by military necessity for a matter of weeks; but as the period of detention stretches from months to years, the case for continued detention to meet military exigencies becomes weaker.

Rasul v. Bush, 124 S. Ct. 2686, 2700 (2004).

the case as a strictly statutory matter. Distinguishing the decision in *Johnson v. Eisentrager*,[156] a case that reviewed and rejected *constitutional* claims, Stevens insisted that *Rasul* raised the alternative *statutory* basis for such claims.[157] As a matter of *statutory* authority, Stevens adopted a broad interpretation of the authorization to hear cases "within their respective jurisdictions" to rule that the Guantanamo Bay prisoners were entitled to judicial review under 28 U.S.C. § 2241. Emphasizing *Braden v. 30th Judicial Circuit Court of Kentucky*[158] as the controlling precedent, Stevens read the terms as allowing the exercise of jurisdiction as long as "the custodian can be reached by service of process."[159] While there will remain a roaring debate over true precedent before *Rasul*,[160] Stevens adopted a clear test as to future petitions for review, a test that focuses not on the location of the custody but on the custodian.

This clarity was quickly lost, however, when Stevens attempted to conform such a view to the Court's general presumption against extraterritoriality. Stevens resolved the tension, but insisted that *Rasul* was not an extraterritorial but rather a strictly territorial case. Since Guantanamo Bay was a military base under the *control* of the United States, he construed the locus to be territory *of* the United States.[161] Like the opinion of Souter and Ginsburg in *Hamdi*, the opinion of Stevens in *Rasul* was clear (albeit controversial) until the final pages, at which point Stevens shifted to a convenient rationale. The opinion seemed to confine the new ruling to the facts of Guantanamo Bay, suggesting that, in the absence of the fairly unique language of the 1903 lease agreement, the question remains open.[162] At the same time, when he declined to speculate about "[w]hatever traction the presumption against extraterritoriality might have in other contexts,"[163] Stevens seemed to suggest that the *Rasul* decision

[156]339 U.S. 763 (1950).

[157]Rasul, 124 S. Ct. at 2694.

[158]410 U.S. 484 (1973).

[159]Rasul, 124 S. Ct. at 2695.

[160]*Id*. at 2703 ("To do so neatly and cleanly, it must either argue that our decision in *Braden* overruled *Eisentrager*, or admit that *it* is overruling *Eisentrager*.") (Scalia, J., dissenting).

[161]*Id*. at 2691.

[162]*Id*. at 2696.

[163]*Id*.

may indeed be expanded. Such judicial minimalism can be easily justified on the institutional preference to rule on the narrowest possible ground, but it seems more the product of a deeply divided Court. *Rasul* was a case calling for a holistic and complete decision. It makes little sense to focus on the lease agreement if the test is one of control over the custody of an individual. Whether a detainee is held at the Bagram Air Base in Afghanistan or at Camp X-Ray at Guantanamo Bay, the status of the custodian does not appear materially different.

*Rasul* was framed not by what was included in the opinion but by what was consciously omitted. There is no analysis of the fundamental implications for the separation-of-powers doctrine. The Court is silent on the threat to a tripartite system if the president can create a fully functioning independent judicial system just beyond the border.[164] It is silent on the distortion arising from the presumption against extraterritoriality. If Congress did mean for § 2241 to be read expansively so that jurisdiction would follow the custodian, it is unclear why the presumption is even relevant or why it would trump such an intent.[165]

With such core issues missing from the case, *Rasul* looks like a Jim Dine painting. Dine's *Self-Portrait* was a picture of the artist's clothing, but he was missing. One was left looking at the suit and

---

[164]Stevens declined to incorporate separation of powers rationales even when pressed by Scalia. Scalia challenged the Court "to explain why our almost categorical rule of *stare decisis* in statutory cases should be set aside in order to complicate the present war, *and*, having set it aside, to explain why the habeas statute does not mean what it plainly says." *Id.* at 2704. Putting aside the questionable suggestion that hearings would "complicate the present war," one factor that may have influenced the Court to adopt a broader interpretation is the threat posed by the president's policies to separation of powers. Here, the president had forced the issue by capitalizing on a possible gap in federal jurisdiction to create his own alternative judicial system. Absent an express limitation in the statutory language, the extreme assertion of presidential power can inform the Court's statutory interpretation—even if the Court is not deciding on constitutional grounds.

[165]As noted in an earlier work, the Court has accepted that the presumption against extraterritoriality is no longer relevant to some types of statutes, particularly antitrust and "market" statutes, Turley, When in Rome, *supra* note 153. In the same fashion, the globalization of the war on terror may have made the presumption a legal anachronism. President Bush has repeatedly stressed that borders have little contemporary meaning in the war on terror. See, e.g., Joseph Curl, You Will Pay a Serious Price, Bush Tells Aggressor Nations, Washington Times, Oct. 18, 2001, at A1.

wondering about the man. This technique makes for intriguing art, but poor law. What was missing in *Rasul* was the Court itself. The case dealt vaguely with hearings and habeas but not the necessary and independent role of the judiciary at a time of war. Once again the Court had succeeded in resolving a dispute, but done little to create a coherent and unified theory of judicial review for foreign nationals held beyond our borders. Stevens completes this picture of omission in his final paragraph:

> Whether and what further proceedings may become necessary after respondents make their response to the merits of petitioners' claims are matters that we need not address now. What is presently at stake is only whether the federal courts have jurisdiction to determine the legality of the Executive's potentially indefinite detention of individuals who claim to be wholly innocent of wrongdoing.[166]

This has now become a standard signature for this divided Court: leaving any and all potentially divisive issues for a later case—and leaving both the detainees and lower courts with years of litigation.[167]

---

[166]Rasul, 124 S. Ct. at 2699.

[167]This habit has led to massive and avoidable confusion, as in the recent decision in *Blakely v. Washington*, 124 S. Ct. 2531 (2004), that suggested (but did not rule) that the federal guidelines may be unconstitutional in whole or in part—producing national confusion among the circuits and uncertainty as to the status of a significant percentage of federal cases. United States v. Curtis, No. 02-16224, 2004 U.S. App. LEXIS 16432 (11th Cir. August 10, 2004) (holding that *Blakely* does not apply to sentences under the Federal Sentencing Guidelines); United States v. Booker, 375 F.3d 508 (7th Cir. 2004) (holding that *Blakely* applies to sentences imposed under the Federal Sentencing Guidelines); United States v. Ameline, 376 F.3d 967 (9th Cir. 2004) (holding that *Blakely* applies to sentences imposed under the Federal Sentencing Guidelines); United States v. Mooney, No. 02-3388, 2004 WL 1636960 (8th Cir. July, 23 2004) (holding the Federal Sentencing Guidelines unconstitutional under *Blakely*); United States v. Pineiro, No. 03-30437, 2004 WL 1543170 (5th Cir. July 12, 2004) (holding that *Blakely* does not apply to sentences imposed under the Federal Sentencing Guidelines); and United States v. Hammoud, No. 03-4253, 2004 WL 1730309 (4th Cir. Aug. 2, 2004) (en banc) (holding that *Blakely* does not overturn sentences under the Federal Guidelines). This confusion and alarm was so great that a question was certified for the Court to clarify its earlier opinion, by the Second Circuit. See United States v. Penaranda, 375 F.3d 238 (2d Cir. 2004) (certifying question of *Blakely's* application to the Supreme Court). As in *Hamdi* and *Rasul*, *Blakely* should be an embarrassing failure of the Court to satisfy the minimal requirement of judicial review—to clarify rather than confuse the legal issues raised by litigants.

There is certainly a value in allowing lower courts to develop such issues before the Supreme Court issues a ruling. However, as in its fatally ambiguous rulings in *Blakely v. Washington*,[168] the failure to give any guidelines to judges inevitably leaves a vacuum of authority and confusion. With hundreds of men deprived of their liberty without judicial review, the Court's inclination to leave such an important question to a later date is a reckless habit.[169] Indeed, the administration has already expanded on the gaps in *Rasul* and *Hamdi* in an attempt to minimize the significance of the decisions—including conducting hearings at Guantanamo Bay that lack basic due process protections.[170]

The dissent by Justice Scalia artfully deconstructs the majority opinion and criticizes each effort to brush over conflicting precedent or gaps in analysis. But Scalia also declines to offer substantive analysis on the implications of the Bush policies for the separation of powers, despite his criticism of the constitutional/statutory distinction. Moreover, Scalia does not question the continued relevance of a territorial presumption in the age of global anti-terrorism rules. Finally, Scalia places great emphasis on the different constitutional status of citizens versus non-citizens. This is perfectly consistent with Scalia's dissent in *Hamdi*. In *Hamdi*, O'Connor dismissed the relevance of citizenship for enemy combatants.[171] Yet, in *Rasul*, the dissenting justices cite the hypocritical statement of the solicitor general that "citizens of the United States, because of their constitutional circumstances, may have greater rights with respect to the scope and reach of the habeas statute as the Court has or would interpret it."[172] Suddenly, the impressionists of *Hamdi* were reconverted into more classic judicial artists when the latter style served to support the president's anti-terror policies.

---

[168]124 S. Ct. 2531 (2004).

[169]This is not to say that this is a recently adopted habit, only an increasing habit. Indeed, in *Youngstown*, Jackson complained that "court decisions are indecisive because of the judicial practice of dealing with the largest questions in the most narrow way." Youngstown Sheet & Tube Co. v. Sawyer, 343 U.S. 579, 635 (1952) (Jackson, J., concurring).

[170]Melissa Block, Federal Government Files Brief Stating They Believe Guantanamo Bay Detainees Should Not Be Granted Access to Legal Counsel Despite Supreme Court Ruling Allowing Them Court Access (NPR Broadcast, Aug. 3, 2004).

[171]Hamdi v. Rumsfeld, 124 S. Ct. 2633, 2640 (2004).

[172]Rasul v. Bush, 124 S. Ct. 2686, 2708 (2004) (quoting Transcript of Oral Argument at 40, Rasul v. Bush, 124 S. Ct. 2684 (2004) (03-334) (argument of solicitor general)).

Despite these criticisms, it is important to observe that the Stevens and Scalia opinions in *Rasul* were significantly more thoughtful and honest in their analysis than the Court's opinion in *Hamdi*. Moreover, the effort of the Court to extend jurisdiction to the detainees was a corrective measure, albeit on statutory rather than on constitutional grounds. Yet, it is also important not to overplay *Rasul*, *Hamdi*, or *Padilla*. After all, even *Quirin* granted review of the basis for the detention and trial of the saboteurs. Missing are the details that define due process. As the Bush military tribunal proceedings illustrate, it is of little value to have a "hearing" when it is structured to virtually guarantee whatever outcome is demanded by the administration. Indeed, it may be worse, as in *Hamdi*, to grant hearings but allow them to be conducted without basic procedural protections. Such hearings amount to superficial reproductions of a legitimate judicial system—lending an appearance of legitimacy without the substance of true adversarial proceedings. In many ways, proceedings like those being conducted at Guantanamo Bay (or likely to be conducted under the *Hamdi* decision) are the legal version of the Potemkin Village. The legend has it that Prince Grigory Aleksandrovich Potemkin hired artists to create realistic facades of actual villages to give the appearance of progress as Catherine II made her grand tour of Ukraine and the Crimea in 1787. It now appears that detainees are likely to be moved through Potemkin proceedings, where a facade of courts, judges, and rules will hide the lack of substance demanded by fundamental principles of due process.

## IV. Conclusion

The analogy of changing methodologies of the Supreme Court to different artistic styles reflects common elements between the law and art. Both are creative and interpretative enterprises. Even more classic narrative artists like Wyeth are engaged in interpretation or translation of their subjects. Artistic works are not photographic pieces but the translation of an object through the lens of an artistic eye. Nevertheless, there are radically different artistic views on how to honor the original object, a spectrum from a more narrative style to complete abstraction. In the same way, legal theories of interpretation spread across a similar spectrum from more narrative to abstract translations. Textualism comes closest to classic schools of painting, where the faithful depiction of the object is at the core of the artistic effort. Intentionalism comes closest to modern painters like Wyeth who remain largely faithful to the object but allow some interpretative expansion on the object. New theories of legal interpretation like those of hermeneutics come closest to abstract art where the object has the least hold on the creative enterprise. These more abstract theories of interpretation are distinctly reader-centered rather than text-centered and share a certain affinity to the works of artists like Picasso or Kandinsky.

The analogy to these art forms is intended to differentiate between true judicial artistic expression and faux styles adopted for the convenience of the moment. Obviously, the use of this vehicle to examine the trilogy of national security cases reveals a highly negative view of the quality and consistency of the Court's opinions. This is certainly the case with the plurality decision in *Hamdi* and the jurisprudence of Justice O'Connor. However, it reflects something more profound than an admittedly peevish take on the cases. The Supreme Court as an institution has proven to be deeply flawed during these critical times. Moreover, the Court's increasing use of vague opinions is due to a dysfunctional split on the Court that robs any majority or plurality author of the ability to go beyond the most minimalist expression. In my view, this latter problem is due in part to the size of the Court itself. Decisions like *Rasul* reflect the long-standing split on the Court. The Court often (as is shown in all three cases) opts to leave major and relevant questions unresolved to maintain a plurality or a five-justice majority.[173] The nine-member Court is particularly susceptible to such divisions and produces other negative consequences for the Court.[174] While such sharp divisions would not be eliminated on a nineteen-member court (any more than such divisions are eliminated on courts of appeal), I believe that an expansion of the Court is long overdue and badly needed. The low quality of these decisions should focus attention not just on their implication for detainees but their implication for the institution itself. I submit that it is time to have a good-faith debate about the optimal structure and size of the Supreme Court.

[173]See Jonathan Turley, Justice O'Connor Wields A Mighty Vote, Los Angeles Times, July 4, 2002, at A17.

[174]See generally Turley, Unpacking the Court, *supra* note 7, at 155.

Putting aside my annual call for an expansion of the Court, the trilogy of national security cases offers reason for both hope and alarm. While Justices Souter and Ginsburg sought, curiously, to join in concurrence with the plurality in *Hamdi* (despite their fundamental disagreement with that decision), there was no blind insistence of unanimity on any possible ground that we saw in *Quirin*. However, these cases reaffirm the fragility of our constitutional rights and the uncertain commitment of the Supreme Court as their final line of defense. There remain four or five justices who seem willing, if not eager, to yield core protections to the exigencies of the moment. It seems tragically similar to Andre Breton's description of abstract artists' "discontent with [their] destiny."[175] The Constitution was designed for this very moment in time; it was designed for that moment when the Court stood in the path of a president seeking tyrannical or autocratic power. Given the natural inclination of the powerful to exceed their limitations, it was a moment that the Framers knew was likely to occur not once but repeatedly through the life of this Republic. In that moment is the destiny of the Court, a moment that defines it and explains the extraordinary steps taken to create it and to protect it as an institution. The refusal to carry out that destiny reflects a corruption of the Court that began long ago in the national security area and persists in such cases as *Hamdi*. Through balancing tests and fluid interpretations of provisions like the Suspension Clause, the Court has been unwilling to be confined by the text and first principles in the Constitution. Instead, it has asserted the right to determine its own destiny, defining a new reality, a constitutional surreality.

---

[175] Andre Breton, Surrealist Manifesto 10 (1924).

# Making a Federal Case Out of It:
## *Sabri v. United States*
## and the Constitution of Leviathan

*Gary Lawson**

## I. Introduction

The popular expression "Don't make a federal case out of it!"[1] only makes sense if federal involvement is something unusual or special that is reserved for matters of urgent national interest. It assumes that a "federal case" is, or at least ought to be, something relatively rare and noteworthy.

For the founding generation, federal involvement in people's affairs, especially through the criminal law, was in fact a relatively rare and noteworthy event. In *The Federalist*, James Madison told the citizens of New York that the powers of the proposed new national government "will be exercised principally on external objects, as war, peace, negotiation, and foreign commerce," while the states would be primarily responsible for "all the objects which, in the ordinary course of affairs, concern the lives, liberties, and properties of the people, and the internal order, improvement, and prosperity of the State."[2] The first congressional statute devoted to defining federal crimes, enacted in 1790, largely vindicated Madison's prediction. It was limited to such matters as treason; murder,

---

*Much of this article is based on a brief filed by the Cato Institute as an amicus curiae in *Sabri v. United States*. I am grateful to Roger Pilon and Bob Levy for giving me the opportunity to work on that brief and for their invaluable comments and guidance in its production.

[1] The expression evidently emerged in the middle of the twentieth century. See Eric Partridge, A Dictionary of Catch Phrases 52 (1977) (identifying 1950 as the expression's date of origin) (cited in Judith Resnik, Constricting Remedies: The Rehnquist Judiciary, Congress, and Federal Power, 78 Ind. L.J. 223, 285 (2003)).

[2] The Federalist No. 45, at 292–93 (James Madison) (Clinton Rossiter ed., 1961). Federal tax collectors, Madison further predicted, "will be principally on the seacoast, and not very numerous." *Id.*

manslaughter, or larceny on federal territory; crimes on the high seas; counterfeiting; stealing or falsifying federal court records, bribery of federal judges, perjury, and interference with federal service of process; interference with foreign ambassadors; misprision of felony with respect to federal crimes; attempts to rescue accused traitors before trial; and (my personal favorite) attempting to rescue the dead body of an executed murderer that had been given over to medical professionals for dissection.[3] Federal criminal law remained confined to such topics until the Civil War, and it really did not begin to take anything resembling its present shape until the New Deal.[4] For much of the nation's history, making a federal case out of it was indeed an extraordinary event.

The Supreme Court's unanimous decision in *Sabri v. United States*,[5] issued on May 17, 2004, demonstrates that modern lexicographers may have to perform some major surgery on that old expression. Basim Sabri was federally indicted for attempting to bribe a state official in connection with the administration of a state program. The only federal involvement in the events giving rise to the indictment was that the entity for which the state official worked received some federal funds. The statute under which Sabri was indicted did not require the attempted bribe to *involve* those federal funds in any way, but required only that a portion of the state agency's multi-million dollar budget come from federal funds. The Supreme Court thought it obvious that this statute was constitutional. A federal case just ain't what it used to be.

The story of how attempted bribery of state officials, with no claim that the bribe concerned the use of federal money, has come to be regarded as uncontroversially within the constitutional scope of federal power highlights virtually all of the myriad ways in which the government envisioned by Madison has developed into precisely the Leviathan that Anti-federalist opponents of the Constitution

---

[3] Act of Apr. 30, 1790, ch. IX, 1 Stat. 112–19.

[4] For a concise history of the development of federal criminal law, see Kathleen F. Brickey, Criminal Mischief: The Federalization of American Criminal Law, 46 Hastings L.J. 1135, 1137–41 (1995). For a longer version, see Thomas J. Maroney, Fifty Years of Federalization of Criminal Law: Sounding the Alarm or "Crying Wolf"?, 50 Syracuse L. Rev. 1317 (2000).

[5] 124 S. Ct. 1941 (2004).

feared. The statute at issue in *Sabri* is a microcosm of almost everything that has gone wrong in constitutional law over the nation's history with respect to the scope of national powers. In order for the national government to claim jurisdiction over the kinds of offenses with which Sabri was charged, one must simultaneously misinterpret the scope and/or sources of the federal government's power to spend money, power to regulate interstate commerce, and power to implement its enumerated authority through the promulgation of criminal laws. As *Sabri* demonstrates, a long string of Congresses, presidents, and Supreme Courts have all been more than up to this considerable task.

Perhaps mercifully, however, the *Sabri* case did not cleanly present these fundamental issues for decision by the Court. The case arose in a procedural context that left many of those constitutional questions in the background. Furthermore, the constitutional claims made by the parties shifted several times during the course of Sabri's appeals, which makes it difficult to determine exactly what was at issue at each stage of the proceedings. Accordingly, Part II of this article describes at length the somewhat convoluted legal maneuverings that led up to the Supreme Court's *Sabri* decision and the procedural wrinkles that significantly skewed the presentation and decision of the case. Part III then looks beyond the technicalities to identify the faulty constitutional principles concerning national power that the Court in *Sabri* either adopted or simply took for granted. Some of those faulty principles are so deeply ingrained in modern jurisprudence that they were not challenged, or even identified, by the parties to the case. Part IV briefly reflects on *Sabri's* long-term implications for limited government.

## II. The *Sabri* Litigation

Basim Omar Sabri is a Minnesota real estate developer.[6] In 2001, Sabri was planning some commercial development in the city of Minneapolis for which he sought city help in the form of regulatory and financial assistance.[7] During this time, Brian Herron was a member of the Minneapolis City Council and a member of the Board of Commissioners of the Minneapolis Community Development Agency

[6] *Id.* at 1944.
[7] *Id.*

(MCDA), a municipal agency that has authority to provide loans and grants to business development projects.[8] A federal criminal indictment charged Sabri with attempting to bribe Herron to help secure needed regulatory approvals, induce property owners to sell their land to Sabri through threats of eminent domain, and obtain financial assistance from the city of Minneapolis and the MCDA.[9]

If these claims are true,[10] one can understand why the city of Minneapolis and the state of Minnesota would be concerned. One would expect bribery and corruption charges to be brought by local or state prosecutors against both Sabri and Herron. It is less obvious why the federal government would get involved in this matter. Sabri, after all, was not accused of trying to bribe federal officials. The federal government had nothing to do with the land deals that he was trying to execute. There was no federal official who could help him, corruptly or otherwise.

The indictment identified the following basis for federal criminal jurisdiction: During 2001, the city of Minneapolis was expected to receive about $28.8 million in federal aid, and the MCDA was expected to receive about $23 million in federal aid.[11] There was no claim in the indictment that any of Sabri's activities involved any of these federal funds.[12] The claim was simply that Herron, the alleged target of Sabri's bribes, worked for local governmental entities that received some form of federal financial assistance in some of their operations.[13]

The statute under which Sabri was charged, section 666(a)(2) of Title 18 of the United States Code, does not require the federal government to claim anything more than it did. The statute, entitled "Theft or bribery concerning programs receiving Federal funds," provides that if a state governmental organization receives more

[8] Id.

[9] Id.

[10] There has not yet been a trial, so the truth of the indictment's allegations has not been tested. That is because Sabri challenged the adequacy of the indictment, and courts must assume that the indictment's allegations are true for purposes of ruling on that challenge.

[11] 124 S. Ct. at 1944.

[12] United States v. Sabri, 326 F.3d 937, 938 (8th Cir. 2003) (reciting allegations of the indictment).

[13] Id.

than $10,000 in federal benefits in a given year, then anyone who "corruptly gives, offers, or agrees to give anything of value to any person, with intent to influence or reward an agent of [such] an organization . . . or any agency thereof, in connection with any business, transaction, or series of transactions of such organization, government, or agency involving anything of value of $5,000 or more; shall be fined under this title, imprisoned not more than 10 years, or both."[14] Put simply, the statute criminalizes attempted bribery of state or local officials provided that the state or local agency receives nontrivial federal benefits in connection with some facet of its operations. If, for example, Minneapolis received federal benefits solely for training police dogs, that would be enough to make it a federal crime for someone like Sabri to attempt to bribe a Minneapolis city official in connection with local land-use decisions.

## A. Litigation in the Lower Courts

Sabri challenged the legal sufficiency of the indictment in the federal district court in Minnesota on two grounds. First, he claimed that section 666(a)(2) should be interpreted to require proof of some connection between the federal benefits received by the state entity and the conduct that is the subject of the indictment. That claim had been successful in some courts,[15] but was rejected by the district court because "[t]he text of § 666(a)(2) cannot support the existence of a 'connection' requirement as one of the elements of the offense . . . ."[16] The Eighth Circuit court of appeals affirmed on this point of statutory interpretation.[17] Sabri also argued that if the statute does not require any such connection between the offense and the federal

---

[14] 18 U.S.C. § 666(a)(2) (2000). The requirement that the agency receive more than $10,000 in federal benefits in a given year comes from section (b) of the statute. See *id.* § 666(b) ("The circumstance referred to in subsection (a) of this section is that the organization, government, or agency receives, in any one year period, benefits in excess of $10,000 under a Federal program involving a grant, contract, subsidy, loan, guarantee, insurance, or other form of Federal assistance."). For comprehensive studies of the legal issues surrounding this statute, see George D. Brown, Stealth Statute—Corruption, the Spending Power, and the Rise of 18 U.S.C. § 666, 73 Notre Dame L. Rev. 247 (1998); Richard W. Garnett, The New Federalism, the Spending Power, and Federal Criminal Law, 89 Cornell L. Rev. 1 (2003).

[15] See United States v. Zwick, 199 F.3d 672, 681–87 (3d Cir. 1999); United States v. Santopietro, 166 F.3d 88, 93 (2d Cir. 1999).

[16] United States v. Sabri, 183 F. Supp. 2d 1145, 1153 (D. Minn. 2002).

[17] See United States v. Sabri, 326 F.3d 937, 945 (8th Cir. 2003).

funds received by the agency, then the statute exceeds Congress's constitutional powers. On that point, the district court and the Eighth Circuit parted ways.

The district court held that section 666(a)(2) was not a valid exercise of Congress's power under the Constitution's Spending Clause, which courts, for nearly seventy years, have maintained authorizes the federal government to spend funds for virtually any purpose and to attach regulatory conditions on the receipt of those funds.[18] The court said that section 666(a)(2) could not be justified under the Spending Clause because it required no connection between funds disbursed to local government and the conduct that is subject to the statute.[19] Furthermore, said the court, section 666(a)(2) is not a valid condition placed on the recipient of federal funds because it regulated private third parties rather than the funding beneficiary.[20] The court did not discuss any other possible constitutional basis for the statute, nor is there any indication that the federal government offered any other possible basis for the statute in its argument.

On appeal to the Eighth Circuit, the government contested the district court's constitutional judgment *solely* on the ground that the Spending Clause, and its concomitant authority to attach conditions on the receipt of federal funds, justified the enactment of section 666(a)(2). The court of appeals unanimously agreed with Sabri and the district court that section 666(a)(2) could not be sustained as a condition on a spending statute because the so-called "conditions"— criminal liability for attempted bribery—were imposed on third parties such as Sabri rather than on the beneficiary of the spending statute.[21] Nonetheless, the Eighth Circuit held the statute constitutional on the basis of a theory that had not been advanced by the government.

Article I, section 8, clause 18 of the Constitution gives Congress authority "[t]o make ... all Laws which shall be necessary and proper for carrying into Execution the foregoing Powers, and all other Powers vested by this Constitution in the Government of

---

[18] If the reader is eagerly awaiting a citation to the Constitution's Spending Clause, on which the federal government relied in *Sabri*, a little patience will yield large rewards. See Part III-A *infra*.

[19] See 183 F. Supp. 2d at 1157–58.

[20] See *id.* at 1155–56.

[21] See 326 F.3d at 940–45; *id.* at 953 (Bye., J., dissenting).

the United States, or in any Department or Officer thereof."[22] It is conventional today to call this provision the "Necessary and Proper Clause," but the founding generation knew it as the "Sweeping Clause,"[23] and I will henceforth use the original label. The Eighth Circuit held that section 666(a)(2) was a valid exercise of power under the Sweeping Clause as a means for carrying into execution the Spending Clause.[24] That is, according to the Eighth Circuit, the Spending Clause authorized Congress to appropriate funds to benefit the city of Minneapolis and the MCDA, and the Sweeping Clause authorized the enactment of laws to protect the integrity of the funded programs. The court was untroubled by the fact that the federal government's lawyers specifically disavowed any reliance on the Sweeping Clause as support for section 666(a)(2).[25] The court was also untroubled by the absence in section 666(a)(2) of any required connection between the prohibited conduct (attempted bribery) and the expenditure of federal funds. The Sweeping Clause gives Congress power to enact laws that are, *inter alia*, "necessary" for executing other federal powers. The Eighth Circuit concluded that a law could be "necessary" if the congressionally-chosen means were—and the court used this phrase three times—"rationally related"[26] to a legitimate legislative end. In constitutional parlance, a "rationally related" standard of inquiry is barely one step removed from no inquiry at all; it represents the highest, most extreme form of deference to legislative decisionmaking.[27] Under this deferential standard, it is readily permissible for Congress to police "the integrity of the entire organization that receives federal benefits"[28] in

---

[22] U.S. Const. art. I, § 8, cl. 18.

[23] See, e.g., The Federalist No. 33, *supra* note 2, at 203 (Alexander Hamilton) (discussing "the sweeping clause, as it has been affectedly called").

[24] See 326 F.3d at 949–53.

[25] See *id.* at 957 (Bye, J., dissenting) ("the government disavowed reliance on the Necessary and Proper Clause when the question first arose at oral argument").

[26] *Id.* at 949, 950, 951.

[27] See, e.g., Nordlinger v. Hahn, 505 U.S. 1, 11–12 (1992) (discussing "rational basis" review under the Equal Protection Clause of the Fourteenth Amendment). See also Garnett, *supra* note 14, at 82 ("It is difficult to see how the extent of federal regulatory power authorized by this doubly deferential scrutiny [adopted by the Eighth Circuit in *Sabri*] is anything but 'limitless.'").

[28] 326 F.3d at 951.

order to guard against the possible misuse of federal funds in some settings.

Judge Bye dissented on the ground that, once the Eighth Circuit majority had brought the Sweeping Clause into the case over the parties' objections, the majority had applied only part of the clause while ignoring some of its most important language. The Sweeping Clause requires congressional laws to be both "necessary" and "proper" for carrying into execution federal powers. Drawing on work by the present author,[29] Judge Bye concluded that even if section 666(a)(2) was "necessary" in order to protect federal funds despite the absence of any connection between the prohibited conduct and the use of federal money, it was not a "proper" means for doing so because it interjected federal power into matters of purely local concern.[30]

## B. Sabri *in the Supreme Court*

The Supreme Court did *not* agree to hear this case in order to address constitutional questions. Rather, the Court granted certiorari in order to resolve the question of statutory interpretation on which the district court and the Eighth Circuit had agreed but which had divided other lower courts: whether section 666(a)(2) should be construed to require some connection between the charged conduct and the misuse of federal funds.[31] But although this statutory question was the only issue raised by Sabri's petition for a writ of certiorari,[32] the Supreme Court's opinion made only one backhanded reference to that issue.[33] The bulk of its brief opinion was instead devoted

---

[29] See *id.* at 954 (citing Gary Lawson & Patricia B. Granger, The "Proper" Scope of Federal Power: A Jurisdictional Interpretation of the Sweeping Clause, 43 Duke L.J. 267 (1993)).

[30] See 326 F.3d at 954–56.

[31] See Sabri v. United States, 124 S. Ct. 1941, 1945 (2004).

[32] See Petition for a Writ of Certiorari, Sabri v. United States, 124 S. Ct. 1941 (2004) (No. 03-44), available at 2003 WL 22428473.

[33] See 124 S. Ct. at 1946 ("It is true, just as Sabri says, that not every bribe or kickback offered or paid to agents of governments covered by § 666(b) will be traceably skimmed from specific federal payments or show up in the guise of a *quid pro quo* for some dereliction in spending a federal grant."). Cf. Salinas v. United States, 522 U.S. 52, 56–57 (1997) ("The expansive, unqualified language of the statute does not support the interpretation that federal funds must be affected to violate § 666(a)(1)(B))."). The reference strongly suggests that the Court saw no requirement of a connection in section 666(a)(2) between the charged conduct and the misuse of federal money.

to two other issues. First, it approved the Eighth Circuit's view that section 666(a)(2) was constitutional as a "necessary" means for carrying into execution the federal spending power, essentially for the same reasons given by the Eighth Circuit. The Court did not mention Judge Bye's concern that section 666(a)(2) might not be "proper." Second, the Court focused heavily on a technical issue that sharply limits the decision's reach and that therefore must be addressed and understood. The issue is confusing even to legal scholars, so I plead for indulgence from non-lawyers.

### 1. The "Facial" Challenge to Section 666(a)(2)

Sabri challenged the sufficiency of his indictment before there was a trial. He claimed, in other words, that even if one accepts everything contained in the government's indictment as true, the indictment did not describe an offense within the constitutional power of Congress to proscribe. This is known in legal jargon as a "facial" challenge to a statute: a challenge that does not depend on the particular facts pertaining to the litigant. If there had been a full trial, with factual findings by the district court, and Sabri had then challenged the constitutionality of the statute on the basis of the record developed at trial, his claim would be called an "as-applied" challenge, meaning that the statute, even if constitutional in some contexts, could not properly be applied to him on the facts of his specific case.

Facial challenges pose special problems for litigants. As a matter of pure theory, a "facial" challenge must claim, in essence, that there is no conceivable set of facts to which the statute can constitutionally be applied.[34] After all, when a court says that a statute is unconstitutional, it does not erase the statute from the pages of the United

---

[34]Justice Scalia has made the theoretical case against facial challenges that do not meet this demanding standard at length in a dissenting opinion. See Chicago v. Morales, 527 U.S. 41, 74–83 (1999) (Scalia, J., dissenting). The Court has occasionally seemed to adopt this strict position against facial challenges, see United States v. Salerno, 481 U.S. 739, 745 (1987) ("[a] facial challenge to a legislative Act is, of course, the most difficult challenge to mount successfully, since the challenger must establish that no set of circumstances exists under which the Act would be valid"), but the Court's general practice has been considerably, if inconsistently, more generous towards such challenges. For a detailed (and generally approving) discussion of the Court's wavering standards for judging and applying facial challenges, see Michael C. Dorf, Facial Challenges to State and Federal Statutes, 46 Stan. L. Rev. 235 (1994), and for a bold attempt to bring some conceptual order to a confused and confusing topic, see Richard H. Fallon, Jr., As-Applied and Facial Challenges and Third-Party Standing, 113 Harv. L. Rev. 1321 (2000).

States Code. It simply says that the statute cannot be applied as law in the case before it, which leaves open the possibility that the statute *could* be applied as law in some other proceeding with different facts. Thus, if section 666(a)(2) constitutionally could be applied to Sabri, then it should be irrelevant whether the statute would be unconstitutional if applied to someone else; that abstract "unconstitutionality" in some different case would not make the statute disappear from the legal world or from Sabri's case. On this procedural understanding, Sabri would have to prove that section 666(a)(2) could *never* be applied to *anyone* in any proceeding in order to challenge the statute before trial.

Sabri had no chance of succeeding if that was the standard for facial challenges to statutes. If Sabri had bribed a local official directly with respect to administration of a federal grant—for example, to steer a federal grant to Sabri[35]—it would be very hard to argue that federal regulation of such bribery was not "necessary and proper" for carrying into execution the federal grant program.[36] Surely the federal government can police the direct spending of its own money. The putative problem with section 666(a)(2) is that it *also* covers conduct that *does not* directly involve the use of federal funds. Thus, there are certainly some circumstances in which section 666(a)(2) could constitutionally be applied, and a pure facial challenge to the statute should therefore fail. That does not mean that Sabri could never challenge the constitutionality of the statute. But he would have to await the outcome of the trial and then, if convicted, would have to argue that no connection to federal funds had been proven and that the circumstances of his case therefore did not fall within the range of constitutionally permissible applications of the statute. His challenge to the indictment jumped the gun.

An alternative route for Sabri that would attempt to circumvent the theoretical problems with facial challenges to statutes would be to claim that the indictment itself had to allege facts directly connecting Sabri's conduct to the administration of federal funds and that

---

[35] This is precisely what the government argued had happened. See Brief for the United States in Opposition at 10, Sabri v. United States, 124 S. Ct. 1941 (2004) (No. 03-44), available at 2003 WL 22428474.

[36] This assumes, of course, that the federal government has power to appropriate funds to local government agencies for economic development. Sabri never challenged this power. I will do so shortly. See Part III-A *infra*.

the statute itself must identify those connections to federal funds as an element of the offense. Under this approach, Sabri would not have to wait for trial to raise his constitutional claim, because even if one accepted all of the government's allegations in its indictment as true, no connection between Sabri's conduct and federal funds was alleged. This was essentially how the Supreme Court construed Sabri's argument.[37] But that claim was doomed. As the Court explained, the position that "proof of the congressional jurisdictional basis must be an element of the statute . . . is of course not generally true at all."[38] In other words, if the government is able to prove at trial the facts necessary to establish federal criminal jurisdiction, the absence of those facts from the statute or indictment is not fatal to its case.

Thus, if the Court strictly applied the theoretical rules for challenging criminal statutes before trial, there would be no occasion to consider any constitutional issues in Sabri's case. Sabri would lose even if section 666(a)(2) was, in some theoretical sense, unconstitutional. The Court, however, does not strictly apply those rules. In general, the Court allows facial challenges to statutes even when those statutes might have some constitutional applications if it is worried that potentially overbroad application of statutes might "chill" legitimate activity for fear of prosecution, if the statutes are ambiguous, or (and there is no better way to describe this) if the Court really, really wants to make a broad constitutional pronouncement about a "hot button" issue such as abortion. None of those concerns was strictly presented by section 666(a)(2). Section 666(a)(2) does not involve any "hot button" issues and is not ambiguous. Concerns about "overbreadth" are generally invoked with respect to statutes whose broad application might threaten freedom of expression, which again is not the case with section 666(a)(2).

### 2. The Court's Opinion

So on what basis, and in what context, did the Court in *Sabri* consider the constitutionality of section 666(a)(2)?

The key paragraph in the opinion reads as follows:

---

[37] See 124 S. Ct. at 1945.
[38] *Id.* at 1948.

We can readily dispose of this position that, to qualify as a valid exercise of Article I power, the statute must require proof of connection with federal money as an element of the offense. We simply do not presume the unconstitutionality of federal criminal statutes lacking explicit provision of a jurisdictional hook, and there is no occasion even to consider the need for such a requirement where there is no reason to suspect that enforcement of a criminal statute would extend beyond a legitimate interest cognizable under Article I.[39]

In the context of that observation concerning the extent to which statutes (and indictments) must contain elements establishing federal jurisdiction over alleged crimes, the Court brusquely affirmed Congress's constitutional authority to enact section 666(a)(2). It said that Congress "has authority under the Spending Clause to appropriate federal monies to promote the general welfare, and it has corresponding authority under the Necessary and Proper Clause to see to it that taxpayer dollars appropriated under that power are in fact spent for the general welfare, and not frittered away in graft . . . ."[40] Section 666(a)(2), the Court maintained, "addresse[d] the problem at the sources of bribes, by rational means . . . ."[41] The Court acknowledged, as Sabri argued, that not every action covered by section 666(a)(2) "will be traceably skimmed from specific federal payments or show up in the guise of a *quid pro quo* for some dereliction in spending a federal grant . . . [,] [b]ut this possibility portends no enforcement beyond the scope of federal interest."[42] The Court reasoned that "[m]oney is fungible, bribed officials are untrustworthy stewards of federal funds, and corrupt contractors do not deliver dollar-for-dollar value. Liquidity is not a financial term for nothing; money can be drained off here because a federal grant is pouring in there. And officials are not any the less threatening to the objects behind federal spending just because they may accept general retainers."[43]

---

[39] *Id.* at 1945–46.

[40] *Id.* at 1946.

[41] *Id.*

[42] *Id.*

[43] *Id.*

The Court also briefly dismissed two other arguments made by Sabri. It maintained, as had the district court and the Eighth Circuit before it, that section 666(a)(2) did not impose impermissible conditions on recipients of federal funds because the statute imposes no conditions at all on such recipients; it directly regulates non-recipients such as Sabri.[44] The Court also rejected Sabri's suggestion that some recent decisions limiting the scope of Congress's power under the Commerce Clause were relevant to the constitutionality of section 666(a)(2).[45]

The majority added "an afterword on Sabri's technique for challenging his indictment by facial attack on the underlying statute"[46] that emphasized that facial challenges "are best when infrequent," "are especially to be discouraged," and are valid "in relatively few settings, and, generally, on the strength of specific reasons weighty enough to overcome our well-founded reticence."[47]

Justice Kennedy and Justice Scalia joined most of the opinion but did not join the "afterword" discussing facial challenges. Their four-sentence concurrence said only that certain prior decisions involving the constitutional power of Congress under the Commerce Clause were unaffected by the decision in *Sabri*.[48]

Justice Thomas concurred in the judgment. He agreed with the majority that section 666(a)(2) was constitutional, but he did not agree that the Sweeping Clause was the appropriate source of constitutional authority. He thought that the majority's discussion of the Sweeping Clause, which assumed that the clause required only a

---

[44] *Id.* at 1947–48.

[45] See *id.* at 1947.

[46] *Id.* at 1948.

[47] *Id.*

[48] See *id.* at 1949 (Kennedy, J., concurring) ("The Court . . . does not specifically question the practice we have followed in cases such as *United States v. Lopez* [514 U.S. 549 (1995)] and *United States v. Morrison* [529 U.S. 598 (2000)]. In those instances the Court did resolve the basic question whether Congress, in enacting the statutes challenged there, had exceeded its legislative power under the Constitution."). It is hard to figure out the purpose of this concurrence. My best guess—and it is purely speculation—is that Justices Kennedy and Scalia were concerned that Justice Souter, the author of the majority opinion, was trying to plant some seeds to undermine the authority of the *Lopez* and *Morrison* decisions, of which Justice Souter has been a persistent and vocal critic.

"'means-ends rationality' test,"[49] misinterpreted the constitutional meaning of the word "necessary," which he thought requires a plainer and more direct connection between means and ends than the majority suggested.[50] Instead, he would have upheld section 666(a)(2) as valid under the Court's case law concerning the Commerce Clause.[51] He reiterated his long-standing doubts about whether the modern Court has correctly interpreted the Commerce Clause, but observed that no one in *Sabri* challenged those precedents.[52]

In the final analysis, Sabri brought his challenge too soon to raise cleanly the constitutional issues concerning section 666(a)(2). If he had been convicted after a trial, at which the government failed to prove any connection between his conduct and the administration of federal funds, his case would have squarely presented issues about the power of Congress to reach such conduct. As the case was presented, however, Sabri was a likely loser *even if section 666(a)(2) is in fact unconstitutional* over a range of cases, perhaps including his own.

### III. The Constitutional Principles at Stake in *Sabri v. United States*

One can understand why someone in Sabri's position would be quick to challenge the constitutionality of section 666(a)(2). How could attempted bribery of local officials involving local land-use decisions possibly be the business of the federal government? One can perhaps imagine why the federal government would be concerned about allegations that federal grants were being misappropriated, but two of the three counts in the indictment against Sabri involved nothing more than the local regulatory approval and eminent domain processes. How does the receipt of federal money by the city of Minneapolis convert every transaction involving city employees into a potential federal crime?

---

[49] *Id.* (Thomas, J., concurring in the judgment).

[50] See *id.* at 1949–51.

[51] See U.S. Const. art. I, § 8, cl. 3 (granting Congress power "[t]o regulate Commerce ... among the several States").

[52] See 124 S. Ct. at 1949.

The grounds on which section 666(a)(2) was defended by the government and/or upheld by the courts have been shifting and varied, ranging from the spending power to the commerce power to the Sweeping Clause. In the end, none of these sources provides the categorical support for section 666(a)(2) sought by the government or suggested by the Court in *Sabri*. A study of the possible constitutional bases for section 666(a)(2) demonstrates how far from the original constitutional design our world has strayed.

*A. The Elusive Spending Power*

The constitutional problems with section 666(a)(2) actually run deeper than the parties to the case, or any of the judges involved, were able to acknowledge under the current state of the law. As Justice Thomas (and Judge Bye on the Eighth Circuit) recognized, it is far from obvious how it can be "necessary," much less "proper," for the federal government to criminalize attempted bribery of local officials that may have nothing to do with the administration of federal money. I will address those issues about the scope of Congress's power under the Sweeping Clause in due course. But there is an even more basic problem with section 666(a)(2) that was never noted by any of the parties or judges. The Sweeping Clause is not a free-standing, self-contained grant of power. The Sweeping Clause only gives Congress power to pass necessary and proper laws "for carrying into Execution . . . Powers vested by this Constitution in the Government of the United States, or in any Department or Officer thereof." Every exercise of power under the Sweeping Clause must be tied to the exercise of some other enumerated federal power. If a law enacted pursuant to the Sweeping Clause is not enacted "for carrying into Execution" a granted federal power, it does not matter how "necessary and proper" the law may be. So exactly which federal power does section 666(a)(2) "carry[] into execution"?

The seemingly obvious answer is the federal spending power. The jurisdictional "hook" for section 666(a)(2) is the provision of federal financial benefits to local governments, such as federal funds provided to the city of Minneapolis or the MCDA for local economic development. When Congress spends money, can't it be necessary and proper for Congress to try to ensure that the money is spent for the appropriated purposes and no others?

Of course Congress can police the uses of appropriated funds through the Sweeping Clause (though I will discuss later whether it can do so through the specific mechanisms employed by section 666(a)(2)). The more basic question, however, is whether Congress has the constitutional power to make the *kinds* of appropriations that form the jurisdictional basis for section 666(a)(2). If Congress simply has no constitutional authority to hand over federal money to an entity such as the MCDA, then one never reaches the question of the extent to which Congress can police the uses of those funds once they reach their target. There would be no valid federal power for section 666(a)(2) to help carry into execution.

Sabri never raised this deeper issue about the federal spending power for an obvious reason: Modern law decrees constitutional challenges to these kinds of appropriations to be hopeless—possibly to the point of being sanctionably frivolous. But the truth is that section 666(a)(2) is a symptom of a very advanced constitutional disease. From the standpoint of the Constitution's true meaning, the most important issue concerning section 666(a)(2) is not that it reaches conduct that does not directly concern federal funds, but that it reaches conduct that does in fact directly concern federal funds that should never have been appropriated in the first place. It is like a statute that provides for congressional removal of the commissioners of a certain federal agency, where the agency's mission is to pre-screen all newspaper editorials to make sure that they conform to official governmental policy. One can surely raise a constitutional challenge to the procedure for removal of the commissioners,[53] but such a challenge somewhat misses the point. Accordingly, the first issue that ought to be raised by section 666(a)(2) is where, if anywhere, does Congress get the authority to hand over federal money to entities such as the city of Minneapolis or the MCDA?

The Court's opinion in *Sabri* blandly noted that "Congress has authority under the Spending Clause to appropriate federal monies to promote the general welfare, Art. I, § 8, cl. 1,"[54] which authority could then be effectuated through the Sweeping Clause. The constitutional provision identified by the Court as the "Spending Clause," which allegedly contains the authority to spend for the general

---

[53] See Bowsher v. Synar, 478 U.S. 714 (1986) (holding that Congress cannot reserve to itself statutory power to remove federal officers).

[54] Sabri v. United States, 124 S. Ct. 1941, 1946 (2004).

welfare that forms the predicate for section 666(a)(2), says that "[t]he Congress shall have Power To lay and collect Taxes, Duties, Imposts and Excises, to pay the Debts and provide for the common Defence and general Welfare of the United States; but all Duties, Imposts and Excises shall be uniform throughout the United States."[55] For almost three-quarters of a century, modern law has acted as though this clause affirmatively authorizes Congress to spend money to promote the general welfare.[56] For almost three-quarters of a century, modern law has been egregiously wrong.

The only power granted to Congress by the first clause of Article I, section 8 is the power to lay and collect taxes, duties, imposts, and excises (which I will henceforth collectively call "taxes," although the various revenue measures were distinct entities to the founding generation).[57] Everything else in the clause—which is properly called the Taxing Clause rather than the Spending Clause—clarifies, qualifies, or limits the taxing power. The final portion of the clause makes clear that duties, imposts, and excises must be uniform throughout the country; Congress cannot enact a duty that makes imports into New York less costly than imports into Boston.[58] The phrase "to pay the Debts and provide for the common Defence and general Welfare of the United States" identifies the *purposes* for which revenue measures may be laid and for which revenue may be collected but does not grant any power independent of the basic power to lay and collect taxes. People have from time to time tried to argue that this

---

[55] U.S. Const. art. I, § 8, cl. 1.

[56] See United States v. Butler, 297 U.S. 1, 64–66, 78 (1936); Helvering v. Davis, 301 U.S. 619, 640 (1937). For an entire symposium devoted to this so-called Spending Clause, which nowhere seriously questions whether Article I, section 8, clause 1 really is a spending clause, see Spending Clause Symposium, 4 Chapman L. Rev. 1-230 (2001).

[57] On the differences among taxes, duties, imposts, and excises, see Joseph A. Story, A Familiar Exposition of the Constitution of the United States § 156 (1833).

[58] The word "taxes" was not included in this uniformity provision because the original Constitution elsewhere required (direct) taxes to be "apportioned among the several States which may be included within this Union, according to their respective Numbers." U.S. Const. art. I, § 2, cl. 3. This apportionment provision was abrogated by the Sixteenth Amendment in 1916. See *id.* amend. XVI ("The Congress shall have power to lay and collect taxes on incomes, from whatever source derived, without apportionment among the several States, and without regard to any census or enumeration.").

clause grants Congress an independent legislative power to "provide for the . . . general Welfare of the United States,"[59] but such an argument makes no textual or structural sense. The grammar of the clause does not support such a reading, and a free-standing "general Welfare" power would transform Congress into a general legislature and thereby make hash out of the rest of Article I.[60] The "general Welfare" is a permissible object of the federal taxing power, but it is not an object of general federal legislative authority.

This identification in the Taxing Clause of the permissible purposes for federal taxation serves some important functions. First, as a purely rhetorical device, it seeks to assure a populace suspicious of federal taxes that such taxes will only be imposed for good cause. Second, and more important, the reference to the "general Welfare" as a permissible purpose for taxation makes clear that taxes may be levied for appropriate regulatory purposes and not simply to raise revenue. As Professor Jeffrey Renz has detailed, this was a matter of special concern to the founding generation, which saw tax policy as an important regulatory tool.[61] For example, the second statute enacted by the First Congress in 1789 imposed duties on imports and described those duties as "necessary for the support of government, for the discharge of the debts of the United States, and *the encouragement and protection of manufactures.*"[62] All three stated purposes for the duties are legitimized by the Taxing Clause; the third purpose would arguably not be permissible without the reference

---

[59] See, e.g., 12 Annals of Cong. 473 (1803) (statement of Rep. Rodney).

[60] For an exhaustive and detailed dissection of the untenable claim that Congress has an enumerated power to promote the general welfare, see Jeffrey T. Renz, What Spending Clause? (Or the President's Paramour): An Examination of the Views of Hamilton, Madison, and Story on Article I, Section 8, Clause 1 of the United States Constitution, 33 J. Marshall L. Rev. 81 (1999).

[61] See id. at 87.

[62] Act of July 4, 1789, ch. II, § 1, 1 Stat. 24 (emphasis added). For those who are curious: The very first statute enacted by the First Congress prescribed the form of the oath of office for government officials other than the president. Act of June 1, 1789, ch. I, 1 Stat. 23. The Constitution requires all federal and state governmental officials to be "bound by Oath or Affirmation, to support this Constitution," U.S. Const. art. VI, cl. 3, but the president is the only official for whom the Constitution specifically prescribes the content of the oath. See id. art. II, § 1, cl. 7. Oaths, in those days, were serious business. For a modest attempt to revive their importance, see Gary Lawson, Everything I Need to Know About Presidents I Learned from Dr. Seuss, 24 Harv. J.L. & Pub. Pol'y 381 (2001).

in the Taxing Clause to the "general Welfare." Thus, the Taxing Clause grants Congress the power to impose taxes for a broad range of purposes. But the only power granted by the clause is the power to tax.

When push comes to shove, very few people actually argue that the Taxing Clause directly grants to Congress the power to spend, for the general welfare or otherwise. That is not surprising, as neither the word "spend" nor any remote synonym appears anywhere in the clause. Instead, modern law has reasoned that a power to spend for the general welfare can be *inferred* from the Taxing Clause. As the Supreme Court argued in 1936 in *United States v. Butler*, which is the seminal modern case on the congressional spending power:

> The Congress is expressly empowered to lay taxes to provide for the general welfare. Funds in the Treasury as a result of taxation may be expended only through appropriation. They can never accomplish the objects for which they were collected unless the power to appropriate is as broad as the power to tax. The necessary implication from the terms of the grant is that the public funds may be appropriated "to provide for the general welfare of the United States." These words cannot be meaningless, else they would not have been used.[63]

There is a great deal wrong with this inference. First, it would be bizarre if the national government's power to spend rested on nothing more than an inference from a taxing provision. One would expect something as basic as the power to appropriate funds to have a cleaner textual basis—which, as I will shortly demonstrate, is precisely the case. Second, there is no structural ground for expecting the federal government's taxing and spending powers to come from the same source. "Indeed, one might well expect the contrary if one thinks that there are likely to be different internal limitations on taxing and spending authority; there is no reason, for instance, to suppose that the Constitution would impose a uniformity requirement on spending in the same manner that it imposes a uniformity requirement on taxation."[64] Third, as scholars have pointed out for

[63] 297 U.S. 1, 65 (1936).

[64] Gary Lawson & Guy Seidman, The Constitution of Empire: Territorial Expansion and American Legal History 26 (2004).

many years, the inference from taxing power to spending power overlooks the fact that taxes are not the federal government's only source of revenue. Money can also be raised by borrowing or by selling land or other property.[65] As David Engdahl has pointed out, "nothing in the Taxing Clause even implicitly contemplates spending such funds [from land sales],"[66] and "the spending allusion in the Taxing Clause does not even colorably reach borrowed sums."[67] Does that mean that borrowed funds or proceeds from land sales cannot be spent—or can only be spent for different purposes than funds raised through taxation? If the language in the Taxing Clause truly generates spending authority, these absurd conclusions are difficult to avoid.[68] Fourth, the language in the Taxing Clause concerning the "general Welfare" is hardly rendered surplusage if one declines to use it to generate spending authority. As has already been discussed, that language assures that the federal taxing power may be used for regulatory as well as revenue-raising purposes. The modern inference of a power to spend for the general welfare rests on nothing.

So where does Congress get the undoubted power to spend money? The obvious answer is: from the same place that it gets the undoubted power to create federal offices, enact criminal statutes, and regulate federal court procedures. The federal spending power comes from the Sweeping Clause. An appropriations act is constitutionally authorized whenever it is "necessary and proper for carrying into Execution" some other federal power.

Important consequences flow from grounding the federal spending power in the Sweeping Clause. Any law enacted pursuant to the Sweeping Clause must "carry[] into Execution" some power vested in an institution of the national government. Spending authority under the Sweeping Clause is therefore limited by the enumerations of substantive powers elsewhere in the Constitution. The

[65] See U.S. Const. art. I, § 8, cl. 2 (granting power "[t]o borrow Money on the credit of the United States"); id. art. IV, § 3, cl. 2 (granting power "to dispose of . . . the Territory or other Property belonging to the United States").

[66] David E. Engdahl, The Spending Power, 44 Duke L.J. 1, 49 (1994).

[67] David E. Engdahl, The Basis of the Spending Power, 18 Seattle U. L. Rev. 215, 222 (1995).

[68] See Charles Warren, Congress As Santa Claus or National Donations and the General Welfare Clause of the Constitution 28–29 (1932).

Sweeping Clause does not generate a free-standing spending power that extends to some conception of the "general Welfare of the United States."[69]

In the context of *Sabri*, the question would be: What enumerated federal power is "carr[ied] into Execution" by an appropriations act dispensing federal grant money to the city of Minneapolis or the MCDA? If the answer is (as it certainly appears to be) "none," then there is nothing for section 666(a)(2) to do in Sabri's case. Section 666(a)(2) can only "carry[] into Execution" the federal appropriation power if that appropriation power is itself properly exercised.

It is a telling indictment of our current constitutional situation that no lawyer in his or her right mind would challenge section 666(a)(2) on this basis. The result would be ridicule at best and legal sanctions at worst. The federal spending power has been running out of control, unconnected to its constitutional moorings, for many decades, and there is no sign that this will change in the foreseeable future.

## B. *The Ubiquitous Commerce Power*

If challenged to produce an enumerated power that federal grants to cities and local development agencies could plausibly be said to "carry[] into Execution," a modern lawyer would likely shoot back, without much hesitation, "the Commerce Clause." That clause grants Congress power "[t]o regulate Commerce with foreign Nations, and among the several States, and with the Indian Tribes."[70] Modern law, notwithstanding a few recent blips, generally treats the clause as a carte blanche for federal authority that is very hard to distinguish from a broad power to promote the "general Welfare of the United States."[71] Indeed, Justice Thomas in *Sabri* thought

---

[69] David Engdahl has argued at some length that a free-standing spending power can be generated from the Property Clause, U.S. Const. art. IV, § 3, cl. 2, which gives Congress power to "dispose of . . . Property belonging to the United States." See Engdahl, *supra* note 66. I have elsewhere outlined the structural case against this position. See Lawson & Seidman, *supra* note 64, at 27–30.

[70] U.S. Const. art. I, § 8, cl. 3.

[71] See, e.g., Perez v. United States, 402 U.S. 146 (1971) (Congress can regulate local loan sharking under the Commerce Clause); Katzenbach v. McClung, 379 U.S. 294 (1964) (Congress can regulate racial discrimination in restaurants under the Commerce Clause). The few modern "blips" concern attempts by Congress to use the Commerce Clause to regulate matters of an obviously noneconomic nature, such as gun possession near a school, see United States v. Lopez, 514 U.S. 549 (1995), or violence against

that the Court's Commerce Clause decisions would *directly* sustain section 666(a)(2), without need for recourse to the Sweeping Clause.[72] If that is even close to being true, then economic development grants to local governments could easily be seen as "carrying into Execution" the commerce power, and section 666(a)(2) could easily be seen as "carrying into Execution" the ensuing federal grant authority.

A detailed treatment of the Commerce Clause is beyond my mission here. The clause has been more than ably analyzed by Randy Barnett, who has elegantly dissected the many modern misconceptions about the original meaning of the power to "regulate commerce . . . among the several States,"[73] including the prevalent misconception that the word "commerce" as it appears in the Constitution refers to all gainful human activity. But if one simply looks at the Constitution, without trying to accommodate modern doctrines or (mis)understandings, the idea that the Commerce Clause can ground a statute such as section 666(a)(2) becomes absurd. A bribe that occurs within the city of Minneapolis is hardly "commerce . . . among the several States," so the Commerce Clause cannot directly authorize section 666(a)(2) as it applies to persons such as Sabri. Nor is a federal grant to the city of Minneapolis a regulation of interstate commerce. Such grants may (or, more likely, may not) ultimately increase the amount of interstate commerce by encouraging economic development, but not everything that increases the amount of commerce is a regulation thereof. The power to *regulate* commerce is not the same as the power to *promote* commerce; the framing generation, after all, knew how to use the word "promote."[74] Nor is it a power to regulate everything that touches on anything that

---

women, see United States v. Morrison, 529 U.S. 598 (2000). And even these modest constraints on national power generated hotly contested 5-4 decisions.

[72] Sabri v. United States, 124 S. Ct. 1941, 1949 (2004) (Thomas, J., concurring). Accord: Peter J. Henning, Federalism and the Federal Prosecution of State and Local Corruption, 92 Ky. L.J. 75, 123 (2003–04) ("Congress clearly could make bribery and embezzlement involving state and local officials a federal crime under the Commerce Clause . . . . Corruption is largely an economic offense . . . .").

[73] See Randy E. Barnett, New Evidence of the Original Meaning of the Commerce Clause, 55 Ark. L. Rev. 847 (2003); Randy E. Barnett, The Original Meaning of the Commerce Clause, 68 U. Chi. L. Rev. 101 (2001).

[74] See, e.g., U.S. Const. art. I, § 8, cl. 8 (giving Congress power to "promote the Progress of Science and useful Arts, by securing for limited Times to Authors and Inventors the exclusive Right to their respective Writings and Discoveries").

is economic; commerce is a subset of economic activity rather than the entire universe. And if the federal government had no power to hand over money to the city of Minneapolis and the MCDA, it had no power to police Sabri's activities with respect to employees of those entities.

## C. *The Not-Quite-So-Sweeping Sweeping Clause*

The federal government in *Sabri* initially defended section 666(a)(2) as a valid exercise of so-called conditional spending authority: Assuming (as modern law unquestionably does) that federal grants to local government agencies are permissible, Congress is permitted to attach conditions to those grants as long as those conditions are not unduly coercive.[75] All three of the courts that heard Sabri's case resoundingly—and correctly—rejected this argument on the simple ground that section 666(a)(2) is not a condition on spending. It does not direct recipients of federal benefits to take or refrain from any action. Instead, it regulates non-recipients of federal funds who deal with agents of recipient entities. No agreement, tacit or express, by entities that receive federal benefits can explain or justify the extension of federal criminal liability to non-recipients who merely transact with those entities.[76]

The Eighth Circuit upheld the constitutionality of section 666(a)(2) on the ground (which the government specifically disavowed) that the statute was a "necessary and proper" means for carrying into execution the federal spending power. The Supreme Court in *Sabri* affirmed the constitutionality of section 666(a)(2) on the same basis. For purposes of analyzing this claim, let us counterfactually assume that the federal government has the power (from whatever source) to make grants to agencies such as the city of Minneapolis and the MCDA. Is section 666(a)(2) "necessary and proper for carrying into Execution" that assumed power? This question really poses two separate questions: Is the statute "necessary" for that purpose and is it "proper" for that purpose? I will consider each question in turn.

---

[75] See South Dakota v. Dole, 483 U.S. 203 (1987).

[76] The rejection of this "conditional spending" rationale for section 666(a)(2) now seems fairly universal. See, e.g., Henning, *supra* note 72, at 116–17; Garnett, *supra* note 14, at 84.

*1. Necessary Connections*

The word "necessary" as it appears in the Sweeping Clause describes a required causal, or telic,[77] connection between legislative means and ends. If section 666(a)(2) prohibited bribery or attempted bribery of federal officials who administer grant programs, no one would doubt that the statute was well tailored for carrying into execution whatever constitutional power justified the grant program. The same would be true if the statute prohibited bribery or attempted bribery of state or local officials in direct connection with the administration of federal funds. The problem with section 666(a)(2) is that it reaches conduct that does not directly involve the administration of federal funds, such as an attempt to bribe a city official to obtain local regulatory clearances or the exercise of local eminent domain authority.

The only causal link between federal spending and the prohibited conduct in such a case is the "money is fungible" argument advanced by the Supreme Court in *Sabri*:

> Money is fungible, bribed officials are untrustworthy stewards of federal funds, and corrupt contractors do not deliver dollar-for-dollar value. Liquidity is not a financial term for nothing; money can be drained off here because a federal grant is pouring in there. And officials are not any the less threatening to the objects behind federal spending just because they may accept general retainers.[78]

As causal connections go, this one is not completely laughable. Neither is it airtight. The question raised starkly by section 666(a)(2) is thus how tight the connection between ends (ensuring that federal funds are spent for their appropriated purposes) and means (penalizing attempted bribery of any employee of any entity that receives federal funds whether or not the bribe directly concerns federal funds) must be under the Constitution. How "necessary" does a law have to be in order to be "necessary and proper for carrying into Execution" federal powers?

The question, in its most general form, has a long and famous history. In *McCulloch v. Maryland*,[79] the state of Maryland argued

---

[77] See David E. Engdahl, Constitutional Federalism in a Nutshell 20 (2d ed. 1987).

[78] Sabri v. United States,124 S. Ct. 1941, 1946 (2004).

[79] 17 U.S. (4 Wheat.) 316 (1819).

that a law could only be "necessary" within the meaning of the Sweeping Clause if it was "indispensably requisite"[80] to the effectuation of some enumerated power. This was also the view of Thomas Jefferson, who understood the Sweeping Clause to authorize only the use of "means without which the grant of the power would be nugatory."[81] This strict definition of the word "necessary" was echoed by other members of the founding generation,[82] and it conforms elegantly to the meanings reported in Samuel Johnson's thencontemporary *Dictionary of the English Language*, which in both the 1755 and 1785 editions defined "necessary" as "1. Needful; indispensably requisite. 2. Not free; fatal; impelled by fate. 3. Conclusive; decisive by inevitable consequence."[83] That linguistic understanding of "necessary" has continued into modern times; the 1933 edition of the *Oxford English Dictionary* defined the term as "Indispensable, requisite, essential, needful; that cannot be done without" and "closely related or connected; intimate."[84]

Other founding-era figures took a very different approach. Alexander Hamilton's position, for instance, was reflected in the preamble to the bill for the first Bank of the United States, which maintained that a law was "necessary" if it "might be conceived to be conducive" to achieving legislative ends,[85] which translates into so-called "rational basis" scrutiny under modern equal protection doctrine.[86]

James Madison took a third view. In his 1791 remarks in Congress opposing the first Bank of the United States, he cast doubt on the strict Jeffersonian understanding of "necessary" as the term appears in the Sweeping Clause:

---

[80] *Id.* at 367 (argument of Mr. Jones).

[81] Opinion on the Constitutionality of the Bill for Establishing a National Bank, in 19 The Papers of Thomas Jefferson 275, 278 (Julian P. Boyd ed., 1974).

[82] See Randy E. Barnett, The Original Meaning of the Necessary and Proper Clause, 6 U. Pa. J. Const. L. 183, 188–96 (2003).

[83] These dictionaries were not numerically paginated.

[84] 7 Oxford English Dictionary 60–61 (1933).

[85] 1 Annals of Cong. 1948 (1791) (statement of James Madison quoting the preamble to the first Bank Bill).

[86] See, e.g., Nordlinger v. Hahn, 505 U.S. 1, 11–12 (1992) ("the Equal Protection Clause is satisfied so long as . . . the relationship of the classification to its goal is not so attenuated as to render the distinction arbitrary or irrational").

Those two words ["necessary" and "proper"] had been, by some, taken in a very limited sense, and were thought only to extend to the passing of such laws as were indispensably necessary to the very existence of the government. He was disposed to think that a more liberal construction should be put on them . . . for very few acts of the legislature could be proved essentially necessary to the absolute existence of government.[87]

At the same time, Madison warned against too generous a reading of the means-ends requirement for executory laws:

The essential characteristic of the government, as composed of limited and enumerated powers, would be destroyed; if instead of *direct and incidental* means, any means could be used, which in the language of the preamble to the bill, "might be conceived to be conducive to the successful conducting of the finances, or might be conceived to tend to give facility to the obtaining of loans."[88]

Madison explained his intermediate position nearly three decades after the first debate on the bank bill. After *McCulloch* had been decided, Madison said in a letter to Spencer Roane that "[t]here is certainly a reasonable medium between expounding the Constitution with the strictness of a penal law, or other ordinary statute, and expounding it with a laxity which may vary its essential character. . . ."[89] That reasonable medium, in the context of the Necessary and Proper Clause, is to require of executory laws "a definite connection between means and ends," in which the executory law and the executed power are linked "by some obvious and precise affinity."[90]

---

[87] 4 The Debates in the Several State Conventions on the Adoption of the Federal Constitution 417 (Jonathan Elliot ed., 1836).

[88] 1 Annals of Cong. 1947–48 (emphasis added).

[89] Letter of Sept. 2, 1819 to Spencer Roane, in 8 The Writings of James Madison 447, 451–52 (Gaillard Hunt ed., 1908).

[90] *Id.* at 448.

In *McCulloch*, the Court's opinion by Chief Justice Marshall famously rejected the strict Jeffersonian view of "necessary."[91] The Court relied on several considerations to reach this conclusion, but the most powerful argument was the intratextual comparison of the Sweeping Clause with the Imposts Clause of Article I, section 10. The Imposts Clause forbids a state from laying import or export duties without congressional consent "except what may be *absolutely necessary* for executing its inspection laws."[92] The Court reasoned, with considerable plausibility, that the pairing of "necessary" with the qualifier "absolutely" supports the view that the unqualified word "necessary" in the Sweeping Clause means something less restrictive than "those single means, without which the end would be entirely unattainable."[93]

It is less clear what standard for necessity the Court in *McCulloch* actually adopted. The Court in *McCulloch* considered whether Congress had power to incorporate a bank as a means "necessary and proper for carrying into Execution" various enumerated fiscal powers of the federal government. In upholding the constitutionality of the bank statute, Chief Justice Marshall articulated the now-standard formulation of the meaning of the Sweeping Clause: "Let the end be legitimate, let it be within the scope of the constitution, and all means which are appropriate, which are plainly adapted to that end, which are not prohibited, but consist with the letter and spirit of the constitution, are constitutional."[94] If one had to associate that formulation with Jefferson, Hamilton, or Madison, one would probably choose Madison. A requirement that a law be "appropriate" and "plainly adapted" to a permissible end and "consist with the

---

[91] I include the following lengthy discussion of *McCulloch* for historical context and for the issues and arguments that it highlights, not because I regard it, or any other Supreme Court pronouncement, as authoritative on the meaning of the Constitution. The Constitution means what it means, regardless of what Founders, judges, or scholars may say about it. For more on my decidedly idiosyncratic disregard for the authority of precedent, see Gary Lawson, The Constitutional Case Against Precedent, 17 Harv. J.L. & Pub. Pol'y 23 (1994). For more on my less-decidedly idiosyncratic approach to constitutional interpretation, which focuses on what a reasonable original observer would have concluded after considering all relevant evidence, see Lawson & Seidman, *supra* note 64, at 7–12.

[92] U.S. Const. art. I, § 10, cl. 2 (emphasis added).

[93] McCulloch v. Maryland, 17 U.S. (4 Wheat.) 316, 414 (2004).

[94] *Id.* at 421.

letter and spirit of the constitution" does not read like an endorse-ment of a Hamiltonian rational basis test. To the contrary, a law that is "plainly adapted" to an end is a law that has more than a remote, hypothetical relationship to the desired end. Otherwise, the adaptation would not be "plain[]."

The Court's application of its standard to the question before it in *McCulloch* also had a Madisonian ring:

> If a corporation may be employed indiscriminately with other means to carry into execution the powers of the govern-ment, no particular reason can be assigned for excluding the use of a bank, *if required for its fiscal operations*. To use one, must be within the discretion of Congress, *if it be an appropriate mode of executing the powers of government*. That it is a conve-nient, a useful, *and essential* instrument in the prosecution of its fiscal operations, is not now a subject of controversy. All those who have been concerned in the administration of our finances, have concurred in representing its *importance and necessity*; and so strongly have they been felt, that statesmen of the first class, whose previous opinions against it had been confirmed by every circumstance which can fix the human judgment, have yielded those opinions to the exigencies of the nation. Under the confederation, Congress, justifying the measure by its necessity, transcended, perhaps its powers to obtain the advantage of a bank; and our own legislation attests the *universal conviction of the utility* of this measure. The time has passed away, when it can be necessary to enter into any discussion in order to prove the *importance* of this instrument, as a means to effect the legitimate objects of the government.[95]

The emphasized language demonstrates that the Court perceived significantly more than a rational connection between the bank and governmental ends. One can fault the Court for taking judicial notice of contested facts about the importance of a national bank, but given the thirty-year history of the bank struggle up to that point, the Court's shorthand reference to that history is understandable.

There is other language in *McCulloch*, however, that suggests a looser means-ends standard more in line with Hamilton. The Court declared at one point that "[t]o employ the means necessary to an

---

[95] *Id.* at 422–23 (emphasis added).

end, is generally understood as employing *any means calculated to produce the end*, and not as being confined to those single means, without which the end would be entirely unattainable."[96] Elsewhere, the Court stated that federal powers could not be beneficially executed "by confiding the choice of means to such narrow limits as not to leave it in the power of Congress to adopt any which might be appropriate, and which were conducive to the end."[97] While the primary focus of these passages was to reject the strict view advanced by the state of Maryland, they do suggest a highly relaxed requirement for tailoring legislative means to ends.

The Eighth Circuit in *Sabri* took this loose Hamiltonian view that requires only a minimal connection between legislative means and ends. This reflected the clear modern consensus about the meaning of *McCulloch* among lower courts and commentators,[98] though Supreme Court decisions between *McCulloch* and *Sabri* were in fact a bit more equivocal than that consensus suggested.[99] The Supreme

[96] *Id.* at 413–14 (emphasis added).

[97] *Id.* at 415.

[98] See, e.g., United States v. Edgar, 304 F.3d 1320, 1325–26 (11th Cir. 2002); United States v. Wang Kun Lue, 134 F.3d 79, 84 (2d Cir. 1998); Laurence H. Tribe, American Constitutional Law § 5-3, at 805 (3d ed. 2000).

[99] Some modern decisions, for example, clearly endorsed a rational basis test, see, e.g., Hodel v. Virginia Surface Mining & Reclamation Association, 452 U.S. 264, 276 (1981); United States v. Darby, 312 U.S. 100, 121 (1941), but those decisions were so closely tied to broad views of the commerce power that it is hard to know whether the Commerce Clause or the Sweeping Clause was doing most of the hard work in those cases. Decisions applying the enforcement provisions of the Civil War Amendments, which authorize Congress to enforce the substantive provisions of those amendments through "appropriate legislation," U.S. Const. amend. XIII, § 2; *id.* amend. XIV, § 5; *id.* amend. XV, § 2, sometimes articulated something that resembles a rational basis test while linking those enforcement provisions to the Sweeping Clause, see, e.g., Katzenbach v. Morgan, 384 U.S. 641, 650–51 (1966); South Carolina v. Katzenbach, 383 U.S. 301, 324 (1966), but it is doubtful whether "rational basis" accurately describes the connection between congressional means and ends required under current caselaw for enforcement of those amendments. See, e.g., Boerne v. Flores, 521 U.S. 507, 533–34 (1997). A recent application of the Sweeping Clause, which upheld a statute that tolls state statutes of limitations while claims over which federal courts have supplemental jurisdiction are pending in federal court, made no specific mention of the test for necessity but conducted a very careful analysis of the statute's relation to Congress's powers over the federal courts that is hard to square with a rational basis test. See Jinks v. Richland County, 583 U.S. 456 (2003).

The strongest pre-*Sabri* decision in favor of a rational basis test held, with respect to Congress's power to regulate court procedures under the Sweeping Clause, that Congress may "regulate matters which, though falling within the uncertain area

Court in *Sabri* went out of its way to endorse the Eighth Circuit's position. The Court said that "[s]ection 666(a)(2) addressed the problem at the sources of bribes, *by rational means*, to safeguard the integrity of the state, local, and tribal recipients of federal dollars."[100] More tellingly, the only cases cited by the Court to describe the necessity requirement under the Sweeping Clause were the two cases that probably took the broadest views of necessity in the Court's history[101] and *McCulloch*, which the Court characterized as "establishing review for *means-ends rationality* under the Necessary and Proper Clause."[102] According to the Court in *Sabri*, the phrase "necessary" in the Sweeping Clause effectively means "believed by Congress to be helpful."

This position makes no constitutional sense. As a matter of text, structure, and history, the Madisonian position is the most plausible, though there is a nonfrivolous case for the strict Jeffersonian view. The one position for which there is no credible constitutional basis is the view that "necessary" means "believed by Congress to be helpful."

Textually, while the word "necessary" in the Sweeping Clause perhaps means something less than "indispensable," it surely means more than "rationally related." Each of the definitions of "necessary" found in Samuel Johnson's eighteenth-century dictionary reflects a far stricter understanding of the term than a mere rational relationship between means and ends. That may not be enough to establish

---

between substance and procedure, are rationally capable of classification as either." Hanna v. Plumer, 380 U.S. 460, 472 (1965). The strongest decisions against such a standard rejected claims that Congress's power "[t]o make Rules for the Government and Regulation of the land and naval Forces," U.S. Const. art. I, § 8, cl. 14, allowed Congress to extend court martial jurisdiction to servicepeople who have left the service or to dependents of servicepeople who live on overseas military bases. See Kinsella v. United States, 361 U.S. 234, 247–48 (1960) (no court martial jurisdiction over civilian dependents for non-capital crimes); Reid v. Covert, 354 U.S. 1, 20–22 (1957) (plurality opinion) (no court martial jurisdiction over civilian dependents for capital crimes); United States ex rel. Toth v. Quarles, 350 U.S. 11, 21–22 (1955) (no court martial jurisdiction over ex-servicepeople even for crimes committed while in the service). Under a rational basis standard, those congressional judgments respecting military security should have been easy winners.

[100] Sabri v. United States, 124 S. Ct. 1941, 1946 (2004) (emphasis added).

[101] See *id.* (citing Hodel v. Virginia Surface Mining & Reclamation Association, 452 U.S. 264, 276 (1981), and Hanna v. Plumer, 380 U.S. 460, 472 (1965)).

[102] 124 S. Ct. at 1946 (emphasis added).

that Jefferson's interpretation of the Sweeping Clause was correct, but it is more than enough to show that Hamilton's "rationally related" interpretation was wrong.

In one of *McCulloch*'s most famous passages, Chief Justice Marshall questioned this textual argument by declaring of the word "necessary": "If reference be had to its use, in the common affairs of the world, or in approved authors, we find that it frequently imports no more than that one thing is convenient, or useful, or essential to another."[103] Putting aside the seeming oddity of equating the word "essential" with the words "convenient" and "useful": Marshall did not identify any of the "approved authors" of whom he spoke, nor did he provide any examples of usages that conformed to his suggested loose meaning for "necessary." In fact, Marshall was simply echoing Alexander Hamilton's famous observation in his opinion to President Washington concerning the first Bank of the United States that "[i]t is a common mode of expression to say, that it is *necessary* for a government or a person to do this or that thing, when nothing more is intended or understood, than that the interests of the government or person require, or will be promoted by, the doing of this or that thing."[104] Hamilton provided no more support for his contention than did Marshall nearly three decades later.

While it would require a professional linguist, a professional historian, or both (and I am neither) to pronounce definitively upon Hamilton's and Marshall's position, a humble lawyer can make two pertinent observations. First, Samuel Johnson's dictionary provides no support whatsoever for the Hamilton/Marshall view of "necessary." If one is looking for reliable authorities concerning common founding-era usage of the word "necessary," Johnson the lexicographer would seem to have more than a modest advantage over a secretary of the treasury and a Supreme Court justice with notorious political interests in the outcome of the inquiry. Second, I have examined every usage of the word "necessary" contemporaneous with or prior to the decision in *McCulloch* that appears in the substantial database contained in the *American Freedom Library* CD-ROM

---

[103] 17 U.S. (4 Wheat) 316, 413 (1819).

[104] Opinion on the Constitutionality of an Act to Establish a Bank, in 8 The Papers of Alexander Hamilton 97, 102 (Harold C. Syrett & Jacob E. Cooke eds., 1965).

collection, and none of those usages even remotely approaches "convenient" or "useful." If I may risk the conceit of self-quotation, the Hamilton/Marshall position on this point "appears to be blather."[105] Structurally, the case against the "rational basis" interpretation of the word "necessary" is strongly reinforced by two important intratextual comparisons within the Constitution. First, if one plugs the Hamiltonian understanding of "necessary" into the Imposts Clause, the result is gibberish: "No State shall, without the Consent of Congress, lay any Imposts or Duties on Imports or Exports, except what may be *absolutely* [rationally related to or believed by Congress to be helpful] to executing its inspection Laws." The qualifier "absolutely" is nonsensical on such an interpretation. In order for the Imposts Clause to make sense, the word "necessary" must involve a direct and substantial connection between means and ends, with the word "absolutely" *amplifying* but not changing the basic character of that connection.

Second, the Constitution's uses of the words "necessary" and "needful" are also instructive. Samuel Johnson's founding-era dictionary cross-defined "necessary" and "needful" as synonyms: One of Johnson's definitions of "necessary" was "needful," and Johnson's entire definition of "needful" was simply "necessary; indispensably requisite." On two separate occasions—the Territories Clause and the District Clause, the latter of which immediately precedes the Sweeping Clause in Article I, section 8—the Constitution uses the term "needful" to define Congress's powers.[106] Both usages of "needful" involve contexts—federal territory and federal enclaves—in which Congress acts with the powers of a general government. If there were ever going to be occasion for giving terms such as "needful" or "necessary" a relatively loose construction, it would occur when defining the legislative powers of a general government rather than when defining the legislative powers of a limited government. Again, this may not be enough to sustain the

---

[105] Gary Lawson, Discretion As Delegation: The "Proper" Understanding of the Nondelegation Doctrine, 73 Geo. Wash. L. Rev. (forthcoming 2005).

[106] See U.S. Const. art. I, § 8, cl. 17 (giving Congress power of exclusive legislation over all land acquired from States "for the Erection of Forts, Magazines, Arsenals, dock-Yards, and other needful Buildings"); *id.* art. IV, § 3, cl. 2 (authorizing Congress to make "all needful Rules and Regulations respecting" federal territory or property).

view that "necessary" means "indispensable," but it certainly defeats the claim that "necessary" means "rationally related."

Historically, the Hamiltonian rational basis standard is inconsistent with the circumstances of the founding. During the ratification debates, the Sweeping Clause was a frequent target of attack as a threat to liberty. The Constitution's advocates responded that the Sweeping Clause simply made explicit what would have been implicit in the absence of such a clause.[107] In a government of limited and enumerated powers, one could hardly imply a congressional power to pass all laws "rationally related" to the enumerated powers in the absence of the Sweeping Clause.

Madison's standard, which requires a direct, obvious, and precise connection between legislative means and ends, best conforms to the Constitution's text, structure, and history. Textually, Madison's formulation conforms to the ordinary meaning (then and now) of the word "necessary," which is not a term that one would likely use to describe remote and attenuated connections. Structurally, it makes sense of the Imposts Clause; under a Madisonian view of "necessary," the phrase "absolutely necessary" in the Imposts Clause of Article I, section 10 means that without congressional consent, states can only tax imports or exports if their inspection laws would otherwise be unenforceable, which makes good structural sense. And historically, if there were no Sweeping Clause, one would likely infer something very much like Madison's standard as an implication from the grant of enumerated powers. The best understanding of the word "necessary" as it appears in the Sweeping Clause is that congressional legislation under that clause must have a direct, obvious, and precise connection to appropriate legislative ends.

---

[107] See The Federalist No. 33, *supra* note 2, at 202 (Alexander Hamilton) (the Sweeping Clause is "only declaratory of a truth which would have resulted by necessary and unavoidable implication from the very act of constituting a federal government and vesting it with certain specified powers"); The Federalist No. 44, *supra* note 2, at 285 (James Madison) ("Had the Constitution been silent on this head, there can be no doubt that all the particular powers requisite as means of executing the general powers would have resulted to the government, by unavoidable implication."); see also 1 Annals of Cong. 1951 (Joseph Gales ed., 1791) (statement of James Madison) ("The explanations in the State Conventions all turned on the . . . principle that the terms necessary and proper gave no additional powers to those enumerated.").

It is, of course, one thing to say that the Sweeping Clause requires a direct, obvious, and precise connection between legislative means and ends. It is another thing to explain how to apply that standard to specific circumstances. Just as one cannot specify in advance all of the means that Congress might try to employ to effectuate federal powers, one cannot specify in advance exactly which fits between means and ends will be unconstitutional. Madison, for instance, may well have been wrong about the application of his own standard to the Bank of the United States; the causal connection between the Bank and the federal borrowing power is hardly remote.

With respect to section 666(a)(2), however, the case against the statute is easy. The statute criminalizes bribery attempts in connection with any transaction involving $5,000 or more as long as the bribe's intended target is "an agent of an organization or of a State, local or Indian tribal government, or any agency thereof" that receives at least $10,000 in federal assistance within one year of the alleged crime. There is no requirement that the attempted bribe have anything to do with any particular federally funded program. The statute simply polices the honesty of everyone who deals with any recipient of the statutorily required amount of federal financial assistance. This falls far short of the constitutional requirements of the Sweeping Clause.

Congress could surely penalize misappropriation of federal funds by their recipients. Such a statute would plainly have a "definite connection" to and "obvious and precise affinity" with the underlying federal program. For similar reasons, Congress could also penalize the acceptance of bribes by recipients of federal funds when the bribes concern the operation of federally-funded programs. Indeed, Congress can possibly penalize such bribes even if they are not shown specifically to affect the disposition of federal funds.[108] In this circumstance, the connection between the penal statute and the execution of an underlying federal power is not as definite, obvious, and precise as in the case of the misappropriation of federal funds, but to require the narrowest possible tailoring of implementing statutes might move too far toward the view that "necessary" means

---

[108] See Salinas v. United States, 522 U.S. 52 (1997); cf. Westfall v. United States, 274 U.S. 256 (1927) (Congress may prohibit bank fraud perpetrated on state banks in the Federal Reserve System without showing that any of the Federal Reserve Banks suffered a specific loss).

"indispensable." Congress can ensure the integrity of the programs that it funds through general laws, even if those laws sometimes sweep beyond their central concerns. It is more doubtful whether Congress could prohibit persons who do not themselves receive federal benefits from offering bribes to persons who do receive such benefits, even when the bribes concern the operation of a federally-funded program: It is unclear how a federal program is definitely or obviously affected simply because temptation is placed in the path of federal funding recipients, given that those recipients can always be punished if they yield to the temptation. But section 666(a)(2) goes far beyond any remotely plausible connection to the execution of federal powers.

Section 666(a)(2) does not require any showing that the alleged bribery have any connection to any federally funded program. All that must be shown is that the target of the bribe received federal assistance of some kind in the amount of $10,000 and that the attempted bribe concerned a transaction involving at least $5,000. This amounts to saying that Congress has an interest in ensuring that recipients of federal benefits not face undue temptation in areas of their lives other than the administration of federal benefits, for fear that they might yield in those other areas and subsequently yield with respect to federal funds as well. If that is "necessary . . . for carrying into Execution" federal powers, so would be a statute prohibiting, for example, solicitation of adultery in connection with recipients of federal funds. The same considerations defeat the Supreme Court's argument that "money is fungible." Federal funding may perhaps increase the possible scope for bribery by increasing the budgets of the funded agencies, but to call that a "definite," "obvious" or "precise" connection between criminal liability and the federal funding power is to reduce those words to a rational basis test. Section 666(a)(2) does not represent a "definite," "obvious," and "precise" means for carrying federal powers into execution.

### 2. Proper Behavior

I have spent a good portion of my professional life arguing that the words "necessary" and "proper" in the Sweeping Clause represent distinct constitutional requirements, so that even if a statute is "necessary . . . for carrying into Execution" federal powers, it is still beyond Congress's powers under the Sweeping Clause if it is not "proper" for that purpose. The argument for this proposition is set out at great length elsewhere,[109] and I cannot replicate that argument here. For those who are disinclined to read two long law review articles, and the commentary thereon, in order to discover for themselves whether my position on the meaning of the word "proper" is, as one set of critics has claimed, "idiosyncractic" and "dramatic"[110]: Although many people disagree with the content that I would attribute to the word "proper" in the Sweeping Clause, the basic view that the words "necessary" and "proper" in the Sweeping Clause have distinct meanings approaches conventional wisdom among informed commentators;[111] was the foundation for Judge Bye's dissenting opinion in *Sabri* in the Eighth Circuit;[112] and has been specifically endorsed by the Supreme Court on at least three occasions in the past decade. In two cases, the Supreme Court has specifically held that congressional statutes were unconstitutional because they were not "proper" means for executing federal powers,[113] and in a third, the Court treated as too obvious for discussion that congressional statutes under the Sweeping Clause must be analyzed separately for necessity and propriety.[114] In my academic career, I have advanced plenty of positions that deserve to be called idiosyncratic, including more than a few in this article, but the view that the words "necessary" and "proper" in the Sweeping Clause serve distinct constitutional functions is not one of them.

The word "necessary" in the Sweeping Clause regulates the "'fit'" between means and ends that must be exhibited by executory legislation. The word "proper" serves a different function. A "'proper'"

---

[109] See Lawson, *supra* note 105; Lawson & Granger, *supra* note 29.

[110] Eric A. Posner & Adrian Vermeule, Interring the Nondelegation Doctrine, 69 U. Chi. L. Rev. 1721, 1728 n.20 (2002).

[111] See, e.g., Randy E. Barnett, Constitutional Legitimacy, 103 Colum. L. Rev. 111, 145 (2003); Steven G. Calabresi & Saikrishna Prakash, The President's Power to Execute the Laws, 104 Yale L.J. 541, 587 (1994); Stephen Gardbaum, Rethinking Constitutional Federalism, 74 Tex. L. Rev. 795, 814 (1996); Garnett, *supra* note 14, at 79; Michael Stokes Paulsen, Abrogating Stare Decisis By Statute: May Congress Remove the Precedential Effect of Roe and Casey?, 109 Yale L.J. 1535, 1568 (2000); Saikrishna Prakash, The Essential Meaning of Executive Power, 2003 U. Ill. L. Rev. 701, 737 (2003).

[112] See United States v. Sabri, 326 F.3d 937, 954–57 (8th Cir. 2003) (Bye, J., dissenting).

[113] See Alden v. Maine, 527 U.S. 706, 732–33 (1999); Printz v. United States, 521 U.S. 898, 923–24 (1997).

[114] See Jinks v. Richland County, 538 U.S. 456 (2003).

law, reflecting the principal meaning of the word "proper" identified by Samuel Johnson in 1785,[115] must respect the *peculiar and distinctive jurisdictional arrangements set forth in the Constitution*. More specifically:

> [T]he authority conferred by executory laws must distinctively and peculiarly belong to the national government as a whole and to the particular institution whose powers are carried into execution. In view of the limited character of the national government under the Constitution, Congress's choice of means to execute federal powers would be constrained in at least three ways: first, an executory law would have to conform to the "proper" allocation of authority within the federal government; second, such a law would have to be within the "proper" scope of the federal government's limited jurisdiction with respect to the retained prerogatives of the states; and third, the law would have to be within the "proper" scope of the federal government's limited jurisdiction with respect to the people's retained rights.[116]

---

[115]See 2 Samuel Johnson, Dictionary of the English Language (1785) ("proper" means "1. Peculiar; not belonging to more; not common").

[116]Lawson & Granger, *supra* note 29, at 297. This "jurisdictional" understanding of the word "proper" has a firm linguistic grounding in founding-era usages, both generally with respect to the allocation of governmental powers, see *id.* at 291–97, and specifically with respect to the Sweeping Clause, see *id.* at 298–308. Two intratextual comparisons indicate that such a usage was incorporated into the Constitution. First, the Recommendation Clause instructs the president to recommend to Congress such measures "as he shall judge *necessary and expedient*." U.S. Const. art. II, § 3 (emphasis added). If the Constitution's drafters wanted a term to accompany "necessary" that simply referred to a law's suitability or aptness, they had a ready model at hand in the term "expedient." Instead, they used the word "proper" as the companion term in the Sweeping Clause; the contrast between "necessary and proper" and "necessary and expedient" highlights the jurisdictional meaning of "proper." Second, the Territories Clause of Article IV gives Congress power to "make all needful Rules and Regulations respecting the Territory or other Property belonging to the United States," U.S. Const. art. IV, § 3, cl. 2, with no requirement that such laws be "proper." Again, the contrast with the Sweeping Clause highlights the jurisdictional component of the latter. When Congress legislates for the territories, it has the powers of a general government; it is not limited by the scheme of enumerated powers. It makes perfect sense to place a jurisdictional restriction in the Sweeping Clause, which applies to Congress in its guise as a limited-government legislature, but not in the Territories Clause, which applies to Congress in its guise as a general-government legislature. Additional, generally unarticulated evidence of this understanding of the word "proper" can be found in events from the founding era. See Lawson & Granger, *supra* note 29, at 315–26. Finally, the jurisdictional understanding of the word "proper" harmonizes with the *principle of reasonableness* that grounded eighteenth-century views of delegated power. See Lawson, *supra* note 105.

The Eighth Circuit majority rejected Judge Bye's argument that section 666(a)(2) was not "proper" because it believed that a law can only fail to be "proper" under the Sweeping Clause when Congress directly regulates states in violation of constitutional principles of federalism.[117] Although the two recent Supreme Court cases that invalidated congressional statutes on the ground that they are not "proper" both involved direct regulation of states in their sovereign capacities, this hardly exhausts the circumstances under which executory laws can be improper.

If Congress sought to direct the outcome of a specific court case, such a statute would not be "proper for carrying into Execution" the federal judicial power.[118] If Congress sought to give itself power to remove executive officers by means other than impeachment, such a statute would not be "proper for carrying into Execution" any federal powers.[119] In 1790, before ratification of the Fourth Amendment, if Congress had sought to authorize the use of general warrants to enforce the tariff laws, such a statute would not have been "proper for carrying into Execution" the taxing power.[120] Laws can be improper under the Sweeping Clause without regulating or involving the states. A "proper" law must respect the Constitution's basic structure in all respects.

The Constitution's most basic structural feature is the principle of enumerated power. A statute enacted pursuant to the Sweeping Clause that threatens to unravel that principle is not "proper for carrying into Execution" federal powers. This point was acknowledged by (of all people) Alexander Hamilton, writing as Publius in *The Federalist*:

> But it may be again asked, Who is to judge of the *necessity* and *propriety* of the laws to be passed for executing the powers of the Union? ... The propriety of a law, in a constitutional light, must always be determined by the nature of the powers

---

[117]See United States v. Sabri, 326 F.3d 937, 949 n.6 (8th Cir. 2003).

[118]See United States v. Klein, 80 U.S. (13 Wall.) 128, 146 (1871).

[119]See Bowsher v. Synar, 478 U.S. 714, 726 (1986).

[120]See 1 Annals of Cong. 438 (1791) (statement of James Madison) (suggesting that in the absence of a bill of rights, Congress might misconstrue its powers under the Sweeping Clause and wrongly enact laws, such as laws providing for general warrants, "which laws in themselves are neither necessary nor proper").

upon which it is founded. Suppose, by some forced constructions of its authority (which, indeed, cannot easily be imagined), the Federal legislature should attempt to vary the law
of descent in any State, would it not be evident that, in
making such an attempt, it had exceeded its jurisdiction, and
infringed upon that of the State?[121]

One must accordingly ask whether section 666(a)(2) is consistent
with the Constitution's overall distribution of governmental authority.

The Sweeping Clause is a vehicle for executing federal powers. It
is not a vehicle for circumventing the Constitution's enumeration of
Congress's legislative jurisdiction. The Sweeping Clause, of course,
is part of that enumerated legislative jurisdiction, and there are
accordingly many subjects that Congress can reach by virtue of that
clause that otherwise would not be within its power. The power to
create federal offices, the power to regulate court procedures, the
power to condemn property, and the power to punish offenses other
than counterfeiting, maritime offenses, or violations of the law of
nations are all powers beyond those enumerated elsewhere in the
Constitution that Congress possesses under the Sweeping Clause.

That does not mean, however, that the means constitutionally
available to Congress are infinite, even limiting oneself only to those
means that are "necessary" within the meaning of the Sweeping
Clause. There is a difference between laws that execute or implement
federal powers (by creating offices, condemning property for public
purposes, specifying court procedures, etc.) and laws that regulate.
Congress's regulatory authority is carefully defined by the enumerations of subjects over which Congress is competent. Those enumerations define what might be termed Congress's "subject matter jurisdiction," which can be effectuated by means of laws pursuant to
the Sweeping Clause. But a law that is presented as a means for
carrying into execution federal powers that in fact regulates an area
beyond the specific enumerations of Congress's regulatory authority
is not "proper." It is not a law that is distinctively and peculiarly
within the jurisdiction of Congress.

---

[121] The Federalist No. 33, *supra* note 2, at 203–04 (Alexander Hamilton) (emphasis
in original).

Section 666(a)(2) is such a law. Congress has authority to promulgate a general criminal code for the territories, the District of Columbia, and federal enclaves, but it has no such authority with respect to territory within the jurisdiction of the states. Rather, in that context, Congress only has authority to promulgate criminal laws that are "necessary and proper for carrying into Execution" enumerated federal powers. Even a criminal law that is "necessary" for that purpose—and section 666(a)(2) fails that test—is beyond Congress's constitutional power if it disrupts a "proper" allocation of authority between state and federal authority. Section 666(a)(2) criminalizes the conduct of persons who simply come into contact with recipients of federal funds. That is precisely the kind of general legislative authority that Congress is denied by the enumerations of legislative competence in Article I, section 8. It is precisely the kind of authority that is not "proper" for Congress to exercise when executing federal powers.

The Supreme Court in *Sabri* did not discuss at all the question whether section 666(a)(2) was "proper" legislation under the Sweeping Clause. Perhaps this is because Sabri's counsel did not highlight the argument. For whatever reason, the issue went unaddressed, even by Justice Thomas.

## IV. *Sabri's* Implications For Limited Government

It is doubtful whether the Supreme Court's decision in *Sabri* will be long remembered. Because Sabri brought a facial challenge to the statute, virtually everything that the Court said about the Constitution is colored by the Court's general distaste for such facial challenges, especially when obviously constitutional applications of the statute are readily at hand. The Court did make some very bad law when it affirmed that the governing test for necessity under the Sweeping Clause is a rational relationship test, but no one was startled by that conclusion, which simply confirmed long-held assumptions about the Court's inclinations. The Court avoided altogether the crucial question whether section 666(a)(2) is "proper" under the Sweeping Clause. Perhaps if the government fails at Sabri's trial to prove any connection between Sabri's activities and the administration of federal funds, the case will reappear in a more appropriate procedural posture with full briefing of the question of section 666(a)(2)'s propriety.

Given the near-limitless scope granted by the Court to congressional spending power, the broad authority granted by the Court to Congress under the Commerce Clause, and the Court's apparent unwillingness to police the boundaries of necessity under the Sweeping Clause, advocates of limited government probably should not look forward to the next case involving section 666(a)(2).

# Tennessee v. Lane: How Illegitimate Power Negated Non-Existent Immunity

*Robert A. Levy*

## Overview

*Tennessee v. Lane* is about sovereign immunity and congressional power. On the immunity question, the Court got it right, for the wrong reason. Tennessee was not entitled to immunity—not because its claim to immunity was abrogated by Congress, but because the Eleventh Amendment does not confer immunity in federal question cases. On the congressional power question, the Court mistakenly found legislative authority under section 5 of the Fourteenth Amendment to enact Title II of the Americans with Disabilities Act. Given the facts in *Lane*, that power does not exist. Nor is there a constitutional pedigree to be found for Title II within any reasonable understanding of the Commerce Clause.

## I. Introduction

Would you believe, nine sovereign immunity decisions in the past eight years? That's right, the Supreme Court has muddled through a remarkable series of cases that has distended and distorted the Eleventh Amendment's immunity doctrine, now wholly unleashed from its crystal-clear text. *Tennessee v. Lane*[1] is the latest in the litany—a 5–4 opinion by Justice Stevens that affirmed Congress's power to abrogate state immunity from most private claims for money damages. After a string of federalism cases that repudiated Congress's power to override state immunity, the Court appears to have curbed its enthusiasm.

Justice O'Connor joined the liberal bloc as she did in last year's immunity controversy, *Nevada Department of Human Resources v. Hibbs*,[2] the first Court case in recent memory to uphold congressional

---

[1] 124 S. Ct. 1978 (2004).
[2] 538 U.S. 721 (2003).

power to supersede the Eleventh Amendment. After a brief apostasy in *Hibbs*, Chief Justice Rehnquist dissented in *Lane* and reaffirmed his brand of federalism. He was joined by Justices Kennedy and Thomas. Justice Scalia dissented separately.[3]

The underlying statute at issue in *Lane* was the Americans with Disabilities Act of 1990 (ADA),[4] which states in Title II that "no qualified individual with a disability shall, by reason of such disability, be excluded from participation in or denied the benefits of the services, programs or activities of a public entity."[5] Plaintiffs Beverly Jones and George Lane, both paraplegics, sued the state of Tennessee, contending that they were refused access to, and the services of, the state court system on account of their disability.[6] Jones is a court reporter who asserted that she lost work because some county courthouses are not wheelchair-accessible. Lane alleged more agonizing facts. He was charged with a criminal traffic offense and had to crawl up two flights of stairs to reach the courtroom. At a subsequent hearing, he declined a second opportunity to crawl or be carried, and then rejected an offer to move all proceedings to a handicapped-accessible courtroom in a nearby town. As a result, Lane was arrested and jailed for failing to appear at his hearing.

The trial court denied Tennessee's motion to dismiss claims by Jones and Lane on immunity grounds. Tennessee then asked the U.S. Court of Appeals for the Sixth Circuit to reverse. At first, the Sixth Circuit delayed review until the Supreme Court could rule in a then-pending Eleventh Amendment case, *Board of Trustees of the University of Alabama v. Garrett*,[7] which also involved the ADA (albeit Title I,[8] prohibiting employment discrimination against the disabled.) But then the Sixth Circuit changed its mind: The court of appeals decided that *Garrett* did not control the outcome in *Lane*

---

[3] Also filed, but not discussed here: a dissent by Justice Thomas, 124 S. Ct. at 2013; a concurrence by Justice Souter, joined by Justice Ginsburg, 124 S. Ct. at 1995; and a concurrence by Justice Ginsburg, joined by Justices Souter and Breyer, 124 S. Ct. at 1996.

[4] 42 U.S.C. § 12101 et seq.

[5] 42 U.S.C. § 12132.

[6] Four other plaintiffs later joined the lawsuit, but the Court cites only the claims by Lane and Jones.

[7] 531 U.S. 356 (2001).

[8] 42 U.S.C. § 12111 et seq.

after all. That's because *Garrett* was an equal protection case alleging employment discrimination against a particular class—the disabled—in violation of the ADA's Title I. *Lane*, by contrast, was a Title II case based on denial of courtroom access, which was deemed to be a due process issue. Based in part on that distinction, the Sixth Circuit upheld the trial court's refusal to dismiss *Lane*.

The Supreme Court agreed with the Sixth Circuit. Essentially, the Supreme Court adopted this logic:

- Under the Eleventh Amendment, Tennessee is entitled to sovereign immunity against suits for money damages.
- Congress can abrogate Tennessee's sovereign immunity if, among other things, it clearly expresses an intent to do so. The Court found that Congress had unambiguously declared its intent in the ADA.
- However, Congress also must base its abrogation of immunity on some constitutional authority. When it passed the ADA, Congress cited both the Commerce Clause and the Fourteenth Amendment as its source of authority.[9] But an earlier Supreme Court case[10] held that Congress, when it enacts legislation under the Commerce Clause, cannot abrogate Eleventh Amendment immunity.[11] The Court, therefore, turned to section 5 of the Fourteenth Amendment.
- The Court held Congress *can* abrogate immunity when it enacts legislation to enforce the Fourteenth Amendment's Due Process and Equal Protection Clauses, provided that the means adopted are "congruent and proportional" to the underlying harm.[12] In *Lane*, said the Court, those conditions were met by Title II of the ADA.

In Part II below, I summarize Justice Stevens's majority opinion. Part III explores whether Tennessee can legitimately claim Eleventh Amendment immunity, and concludes that no immunity exists because the Eleventh Amendment does not apply to this case. That

---

[9] 42 U.S.C. § 12101(b)(4).

[10] Seminole Tribe v. Florida, 517 U.S. 44 (1996).

[11] *Id.* at 73 ("Article I cannot be used to circumvent the constitutional limitations placed upon federal jurisdiction.").

[12] See Boerne v. Flores, 521 U.S. 507, 520 (1997).

means the Court did not need to scrutinize Congress's power to abrogate immunity under the Fourteenth Amendment.

Nonetheless, the Court incorrectly perceived a need to abrogate immunity and looked, therefore, to the Fourteenth Amendment for a congressional power to do so. Part IV addresses whether the enactment of Title II was authorized under section 5 of that amendment. A majority of the justices said yes. Four justices disagreed. I review the two major dissenting opinions and decide that the dissenters have the better of the argument. The Court's "congruence and proportionality" criteria for validating federal intervention to enforce the Fourteenth Amendment were not fulfilled in this case.

Then, in Part V, I comment on what the Court should have held if it had sought to justify federal intervention under the Commerce Clause. I find that the commerce power affords no authority for Title II of the ADA—a statute that creates a private cause of action for disabled persons who claim to have been excluded from the benefits of state services. Even if it were demonstrated that the plaintiffs in *Lane* were in fact denied access to a state court, such access is not commerce; it is not interstate; and it is not, then, a fit subject for the Commerce Clause, the primary purpose of which is to ensure the free flow of trade among the several states.

## II. The Majority Opinion

The issue tackled by the Court in *Lane* was whether Congress, legislating under section 5 of the Fourteenth Amendment, could force states to provide access by disabled persons to public facilities. The majority held that the legislation, Title II of the ADA, is constitutional if the access at issue is a fundamental right, such as access to the courts. Access to other, presumably less vital, public facilities—such as a public swimming pool—might not be guaranteed, depending on future Court rulings.

Advocates for the disabled, supported by the Bush administration, wanted a more expansive ruling that would have ensured access to a wide range of public services and activities. But Justice Stevens limited the Court's holding "to the class of cases implicating the fundamental right of access to the courts."[13] According to Tony Coelho, the former House majority whip (D-Calif.) who played a

---

[13] Tennessee v. Lane, 124 S. Ct. 1978, 1994 (2004).

leading role in drafting the ADA, the majority focused on the issue of court access "in order to get Justice O'Connor's vote."[14]

*New York Times* reporter Linda Greenhouse agreed. She wrote that "it was clearly more important for Justice Stevens and his usual three allies to win Justice O'Connor's support than to set out a far-reaching critique of the 2001 disability decision [referring to *Garrett*] or of others she had joined on the states'-rights side."[15] Greenhouse observed that the "majority's focus on the 'basic right' of access to court . . . served its purpose without prejudging future cases."[16] The Court's fragile 5–4 majority, she concluded, "managed to carve out one disputed application of the law and uphold it in the face of Tennessee's claim of constitutional immunity"—"a development with potentially broad implications."[17]

Indeed, Stevens managed to leave the door half-opened. He cited evidence of additional problems faced by the disabled—going beyond access to the courts and touching on areas such as voting, marriage, jury duty, treatment of the retarded, and public educa-tion.[18] Those citations have given activists hope that *Lane* might be useful ammunition if other Title II cases reach the high Court.

The scope of the evidence considered by Stevens also helped the Court distinguish between *Lane* and *Garrett*, the 2001 case in which the Court told Congress it could not enforce the anti-discrimination provisions of Title I of the ADA against state employers. University of California (Hastings) law professor Vikram David Amar points out that the Court, by reviewing more evidence in *Lane*, "was able to characterize the congressional demonstration of state constitutional violations as more egregious."[19]

Amar speculates that *Garrett* might have gone the other way if the evidentiary lens had been as wide as the one used in *Lane*. He

[14] Quoted in Charles Lane, Disabled Win Right to Sue States over Court Access, Washington Post, May 18, 2004, at A1.

[15] Linda Greenhouse, Justices Find States Can Be Liable for Not Making Courthouses Accessible to Disabled, New York Times, May 18, 2004, at A20.

[16] *Id.*

[17] *Id.*

[18] Lane, 124 S. Ct. at 1989.

[19] Vikram David Amar, The Supreme Court Hands Down a Key Federalism/Disabil-ity Law Decision, and Surprises Some Observers with Its Result, Findlaw's Legal Commentary (May 27, 2004), at http://writ.news.findlaw.com/amar/20040527.html.

noted two major differences. First, *Garrett* had considered only state employers, not county and city employers. By contrast, *Lane* took into account courtrooms run by municipal and county officials. Second, *Garrett* was an employment case and did not examine state discrimination in other contexts. *Lane*, on the other hand, looked at settings outside the courtroom, even though the Court's holding applied only to courtroom access.[20]

In addition to parsing the evidence, the Court's legal analysis in *Lane* went like this: To determine if Congress can abrogate a state's Eleventh Amendment immunity, the threshold question is whether the underlying federal legislation unequivocally states an intent to abrogate. In *Lane*, that was not a disputed issue. The ADA specifically provides: "A State shall not be immune under the eleventh amendment . . . from an action in Federal or State court."[21]

The second question for the Court was more difficult: Did Congress act pursuant to a valid grant of constitutional authority? Under section 5 of the Fourteenth Amendment, said the Court, Congress's enforcement power includes authority both to remedy and to deter violations. That means Congress can prohibit "a somewhat broader swath of conduct, including that which is not itself forbidden by the Amendment's text."[22] In other words, Congress can legislate prophylactically to prevent unconstitutional conduct even if, in the process, it prohibits acts that are not themselves unconstitutional. In *Hibbs*, for example, the Court upheld the Family and Medical Leave Act of 1993,[23] which invalidated a state's medical leave policy because it had a discriminatory effect, even though the state policy had not been adopted with an unconstitutional discriminatory purpose.

The *Lane* Court cautioned, however, that the measures adopted by Congress under section 5 are not unlimited; they "may not work a 'substantive change in the governing law.'"[24] That said, the line between a remedy and a substantive change is not easy to draw.

---

[20] *Id.*

[21] 42 U.S.C. § 12202.

[22] Lane, 124 S. Ct. at 1985 (citation omitted).

[23] 29 U.S.C. § 2601 et seq.

[24] Lane, 124 S. Ct. at 1986 (citing Boerne v. Flores, 521 U.S. 507, 519 (1997)).

The touchstone, under *Boerne v. Flores*,[25] is that the means chosen by Congress must be congruent and proportional to the injury to be prevented or remedied.[26]

For example, in *Garrett*, the Court held that Title I of the ADA, which barred discrimination in employment against the disabled, was not a valid enforcement of the Fourteenth Amendment's Equal Protection Clause. That conclusion was reached, in part, because Congress could not point to any history of unconstitutional discrimination by public employers. Instead, Congress had spotlighted employment discrimination in the *private* sector.[27] As a result, the Court concluded Congress had not adequately shown any basis in fact for abrogating state immunity. Put another way, the sweep of the statute was too broad; its remedies were not targeted at the identified harms.

But the *Lane* Court treated Title II differently. That's because Lane sought access to rights that are secured by the Due Process Clause. Lane is entitled under that clause to be present at his trial, heard by the court, and judged by a jury of his peers.[28] Abridgement of those rights is subject to "more searching judicial review" than in *Garrett*, where unequal treatment of the disabled was not constitutionally "suspect" and did not therefore trigger heightened scrutiny.[29] In *Lane*, "Congress enacted Title II against a backdrop of pervasive unequal treatment in the administration of state services and programs, including systematic deprivation of fundamental rights."[30] The Court concluded that the right of access to courts called for "a standard of judicial review at least as searching, and in some cases more searching, than the standard that applie[d] to sex-based classifications" in last term's *Hibbs* case.[31]

In applying that heightened standard, the *Lane* Court still had to determine whether Title II was an appropriate response to the history

---

[25] *Supra* note 12.
[26] Lane, 124 S. Ct. at 1986 (citing Boerne, 521 U.S. at 520).
[27] Board of Trustees of the University of Alabama v. Garrett, 531 U.S. 356, 371–72 (2001).
[28] Lane, 124 S. Ct. at 1989.
[29] *Id.* at 1992.
[30] *Id.* at 1989.
[31] *Id.* at 1992.

and pattern of treatment that had been documented. The key to that question lay in the Court's pronouncement that *Lane* is an "as applied" constitutional challenge rather than a "facial" challenge— a subject to which we will return in Part IV, which discusses Justice Rehnquist's dissent. For now, it's important to recall that Justice Stevens decided *Lane* narrowly—limiting its holding to courtroom access, not the full scope of activities covered by Title II. As Stevens put it: "[T]he question presented in this case is not whether Congress can validly subject the States to private suits for money damages for failing to provide reasonable access to hockey rinks, or even to voting booths, but whether Congress had the power under § 5 to enforce the constitutional right of access to the courts."[32]

The assessment of the *Lane* majority was that "Congress's chosen remedy . . . , Title II's requirement of program accessibility, is congruent and proportional to its object of enforcing the right of access to the courts."[33] The only qualification, volunteered Stevens, is that the states need not employ any and all means to ensure courtroom access. All that is necessary are "'reasonable modifications' that would not fundamentally alter the nature of the services provided, and only when the individual seeking modification is otherwise eligible for the service."[34] In no event, he added, "is the entity required to undertake measures that would impose an undue financial or administrative burden [or] threaten historic preservation interests."[35]

With that background, we turn next to an analysis of the majority opinion from two perspectives: first, whether Tennessee's claim of Eleventh Amendment immunity is supportable in a federal question case; second, whether Title II of the ADA rests on a sound constitutional footing.

### III. The Case Against Sovereign Immunity

*A. What the Courts Have Said*

Beginning in 1890 and concluding with an unbroken string of seven cases from 1996 through 2002, the Supreme Court enlarged the

---

[32] *Id.* at 1993.
[33] *Id.*
[34] *Id.*
[35] *Id.* at 1994.

doctrine of sovereign immunity, which bars most private lawsuits against non-consenting state governments for money damages.[36] Along the way, the Court ignored the plain text of the Eleventh Amendment: "The Judicial power of the United States shall not be construed to extend to any suit in law or equity, commenced or prosecuted against one of the United States by Citizens of another State, or by Citizens or Subjects of any Foreign State."[37]

In its earliest case, *Hans v. Louisiana*,[38] despite the Eleventh Amendment's clear mandate that the litigants be from different states, the Court held that sovereign immunity applies to suits against a state by its own citizens. More than a century later, in 1996, the Court immunized states against actions brought under federal question, not just diversity, jurisdiction.[39] Then in 1999, the Court extended immunity to suits in state courts.[40]

The Court has acknowledged only one new exemption from its ballooning immunity doctrine: States remain vulnerable to private suits pursuant to federal laws that enforce the Fourteenth Amendment. But then, in four cases from 1999 through 2001, the Court steadily chipped away at that exemption. Two of those cases were near-replicas of *Lane*. In *Kimel v. Florida Board of Regents*,[41] the Court concluded that Congress's attempted abrogation of state immunity in the Age Discrimination in Employment Act[42] exceeded its authority to enforce the Fourteenth Amendment.[43] Age, the Court said, is not a "suspect class," so states have more leeway to discriminate by age than by, say, race.[44] Thirteen months later, the Court decided

---

[36] This section has been extracted in part from Robert A. Levy, People v. State: The Law Should Protect Citizens' Dignity, Not States' Immunity, Legal Times, June 16, 2003, at 74. See also Robert A. Levy, When State Dignity Trumps Individual Rights, 2001–2002 Cato Sup. Ct. Rev. 31 (2002).

[37] U.S. Const. amend. XI.

[38] 134 U.S. 1 (1890).

[39] Seminole Tribe v. Florida, 517 U.S. 44, 66–67, 72 (1996) (overruling *Pennsylvania v. Union Gas Co.*, 491 U.S. 1 (1989), which had held that Congress is empowered to abrogate state sovereign immunity when legislating under the Commerce Clause).

[40] Alden v. Maine, 527 U.S. 706, 755 (1999).

[41] 528 U.S. 62 (2000).

[42] 42 U.S.C. § 6101 et seq.

[43] Kimel, 528 U.S. at 82–83.

[44] *Id.* at 83.

*Garrett*, upholding state immunity from suit under Title I of the ADA. Disability, like age, is not a suspect class.[45]

Lastly, the Court's ever-widening immunity doctrine was broadened to bar suits by private parties against a state in a federal administrative agency. The conservative majority in that case, *Federal Maritime Commission v. South Carolina State Ports Authority*,[46] asserted that the "central purpose" of sovereign immunity "is to accord the States the respect owed them as joint sovereigns."[47] In other words, the primary reason for immunity is to give the states the dignity that their sovereign status entails.

But if state dignity is the justification for sovereign immunity, what can explain the numerous exceptions that have been carved out? A state can be sued by the federal government or another state. Political subdivisions, school boards, and municipalities, which are creations of the state, can be sued under the Eleventh Amendment.[48] So can state officials in their personal capacity.[49] And both *Hibbs* (2003) and *Lane* (2004) now confirm that a state can be sued by private individuals in certain enforcement actions under the Fourteenth Amendment.

The relevant legislation in *Hibbs* was the Family Medical Leave Act (FMLA),[50] which grants unpaid leave when an employee's parent, child, or spouse is seriously ill. The FMLA was designed to address lingering gender discrimination in the workplace. Congress found that women were disproportionately burdened by having to take care of sick family members. Because the alleged discrimination was based on gender, which the Court gives heightened review, not

---

[45]In two other 1999 cases, the Court rejected congressional attempts to abrogate Eleventh Amendment immunity by invoking the Fourteenth Amendment. See Florida Prepaid Postsecondary Education Expense Board v. College Savings Bank, 527 U.S. 627, 642–43, 645–46 (1999); College Savings Bank v. Florida Prepaid Postsecondary Education Expense Board, 527 U.S. 666, 672–75 (1999). For further details, see Levy, When State Dignity Trumps Individual Rights, *supra* note 36, at 37–38.

[46]535 U.S. 743 (2002).

[47]*Id.* at 765 (internal quotation omitted).

[48]See, for example, Mt. Healthy City School District Board of Education v. Doyle, 429 U.S. 274 (1977).

[49]Ex parte Young, 209 U.S. 123 (1908).

[50]*Supra* note 23.

the minimal scrutiny applied to age- or disability-based discrimination, "it was easier for Congress to show a pattern of state constitutional violations."[51]

Like *Hibbs*, *Lane* was a case in which the Court had an easier time finding state misconduct that rose to the level of a constitutional infraction. In *Lane*, however, the Court's heightened scrutiny was not attributable to discrimination on the basis of a suspect class. Instead, the Court's rationale was based on due process, and the increased scrutiny derived from alleged denial of a "fundamental" right—access to the court.

## B. The Trouble With Sovereign Immunity

By abrogating Tennessee's sovereign immunity, *Lane* produced the right result—even though for the wrong reason. Regrettably, the Court missed its ninth opportunity in eight years to affirm that compensating injured parties and deterring state misbehavior takes precedence over safeguarding government bank accounts. A free society cannot subordinate the rights of individuals to the "dignity" of state governments—not even with the noble aim of inhibiting federal power.

A proper understanding of the role of government dictates that the Eleventh Amendment be construed narrowly. Clearly, that is not what the Court had done pre-*Hibbs*. By its extra-textual reading of the amendment, the Court took the common law concept of sovereign immunity, dubious on its own terms,[52] and constitutionalized it. Concern for state dignity superseded the rights of individuals, relegated by judicial edict to the bottom of the pecking order. Essentially, the Rehnquist Court had embraced the appalling notion that states can violate individual rights without being held accountable for monetary losses associated with personal injuries.

In its defense, the Court proceeded with the best of intentions—to restrain a Congress that has flouted the doctrine of enumerated powers and established a pervasive regulatory and redistributive state that threatens individual liberty. The federal government has

---

[51] Nevada Department of Human Resources v. Hibbs, 538 U.S. 721, 736 (2003).

[52] See, e.g., Seminole Tribe v. Florida, 517 U.S. 44, 95 (1996) (Souter, J., dissenting) (noting that the common law doctrine of sovereign immunity rested on the "absurd" belief that "the King can do no wrong").

wormed its way into virtually every aspect of our lives—imposing rules to control a broad array of human endeavor, exacting tribute from anyone, for almost any purpose, then dispensing the proceeds to anyone else. No doubt, the Court's steps to curtail Congress's seemingly boundless powers were long overdue.

But, while the Rehnquist Court justifiably tried to slow down the federal juggernaut, it went about it in the wrong manner. The proper remedy is to attack unconstitutional statutes on their merits, not to pretend that federal law can't be invoked by individuals against state governments when damages are sought.

The real culprit was the 1996 *Seminole* case, in which the Court extended sovereign immunity to cover cases brought against states under *federal* law. Bear in mind that Article III of the Constitution provides that federal courts can decide two types of lawsuits: those concerning federal law,[53] and those involving citizens of different states.[54] The text of the Eleventh Amendment covers the second type (so-called diversity of citizenship cases) but not the first type (so-called federal question cases.) That didn't stop the Supreme Court in *Seminole*, not even the Court's conservatives. The textualist approach to constitutional interpretation, presumably favored by the conservatives, provides no support for *Seminole* or any of the other cases that have stretched the Eleventh Amendment.

Indeed, the holding in *Seminole* flies in the face of the Supremacy Clause of Article VI. There, the Constitution provides that "the Laws of the United States . . . shall be the supreme Law of the Land."[55] The hierarchy laid out in Article VI places the laws of the United States above the laws of any state—even above a state constitution. But in *Seminole*, sovereign immunity, which is basically a common law doctrine, is accorded a status above that of a federal statute. As for individuals, they are last in line—sending a message that individuals are subordinate to states rather than the other way around.

The effect of sovereign immunity is to place the government above the law and to ensure that some individuals will be unable to obtain redress for injuries. That's simply not acceptable. In a free society,

[53] U.S. Const. art. III, § 2, cl. 2.
[54] U.S. Const. art. III, § 2, cl. 1.
[55] U.S. Const. art. VI, cl. 2.

the "dignity" of state governments cannot be permitted to trump the rights of individual Americans.

Perhaps the Constitution would be a more liberating document if the Eleventh Amendment had never been ratified. But, of course, it was ratified in 1795, and the Court is stuck with it. That does not, however, obligate the Court to extend the reach of the amendment by reading more into it than can possibly be justified by its unambiguous text.

## IV. Congressional Power: The Dissenters' Case Against the Fourteenth Amendment

Notwithstanding the compelling arguments against Eleventh Amendment immunity in federal question cases, the Supreme Court has been unwilling to revisit *Seminole*. Yet the Court now seems disposed to permit congressional abrogation of state immunity under the Fourteenth Amendment. That's the lesson of *Hibbs*, where the Court applied heightened equal protection scrutiny because of perceived gender discrimination by the state; and *Lane*, where the Court applied heightened due process scrutiny because of perceived denial of courtroom access—a "fundamental" right—by the state.

Not all of the justices agreed with those results. In *Hibbs*, Justice Kennedy, joined in dissent by Justices Scalia and Thomas, questioned whether the states had "engaged in a pattern of unlawful conduct which warrants the remedy of opening state treasuries to private suits."[56] He remarked on the Court's inability to adduce evidence of alleged discrimination and on "the inescapable fact that the federal scheme is not a remedy but a benefit program."[57] Justice Scalia, in a separate dissent, warned against "guilt by association, enabling the sovereignty of one State to be abridged . . . because of violations by another State . . . or even by 49 other States."[58]

The same three justices dissented in *Lane*, along with Chief Justice Rehnquist. I discuss in turn the two major dissents—the first by Chief Justice Rehnquist, the second by Justice Scalia.

---

[56]Nevada Department of Human Resources v. Hibbs, 538 U.S. 721, 745 (2003) (Kennedy, J., dissenting).

[57]*Id.*

[58]*Id.* at 741–42 (Scalia, J., dissenting).

## A. Rehnquist's Dissent

Rehnquist, joined by Kennedy and Thomas, argued that Title II of the ADA is not a valid section 5 enforcement action. Instead, like Title I in *Garrett*, Title II substantively redefines the rights protected by the Fourteenth Amendment. In reaching that conclusion, Rehnquist goes through the three-step process spelled out in *Boerne*: first, identify the rights at issue; second, examine the evidence cited by Congress to establish a pattern of violations; and third, consider whether the remedies created by Title II are congruent and proportional to the documented violations.

With respect to the rights at issue, Rehnquist observed that Title II goes beyond the equal protection concerns of Title I, which protects the disabled against irrational discrimination. Title II also purports to safeguard rights—such as courtroom access—that fall under the Due Process Clause. Specifically, Rehnquist pinpointed four due process rights cited by the majority: "(1) the right of the criminal defendant to be present at all critical stages of the trial; (2) the right of litigants to have a meaningful opportunity to be heard in judicial proceedings; (3) the right of the criminal defendant to trial by a jury composed of a fair cross section of the community; and (4) the public right of access to criminal proceedings."[59]

Next, Rehnquist asked whether Congress had found a history and pattern of violations. His answer: an unequivocal "no." Although Congress, when it enacted the ADA, offered a wide-ranging account of societal discrimination against the disabled, the bulk of the evidence—mostly unexamined and anecdotal—concerned non-state government acts, which had been deemed irrelevant in prior sovereign immunity cases like *Garrett* and *Kimel*. Some of that evidence might be relevant, stated Rehnquist, if the Court were reviewing Title II as a whole. But the Court had rejected that approach, preferring a narrower "as-applied" inquiry that focused only on courtroom access.[60]

Even if Title II is viewed narrowly, Rehnquist insisted, "the mere existence of an architecturally 'inaccessible' courthouse . . . does not state a constitutional violation. A violation of due process occurs

---

[59]Tennessee v. Lane, 124 S. Ct. 1978, 1998–99 (2004) (Rehnquist, C.J., dissenting) (internal quotation and citations omitted).

[60]*Id.* at 1999.

only when a person is actually denied the constitutional right to access a given judicial proceeding. We have never held that a person has a *constitutional* right to make his way into a courtroom without any external assistance."[61]

Finally, Rehnquist explored the congruence and proportionality of Title II's remedial provisions. In its findings, Congress had made it clear that Title II attacked discrimination in all areas of public services, as well as the "discriminatory effect" of "architectural, transportation, and communication barriers."[62] Rehnquist maintained that those broad terms go beyond arguable constitutional violations. Title II is not tailored to protect *just* courtroom access. Instead, it covers all services, programs, and activities provided by a public entity. As Rehnquist noted, a "requirement of accommodation for the disabled at a state-owned amusement park or sports stadium . . . bears no permissible prophylactic relationship to enabling disabled persons to exercise their fundamental constitutional rights."[63]

Put somewhat differently, Rehnquist considered the coverage of Title II to be massively overbroad—a problem that the majority claimed to have cured with its "as-applied" approach, limited to courtroom access. Rehnquist would sooner have invalidated Title II on a "facial" basis because of its many unconstitutional applications, even if he were to concede that Title II's application to Lane's particular challenge might be constitutional.

To be sure, the Court typically disfavors facial, or overbreadth, challenges—preferring to avoid constitutional confrontations by contracting the reach of congressional statutes. In this instance, however, Rehnquist argued persuasively that the Court's as-applied test cannot be harmonized with *Boerne*'s test for congruence and proportionality. After all, how can the majority assert, on one hand, that Title II must be construed narrowly because it would otherwise restrict state conduct that is constitutionally permissible; then, on the other hand, assert that the remedies provided by Title II are congruent and proportional to documented violations of constitutional rights?

---

[61] *Id.* at 2002.
[62] 42 U.S.C. §§ 12101(a)(3), (a)(5).
[63] *Lane*, 124 S. Ct. at 2004 (Rehnquist, C.J., dissenting).

The majority gets away with that legerdemain by positing "a hypothetical statute, never enacted by Congress, that applies only to courthouses. The effect is to rig the congruence-and-proportionality test by artificially constricting the scope of the statute to closely mirror a recognized constitutional right."[64] That bogus approach, said Rehnquist, becomes a test of whether the Court can visualize an imaginary statute that is narrow enough to constitute valid prophylactic legislation.

## B. Scalia's Dissent

Justice Scalia agreed with the chief justice. He too believed that the majority flouted the congruence and proportionality standard. But he filed a separate dissent in *Lane* to push that message further than the other dissenters were willing to go. Despite joining the Court's opinion in *Boerne*, Scalia rejected the congruence and proportionality test—not only because it is incompatible with the Court's as-applied maneuver in *Lane*, but also because he does not approve of "such malleable standards as 'proportionality,' because they have a way of turning into vehicles for the implementation of individual judges' policy preferences."[65]

Scalia claimed to have yielded to the "lessons of experience. The 'congruence and proportionality' standard, like all such flabby tests, is a standing invitation to judicial arbitrariness and policy-driven decisionmaking . . . . Under it, the courts . . . must regularly check Congress's homework to make sure that it has identified sufficient constitutional violations to make its remedy congruent and proportional."[66]

In its place, Scalia would substitute a different test, which appears in the text of section 5 of the Fourteenth Amendment. He would require Congress to "enforce" section 5, not to "go *beyond* the provisions of the Fourteenth Amendment to proscribe, prevent, or 'remedy' conduct that does not *itself* violate any provision of the Fourteenth Amendment." "So-called 'prophylactic legislation,'" states Scalia, "is reinforcement rather than enforcement."[67]

---

[64] *Id.* at 2005.
[65] *Id.* at 2007–08 (Scalia, J., dissenting).
[66] *Id.* at 2008–09.
[67] *Id.* at 2009.

Scalia conceded just two exceptions to his far-reaching proposal. First, he would authorize legislation that imposes rules directly related to the facilitation of enforcement—like reporting requirements, for example. Second, he would respect past decisions now well-settled in law and allow, on *stare decisis* grounds, prophylactic measures to combat racial discrimination alone. That single practice, according to Scalia, was the issue in dispute when the Court expansively interpreted section 5. When congressional legislation was targeted at discrimination in other areas, the Court was more restrained.

Hereafter, advised Scalia, he will "leave it to Congress, under constraints no tighter than those of the Necessary and Proper Clause, to decide what measures are appropriate under § 5 to prevent or remedy racial discrimination by the States."[68] But even in race cases, Scalia will insist that Congress can impose prophylactic legislation on those *particular* states, and no others, that have a history of relevant constitutional violations. In cases not directed at racial discrimination, Scalia will uphold only those statutes that enforce the provisions of the Fourteenth Amendment—that is, legislation that addresses actual or imminent constitutional violations, and does not proscribe state conduct that itself is constitutional, even to deter other conduct that may not be.

Although Rehnquist, Thomas, and Kennedy did not subscribe to Scalia's recommended overhaul of section 5 jurisprudence, the four

---

[68] *Id.* at 2013. Scalia's replacement of "congruent and proportional" with "necessary and proper" may be based on constitutional text, but his new test is unlikely to provide much comfort to advocates of limited federal government. The permissive "necessary and proper" standard that Scalia proposes is the one first enunciated by Chief Justice John Marshall in *McCulloch v. Maryland*, 17 U.S. (4 Wheat.) 316 (1819), which defines "necessary" as "convenient" and offers little illumination of "proper." *Id.* at 413. In practice, "necessary and proper" has meant no more than rational basis scrutiny. This term, in *Sabri v. United States*, 124 S. Ct. 1941 (2004), the Court unanimously declined an opportunity to redefine the "Necessary and Proper Clause." Only Justice Thomas, in a concurring opinion, urged the Court to consider Marshall's proviso that "necessary" requires not merely a rational link between means and ends, but a link that is "appropriate" and "plainly adapted"—perhaps something closer to an obvious, simple, and direct relationship. *Id.* at 1949 (Thomas, J., concurring). As for "proper," it should, but has not been interpreted to, suggest a consistency with principles of federalism, separation of powers, and "the background rights retained by the people." See Randy E. Barnett, Restoring the Lost Constitution: The Presumption of Liberty 186 (2004).

dissenters in *Lane* got the main question right. There is no constitutional power under section 5 of the Fourteenth Amendment to compel states to provide access by disabled persons to all of the "services, programs or activities of a public entity."[69] That's what Title II is about, and to interpret it narrowly—as if it meant access only to courtrooms—is to ignore its text and eviscerate the mandate in *Boerne* that section 5 legislation must be congruent and proportional to asserted injuries.

Still, rejection of the Fourteenth Amendment as a legitimate source of authority is not the final word. Recall that Congress in enacting the ADA also relied on the Commerce Clause.

## V. Congressional Power: The Case Against the Commerce Clause

*Lane* is not a Commerce Clause case. But it might have been. Suppose, for example, that the United States, not Lane, had sued Tennessee for noncompliance with Title II of the ADA; or Lane had sued under *Ex parte Young*[70] for injunctive relief only; or the Supreme Court suddenly realized that the Eleventh Amendment does not immunize states against money damages in federal question cases. Under any of those scenarios, Lane would not have been required to establish that sovereign immunity had been abrogated. Consequently, the Court might have circumvented *Seminole's* proscription and looked at the Commerce Clause rather than the Fourteenth Amendment as a source of congressional authority.

Indeed, that is what Justice Stevens advocated in his *Hibbs* concurring opinion. He first conceded uncertainty about whether the FMLA "was truly needed to secure the guarantees of the Fourteenth Amendment."[71] But he did not have to resolve that question. Even without a Fourteenth Amendment lineage, declared Stevens, the FMLA fit comfortably under the Court's modern Commerce Clause jurisprudence.[72] And on the sovereign immunity question, Stevens correctly noted that "The Eleventh Amendment poses no barrier to

[69] 42 U.S.C. § 12132.

[70] *Supra* note 49.

[71] Nevada Department of Human Resources v. Hibbs, 538 U.S. 721, 741 (2003) (Stevens, J., concurring) (internal quotation omitted).

[72] Tennessee v. Lane, 124 S. Ct. 1978, 1985 (2004) (citing Fitzpatrick v. Bitzer, 427 U.S. 445, 458 (1976) (Stevens, J., concurring)).

the adjudication of this case because the respondents are citizens of Nevada."[73]

Consider also the parallel ADA provisions of Title I (employment) and Title III (public accommodations),[74] both of which regulate private activities that do not implicate the Fourteenth Amendment. Title III in particular covers many privately operated facilities that are analogous to the publicly operated facilities that come under Title II—for example, concert halls, stadiums, convention centers, hospitals, museums, libraries, transportation terminals, parks, schools and homeless shelters.[75] Each of those facilities "affect" commerce and would presumably be scrutinized under the Commerce Clause, whether privately or publicly operated.[76]

What, then, would have been the outcome if the Court had relied on the Commerce Clause as the enumerated congressional power that underlies Title II? Well, imagine if a congressman proclaimed before the House of Representatives: "In order to guarantee that trade among the states remain free and unfettered, Congress must direct the states to provide unobstructed physical access to all of their courtrooms by disabled persons accused of criminal traffic violations." To ponder that statement is to realize how utterly daft it is.

Still, the Court would probably have found Title II to be a legitimate exercise of Congress's unbounded Commerce Clause power. That's because Congress and the courts have shamelessly inflated the Commerce Clause—detaching it from the operative word "commerce" and allowing the federal government to assume dominion over nearly all manner of human conduct.

---

[73] *Id.*

[74] Title III prohibits discrimination on the basis of disability by privately operated public accommodations, and requires places of public accommodation and commercial facilities to be designed, constructed, and altered in compliance with certain accessibility standards. 42 U.S.C. § 12181.

[75] The facilities listed are among those expressly identified as public accommodations covered by Title III. See 42 U.S.C. § 12181(7). Under *Garcia v. San Antonio Metropolitan Transit Authority*, 469 U.S. 528 (1985), Congress can regulate state activities that affect commerce as long as the regulations are generally applicable—i.e., they are also imposed on analogous non-state activities. *Id.* at 554. Titles II and III of the ADA, taken together, seem to meet that requirement.

[76] See, e.g., United States v. Morvant, 898 F. Supp. 1157, 1167 (E.D. La. 1995) ("As Congress has not invoked the Fourteenth Amendment with respect to Title III of the ADA, the Court will only address its constitutionality under the Commerce Clause.").

As the country grew, some people believed that many of its problems required national regulatory solutions. So Congress earmarked a specific constitutional power to justify its ambitious federal agenda. The Commerce Clause was the vehicle of choice. But the Framers' central reason for placing the clause in the Constitution was quite different. Under the Articles of Confederation, the national government lacked the power to regulate interstate commerce. Each state was able to advance local interests and create barriers to trade, without regard to prejudice against out-of-state interests. The hoped-for solution was a constitutional convention at which, according to Justice William Johnson, "If there was any one object riding over every other . . . it was to keep the commercial intercourse among the States free from all invidious and partial restraints."[77]

Thus, the original purpose of the Commerce Clause was functional: to secure the free flow of trade among the states. That meant Congress could act affirmatively whenever actual or imminent state regulations impeded that purpose, or whenever it was clear that uniform national regulations were essential toward that purpose. More concretely, Congress could regulate channels and vehicles of interstate trade, like waterways, airways, and railroads; bar discrimination by a state against out-of-state business interests; and prohibit acts by a state that shape commercial transactions outside the state's borders (e.g., in a modern context, state rules governing national stock exchanges, communications, or the internet.)

Today, however, instead of serving as a shield against interference by the states, the commerce power has become a sword wielded by the federal government in pursuit of an endless array of socioeconomic programs. The defining cases came during the New Deal, and when the Court was through, Congress could regulate anything that "affected" interstate commerce. At some level, everything affects interstate commerce; so the floodgates were opened and the modern regulatory state poured through.

Only in the last decade has the Supreme Court taken modest steps to bind the Congress in the chains of the Constitution. In the 1995 *Lopez* case, Chief Justice Rehnquist said that "[w]e start with first

---

[77]Gibbons v. Ogden, 22 U.S. (9 Wheat.) 1, 231 (1824) (Johnson, J., concurring).

principles. The Constitution creates a Federal Government of enumerated powers."[78] But that ringing endorsement of limited government yielded no more than an incremental change in the Court's Commerce Clause jurisprudence. Lopez was accused of violating a federal law that banned possession of a gun within 1,000 feet of a school.[79] The Court invalidated that law because the banned conduct was not an economic activity that might, through repetition, have a *substantial* effect on interstate commerce.[80]

Five years later, in *United States v. Morrison*,[81] the Court took another mini-step forward—overturning a federal statute that created a private cause of action for victims of gender-motivated violence. In that case, the Court declared that Congress cannot regulate *noneconomic* acts merely because, in the aggregate, they may affect interstate commerce.[82] While both *Lopez* and *Morrison* are welcome developments, the Court left in place its essential Commerce Clause precedents, including its notorious holding in *Wickard v. Filburn*,[83] which upheld an act of Congress regulating agricultural products grown for personal consumption—supposedly an economic act— because of the aggregate effect on interstate markets.[84]

The real test of the Supreme Court's stance on the Commerce Clause will come in major cases now percolating through the lower courts. All eyes will be on a key case to be argued next term, *Ashcroft v. Raich*,[85] in which the Court will decide whether the Controlled Substances Act[86] exceeds Congress's commerce power as applied to intrastate cultivation, possession, distribution and cost-free use of "medical marijuana." The U.S. Court of Appeals for the Ninth Circuit

---

[78] United States v. Lopez, 514 U.S. 549, 552 (1995).

[79] *Id.* at 551.

[80] *Id.* at 549 ("'Congress' commerce authority includes the power to regulate those activities having a substantial relation to interstate commerce.").

[81] 529 U.S. 598 (2000).

[82] *Id.* at 617–18 ("We . . . reject the argument that Congress may regulate noneconomic, violent criminal conduct based solely on that conduct's aggregate effect on interstate commerce.").

[83] 317 U.S. 111 (1942).

[84] *Id.* at 128 ("Home grown wheat . . . competes with wheat in commerce.").

[85] 352 F.3d 1222 (9th Cir. 2003), cert. granted, 124 S. Ct. 2909 (June 28, 2004) (No. 03-1454).

[86] 21 U.S.C. § 801 et seq.

has ruled that federal criminal laws against marijuana are unconstitutional when applied to sick people who use the drug with their doctor's approval in accordance with state law.[87] Ultimately, the case could resolve whether *Wickard* remains valid in the light of *Lopez* and *Morrison*.

Meanwhile, the federal government's power "[t]o regulate Commerce . . . among the several States" cannot reasonably be extended to cover courtroom access by disabled persons facing criminal traffic charges. According to constitutional scholar Randy Barnett,[88] the text of the Commerce Clause raises three obvious questions: What is commerce? What is "among" the states? What is "to regulate"? Barnett argues that "commerce" means the exchange of goods, including their transportation. "Among the states" means between persons of one state and another. And "to regulate" means to make regular; that is, to decide how transactions can occur in an environment freed of state-imposed prohibitions.[89]

Suppose we reject those definitions, Barnett continues, and adopt the broadest possible meanings. Suppose "commerce" means any gainful activity. "Among the states" means anywhere in the nation, even wholly within a single state. And "to regulate" means to impose federal prohibitions. Applying the new definitions, the Commerce Clause would allow regulation or prohibition of any gainful activity anywhere in the country. But still, the commerce power would not stretch to include *noncommerce*—like criminal defendants' access to state courtrooms.

## VI. Conclusion

Presumably applying time-honored principles of federalism, the Supreme Court began in 1996 to invalidate congressional statutes on the ground that they were trumped by sovereign immunity. The Fourteenth Amendment, which postdated the Eleventh Amendment by almost three-quarters of a century, was narrowly construed in successive cases not to authorize private causes of action against the states for money damages. At first blush, that was an appealing outcome for fans of federalism, concerned about the post-New Deal

---

[87] Raich v. Ashcroft, 352 F.3d 1222 (9th Cir. 2003).

[88] See Barnett, *supra* note 68.

[89] *Id.* at 278, 313.

avalanche of legislation allowing Congress to regulate anything and everything.

But last year in *Hibbs* and this year in *Lane*, the Court expressed some reservations about its prior sovereign immunity decisions. In those two cases, the reach of the Fourteenth Amendment was extended—first, because *Hibbs* involved alleged discrimination by gender, a "semi-suspect" class; second, because *Lane* involved physical access to courtrooms, a so-called fundamental right. The result: no state immunity from money claims by private parties as long as federal legislation authorizing the suit was enacted to enforce the Fourteenth Amendment, and the means adopted were congruent and proportional to the asserted injuries.

On the surface, that too should have appealed to federalists. Not because they necessarily approve of expanded national powers, but rather because federalism is about *dual* sovereignty, with Congress occasionally called on to redress abuses of power by the states. In other words, federalism is a two-way street: The Tenth Amendment reserves powers to the states that are not enumerated and delegated to the national government; but the Fourteenth Amendment grants power to Congress if the states violate rights that are secured by the federal Constitution.

Nonetheless, a deeper look suggests federalism (understood as *dual* sovereignty) has actually taken a consistent beating. The problem with pre-*Hibbs* immunity cases was that the Supreme Court attempted to curtail federal powers through a backdoor, ill-conceived, extra-textual distention of the Eleventh Amendment, in the process denying private citizens the right to pursue monetary redress for injuries suffered at the hands of the state. The Court refused to recognize that Eleventh Amendment immunity is, quite simply, not available in federal question cases. Rather than apply that straightforward proposition, the Court invented immunity where none existed and then, until last year, struck down federal statutes that were not properly crafted to abrogate immunity.

Happily, in *Hibbs* and *Lane*, the scope of the immunity doctrine has been modestly narrowed. But the Court's new approach is no less problematic: The Court has suddenly discovered broader powers within the Fourteenth Amendment. By toying with semi-suspect classes, fundamental rights, and tiered levels of scrutiny as bases for abrogating immunity,[90] the Court threatens to create expansive new federal powers—a wrongheaded remedy for government bloat. The proper resolution of the sovereign immunity mishmash involves two steps. First, restrict the purview of the Eleventh Amendment to diversity cases in federal court. Second, ensure that each piece of federal legislation is consistent with principles of federalism, separation of powers, and individual liberty; and has an obvious and direct relationship to the specific constitutional power that the legislation purports to execute. That means a frontal assault on overarching central government—confining Congress to those functions that are limited by and enumerated in the Constitution.

[90] Despite a one-case respite in *Lawrence v. Texas*, 539 U.S. 558 (2003), the Court seems fixated on hierarchical rights—each tier commanding different scrutiny when legislation is subjected to judicial review. In *Lawrence*, the Court tried to dodge its post-New Deal case law, which presumes the constitutionality of statutes abridging "non-fundamental" rights. Justice Kennedy, in a 5–4 opinion, held that states may not criminalize private, consensual sodomy—not because such acts are fundamental, but rather because they are an exercise of liberty, the circumscription of which the state had not justified. See generally Randy E. Barnett, Justice Kennedy's Libertarian Revolution: Lawrence v. Texas, 2002–2003 Cato Sup. Ct. Rev. 21 (2003). That's progress. The Court has yet to announce a coherent and principled theory of rights—including those rights implicit in the Ninth Amendment—by which to conclude that access to a courtroom is fundamental while access to, say, a public library might not be.

# The *Cheney* Decision—A Missed Chance to Straighten Out Some Muddled Issues

*Vikram David Amar*

The Supreme Court's ruling in *Cheney v. United States District Court for the District of Columbia*[1] was not really surprising; in some ways it was fully in keeping with this term's big theme—deciding not to decide. As predictable as it may have been, though, the Court's opinion in *Cheney* represents a missed opportunity for the Court to educate and clarify on two confusing subjects: so-called executive privileges and immunities, and the complex office of the vice presidency.

## I. The *Cheney* Litigation and the Court's Decision to Remand

The *Cheney* litigation began when various public interest groups sued Vice President Richard Cheney and the National Energy Policy Development Group (NEPDG) that President Bush directed him to head. The plaintiffs, relying on the Federal Advisory Committee Act (FACA),[2] sought to obtain records of the group's meetings. FACA's disclosure requirements were enacted by Congress to enable the public "to monitor the 'numerous committees, boards, commissions, councils and similar groups [that] advise officers and agencies in the [] Federal Government,' and to prevent 'wasteful expenditure of public funds' that may result from their proliferation."[3] Vice President Cheney and other defendants objected to disclosure of these records and moved to dismiss the case against them.[4] Specifically, they pointed to an exception in the FACA itself, which states that the Act's public disclosure and other requirements need not be

---

[1] 124 S. Ct. 2576 (2004).
[2] 5 U.S.C. App. § 2, pt. 1.
[3] 124 S. Ct. at 2583 (internal citations omitted).
[4] *Id.* at 2582 (summarizing case history).

met if the commission in question is "composed wholly of full-time, or permanent part-time, officers or employees of the Federal Government."[5] The *Cheney* defendants argued that since—under the president's memorandum establishing the NEPDG to generate policy proposals—the task force was supposed to consist only of the vice president and "other officers of the Federal Government," the FACA simply didn't apply.[6] They also asserted that applying FACA to the vice president under these circumstances would be problematic in any event under separation-of-powers/executive privilege-type doctrines.[7]

The plaintiffs responded that, regardless of the president's intent to limit the NEPDG to government employees, the task force *in reality* had included private lobbyists and other outsiders who so regularly attended and fully participated in non-public meetings that these other persons were "de facto" members of the group, bringing it within the disclosure requirements of the FACA.[8] After reviewing these arguments, the federal district court, applying earlier decisions from the U.S. Court of Appeals for the D.C. Circuit recognizing the likely existence of a "de facto membership" doctrine, declined to dismiss the *Cheney* lawsuit.[9] Instead, the trial court allowed the plaintiffs to conduct some preliminary "discovery"—formal information sharing by the defendants—to enable the court to decide whether, in fact, non-federal employees had participated in the group's proceedings in a manner that triggered the FACA.[10] Ironically, as both the court of appeals and the Supreme Court later noted, the discovery approved by the district court actually entitled the plaintiffs to receive far *more* information than the defendants would be required to disclose under the FACA itself if the district court had concluded that the Act applied to the task force—the very question the court said it needed more information in order to

---

[5] 5 U.S.C. App. § 3(2).

[6] See, e.g., Cheney, 124 S. Ct. at 2582; see also Judicial Watch, Inc. v. National Energy Policy Development Group, 219 F. Supp. 2d 20, 44 (D.D.C. 2002).

[7] Judicial Watch, 219 F. Supp. 2d at 67–68.

[8] Cheney, 124 S. Ct. at 2582 (discussing Judicial Watch Complaint); Judicial Watch, 219 F. Supp. 2d at 43–44 (discussing plaintiffs' allegations).

[9] Judicial Watch, 219 F. Supp. 2d at 54–55.

[10] *Id.* at 54.

resolve.[11] Nonetheless, the district court ordered the defendants to comply with the overly broad discovery requests made by the plaintiffs, and to assert objections only to specific information requests with which they did not want to comply.[12]

Having effectively lost in the trial court, the defendants then moved to the court of appeals. An ordinary appeal, however, was not possible. A case usually cannot be reviewed by an appellate court in the federal system until it reflects a "final judgment" by the district court—that is, a final resolution by the district court of *all* matters comprising the case.[13] In the *Cheney* litigation, the district court's discovery orders to the defendants did not end the district court's involvement—but rather merely preceded the district court's determination, still to come, of whether the FACA's *de facto* membership doctrine applied to the NEDPG. The case was thus not ripe for ordinary appellate review. For that reason, defendants sought in the court of appeals the extraordinary remedy of "mandamus"—a special judicial order directed to a lower court (or other government official) to stop abusing official power or discretion. (The request for mandamus explains the unusual caption in this case, where the district court is itself seemingly being sued by Vice President Cheney; when mandamus is requested, the "defendant" in the action becomes the court or other government entity against whom the order of mandamus is sought.) To obtain mandamus, a party must establish that his right to relief is clear and indisputable, and that no less extraordinary a remedy would suffice.[14]

The court of appeals rejected the vice president's bid for mandamus, concluding that to the extent the vice president and other defendants are constitutionally harmed by complying with the discovery orders, they can and should invoke "executive privilege" to refuse to comply with particular and specific information requests.[15]

---

[11]See, e.g., Cheney, 124 S. Ct. at 2585 ("The majority [of the appeal panel] acknowledged the scope of respondents' requests is overly broad, because it seeks far more than the 'limited items' to which respondents would be entitled if the 'district court ultimately determines that the NEPDG is subject to FACA.' ").

[12]Order Approving Discovery Plan at 2 (D.D.C. Aug. 2, 2002) (quoted at Cheney, 124 S. Ct. at 2585).

[13]See, e.g., Liberty Mutual Insurance Co. v. Wetzel, 424 U.S. 737 (1976).

[14]Kerr v. U.S. Dist. Court for Northern Dist. of Cal., 426 U.S. 394, 403 (1976).

[15]In re Cheney, 334 F.3d 1096, 1105 (D.C. Cir. 2003).

Such particularized objections would allow the defendants to protect their constitutional interests, and at the same time enable the district court to evaluate the defendants' actual and specific need for secrecy.[16] After the court of appeals ruled, the defendants sought review in the Supreme Court, on the question whether the court of appeals should have directed a writ of mandamus telling the district court not to enforce the discovery orders. Separation of powers and executive privacy, the defendants argued, should have led the court of appeals to conclude that FACA cannot apply here, and that mandamus was appropriate.[17]

The Supreme Court ruling, handed down in June, did not really resolve these statutory and constitutional questions. Instead, the Court said that the court of appeals was wrong for thinking that specific and particularized invocations of executive privilege are always required before the executive branch's constitutional arguments should be heard.[18] Accordingly, the high Court simply remanded the case to the court of appeals, although it did send some strong signals that on remand the lower courts should now be open and attentive to the arguments that Vice President Cheney was making about the need for secrecy. As the Court put it:

> Contrary to the District Court's and the Court of Appeals' conclusions, [the] executive Branch [is not left with the sole option of] invok[ing] executive privilege while remaining otherwise powerless to modify a party's overly broad discovery requests . . . . All courts should be mindful of the burdens imposed on the executive Branch in any future proceedings. Special considerations applicable to the President and the Vice-President suggest that the courts should be sensitive to requests by the Government for [immediate] appeals to

[16]*Id.* at 1108 ("Petitioners have yet to invoke executive privilege, which is itself designed to protect the separation of powers, and the narrow discovery we expect the district court to allow may avoid the need for petitioners to even invoke the privilege.").

[17]Petition for Writ of Certiorari at 6, Cheney v. U.S. Dist. Court for the Dist. of Columbia, 124 S. Ct. 2576 (2004) (No. 03-475) ("These cases present fundamental separation-of-powers questions arising from the district court's orders compelling the Vice President and other close presidential advisers to comply with broad discover requests by private parties.").

[18]Cheney v. U.S. Dist. Court for the Dist. of Columbia, 124 S. Ct. 2576, 2592 (2004).

reexamine, for example, whether the [FACA really does] embod[y] the de facto membership doctrine. [19]

In other words, Advantage: Cheney. But the game is not completely over. Further proceedings will occur in the lower courts, and it is possible these courts won't fully take the Supreme Court's hint, in which case the litigation could make its way back to the high Court eventually.

## II. *Cheney* in Context: Sending Signals, Rather Than Resolving Questions Finally, Was Par for the Course This Term

The failure to fully and finally resolve legal questions was quite common in cases this Supreme Court term. Consider, for example, *Vieth v. Jubelirer*[20]—where plaintiffs had challenged the drawing of Pennsylvania's congressional districts on the ground that it was done in an excessively partisan way. In *Vieth*, the Court ruled only that there are no judicially manageable standards *at this time* to resolve such claims.[21] Justice Kennedy's crucial fifth vote, accompanied by a separate concurring opinion he penned, held open the possibility that judicially administrable standards could in fact be developed later.[22] In effect, then, the Court simply put off the question whether it will ever police overly zealous political gerrymandering.

The Court decided not to make a decision again in the well-publicized "one nation under God"/Pledge of Allegiance case—*Elk Grove Unified School District v. Newdow.*[23] In its opinion there, the Court held only that, under California law, Mr. Newdow's custodial arrangement with his daughter was so complicated as to make federal court adjudication of his constitutional claim imprudent.[24] As a result of this disposition, the Court was able to undo the thorny

---

[19] *Id.* at 2592–93.

[20] 124 S. Ct. 1769 (2004).

[21] *Id.* at 1792 ("for the time being . . . this matter is nonjusticiable").

[22] *Id.* at 1796 (Kennedy, J., concurring) ("That no such standard has emerged in this case should not be taken to prove that none will emerge in the future.").

[23] 124 S. Ct. 2301 (2004).

[24] *Id.* at 2312.

Ninth Circuit ruling that had invalidated the reference to God, without having to deal with the tricky Establishment Clause issue Mr. Newdow raised.

It is worth noting, however, that—just as in *Cheney*—various justices in *Newdow* did try to send some messages to the lower courts even though the majority of the Court issued no formal ruling of the merits. Four justices in particular—Justice Scalia who recused himself because he had expressed his views on the merits while the case was pending in the lower courts, and three other justices who wrote separately in *Newdow* to reject the father's Establishment Clause challenge directly—have clearly indicated that they believe the phrase "one nation under God" poses no constitutional problem.[25] Future challengers to this aspect of the Pledge therefore will start with a 4–0 handicap. And that handicap, in turn, may (and should) influence how receptive lower courts are to any such challenges.

Even the cases handed down this term concerning the so-called "War on Terror" (cases that the Court had no choice but to take) were, doctrinally speaking, rather narrow and somewhat cryptic. To be sure, the justices definitely sent some messages to the administration and the rest of the world about the necessity and inevitability of judicial involvement. Nonetheless, one could argue that these rulings created as many legal questions as they answered. The *Hamdi* decision[26] held that U.S. citizen Yaser Hamdi, arrested in a combat zone abroad, was entitled to a hearing on his "enemy combatant" status in front of a neutral decisionmaker, according to fair procedures.[27] But the *Padilla* case,[28] which involved a U.S. citizen arrested in the U.S, was dismissed outright on technical jurisdictional grounds. (The Court held the New York venue was improper.)[29] Plainly, the *Hamdi* precedent will benefit Jose Padilla; he, too, ought now to have a process in which to challenge his "enemy combatant" status. But Padilla's case also arguably raised additional questions— such as whether a U.S. citizen captured within the U.S. can *ever*

---

[25] *Id.* at 2312–33 (Rehnquist J., joined by O'Connor, J., and Thomas, J., concurring).

[26] Hamdi v. Rumsfeld, 124 S. Ct. 2633 (2004).

[27] *Id.* at 2651–52.

[28] Rumsfeld v. Padilla, 124 S. Ct. 2711 (2004).

[29] *Id.* at 2724.

be characterized as an enemy combatant—that, for now, remain unanswered.

Meanwhile, the cases brought by Guantanamo prisoners challenging the legality of their detention were decided, yet they too were resolved only on very narrow jurisdictional grounds. Specifically, the Court ruled that those being held in Guantanamo could contest the lawfulness of their imprisonment by seeking writs of habeas corpus from federal judges.[30] But the Court gave no real hint of what standards—procedural or substantive—should govern those habeas proceedings to come.

Perhaps it is not entirely surprising, or inappropriate, that incrementalism (and perhaps even avoidance) to some extent characterize the term that just ended. Last year's term, after all, was truly pathbreaking, with cases like *Grutter*,[31] the ruling upholding University of Michigan Law School's race-based affirmative action policy; *Lawrence*,[32] the Texas case invalidating a criminal prohibition on gay sex; and *McConnell*,[33] the case rejecting a broad challenge to the Bipartisan Campaign Finance Reform Act. After a year of such doctrinal importance, the Court may have wanted to generate less law than it could have—to do less with its high-profile docket than it might have—this term, especially given the pendency of what will very likely be a contentious presidential election campaign.

However predictable (and understandable) the Court's reluctance to resolve many tough questions this year may be, it remains somewhat problematic. Take, for example, the *Newdow* ruling. I suspect I know *why* a majority of justices dodged the vexing Establishment Clause question there. Writing a coherent and *narrow* opinion either way—that is, either upholding or invalidating the reference to God—would be tough, and the Court is understandably reluctant to give either side in the battle over how much religion there can

---

[30] See, e.g., Rasul v. Bush, 124 S. Ct. 2686 (2004).

[31] Grutter v. Bollinger, 539 U.S. 306 (2003).

[32] Lawrence v. Texas, 539 U.S. 558 (2003).

[33] McConnell v. FEC, 540 U.S. 93 (2003). By characterizing *McConnell* as entirely a 2002–2003 term case, I'm cheating a bit. Technically, *McConnell* was argued during the 2002–2003 term (in September 2003, before the new term began in October), but decided in the 2003–2004 term, in December 2003. But *McConnell* really was a holdover from the 2002–2003 term, and since it was handed down before the election year of 2004, I consider it psychologically part of the earlier Court cycle.

be in public life too broad and powerful a weapon with which to bludgeon the other side. But the Court's reasoning in getting rid of the case was less than ideal—for it did not seem to accord full respect to California case law and the California judiciary. If Mr. Newdow's family law status in California was uncertain at all, the Court had another option: It could have certified state law questions to the California courts, and then decided whether to proceed after getting answers to those questions. ("Certification" is a process by which federal courts can request from states' highest courts answers to unclear questions of state law. It aims to preserve the role of each state's highest court as the ultimate arbiter of the law of its respective state.) Pursuing this option would, of course, have meant that the Establishment Clause issue might have been back before the justices after certification—a prospect I'm sure none of them relished.

## III. The Missed Opportunities in the *Cheney* Case

The Court's failure to fully resolve the *Cheney* litigation is also unsatisfying, because there are two big legal topics that are at present very misunderstood, both of which would have benefited from the kind of sustained and meaningful analysis that a final ruling in the *Cheney* case might have required and provided.

### A. The Messed-Up Law of Executive Privilege and Immunity

First is the huge question of executive privileges and immunities. There have been three landmark cases issued by the Supreme Court during the last generation over the extent to which the presidency and the executive branch should be immune from legal and judicial processes and orders that would require disclosure of executive information and/or consumption of executive time: the famous Nixon Tapes case, *United States v Nixon*;[34] the so-called "Independent Counsel" case, *Morrison v. Olson*;[35] and Paula Jones's case against then-President Bill Clinton, *Clinton v. Jones*.[36] In each case, the president and his underlings made plausible arguments that the need for executive secrecy and autonomy militated against subjecting executive branch officials to ordinary legal processes. And—perhaps to avoid the impression in a post-Watergate world that the president

[34] 418 U.S. 683 (1974).
[35] 487 U.S. 654 (1988).
[36] 520 U.S. 681 (1997).

is above the law—the Supreme Court rejected all of these plausible claims of executive immunity or privilege, by an aggregate and whopping margin of 24–1 votes. The imperial presidency is surely dead.

But is the way it died something over which to rejoice, or grieve? Consider first the *Nixon* case. There, Richard Nixon refused to turn over White House tapes that recorded conversations between the president and various White House aides. The tapes were sought by the special Watergate prosecutor—Leon Jaworski—in order to prosecute some of the aides who had been indicted by Jaworski's grand jury. President Nixon, arguing that the executive branch's interest in confidentiality outweighed the need to obtain information that would incriminate, and facilitate prosecution of, the indicted defendants, balked at a lower court order. The Supreme Court unanimously rejected Nixon's claim.[37] The Court did purport to recognize a limited privilege for private Oval Office communications, but concluded that this executive privilege had to be balanced against the judicial need for evidence.[38] According to the Court, when this free-form balance is performed, the necessity for confidentiality will ordinarily be outweighed (absent national security concerns) so long as the evidence sought for a criminal proceeding is specific, admissible, and relevant to a criminal proceeding.[39] Obviously, saying a privilege can be overcome so long as the information sought is specific, relevant and admissible means there is not much of a privilege. Indeed, if information is *not* specific or relevant or admissible, one often does not need a privilege in order to resist its disclosure.

In minimizing the president's right to keep confidential conversations secret, the Court said a number of bizarre things. As one commentator (who happens to be my brother) has pointed out:

> Chief Justice Warren Burger's unanimous opinion began by inaptly analogizing the dispute to one "between two congressional committees." Two committees are presumptively

[37] Nixon, 418 U.S. at 713.

[38] *Id.* at 706–13.

[39] *Id.* at 712–13 ("A President's acknowledged need for confidentiality in the communications of his office" must give way to the "constitutional need for production of relevant evidence in a criminal proceeding"; "[w]ithout access to specific facts a criminal prosecution may be totally frustrated.").

coordinate authorities; Nixon and Jaworski were not. Constitutionally, Nixon was President and Jaworski was his inferior. Democratically, Nixon had been elected by the nation, and Jaworski had not even been confirmed by the Senate. Their dispute was more like one between the Senate and a staffer, or the Court and a law clerk.

. . .

. . . Next, Burger invoked a Nixon Administration regulation in which Nixon promised Jaworski a free hand in his investigation, and further promised not to fire Jaworski without the concurrence of various Congressional barons . . . . This regulation, said Burger, had "the force of law," empowering executive inferior Jaworski to contest Chief Executive Nixon. Because of this "law," Burger declared his Court free to decide who was right and ignore who was boss. But this regulation-as-law gambit was hard to maintain with a straight face: any truly legally binding regulation would have been flatly unconstitutional. As President Washington and Congressman Madison established at the Founding, the President alone decides whom to fire within the executive branch; Congress members can jawbone, but cannot legally obstruct any purely executive-branch removal . . . .

. . .

. . . Even if the regulation somehow counted as law, the Court also conceded that the Nixon Administration was free simply to rescind the regulation unilaterally—and then, Nixon could tell Jaworski what to do or where to go. But this concession by the Court raised obvious questions: Why were the Justices insisting that Nixon first rescind, and only then countermand Jaworski? Why wasn't it enough that in their very courtroom, the President was clearly saying that he disagreed with his inferior about the proper discharge of executive-branch business?[40]

Clearly, even if the *Nixon* case reached the right and just result—because Richard Nixon was an unindicted co-conspirator engaged in ongoing wrongdoing who thus should not have enjoyed the benefit of privileges that people not currently engaged in wrongdoing enjoy—the Court made a hash of the law of executive privacy and autonomy.

[40] Akhil Reed Amar, Nixon's Shadow, 83 Minn. L. Rev. 1405, 1406–07 (1999).

The next major case in the grouping involved a challenge to the now infamous "Independent Counsel Act" passed after Watergate— the Act under which Ken Starr operated. In *Morrison v. Olson*,[41] the Court rejected the idea that an unelected and essentially unremovable "independent" investigator (in that case Alexia Morrison) rooting around into the affairs of high-level executive officials could disrupt the ability of the president and the executive branch to discharge their constitutional and statutory obligations. In spite of the concerns raised by the president, seven justices voted to uphold the Act, reasoning that the effective functioning of the executive branch would not in practice be compromised by independent counsels operating in their midst.[42] In reaching this result, "*Morrison* winked at the word 'inferior' [in the Constitution], slighted the fact that Article II vests all executive power in the President, and disregarded the objection that judges were performing plainly executive tasks. In each of these respects, *Morrison* followed *Nixon*."[43] Only Justice Scalia dissented.[44]

The last case in the trilogy is *Clinton v. Jones*.[45] There, President Bill Clinton argued that the civil damage lawsuit filed against him by Paula Jones for sexual harassment should have been delayed until after he left the Oval Office, on the ground that discovery and other aspects of civil litigation against him could distract him and his administration from fulfilling constitutional duties.[46] The Court, unanimous as it was in *Nixon*, rejected the president's claim for executive immunity, reasoning that a wise and sound district court judge can manage discovery and other aspects of a civil lawsuit so as to prevent it from disrupting the affairs of the executive branch.[47] The Monica Lewinsky fiasco, which, it must always be remembered,

---

[41]*Supra* note 35.

[42]Morrison v. Olson, 487 U.S. 654, 695 (1988).

[43]Amar, *supra* note 40, at 1414.

[44]Morrison, 487 U.S. at 699 (Scalia, J., dissenting).

[45]*Supra* note 36.

[46]Clinton v. Jones, 520 U.S. 681, 697–98 (1997).

[47]*Id.* at 707 ("potential" burdens on the president "are appropriate matters for the District Court to evaluate in its management of the case. . . . If and when that should occur, the court's discretion would permit it to manage those actions in such fashion (including deferral of trial) that interference with the President's duties would not occur.").

came to light only as a byproduct of discovery conducted in the Paula Jones civil case, makes such a belief today look quite quaint. That is where we were at before this term. The *Cheney* Court had important things to say that bear on each of these three seminal cases, but the *Cheney* majority opinion does not itself connect any of the dots, thus leaving all of us to speculate about where things stand today. Let us start with *Cheney*'s effect on *Nixon*. The justices in *Cheney* did discuss the *Nixon* precedent at some length, reading that 1974 case narrowly.[48] Limiting a badly done earlier ruling is a good thing. But limiting it in a way that perpetuates the weaknesses of the earlier ruling is not such a good thing.

In essence, the *Cheney* Court said that *Nixon* was different because *Nixon*—unlike *Cheney*—involved a criminal proceeding.[49] It is certainly true that the *Nixon* opinion highlighted the criminal facets of Mr. Jaworski's investigation.[50] And "[t]he distinction [*Nixon* drew] between criminal and civil proceedings is not just a matter of formalism."[51] A criminal proceeding, the Court noted in both *Nixon* and again in *Cheney*, is generally more important than a civil proceeding, and getting relevant information out on the table is crucial to reaching the right result in a criminal case.[52] Thus, the importance of executive privilege in *Nixon* was outweighed by the need to obtain "every man's evidence."[53] That is not true here, where the FACA statute is completely civil in character: "Even if FACA embodies important congressional objectives, the only consequence from [plaintiffs'] inability to obtain the discovery they seek is that it would be more difficult for private complainants to vindicate Congress's policy objectives under the FACA."[54]

But can the criminal nature of the *Nixon* case really explain the result in that dispute as easily as the *Cheney* Court suggests? I am

---

[48] Cheney v. U.S. Dist. Court for the Dist. of Columbia, 124 S. Ct. 2576, 2588–2593 (2004) (discussing *Nixon*).

[49] *Id.* at 2489 ("the need for information in the criminal context is much weightier" than in the civil context).

[50] *Id.* at 2589.

[51] *Id.*

[52] *Id.* (distinguishing *Nixon* based on the " 'fundamental' and 'comprehensive' need for 'every man's evidence' in the criminal justice system").

[53] *Id.*

[54] *Id.*

doubtful, for a few reasons. First, the desire for "every man's evidence" in criminal cases is usually implemented somewhat asymmetrically: A criminal defendant has a right to obtain and use all exculpatory evidence, but the government is rarely able to gather *all* possibly incriminating evidence. The Fifth Amendment's protection against compelled self-incrimination is an example of this asymmetry—under current doctrine a defendant does not have to produce testimonial evidence, however relevant to the truth, that would hurt him.[55] This point seemed to have been lost on the Court in *Nixon* (and then again in *Cheney*); Chief Justice Burger in *Nixon* invoked both the Fifth and Sixth Amendments as bases for making President Nixon turn over the tapes,[56] but those amendments protect the accused, not the government, *which was seeking the incriminating information* in *Nixon*. Thus, notwithstanding the *Cheney* Court's reasoning, the criminal character of the *Nixon* case should not have been a big plus in favor of Jaworski and against President Nixon.

Relatedly, throwing bad guys in jail is not the only important government interest. In *Nixon*, the president's argument was that executive confidentiality would preserve the executive branch's long-term ability to enforce laws. Executive branch officials often do unpleasant things in disposing of particular criminal cases—like cutting deals with guilty defendants, immunizing guilty witnesses, etc.—in the name of future and more important executive branch goals. President Nixon's decision to keep White House conversations private might make prosecution of the Watergate criminals harder, but it might also enable future presidents to communicate with their staffs in a way that makes all law enforcement—including criminal law enforcement—more effective. So, again, it simply can't be that *Nixon* should sensibly be read for the idea the executive privilege has little or no place in criminal cases.

Third, just as the *Cheney* Court overstates the case against executive privilege in the criminal context, it understates the case against executive privilege in some civil contexts. Take the FACA itself. Early in the opinion, the Court properly identifies FACA as a law designed to prevent waste and abuse of federal resources by public-private groups that may become captured by narrow rent-seeking

---

[55] See, e.g., Kastigar v. United States, 406 U.S. 441 (1972).
[56] United States v. Nixon, 418 U.S. 683, 709, 711 (1974).

interests.[57] Making sure that government-sponsored commissions in fact serve the public interest—making sure, in other words, that the people can police the government—can often be as important as making sure the government can police the people. So the interest on the "disclosure" side of the executive privilege balance is not weak simply because the statute under which disclosure is sought happens not to be criminal.[58] In the end, the Court would have done better to explain the *Nixon* case by reference to the person of Richard Nixon rather than to explain it exclusively by reference to a criminal/ civil distinction. (In particular, as noted earlier, the Court might have justified ruling against Mr. Nixon by pointing out that he was himself engaged in ongoing criminal activity, and that therefore any privileges afforded persons who are not currently engaged in crime do not apply.)

With respect to the continued vitality and meaning of the other two seminal executive immunity/privilege cases—*Morrison* and *Jones*— the Court in *Cheney* also made important, albeit under-explained, remarks. For example, in further unpacking the criminal/civil dichotomy, the Court made the following assertion:

> The observation in *Nixon* that production of confidential information would not disrupt the functioning of the executive Branch cannot be applied in a mechanistic fashion to civil litigation. In the criminal justice system, there are various constraints, albeit imperfect, to filter out insubstantial legal claims. The decision to prosecute a criminal case, for example, is made by a publicly accountable prosecutor subject to budgetary considerations . . . .[59]

Fair enough. This might even explain why Leon Jaworski—the prosecutor in the Nixon case—should have been given some slack; after all, as pointed out earlier, President Nixon technically could have fired him or cut off his funding if his actions really had been interfering with executive functions.

---

[57] Cheney, 124 S. Ct. at 2582.

[58] Indeed, the interest served by disclosure in *Cheney* was greater than the plaintiff's interest at stake in *Jones*, which involved only private redress, not government accountability. And yet in *Jones* the president lost.

[59] Cheney, 124 S. Ct. at 2590.

But what about "independent" counsel Alexia Morrison or Ken Starr? They were not "publicly accountable," nor subject to meaningful "budgetary considerations."[60] Thankfully, the Independent Counsel Act has died a quiet legislative death. But should we take the language from *Cheney* to mean that the *Cheney* majority would no longer agree with the reasoning of the *Morrison* majority? One can hope so, but one would also have hoped that the Court would have been less vague and more elaborate here.

More explicit discussion of *Jones* would similarly have been helpful. The *Cheney* Court did observe, after talking about the accountability—and therefore trustworthiness—of prosecutors, that,

> In contrast, there are no analogous checks in the civil discovery process here. Although under Federal Rule of Civil Procedure 11, sanctions are available, and private attorneys owe an obligation of candor to the judicial tribunal, these safeguards have proved insufficient to discourage filing of meritless claims against the Executive Branch. In view of the visibility of the Offices of the President and the Vice President and the effect of their actions on countless people, they are easily identifiable targets for suits for civil damages.[61]

Again, sounds reasonable. But where was this reasonableness in *Jones*? In *Jones*, the Court effectively said, trust district court judges—they will manage things nicely. Where is the trust for the district court judge in *Cheney*? Lest I be misunderstood, I do not think trusting the judicial process is necessarily the right answer to these questions. I simply see deep inconsistency between the reasoning of *Cheney* and *Jones* (just as there is inconsistency between *Cheney's* analysis and *Morrison's*.) Inconsistency itself is not bad—*Brown's* inconsistency with *Plessy* was quite good. Unnoticed and unexplained inconsistency, on the other hand—the kind we have here— is a recipe for more doctrinal confusion.[62]

---

[60] Ken Starr's overall expenditures, for example, exceeded $70 million. See Joshua Micah Marshall, "Kenneth Starr's $70 Million Bag Of Garbage," posted at http://www.salon.com/politics/feature/2002/03/12/ray/index_np.html.

[61] Cheney, 124 S. Ct. at 2590 (internal quotations and citations omitted).

[62] This doctrinal confusion might explain why the Bush administration's invocation of executive privilege has, at times, seemed quite screwy. See, e.g., Vikram David Amar, Executive Privilege: Often Valuable to Protect the Presidency, But Misunderstood by President Bush in the Condoleezza Rice Case, Findlaw.com (April 16, 2004), available at http://writ.news.findlaw.com/amar/20040416.html.

*B. The Uncertain "Executive" Office of the Vice Presidency*

In addition to complicating, rather than clarifying, the essence of executive privilege in the context of the three important decisions that precede it, the *Cheney* ruling also missed a golden chance to explain how, or even why, executive privilege applies to the peculiar office of the vice presidency (an office at issue in *Cheney* but not in any of the earlier cases.) The *Cheney* Court repeatedly and reflexively lumps the vice presidency together with the presidency, and talks as if executive privilege concepts necessarily play out identically for to both offices. For example, the Court states that "[w]ere the Vice President not a party in this case, the argument that the Court of Appeals [erred] might present different considerations."[63] In a similar vein is the Court's closing remark that there are "special considerations applicable to the President and Vice President."[64] And in the passage quoted above in connection with the *Jones* discussion, the Court lumps the offices of the president and vice president together as of particularly high "visibility." But does this merging of the two offices make sense for executive privilege purposes? Should veeps even be considered members of the executive team for executive privilege purposes? It turns out that the answer to this question is far more complicated than most would ever imagine.

When one looks first at the text of the original Constitution, one finds that the vice president is not formally given any executive responsibilities. The Constitution of 1787 specified only two real jobs for vice presidents. One is to wait around in case the president is unable to discharge his duties.[65] The other is to preside over the Senate in the meantime.[66] Neither one of these functions seems quintessentially executive. Indeed, the function of presiding over the Senate—and casting its tie-breaking vote—seems downright legislative. It is worth noting here as well that the Constitution's text does not give the president the power to remove a vice president, in the way that the constitutional power to appoint cabinet members and other executive officers has been construed to carry with it a presidential power to remove such persons.

---

[63] Cheney, 124 S. Ct. at 2587.
[64] *Id.* at 2593.
[65] U.S. Const. art. II, § 1.
[66] U.S. Const. art. I, § 3.

If we move from constitutional text to founding history, the question whether the vice president should be considered a high-level executive insider for executive privilege purposes gets even muddier. The primary reason for that is the clear (albeit little known) fact that both the Framers and later generations of Americans gave rather little thought to the vice presidency and its role in executive administration.[67]

The very idea of a vice presidency was dreamed up in the closing days of the Philadelphia Convention of 1787, and its chief value was as one cog in an intricate electoral college contraption regulating presidential elections. Delegates worried that after George Washington left the political scene, each state might simply cast all its electoral votes for its own favorite son. But then this scattering of electoral votes would deny any one candidate a majority and thus throw every presidential election into Congress, in which case the executive might become overly dependent on the legislature.

The Philadelphia delegates' ingenious solution was to require each state to vote for two persons—one of whom must be an out-of-stater—with the top vote-getter winning the presidency.[68] This rule would give a boost to national candidates—respected statesmen who might be everyone's second choice after the local favorite son. Meanwhile, to discourage states from gaming the system by wasting their second (out-of-state) vote—thereby cycling back to a fractured world of favorite sons—the Framers created an office called the vice presidency and provided that this office would go to the runner-up

---

[67] Many of the paragraphs that follow build on and borrow heavily from two earlier works that my brother Akhil Reed Amar and I have produced—Akhil Reed Amar and Vikram David Amar, Constitutional Vices: Some Gaps in the System of Presidential Succession and Transfer of Executive Power, Findlaw.com (July 26, 2003), available at http://writ.news.findlaw.com/amar/20020726.html and Akhil Reed Amar and Vik Amar, President Quayle, 78 Va. L. Rev. 913 (1992). Interested readers should consult each of these other two sources for more analysis.

[68] U.S. Const. amend XII provides as follows:
The electors shall meet in their respective states and vote by ballot for President and Vice-President . . . [T]hey shall name in their ballots the person voted for as President, and in distinct ballots the person voted for as Vice-President, . . . The person having the greatest number of votes for President, shall be the President. . . . The person having the greatest number of votes as Vice-President, shall be the Vice-President.

in the presidential race.[69] Thus states would have strong incentives to take their second (out-of-state) vote seriously.

When Elbridge Gerry (who, ironically enough, would one day serve as vice president) complained about this odd office and proposed eliminating it, another delegate candidly responded that "such an officer as the Vice President was not wanted. He was introduced only for the sake of a valuable mode of election which required two to be chosen at the same time."[70] In light of this history, it is hardly surprising that the Founders' Constitution neglected to specify certain critical details concerning the vice presidency and its relationship to the presidency itself and the rest of the executive branch.

The circumstances culminating in the passage of the Twelfth Amendment in 1804 serve to underscore the inherent ambiguity of the vice presidency as a member of the president's team at the founding and in the early Republic. To understand the Twelfth Amendment, one must begin by recognizing that the original Constitution did not permit electors to specify their votes for the two offices of president and vice president separately—instead, each elector simply cast two votes.[71] Of course, electoral collegians, and the states and parties whom they represented, did have strong views about which of the two persons voted for should occupy the presidency. But electors who wanted to elect a president and vice president of the same party were confronted with a dilemma: If all of the party's electors named the same two individuals on the ballot, and if that party constituted a majority of electors at the electoral college, then a tie would result between the two top vote-getters. And under the terms of Article II of the Constitution, the election would then be resolved by the House of Representatives, where the party risked "inversion" of the two candidates. That is, the House might vault

---

[69] See U.S. Const. art II, § 1, cl. 1–3:
The Electors shall meet in their respective States, and vote by Ballot for two Persons. . . . The Person having the greatest Number of Votes shall be the President, . . . and if there be more than one who . . . have an equal Number of Votes, then the House of Representatives shall immediately chuse [sic] by Ballot one of them for President. . . . In every Case, after the Choice of the President, the Person having the [next] greatest Number of Votes of the Electors shall be the Vice President.

[70] See 2 The Records of the Federal Convention of 1787, at 537 (Max Farrand ed., 1937) (statement of delegate Williamson).

[71] U.S. Const. art. II, § 1, cl. 1–3.

a party's vice presidential candidate above the party's presidential candidate. This was especially possible because the party controlling the House was not necessarily going to be the same party that generated the top two presidential election vote-getters.

To avoid such possible inversion, early party leaders began "sloughing" votes off the party's vice presidential choice. Party bigwigs would convince a few electors from a few states to delete the party's preferred vice presidential candidate from the two-person ballots cast at the electoral college, naming someone else instead.[72] By this device, a tie between the majority party's two top choices could be avoided. But this technique effectively created a window that allowed the minority party to elect its most popular, or presidential, candidate to the vice presidency by coming in second, ahead of the majority party's vice presidential choice.

This happened, in fact, in 1796. John Adams—a Federalist—finished first. But because Federalist electors sloughed off some votes for their preferred vice presidential choice, Thomas Pinckney (in order to avoid a Pinckney-Adams tie), Thomas Jefferson, a Republican, was able to finish second, ahead of Pinckney, and become Adams's vice president.[73]

Significantly, the outcome of the 1796 election—where the vice president was not a member of the president's executive team but rather a member of the opposition party—did not stir up any real movement to amend the selection method set forth in Article II. The leaders at the time did not see the original Constitution's selection method's bias in favor of a "split party" White House as a major drawback.[74] Jefferson himself believed that the vice president would act only as a legislative and not as an executive agent.[75] Moreover, some who would later unsuccessfully oppose the Twelfth Amendment saw a great deal of virtue in having an intrabranch check within the White House. As Representative James Hillhouse of Connecticut would later urge, the president and vice president should be of different parties "to check and preserve in temper the over-heated

---

[72] See Lolabel House, Twelfth Amendment of the Constitution of the United States 20–40 (1901) (unpublished Ph.D. dissertation, University of Pennsylvania).

[73] *Id.* See also Jules Witcover, Crapshoot: Rolling the Dice on the Vice Presidency 5 (1992).

[74] House, *supra* note 72, at 39 (citing draft amendments prepared by Jefferson).

[75] Letter from Thomas Jefferson to James Madison (Jan. 22, 1797), in The Writings of Thomas Jefferson 108 (Paul L. Ford ed., 1896).

zeal of party. . . . If we cannot destroy party, we ought to place every check upon it."[76]

Real interest in constitutional reform would be stirred only after the election of 1800. In that year, the sloughing-off device failed to work, and a tie between the top two Republican candidates, Jefferson and Aaron Burr, resulted in the election being thrown into the House. Federalists, however, controlled the House, and threatened to make Burr president instead of Jefferson—largely to spite Jefferson—even though no Republican wanted Burr to be anything other than vice president. The intractable "inversion" problem—and not the possibility or likelihood of the president and vice president being of opposite teams—is what led to the Twelfth Amendment, the terms of which now require electors to designate separately votes for the president and the vice president.[77] As Gouverneur Morris from New York wrote in a letter in 1802, the primary "evil . . . in the [original] mode of selection" is the possibility that "at some time or other a person admirably fitted for the office of President might have an equal vote with one totally unqualified, and that, by the predominance of faction in the House of Representatives, the latter might be preferred."[78] Indeed, as noted earlier, some political leaders thought the "split" White House tendency of Article II as originally drafted to be its main virtue. These leaders saw the loss of this tendency as a cost to be borne in order to remedy the inversion problem, rather than a benefit to be obtained as a result of the new amendment.

None of this is to say, however, that the Framers of the Twelfth Amendment did not recognize that it would enable one party—one team, if you will—to more easily capture both the presidency and the vice presidency. Clearly they did.[79] But recognizing the inevitable and being happy about it are entirely different things. So even after the Twelfth Amendment, the extent to which vice presidents should be seen as executive agents of the president, and thus beneficiaries of any executive privilege, would seem quite open.

That the Twelfth Amendment didn't really clarify and improve the office of the vice president was not surprising. After all, the

[76] House, *supra* note 72, at 50 (quoting Hillhouse's speech).

[77] *Id.* at 50–51; Witcover, *supra* note 73, at 25.

[78] Witcover, *supra* note 73, at 24 (quoting an 1802 letter from Gouveneur Morris to the president of the New York Senate).

[79] House, *supra* note 72, at 50.

Twelfth Amendment itself focused far more on selection of the president than on the number two slot. Indeed, critics predicted that the amendment would diminish the quality of future vice presidents, who would no longer be major presidential candidates in their own right, but merely second-fiddles to party leaders.[80] This criticism proved prescient. So long as presidents stayed healthy in office—as did the first eight presidents spanning the Constitution's first half century—the vice presidency received rather little attention.

In fact, for much of American history—around thirty-seven of the Constitution's first 180 years—the country did without a vice president entirely, yet few seemed to notice. The first vacancies occurred in James Madison's presidency, when his first term vice president George Clinton died in 1812 and his second term vice president Elbridge Gerry died in 1814. Under the Philadelphia Constitution, no mechanism existed to fill a vice presidential vacancy—yet another signal of the low status of the office in early America.

At critical moments in American history when presidents died or became disabled, the inattention to the vice presidency in the Founders' Constitution became more visible, and more problematic. In 1841, William Henry Harrison became the first chief executive to die in office, and Vice President John Tyler assumed the reins of power. A nice constitutional question then arose: Was Tyler merely the vice president acting as president, or did he instead actually become president upon Harrison's death?

The relevant constitutional text of Article II, section 1, could be read either way: "In Case of the Removal of the President from Office, or of his Death, Resignation, or Inability to discharge the Powers and Duties of the said Office, the Same shall devolve on the Vice President . . ."[81] Did "the Same" mean the office itself, or merely the powers and duties of the office? If the former was the case, an ascending vice president was entitled to the honorific title of "president." (Formal titles mattered a great deal in the old days. George Washington had wanted to be addressed as "His High Mightiness, the President of the United States and Protector of their Liberties," but the First Congress ultimately opted for the less monarchical "Mister President.")[82] More important, if an ascending vice

---

[80] See, e.g., *supra* note 76 and accompanying text.

[81] U.S. Const. art. II, § 1.

[82] See Akhil Reed Amar, America's Constitution: A Guided Tour (forthcoming 2005).

president indeed became president rather than just assuming presidential powers and duties, he could claim a president's salary, which was both higher than a vice president's, and also immune from congressional tampering under the rules of Article II. In turn, such immunity would enable him to wield the veto pen and other executive powers with greater independence from the legislature than would be the case if he were beholden to Congress for his very bread.

Unsurprisingly, Tyler resolved the constitutional ambiguity in his own favor, claiming that he was indeed the president, and not simply the vice president acting as president.[83] Following Tyler, later vice presidents regularly proclaimed themselves presidents upon the deaths of their running mates, with Millard Fillmore replacing Zachary Taylor in 1850 and Andrew Johnson succeeding Abraham Lincoln in 1865.

The Twenty-Fifth Amendment, proposed and ratified after John Kennedy's assassination, fills many of the gaps left open by the Founders.[84] For starters, the amendment resolves the question John Tyler confronted by making clear that when the president dies or resigns or is removed from office, then—and only then—the vice president does in fact "become President."[85] Otherwise, if the president is merely disabled (perhaps only temporarily) from exercising the powers and duties of his office, then the vice president may step in and "assume the powers and duties of the office as Acting President" without prejudice to the president's ability to resume his post if and when he has recovered from his disability.[86] That, by the way, is exactly what Dick Cheney did a few years back when George Bush was under anesthesia.

The amendment also provides a clearer framework for determining whether the president is in fact disabled, and for how long. This framework specifies the precise roles of the president, the vice president, the cabinet, and the Congress in resolving questions about

---

[83] *Id.*

[84] U.S. Const. amend. XXV.

[85] *Id.* § 1: "In the case of the removal of the President from office or of his death or resignation, the Vice President shall become President."

[86] *Id* § 4: "Whenever the Vice President and a majority of either the principal officers of the executive departments or of such other body as Congress may by law provide, transmit to the President pro tempore of the Senate and the Speaker of the House of Representatives their written declaration that the President is unable to discharge the powers and duties of his office, the Vice President shall immediately assume the powers and duties of the office as Acting President."

possible disability.[87] In some ways, the vice president is treated in this process as the head of the cabinet for assessing whether the president is disabled. Yet another provision of the amendment allows a president, with congressional approval, to fill a vice presidential vacancy. Through this amendment, Richard Nixon named Gerald Ford to the vice presidency when Spiro Agnew left office in 1973; and Ford in turn appointed Nelson Rockefeller in 1974 when Ford himself became president upon Nixon's resignation.

All these changes brought by the Twenty-Fifth Amendment might have important consequences for the issue of executive privilege. By formalizing succession, by making the vice president part of (and indeed a leader of) the cabinet for purposes of determining presidential disability, and by making clear that the president gets to choose persons to fill vice presidential vacancies—making succession apostolic, if you will—the amendment strongly suggests that, today at least, the vice president is a full member of the president's executive team. This amendment, much more so than the Twelfth, then, formally concretizes an evolving importance of the vice presidency to the executive branch. As a result, it *might* provide a possible basis *today* for a somewhat broad claim of executive privilege on the part of the vice president.

## IV. Conclusion

So there was much—concerning the executive privilege and the vice presidency's place within it—that the *Cheney* Court could and should have discussed; the analysis I have presented here has been designed to provoke questions rather than to definitively resolve them.[88] Less, it is said, is sometimes more. But here, at least, more would have been more, and would have been more helpful for us all.

---

[87] See generally *id.* § 4.

[88] There are other tricky aspects of the *Cheney* dispute that also warrant significant attention. For example, even if vice presidents do today ordinarily partake of executive privilege, what about the fact that the NEDPG was gathering data largely for *legislative* proposals, rather than executive actions? Also, what about the fact that the communications the vice president wants to shield may have involved persons not within the executive branch? In other words, does executive privilege apply with respect to communications between executive officials and persons outside the executive branch, or instead is it limited only to intra-executive communications? Cf. Public Citizen v. Department of Justice, 491 U.S. 440 (1989). These, and other thorny questions, remain to be resolved on remand.

# Old Puzzles, Puzzling Answers: The Alien Tort Statute and Federal Common Law in *Sosa v. Alvarez-Machain*

Mark K. Moller

## I. Introduction

When the Mexican drug cartel abducted, tortured, and murdered DEA undercover agent Enrique "Kiki" Camarena in Guadalajara, Mexico, in 1985, it set in motion a chain of events that culminated in the Supreme Court this term. Unable to obtain the assistance of the Mexican government in the extradition of one Dr. Humberto Alvarez-Machain, thought by U.S. officials to be implicated in the murder, the DEA in 1990 arranged for him to be kidnapped by Mexican bounty hunters and brought to the United States. The government's subsequent prosecution of Alvarez-Machain failed spectacularly, whereupon he returned to Mexico to bring suit under the arcane and, until recently, long-dormant 1789 Alien Tort Statute, which is said to authorize aliens to sue for torts committed in violation of international law. Alvarez-Machain lost in the Supreme Court, but the issues he raised are far from settled.

Americans, as is often observed, have a decidedly ambivalent view of international institutions and international law. That division of mind has been with us since the founding, when state and federal courts alternated between praising and denouncing international law in equal measure. On the one hand, many early state courts treated international law as a species of "natural law," quoting Vattel and Grotius alongside American reporters and common law treatises.[1] Justice Story, among the most learned of antebellum commentators, suggested that it is "no slight recommendation" that an

---

[1]R.H. Helmholz, Relationships Among Roman Law, Common Law, and Modern Civil Law: Use of the Civil Law in Post-Revolutionary American Jurisprudence, 66 Tul. L. Rev. 1649, 1657–64, 1667, 1671–76 (1992) (discussing sources).

American law is "approved by the cautious learning of Valin, the moral perspicacity of Pothier, and the practical and sagacious judgment of Emerigon."[2]

But others in the nation's early years were less receptive. As legal historian Richard Helmholz has illustrated, early American law books are replete with examples of frontier lawyers' disdain for international law—from the "Kentucky counsel who contrasted the purity of American institutions with the vice" of supposedly authoritarian civil law; to the "Indiana lawyer who stigmatized a law from *ius commune* as a product of 'the gloomy times of popery'"; to the "counsel before the United States Supreme Court who described Bynkershoek's treatment of the law of nations as 'written in blood.'"[3]

*Sosa v. Alvarez-Machain*[4] asks the Court to address our ambivalence by posing a deceptively simple question: To which branch of government did the Framers commit the decision to incorporate international norms into our domestic legal framework? The answer would seem to be settled by Article I, section 8, clause 10 of the Constitution (the "Define and Punish Clause"), which grants Congress the power to define and punish offenses against the law of nations.[5] But the matter is not so simple. In the last two decades, a number of human rights lawyers have championed a radically different view—namely, that American federal courts have wide-ranging "common law" power to apply international law as a part of "our" law, without any further authorization by Congress. They base their argument on the 1789 "Alien Tort Statute," which authorizes federal jurisdiction over "torts" for violations of international law. Forgotten by American lawyers for nearly two centuries, the statute has surfaced recently in a burgeoning number of innovative "human rights" tort suits.

In *Sosa*, the Court attempted to walk a narrow line: Based on a sketchy historical record, it ruled that the Alien Tort Statute authorizes federal courts to remedy offenses against "universal" and "definite" norms of international law, but warned that lower courts must

---

[2]*Id*. at 1681–82 (citing Peele v. Merchants' Insurance Co., 19 F. Cas. 98, 102 (C.C.D. Mass. 1822) (Story, J.)).

[3]Helmholz, *supra* note 1, at 1656 & notes 27–29 (citing sources).

[4]124 S. Ct. 2739 (2004).

[5]U.S. Const. art. I, § 8, cl. 10.

use this power with "great caution."[6] The decision leaves elaboration of the kinds of international norms that may be enforceable to future cases, ruling only that the discrete claims advanced in *Sosa* do not qualify for judicial recognition.

This article addresses the merits of the opinion and its likely implications. In Part II, I set forth in somewhat more detail the background of the *Sosa* litigation. In Part III, I examine the merits of the claim that the Alien Tort Statute permits courts to remedy offenses against international law, concluding that the argument is contrary both to the text and to the structure of the Constitution. In Part IV, I examine the Court's opinion in the case: Although unlikely to result in a new wave of successful suits for violations of international rights, it nonetheless raises questions about the Court's commitment to constitutional text and the separation of powers.

## II. The Litigation Odyssey of Humberto Alvarez-Machain

In 1985, members of Mexico's drug cartel abducted, tortured, and murdered DEA undercover agent Enrique "Kiki" Camarena in Guadalajara, Mexico.[7] Camarena died in a vicious, cruel way: His captors tortured him over the course of two days with a cattle prod, a tire iron, and a broomstick.[8] A Mexican farmer found his body a month after his abduction, still bound and gagged, eyes taped shut, in a shallow grave seventy miles outside of Guadalajara.[9]

Camarena's death triggered a diplomatic crisis between the United States and the Mexican government. As then-DEA administrator Jack Lawn has recounted, "We determined that the individuals who at least took Camarena off the street were [Mexican] law enforcement personnel."[10] Worse, claims Lawn, "[e]very effort we made to pursue the investigation was halted by the government of Mexico."[11] As the investigation developed, many DEA officials, including Lawn, suspected that "[t]he Mexican government knew what happened,

---

[6]Sosa v. Alvarez-Machain, 124 S. Ct. 2739, 2761–62, 2763, 2766 (2004).

[7]See Alvarez-Machain v. United States, 331 F.3d 604, 609 (9th Cir. 2003).

[8]*Id.*

[9]*Id.*

[10] Drugs Wars: Interview with Jack Lawn, Frontline, available at http:// www.pbs.org/wgbh/pages/frontline/shows/drugs/interviews/lawn.html (last visited July 20, 2004).

[11]*Id.*

and . . . that the government of Mexico indeed was covering up the assassination."[12]

Unable to apprehend the kingpins who ordered the killing, the U.S. government targeted lower-level alleged conspirators, including Dr. Humberto Alvarez-Machain, a medical doctor; some DEA officials believed that he had injected Camarena with Lidocaine, a heart medication, in order to keep Camarena alive and prolong his torture.[13] The United States sought and received an indictment of Alvarez-Machain from a Los Angeles grand jury.[14] Because Mexican officials proved unwilling to assist in his apprehension, or to grant an extradition request,[15] the DEA hired Mexican nationals, unaffiliated with either the United States or the Mexican government, to apprehend Alvarez-Machain in Mexico and bring him across the border.[16] On April 2, 1990, the bounty hunters kidnapped Alvarez-Machain outside of his office in Guadalajara and, within a period of less than twenty-four hours, carried him to El Paso, Texas, where DEA agents formally arrested him.[17]

After Alvarez-Machain's arrest, a decade-long legal battle ensued, including two trips to the U.S. Supreme Court.[18] In 1992, he appeared

[12]*Id.*

[13]Elka Worner, Guilty Verdict in Camarena Case, United Press International, December 22, 1992 ("Alvarez Machain was accused of injecting Camarena with Lidocaine to keep him awake during a torture session."). See Br. for United States as Respondent Supporting Petitioner at 2, Sosa v. Alvarez-Machain, 124 S. Ct. 2739 (2004) (03-339) ("Eyewitnesses placed respondent Humberto Alvarez-Machain . . . at the house while Camarena-Salazar was being tortured . . . . DEA officials believe that respondent, 'a medical doctor, participated in the murder by prolonging Agent Camarena's life so that others could further torture and interrogate him.'").

[14]Alvarez-Machain v. United States, 331 F.3d 604, 609 (9th Cir. 2003).

[15]Br. for Petitioner at 2, Sosa v. Alvarez-Machain, 124 S. Ct. 2739 (2004) (03-339) ("The DEA attempted to obtain respondent's presence in the United States through informal negotiations with Mexican officials.").

[16]For details of the bounty-hunting agreement, see Alvarez-Machain, 331 F.3d at 609.

[17]Marjorie Miller and Jim Newton, Defendant Freed in Camarena Case Returns to Mexico, Los Angeles Times, Dec. 16, 1992, at A3. During subsequent interrogation in U.S. custody, Alvarez-Machain allegedly told DEA investigators that he served as a family doctor to drug kingpin Rafael Caro Quintero and also "gave authorities a statement in which he said he had been in a Guadalajara house where Camarena was being tortured." *Id.*

[18]For a comprehensive summary of the history of litigation, see Alvarez-Machain, 331 F.3d at 608–10.

before the Court for the first time, arguing that his abduction violated the U.S.-Mexico Extradition Treaty. The Court disagreed, ruling that the abduction did not violate the terms of the treaty (the Court also refused to intervene based on prudential considerations, including the "advantage of a diplomatic approach to the resolution of difficulties between two sovereign nations.")[19] On remand, the case proceeded to trial, where the U.S. government lost in spectacular fashion. The district court granted a motion of judgment of acquittal based on a lack of evidence, and pulled no punches: The government's case, said the Court, was based on "suspicions and . . . hunches but . . . no proof."[20] The government's theories were "whole cloth, the wildest speculation."[21]

The victory freed Alvarez-Machain to return to Mexico, where he commenced civil litigation against the United States. In 1993 he filed a civil action against the bounty hunters, the United States, and four DEA agents, seeking damages for kidnapping, false arrest, and false imprisonment. He sought relief against the United States based on a variety of ordinary tort claims.[22] He also sought relief under international law against one of the bounty-hunters, Jose Francisco Sosa, pursuant to 28 U.S.C. § 1350, the Alien Tort Statute, based on allegations that his kidnapping on Mexican soil and twenty-four-hour detention in Mexico, prior to his formal arrest in El Paso, violated an international "norm" against arbitrary arrest and imprisonment.[23] The litigation dragged on for more than ten years, ending with a defeat for Alvarez-Machain in the Supreme Court—in *Sosa v. Alvarez-Machain.*

## III. The Principles at Stake in *Sosa v. Alvarez-Machain*

Before examining *Sosa v. Alvarez-Machain* in detail, it will be useful to look briefly at the Alien Tort Statute, focusing on the thorny constitutional implications of this arcane provision.

---

[19]United States v. Alvarez-Machain, 504 U.S. 655, 670 (1992).

[20]See Alvarez-Machain v. United States, 331 F.3d 604, 610 (9th Cir. 2003).

[21]*Id.*

[22]28 U.S.C. § 1346(b).

[23]Sosa v. Alvarez-Machain, 124 S. Ct. 2739, 2747 (2004) (summarizing petitioners' claims).

## A. A Brief History of the Alien Tort Statute

The Alien Tort Statute, as amended, provides as follows:

> The district courts shall have original jurisdiction of any civil action by an alien for a tort only, committed in violation of the law of nations or a treaty of the United States.[24]

The statute is simultaneously one of the oldest provisions of American law and one of the most mysterious—a "kind of legal Lohengrin," in the memorable phrase of Judge Henry Friendly, who noted, accurately, that "no one seems to know whence it came."[25] This much we know: The provision was added by the first Congress to the first Judiciary Act,[26] which created the lower federal courts, only to be forgotten for nearly two centuries by federal litigants. Such was the obscurity of the statute in 1975, when Judge Friendly encountered it, that he had trouble locating reported federal cases involving a successful damage suit under its auspices.[27]

But in 1980 the Alien Tort Statute gained a new purchase on American law when the Second Circuit decided *Filartiga v. Pena-Irala*,[28] a landmark decision that transformed federal courts' understanding of international law's role in U.S. federal courts.[29] The plaintiffs in *Filartiga*—Paraguayan citizens Dr. Joel Filartiga and his daughter Dolly Filartiga—actively opposed the dictatorial regime of then-president of Paraguay Alfredo Stroessner. Plaintiffs contended that Americo Pena-Irala, the police inspector general of the city of

---

[24]28 U.S.C. § 1350. The original provision provided that federal courts "shall have cognizance, concurrent with the courts of the several States, or the circuit courts, as the case may be, of all causes where an alien sues for a tort in violation of the law of nations or a treaty of the United States." See Judiciary Act, ch. 20, 9, 1 Stat. 73, 77 (1789).

[25]IIT v. Vencap, Ltd., 519 F.2d 1001, 1015 (2d Cir. 1975) ("This old but little used section is a kind of legal Lohengrin; although it has been with us since the first Judiciary Act, no one seems to know whence it came.").

[26]Judiciary Act of 1789, § 9, 1 Stat. 73, 77 (1789).

[27]Vencap, 519 F.3d at 1015 ("We dealt with [the ATS] some years ago . . . . At that time we could find only one case where jurisdiction under it had been sustained, in that instance a violation of a treaty; there is now one more.").

[28]630 F.2d 876 (1980).

[29]See Harold Hongju Koh, Transnational Public Law Litigation, 100 Yale L.J. 2347, 2366 (1991) ("In *Filartiga*, transnational public law litigants finally found their *Brown v. Board of Education*.").

Asuncion, Paraguay, had ordered Dr. Filartiga's son kidnapped and tortured to death in retaliation for the family's anti-government views. The Filartigas fled to the United States and sued Pena-Irala in federal court under the Alien Tort Statute, seeking compensatory and punitive damages totaling $10 million.[30]

Dr. Filartiga did not seek redress based on a substantive U.S. statute or treaty. Rather, the Filartigas asserted their claims under "customary international law" (CIL), a strange creature in American jurisprudence. CIL is not derived from any positive U.S. law—such as a statute, a treaty, or the Constitution. The term is a label for a number of judge-made doctrines that some courts independently have developed to settle international disputes. As Professors Jack Goldsmith and Eric Posner put it, CIL is "unwritten; it is said to arise spontaneously from the decentralized practices of nations; the criteria for its identification are . . . unclear; and it is said to bind all nations in the world."[31]

The *Filartiga* plaintiffs argued that CIL regulates the conduct of foreign states toward their own citizens. Under their theory, modern CIL is composed of norms of such universality that they should be treated as "law" binding on state actors, regardless of the content of domestic state constitutions or legal enactments. Crucially, the Filartigas argued that the Alien Tort Statute provides "jurisdiction" for courts to enforce these "international" norms in U.S. courts.[32]

Their theory supposed implicitly that the Alien Tort Statute authorizes federal courts to discover and apply new "customary" international legal rules, and to award damages to aliens whose "international rights" have been violated. In effect, under their theory, the Alien Tort Statute operates in the international realm in a fashion roughly similar to the Sherman Act: that is, as a standing order to U.S. courts to articulate the rules governing the conduct of foreign states, and to police the conduct of other states vis-à-vis their citizens, much as federal antitrust statutes delegate to judges the freewheeling power to police accumulations of economic power in the domestic marketplace.

---

[30]Filartiga, 630 F.2d at 878–79.

[31]Jack L. Goldsmith & Eric A. Posner, A Theory of Customary International Law, 66 U. Chi. L. Rev. 1113, 116 (1999).

[32]Filartiga, 630 F.2d at 879.

The Second Circuit agreed on all counts: "It is clear that courts must interpret international law not as it was in 1789, but as it has evolved and exists among the nations of the world today."[33] To make this determination, the Second Circuit provided that district courts may look to a number of sources as "evidence" of international norms, including (controversially) U.N. resolutions that were not independently enforceable in U.S. courts.[34] Most important, the Second Circuit construed the Alien Tort Statute (in particular, its grant of "jurisdiction" over "torts in violation of the law of nations") to permit federal courts to enforce this "evolving . . . . international law" as "our law."[35]

*Filartiga* was a watershed moment in the history of the Alien Tort Statute. As Professor Curtis Bradley has noted, "International human rights litigation in U.S. courts largely began in 1980, with the Second Circuit's decision in *Filartiga*."[36] Over the 1980s and 1990s, federal lawsuits under the Alien Tort Statute proliferated. Notable examples include claims against the Nigerian government and Royal Dutch Petroleum for persecution of the minority Ogoni people,[37] against South Africa for the extrajudicial killing of black dissidents during the apartheid regime,[38] and, most recently, against the Unocal Corporation for allegedly participating in the human rights abuses of Myanmar's military junta.[39]

## B. Constitutional Problems with the Alien Tort Statute: An Overview

It is certainly true that the kinds of human rights abuses the *Filartiga* Court addressed deserve our attention and condemnation. But, under our constitutional system of separated powers, is the Alien Tort Statute a sufficient basis for federal courts of limited

---

[33]*Id.* at 881 (citing Ware v. Hylton, 3 U.S. (3 Dall.) 199 (1796)).

[34]Filartiga, 630 F.2d at 884.

[35]*Id.* at 885–88.

[36]Curtis A. Bradley, The Costs of International Human Rights Litigation, 2 Chi. J. Int'l L. 457, 457 (2001).

[37]Wiwa v. Royal Dutch Petroleum Co., 226 F.3d 88 (2d Cir. 2000).

[38]See, e.g., In re South African Apartheid Litigation, 238 F. Supp. 2d 1379 (J.P.M.L. 2002).

[39]John Doe I v. Unocal Corp., Nos. 00-56603, 00-57197, 00-56628, 00-57195, 2002 U.S. App. LEXIS 19263 (9th Cir. Sept. 18, 2002).

jurisdiction to define and enforce such rights? Surely, an interpretation of the Alien Tort Statute that gives courts that extraterritorial power in the first instance, without any further direction from the political branches, raises serious questions about constitutional structure and the principle that Article III courts are courts of limited jurisdiction.

### 1. A Short Note on Interpretation

At the outset, the Alien Tort Statute presents a "difficult" problem of statutory interpretation.[40] The statute, very old and little used, is a rarity. There is little or no legislative history concerning its enactment,[41] and the history that does exist is conflicting and impressionistic.[42] Similarly, there is little recorded discussion of international law in the records of the Constitutional Convention and no consensus among legal historians concerning the Founders' views about the domestic judicial application of international law in U.S. courts.[43]

---

[40]David P. Currie, The Constitution in Congress: The Federalist Period, 1789–1801, at 52 (1997).

[41]Br. of United States as Respondent Supporting Petitioner at 17, Sosa v. Alvarez-Machain, 124 S. Ct. 2739 (2004) (No. 03-339) ("Although a great deal has been written about the history of Section 1350 since the Second Circuit's decision in *Filartiga*, not much is known for certain about the origins or original purpose of the law. Neither the record history of the Judiciary Act of 1789 nor the private writings of the Members of the First Congress expound in any depth on the provision.").

[42]Compare Br. of Professors of Federal Jurisdiction and Legal History as Amici Curiae in Support of Respondents at 6–8, Sosa v. Alvarez-Machain, 124 S. Ct. 2739 (2004) (No. 03-339) (the Alien Tort Statute enacts the 1781 recommendations of Oliver Ellsworth, a leading proponent of creating a "tribunal . . . [to] decide on offences against the law of nations" that were not enumerated in the statutory code; Ellsworth played a principal role in drafting the Judiciary Act of 1789), with Br. of Professors of International Law, Federal Jurisdiction, and Foreign Relations Law in Support of Petitioner at 28, Sosa v. Alvarez-Machain, 124 S. Ct. 2739 (2004) (No. 03-339) ("Congress may have thought that what is now § 1350 was necessary to ensure that admiralty courts heard not only disputes over the ownership of property, including salvage, but also all torts, including personal injuries, occurring within the maritime jurisdiction of the United States.").

[43]Compare Br. of Professors of Federal Jurisdiction and Legal History as Amici Curiae in Support of Petitioner at 13, Sosa v. Alvarez-Machain, 124 S. Ct. 2739 (2004) (No. 03-339) ("As common law, the law of nations applied in both state and federal courts . . . . [B]ecause it was part of the common law, the law of nations required no legislative enactment to be effective."), with Curtis A. Bradley & Jack L. Goldsmith III, The Current Illegitimacy of International Human Rights Litigation, 66 Fordham L. Rev. 319, 332–33 (1997) ("[O]ne of the Framers' primary concerns was the inability

Nevertheless, there are a number of interesting theories about the original understanding of the Alien Tort Statute. Perhaps the most compelling has been advanced by Bradley.[44] In barest outline, he notes that Article III of the Constitution enumerates a number of circumstances in which federal courts of limited jurisdiction may entertain a lawsuit. Some of those circumstances turn on the identity of the parties. The most common such basis is "diversity jurisdiction"—so-called because it arises when the plaintiff and defendant are citizens of different ("diverse") states. Diversity jurisdiction, like all other sources of federal jurisdiction, is based on the text of Article III—specifically, its direction that the federal "judicial power" shall extend to "controversies" between "citizens of different states."[45] Another party-specific source of federal jurisdiction is "alienage jurisdiction," which is based on Article III's proviso that federal courts may hear lawsuits "between a State, or the Citizens thereof, and foreign States, citizens, or subjects."[46] Alienage jurisdiction exists when a citizen of the United States is on one side of a lawsuit and a citizen of a different country is on the other side.

It has been understood since the founding that federal courts may hear nonconstitutional cases only if they possess both constitutional jurisdiction under Article III and a statutory basis for jurisdiction.[47] According to Professor Bradley, the Alien Tort Statute was intended to provide the statutory basis for Article III "alienage jurisdiction." As he hypothesizes:

---

of the federal government during the Articles of Confederation period to punish infractions of international law, and one of their primary aims was to establish a constitutional structure that would allow for uniform federal enforcement of CIL. But, as we noted . . . this uniformity was not guaranteed by the automatic incorporation of CIL into federal law. Rather uniformity was promoted by empowering the political branches to enact the federal law necessary to carry out international obligations.").

[44] Curtis A. Bradley, The Alien Tort Statute and Article III, 42 Va. J. Int'l L. 587 (2002).

[45] U.S. Const. art. III, § 2, cl. 7.

[46] U.S. Const. art. III, § 2, cl. 9.

[47] See, e.g., David P. Currie, The Constitution in Congress: The First Congress and the Structure of Government, 1789–1791, 2 U. Chi. L. Sch. Roundtable 161 (1982) (noting the first Judiciary Act "clearly reveals Congress's conviction that nothing in the Constitution required it give federal trial courts jurisdiction over all the cases and controversies enumerated in Article III. For apart from civil and criminal cases brought by the Government, the district courts were to sit basically in admiralty, and the circuit courts in diversity and alienage cases involving more than $500. There was no general grant of federal-question jurisdiction.").

The alien tort statute in Section 9 [of the first Judiciary Act] can . . . be construed as referring implicitly to suits brought by aliens against U.S. citizens. Understood this way, the alien tort clause is a subset of the First Congress's general grant of alienage diversity jurisdiction in Section 11 [of the Judiciary Act], but without a jurisdictional amount requirement . . .

. . .

. . . [This] construction of the Statute is consistent with the law of international responsibility in the late 1700s . . . . Blackstone . . . stated in his Commentaries that "where the individuals of any state violate this general law [of nations], it is then the interest as well as duty of the government under which they live, to animadvert upon them with a becoming severity."[48]

According to Bradley, the first Congress assumed that federal courts would apply the law of nations as a rule of decision under the Alien Tort Statute without further authorization from Congress. As he says, "The law of nations was considered at that time to be part of the general common law, which could be applied by courts in the absence of controlling positive law to the contrary . . . . As a result, for those situations in which the law of nations in 1789 regulated tortious conduct, the First Congress would not have perceived a need to supplement this law with a[n] [additional] federal statutory cause of action."[49]

---

[48]Bradley, *supra* note 44, at 629–30.

[49]*Id.* at 596. Note that, if Bradley's theory is right, it means that disputes like that in *Filartiga*, which involve no U.S. citizens, are not proper subjects of federal jurisdiction under the Alien Tort Statute. It also suggests that the U.S. government, as an entity, is not a proper defendant under the Alien Tort Statute. *Id.* at 618.

While Bradley does not directly suggest the possibility, there is another, even more restrictive interpretation: During the Articles of Confederation period, a number of states enacted statutes authorizing causes of action for damages in cases where foreigners have been injured by another person on U.S. soil. See note 93 *infra*. The Alien Tort Statute arguably may have been enacted to ensure that litigants could prosecute these actions under these *state* statutes in *federal* courts, without regard to amount in controversy requirements imposed under the first diversity statute, and subject to subsequent supervening congressional enactments. Federal tribunals presumably would have been more amenable to foreign interests. That reading is consistent with a strict reading of the original Rules of Decision Act, which did not explicitly mention "the law of nations" as a basis for decision in diversity cases. Judiciary Act of 1789, ch. 20, § 34, 1 Stat. 73, 92 (currently codified at 28 U.S.C. § 1652 (1976)). That interpretation, of course, assumes that Justice Story was wrong when he read an

Bradley's argument is compelling, and supported by solid evidence, but it is not conclusive. There appears to be some dissent from his view even among members of the founding generation. Take the opinion of Thomas Jefferson's attorney general, Levi Lincoln. As Bradley describes:

> In [an 1802] opinion, Lincoln discussed the implications of an insult to the Spanish minister, which Lincoln described as involving "a high-handed breach of the peace, an outrageous riot, and an aggravated violation of the law of nations." Lincoln stated that he could "find no provision in the Constitution, in any law of the United States, or in the treaty with Spain which reaches the case." Rather, he said that the case was governed by the law of nations, which forms "part of the municipal body of each State." Lincoln *therefore "doubted the competency of the federal courts, there being no statute recognizing the offence."*[50]

Lincoln's interpretation—200 years closer to the statute's enactment—would appear to be in some tension with Bradley's.[51] But the problem is not simply that there is some contrary evidence: The evidentiary record as a whole is sparse, making the task of interpretation an exercise in educated guesswork. As Bradley himself notes, "there was essentially no discussion of the Statute in the recorded debates of the First Congress."[52] Worse, the statute, soon after its passage, lapsed into desuetude (which is itself suggestive); as a result, there is almost no authoritative judicial interpretation of the

---

exception for "general common law" into the Rules of Decision Act in *Swift v. Tyson*, 41 U.S. (16 Pet.) 1, 18–19 (1842). See notes 69 to 93 *infra*.

[50]Bradley, *supra* note 44, at 615 (emphasis added).

[51]While it is possible Lincoln may have only federal criminal prosecutions in mind, Lincoln's denial that any "statute" "reaches" the case is sweeping and appears on its face to embrace any federal remedial power. See generally 5 Op. Att'y Gen. 691 (1802). Given that the fact pattern—an "outrageous riot" that insulted the ambassador—sounds in tort, and may have been actionable at common law, (see J.H. Baker, An Introduction to English Legal History 504 (2d ed. 1990) (discussing treatment of insults under the eighteenth century tort of defamation)), the attorney general's silence about the availability of a federal civil remedy, coupled with his suggestion that the wrongdoers may be held "liable in law" in Pennsylvania, suggests it may have been Lincoln's view that federal civil intervention requires statutory authorization. *Id.*

[52]Bradley, *supra* note 44, at 623.

statute.[53] Nor does the background legal "context" provide a sure clue. While it is true that early lawyers treated the "law of nations" as part of the general "common law," the role of the *federal* government in "enforcing" the "law of nations" was a matter of great controversy. Here is Bradley again, describing the 1787 Constitutional Convention:

> The Federalists argued that the federal courts should have jurisdiction over cases involving foreign citizens because of potential bias in state courts. So great was this concern that at least two proposed drafts of the Constitution—the initial Virginia plan and Hamilton's plan—would have allowed the federal courts jurisdiction over any case concerning a foreign citizen.
>
> . . . In response to these arguments, the Anti-Federalists had argued that state courts could be trusted with these cases and that foreign citizens should not have greater access to federal court than in-state citizens. For example, George Mason argued during the Virginia ratification debates:
>
> A dispute between a foreign citizen or subject, and a Virginian cannot be tried in our own Courts, but must be decided in the Federal Court. Is this the case in any other country? Are not men obliged to stand by the laws of the country where the disputes are? . . . . [The Federalist proposal] will annihilate your State judiciary: It will prostrate your Legislature.[54]

This evidence—drawn from Bradley's piece—is offered not as a refutation of his historical argument, but to emphasize that the record with which scholars must work is materially incomplete.

The nature of the historical record is not a bar to scholarly investigation, but it does raise a practical question for courts: After two centuries of neglect, should courts interpret the statute based on speculation about the subjective original understanding of the first Congress? True, original understanding is an important interpretive source. However, in this case, while there is much fodder for learned

---

[53]*Id.* at 588 (noting that before 1980, jurisdiction had been upheld under the Alien Tort Statute in only two reported cases).

[54]*Id.* at 623.

speculation, there is relatively little in the way of direct source material. That makes the use of history as the guide to interpretation of the statute problematic. Are there any compelling alternatives?

Professor Randy Barnett suggests, without necessarily endorsing, one answer. When interpreting text, he says, sometimes we may be forced to look to "a sort of 'objectified' intent—the intent that a reasonable person would gather from the text of the law, placed alongside the remainder of the *corpus juris*."[55] Objective textualism makes the ambiguous text "the best it can be" by harmonizing our interpretation of the statute with our best understanding of the textual implications of the Constitution and its separation-of-powers framework. That approach may not be appropriate in every case, but arguably has a significant claim to guide interpretation here, where the historical record of an ancient, obscure, forgotten, and largely superfluous[56] statute is too spotty and conflicting to provide definitive guidance.

Viewed that way, the interpretive problem posed by the Alien Tort Statute is much less difficult than it first appears: As a textual matter, the Constitution is filled with evidence that Congress, not federal courts, is the preferred expositor of "international" law. That textual preference has interpretive implications: As the Supreme Court has repeatedly underscored, a robust commitment to separation of powers means that federal courts are courts of limited jurisdiction, and as such must narrowly interpret their statutory authority in areas constitutionally committed to Congress's oversight in the first instance. That leads to one conclusion: That the long-dormant Alien Tort Statute depends on further direction from Congress before federal courts may affirmatively remedy specific violations of international law.[57]

---

[55]Randy Barnett, An Originalism for Non-Originalists, 45 Loy. L. Rev. 611, 620–21 (1999).

[56]Congress, like courts and litigants, also seems to have forgotten the statute: Modern alienage jurisdiction now rests on another statutory provision, 28 U.S.C. § 1332(a) (1976).

[57]In some cases, Congress has already provided that direction. See Torture Victims Protection Act, 28 U.S.C. § 1350 note (1992).

## 2. Objective Textualism and the Alien Tort Statute

### a. The Define and Punish Clause

The Constitution is not silent about which branch is entrusted to define offenses against the law of nations. To the contrary, textual evidence suggests *Congress* has the primary power to incorporate international law into our domestic law. Here is an overview of the argument:

The "law of nations" makes only one appearance in the Constitution—in Article I, section 8, which enumerates the powers of Congress: Congress "shall have Power . . . To define and punish Piracies and Felonies committed on the high Seas, and Offences against the Law of Nations."[58] By contrast, Article III, which governs the federal judiciary, contains no corresponding reference to the law of nations. Indeed, on its face, Article III's enumeration of federal sources of law appears to include only *domestic* sources—that is i.e., "cases, in Law and Equity, arising under this Constitution, the Laws of the United States, and Treaties made . . . under their Authority."[59] Similarly, the Supremacy Clause of Article VI does not include a reference to the law of nations: It provides that the "Constitution, and the Laws of the United States which shall be made in Pursuance thereof; and all Treaties made, or which shall be made, under the Authority of the United States" are alone part of the "supreme" federal law.[60] The explicit inclusion of the law of nations in Article I, and its absence in Articles III and VI, suggests the definitional power over the law of nations is committed to Congress in the first instance.[61]

This conclusion is bolstered by the rule that specific textual enumerations are evidence that "unmentioned, open-ended, 'equitable'

---

[58]U.S. Const. art I, § 8, cl. 10. While some scholars have suggested that the Define and Punish Clause is directed only to criminal "offences," Professor Beth Stephens has made a compelling case that the clause also encompasses the power to regulate civil remedies. Beth Stephens, Federalism and Foreign Affairs: Congress's Power to "Define and Punish . . . Offenses Against the Law of Nations," 42 Wm. and Mary L. Rev. 447, 523–32 (2000).

[59]U.S. Const. art. III, § 2, cl. 1.

[60]U.S. Const. art VI, cl 2.

[61]For a lengthy and convincing refutation of the argument that the "Laws of the United States" under Article III and VI implicitly include the law of nations, see Bradley, *supra* note 44, at 601–608.

exceptions" to that enumeration may not be implied.[62] The Vesting Clause of Article I suggests that that canon is appropriate here: It provides that *"all* legislative Powers herein granted *shall* be vested" in Congress.[63] Because Article I, section 8's reference to the law of nations takes the form of a grant, the Vesting Clause creates a strong presumption that that grant is a *legislative* power within the scope of the Vesting Clause, and that the *entire* quantum of that enumerated power ("all [of that] legislative power") is vested in Congress, rather than shared among the branches.

The Supreme Court's interpretation of the federal courts' criminal common law power compels a similar conclusion. Article I enumerates a number of discrete and narrowly defined areas of federal criminal jurisdiction. The Supreme Court has long held that enumeration of *specific* areas of federal criminal jurisdiction in Article I implicitly bars federal courts from recognizing a general, unenumerated "common law" criminal jurisdiction over that same subject matter. As the Supreme Court put it in *United States v. Hudson & Goodwin*,[64] the natural implication of Article I, section 8's treatment of federal crimes is that the "legislative authority of the Union . . . must first make an act a crime, affix a punishment to it, and declare the Court that shall have jurisdiction of the offence," before a Court can "punish" a person for a federal crime.[65]

The Define and Punish Clause is similarly specific: It takes the form of a precisely delineated grant of power to "define" "offenses" and to "punish"—concepts ordinarily associated with courts. By carefully choosing those words to accomplish the grant, the Define and Punish Clause again suggests congressional primacy.

The textual implications of the Define and Punish Clause also are bolstered by a structural concern: It would make little sense for the Constitution to require agreement between political branches—the executive and the Senate—to ratify treaties, but to permit the judiciary carte blanche to incorporate the customary law of nations domestically, without any assent from either political branch. The Treaty Power strongly suggests that elaboration of international

[62]United States v. Brockamp, 519 U.S. 347, 352 (1997).
[63]U.S. Const. art I, § 1 (emphasis added).
[64]11 U.S. (7 Cranch) 32 (1812).
[65]*Id.* at 34.

legal obligations must be subject to structural checks and balances, and to democratic oversight.

Finally, the drafting history of the Define and Punish Clause, while far from clear, offers some further support for congressional primacy. As Bradley describes:

> [S]ome of the proposed drafts of the Constitution would have included cases arising under the law of nations within the federal courts' jurisdiction. The Pickney Plan would have given the Supreme Court appellate jurisdiction over state court decisions "in all Causes wherein Questions shall arise . . . on the Law of Nations." Similarly, although the record is not entirely clear, there is evidence suggesting that the New Jersey Plan would have given the federal judiciary the authority to hear, on appeal, all cases "which may arise . . . on the Law of Nations, or general commercial or marine Laws." But that proposed language was never adopted. Instead, the draft that emerged from the Convention's Committee of Detail listed specific cases and controversies, some which, like admiralty cases and controversies involving ambassadors, would be likely to involve the law of nations. The Founders' delineation of these specific cases and controversies, combined with their decision not to adopt proposed language mentioning the law of nations, suggests that they were not implicitly granting a general law of nations jurisdiction in the "Laws of the United States" language in Article III.[66]

To be sure, that history is consistent with the proposition that the Framers envisioned that the law of nations would serve as a source of decision in certain federal enclaves, including, it should be stressed, disputes between American citizens and foreign citizens. Nonetheless, the Framers' refusal to expressly authorize a *general* law of nations jurisdiction under Article III, and their corresponding decision to grant that general definitional power to Congress, reinforces the conclusion that Congress has a special claim to predominance. This is not a claim that Congress's power is exclusive, only that the interests of Congress deserve special attention when litigants ask

[66]Bradley, *supra* note 44, at 598.

courts, as a matter of first impression, to take on the role of "defining" offenses against the law of nations.[67]

*b. Implications for Interpretation of the Alien Tort Statute*

Congressional primacy over the law of nations has powerful interpretive implications. To see why it's important, consider two sets of precedents—*Erie Railroad Co. v. Tompkins*[68] and the modern law of federal statutory interpretation. Both suggest that structural separation-of-powers concerns should militate against reading a broad federal judicial power under the Alien Tort Statute, absent congressional enactment of positive offenses against the law of nations.

*Erie* involved an ordinary domestic tort claim between Tompkins, a citizen of Pennsylvania, and the Erie Railroad, a corporate citizen of New York,[69] and so raised a choice-of-law question about the source of law applied by federal courts exercising diversity jurisdiction. In *Swift v. Tyson*, a century earlier, Justice Joseph Story held that federal courts exercising diversity jurisdiction over common law claims "need not . . . apply the unwritten law of the State as

[67]There may be a number of cases where constitutional structure and history clearly indicate a "common-law-making" role in areas that implicate international law, regardless of *Erie* (see Section III.B.2.b *infra*). For example, the "law of nations" under Article I, section 8 clearly encompasses admiralty law, and the federal courts—based on a grant of admiralty jurisdiction in Section 9 of the federal Judiciary Act—did, and still do, exercise a federal common law power in admiralty despite the commitment of the power to "define" offenses against the law of nations to Congress. American Dredging Co. v. Miller, 510 U.S. 443, 455 (1994) ("there is an established and continuing tradition of federal common lawmaking in admiralty"). However, given its long history, and the relative lack of controversy surrounding its implementation, admiralty jurisdiction does not pose the same interpretive dilemma posed by the Alien Tort Statute, a statute given conflicting interpretations by early commentators, and then quickly forgotten. Given its unique history of controversy and neglect, the textual claims of Congress to predominance are unique and powerful in this context. And, as discussed in Section III.B.2.b below, that predominance has interpretive implications when federal courts, two centuries after its passage, belatedly take up the interpretive oar today. For discussion of discrete areas, besides admiralty, where there is sufficient countervailing evidence to support limited common-law power in the shadow of international law, see Bradford P. Clark, Federal Common Law: A Structural Reinterpretation, 144 U. Pa. L. Rev. 1245, 1292–1306 (1996) (arguing that structural separation-of-powers considerations suggest reasons for a more vigorous judicial law-making role in the discrete areas of public international law—e.g., the act-of-state doctrine—and providing examples).

[68]304 U.S. 64 (1938).

[69]*Id.* at 69.

declared by its highest court."[70] Instead, he said, "they are free to exercise an independent judgment as to what the common law of the State is—or should be."[71] *Erie* overturned *Swift.* "There is," said the Court, "no federal common law":

> Congress has no power to declare substantive rules of common law applicable in a State whether they be local in their nature or 'general,' be they commercial law or a part of the law of torts. And no clause in the Constitution purports to confer such a power upon the federal courts.[72]

*Erie* is best understood as a separation-of-powers case. Quoting Justice Field, the Court warned that "[s]upervision over either the legislative or the judicial action of the States is in no case permissible except as to matters . . . authorized or delegated to the United States" by the Constitution.[73] Put another way, *Erie* redirected lower courts to *constitutional* restraints on judicial power—and, in particular, on the materiality of textual "authoriz[ations]" or "delegat[ions]" of constitutional authority.[74] *Erie,* understood this way, is an application of the principle that a branch cannot act to "increase its own powers" beyond that provided by the Constitution.[75] *Erie* is also a subsidiary affirmation that respect for the structure of checks and balances requires respect for the written-ness of the Constitution when resolving disputes about the proper scope of judicial authority.

It is important to note that *Erie,* on its face, is not inherently opposed to a robust judicial role, where appropriate. After all, *Erie's* separation-of-powers analysis relies heavily on an earlier dissenting opinion by Justice Field,[76] who was a key dissenter in the *Slaughter-House Cases,*[77] where he argued that the Privileges or Immunities

---

[70]*Id.* at 71 (discussing *Swift*).

[71]*Id.*

[72]*Id.* at 78.

[73]*Id.* at 78–79.

[74]*Id.* at 79.

[75]Morrison v. Olson, 487 U.S. 654, 693 (1988) ("the system of separated powers and checks and balances established in the Constitution was regarded by the Framers as 'a self-executing safeguard against the encroachment or aggrandizement of one branch at the expense of the other'") (quoting Buckley v. Valeo, 424 U.S. 1, 122 (1976)).

[76]Erie, 304 U.S. at 78–79 (quoting Baltimore & Ohio R. Co. v. Baugh, 149 U.S. 368, 401 (1893) (Field, J., dissenting)).

[77]The Slaughter-House Cases, 83 U.S. 36 (1873).

Clause of the Fourteenth Amendment authorizes federal courts to strike down positive laws that interfere with common-law rights of property and contract.[78] The principle that courts must look to constitutional text for their authority, properly understood, means only this: Constitutional text must be respected, both in cases where text authorizes courts to take an active role, and in cases where the text does not.

As discussed, the Define and Punish Clause suggests that application of the "law of nations" is one instance where the Constitution gives Congress a predominant role, while envisioning a more restrained role for federal courts. To be sure, the Alien Tort Statute grants federal courts "jurisdiction" over certain civil actions alleging violations of international law. But that should not be construed as a wholesale delegation to courts of Congress's power to define and punish offenses against the law of nations. In *Erie*, after all, federal courts also had the benefit of a "jurisdictional" grant—of diversity jurisdiction. *Erie* implicitly suggests that, under our separation-of-powers framework, a legislative grant of jurisdiction—absent some source of authority (for example, *constitutional* authority)—does not authorize a general common-law power.

That reading is confirmed by the modern law of statutory interpretation, which has grown up in the shadow of *Erie*'s separation-of-powers concerns. The post-*Erie* Court has emphasized that courts, in cases where their authority rests on a statute and not on the Constitution, must construe their statutory authority narrowly. As the Court has put it: "Raising up causes of action where a statute has not created them may be a proper function for common-law courts, but not for federal tribunals."[79]

---

[78]*Id.* at 89 (Field, J., dissenting) ("The question presented is, therefore, one of the gravest importance, not merely to the parties here, but to the whole country. It is nothing less than the question whether the recent amendments to the Federal Constitution protect the citizens of the United States against the deprivation of their common rights by State legislation. In my judgment the fourteenth amendment does afford such protection, and was so intended by the Congress which framed and the States which adopted it."). See Kimberly C. Shankman and Roger Pilon, Reviving the Privileges or Immunities Clause to Redress the Balance Among States, Individuals, and the Federal Government (Cato Policy Analysis No. 326, 1998).

[79]Alexander v. Sandoval, 532 U.S. 275, 287 (2001). Of course, this proviso should be qualified: Raising up causes of action where a statute has not created them is not a proper role for federal tribunals—*unless* the cause of action is for a violation of our *constitutional* rights.

The text of a statute is paramount when interpreting whether a statute authorizes courts to grant relief.[80] As the Court has directed, if the text clearly does not evidence any intent to create a private right of action, analysis can "begin . . . and end" with the "text and structure" of the statute interpreted.[81] Arguments based on enacting Congress's "expectation . . . formed in light of the 'contemporary legal context' "[82] are not dispositive: "We have never," said the Court in *Alexander v. Sandoval*,[83] "accorded dispositive weight to context shorn of text."[84]

In the absence of a clear authorization, courts must decide whether that intent may be inferred. A court may infer a private right of action from a statutory creation of a "remedial scheme"—including provision for damages, and provisions governing statutes of limitations or affirmative defenses to liability.[85] The absence of a remedial scheme, however, is not necessarily dispositive. In some cases, the "substantive provisions" of a statute may suggest "legal consequences" at such a low level of specificity that the language a fortiori implies a power of judicial enforcement. For example, in *Transamerica Mortgage Advisors, Inc. v. Lewis*,[86] the Court held that a provision of federal securities law that declared certain contracts void "implie[d] a right to specific and limited" contractual relief that ordinarily attends contractual rescission.[87]

However, a simple *jurisdictional* provision that includes *no* remedial provision, *no* specific substantive proscriptions, and *no* announcement of a legal effect in discrete cases, categorically does *not* entitle a plaintiff to a remedy. In *Touche Ross & Co. v. Redington*,[88] the Court considered a plaintiff's claim that Section 27 of the Securities Exchange Act of 1934, which creates "exclusive [federal] jurisdiction" over violations of the Exchange Act, did not implicitly authorize courts to remedy violations.[89] "Section 27," said the Court,

---

[80]*Id.* at 287.
[81]*Id.* at 288.
[82]*Id.* at 287.
[83]*Supra* note 79.
[84]Sandoval, 532 U.S. at 288.
[85]Transamerica Mortgage Advisors, Inc. v. Lewis, 444 U.S. 11 (1979).
[86]*Supra* note 85.
[87]444 U.S. at 18.
[88]442 U.S. 560 (1979).
[89]See, e.g., 15 U.S.C. § 77a (1934).

"grants jurisdiction to the federal courts .... It creates no cause of action of its own force and effect ...."[90]

The distinction between a decision on the merits and a decision on "jurisdiction," while technical, is important. Separation-of-powers concerns dictate that courts must construe their statutory authority narrowly. Where the basis for judicial action comes from Congress, and not the Constitution, Congress's grant of statutory jurisdiction alone is *limited* and does *not* (in the general run of statutory cases) include the power to grant relief. This distinction reflects the fact that federal courts are disciplined by the separation-of-powers framework.

These principles argue against recognition of judicial power to apply the law of nations under the Alien Tort Statute, absent further legislative direction. The statute does not contain remedial provisions. It does not contain any specific substantive proscriptions. It does not declare any legal outcome in a particular class of cases. It does not even create exclusive federal jurisdiction over claims arising under the law of nations.[91] The statute creates only "jurisdiction" over a class of cases. In the words of *Touche Ross*, "If there is to be a federal damages remedy under these circumstances, Congress must provide it."[92]

Again, I am not making a broad claim that federal courts generally should be deferential to the legislature, or simply inactive. When the Constitution envisions a robust judicial role, as in many cases it does, that role must be respected. But here the text of the Constitution gives Congress primacy over the articulation of the law of nations. Respect for Congress's role, and the separation-of-powers framework in which Congress and the courts operate, mandates that courts

---

[90]Touche Ross, 442 U.S. at 577.

[91]See *supra* note 24 (quoting original text).

[92]Touche Ross, 442 U.S. at 579 (internal quotations omitted). It is instructive to compare the Alien Tort Statute with early pre-1789 state statutes authorizing private remedies for violations of the law of nations under state law. Those statutes explicitly authorize liability and an award of damages. See, e.g., 4 The Public Records of the State of Connecticut for the Year 1782, at 156–57 (Leonard Woods Labaree ed., 1942): "That if any Injury shall be offered and done by any Person or Persons whatsoever, to any foreign Power, or to the Subjects thereof, either in their Persons or Property, by means whereof any Damage shall or may any ways arise, happen or accrue, either to any such foreign Power, to the said United States, to this State, or to any particular Person; the Person or Persons offering or doing any such Injury, shall be liable to pay and answer for all such Damages as shall be occasioned thereby."

must wait for further legislative direction before they can make use of the long-dormant "jurisdiction" granted by the Alien Tort Statute. Nor do I contend that cases like *Erie, Sandoval,* or *Touche Ross* provide insight into the subjective intent of the drafters of the Alien Tort Statute. The understanding of "jurisdiction" articulated above, while consistent with the objective implications of separated powers, may be anachronistic when applied over a gap of centuries. But, even so, the subjective intent of the statute's drafters may be unrecoverable. If that is the case, we are left to make an objective interpretation of this forgotten statute. Weighed against the spotty historical record, the natural implications of constitutional text and separation of powers have a powerful claim to govern that interpretation.

## IV. The Court's Opinion in *Sosa v. Alvarez-Machain*: A Critique

In a 9–0 decision, with Justice Scalia in partial dissent, the Supreme Court purported to narrowly construe the Alien Tort Statute. The Court did so in a way that paid lip service to the structural restraints the Constitution, *Erie*, and canons of statutory interpretation place on judicial power. But the Court equivocated, leaving key questions unresolved.

### A. What the Court Said

The Court's opinion argues in two steps. First, it considers whether the grant of "jurisdiction" in the Alien Tort Statute implicitly authorizes federal courts to "define" offenses against the law of nations, answering in the affirmative. Second, it considers the degree of interpretive discretion federal courts possess when exercising that jurisdiction.

### 1. The Birth of the New Federal Common Law

The Court began promisingly enough. Justice Souter, writing for the Court, underscored that "[t]here is no record of congressional discussion about private actions that might be subject to . . . the provision"; that the statute's historical use is nearly non-existent; and that the historical record is fodder for "radically different historical interpretations."[93] Nonetheless, the Court ventured this: The argument of respondent Alvarez-Machain is "implausible."[94] "Alvarez says that the ATS was intended not simply as a jurisdictional

---

[93]*Sosa v. Alvarez-Machain*, 124 S. Ct. 2739, 2755, 2758 (2004).
[94]*Id.* at 2755.

grant, but as authority for the creation of a new cause of action for torts in international law."[95] Yet, "[a]s enacted in 1789, the ATS gave the district courts 'cognizance' of certain causes of action, and that term bespoke a grant of jurisdiction, not power to mold substantive law."[96]

So far so good. But the opinion did not end there: "Holding the ATS jurisdictional," said the Court, "raises a new question" . . . to wit, whether "federal courts could entertain claims once the jurisdictional grant was on the books, because torts in violation of the law of nations would have been recognized within the common law of the time."[97] To answer that ultimate question, the Court looked to pre-*Erie* "history and practice."[98]

Given the patchwork nature of sources illustrating the early understanding of the Alien Tort Statute, the Court relied on a motley assortment of authority, including:

- the views of Oliver Ellsworth, the member of Congress who chaired the committee that reported the 1789 Judiciary Act and, during the Articles of Confederation, had recommended that states enact statutes to authorize damage suits under the law of nations in cases affecting ambassadors;[99]
- scattered statements of Blackstone, which the Court said demonstrated that the content of the early law of nations was "definite and actionable";[100]
- the interpretation of the Alien Tort Statute by Attorney General William Bradford, who suggested the statute authorizes private actions in federal court for damages.[101]

Based on these sources, the Court concluded that "Congress did not intend the ATS to sit on the shelf."[102] The statute, said Souter,

[95] *Id.*
[96] *Id.*
[97] *Id.*
[98] *Id.*
[99] *Id.* at 2758.
[100] *Id.* at 2759.
[101] *Id.*
[102] *Id.* at 2761.

authorizes the Court to unilaterally remedy offenses against international law.[103]

## 2. The New Federal Common Law Defined

Having decided that the Alien Tort Statute authorizes courts to apply at least part of the "law of nations" as a kind of federal common law, the Court faced another question: What part of the "law of nations" may federal courts apply as federal common law?

Here the Court turned to post-*Erie* precedent. "A series of reasons," said the Court, "argue for judicial caution."[104] The first reason? *Erie*. *Erie*, said the Court, reflects a "general understanding" that federal law "is not so much found or discovered as it is . . . made or created."[105] That "understanding" entails a "general practice" of "look[ing] for legislative guidance" before "exercising innovative authority over substantive law."[106]

The second reason? The modern principles of statutory interpretation. "[T]his Court has recently and repeatedly said that a decision to create a private right of action is one better left to legislative judgment in the great majority of cases."[107] Accordingly, said the Court, courts should be "reluctant" to infer the existence of a private cause of action "where the statute does not supply one expressly."[108]

The third reason? The "collateral consequences" that a private right of action to enforce international law may create: "It is one thing for American courts to enforce constitutional limits on our own State and Federal governments' power, but" it is quite another to "consider suits under rules that would go so far as to claim a

---

[103]Justice Scalia dissented from this part of the opinion, and would have harmonized the statute with the post-*Erie* understanding that jurisdiction alone does not permit courts to apply general common law. See, e.g., 124 S. Ct. at 2769, 2773 (Scalia, J., dissenting) ("The general common law was the old door. We do not close that door today, for the deed was done in *Erie*. Federal common law is a new door. The question is not whether that door will be left ajar, but whether this Court will open it . . . . These considerations . . . are reasons why courts cannot possibly be thought to have been given . . . federal-common-law-making powers with regard to the creation of private rights of action for violations of customary international law.").

[104]*Id.* at 2762.

[105]*Id.*

[106]*Id.*

[107]*Id.* at 2762–63.

[108]*Id.* at 2763.

limit on the power of foreign governments" under "modern international law."[109]

These considerations, said the Court, compel a single rule of recognition for enforceable international norms: "definiteness." "Whatever the ultimate criteria for accepting a cause of action" under the Alien Tort Statute, said the Court, "federal courts should not recognize private claims under federal common law for violations of any international law norm with less definite content and acceptance among civilized nations than the historical paradigms familiar" when the Alien Tort Statute "was enacted."[110] The Court added one further caveat: "[T]he determination whether a norm is sufficiently definite to support a cause of action should (and, indeed, inevitably must) involve an element of judgment about the practical consequences of making that cause available to litigants in the federal courts."[111]

### 3. Alvarez-Machain's Suit Dismissed

With this understanding of the Alien Tort Statute in hand, the Court ruled that the claims of Alvarez-Machain for "arbitrary arrest" must be dismissed. The Court reached that ruling for three reasons:

First, the Court rejected Alvarez-Machain's contention that the Universal Declaration of Human Rights and the International Covenant on Civil and Political Rights were appropriate sources for recognizing a customary international norm. "[T]he Declaration does not of its own force impose obligations as a matter of international law. . . . And, although the Covenant does bind the United States as a matter of international law, the United States ratified the Covenant on the express understanding it was not self-executing and so did not itself create obligations enforceable in the federal courts."[112]

Second, the Court reasoned that recognition of an international norm against arbitrary detention would supplant domestic law: The norm "would create a cause of action for any seizure of an alien in

---

[109] Id.

[110] Id. at 2765.

[111] Id. at 2766.

[112] Id. at 2767.

violation of the Fourth Amendment, supplanting actions under § 1983 and *Bivens v. Six Unknown Fed. Narcotics Agents.*[113]

Third, the Court noted that the nature of the injury was relatively slight: "It is enough to hold that a single illegal detention of less than a day, followed by transfer of custody to lawful authorities and a prompt arraignment, violates no norm of customary international law so well defined as to support creation of a federal remedy."[114]

## B. Implications

Too often, a properly assertive judicial role is derided as "usurpation" of Congress's "lawmaking" power. In many cases, an active judicial role is compelled by analysis of constitutional text, and consistent with the role of the judiciary in the system of checks and balances. Here, however, the charge has some force. Below I briefly outline what the Court's analysis says about the method of the Court and then briefly consider some real-world consequences.

### 1. Method

*Sosa v. Alvarez-Machain* engages in a puzzling inversion: An ephemeral historical record is given enormous weight, while the tangible implications of constitutional text and separation of powers are given short shrift.

Indeed, the Define and Punish Clause makes no appearance in the opinion. *Erie* and the modern principles of statutory interpretation enter into the Court's analysis only *after* the Court has established that the Alien Tort Statute implicitly authorizes courts to recognize "common law causes of action" for violations of international law. When those sources do enter the picture, they are unmoored from their origin in an articulated understanding of the Constitution's text and its structure of checks and balances. Under *Sosa, Erie* is merely a "general understanding" of judicial power—rather like a habit of thought. Similarly, the modern canons of statutory interpretation are no longer linked to the constitutional principle that federal courts are courts of limited jurisdiction. Instead, the

---

[113]*Id.* at 2768.
[114]*Id.* at 2769.

Court appears to suggest that the canons reflect prudential judgments about legislative competence and the "collateral consequences" of statutory interpretation. Obscured in this analysis is the notion that federal courts, as courts of limited jurisdiction, must base their authority on a clear textual "authorization" or "delegation" contained either in the Constitution, or in legislation enacted pursuant to constitutional authority.[115]

In place of constitutional text and structure, the Court turns to a historical examination of ephemeral early judicial practice as it existed in a brief window of time at the very cusp of the founding. The Court never articulates why this history (or, in the Court's words, the "ambient law of the era")[116] should trump constitutional text and structure. Indeed, the Court's description of the record seems to present a compelling case for the *in*conclusiveness of the historical record. The Court itself admits that the historical record is "poor";[117] that contemporaneous legal sources are "sparse";[118] that there is no "congressional discussion about private actions that might be subject to jurisdictional provision";[119] that "there is no record even of debate on the section";[120] and that the provision has "remained largely in the shadow for much of the prior two centuries."[121]

Nor are the historical fragments upon which the Court relies probative. First, as the Court itself notes, historians have reached diametrically opposed interpretations of the Alien Tort Statue on the very same thin body of evidence. Moreover, the particular fragments of this record adduced by the Court are not new to the debate and shed no new light on the material questions here: that is, the views of the enacting Congress, and the intent of the Framers with respect to the key constitutional text at issue, the Define and Punish Clause.

For example, the statements of Oliver Ellsworth adduced by the Court concern the desirability of private damages actions in *state*

---

[115]Erie Railroad Co. v. Tompkins, 304 U.S. 64, 78–79 (1938).

[116]124 S. Ct. 2739, 2755 (2004).

[117]*Id.* at 2758 (noting "poverty" of the drafting history of the Alien Tort Statute).

[118]*Id.* at 2759.

[119]*Id.* at 2758.

[120]*Id.*

[121]*Id.* at 2762.

courts during the Articles of Confederation period; those statements were ventured nine years before the Alien Tort Statute was enacted into law; were directed at the role of international law under a different constitutional regime (the Articles of Confederation); and were made without consideration of the U.S. Constitution's subsequent commitment of the power to "define" "offenses" against the "law of nations" to Congress. The views of Attorney General Bradford are counterbalanced by those of Attorney General Levi Lincoln.[122] The views of Blackstone about the "definite" nature of the early law of nations—while an authoritative statement of the law of nations under English law—do not shed any light on the locus of definitional power over international law posed by *our* constitutional text.

*Sosa* is, in effect, an anti-textualist opinion, in which history is used not to clarify, but to evade the implications of text and constitutional structure. This is the originalism of convenience, not of principle.

### 2. Consequences

Should we be alarmed by *Sosa*? At the most fundamental level, the case is troubling for what it reflects about the Court's fidelity to the rule of law. In *Sosa*, the written-ness of the Constitution—so central to a mature understanding of our separation-of-powers framework—seems to have evaporated as a meaningful source of judicial *self*-regulation. Nor is the Court's decision to downplay a structural interpretation of *Erie* an isolated hiccup. The Court's jurisprudence, with a few notable exceptions, generally has evidenced a disturbing trend away from text as a guide for courts: a trend evidenced in the textually *over*-broad reading of the Eleventh Amendment and the Necessary and Proper Clause this term, or the textually *under*-broad reading of the Equal Protection Clause last term. *Sosa*, which is inconsistent with a separation-of-powers reading of *Erie*, reinforces that trend—and is one more step in the wrong direction.

Like many methodologically problematic decisions, *Sosa* may also result in unpleasant policy consequences that could have been avoided by more disciplined analysis. Below, I identify three possible problems. The first is a false alarm; the other two are real.

---

[122]See *supra* notes 50–51 and accompanying text.

*Government Liability.* Some conservative critics have claimed that *Sosa v. Alvarez-Machain* will unleash huge liability risks against the U.S. government when it takes vigorous action in defense of the United States abroad. That concern can be taken too far: There may be cases (like torture) in which we might favor *more* government liability than current law allows. Nonetheless, there is some reason to think that large liability risks under the Alien Tort Statute might translate into less vigorous protection of our security interests than we might want. Even so, on the face of the *Sosa* opinion, this concern is likely overblown.

Consider the record of Alien Tort Statute litigation following *Filartiga*: While claims against state actors have proliferated, few if any of these suits have proven successful.[123] Most of these suits are dismissed based on technical jurisdictional and venue concerns (including personal jurisdiction, forum non conveniens, exhaustion, standing, statute of limitations, and sovereign immunity). If the restrictive spirit of the *Sosa* opinion is honored in subsequent cases, those technical limitations may prove to be as much, if not more, of a barrier in post-*Sosa* litigation.[124]

That is especially the case where litigation concerns the federal government and its agents. In particular, the Court appeared to suggest that the Alien Tort Statute cannot be used to "supplant" preexisting statutory causes of action, including 18 U.S.C. § 1983 (the statutory provision that provides a cause of action for official

---

[123]See, e.g., Beth Stephens, Upsetting Checks and Balances: The Bush Administration's Efforts to Limit Human Rights Litigation, 17 Harv. Hum. Rts. J. 169, 177 (2004) ("Most of the post-*Filartiga* cases have been dismissed, most often for failure to allege a violation of international [sic] recognized human rights, for *forum non conveniens*, or because of the immunity of the defendant.").

[124]That is not to say that these barriers could not be overcome. Professor Bradley has outlined some of the mechanisms for expansion. See Bradley, The Costs of International Human Rights Litigation, *supra* note 36, at 470–73. Moreover, the biggest litigation threat may be directed at multinational *corporate* defendants. While that problem is not addressed in this article, which focuses on liability for state actors, the prospect that the Alien Tort Statute, in conjunction with federal class action procedures, may abet the rise of extortionate "international mass tort" litigation in U.S. courts is substantial and worrisome. See generally Beth Van Schaack, Unfulfilled Promise: The Human Rights Class Action, 2003 U. Chi. Legal F. 279 (2003) (discussing possibility of harnessing customary international law and class action procedures to compel settlements against corporate "human-rights" abusers).

deprivations of rights under color of U.S. law).[125] A natural implication of that ruling is that the statute must be applied with respect
for the scope of *Bivens* and 18 U.S.C. § 1983: After all, if the Alien
Tort Statute is applied in such a way that it provides a more liberal
source of remedies against the government than *Bivens* or Section
1983, then litigants are likely to use the Alien Tort Statute as a
remedial vehicle of choice, thereby "supplanting" these other
sources of a remedy.[126]

If true, that means *Sosa* is likely to have little immediate effect on
government policy. Both the U.S. government as a legal entity and
its agents may assert sovereign immunity and qualified immunity
as defenses to *Bivens* litigation and under § 1983. If the Alien Tort
Statute may not be used to preempt or supercede domestic law,
then those same grants of immunity a fortiori will likely be found
to apply to any Alien Tort Statute claims against the federal government or its agents, absent legislative direction otherwise. In practical
terms, that grant of immunity is an effective bar, if not to litigation,
then to any actual liability. In the *Bivens* context, for example, actual
recovery for constitutional violations is "extraordinarily rare."[127] To

---

[125]While there are colorable arguments that violations of *jus cogens* norms (of which
torture is likely one example) effectively repeal sovereign immunity as a matter of
international law, the *Sosa* Court's express holding that an Alien Tort Statute claim
cannot be used to supercede American domestic law would appear to implicitly
reject the notion that international rules of sovereign immunity may trump domestic
sovereign immunity.

[126]Use of the word "supplant" this way is similar to some interpretations of the
McCarran-Ferguson Act, 15 U.S.C. §§ 1011–15, which preempts federal laws that
would "invalidate, impair, or supercede" state insurance laws. See, e.g., Ambrose v.
Blue Cross & Blue Shield of Virginia, Inc., 891 F. Supp. 1153, 1165 (E.D. Va. 1995)
(federal statutes, like RICO, that provide greater remedies for insurance fraud than
state law allows "supercede the state laws at issue").

[127]See Cornelia T.L. Pillard, Taking Fiction Seriously: The Strange Results of Public
Officials' Individual Liability Under Bivens, 88 Geo. L.J. 65, 65 (1999) ("[i]ndividual
liability under *Bivens* is fictional"). Nor do the administration's recent "torture
memos" change that equation in the torture context. Those memos, which analyze
the legal definition of torture under the restrictive definitional standards of the statute
implementing the Geneva Convention Against Torture, may seem repugnant to moral
sensibilities; but there is good reason to believe the memos will bolster the qualified
immunity *defense* of federal officials accused of torture (indeed, that may have been
among their principal purposes). Under qualified immunity doctrine, an official is
entitled to immunity, even if he violated the law as declared by the court, only if
the right the official is alleged to have violated is clearly established in the sense that
the fact-specific application of the right is governed by a clear, definitive, analogous

be sure, the ineffectual nature of *Bivens* is not reason for celebration: In general, government should be held far *more* accountable for wrongs than it is. Nor should sovereign immunity be held out as an "answer" to an overbroad reading of the Alien Tort Statute: The proper answer to that problem is a proper reading of the statute, one that is consistent with separation of powers. But, even so, this analysis does underscore that it is possible to be too alarmist about the *Sosa* decision.

There are, however, at least two concrete reasons for immediate practical concern. I sketch each briefly below:

*Transnational Jurisprudence.* First, the decision may give impetus to judicial use of international law to construe the content of substantive constitutional, or statutory, rights. In recent years, Justices Breyer and Ginsburg have both advocated what Harold Hongju Koh calls a "transnationalist jurisprudence"—that is, a jurisprudence that looks to "developments internationally" when interpreting the Constitution.[128] For example, in last term's *Grutter v. Bollinger*[129]decision, Justice Ginsburg, joined by Justice Breyer, argued that the International Convention on the Elimination of All Forms of Racial Discrimination is relevant to the interpretation of the Equal Protection Clause and supports upholding time-limited affirmative action programs.[130] Similarly, in *Printz v. United States*,[131] Justice Breyer argued that

---

precedent that bars the action. See, e.g., Jenkins by Hall v. Talladega City Board of Education, 115 F.3d 821, 823 (11th Cir. 1997) (holding that clearly invasive strip searches, which were illegal under the Fourth Amendment, nonetheless did not rise to the level of a violation that obviates qualified immunity, because there was no specifically on-point factual precedent that "dictate[s], that is, truly compels" the conclusion). The torture memos—which, whatever may be said of them, engage in a careful interpretation of the strict letter of the Geneva Convention's implementing statutes—may be used to show that, at this point in the development of American law, reasonable legal opinions may differ concerning the definition of torture, and therefore, perversely, may create a defense to liability—even if a court ultimately disagrees with their content. See, e.g., Memorandum for Alberto R. Gonzales Regarding Standards of Conduct for Interrogations under 18 U.S.C. §§ 2340–2340A, Office of Legal Counsel, Department of Justice (August 1, 2002).

[128]Harold Hongju Koh, The United States Constitution and International Law: International Law as Part of Our Law, 98 A.J.I.L. 43, 52–53 (2004).

[129]539 U.S. 306 (2003).

[130]*Id.* at 342 (Ginsburg, J., concurring).

[131]521 U.S. 898 (1997).

the international experience of European federated states supports broad federal power to direct the conduct of state officials:

> At least some other countries, facing the same basic problem, have found that local control is better maintained through application of a principle that is the direct opposite of the principle the majority derives from the silence of our Constitution. The federal systems of Switzerland, Germany, and the European Union, for example, all provide that constituent states, not federal bureaucracies, will themselves implement many of the laws, rules, regulations, or decrees enacted by the central "federal" body.[132]

Judicial willingness to "harmonize" our domestic supreme law with international practice is problematic. As Richard Posner has noted:

> [One] problem with citing foreign decisions in U.S. courts is that they emerge from a complex socio-historico-politico-institutional background of which our judges, I respectfully suggest, are almost entirely ignorant. (Do any of the Supreme Court justices know any foreign languages well enough to read a judicial decision that is not written in English? And are translations of foreign decisions into English reliable?)
>
> . . .
>
> To know how much weight to give to, say, the decision of the German Constitutional Court in an abortion case, you would want to know such things as how the judges of that court are appointed and how German constitutional judges conceive of their role.[133]

*Sosa* gives "transnational jurisprudence" more, and not less, momentum. If courts have an institutional capacity to apply international law directly, then it is arguable courts also have authority to undertake the relatively more modest task of interpreting preexisting statutes with reference to international practice. To be sure, Souter's opinion is suffused with cautionary language; but much of the cautionary language is narrowly targeted toward the collateral *political*

---

[132]*Id.* at 976 (Breyer, J., concurring).

[133]Richard A. Posner, "No Thanks, We Already Have Our Own Laws," *Legal Affairs*, available at http://www.legalaffairs.org/issues/July-August-2004/feature_-posner_julaug04.html (last checked July 29, 2004).

consequences of creating a *direct* remedy for violation of international norms, not the indirect use of international law advocated by fans of "transnational jurisprudence."

An expansion of "transnational jurisprudence" would be cause for concern. Many foreign governments are, indeed, far less inclined to entertain the concerns of civil libertarians than our own. The U.K., for example, has proven willing to dispense with many criminal procedural protections we consider fundamental in the name of security.[134] The U.K. operates, however, without a written constitution and under a government structure that is far more centralized than our own. Interpreting, say, the Fourth Amendment's "reasonableness" requirement in light of U.K. practice, or that of an analogous state operating in a similarly permissive constitutional climate, surreptitiously denudes the Fourth Amendment from the written structural constitutional context in which it operates and must be interpreted.

*Moral Hazard Problems.* Second, *Sosa v. Alvarez-Machain* creates "moral hazard" problems for the enforcement of important human rights norms against U.S. officials. The textual commitment of the power to "define" offenses against the law of nations is, in part, an invitation—to us, as a democratic political community, to decide what kind of country we want to be in places where the Constitution may not reach. Part of the force of that invitation lies in the clarity of the Constitution's commitment of ultimate responsibility. That is an invitation, and an assignment of responsibility, that may lose force, clarity, and momentum if Congress assumes private litigants and trial judges will take up its slack.

The administration's response to the recent furor over the use of torture is instructive in this regard. Asked if the administration will abide by norms against torture, President Bush responded, "The instructions went out to our people to adhere to law. That ought to comfort you."[135] In fact, as the Office of Legal Counsel's memos

[134]See, e.g., Michael P. O'Connor & Celia P. Rumann, Into the Fire: How to Avoid Getting Burned by the Same Mistakes Made Fighting Terrorism in Northern Ireland, 24 Cardozo L. Rev. 1657 (2003); Fionnuala Ni Aolin, The Fortification of an Emergency Regime, 56 Alb. L. Rev. 1353 (1996) (discussing history of emergency powers assumed by the British government in Northern Ireland).

[135]See "Rules As Solid As Sand: Bush's Legalistic Evasions Set A Dangerous Example For U.S. Forces And The World," AJC.com, June 16, 2004, at www.ajc.com/opinion/content/opinion/0604/16torture.html.

on torture subsequently illustrated, the administration has taken a narrow view of what constitutes "torture," based on a restrictive textual reading of the acts that constitute "severe" pain and suffering within the meaning of the statute implementing the Geneva Convention Against Torture.[136] The "torture memo" underscores that interpretation of international law is susceptible to highly formalistic legal constructions—a threat created in part by the diffuse and ephemeral nature of international legal "norms" themselves. The Define and Punish Clause reminds us that our international obligations aren't something that lawyers can look up in a book. Rather, the act of "defining" international obligations, and our level of commitment to those norms, is something for which we as a political community must take *moral* responsibility—a responsibility that may require us to give those norms more force than the wranglings of government lawyers might permit. Unfortunately, *Sosa v. Alvarez-Machain* gives lawyers—and, presumably, government lawyers—a leading role in defining those obligations, and so risks diluting that message.

## V. Conclusion

Of course, as with all Court decisions that reflect a shift in legal-thinking while leaving key details undefined, the ultimate endgame remains guesswork. As Justice Scalia said in his partial dissent, the majority opinion leaves the door "open" to mischief.[137] It has not yet pushed us through. But, given the *Sosa* Court's lack of discipline, that is only a very small comfort.

---

[136]See, e.g., Memorandum for Alberto R. Gonzales Regarding Standards of Conduct for Interrogations under 18 U.S.C. §§ 2340–2340A, Office of Legal Counsel, Department of Justice (August 1, 2002).

[137]Sosa v. Alvarez-Machain, 124 S. Ct. 2739, 2774 (2004) (Scalia J., dissenting).

# McConnell v. FEC: Rationing Speech to Prevent "Undue" Influence

*Erik S. Jaffe*

## I. Overview

In upholding one of the most sweeping expansions of campaign finance restrictions in decades, *McConnell* v. *FEC*,[1] the Supreme Court continued in a direction that strikes at the heart of First Amendment protection for freedom of speech, and in particular the jealous protection for core political speech. The decision sanctioned expansive restrictions on political speech by engineering two substantial shifts in its approach to such issues.

First, the Court took pains to dissociate political speech from the money used to generate the speech. Focusing on the money itself, rather than the speech that resulted from spending the money, the Court devalued the First Amendment interests at stake and strengthened a rhetorical similarity between campaign spending and bribery. Based on the operative notion that money influences politics—rather than that speech influences politics—the Court applied a diluted standard of First Amendment scrutiny that allowed it to uphold restrictions that would never pass strict scrutiny.

Second, the Court expanded upon its notion of what constitutes corruption of government officials, sweeping in candidate gratitude, responsiveness, and accessibility to those who provide political support through contributions or expenditures for speech. The Court also expanded on the notion that influence gained through substantial spending on political speech could be "undue," and hence corrupt. That suggests an appropriate baseline amount of political speech—and hence gratitude and influence—that echoes the one-person-one-vote principle in the voting context. But the notion that persons and groups have some hypothetically "due" amount of

[1] 124 S. Ct. 619 (2003).

speech and influence smacks of a false egalitarianism, which has no place in a system predicated upon *freedom* of speech. The end-point of substituting equality for freedom is the rationing of speech so that each person and group has no more than their "due" share. That is the direction in which our campaign finance laws are moving, and it is the direction that the *McConnell* opinion sadly endorses. The Supreme Court has thus handed Congress a significant weapon against speech, and both freedom and the First Amendment will be the victims.

Section I of this Article provides some background to the *McConnell* opinion, summarizing the statutory provisions at issue in the case and briefly commenting on the lower court's decision. Section II then examines the key opinions that the Supreme Court released on December 10, 2003. That's followed by an extended Section III, which discusses two of the fundamental issues raised by the *McConnell* decision and their profound implications. Readers who are broadly familiar with the statute and the Court's opinions may wish to proceed directly to the discussion section.

## II. Background

The Bipartisan Campaign Finance Reform Act of 2002 (BCRA)[2] is the most significant overhaul of campaign finance legislation in a generation. In it, Congress significantly curbs the use of so-called "soft money"—i.e., money not previously subject to federal regulation—for expressive activities that might influence federal elections, and regulates spending on supposedly "sham" issue ads that are intended to influence federal elections.

The BCRA amended the Federal Election Campaign Act of 1971 (FECA), the Communications Act of 1934, and other portions of the United States Code. The *McConnell* opinions address various portions of BCRA Titles I, II, III, and V. Title I regulates the use of soft money by political parties, officeholders, and candidates. Title II generally prohibits corporations and labor unions from using their own funds for certain communications that could influence federal elections. Title III contains miscellaneous provisions modifying contribution limits, imposing burdens on attack ads, and prohibiting

---

[2] 116 Stat. 81.

contributions by minors. Title V imposes various recordkeeping requirements on broadcasters regarding requests to broadcast political messages. The sections of the BCRA most relevant to the *McConnell* decision and this article are described below.

## A. BCRA Title I

The central element of BCRA Title I is the creation of new FECA § 323(a), which makes it illegal for national party committees and their agents to "solicit, receive, . . . direct . . ., or spend any funds . . . that are not subject to [FECA's] limitations, prohibitions, and reporting requirements."[3] In short, § 323(a) means that *all* funds used by national parties must now be heavily regulated "hard money." The remainder of new FECA § 323 shuts down a variety of other avenues for soft money that might see increased use once the funds available to national parties are reduced and regulated.

New FECA § 323(b) prohibits state and local parties from using soft money for activities affecting federal elections.[4] Such "federal election activit[ies]," defined in new FECA § 301(20)(A), include (1) voter registration activity during the 120 days before a federal election; (2) voter identification, get-out-the-vote and generic campaign activity in connection with elections where federal offices are at stake; (3) any "public communication" promoting, supporting, attacking, or opposing a "clearly identified [federal] candidate"; and (4) the services of any state-party employee dedicating a portion of his paid time to "activities in connection with a Federal election."[5] A limited exception created by the so-called Levin Amendment allows state and local parties to use some less regulated funds for certain activities targeted at state and local candidates running in the same election cycle as federal candidates.[6]

New FECA § 323(d) makes it illegal for national, state, and local party committees and their agents to "solicit any funds for, or make or direct any donations" to § 501(c) tax exempt organizations that make expenditures in connection with a federal election, and to certain § 527 political organizations.[7]

[3] 2 U.S.C. §§ 441i(a)(1)–(2).
[4] 2 U.S.C.A. § 442i(b).
[5] 2 U.S.C. §§ 431(20)(A)(i)–(iv).
[6] 2 U.S.C. §§ 441i(b)(2)(B)(i)–(ii).
[7] 2 U.S.C. § 441i(d)

New FECA § 323(e) restricts federal candidates and officeholders from receiving, spending, or soliciting soft money in connection with federal elections and limits their ability to do so in connection with state and local elections.[8]

Finally, new FECA § 323(f) prohibits state and local candidates from raising and spending soft money to fund advertisements and other public communications that promote or attack federal candidates.[9]

## B. BCRA Title II

BCRA Title II generally targets non-party expenditures for election-related communications. It expands upon various reporting requirements and restrictions by increasing the range of persons and communications subject to such restrictions.

BCRA § 201 amends FECA § 304, which requires political committees to file detailed periodic financial reports with the FEC. The BCRA expands the FECA's reporting requirements to the broader category of "electioneering communication[s]," which includes any broadcast, cable, or satellite communication that clearly identifies a candidate for federal office, airs within thirty days of a primary or sixty days of a general election, and is targeted to the relevant electorate.[10] The definition expressly excludes news items and editorial commentary.

BCRA § 202 expands the scope of so-called "coordinated" expenditures that will be considered "contributions" to candidates or parties.[11]

BCRA § 203 extends to all electioneering communications FECA § 316(b)(2)'s restrictions on corporations and unions using their own funds for political speech, previously restricted only in the case of "express advocacy" of the election or defeat of federal candidates.[12] Those entities may still organize and administer segregated funds, or Political Action Committees (PACs) for election-related speech.

---

[8] 2 U.S.C. § 441i(e).
[9] 2 U.S.C.A. § 441i(f).
[10] 2 U.S.C. § 434(f)(3)(A)(i).
[11] 2 U.S.C. § 441a(a)(7)(C).
[12] 2 U.S.C. § 441b(b)(2).

BCRA § 204, extends to nonprofit corporations the prohibition on the use of their own general funds to pay for electioneering communications.

BCRA § 213 requires political parties to choose between coordinated and independent expenditures during the postnomination, preelection period.[13]

And finally, BCRA § 214 reinforces the rule of BCRA § 202 restricting coordinated expenditures by directing the FEC to promulgate new regulations that do not "require agreement or formal collaboration to establish coordination."[14]

## C. BCRA Title III

BCRA Title III contains miscellaneous provisions adjusting various campaign-related speech and contribution restrictions.

BCRA § 305 amends the Communications Act of 1934,[15] which requires broadcast stations to give favorable pricing—the so-called lowest-unit-charge rule—for candidate ads in the lead-up periods to primary or general elections, by denying such benefit to ads that "make any direct reference to another candidate for the same office," without the candidate clearly identifying himself at the end of the broadcast and stating that he approves of the broadcast.[16]

BCRA § 307 amends FECA § 315(a)(1) to increase and index for inflation certain FECA contribution limits.

BCRA §§ 304, 316, and 319, known as the "millionaire provisions," increase or eliminate certain contribution and coordinated expenditure limits if a candidate's (wealthy) opponent spends more than certain triggering amounts of his personal funds.

BCRA § 311 extends to electioneering communications FECA § 318's requirement that certain communications clearly identify whether they were "authorized" by a candidate or his political committee or, if not so authorized, identify the payor and announce the lack of authorization.[17]

---

[13]2 U.S.C. § 441a(d)(4).

[14]2 U.S.C. § 441a(a) note.

[15]§ 315(b), 48 Stat. 1088, as amended, 86 Stat. 4.

[16]47 U.S.C. §§ 315(b)(2)(A), (C).

[17]2 U.S.C. § 441d.

Finally, BCRA § 318 adds FECA § 324, which prohibits individuals "17 years old or younger" from making contributions to candidates or political parties.[18]

## D. BCRA Title V

BCRA Title V adds various recordkeeping requirements for broadcaster stations, including the obligations to keep public records of requests for broadcast time by candidates for public office ("candidate requests"), requests by any person seeking to broadcast messages that refer either to a candidate or to any election to federal office ("election message requests"), and requests by any person seeking to broadcast messages related to a "national legislative issue of public importance" or otherwise relating to a "political matter of national importance" ("issue requests").[19]

## E. The Lower Court Opinion

The initial challenges to the BCRA were consolidated and heard before a three-judge panel of the U.S. District Court for the District of Columbia. The panel was composed of District Judges Koleen Kollar-Kotelly and Richard Leon and Circuit Judge Karen Henderson. The three-judge panel produced four different decisions totaling over 1,500 pages.[20] The various configurations of judges produced a mixture of results; upholding some provisions, striking down others, and declining to reach a variety of challenges based on the lack of ripeness or standing. In general, however, the BCRA's supporters seemed to get the better of the mix.

## III. The Supreme Court's Opinions

On December 10, 2003, following expedited briefing and a special four-hour argument held before the start of the Supreme Court's October 2003 term, the Supreme Court issued its decision in *McConnell*. Through various combinations of justices across three different majority opinions, the Court upheld the BCRA against substantially all of the significant challenges and declined to reach a number of other challenges.

[18]2 U.S.C. § 441k.
[19]47 U.S.C. §§ 315(e)(1)(A)–(B).
[20]251 F. Supp. 2d 176 (D.D.C. 2003).

McConnell v. FEC: *Rationing Speech to Prevent "Undue" Influence*

The principal opinion in the case was jointly written by Justices Stevens and O'Connor, joined by Justices Souter, Ginsburg, and Breyer, and upheld virtually all of the challenged provisions of BCRA Titles I and II.

During a brief introductory history of Congress's ever-expanding regulation of campaign speech and financing,[21] the Court identified the central target of such regulation as "the political potentialities of wealth and their untoward consequences for the democratic process."[22] Turning to the more recent phenomenon of soft-money contributions, and observing that the largest corporate donors of soft money often gave to both major political parties, the Court drew the inference that such contributions "were motivated by a desire for access to candidates and a fear of being placed at a disadvantage in the legislative process relative to other contributors, rather than by ideological support for the candidates and parties."[23] Adopting a theme that would repeatedly echo throughout the opinion, the Court concluded that soft money contributions "enabled parties and candidates to circumvent [existing] limitations on the source and amount of contributions in connection with federal elections."[24]

The Court likewise described "issue" ads—those not using words of express advocacy, and hence not previously treated as contributions—as yet another means of circumventing contribution limits. Discussing the distinction drawn in *Buckley* v. *Valeo*[25] between "issue ads" and "express advocacy," the Court observed that the two were "functionally identical in important respects" in that they were both used to advocate election or defeat of specifically identified candidates, regardless of whether they used any "magic words" of express advocacy like "vote for" or "defeat." Both issue ads and express advocacy, insisted the Court, are specifically intended to influence election results given the timing of almost all of the ads in the sixty days preceding an election.[26]

---

[21] McConnell v. FEC, 124 S. Ct. 619, 644–648 (2003).

[22] *Id.* at 644.

[23] *Id.* at 649 (footnote omitted).

[24] *Id.* at 650.

[25] 424 U.S. 1 (1976).

[26] McConnell, 124 S. Ct. at 650–651.

Following that ominous introduction, the primary opinion proceeded to uphold virtually all of the challenged provisions of BCRA Title I.

## A. Level of Scrutiny

The Court began its analysis by endorsing its prior cases reviewing contribution limits using something less than the strict scrutiny ordinarily applied to restrictions on political speech. The Court embraced the frequently criticized reasoning from *Buckley* that the First Amendment value of contributions involves only the "'undifferentiated, symbolic act of contributing,'" that "'the transformation of contributions into political debate involves speech by someone other than the contributor,'" and that limitations on contributions "'thus involves little direct restraint on [the contributor's] political communication, for it permits the symbolic expression of support evidenced by a contribution but does not in any way infringe the contributor's freedom to discuss candidates and issues.'"[27]

Although recognizing that contribution limits "may bear 'more heavily on the associational right than on freedom to speak,'" by limiting like-minded persons from affiliating with a candidate and from pooling their resources, the Court claimed that unlike expenditure limits, which "'preclud[e] most associations from effectively amplifying the voice of their adherents,' contribution limits both 'leave the contributor free to become a member of any political association and to assist personally in the association's efforts on behalf of candidates,' and allow associations 'to aggregate large sums of money to promote effective advocacy.'"[28] According to the Court, contribution limits "'merely . . . require candidates and political committees to raise funds from a greater number of persons.'"[29]

The Court also justified the lower level of scrutiny for contribution limits as reflecting the importance of the "'interests in preventing 'both the actual corruption threatened by large financial contributions and the eroding of public confidence in the electoral process

---

[27] *Id.* at 655 (quoting Buckley, 424 U.S. at 21).
[28] McConnell, 124 S. Ct. at 656 (citations omitted).
[29] *Id.* (citation omitted).

through the appearance of corruption."'[30] It concluded with an invitation for yet more regulation by Congress: "The less rigorous standard of review we have applied to contribution limits . . . provides Congress with sufficient room to anticipate and respond to concerns about circumvention of regulations designed to protect the integrity of the political process."[31]

### B. Application to Title I

Applying that more lenient standard of review to the restrictions of Title I, the Court proceeded to uphold the challenged new provisions of FECA § 323.

#### 1. The First Amendment and Governmental Interests Implicated by New FECA § 323

Addressing new § 323 in general, the Court held that, like prior contribution limits, it had "only a marginal impact on the ability of contributors, candidates, officeholders, and parties to engage in effective political speech," finding that it "does little more than regulate the ability of wealthy individuals, corporations, and unions to contribute large sums of money to influence federal elections, federal candidates, and federal officeholders."[32] The Court held that the restrictions on *soliciting* large contributions "in no way alters or impairs the political message 'intertwined' with the solicitation" and would tend "to increase the dissemination of information by forcing parties, candidates, and officeholders to solicit from a wider array of potential donors."[33]

The Court also found that new FECA § 323 had only a "modest impact" on the ability of party committees to associate with each other and that such burden as it created would be accounted for "in the application, rather than the choice, of the appropriate level of scrutiny."[34]

Turning to the government interests justifying the new restrictions, the Court reiterated its prior conceptions of a government interest in preventing corruption and the appearance of corruption.

[30] *Id.* (citation omitted).
[31] *Id.* at 656–657.
[32] *Id.* at 657 (citation omitted).
[33] *Id.* at 658 (citations omitted).
[34] *Id.* at 659.

Its concern, it said, was "'not confined to bribery of public officials, but extend[ed] to the broader threat from politicians too compliant with the wishes of large contributors.'"[35] The government could properly direct its attention "to curbing 'undue influence on an officeholder's judgment'" and the acquisition of preferential "access to high-level government officials" regardless of whether such access resulted in any "actual influence."[36]

And it reiterated an "almost equal" interest "in combating the appearance or perception of corruption engendered by large campaign contributions," finding that "the cynical assumption that large donors call the tune could jeopardize the willingness of voters to take part in democratic governance."[37] Such interests were deemed "sufficient to justify not only contribution limits themselves, but laws preventing the circumvention of such limits."[38]

Extending the notion of candidate and officeholder gratitude to contributors as the crux of corruption, the Court held that "contributions to a federal candidate's party in aid of that candidate's campaign threaten to create—no less than would a direct contribution to the candidate—a sense of obligation."[39] Given the supposedly "special relationship and unity of interest" between politicians and national parties, such parties were deemed to be "in a unique position, 'whether they like it or not,' to serve as 'agents for spending on behalf of those who seek to produce obligated officeholders.'"[40] Observing that national parties often facilitate contacts between politicians and party contributors, the Court viewed the parties as "'necessarily the instruments of some contributors whose object is . . . to support a specific candidate for the sake of a position on one narrow issue, or even to support any candidate who will be obliged to the contributors.'"[41]

---

[35] *Id.* at 660 (citation omitted).
[36] *Id.* at 664 (citations omitted).
[37] *Id.* at 660–61 (citations and internal quotations omitted).
[38] *Id.* at 661.
[39] *Id.*
[40] *Id.* (quoting FEC v. Colorado Republican Federal Campaign Committee, 533 U.S. 431 (2001)[hereinafter "Colorado II"]).
[41] McConnell, 124 S. Ct. at 664 (quoting Colorado II, 533 U.S. at 451–452).

Turning to the specifics of BCRA Title I, the Court rejected a variety of challenges to the manner in which the BCRA sought to suppress soft-money.

### 2. New FECA § 323(a)'s Restriction on Spending and Receiving Soft Money

Regarding the restriction on national party receipt or use of *any* soft money, regardless of what speech such money funded, the Court rejected an overbreadth challenge by reasoning that "it is the close relationship between federal officeholders and the national parties, as well as the means by which parties have traded on that relationship, that have made *all* large soft-money contributions to national parties suspect."[42] Such contributions, said the Court, "are likely to buy donors preferential access to federal officeholders no matter the ends to which their contributions are eventually put."[43]

Having upheld the central elements of new FECA § 323(a), the Court readily upheld its further restrictions on national parties' solicitation or direction of soft money to others. Once again extending the causal chain—linking candidate gratitude with *party* gratitude—the Court viewed such restrictions as basic anti-circumvention measures because a "national committee is likely to respond favorably to a donation made at its request regardless of whether the recipient is the committee itself or another entity."[44]

The Court also rejected the claim that § 323(a)'s prohibition on spending or directing the use of soft money by others imposed an undue associational burden by limiting national and state/local party interaction. It instead found that "[n]othing on the face of § 323(a) prohibits national party officers, whether acting in their official or individual capacities, from sitting down with state and local party committees or candidates to plan and advise how to raise and spend soft money," and that § 323(a) permits a wide range of

---

[42]McConnell, 124 S. Ct. at 667 (emphasis added).

[43]*Id.* at 668.

[44]*Id.* The Court also upheld the facial application of new § 323(a) to minor parties, observing, first, that regardless of the number of legislators a party managed to elect, the interest in avoiding corruption or its appearance is the same and, second, that any national party with official status gains "significant benefits" for its members. 124 S. Ct. at 669. The Court left open the possibility that a struggling minor party could "bring an as-applied challenge if § 323(a) prevents it from 'amassing the resources necessary for effective advocacy.'" *Id.* (quoting Buckley v. Valeo, 424 U.S. 1, 21 (1976)).

joint planning and electioneering activity."[45] The seemingly subtle distinction between "planning" or "advising" and "directing" the use of soft money—and the likelihood that such supposedly available activities would be deemed "circumvention" of § 323(a)—was left unexplored.

### 3. New FECA § 323(b)'s Restrictions on State and Local Party Committees

The BCRA's various restrictions on state and local party activity that could affect federal elections were also upheld as anti-circumvention measures based on the purportedly "close ties between federal candidates and state party committees."[46] Endorsing Congress's conclusion that soft-money contributions to state and local parties had been and would be used to try to influence federal candidates, the Court concluded that such candidates and officials would feel or appear to feel a corrupting gratitude for contributions to state and local parties used for even basic political activities—voter registration, get-out-the-vote efforts, and generic campaigning—that could influence federal races held simultaneously with state races.[47]

Again emphasizing the broad sweep of its gratitude-is-corrupting rationale, the Court gave "substantial deference" to Congress's views that "federal candidates would be just as indebted to" contributors who shifted their giving to state and local parties "as they had been to those who had formerly contributed to the national parties."[48] The restrictions of § 323(b), said the Court, were narrowly tailored to Congress's interests because they targeted only "those contributions to state and local parties that can be used to benefit federal candidates directly."[49]

---

[45] McConnell, 124 S. Ct. at 670.

[46] Id.

[47] Id. at 671–73.

[48] Id. at 673.

[49] Id. at 674. The Court similarly upheld the Levin Amendment's convoluted rules regarding funding of certain state-party activities with at best a tenuous connection to federal candidates—noting that "not every minor restriction on parties' otherwise unrestrained ability to associate is of constitutional dimension," and that given "the delicate and interconnected regulatory scheme at issue here, any associational burdens imposed by the Levin Amendment restrictions are far outweighed by the need to prevent circumvention of the entire scheme." Id. at 676–77

Finally, the Court dismissed as "speculative" the claim that § 323(b) would prevent state and local parties from engaging in effective advocacy. With seemingly unintended irony, the Court observed that "[i]f the history of campaign finance regulation discussed above proves anything, it is that political parties are extraordinarily flexible in adapting to new restrictions on their fundraising abilities."[50] (Such flexibility, of course, is consistently abhorred in the remainder of the opinion as "circumvention" of existing restrictions and as a justification for still further restrictions.) More troubling, however, was the Court's disparagement of the First Amendment significance of any speech-reducing consequences of § 323(b): "[T]he mere fact that § 323(b) may reduce the relative amount of money available to state and local parties to fund federal election activities is largely inconsequential. The question is not whether § 323(b) reduces the amount of funds available over previous election cycles, but whether it is 'so radical in effect as to . . . drive the sound of [the recipient's] voice below the level of notice.'"[51] Apparently the First Amendment now only protects speech up to some *de minimis* level needed to get noticed, but little more.

### 4. New FECA § 323(d)'s Restrictions on Parties' Solicitations for, and Donations to, Tax-Exempt Organizations

The prohibition in new FECA § 323(d) barring all political party committees from soliciting, directing, or donating funds to certain tax exempt organizations that engage in speech related to federal elections was likewise upheld as a valid anti-circumvention measure.[52] The Court found that "[d]onations made at the behest of party committees would almost certainly be regarded by party officials, donors, and federal officeholders alike as benefiting the party as well as its candidates"; thus, those donations pose the same threat of corruption and the appearance of corruption as national-party soft-money contributions.

In one of the few nods to the First Amendment, however, the Court narrowed the application of § 323(d) to permit party donations of hard money, holding that a "complete ban on donations prevents

---

[50] *Id.* at 677.

[51] *Id.* (citation omitted).

[52] *Id.* at 678.

parties from making even the 'general expression of support' that a contribution represents," and that banning hard-money donations "does little to further Congress' goal of preventing corruption or the appearance of corruption of federal candidates and officeholders."[53]

### 5. New FECA § 323(e)'s Restrictions on Federal Candidates and Officeholders

The Court also upheld new FECA § 323(e)'s general prohibition on federal candidates and officeholders "solicit[ing], receiv[ing], direct[ing], transfer[ring], or spend[ing]" any soft money in connection with federal, state, and local elections.[54]

The Court held that the restrictions were "valid anticircumvention measures" because the value of—and hence the candidate's gratitude for—such donations to nonprofits "is evident from the fact of the solicitation itself," and because the various exceptions adequately accommodated "the individual speech and associational rights of federal candidates and officeholders."[55]

### 6. New FECA § 323(f)'s Restrictions on State Candidates and Officeholders

Finally, the Court upheld new FECA § 323(f)'s prohibition on state and local candidates and officeholders spending soft money to fund "public communications" that "refer[] to a clearly identified candidate for Federal office . . . and that promote[] or support[] a candidate for that office, or attack[] or oppose[] a candidate for that office" except where the communication refers only to the candidate himself or his opponents for the same office.[56] The Court found it "eminently reasonable" that Congress expected that "state and local candidates

---

[53]Id. at 681 (quoting Buckley v. Valeo, 424 U.S. 1, 21 (1976)).

[54]2 U.S.C. § 441i(e). Various exceptions to the prohibition allow federal candidates and officeholders to speak or be guests at state or local party fundraising events, to solicit contributions to certain non-profits that do not engage in federal election activities, and to solicit limited amounts from individuals to non-profits that do engage in such activities. 2 U.S.C. §§ 441i(e)(3) & (4).

[55]McConnell, 124 S. Ct. at 683.

[56]2 U.S.C. § 441i(f), § 431(20)(A)(iii).

and officeholders will become the next conduits for the soft-money funding of sham issue advertising."[57]

## C. BCRA Title II

Turning to BCRA Title II, involving expenditures for speech by groups and individuals other than candidates, the Court once again rejected virtually all of the constitutional challenges to the law.

### 1. BCRA § 201's Definition of "Electioneering Communication"

The most significant element of Title II is its definition of a new category of regulated speech—electioneering communications— that had previously been immune from regulation under *Buckley*. BCRA § 201 modified FECA § 304 and expanded the category of regulated expenditures to include outlays for any "broadcast, cable, or satellite communication" that refers to a clearly identified candidate for federal office, is made within thirty days of a primary, convention, or caucus or within sixty days of a general election, and is targeted to the relevant electorate.[58]

In upholding Congress's authority to regulate that broader category of speech, the Court rejected the argument that the First Amendment required it to maintain *Buckley's* distinction between express advocacy (treated like a contribution) on the one hand and other forms of political speech (protected from regulation) on the other. Instead, the Court held that *Buckley's* express advocacy line was merely one possible solution to a vagueness problem in the language of the prior statute, and that other definitions of speech to be regulated could satisfy the First Amendment.[59]

Addressing the deficiencies of the express-advocacy line, the Court held that "the presence or absence of magic words cannot meaningfully distinguish electioneering speech from a true issue ad," and

---

[57] McConnell, 124 S. Ct. at 684. The Court quickly disposed of claims that Title I exceeded Congress's Election Clause authority, U.S. Const art. I, § 4, and violated the Tenth Amendment by impairing the authority of the states to regulate their own elections. 124 S. Ct. at 685. The Court also rejected an equal protection argument premised on the supposed discrimination against political parties and in favor of special interest groups. *Id.* at 685–86.

[58] 2 U.S.C. § 434(f)(3)(A)(i).

[59] McConnell, 124 S. Ct. at 687.

that "*Buckley*'s magic-words requirement is functionally meaningless."[60] Finding that the new definition of electioneering communications "raises none of the vagueness concerns that drove [the Court's] analysis in *Buckley*," the Court rejected the general challenge to the definition.[61]

### 2. BCRA § 201's Disclosure Requirements

Turning to the application of various disclosure provisions to the broader category of electioneering communications, the Court readily upheld FECA § 304's requirement that if "any person makes disbursements totaling more than $10,000 during any calendar year for the direct costs of producing and airing electioneering communications, he must file a statement with the FEC identifying the pertinent elections and all persons sharing the costs of the disbursements," including, in some instances, all persons who contributed $1,000 or more to the account or the person or fund paying for the communication.[62]

According to the Court, such requirements furthered the important interests of "providing the electorate with information, deterring actual corruption and avoiding any appearance thereof, and gathering the data necessary to enforce more substantive electioneering restrictions."[63] Elevating the public's interest in information above the First Amendment interest in speaker anonymity, the Court held that the evidence did not establish that forced disclosure would cause "the requisite 'reasonable probability' of harm to any plaintiff group or its members" that might serve to chill such speech.[64] The Court left open, however, possible future as-applied challenges where a particular threat from disclosure could be demonstrated.[65]

---

[60]*Id.* at 689.

[61]*Id.*

[62]2 U.S.C.A. §§ 434(f)(2)(A)–(B), (D)–(F).

[63]McConnell, 124 S. Ct. at 690.

[64]*Id.* at 691–92. The Court likewise upheld new FECA § 304(f)(5)'s application of the disclosure requirement to *executory* contracts for electioneering communications, finding that "the interest in assuring that disclosures are made promptly and in time to provide relevant information to voters is unquestionably significant." McConnell, 124 S. Ct. at 693.

[65]McConnell, 124 S. Ct. at 693.

### 3. BCRA § 202's Treatment of "Coordinated Communications" as Contributions

BCRA § 202's treatment of coordinated electioneering communications as contributions was readily upheld by the Court with the brief observation that there "is no reason why Congress may not treat coordinated disbursements for electioneering communications in the same way it treats all other coordinated expenditures."[66]

### 4. BCRA § 203's Prohibition of Corporate and Labor Expenditures on Electioneering Communications

The Court also upheld BCRA § 203's ban on corporations or unions using their own funds for electioneering communications and the requirement that any such speech be funded through separate segregated funds—i.e., PACs—that can be raised only through limited contributions from narrow categories of persons directly affiliated with the corporations or unions. The Court reasoned—and claimed that the challengers had conceded—that the "'PAC option allows corporate political participation without the temptation to use corporate funds for political influence, quite possibly at odds with the sentiments of some shareholders or members, and it lets the government regulate campaign activity through registration and disclosure without jeopardizing the associational rights of advocacy organizations' members.'"[67]

Such restrictions, the Court held, furthered the compelling interest in controlling the "'corrosive and distorting effects of immense aggregations of wealth that are accumulated with the help of the corporate form and that have little or no correlation to the public's support for the corporation's political ideas,'" and hedged "against 'circumvention of [valid] contribution limits.'"[68]

Reiterating its view that express advocacy and electioneering communications were functionally equivalent, and accepting that both were core political speech entitled to the "'fullest and most urgent'" protection of the First Amendment, the Court held that the justifications for regulating express advocacy apply equally to electioneering

---

[66]*Id.* at 694.
[67]*Id.* at 694–95 (citation omitted).
[68]*Id.* at 695–96 (citations omitted).

communications.[69] What once had been a narrow exception allowing regulation of express advocacy having a supposedly greater potential for corruption thus is now a general rule that any speech with the possibility of influencing an election can be regulated.

Rejecting the claimed overbreadth of the restrictions, the Court held that they had ample legitimate applications given that most issue ads were merely sham attempts to influence elections and given that any supposedly "genuine" issue ads—which the Court *assumed* might be constitutionally protected—could still be run by corporations or unions by avoiding any reference to a specific federal candidate.[70]

The Court likewise rejected the claim that the restriction was under-inclusive—and hence not properly tailored—in that it does not apply to print or internet advertising or to news stories, commentary, and editorials aired by certain broadcasters.[71] In a disturbing echo of rational basis scrutiny, the Court held that "'reform may take one step at a time, addressing itself to the phase of the problem which seems most acute to the legislative mind,'" and that there was a "'valid distinction'" between "'the media industry and other corporations that are not involved in the regular business of imparting news to the public.'"[72]

### 5. BCRA § 204's Application to Nonprofit Corporations

Regarding BCRA § 204's application of the corporate speech restrictions to non-profit corporations, the Court reaffirmed the line drawn in its previous cases between so-called *MCFL* corporations— those that are formed for the express purpose of promoting political ideas, do not engage in business activities, have no shareholders or affiliated persons with claims on their assets, and were neither established by nor accept contributions from business corporations

---

[69] *Id.* at 696 (citation omitted).

[70] *Id.* at 696–97.

[71] 2 U.S.C § 434(f)(3).

[72] McConnell, 127 S. Ct. at 697 (quoting Buckley v. Valeo, 424 U.S. 1, 105 (1976) (internal quotation marks and citations omitted by the Court) and Austin v. Michigan State Chamber of Commerce, 494 U.S. 652, 668 (1990)).

or labor unions—and all other non-profits.[73] The defining characteristics of *MCFL* corporations were claimed, first, to ensure that "'political resources reflect political support'"; second, that "persons connected with the organization will have no economic disincentive for disassociating with it if they disagree with its political activity"; and, third, to prevent "such corporations from serving as conduits" for otherwise restricted expenditures by business corporations and unions.[74]

Because the new FECA § 316(c)(6) did not contain any exception for *MCFL* corporations, however, the Court upheld the provision only by imposing a limiting construction that "presume[d]," despite plain language to the contrary, "that the legislators who drafted § 316(c)(6) were fully aware that the provision could not validly apply to *MCFL*-type entities."[75]

### 6. BCRA § 212's Reporting Requirement for $1,000 Expenditures

The Court next upheld BCRA § 212, which requires persons making independent expenditures (defined to include executory contracts) of $1,000 or more during the twenty-day period before an election to report such expenditures.[76] Only the timing of such disclosures—in some cases before the actual speech occurred—was challenged, and the Court rejected the challenge for the same reason it upheld similar pre-speech disclosures under new FECA § 304(f).[77]

### 7. BCRA § 213's Requirement that Political Parties Choose Between Coordinated and Independent Expenditures After Nominating a Candidate

One of the few provisions of the BCRA invalidated by the Court was the requirement imposed by BCRA § 213 that appeared to "require political parties to make a straightforward choice between using limited coordinated expenditures or unlimited independent

[73]McConnell, 124 S. Ct. at 699 (citing FEC v. Massachusetts Citizens for Life, Inc., 479 U.S. 238, 252–53, 256–60 (1986) [hereinafter "MCFL"]).

[74]McConnell, 124 S. Ct. at 699 (quoting MCFL, 479 U.S. at 264).

[75]McConnell, 124 S. Ct. at 699.

[76]*Id.*

[77]See *supra* note 64.

expenditures to support their nominees" during the post-nomination, pre-election, period.[78] The Court read the section more narrowly, however, as imposing a choice only between coordinated expenditures and independent *express advocacy*—but not limiting independent expenditures for the broader category of electioneering communications that did not use the magic words urging a particular vote. As thus narrowed, however, the Court held that even express advocacy was entitled to protection and that the government's interest was illusory given that limiting the restriction to express advocacy was "functionally meaningless" and hence "woefully inadequate" to serve the alleged purpose.[79]

### 8. BCRA § 214's Changes in FECA's Provisions Covering Coordinated Expenditures

Finally, the Court upheld BCRA § 214's modification of FECA § 315's definition of "coordinated" expenditures that are treated as contributions, allowing expenditures to be deemed coordinated even without any formal agreement or collaboration.[80] The Court held that while "wholly independent" expenditures "'are poor sources of leverage for a spender, . . . expenditures made after a 'wink or nod' often will be 'as useful to the candidate as cash.'"[81] Rejecting the argument that the broader definition of coordination was vague, the Court noted that the FEC's existing regulatory definition of coordination did not require an agreement and that the long application of that definition "'delineates its reach in words of common understanding.'"[82]

### D. BCRA Title III

A second opinion for the Court, holding that various plaintiffs lacked standing to challenge miscellaneous provisions in BCRA Title III, was written by Chief Justice Rehnquist, joined in full by Justices O'Connor, Scalia, Kennedy, and Souter. Justices Stevens, Ginsberg,

---

[78] McConnell, 124 S. Ct. at 700.

[79] *Id.* at 703.

[80] *Id.* at 704–05.

[81] *Id.* at 705 (citations omitted).

[82] *Id.* at 706 (citations omitted). The Court declined to reach certain challenges to the regulations that would implement the expanded definition, holding that such challenges were not ripe. *Id.*

and Breyer joined most of the opinion, except with regard to BCRA § 305. Justice Thomas also joined most of the opinion.

### 1. BCRA § 305

Regarding Senator McConnell's challenge to BCRA § 305, which, in order to discourage attack ads, denies candidates the benefit of receiving the "lowest unit charge" for broadcast time prior to an election or primary if the ads fail various content requirements, the Court held that Senator McConnell lacked standing to bring the challenge. Because he could not be affected by the provision until 2008, the Court found that his "alleged injury in fact is too remote temporally to satisfy Article III standing."[83]

### 2. BCRA § 307

A variety of plaintiffs, including voters, voter organizations, and candidates challenged BCRA § 307, which increases and indexes for inflation certain FECA contribution limits. The Court again concluded that the challengers lacked standing, finding that their claimed injury of a loss "of an equal ability to participate in the election process based on their economic status"—i.e., they could not afford to contribute up to the higher limits—did not constitute "an invasion of a concrete and particularized legally protected interest."[84] The Court noted that "'[p]olitical "free trade" does not necessarily require that all who participate in the political marketplace do so with exactly equal resources.'"[85] The Court also found that the candidate-plaintiffs lacked standing to challenge the higher limits because their alleged competitive injury—based on their concern over appearing corrupt and their unwillingness to solicit or accept contributions up to the BCRA's higher limits—was not "'fairly traceable' to BCRA § 307."[86] Such injury, said the court, "stems not from the operation of § 307, but from [the candidates'] own personal 'wish' not to solicit or accept large contributions, i.e., their personal choice."[87]

---

[83] *Id.* at 708.
[84] *Id.*
[85] *Id.* (citation omitted).
[86] *Id.* at 709 (citation omitted).
[87] *Id.*

Finally, the Court found that certain plaintiffs lacked standing to bring a Free Press challenge based on alleged discrimination in the law favoring the "institutional media" given that "if the Court were to strike down the increases and indexes established by BCRA § 307, it would not remedy the . . . plaintiffs' alleged injury because both the limitations imposed by FECA and the exemption for news media would remain unchanged."[88]

### 3. BCRA §§ 304, 316, and 319

The Court also found that certain plaintiffs lacked standing to challenge the so-called "millionaire provisions," BCRA §§ 304, 315, and 316, which partially exempt candidates from certain contribution and coordinated expenditure restrictions if the candidate's opponent spends certain triggering amounts of his personal funds. The Court held that the alleged injuries were the same as with BCRA § 307 and were not "fairly traceable" to BCRA.[89] Furthermore, because none of the plaintiffs was "a candidate in an election affected by the millionaire provisions," the Court agreed with the district court that "'it would be purely "conjectural" for the court to assume that any plaintiff ever will be.'"[90]

### 4. BCRA § 311

The Court next upheld the disclosure requirements of BCRA § 311, which extended to "electioneering communications" the existing FECA § 318 requirement that certain communications "authorized" by a candidate or his political committee clearly identify the candidate or committee or, if not so authorized, identify the payor and announce the lack of authorization.[91] The Court found that the required disclosure "bears a sufficient relationship to the important governmental interest of 'shed[ding] the light of publicity' on campaign financing," assuming, as the Court thought it must, that the FECA's existing disclosure provisions were otherwise valid.[92]

---

[88] Id.
[89] Id. at 710.
[90] Id. (citation omitted).
[91] 2 U.S.C. § 441d.
[92] McConnell, 124 S. Ct. at 710.

## 5. BCRA § 318

Finally, in the last of the few defeats dealt the government, the Court struck down BCRA § 318, which forbids individuals "17 years old or younger" to make contributions to candidates and political parties.[93] Rejecting the government's claim that the provision "protects against corruption by conduit"—*i.e.*, parents circumventing contribution limits by giving through their children—the Court found "scant evidence of this form of evasion."[94] Noting that FECA § 320 already prohibited such circumventing contributions made in the name of another person and that the states had adopted narrower means of addressing any problems regarding minors, the Court held that "[a]bsent a more convincing case of the claimed evil, this interest is simply too attenuated" and "the provision here sweeps too broadly."[95]

## E. BCRA Title V

A final opinion for the Court, upholding BCRA § 504, was written by Justice Breyer and joined by Justices Stevens, O'Connor, Souter, and Ginsburg.

BCRA § 504 requires broadcasters to keep publicly available records of broadcasting requests (1) by or on behalf of a candidate; (2) by any person where the message will refer to a candidate or a federal election; and (3) by any person where the message is related to a "national legislative issue of public importance" or to a "political matter of national importance."[96] The Court found that the "candidate request" requirement was similar to an existing FCC regulation, would impose on each broadcaster only six to seven hours of work per year, and thus constituted a "microscopic" burden on broadcasters relative to their revenues from candidates and relative to existing recordkeeping requirements.[97] The Court also found that the requirements served important government interests in aiding verification of broadcasters'

---

[93]2 U.S.C. § 441k.
[94]McConnell, 124 S. Ct. at 711.
[95]*Id.*
[96]47 U.S.C. §§ 315(e)(1)(A)–(B).
[97]McConnell, 124 S. Ct. at 712–14.

"equal time" and "lowest unit charge" obligations toward candidates, in helping the government and the public evaluate whether broadcasters were being even-handed toward candidate requests for time, and in providing an independent set of data for verifying compliance with the various disclosure and funding limitations of the BCRA and the FECA.[98] The Court also found a curious further interest in making "the public aware of how much money candidates *may be prepared to spend* on broadcast messages."[99] Regarding "election message requests" by any person, the Court again found "only a small incremental burden" and important interests in helping, first, "both the regulatory agencies and the public evaluate broadcasting fairness, and determine the amount of money that individuals or groups, supporters or opponents, intend to spend to help elect a particular candidate"; and, second, the FCC determine "whether a broadcasting station is fulfilling its licensing obligation to broadcast material important to the community and the public."[100]

Finally, regarding the "issue request" requirements, the court found important interests in helping "the FCC determine whether broadcasters are carrying out their 'obligations to afford reasonable opportunity for the discussion of conflicting views on issues of public importance,' and whether broadcasters are too heavily favoring entertainment, and discriminating against broadcasts devoted to public affairs."[101]

The Court rejected the claim that the definition of issue requests was unconstitutionally vague and overbroad, finding instead that the "language is no more general than the language that Congress has used to impose other obligations upon broadcasters." Further, declared the Court, the FCC could interpret the provision in a way that "may limit, and make more specific, the provision's potential linguistic reach."[102] The Court left open the possibility of a future as-applied challenge or a challenge to any subsequent FCC regulations.[103]

---

[98] *Id.* at 714.
[99] *Id.* (emphasis added).
[100] *Id.* at 715.
[101] *Id.* at 716.
[102] *Id.* at 716–17.
[103] *Id.* at 717.

The Court also rejected the claim that the "issue request" requirement will force speakers to reveal their political strategies to opponents, sometimes prior to any broadcast. Assuming, "purely for
argument's sake," that the Constitution offered some protection
against forcing premature disclosure of campaign strategies, the
Court argued that the statute did not require disclosure of the substantive content of the message to be broadcast, that the FCC could
issue regulations avoiding any premature disclosures that might be
forbidden by the Constitution, and that it saw no evidence of any
"strategy-disclosure" problem under the FCC's previously existing
candidate request requirement.[104]

### F. The Concurring and Dissenting Opinions

In addition to the three majority opinions, there were five separate
decisions concurring in part and dissenting in part. Four of those
decisions would have struck down the bulk of the BCRA's new
restrictions, and concurred, to varying degrees, only with regard to
certain disclosure requirements or with the decision not to resolve
various of the challenges to Title III. One of the opinions, however,
would have gone further and upheld BCRA § 305's content-based
restrictions on the lowest-unit-charge rule for candidate ads, the
challenge to which the majority avoided by finding that Senator
McConnell lacked standing to raise the issue.

### 1. Justice Scalia's Opinion

Justice Scalia's concurring and dissenting opinion[105] in general
sided with the challengers and would have struck down much of
the BCRA.

Justice Scalia began by reiterating his view that *Buckley* "was
wrongly decided."[106] He then expressed dismay that the same Court
that "has sternly disapproved of restrictions upon such inconsequential forms of expression as" virtual child pornography, tobacco
advertising, dissemination of illegally intercepted communications,
and sexually explicit cable programming, "would smile with favor
upon a law that cuts to the heart of what the First Amendment is

[104] *Id.*
[105] *Id.* at 720–30 (Scalia, J., dissenting).
[106] *Id.* at 720.

meant to protect: the right to criticize the government."[107] The BCRA, he said, "prohibits the criticism of Members of Congress by those entities most capable of giving such criticism loud voice: national political parties and corporations, both of the commercial and the not-for-profit sort."[108]

The nominal evenhandedness of the restrictions on all candidates was illusory, he maintained, because "*any* restriction upon a type of campaign speech that is equally available to challengers and incumbents tends to favor incumbents."[109] And, Justice Scalia observed, many of the restrictions contained in the BCRA were especially favorable to incumbents, who generally have an easier time raising the types of funds least restricted by the law.[110] He found it difficult to believe that such imbalance was "mere happenstance."[111]

Addressing three propositions that he believed underlay the BCRA's restrictions and the Court's decision, Justice Scalia rejected each in turn.

As to the proposition that money is not speech, he condemned the Court's "cavalier attitude toward regulating the financing of speech" because in "any economy operated on even the most rudimentary principles of division of labor, effective public communication requires the speaker to make use of the services of others."[112] While general commercial regulations that impact funds for speech are acceptable if the government "applies them evenhandedly to those who use money for other purposes," where "the government singles out money used to fund speech as its legislative object, it is acting against speech as such, no less than if it had targeted the paper on which a book was printed or the trucks that deliver it to the bookstore."[113]

Rather than mere indirect burdens on speech, therefore, Justice Scalia found it "obvious, then, that a law limiting the amount a

---

[107] *Id.*
[108] *Id.*
[109] *Id.* at 721.
[110] *Id.*
[111] *Id.*
[112] *Id.* at 722.
[113] *Id.*

person can spend to broadcast his political views is a direct restriction on speech."[114] And he found it "equally clear that a limit on the amount a candidate can *raise* from any one individual for the purpose of speaking is also a direct limitation on speech," no different from "a law limiting the amount a publisher can accept from any one shareholder or lender, or the amount a newspaper can charge any one advertiser or customer."[115]

Justice Scalia next rejected the proposition that "the First Amendment right to spend money for speech does not include the right to combine with others in spending money for speech."[116] Just as it would be an "obvious violation of the First Amendment" for Congress to require "newspapers to be sole proprietorships, banning their use of partnership or corporate form," he found it "incomprehensible why the conclusion should change when what is at issue is the pooling of funds for the most important (and most perennially threatened) category of speech: electoral speech."[117]

Finally, Justice Scalia challenged the notion that "the particular form of association known as a corporation does not enjoy full First Amendment protection," and repeated his view that the decision in *Austin v. Michigan Chamber of Commerce*[118] was in error.[119] Because corporations are the most common means for people to "associate," i.e., pool their financial resources, "for economic enterprise" and, increasingly, "to defend and promote particular ideas" as in the cases of the NRA and the ACLU, Justice Scalia rejected the prospect that a candidate could be "insulated from the most effective speech" by such major economic participants and interest groups.[120]

Justice Scalia found inadequate the Court's reliance on the supposed "danger to the political system posed by 'amassed wealth,'" noting that bribery is already criminalized and finding the use of wealth to speak "unlikely to 'distort' elections—*especially* if disclosure requirements *tell* the people where the speech is coming

---

[114]*Id.* at 724.
[115]*Id.*
[116]*Id.*
[117]*Id.* at 725.
[118]494 U.S. 652 (1990).
[119]McConnell, 124 S. Ct. at 725.
[120]*Id.* at 726.

from."[121] Given that the "premise of the First Amendment is that the American people are neither sheep nor fools," said Justice Scalia, "there is no such thing as *too much* speech."[122]

As for candidate gratitude toward contributors or supportive speakers, Justice Scalia noted that any "*quid-pro-quo* agreement for votes" again would already be a crime and that enhanced access for, or a general tendency to favor, supporters is simply "the nature of politics," equally non-corrupt as to corporate and non-corporate allies alike.[123] He found that so long as disclosure rules exist, undue influence would be sufficiently checked "by the politician's fear of being portrayed as 'in the pocket' of so-called moneyed interests," and that the First Amendment assumes that any supposed benefits from restricting speech are "more than offset by loss of the information and persuasion that corporate speech can contain."[124]

Justice Scalia also ridiculed the "notion that there is too much money spent on elections," noting that such spending—mostly on brief television ads—are apparently effective at persuading voters and that it is not the proper role of government to judge what campaign speech is valuable "and to abridge the rest."[125] And he deemed the total amount spent on campaign speech minor as compared to total spending on other items such as movies, cosmetics, and "pork (the nongovernmental sort)."[126]

Justice Scalia concluded that BCRA was about "preventing criticism of the government," and that the Court had abandoned the First Amendment's "fundamental approach" of rejecting the regulation of political speech "for fairness' sake."[127] He deemed the *McConnell* decision "merely the second scene of Act I of what promises to be a lengthy tragedy. In scene 3 the Court, having abandoned most of the First Amendment weaponry that *Buckley* left intact, will be even less equipped to resist the incumbents' writing of the rules of political debate."[128]

---

[121] *Id.* (emphasis in original).

[122] *Id.* (emphasis in original).

[123] *Id.*

[124] *Id.* at 726–27.

[125] *Id.* at 727–28.

[126] *Id.* at 728.

[127] *Id.* (citation and quotation marks omitted).

[128] *Id.* at 729.

McConnell v. FEC: *Rationing Speech to Prevent "Undue" Influence*

*2. Justice Thomas's Opinion*

Justice Thomas, joined in part by Justice Scalia, also filed a concurring and dissenting opinion that generally would have struck down much of the BCRA.[129]

Describing the BCRA as "the most significant abridgment of the freedoms of speech and association since the Civil War," Justice Thomas mourns the casting aside of fundamental First Amendment principles "in the purported service of preventing 'corruption,' or the mere 'appearance of corruption.'"[130] Arguing that the BCRA should be reviewed under strict scrutiny, he viewed bribery laws and disclosure laws as "'less restrictive means of addressing [the Government's] interest in curtailing corruption.'"[131]

Justice Thomas then charged the majority with continuing and building upon the errors of *Buckley* "by expanding the anticircumvention rationale beyond reason."[132] Noting that each new restriction on speech has been justified as a means of preventing circumvention of the previous restriction, Justice Thomas thought it "not difficult to see where this leads. Every law has limits, and there will always be behavior not covered by the law but at its edges; behavior easily characterized as 'circumventing' the law's prohibition. Hence, speech regulation will again expand to cover new forms of 'circumvention,' only to spur supposed circumvention of the new regulations, and so forth" in a "never-ending and self-justifying process."[133]

Justice Thomas then offered an extended critique of the supposed evidence of improper influence, concluding that it consisted of "nothing more than vague allegations of wrongdoing" and "'at best, [the Members of Congress's] personal conjecture regarding the impact of soft money donations on the voting practices of their present and former colleagues.'"[134]

Justice Thomas next rejected the majority's continuation of the "disturbing trend" of decreasing "the level of scrutiny applied to restrictions on core political speech" as in the case of broadly defined

[129]*Id.* at 729–42 (Thomas, J., dissenting).

[130]*Id.* at 729–30.

[131]*Id.* at 730 (citation omitted).

[132]*Id.*

[133]*Id.* at 732.

[134]*Id.* at 732, 733 (quoting Judge Leon's opinion from the district court).

coordinated expenditures and corporate or union speech.[135] As to the latter, Justice Thomas disputed the claim that aggregations of wealth spent on speech that might actually convince voters were corrosive or distorting, and wryly noted that "[a]pparently, winning in the marketplace of ideas" is "now evidence of corruption," a conclusion that "is antithetical to everything for which the First Amendment stands."[136]

Contrary to all of his colleagues, Justice Thomas also took issue with the BCRA's various disclosure requirements, defending the right to anonymous speech and rejecting the sufficiency of an "interest in providing 'information' about the speaker to the public."[137] He also disputed the majority's abandonment of *Buckley*'s "express advocacy" line to allow disclosures and restrictions related to a broader category of speech, noting that the line was drawn "to ensure the protection of the 'discussion of issues and candidates,' not out of some strange obsession of the Court to create meaningless lines."[138] Because any distinction between the two "'may often dissolve in practical application,'" only an unambiguous line would provide adequate protection for the discussion of issues that might overlap with the discussion of candidates.[139]

Justice Thomas concluded with the dire assessment that the "chilling endpoint of the Court's reasoning is not difficult to foresee: outright regulation of the press."[140] Pro-candidate editorials and commentary, no less than political advertising, could engender candidate gratitude; media-corporation wealth are just as unrelated to the public's political views; and media corporations just as desirous of access and influence as any other corporation or union.[141] He found nothing in the majority's reasoning that would "stop a future Congress from determining that the press is 'too influential,' and that the 'appearance of corruption' is significant when media organizations endorse candidates or run 'slanted' or 'biased' news stories"

---

[135] *Id.* at 734.
[136] *Id.* at 735.
[137] *Id.* at 736.
[138] *Id.* at 739.
[139] *Id.* at 740 (quoting Buckley v. Valeo, 424 U.S. 1, 42 (1976)).
[140] McConnell, 124 S. Ct. at 740.
[141] *Id.* at 740–41.

or from "concluding that the availability of unregulated media corporations creates a loophole that allows for easy 'circumvention' of" existing restrictions.[142] "Although today's opinion does not expressly strip the press of First Amendment protection, there is no principle of law or logic that would prevent the application of the Court's reasoning in that setting."[143]

### 3. Justice Kennedy's Opinion

A third, and lengthy, concurring opinion was written by Justice Kennedy, joined in whole or in part by Chief Justice Rehnquist and Justices Scalia and Thomas, again substantially siding with the BCRA's opponents though supporting a variety of the BCRA's restrictions as well.[144]

Arguing that the "First Amendment guarantees our citizens the right . . . to decide for themselves which entities to trust as reliable speakers," he viewed the BCRA as forcing "speakers to abandon their own preference for speaking through parties and organizations," and codifying "the Government's own preferences for certain speakers."[145] Those governmental preferences, said Justice Kennedy, worked to the detriment of new political parties and discriminated "in favor of the speech rights of giant media corporations and against the speech rights of other corporations, both profit and nonprofit."[146]

Justice Kennedy also accused the majority of conflating the anti-corruption rationale with the corporate speech rationale, with the purpose "to cast the speech regulated here as unseemly corporate speech," even where the law failed to draw such distinctions and regulated far broader swaths of speech.[147] Distinguishing *Buckley's* aim as "to define undue influence by reference to the presence of *quid pro quo* involving the officeholder," Justice Kennedy then rejects the Court's conclusion that "access, without more, proves influence is undue," finding that such "new definition of corruption sweeps away all protections for speech that lie in its path."[148]

---

[142] *Id.* at 741.
[143] *Id.* at 742.
[144] *Id.* at 742–77 (Kennedy, J., dissenting).
[145] *Id.* at 742.
[146] *Id.*
[147] *Id.* at 744.
[148] *Id.* at 746.

Rather than access or influence being corrupt, said Justice Kennedy, "[i]t is well understood that a substantial and legitimate reason, if not the only reason, to cast a vote for, or to make a contribution to, one candidate over another is that the candidate will respond by producing those political outcomes the supporter favors. Democracy is premised on responsiveness."[149] Justice Kennedy thus would limit the government's compelling interest in "corruption" to quid pro quo arrangements.[150] And he similarly would evaluate any claimed interest in preventing the "appearance of corruption" based not "on whether some persons *assert* that an appearance of corruption exists," but "on whether the Legislature has established that the regulated conduct has *inherent* corruption potential, thus justifying the inference that regulating the conduct will stem the appearance of real corruption."[151] Justice Kennedy next took issue with the application of lesser scrutiny to various forms of expenditures that the Court treated as if they were contributions.[152] Under *Buckley*'s own terms, he concluded that the BCRA creates "markedly greater associational burdens than the significant burden created by contribution limitations and, unlike contribution limitations, also creates significant burdens on speech itself."[153] He thus argued that strict scrutiny should apply, and found most of Title I lacking.[154]

Finally, Justice Kennedy rejected the restrictions on corporate and union speech in BCRA § 203, explaining at length why he would overrule *Austin v. Michigan Chamber of Commerce*.[155] Rejecting the majority's "endear[ment]" or gratitude theory of corruption, Justice Kennedy found that such a rationale would have "no limiting principle," would give Congress "the authority to outlaw even pure issue ads," and "would eviscerate the line between expenditures and contributions."[156]

---

[149] *Id.* at 748.
[150] *Id.*
[151] *Id.* (emphasis added).
[152] *Id.* at 755–57.
[153] *Id.* at 756.
[154] *Id.* at 757.
[155] *Id.* at 762.
[156] *Id.* at 766.

## 4. *Chief Justice Rehnquist's Opinion*

Chief Justice Rehnquist, joined by Justices Scalia and Kennedy, wrote separately to express his dissenting views regarding Titles I and V.[157]

Chief Justice Rehnquist deemed the BCRA overinclusive in its restrictions on national and state political parties, particularly with regard to the prohibition of national party use of soft money for "pure political speech" that was either unrelated to elections or had "little or no potential to corrupt their federal candidates and officeholders." The chief justice would also have invalidated BCRA restrictions on state-party conduct such as "voter identification, and get-out-the-vote for state candidates even if federal candidates are not mentioned"; "soliciting and donating 'any funds' to nonprofit organizations" like the NRA and the NAACP; and state-candidate television ads that stake out positions opposing presidential policies.[158]

Regardless whether such activities "may *affect* federal elections," said the chief justice, "there is scant evidence in the record to indicate that federal candidates or officeholders are corrupted or would appear corrupted by donations for these activities."[159] And he rejected the Court's conclusion that deference to Congress is justified simply because such "activities *benefit* federal candidates and officeholders, or prevent the circumvention of" other restrictions, observing that newspaper editorials and political talk shows likewise "*benefit* federal candidates and officeholders" and generate gratitude, yet could not be restricted consistent with the First Amendment.[160]

The chief justice tellingly noted the irony in the Court's view that "Congress cannot be trusted to exercise judgment independent of its parties' large donors in its usual voting decisions because donations may be used to further its members' reelection campaigns, but yet must be deferred to when it passes a comprehensive regulatory regime that restricts election-related speech."[161] He found it "no less

---

[157] *Id.* at 777–84 (Rehnquist, C.J., dissenting).

[158] *Id.* at 779.

[159] *Id.* at 780 (emphasis in original).

[160] *Id.*

[161] *Id.* at 780 n.2.

likely that Congress would create rules that favor its Members' reelection chances, than be corrupted by the influx of money to its political parties, which may in turn be used to fund a portion of the Members' reelection campaigns."[162]

The chief justice criticized the Court's broad application of the circumvention rationale by noting that it "ultimately must rest on the circumvention itself leading to the corruption of federal candidates and officeholders."[163] "All political speech that is not sifted through federal regulation circumvents the regulatory scheme to some degree or another," said the chief justice, "and thus by the Court's standard would be a 'loophole' in the current system."[164] He concluded that the Court's "untethering" of its inquiry from "corruption or the appearance of corruption" has "removed the touchstone of our campaign finance precedent and has failed to replace it with any logical limiting principle."[165] The Court's approach, in his estimation, "all but eliminates the 'closely drawn' tailoring requirement and meaningful judicial review."[166]

Finally, the chief justice would have invalidated BCRA § 502 insofar as it required disclosure of mere broadcast "requests," as opposed to disbursements, finding that the provision had no connection to any corruption interests and threatened to burden the First Amendment freedoms of purchasers.[167]

### 5. Justice Stevens' Opinion

In the final separate opinion, Justice Stevens, joined by Justices Ginsburg and Breyer, wrote a brief dissent to the Court's refusal to reach Senator McConnell's challenge to BCRA § 305's new restrictions on the lowest-unit charge rule for candidate advertising.[168] Justice Stevens would have found that Senator McConnell had standing and then upheld the challenged provision as serving an informational interest in shedding light on campaign financing.[169] He rejected

[162] *Id.* at 780.
[163] *Id.*
[164] *Id.* at 780–81.
[165] *Id.* at 781.
[166] *Id.*
[167] *Id.* at 782–84.
[168] *Id.* at 785–86 (Stevens, J., dissenting).
[169] *Id.* at 785.

any characterization of the provisions' focus on attack ads as being "viewpoint-based" by noting that while it targets attacks on one's opponent, it applies equally to the opponent's response.[170]

## IV. Discussion

While reams of paper could be devoted to identifying the numerous problems, large and small, with the *McConnell* decision, this article is limited to two conceptual problems that taint virtually all aspects of the decision.

First, even more than it has in the past, the Court dissociates the money that the BCRA regulates from the speech and expressive activity on which that money is spent. Indeed, the Court barely acknowledges that speech and expressive activity are the grounds on which the money is regulated in the first place. The Court thus undervalues the First Amendment interests at stake and overstates the government's interests by its almost casual treatment of key protected activities from which "influence" is supposedly gained through money.

Second, the Court continues and expands upon a theory of "corruption" that lacks a rational foundation in the core principles of our constitutional democracy. By characterizing as corrupt a candidate's "gratitude" for supportive political speech, and responsiveness to those who support or generate such speech, the Court indicts the fundamental political mechanism—free speech—enshrined in the Constitution. Furthermore, by having the hubris to condemn certain degrees of speech-mediated political influence as "undue," and hence corrupt, the Court implicitly endorses an influence-rationing, and hence speech-rationing, theory of politics that collapses in the end to a revolutionary one-person-one-voice principle alien to our Constitution. Such a principle substitutes the misguided requirement for some rough *equality* of speech—cast in terms of equal opportunity for influence and access to those who benefit from political speech—in place of the constitutionally guaranteed *freedom* of speech.

[170] *Id.* at 785–86.

*A. McConnell Erroneously Dissociates Speech from the Money Used Exclusively to Pay for Such Speech*

A major theme of the *McConnell* decision—carried forward and expanded from the Court's previous decisions starting with *Buckley*—is the denigration of political contributions and expenditures as being primarily about the use of money in politics. That characterization dissociates contributions and expenditures from the political speech they necessarily fund and from the First Amendment value of protecting such essential prerequisites of political speech. The consequence of such dissociation was a consistently trivial degree of scrutiny that seemed barely more rigorous than rational basis scrutiny.

Starting with contributions, the Court endorsed its views from *Buckley* that the First Amendment value of contributions involves only the "'undifferentiated, symbolic act of contributing,'" that the "'the transformation of contributions into political debate involves speech by someone other than the contributor,'" and that limitations on contributions "'thus involves little direct restraint on [the contributor's] political communication, for it permits the symbolic expression of support evidenced by a contribution but does not in any way infringe the contributor's freedom to discuss candidates and issues.'"[171] Those dubious propositions had been used in *Buckley* to establish a false dichotomy between contributions and expenditures, with contributions receiving ever more feeble protection under the First Amendment.

In a pyrrhic victory for consistency, however, the *McConnell* decision eroded that false dichotomy by extending its cavalier attitude towards contributions to a broad variety of expenditures for political speech. To be sure, *Buckley* had drawn a distinction between "express advocacy" and other forms of political speech—yet another false dichotomy. But at least the *Buckley* Court had acknowledged that expenditures for speech were part and parcel of the resulting speech itself and accordingly were to receive full First Amendment protection.[172]

---

[171] *Id.* at 655 (quoting Buckley v. Valeo, 424 U.S. 1, 21 (1976)).

[172] See, e.g., Buckley, 424 U.S. at 43–44 & n.52 (express advocacy treated as a contribution).

Significantly abandoning *Buckley*'s willingness to grant greater protection to most expenditures than to contributions, *McConnell* treats both political acts more consistently. Regrettably, the treatment is consistently wrong, with both contributions and expenditures afforded diminished protection, as they are divorced from the speech they necessarily produced. For example, in upholding BCRA Title I's prohibition on national parties receiving or using soft money, even where such money would neither be transferred nor coordinated with particular candidates, the Court treated larger categories of speech as equivalent to contributions, not expenditures.[173] It also treated limits on solicitation—a direct speech activity—as a contribution restriction, even where the solicitation was for money to third parties, such as nonprofit corporations, entitled to receive such money.[174]

Similarly, in upholding BCRA Title II's restrictions on "electioneering communications," the Court again painted with the same dismissive brush by treating such speech as the equivalent of express advocacy, which had in turn been treated as the equivalent of contributions in *Buckley*.[175] While the Court correctly recognized that many issue ads were functionally indistinguishable from express advocacy and that a magic-words requirements had no substance,[176] it failed to recognize that such equivalence demonstrated the *error* in equating express advocacy to contributions in the first place. Instead, it held that both categories of indisputable core political speech could be regulated, eliminating one of *Buckley*'s false dichotomies by eliminating the protection *Buckley* had maintained for expenditures on non-express advocacy. By turning *Buckley*'s irrational, though mercifully narrow, exception allowing regulation of express advocacy into the general rule for any speech that could influence an election, *McConnell* exacerbated the First Amendment devaluation of political speech begun with *Buckley*'s assault on contributions.

---

[173] McConnell, 124 S. Ct. at 660.

[174] *Id.* at 680. Coordinated expenditures are another example of direct speech and direct association being grouped with and scrutinized as contributions despite the complete absence of the distinguishing features of contributions. *Id.* at 704.

[175] Buckley, 424 U.S. at 43–45 & n.52.

[176] McConnell, 124 S. Ct. at 689.

The expansion of the Court's dissociation of money from the speech it produces is most noticeable, however, in the Court's broad-brush descriptions of the BCRA as a whole, where it implies an equivalence between campaign spending and genuine bribery or vote-buying. "Congress's most recent effort to confine the ill effects of aggregated wealth on our political system," said the Court, is part of its power to " 'safeguard . . . an election from the improper use of money to influence the result.' "[177] "[M]oney is the mother's milk of politics," the Court quotes a former Senator as saying, and then itself later concludes that "[m]oney, like water, will always find an outlet."[178]

What is so deeply troubling about the Court's expanded willingness to treat both contributions and expenditures as involving only money, rather than speech, to influence politics is that it builds upon an illogical foundation used for regulating contributions and then renders the premises *wholly* indefensible as expanded to expenditures. Embracing *Buckley*'s justifications for diluted scrutiny of contribution restrictions, *McConnell* repeated the claims that contributions involve only symbolic speech by the contributor, that any further expression is contingent on "speech by someone other than the contributor,"[179] and that the burden imposed by contribution restrictions are marginal.[180] Those assertions, however, are wrong.

First, contributions involve far more than undifferentiated symbolic speech. As even *Buckley* itself acknowledged that "[m]aking a contribution. . . . enables like-minded persons to pool their resources in furtherance of common political goals."[181] Just as with contributors to other advocacy groups, campaign contributors form part of an expressive association organized around a favored candidate who is both an object of the collective speech as well as a unifying spokesperson or coordinator for such speech.

Contributors thus "speak" not only through the symbolic act of contributing, but also through the speech funded by the contribution.[182] Such speech will indeed vary in both scope and reach according to the amount of contributions. And it will effectively vary in

[177] *Id.* at 706 (citation omitted).
[178] *Id.* at 663, 706 (citation and quotation marks omitted).
[179] Buckley, 424 U.S. at 21.
[180] McConnell, 124 S. Ct. at 655.
[181] 424 U.S. at 22.
[182] NAACP v. Alabama, 357 U.S. 449, 460 (1958) (the NAACP "is but the medium through which its individual members seek to make more effective the expression

content according to the distribution of a contributor's total contributions across multiple candidates and groups.[183]

Furthermore, while dismissing the speech value of contributions as merely symbolic is wrong from the outset, it is entirely nonsensical when expanded to expenditures for express advocacy, electioneering communications, and coordinated speech. Regardless of whether expenditures for such direct speech have a similar potential for obtaining favor from a candidate—an issue related to the government interest involved, not the speech interests at stake—such expenditures are plainly neither symbolic nor undifferentiated.

Second, denigrating contributions as producing only contingent and once-removed speech-by-proxy ignores both the nature of contributions and the nature of virtually all effective speech directed at a large audience. Unlike gifts or bribes, campaign contributions can be spent *only* to support campaign-related expression,[184] and hence implicate purported government interests only when they *are* spent to support such expression. Because contributions, as thus defined, only have value to a candidate when used to support political speech, both sides of the First Amendment balance—government interests and speech interests—turn on the same contingency, whether political speech in fact flows from the contribution. For that reason, the contingency is irrelevant.

And while the candidate may do the literal speaking that results from contributions, it is emphatically *not* true that such speech is *only* that of the candidate, rather than the speech of both the candidate and the contributors combined. That someone other than the

---

of their own views"); see also Buckley, 424 U.S. at 22 (role of associations is to "effectively amplify[ ] the voice of their adherents"); Nixon v. Shrink Missouri, 528 U.S. 377, 415 (2000) (Thomas, J., dissenting) ("a contribution, by amplifying the voice of the candidate, helps to ensure the dissemination of the messages that the contributor wishes to convey").

[183]Giving $2,000 to candidate Smith, $1,000 dollars to candidate Jones, and $10,000 to the Cato Institute allocates the content of the giver's total speech no less than if he spent one day giving speeches praising Smith and his ideas, two days praising Jones and his ideas, and ten days praising the Cato Institute and its ideas. Such decisions regarding both the recipient and the amount given are content-based decisions in precisely the same way that a magazine's editorial decisions about authors and the amount of space devoted to particular articles are the speech and expression of the editors, not merely symbolic acts of association.

[184]BCRA § 313.

multiple contributors utters the final words neither diminishes the expressive interest of the contributors nor distinguishes contributions from other expenditures for speech. Indeed, given the size and geographic dispersion of the voting population—the key listeners for core political speech—and the need to employ costly mass media to have any hope of effective communication, effective political speech almost necessarily requires collective efforts by speakers and hence some use of proxies. The days of a lone orator on a soapbox are long gone, and only the wealthiest among us can afford to purchase mass media time for their own individual speech. Political association and the pooling of resources for speech are the only realistic means of effective advocacy to the electorate.

As extended to contributions, therefore, while the speech-by-proxy rationale is not as literally incoherent as the symbolic speech claim, it instead proves far too much. If speech-by-proxy is indeed a valid basis for diluted First Amendment scrutiny, then *all* expenditures by expressive associations (large or small) are subject to regulations that limit the "contributions" to such associations and hence the resources available for such groups to speak. Indeed, that is precisely what the BCRA has done, and the Court has upheld, in the case of political parties, corporations, and unions, with the only limiting principle seeming to be that Congress cannot constrain their resources to such a degree as to drive their voices *completely* "'below the level of notice.'"[185] But freedom of speech would become a truly pitiful right if all it protected was the minimal ability to get noticed.

---

[185]See McConnell, 124 S. Ct. at 677 (citation omitted). While the Court has given somewhat greater protection to *MCFL* non-profit corporations, given its repeated criticism of the aggregated wealth of both individuals and corporations alike, there is little reason to be sanguine that such protection is secure against the boundless logic of the remainder of the *McConnell* opinion. Like *Buckley*'s express-advocacy line, the *MCFL* line may likewise end up in the dustbin. And given the popular outcry against wealthy individuals financing so-called section 527 entities to engage in political speech, the *MCFL* line may meet its demise sooner rather than later. After all, in terms of their ability to influence federal elections, *MCFL* corporations with wealthy patrons are little different than other large aggregations of wealth. Should Mr. Kerry win the upcoming election and/or the Democrats take back the Senate, both he and the DNC will undoubtedly be quite grateful to Mr. Soros and others, who have done yeoman's work in compensating for the hard-money gap between Kerry and Bush.

Third, claiming that the First Amendment burden of contribution limits is minimal is appalling with regard to the character of the burden and simply wrong with regard to the magnitude of the burden. As for the character of the First Amendment burden, the restrictions are imposed precisely because contributions will (and can only) be used for core political speech—supporting or opposing candidates or otherwise discussing elections and voting. That makes the restrictions content-based and hence among the most offensive types of speech restrictions. And, as Justice Scalia persuasively argues, there is every reason to consider the BCRA's restrictions as viewpoint-discriminatory as well, because even though they are facially viewpoint neutral, they have the predictable—and very likely intended—effect of favoring incumbents and disproportionately burdening those who would challenge existing elected officials.[186] Such content and viewpoint discrimination is more than sufficient to characterize the First Amendment burden here as significant. Even a trifling speech tax discriminatorily imposed on messages critical of the government would be subject to the strictest scrutiny regardless of the quantity of speech, if any, likely to be suppressed.

That the restrictions apply to the raising, rather than the spending, of money for speech does not diminish their offensive nature. In *Buckley* the Court suggested that a contribution limit is merely an "indirect[ ]" burden on campaign speech, "making it relatively more difficult for candidates to raise large amounts of money."[187] *McConnell* echoed that sentiment, arguing that contribution limits '"merely . . . require candidates and political committees to raise funds from a greater number of persons.'"[188] But there is nothing *indirect* in conditioning the amount of a candidate's (or political party's) expression on his ability to raise funds from a greater number of persons, and there is nothing *indirect* in forcing people who would otherwise contribute larger amounts to expend such funds themselves rather than in association with their preferred messenger. Rather, allowing

---

[186]See *id.* at 720–21 (Scalia, J., concurring and dissenting); see also *id.* at 780 n.2 (Rehnquist, C.J., concurring and dissenting) (claimed threat of corruption to gain contributions to fund reelection campaign no more likely than Congress creating campaign finance restrictions that "favor its Members' reelection chances").

[187]Buckley v. Valeo, 424 U.S. 1, 26 n.27 (1976).

[188]McConnell, 124 S. Ct. at 656 (citation omitted).

speakers to raise and pool money only by bits and pieces, and doing so precisely *because* such money will be used for political speech, directly offends the First Amendment and burdens speech and association.[189]

Whether direct or indirect, however, the burden also is substantial, particularly where the aggregation of large amounts of money is essential for access to "expensive modes of communication" such as television, radio, and other mass media, which are "indispensable instruments of effective political speech."[190] Requiring a gardener to water a garden with a thimble rather than a pitcher plainly would burden the production of flowers, and so too with contribution limits and the production of speech. Contribution limits necessarily increase the time and expense a candidate must devote to raising money to support speech and divert such time and expense from the campaign speech itself. And they also increase the burden on contributors, who must search for less effective means of combining in support of a shared message. Those contributors are likely to find numerous alternative avenues of expressive association foreclosed in the name of preventing "circumvention."

As the "minimal burden" rationale is extended to expenditure limits, the above errors are compounded. The content-based nature of the expenditure limits is even more apparent in the various limits on electioneering communications and express advocacy, and the prohibition on corporate and union speech is as direct as can be.[191] Furthermore, the justifications for restricting corporate and union

[189] That the burden is imposed *because* the money is targeted for speech is what distinguishes contribution restrictions from general income taxes or similar financial burdens that have only an incidental effect on speech and thus fall within the analysis of *United States v. O'Brien*, 391 U.S. 367, 377 (1968). But a restriction specifically on raising money for speech and imposed precisely because such money will be spent on speech—*i.e.*, because of its communicative impact—fails the *O'Brien* test. *Id.* at 382.

[190] Buckley, 424 U.S. at 19.

[191] Corporations and unions have the option of forming PACs for such political speech, but that does not alter the character of the burden, which remains substantial in magnitude as well. First, raising funds for a PAC is no minor matter compared with spending a corporation's or union's own funds. Second, the amount that individuals can contribute to PACs is tightly regulated. Third, unlike with national parties and elected officials, the pool from which a corporation or union can solicit PAC funds is extremely limited, thus significantly constraining the total funds a corporation has available for the core political speech restricted by the BCRA.

speech do nothing to mitigate the First Amendment burden, and in some instances actually compound the burden.

Corporations and unions are vital associations based on the shared interests of their members—assuming voluntary purchase of stock by shareholders or payment of membership dues by workers.[192] That their interests are largely economic does nothing to diminish their constitutional status, and given the federal government's pervasive manipulation of the economy, speech from such interests would seem especially important. Political advocacy and speech driven by economic perspectives are likely universal and, in any event, are no different than speech motivated by less worldly concerns.[193]

Claiming that corporations possess an "unfair" advantage because they have characteristics that allow them to accumulate significant capital is no more and no less than a complaint that they are wealthy and that it is somehow wrong to use wealth to support political speech. Furthermore, the very characteristics that help corporations raise money—the liquidity of stock markets and the limited financial risks of stock ownership—also facilitate widespread and voluntary association of all types of citizens through the medium of a corporation.

Insofar as the perceived unfairness of corporate wealth being used for contributions or expenditures is premised on the notion that corporations can generate speech and influence out of proportion to the strength or support behind their ideas and hence beyond the amount of speech and influence they *ought* to have, that is the same criticism leveled against all large contributions, regardless of source,

---

[192]The claim that corporate and union speech is somehow not a valid reflection of the interests of the shareholders or members, FEC v. MCFL, 479 U.S. 236, 258, 260 (1986), simply ignores that such agency issues are inherent to all associations and do not diminish the speech interests involved so long as association is voluntary. All shareholders and members are free to remain affiliated or not, and do so knowing that the entities are authorized to speak in furtherance of the collective economic interests that they represent. That individuals may have other interests that conflict with their economic interests in a corporation or union—and hence conflict with a corporation's or union's speech—simply puts them to the choice of which interests are more important and whether to continue or terminate their association. That same choice is presented by all forms of association.

[193]Cf. NAACP v. Alabama, 357 U.S. 449, 460 (1958) ("it is immaterial whether the beliefs sought to be advanced by association pertain to political, economic, religious or cultural matters").

and begs the same question of what is the "proper" amount of speech and influence. Once again, the notion that the wealthy have too great a voice is not only inadequate as a justification for lesser scrutiny of corporate speech restrictions, it is also a reason itself to invalidate such restrictions. Though failing in its application, *Buckley* at least correctly recognized that government may not "restrict the speech of some elements of our society in order to enhance the relative voice of others."[194] That, said *Buckley*, is "wholly foreign to the First Amendment," the protections of which "cannot properly be made to depend on a person's financial ability to engage in public discussion."[195] Manipulating different groups' relative ability to speak "is a decidedly fatal objective."[196]

*McConnell's* application of lenient judicial scrutiny, initially reserved for contribution restrictions but now extended to many expenditure restrictions, is a particularly treacherous example of the slippery slope at work. The desire to uphold contribution restrictions was so powerful in *Buckley* that it caused the Court to create false dichotomies between contributions and expenditures and between different types of expenditures in order to reach that result. Given the absence of sustainable logic supporting those dichotomies, they were bound to break down.

Instead of finding the common feature of contributions and expenditures to be the resulting speech to which each was integrally and necessarily tied, and hence abandoning *Buckley's* holding as to contributions, the Court went the other way and extended lower scrutiny to more expenditures as well, all in the name of preventing circumvention of the *result* it sought to sustain. Given that *Buckley's* already dubious reasoning regarding contributions is incoherent as applied to expenditures, the Court was forced to take the further step of ignoring the speech that comes from both contributions and expenditures and instead focusing on the facts that money is the common resource that creates such speech and that gratitude and political influence are what can result. It is the connection between money and influence, and a disregard for the core political speech

---

[194] 424 U.S. at 48–49.

[195] *Id.*

[196] Hurley v. Irish-American Gay, Lesbian and Bisexual Group of Boston, 515 U.S. 557, 579 (1995).

involved, that the Court then uses to characterize even expenditures as a mere means to circumvent contribution limits.[197] But while it is correct that both contributions and expenditures can influence elections (though the direction of such influence is often unclear), and can ultimately lead to candidate gratitude if the influence is favorable, ignoring the speech component hides the reason for such influence and potential gratitude. A candidate's appreciation for contributions or expenditures stems not from their monetary value as such, but from their speech value—from the favorable political speech that results and that might persuade voters to elect or reelect the candidate. Money thus serves to amplify and expand the reach of the candidate's and his supporters' message, either as directly expressed by the candidate using contributions or as expressed by his supporters through their expenditures on speech that conveys the same message, praises the candidate's virtues, or criticizes the contrary views of his opponents. It is not money that buys influence, it is effective speech. Money only buys speech, which will be effective or not depending on whether voters are persuaded by the message.[198] As with many rights, exercising the right to speak almost always costs money, especially if the speaker intends to reach a large audience. The right to speak thus necessarily encompasses the right to pay for speech or the distribution of speech, just as the right to counsel encompasses the right to hire a lawyer, and the right to free exercise of religion includes the right to contribute to a church. In each of those cases the expenditure or contribution is protected not because "money is speech," or "money is a lawyer," or "money is

---

[197]It is precisely the distorted view of expenditures for political speech as a means of circumventing contribution limits that has driven the BCRA's further restrictions on electioneering communications. Using contribution limits to bootstrap still further restrictions on speech that might influence candidates caused the unprincipled exception to swallow the First Amendment rule. Even assuming that contributions to candidates are themselves suspect means of gaining influence, effective political speech and association used to influence government are not means of *circumventing* restrictions on supposedly improper influence. Rather, they are the constitutionally favored alternatives for achieving desired ends *without* force, bribery, or other improper means.

[198]In the Court's terms, it is speech, not money, that is the "mother's milk" of politics. Money is merely the milkman (or the breast pump, if one wants to keep the metaphor precise.)

religion," but rather because such targeted use of money is part of the *exercise* of the right to speak, to counsel, or to free exercise of religion. But in no case is such targeted money simply "money" in the generic sense. It is necessarily an integral component of the protected activity and should be analyzed as such. The *McConnell* decision not only ignores that fact, it also goes out of its way to mask it, to devastating effect on the First Amendment.

B. McConnell *Both Misconceives and Vastly Expands the Interests in Preventing Corruption*

A second major theme of the *McConnell* opinion is its characterization of the government's interest in preventing corruption and the appearance of corruption. By characterizing as corrupt not merely such classic wrongdoing as bribery but also virtually any use of concentrated wealth—including its use for *speech*—to influence the political process, the Court deems "corrupt" several fundamental aspects of our constitutional democracy.

The underlying principle inherent in the Court's view of corruption as "undue" influence is an implied baseline of rough equality of political influence that echoes the one-man-one-vote concept but that is totally alien to the First Amendment's protection of the *freedom* of speech. Such forced equality can only be reached by replacing freedom of speech with the rationing of political speech, which is precisely what the BCRA has begun to do and precisely what the Court endorses. Individuals and groups may generate or support only as much speech—and thus gain only as much gratitude, influence, and access—as they are respectively "due." And while the rationing of political speech is not yet complete—Congress has yet to turn its full attention toward the speech and association of wealthy individuals or toward speech seeking to influence the legislative process apart from elections—the opportunities for "undue" influence from concentrated wealth used for speech exist in those contexts as well. The logic of *McConnell* gives Congress all the encouragement it needs to go further.

Following on the path marked by *Buckley* and its progeny, the *McConnell* decision defines corruption as the supposedly undue influence and access gained through the employment of large personal and aggregated wealth in the political process.[199] But whereas

[199] 124 S. Ct. 619, 660 (2004).

*Buckley* had focused on a government interest in preventing "the real or imagined *coercive* influence of large financial contributions on candidates' positions and on their actions if elected to office,"[200] *McConnell* seems to extend that notion to even non-coercive candidate "gratitude" that might create, or be imagined to create, undue influence with or access to elected officials.[201] The asserted interest in preventing "corruption," however, fails to differentiate between acceptable and unacceptable causes of officeholder gratitude and between proper and improper influence on government officials. Without a principled basis for drawing such a distinction, the label "corruption" simply devolves into a generic epithet addressed at any political influence that is contrary to the often unspoken preferences of the person applying the label. There are two essential problems with the Court's conception of corruption.

First, given that the contributions and expenditures said to foster gratitude—and hence influence and access—all achieve that effect only through the mechanism of speech seeking to persuade the public to vote for a candidate, they are intrinsic elements of our constitutional democracy. The resulting tendency of elected officials to be grateful, responsive and accessible to those who aided them in persuading voters is nothing more sinister than democratic responsiveness.

The basis for a distinction between proper and improper influence over elected officials necessarily starts with the recognition that democracy in general, and elections in particular, are, by definition, an exchange between candidates and the citizens that elect them. Every candidate for office necessarily says to voters: "Give me your vote, give me a job as your representative, and I will give you something in return." Different candidates offer different things in exchange for being given their jobs. Some promise to lower taxes, some to provide more social services; some promise to fight for abortion rights, others to fight against abortion; some promise to bring more public works to their jurisdiction, others to reduce "pork" in politics. And every voter says to the candidates in turn: "Give me the policies and laws that I desire and I will give you my vote for a job as my elected representative. Deny me the official actions

[200] 424 U.S. at 1, 25 (1998) (emphasis added).
[201] 124 S. Ct. at 666.

291

I desire and I will vote you out on your ear." The exchange of elective office for desired official conduct, and the influence over government officials that such an exchange necessarily creates, are the essence of representative democracy and neither the exchange nor the influence can be characterized as improper without indicting our democratic system as a whole.[202]

Our constitutional democracy also relies on the core premise, endorsed through the First Amendment, that politicians and the public will be influenced not merely by voting in a vacuum, but also by the political speech of competing interest groups and individuals. The influence exerted through the exchange of supportive political speech for desired official action is an inherent and desirable element of a democracy that relies upon speech and elections, rather than force, to change its laws and leaders.[203] To indict the exchange of political support for official action would brand virtually *all* behavior by elected officials as corrupt and would condemn the Constitution itself.[204]

---

[202] Even where the exchange of elective office support for desired public policy is expressed in terms of an explicit quid pro quo—vote for me and I promise to do X; we will vote for you if you promise to do X—there still is nothing *improper* about that exchange. In fact, the exchange is precisely what we want and expect it to be. Voters are entitled to vote for candidates responsive to their desires, and candidates are entitled to respond to those desires through lawful official action.

[203] Just as with votes, speech is routinely exchanged for the promise and performance of official conduct. A newspaper that says it will only endorse a candidate who pledges to vote for/against abortion rights, a citizens' group that says it will endorse a candidate that pledges not to raise taxes, and a candidate that promises to increase law enforcement in exchange for the endorsement of a respected anti-crime advocate. All are engaged in the same exchange embodied in the election process itself.

[204] The suggestion that soft-money contributions do not involve *genuine* political support because the largest soft-money donors gave to both major parties makes an unwarranted logical leap and is a far cry from demonstrating corruption. Large donors may still show a slight preference in the relative amounts they give to the two parties—does a particular donor prefer free-market Republicans or protectionist Democrats?—and may believe that giving both parties sufficient political support is an important means to allow them to keep each other in check. Avoiding dominance by either party could serve to minimize the ability of extremists in the dominant party to further their agenda. Such a checks-and-balances approach to political donations is a perfectly sensible, and genuine, basis for political support. Furthermore, the largest donors may well have a strong preference for the established two-party system, find much in common between the major parties, and prefer *either* of the traditional alternatives to the third-party prospects that have cropped up in recent years. Donations to both major parties thus may be equally or better explained by an ideological preference for American centrism (in either current flavor) to the occasional varieties of populism.

If the most blatant description of the democratic political exchange—votes and support for official action—is necessarily embodied in the very notion of democracy, then so too is the Court's fuzzier version. Focusing on a politician's vague gratitude for political support mediated by contributions and expenditures for speech changes nothing. Politicians *should* be grateful for the political support that helps them get their message to the public and thus potentially helps them get elected if the message is appealing. They *should* be grateful not only to the large groups of constituents who voted for them but also to the individuals and groups that helped persuade those constituents to vote. That, once again, is merely democratic responsiveness.

The fact that the political support comes in the form of money either contributed for campaign speech or expended directly on political speech does not change the equation in the slightest. The *only* use of campaign contributions or expenditures is to generate political speech and the *only* value to a candidate stems from the prospect that the resulting speech will persuade voters and help the candidate get elected. Contributions that assist the candidate in getting elected through the entirely proper mechanism of generating political speech are no different than endorsements or votes. Because the assistance is ultimately channeled through the protected medium of political speech, it cannot be deemed corrupt.

In contrast to the fundamental democratic exchange of electoral support for desired official conduct, genuine corruption is limited to the exchange of official action for some private advantage. Bribery is the archetype of such corruption: "I'll give you cash for your *personal* benefit if you vote for an upcoming bill." But the element of private gain inherent in the concept of corruption does not and cannot include whatever personal satisfaction and benefit come from being elected to public office. And if the benefit of actually being elected cannot be deemed corrupting, neither can the potential electoral benefit from speech or association in support of a candidate be deemed corrupting. While such speech, like votes themselves, may well be exchanged for official action, such exchanges are the essence of representative democracy and may not be redefined, ipse dixit, as "corrupt."

Given the Court's historic difficulty in identifying any actual or genuine corruption, it continued to rely heavily on the further interest in avoiding a public perception of unproven corruption—the mere "appearance" of corruption—that might shake public confidence in our democratic institutions.[205] But mere public suspicions or misperceptions that the operation of free speech is somehow corrupt are no bases for ignoring the constitutional scheme. Rather, the proper answer to such misperceptions is either more speech, the election of candidates voluntarily practicing the public's notion of virtue, or, ultimately, a constitutional amendment if the existing system cannot hold the public's confidence. In no event are public misperceptions a justification for distorting constitutional provisions set out precisely to resist even the strongly held desires of a temporal majority.

> The very purpose of a Bill of Rights was to withdraw certain subjects from the vicissitudes of political controversy, to place them beyond the reach of majorities and officials and to establish them as legal principles to be applied by the courts. One's right to life, liberty, and property, to free speech, a free press, freedom of worship and assembly, and other fundamental rights may not be submitted to vote; they depend on the outcome of no elections.[206]

Maintaining the public's esteem may be desirable for a government deserving of such esteem, but it is not a sufficient basis for avoiding constitutional requirements.[207] If the danger from exposing or imagining a corrupt government is so great, then there should be ample incentive for more speech to counter such danger. And if more speech is insufficient to mitigate the public's contempt and distrust for the government, and to restore its confidence in our constitutional system, then presumably there will be sufficient support and motivation for a constitutional amendment.

The second problem with the approach in *McConnell* is its notion that while some unspecified degree of influence may be appropriate, influence gained through the application of concentrated wealth for political speech is improper or "undue." But simply characterizing

---

[205]McConnell, 124 S. Ct. at 660.

[206]West Virginia State Board of Education v. Barnette, 319 U.S. 624, 638 (1943).

[207]The government surely could not forbid speech accusing elected officials of corruption because they kowtow to political polls or favor the interests of their home states, regardless whether such criticism caused the public to *believe*—rightly or wrongly—that elected officials were corrupt.

the influence of expressive activities as "undue" is merely an epithet, not an explanation. Many things have an influence—indeed, even a coercive influence—on candidates' positions and actions, yet few would be considered improper.[208] The mere size or force of influence thus is not the measure of whether such influence is corrupt.

What ultimately seems to be the crux of the Court's notion of "undue" influence is influence substantially out of proportion to the somehow valid characteristics of the person or group wielding it. Any indictment of disproportional influence, however, begs the question of how much influence any given person or group *should* have in some idealized construction of the world. While each person has only one *vote*, and hence has limited influence in that sense, we have never imagined that the *speech* of each person or group should be equally influential or that the views of politicians should be based solely on broad opinion polls.

Speech having unequal influence on the public, and hence unequal value to candidates, comes in many shapes—speech by the media, speech by celebrities, speech by religious leaders, and speech by the economically successful. Whether through differences in access, quantity, or credibility, the impact of speech necessarily will vary.[209] But the falsely egalitarian notion that the speech of persons and groups *ought* to have influence in proportion to the voting strength of the speakers, and the assumption that speech in fact will have influence solely in relation to its quantity, represent fundamental misunderstandings of the principles and predicates of the First Amendment.

The *freedom* of speech means that the quantity and substance of speech *ought* to be determined by private choices, not government

---

[208] Public opinion is an obvious example of something that might "coercively" influence a candidate—at least any candidate that takes seriously his or her role as a representative of constituents and who has any interest in being elected or re-elected. Vehement public opposition to a particular policy would exert a tremendously coercive influence on candidates considering such a policy. Yet that influence could not be deemed corrupt.

[209] And if an elected official is more responsive to those constituents that have a greater impact in persuading the public to vote for him or her, that is not corruption—that is simply politics. Disparities in influence are the inevitable consequence of differences in wealth, intelligence, popularity, motivation, and a hundred other factors. Such disparities might be addressed through means such as education, economic opportunity, and the like, but they can never be eliminated in a free society.

control. And the First Amendment assumes that, so long as government stays out of the way, the eventual influence of speech will turn on its substance, not its quantity or initial popularity, and that more speech is superior to restricted speech. Through such assumptions the First Amendment places its trust in the public, not government, to sort it all out in the end. Judge Learned Hand reminds us that the First Amendment "presupposes that right conclusions are more likely to be gathered out of a multitude of tongues, than through any kind of authoritative selection. To many this is, and always will be, folly; but we have staked upon it our all."[210]

Even if disparities in actual or apparent influence are troubling, the government may not attempt to equalize the political strength of different elements in society by restricting the voice of some to enhance the voice of others.[211] The First Amendment uniquely and especially condones political influence mediated through speech and forbids government manipulation of that aspect of the political process. However imperfect or worrisome a system built on such influence may be, it is the system the Constitution established, it is better than the alternatives, and it may not simply be redefined as "corrupt" in order to avoid the First Amendment.

The exchange of political speech and association for desired official action embodies representative government. To have a coherent definition of corruption, the concept must be limited to official action exchanged for some *private* advantage, not simply for the very public advantage of getting elected. Any alleged interest based on contrary assumptions is not compelling, is not substantial, and is not even valid.

## V. Conclusion

The two major themes of the *McConnell* decision discussed in this article—the dissociation of political speech from the money that funds it and the characterization of disproportionate influence and access as corrupt even when such influence is mediated through speech—look to be grim harbingers for First Amendment protection of political speech. Gone is the quaint notion of a "free" marketplace

---

[210]United States v. Associated Press, 52 F. Supp. 362, 372 (S.D.N.Y. 1943), aff'd, 326 U.S. 1 (1945).

[211]Buckley v. Valeo, 424 U.S. 1, 48–49 (1976).

of ideas and the commitment to the principle that more speech is the answer to speech that may trouble us. In their place has arisen a new theory of political speech dedicated to regulating and equalizing the ability of individuals to use speech to influence elections. The new regime takes as its fundamental rationale a need to prevent elected officials from feeling gratitude and being more accessible to those who help them get elected, and thus ushers in a political philosophy that is startlingly different from that embodied in our Constitution.

While the BCRA did not go as far as it might have in regulating political speech, Congress has been given the green light to reach further still. Given the core reasoning of the *McConnell* opinion, it is difficult to find much that will give Congress pause; the logic of the opinion is virtually boundless. It is a sad milestone for the First Amendment.

# Ashcroft v. ACLU II: The Beat Goes On
### Robert Corn-Revere

## I. Introduction

In *Ashcroft v. ACLU*[1] the Supreme Court upheld a 1999 injunction order barring enforcement of the Child Online Protection Act (COPA) and remanded the case for further proceedings to determine the law's constitutionality.[2] The decision put off, for at least two years, a final determination of the constitutionality of the federal government's second attempt to regulate non-obscene, sexually-oriented speech on the internet. Although the 5–4 decision did not finally resolve the important constitutional issues presented by the law, the ruling's narrow practical focus obscures its importance. The majority reaffirmed and clarified some basic principles underlying First Amendment strict scrutiny and set the bar for future regulatory efforts at a high level. The case also highlights a significant doctrinal division on the Court concerning how the First Amendment should be understood and applied.

As an interim ruling that declined to address the ultimate constitutional issues in the case, *Ashcroft II* would not be particularly noteworthy if not for several factors. It was the second time the Court reviewed the federal government's second attempt to regulate speech on the internet, and its nondispositive outcome all but guarantees there will be an *Ashcroft III* (although it will be named for whomever may be the attorney general two years hence). The razor-thin 5–4 vote reflects deep divisions on the Court, but the principle on which the majority based its opinion, that the government has the burden to prove the law is more effective than less burdensome alternatives, promises significant development on remand and when the Court takes up the issue again. Moreover, none of the principal legal problems that various reviewing courts grappled with over

---

[1]Ashcroft v. ACLU, 124 S. Ct. 2783 (2004) (Ashcroft II).

[2]*Id.* at 2795.

299

the past six years are off the table. All of the issues previously addressed in the case, including the relative burdens of speech restrictions on the internet and the appropriate "community standard" for online speech, may yet play a role in the ultimate decision.

## II. Background

### A. The History of the Child Online Protection Act

The federal government has struggled to find a constitutional formulation justifying regulation of non-obscene sexual expression on the internet since 1996. Its first attempt came in the Communications Decency Act (CDA),[3] adopted as part of the Telecommunications Act of 1996, which sought to impose the same standard on the internet that the Federal Communications Commission (FCC) uses to regulate broadcast indecency. That culminated in the Supreme Court's landmark decision in *ACLU v. Reno*,[4] where the Court unanimously struck down a provision prohibiting the display of "indecent" materials online, and voted 7–2 to void a provision that banned the transmission of indecent information to a minor. It held that the internet receives the full protection of the First Amendment, and that the CDA's prohibitions were both vague and overly broad.[5]

The decision prompted Congress to adopt COPA, or "Son of CDA" as some called it.[6] In response to *ACLU v. Reno*, Congress sought to avoid the same fate for the new law by making COPA narrower than its predecessor. Unlike the CDA, COPA does not apply to all sexually-oriented information on the internet, but prohibits making "any communication for commercial purposes" over the World Wide Web that "is available to any minor and that includes any material that is harmful to minors."[7] More specifically, COPA restricts material that "depicts, describes, or represents, in a manner patently offensive with respect to minors, an actual or simulated sexual act or sexual contact, an actual or simulated normal

---

[3]Pub. L. No. 104-104, § 502, 110 Stat. 133, 47 U.S.C. § 223 (1994 ed. Supp. II).

[4]521 U.S. 844 (1997).

[5]*Id.* at 872–74. The parties did not challenge CDA provisions addressed to obscene communications online.

[6]Child Online Protection Act, 112 Stat. 2681–736, codified at 47 U.S.C. § 231 (1998).

[7]47 U.S.C. § 231(a)(1).

or perverted sexual act, or a lewd exhibition of the genitals or post-pubescent female breast."[8] By incorporating the variable obscenity test for material considered "harmful to minors," the Act requires a finding that the average person, applying contemporary community standards, would find that the material, taken as a whole, would appeal to the prurient interest of minors, and that it lacks "serious literary, artistic, political, or scientific value for minors."[9]

The Supreme Court has held that the government may designate some sexually oriented material as "harmful to minors" and may limit the sale or display of such things as "girlie magazines" to children.[10] Under this variable obscenity approach the government cannot unduly limit adult access to the material but may seek to screen out children. Nor may it impose vague restrictions on speech—not even for the benefit of minors—and thereby "reduce the adult population . . . to reading only what is fit for children."[11] Unlike the open-ended indecency standard invalidated in *Reno*, the Court has ruled that the three-part test for obscenity articulated in *Miller v. California*,[12] should be used to determine what material is obscene for minors, but with a slight difference. Reviewing courts must determine whether the average person, applying contemporary community standards, would find that the work, taken as a whole, appeals to the prurient interest *of minors*, and whether the work lacks serious literary, artistic, political, or scientific value *for minors*. Over the years, courts have held that in order to meet this standard, the material must lack serious value for "a legitimate minority of normal, older adolescents,"[13] and the Supreme Court has indicated that regulation is limited to material that is "virtually obscene."[14]

---

[8]47 U.S.C. § 231(e)(6)(b).

[9]47 U.S.C. § 231(e)(6)(c).

[10]Ginsberg v. New York, 390 U.S. 629 (1968).

[11]Butler v. Michigan, 352 U.S. 380, 383–84 (1957). See Bolger v. Youngs Drug Products Corporation, 463 U.S. 60, 73–74 (1983); Erznoznik v. Jacksonville, 422 U.S. 205 (1975); Interstate Circuit v. Dallas, 390 U.S. 676 (1968).

[12]413 U.S. 15 (1973).

[13]American Booksellers Association v. Virginia, 882 F.2d 125, 127 (4th Cir. 1989). See American Booksellers v. Webb, 919 F.2d 1493, 1504–05 (11th Cir. 1990); Davis-Kidd Booksellers, Inc. v. McWherter, 866 S.W.2d 520, 528 (Tenn. 1993).

[14]Virginia v. American Booksellers Association, 484 U.S. 383, 390 (1988).

However, it has not yet attempted to define specifically what material falls in the margin between "adult" and "variable" obscenity.

In addition to limiting its substantive reach, Congress also restricted the range of speakers to which COPA applies. Instead of regulating all who may engage in communication via the internet, as did the CDA, COPA applies to entities "engaged in the business" of making communications over the World Wide Web. The law defines the term broadly to include any entity that "devotes time, attention, or labor to such activities, as a regular course of such person's trade or business, with the objective of earning a profit."[15] The law's restrictions apply to entities that "knowingly" post harmful material to minors on the web, or knowingly "solicit" such materials to be posted on the web.[16] However, it is not required that such postings be "the person's sole or principal source of income" or that the person actually make a profit. Thus, COPA may apply to an online business even where a very small part of its trade involves "harmful" materials.[17]

COPA established criminal sanctions of a $50,000 fine and six months imprisonment for "knowing" violations.[18] It imposed an additional fine of $50,000 for "intentional" violations of the law, and each day of noncompliance is considered a separate violation.[19] The law also established an additional civil fine of $50,000 for each "knowing" violation, again making each day of noncompliance a separate violation.[20] Like the CDA, COPA established various affirmative defenses in the event of a prosecution. If charged with a violation, a defendant may demonstrate that it restricted minors' access by use of a credit card, debit account, adult access code, adult personal identification number, digital certification of age or other "reasonable" measure that is feasible under available technology.[21]

### B. The Litigation

#### 1. Initial Judicial Review

On October 22, 1998, the day President Clinton signed COPA into law, the American Civil Liberties Union (ACLU) filed suit in the

[15] 47 U.S.C. § 231(e)(2)(B).
[16] Id.
[17] Id.
[18] 47 U.S.C. § 231(a)(1).
[19] 47 U.S.C. § 231(a)(2).
[20] 47 U.S.C. § 231(a)(3).
[21] 47 U.S.C. § 231(c).

U.S. District Court for the Eastern District of Pennsylvania challenging the law's constitutionality. Representing various content providers on the World Wide Web, including A Different Light Bookstore and Salon.com, the ACLU argued that COPA infringes upon constitutionally protected speech of both minors and adults, and is unconstitutionally vague. District Judge Lowell A. Reed first issued a temporary restraining order blocking enforcement of COPA, finding that plaintiffs would suffer "serious and debilitating effects" if they attempted to rely on COPA's affirmative defenses.[22] In addition, Judge Reed found that "fears of prosecution under COPA will result in the self-censorship of [some plaintiffs'] online materials in an effort to avoid prosecution.[23] Although the court agreed that the "public certainly has an interest in protecting its minors," it concluded that "the public interest is not served by the enforcement of an unconstitutional law."[24]

Judge Reed reaffirmed his preliminary decision in February 1999 and issued a preliminary injunction.[25] The court found that plaintiffs were likely to succeed on the merits of their constitutional claim— that the law would impose burdens on constitutionally protected speech, that it would chill online speech in general, and that the government had failed to demonstrate that COPA is the least restrictive means of serving its purpose. Significantly, the court considered the burdens of COPA in light of "the unique factors that affect communication in the new and technology-laden medium of the Web."[26] The opinion noted that any barrier erected by web-site operators and content providers to bar access even to some of the content on their sites to minors "will be a barrier that adults must cross as well."[27] Judge Reed added that "perhaps we do the minors of this country harm if First Amendment protections, which they will with age inherit fully, are chipped away in the name of their protection."[28]

---

[22]ACLU v. Reno, No. Civ. A. 98-5591, 1998 WL 813423, at *3 (E.D. Pa. Nov. 23, 1998).
[23]*Id.*
[24]*Id.* at *4.
[25]ACLU v. Reno, 31 F. Supp. 2d 473 (E.D. Pa. 1999).
[26]*Id.* at 495.
[27]*Id.*
[28]*Id.* at 498.

## 2. *Ashcroft I*

The U.S. Court of Appeals for the Third Circuit affirmed Judge Reed's decision, but did so for reasons not found in the district court order and not argued by the parties. Instead, the court of appeals focused on the futility of applying "contemporary community standards" to a global medium. The court found that "web publishers are without any means to limit access to their sites based on the geographic location of particular Internet users."[29] Accordingly, it concluded that that First Amendment analysis was affected dramatically by "the unique factors that affect communication in the new and technology-laden medium of the web."[30]

The court distinguished the way obscenity law applies to other technologies, noting that publishers can choose not to mail unsolicited sexually explicit material to certain locales and phone-sex operators can refuse to accept calls from particular communities. Because the court found that "the Internet 'negates geometry'" and a web publisher "will not even know the geographic location of visitors to its site," it reasoned that application of a First Amendment test based on community standards "essentially requires that every Web publisher subject to the statute [must] abide by the most restrictive and conservative state's community standards in order to avoid criminal liability."[31] It held that "this aspect of COPA, without reference to its other provisions, must lead inexorably to a holding of the likelihood of unconstitutionality of the entire COPA statute."[32] The court based its holding entirely on the probable unconstitutionality of the "community standards" concept in the internet context. The court of appeals made clear that its critique of the "harmful to minors" standard applies equally to the test for obscenity. It stated that *Miller v. California* "has no applicability to the Internet and the Web, where Web publishers are currently without the ability to control the geographic scope of the recipients of their communications."[33] It further noted that "[t]he State may not regulate at all if it turns out that even the least restrictive means of regulation is still

---

[29]ACLU v. Reno, 217 F.3d 162, 175 (3d Cir. 2000).
[30]*Id.* at 174–175.
[31]*Id.* at 169, 175.
[32]*Id.* at 174.
[33]*Id.* at 180.

unreasonable when its limitations on freedom of speech are balanced against the benefits gained from those limitations."[34]

The case advanced to the Supreme Court after the Bush administration came to power and thus became *Ashcroft v. ACLU*.[35] Just as the fortunes of the national political parties shifted after the 2000 election, the unbroken string of internet free-speech cases in which First Amendment rights had been affirmed also came to an end. The Court voted 8–1 to reverse the Third Circuit decision and to remand the case for further proceedings.[36] In doing so, however, it did not disturb Judge Reed's injunction during lower court review.

The near unanimity for the result deflected some attention from the five diverse opinions in *Ashcroft I*, which reopened doctrinal debates that were prominent in the Court's obscenity cases of the 1960s.[37] Although five justices signed onto various portions of the opinion of the Court written by Justice Thomas, the only conclusion with which they could agree was that "COPA's reliance on community standards to identify 'material that is harmful to minors' does not *by itself* render the statute substantially overbroad for purposes of the First Amendment."[38] Beyond that one point of agreement, there was a significant division over how community standards should apply to the internet.

Justice Thomas, joined by Justice Scalia and Chief Justice Rehnquist, took the hardest line in portions of the opinion not joined by a majority, observing that jurors may draw upon personal knowledge of their own communities where the law does not specify a particular geographic area. If, as a result, speakers on the internet must conform to varying local standards, so be it. Those who fear draconian local enforcement can simply avoid using the internet as a means of communication. As Justice Thomas put it, "[i]f a publisher wishes for its material to be judged only by the standards of particular communities, then it need only take the simple step of utilizing a medium that enables it to target the release of its material into

[34]*Id.* at 179–180.

[35]Ashcroft v. ACLU, 535 U.S. 564 (2002) (Ashcroft I).

[36]*Id.* at 566.

[37]See Robert Corn-Revere, Cyberspace Cases Force Court to Reexamine Basic Assumptions of Obscenity and Child Pornography Jurisprudence, 2001–2002 Cato Sup. Ct. Rev. 115, 142–48 (2002).

[38]535 U.S. at 585 (emphasis in original).

those communities."[39] In this view, unreasonable local standards are moderated by the "serious merit" criterion, which enables appellate courts to set "a national floor for socially redeeming value."[40]

Justices O'Connor and Breyer each wrote separately to express their disagreement over which community standard to apply. Although both concurred in the judgment of the Court, they argued that the Constitution requires the use of a national standard to judge speech on the internet. Otherwise, Justice Breyer wrote, "the most puritan of communities" would have "a heckler's Internet veto affecting the rest of the nation."[41] He cited language from COPA's legislative history for support that Congress intended to employ an "adult" standard rather than a "geographic" standard for determining what material is "suitable for minors."[42] Justice O'Connor similarly expressed some concern that the use of local community standards "will cause problems for regulation of obscenity on the Internet, for adults as well as children, in future cases."[43] She suggested that *Miller* allowed the application of local standards but did not mandate their use, and disputed the Court's earlier conclusion that a national standard is "unascertainable."[44]

Justice Kennedy, joined by Justices Souter and Ginsburg, wrote that there is a very real likelihood that COPA ultimately would fail a facial challenge as an overly broad restriction on speech. He suggested that the Court should proceed cautiously in light of Congress's attempt to fashion a narrower law than the CDA, and, for that reason, the Third Circuit's community standards rationale "stated and applied at such a high level of generality" could not be sustained.[45] Nevertheless, Justice Kennedy explained that a range of concerns may invalidate COPA's variable obscenity standard, including the variation in community standards, the question of what constitutes the work "as a whole" on the internet, the type

---

[39]*Id.* at 583

[40]*Id.* at 579, 583 (citation omitted) (plurality op.).

[41]*Id.* at 590 (Breyer, J., concurring).

[42]*Id.*

[43]*Id.* at 587 (O'Connor, J., concurring).

[44]*Id.* at 587–88.

[45]*Id.* at 592 (Kennedy, J., concurring).

and amount of speech restricted by COPA among other factors.[46] Despite "grave doubts that COPA is consistent with the First Amendment," he concluded that the Court should await a more thorough analysis by the Third Circuit.[47]

The sole dissenter was Justice Stevens, author of the Court's opinion in *Reno v. ACLU*.[48] In his view, it is "quite wrong to allow the standards of a minority consisting of the least tolerant communities" to regulate access to the World Wide Web.[49] In the internet context, however, Justice Stevens found that "community standards become a sword rather than a shield" because "[i]f a prurient appeal is offensive in a puritan village, it may be a crime to post it on the World Wide Web."[50] Acknowledging that COPA was an improvement over the CDA, Justice Stevens nevertheless concluded that the changes were insufficient to cure the law's constitutional deficiencies. The elements of COPA's "harm to minors test" did not narrow the law sufficiently, he concluded, because the "patently offensive" and "prurient interests" elements of the standard depended on a community standard.[51] The requirement that the material be "in some sense erotic" similarly did not narrow its scope, since "[a]rguably every depiction of nudity—partial or full—is in some sense erotic *with respect to minors*."[52] Similarly, the "serious value" prong of the test did not narrow COPA's scope, because it requires juries to determine whether the material has serious value for minors.[53] Accordingly, Justice Stevens concluded that the community standards analysis alone doomed COPA.

With these divergent opinions the Supreme Court sent the case back to the Third Circuit with little instruction beyond the clear signal that the circuit court was to broaden analysis beyond the issue of community standards.

---

[46]*Id*. at 592–93.
[47]*Id*. at 592–602 (citations omitted).
[48]*Id*. at 602 (Stevens, J., dissenting).
[49]*Id*. at 612.
[50]*Id*. at 603–04.
[51]*Id*. at 607–08.
[52]*Id*. at 608 (emphasis in original).
[53]*Id*. at 608–09.

On remand, the Third Circuit reaffirmed its earlier decision that the district court had not abused its discretion by preliminarily enjoining enforcement of the law, but this time ruled on broader grounds.[54] Although noting that it was not obliged to determine whether COPA was overly broad and vague, the court of appeals nevertheless did so in order to "touch all bases." It found that it was essential to answer "the vexing question of what it means to evaluate internet material 'as a whole,'" and that "the plain meaning of COPA's text mandates evaluation of an exhibit on the Internet in isolation, rather than in context."[55] As a result, the court concluded that COPA "impermissibly burdens a wide range of speech and exhibits otherwise protected for adults."[56] It also found that the term "minor," as used in COPA, "applies in a literal sense to an infant, a five-year-old, or a person just shy of seventeen."[57] The court held that COPA's application to internet speech for "commercial purposes" was impermissibly broad, and it found that the law's affirmative defenses failed to insulate protected speech from liability. Among other things, the court pointed out that affirmative defenses do not provide freedom from prosecution, and noted that the law "raises serious constitutional difficulties by seeking to impose on the defendant the burden of proving his speech is not unlawful."[58] It also concluded that COPA was not the least restrictive means of addressing the problem, and that voluntary use of filtering software by parents was at least as effective in sheltering children from sexually-oriented materials. Finally, the court returned to the community standards issue that the Supreme Court addressed, and concluded that the law's use of community standards "exacerbates these constitutional problems in that it further widens the spectrum of protected speech that COPA affects."[59]

## III. *Ashcroft II*: Reaffirming Basic First Amendment Principles

### A. *The Majority Opinion*

In its second pass at COPA, the Supreme Court again declined to resolve the law's constitutionality. Justice Kennedy wrote the opinion for the Court, which focused solely on "whether the Court of

[54]ACLU v. Ashcroft, 322 F.3d 240 (3d Cir. 2003).
[55]*Id.* at 253.
[56]*Id.* at 251–53.
[57]*Id.* at 254.
[58]*Id.* at 260.
[59]*Id.* at 261–66, 270.

Appeals was correct to affirm a ruling by the district court that enforcement of COPA should be enjoined because the statute likely violates the First Amendment."[60] In contrast to *Ashcroft I*, where the Court faulted the Third Circuit for focusing on a single issue (albeit one that has not been part of the district court's rationale), the *Ashcroft II* Court itself based its decision on one point—whether the government had satisfactorily proved that the law is the least restrictive means of accomplishing its purpose. Noting that the Third Circuit had construed various statutory terms and had determined that COPA was unconstitutional, the Court observed that "[n]one of those constructions of statutory terminology . . . were relied on by or necessary to the conclusions of the District Court."[61] As a consequence, the Court limited its holding to determining whether the district court's rationale for issuing a preliminary injunction was valid, and it declined "to consider the correctness of the other arguments relied on by the Court of Appeals."[62]

The decision remanded the case to the district court for a trial on the merits, and maintained the interim injunction to avoid chilling free speech through the threat of prosecutions, a threat the Court characterized as an "extraordinary harm."[63] Allowing the preliminary injunction to stand pending further factfinding and review, according to the majority, "require[s] the Government to shoulder its full constitutional burden of proof."[64] The Court was again divided, although not so badly fractured as in *Ashcroft I*. Justice Kennedy's majority opinion was joined by Justices Stevens, Souter, Thomas, and Ginsburg. Justice Stevens wrote a concurring opinion, which was joined by Justice Ginsburg. Justice Scalia filed a dissent, as did Justice Breyer, who was joined by Chief Justice Rehnquist and Justice O'Connor.

Importantly, the majority opinion reaffirmed the high level of constitutional protection that the Court has accorded the internet. This view of technology and the First Amendment fundamentally reverses the approach the Court took regarding speech transmitted

---

[60]Ashcroft v. ACLU II, 124 S. Ct. 2783, 2788 (2004).

[61]*Id.* at 2791.

[62]*Id.*

[63]*Id.* at 2794.

[64]*Id.*

via new communications technologies in the decades before *Reno v. ACLU*.[65] With other media, when they were new, the Court only grudgingly and incrementally extended First Amendment protections. This was true of broadcasting (which has yet to receive full protection),[66] cable television,[67] and, to a certain extent, telecommunications.[68] But with the debut of the internet, the Court stressed that "our cases provide no basis for qualifying the level of First Amendment scrutiny that should be applied to this medium."[69] The Court continued this trend in *Ashcroft II*, holding that the government's burden of proof was compounded by the fact that "[t]he technology of the Internet evolves at a rapid pace."[70] For that reason, and because of the risk of chilling speech in the interim, the Court erred on the side of the First Amendment and upheld the district court's injunction.

Justice Kennedy's majority opinion focused primarily on the technology of internet content filters, which the Court had taken note of in previous cases. In *Reno v. ACLU*, for example, the Court noted that "[s]ystems have been developed to help parents control the material that may be available on a home computer with Internet access."[71] The *Reno* Court was commenting only on the voluntary private use of filters in the home and found that the existence of such technologies exacerbated the CDA's constitutional problems by highlighting the law's overbreadth. In *American Library Association v. Ashcroft*,[72] on the other hand, the Court upheld conditions associated with federal subsidies that require schools and libraries to use internet content filters.[73] Although it acknowledged that filters may both over- and underblock designated websites, the Court concluded that this fact did not violate the First Amendment because libraries

---

[65]*Supra* note 4.

[66]Red Lion Broadcasting Co. v. FCC, 395 U.S. 367 (1969); FCC v. League of Women Voters of California, 468 U.S. 364 (1984).

[67]Los Angeles v. Preferred Communications, Inc., 476 U.S. 488 (1986); Turner Broadcasting System v. FCC, 512 U.S. 622, 644–46 (1994). But see United States v. Playboy Entertainment Group, Inc., 529 U.S. 803 (2000).

[68]Sable Communications of California, Inc. v. FCC, 492 U.S. 115 (1989).

[69]Reno v. ACLU, 521 U.S. 844, 870 (1997).

[70]Ashcroft v. ACLU II, 124 S. Ct. 2783, 2794 (2004).

[71]Reno, 521 U.S. at 854–55.

[72]539 U.S. 194 (2003).

[73]*Id.* at 214

are not designated as "public forums" and because adults may request that filters be disabled.[74]

The Court's renewed emphasis on internet content filters in *Ashcroft II* reveals the government's rather schizophrenic attitude toward the technology in recent cases. In *Reno*, the government had criticized filters as a limited and ineffective alternative to regulation, while in *American Library Association*, it adopted filters as its preferred solution. On the other side of the argument, opponents of the CDA first raised filters as an effective alternative to the law while opposing them as censorship in the library setting. However, the constitutional dispute was never about whether filters necessarily are "good" or "bad," but over who should decide when they must be used. When individuals choose to use content filters on their home computers it is an exercise in parenting, but when government mandates their use it is an effort to control content. In *Ashcroft II*, for example, the government's main complaint about filters was that their use was voluntary and therefore inherently less effective than a mandatory approach to the problem.[75]

In the face of the government's shifting positions on the specific issue of internet content filters, Justice Kennedy's majority opinion sought to clarify the Court's least restrictive means test in First Amendment strict scrutiny cases. The purpose of the test, according to the majority, is "to ensure that speech is restricted no further than necessary," not to consider "whether the challenged restriction has some effect in achieving Congress' goal, regardless of the restriction it imposes."[76] Accordingly, the inquiry does not take the status quo as a given and ask whether the challenged regulation adds some incremental ability to address the problem. Such an approach could be used to justify any restriction on speech, according to the Court. Instead, reviewing courts must ask "whether the challenged regulation is the least restrictive means among available, effective alternatives."[77]

---

[74]*Id.* at 205–06, 208–09.

[75]Brief for the Petitioner, Ashcroft v. ACLU II, 124 S. Ct. 2783 (2004) (No. 03-218), available at 2003 WL 22970843, at *40 ("By contrast, the court of appeals' blocking alternative is voluntary, it does not eliminate all harmful material, it has the effect of blocking material that is not harmful, and it imposes significant costs and burdens on parents.").

[76]Ashcroft v. ACLU II, 124 S. Ct. 2783, 2791 (2004).

[77]*Id.*

In this connection, the *Ashcroft II* opinion made clear that less restrictive alternatives need not be part of some government program, but instead may involve the volitional use of technology that the market makes available. That is, the First Amendment test relates to less restrictive *alternatives* and not necessarily less restrictive *regulations*. The Court specifically rejected the government's complaint that the filtering technology is voluntary, pointing out that "[t]he need for parental cooperation does not automatically disqualify a proposed less restrictive alternative."[78] It also declined to accept the government's characterization of private, market-based filters as an existing feature of the regulatory system that COPA merely supplemented. As a counterpoint to primarily private solutions, the Court also noted that other less restrictive regulations had been adopted since COPA was enacted, including a prohibition on misleading domain names and creation of a "child-friendly" internet domain.[79]

Although the majority opinion suggested that the government might legitimately *encourage* the use of content filters, it did not posit such official measures as a prerequisite to finding that technology can be an adequate alternative to regulation.[80] Indeed, the majority seemed to assume that it would not be constitutionally permissible to require the use of filtering software. Noting that software "is not a perfect solution" because it "may block some materials that are not harmful to minors and fail to catch some that are," the Court nevertheless rejected the argument "that filtering software is not an available alternative because Congress may not require it to be used."[81] It found that the inability to compel the use of blocking technology "carries little weight" in light of the fact that Congress can promote the use of filters, citing the "strong incentives" upheld

---

[78]*Id.* at 2793.

[79]*Id.* at 2790–91 (citing 18 U.S.C. § 2252B (Supp. 2004) and 47 U.S.C. § 941 (Supp. 2004)).

[80]Ashcroft II, 124 S. Ct. at 2793.

[81]*Id.* The mandatory use of internet content filters in the public library setting has been found to violate the First Amendment. Mainstream Loudoun v. Board of Trustees, 24 F. Supp. 2d 552 (E.D. Va. 1998). The Court in *American Library Association* found only that the conditioned subsidies were constitutional to the extent adult library patrons could ask that filters be disabled and access readily permitted to blocked websites. United States v. American Library Association, 539 U.S. 194, 203–09 (2003).

in *American Library Association* and alluding to other measures the government might adopt to encourage the development of filters by industry and use by parents.[82]

The *Ashcroft II* majority explained the nature of the government's burden under the "least restrictive means" test. It emphasized the importance of keeping the "starch in our constitutional standards" because content-based prohibitions "have the constant potential to be a repressive force in the lives and thoughts of a free people."[83] As a consequence, those challenging a law on First Amendment grounds are not required "to introduce, or offer to introduce, evidence that their proposed alternatives are more effective."[84] Instead, the government "has the burden to show they are less so."[85] This constitutional obligation is not discharged by showing that a proposed alternative "has some flaws"; the government must demonstrate that the alternative measures are "less effective" than the law.[86] Measuring the relative benefits of various alternatives is inherently speculative but the comparison among solutions is based on the Court's estimation of the *potential* effect of each alternative. Thus, the question posed in *Ashcroft II* is not whether most parents have in fact installed internet content filters; it is whether filters, if used, would be more or less effective than a legal prohibition.

This reading of the Court's less restrictive means analysis is supported by *United States v. Playboy Entertainment Group, Inc.,*[87] which the majority characterized as the "closest precedent on the general point."[88] In *Playboy* the Court invalidated a government regulation intended to shield children from unsolicited sexually-oriented sounds and images from "signal bleed"—imperfectly scrambled adult cable channels that can be seen in the homes of non-subscribers. Like *Ashcroft II*, the case turned on whether the government had satisfied its burden to show that the law at issue was the least restrictive means of addressing the problem. The *Playboy* Court held

---

[82]Ashcroft II, 124 S. Ct. at 2793.
[83]*Id.* at 2788, 2794.
[84]*Id.* at 2793.
[85]*Id.*
[86]*Id.*
[87]*Supra* note 67.
[88]Ashcroft II, 124 S. Ct. at 2793.

that the government failed to meet its obligation because the law in question provided a voluntary (i.e., "opt-in") blocking option that parents could use in addition to the mandatory restrictions that were challenged on First Amendment grounds.[89] It reached this conclusion despite the fact that "fewer than 0.5% of cable subscribers requested full blocking" during the time the more restrictive prohibition was enjoined and only the voluntary option was available.[90]

The *Playboy* Court noted the "uncomfortable fact" that "the public greeted [voluntary blocking] with a collective yawn" during the time it was the sole blocking alternative.[91] It reasoned, however, that the less than enthusiastic reaction could be explained as readily by the possibility that the problem it sought to address was less of a concern to parents than the government supposed, or that the voluntary option was insufficiently publicized. Either way, it was the government's burden to prove that such plausible explanations for its limited use were wrong and that voluntary blocking suffered from "technological or other limitations."[92] In addition to the less restrictive regulation, the Court also pointed to "market-based solutions" (such as programmable televisions and channel-mapping set-top boxes) that provided less restrictive alternatives.[93]

The Court's emphasis on the theoretical, as opposed to the actual effectiveness of voluntary alternatives measured by the extent of their use, is rooted in the First Amendment philosophy that the "citizen is entitled to seek out or reject certain ideas or influences without Government interference or control."[94] If an effective means of avoiding unwanted speech is readily available, direct restrictions on expression are disfavored even if people have elected not to use the less burdensome option. Justice Kennedy explained that "[t]echnology expands the capacity to choose; and it denies the potential of this revolution if we assume the Government is best positioned to make these choices for us."[95] He continued the same

[89]United States v. Playboy Entertainment Group, Inc., 529 U.S. 803, 816 (2000).
[90]*Id.*
[91]*Id.*
[92]*Id.* at 816, 818–19.
[93]*Id.* at 821.
[94]*Id.* at 818.
[95]*Id.* at 817–18.

line of reasoning in *Ashcroft II*, by focusing on the capacity of internet content filters to block unwanted speech rather than asking how often such software is used. With respect to the latter question Justice Kennedy suggested that filters could be effective if adequately promoted because "COPA presumes that parents lack the ability, not the will, to monitor what their children see."[96]

The Court listed a number of reasons why content filters in the home may be more effective than legal restrictions in shielding children from unwanted sexual images. Whereas COPA applies only to images on the World Wide Web, filters may sift information transmitted via all forms of internet communication, including email. In addition, while COPA limits material available only on U.S.-based websites, filters may block information from any source regardless of its geographic location. According to the Court, this fact alone "makes it possible that filtering software might be more effective in serving Congress' goals," especially since providers of sexually-oriented materials could avoid COPA's reach (if it ultimately were to be upheld) simply by moving their operations overseas. At the same time, the use of filters is obviously less restrictive because they impose only "selective restrictions on speech at the receiving end, not universal restrictions at the source."[97]

On this basis the majority concluded that the Third Circuit was correct in finding that the district court's grant of injunctive relief was not an abuse of discretion. It remanded the case for further findings as to the effectiveness of internet filters, observing that the district court's initial findings of fact were more than five years old. Also noting the rapid rate of development for the internet, the majority suggested "[i]t is reasonable to assume that other technological developments important to the First Amendment analysis have also occurred during that time."[98]

### B. *The Concurring Opinion*

In a brief concurrence, Justice Stevens reiterated his position from *Ashcroft I* that COPA is unconstitutional because it subjects the World

---

[96]Ashcroft v. ACLU II, 124 S. Ct. 2783, 2793 (2004).
[97]*Id.* at 2792.
[98]*Id.* at 2791, 2794.

Wide Web to the community standards of "the least tolerant communities in America."[99] This time, however, he was joined by Justice Ginsburg, who in *Ashcroft I* had joined in an opinion written by Justice Kennedy that expressed "grave doubts that COPA is consistent with the First Amendment"[100] but did not consider the community standards issue dispositive. Justice Stevens stressed the extent to which COPA's criminal penalties were excessively restrictive, concluding that criminal penalties "are, in my view, an inappropriate means to regulate the universe of materials classified as 'obscene' since 'the line between communications which "offend" and those which do not is too blurred to identify criminal conduct.'"[101] He noted that the problem of vagueness was even more problematic with "the novel and nebulous category of 'harmful to minors' speech." Justice Stevens expressed a "growing sense of unease" when the law is used "as a substitute for, or a simple backup to, adult oversight of children's viewing habits."[102] Accordingly, he concluded that COPA's constitutionality should be reviewed with "special care," particularly since "Congress might have accomplished the goal of protecting children from harmful materials by other, less drastic means."[103]

## C. The Dissents

Justice Scalia's dissent was diametrically opposed to the majority's insistence on careful constitutional review. "Nothing in the First Amendment," he wrote, requires "commercial entities which engage in 'the sordid business of pandering'" to be held to strict scrutiny.[104] Quite to the contrary, he articulated the startling proposition that COPA is lawful because "commercial pornographers" could be banned entirely without "constitutional concern."[105] He reached this conclusion despite the fact that adults have a constitutional right to

---

[99]*Id.* at 2796 (Stevens, J., concurring).

[100]Ashcroft v. ACLU I, 535 U.S. 564, 594–602 (2002) (Kennedy, J., concurring) (citations omitted).

[101]Ashcroft II, 124 S. Ct. at 2796 (Stevens, J., concurring) (quoting Smith v. United States, 431 U.S. 291, 316 (1977) (Stevens, J., dissenting)).

[102]Ashcroft II, 124 S. Ct. at 2797 (Stevens, J., concurring).

[103]*Id.* at 2796–97.

[104]*Id.* at 2797 (Scalia, J., dissenting).

[105]*Id.*

access materials considered to be "harmful to minors."[106] Justice Breyer's dissent, on the other hand, accepted the majority's premise that COPA is subject to strict scrutiny. However, joined by Chief Justice Rehnquist and Justice O'Connor, he concluded that COPA is constitutional because it imposes only a "modest" burden on protected speech and that Congress could not have achieved its objective in less restrictive ways.

A central assumption of Justice Breyer's dissent is that COPA's definitions "limit the material it regulates to material that does not enjoy First Amendment protection, namely legally obscene material, and very little more."[107] He characterized the law's "harmful to minors" standard as adopting "the *Miller* standard, virtually verbatim" and suggested that any extension of COPA beyond the category of adult obscenity would reach "only borderline cases."[108] Although the dissent acknowledged that the law's formulation of the three-part *Miller* test for obscenity was qualified by the statements that a work must appeal to the prurient interest "with respect to minors" and lack serious literary, artistic, political, or scientific value "for minors," Justice Breyer discounted these differences as insignificant. Material that appeals to the prurient interests "of adolescents or postadolescents will almost inevitably appeal to the 'prurient inter-est[s]' of some group of adults as well," he reasoned, and the same goes for serious merit: "[O]ne cannot easily imagine material that has serious literary, artistic, political or scientific value for a significant group of adults, but lacks such value for any significant group of minors."[109]

Although he acknowledged that "the obscene and the nonobscene do not come tied neatly into separate, easily distinguishable packages,"[110] Justice Breyer bolstered his claim regarding the narrowness of COPA with a series of examples drawn from the record. He asserted that works of serious merit that included "an essay about a young man's experience with masturbation and sexual shame," a discussion of "homosexuality, . . . or the consequences of prison

---

[106]See, e.g., Virginia v. American Booksellers Association, 484 U.S. 383, 384 (1988).
[107]Ashcroft II, 124 S. Ct. at 2797–98 (Breyer, J., dissenting).
[108]*Id.* at 2799, 2805.
[109]*Id.* at 2799.
[110]*Id.* at 2806.

rape," a "graphic illustration of how to use a condom," or the controversial images of photographer Robert Mapplethorpe would not be restricted by COPA.[111] He concluded that these and other examples of sexual imagery did not fall within the "limited class of borderline material," notwithstanding the "inevitable uncertainty about how to characterize close-to-obscene material."[112] Justice Breyer based this conclusion on an assumption that such materials do not pander to the prurient interest of significant groups of minors and are not without serious value for significant groups of minors. He also noted the requirement that material be evaluated "as a whole" further limits the scope of COPA.[113]

Another limitation on COPA's restrictiveness, according to Justice Breyer, is that it "does not censor the material it covers" but only requires the "providers of 'harmful to minors' material to restrict minors' access to it by verifying age."[114] Recognizing that measures necessary to implement the law would entail monetary costs and certain inconveniences, Justice Breyer described these as "a modest additional burden on adult access to legally obscene material."[115] This analysis did not contemplate the burden that a criminal conviction under COPA would entail, but the dissent rejected Justice Stevens' argument that the line between protected and unprotected speech is too "blurred" to permit the application of criminal law. Justice Breyer concluded simply that removing a "major sanction" would make the statute "less effective."[116]

The heart of Justice Breyer's opinion is a critique of the majority's analysis of the "least restrictive means" requirement. Claiming that "the Constitution does not . . . require the government to disprove the existence of magic solutions," he argued that "the presence of filtering software is not an *alternative* legislative approach to the problem of protecting children."[117] Justice Breyer explained that the Court should not compare COPA and filters against one another

---

[111]*Id.* at 2799–2800.

[112]*Id.* at 2800.

[113]*Id.* at 2799–2800.

[114]*Id.* at 2800.

[115]*Id.* at 2800–01.

[116]*Id.* at 2804.

[117]*Id.* at 2801, 2804 (emphasis in original).

and try to determine which was more effective or less restrictive. Doing nothing, he noted, is always less restrictive than doing something.[118] Instead, he combined the "least restrictive means" prong of the First Amendment analysis with his assessment of the compelling interest in protecting children and his assumption that COPA would materially advance that interest. The result was more organic: COPA is constitutional because, given the status quo (which includes filters), there remains a compelling problem to be solved and the law will help reduce the problem.[119] Justice Breyer discounted the majority's point that a substantial portion of internet pornography originates overseas by suggesting that the amount of material that nevertheless would be regulated is not "insignificant."[120]

The dissent listed four "serious inadequacies" of filtering software "that prompted Congress to pass legislation instead of relying on its voluntary use."[121] These problems include: (1) filters underblock and therefore do not solve the "child protection" problem; (2) software costs money that not every family can afford; (3) filtering depends for its effectiveness on the voluntary actions of parents; and (4) filters "lack precision" and thereby block "a great deal of material that is valuable."[122] These criticisms really boil down to two issues: Voluntary solutions place the burden on parents to take action and filters are an imprecise tool that both over- and underblocks the targeted expression.

In this regard, Justice Breyer's complaints about the inadequacies of filtering software were notable. Citing Justice Stevens' dissent in *American Library Association*, he pointed out that filters do not have the capacity to exclude a precisely defined category of images and therefore "cannot distinguish between the most obscene pictorial image and the Venus de Milo."[123] He also quoted testimony that such software "is simply incapable of discerning between constitutionally protected and unprotected speech" and noted that "[n]othing in

---

[118]*Id.* at 2802.
[119]*Id.*
[120]*Id.* at 2802–03.
[121]*Id.* at 2802.
[122]*Id.* at 2802–03.
[123]*Id.* at 2802.

the District Court record suggests the contrary."[124] Although such concerns about filtering technology may well be warranted, they rest rather uncomfortably with Justice Breyer's own observations in *American Library Association* that filters "'provide a relatively cheap and effective' means of furthering [the government's] goals."[125] While he acknowledged that filters tended to both overblock and underblock the speech targeted by the regulations, he noted that "no one has presented any clearly superior or better fitting alternatives."[126] On remand, the district court will put Justice Breyer's conclusions regarding filters to the test—both those he expressed in *American Library Association* and in *Ashcroft II*.

**IV. Where Do We Go from Here?**

Usually when a case is remanded from the Supreme Court the issues the lower court must address are more focused than in the initial round of litigation. In the very rare instance in which a case is remanded more than once, the remaining issues usually are refined further still. But that is not what happened in *Ashcroft II*. The Court remanded the case to update the factual record on technological developments relevant to its least restrictive means analysis, but none of the issues that relate to the ultimate question of COPA's constitutionality have been resolved.[127] Because the Court affirmed only the district court's decision to issue a preliminary injunction, all of the issues that go to the merits still must be decided. These include a decision on COPA's scope and whether it is overly broad, how to apply the obscenity test in the online context—including determining what constitutes the work "as a whole" and which community standard to use—and whether the law represents the least restrictive means of addressing the government's concerns in light of current technology. Some of these issues, such as the question of community standards, reopen decades-old doctrinal rifts that were put to rest only temporarily by the decision in *Miller v. California*.[128]

[124]*Id.* at 2802–03.

[125]United States v. American Library Association, 539 U.S. 194, 219 (2003) (Breyer, J., concurring).

[126]*Id.* at 219 (citation omitted).

[127]Ashcroft II, 124 S. Ct. at 2795.

[128]For a more complete discussion of this point, see Corn-Revere, *supra* note 37.

The only point about which the Court has achieved near consensus is that regulating expression on the internet in the interest of protecting children requires the government to satisfy strict First Amendment scrutiny. Justice Scalia is the sole holdout for a less rigorous standard of review, and his dissent in *Ashcroft II* harkens back to the era before *Roth v. United States*[129] where the Court made clear that "[a]ll ideas having even the slightest redeeming social importance— unorthodox ideas, controversial ideas, even ideas hateful to the prevailing climate of opinion—have the full protection of the [First Amendment] guarantees."[130] The rest of the justices may agree on which standard is appropriate, but how they apply it in this case is a product of distinctly different worldviews.

The principal doctrinal disagreement among the justices arises from their divergent conceptions of the least restrictive means analysis. Justice Kennedy's majority opinion in *Ashcroft II* conducts this analysis from the perspective of individual choice. In this view, if a particular household has the ability to use technology to screen out unwanted expression, such voluntary action may be an adequate alternative to the use of legal sanctions that apply across the board. This philosophy was articulated in *Playboy Entertainment Group* (with the same 5–4 split), where Justice Kennedy emphasized that the purpose of the First Amendment was to permit citizens "to seek out or reject certain ideas or influences without Government interference or control."[131] Technology provides the means by which individuals may make such choices, and so long as they can be made effectively, there is no need for government intervention.[132]

Justice Breyer's position represents a more collectivist approach to the least restrictive means analysis. In this view, it does not matter that any individual may take steps that effectively protect his or her household from unwanted communications. In the real world it is understood that not everyone will make such choices, so that a voluntary approach is really a "magic solution" and not a true alternative to regulation. Accordingly, the analysis downplays individual choice and assesses the adequacy of alternatives from the

[129]354 U.S. 476 (1957).

[130]*Id.* at 484.

[131]United States v. Playboy Entertainment Group, Inc., 529 U.S. 803, 818 (2000).

[132]*Id.* at 817–18.

perspective of society as a whole. After defining any existing use of filters as a status quo baseline, it asks whether the government still has a compelling interest and if the regulation at issue would provide some incremental benefit. If the answer is yes, then the regulation should be allowed.

The difference between the *Ashcroft II* majority and the dissenters is even more extreme than to say that for one side the glass is half full and for the other it is half empty. The majority position is akin to saying that nothing prevents parents from getting a glass of water if they want one. But to the dissenters, no such thing as a glass exists unless the government provides it. To the extent the "glass" in this metaphor is the existence of internet filtering software, the divergent perspectives of the justices significantly affect their respective evaluations of the technology.

For the majority, filters can be an effective alternative to the extent they can help effectuate individual choices. Justice Kennedy described filters as imposing "selective restrictions on speech at the receiving end, not universal restrictions at the source," and he noted that adults without children can access speech without restriction and that parents can turn off filters whenever they want. He added that filters do not "condemn as criminal any category of speech" and that technology can be configured to reach more of the internet, and more websites, than does the law. A significant virtue of this option, according to the majority, is that the use of filters is voluntary, not mandatory.[133]

What to the majority is a virtue is the principal vice of filtering software according to Justice Breyer. The fact that it is not required for all users means that filters cannot be considered as an alternative "legislative" approach to the problem. For the same reason, his main critique of the effectiveness of filtering software is that it fails to duplicate legal controls. That is, it does not restrict all expression that would legally be considered "harmful to minors" and blocks additional material that would not violate the law.[134] This complaint about filters is revealing, for it shows Justice Breyer's interest in filters is in evaluating their use as a proxy for law, and not as a tool that can empower users and enhance individual choice. Indeed,

[133]Ashcroft v. ACLU II, 124 S. Ct. 2783, 2792 (2004).
[134]*Id.* at 2801–02 (Breyer, J., dissenting).

parents may well want to select filtering software that blocks far more than the law would restrict because they believe that the chosen product is more tailored to their personal philosophies and values. In such a case, inconsistency with the law would make the filter more effective, not less, because it better approximates the personal preferences of the user. Justice Breyer's additional complaint that filters "cost money" fails to recognize that most major Internet Service Providers offer filtering as a feature of their service and that additional filtering software and other user empowerment options are available from numerous sources online.[135]

The communitarian versus individualist perspective permeates other issues on which the majority and dissenters disagree as well. For example, the majority's conclusion that COPA is ineffective because of the existence of foreign websites is predicated on the point of view of the individual user: Even if the law restricted most sexually-oriented websites, any particular child could readily gain access to one or more of the many thousands of offshore sites that COPA cannot reach.[136] Thus, as a practical matter, the law has little if any effect. But Justice Breyer based his conclusion regarding the positive impact of COPA on an analysis of the World Wide Web in the aggregate. He assumed that COPA's impact would be significant because "most" sexually-oriented websites may be subject to the law,[137] even if individuals may still find "harmful to minors" material.

Finally, the opposing evaluations of COPA's censorial effect are colored by the justices' views regarding the extent to which the First Amendment is intended to protect individual rights as opposed to more general societal interests. The majority's effort to keep "the starch in the standards" was explained by its awareness that content restrictions "have the constant potential to be a repressive force in the lives and thoughts of a free people."[138] As Justice Kennedy wrote in *Playboy Entertainment Group*, "[w]e cannot be influenced . . . by the perception that the regulation in question is not a major one because the speech is not very important. The history of the law of

[135]See, e.g., www.getnetwise.org.
[136]Ashcroft II, 124 S. Ct. at 2792.
[137]*Id.* at 2803 (Breyer, J., dissenting).
[138]*Id.* at 2788.

free expression is one of vindication in cases involving speech that many citizens may find shabby, offensive, or even ugly."[139] The central question for First Amendment purposes is one of individual autonomy, for any evaluation of the relative value of expression is a judgment "for the individual to make, not for the Government to decree, even with the mandate or approval of a majority."[140] Justice Breyer, on the other hand, wrote that the impact of COPA in the aggregate would be "modest" and that the burdens on speech are acceptable because only a small subset of publishers would be affected and the expression to be restricted of limited value.[141]

Apart from its strikingly different approach toward the nature of First Amendment protections, Justice Breyer's dissent is remarkable for its unusual reading of the "harmful to minors" standard. His effort to bring a heightened level of precision and to narrow the variable obscenity standard is a worthy goal but the analysis is difficult to follow. For example, Justice Breyer asserts that "harmful to minors" material is virtually indistinguishable from adult obscenity as defined in *Miller* (which relates only to patently offensive depictions of hard core sexual conduct), yet fails to reconcile this conclusion with the statutory language that provides that the lewd exhibition of a "post-pubescent female breast"[142] can violate COPA. While he acknowledges the tension between the standard for obscenity and COPA's definitions, which provide that a work must be evaluated as a whole "with respect to minors" and serious merit evaluated "for minors,"[143] his conclusion that these limiting terms have no effect is not logical.

Justice Breyer recites a litany of edgy but meritorious examples from the record (e.g., Robert Mapplethorpe photographs and discussions of prison rape) that he asserts do not even fall into the "borderline" between protected and nonprotected speech, but provides no supporting analysis for his conclusion that these examples "fall outside that class."[144] Quite to the contrary, Chief Justice Rehnquist and

---

[139]United States v. Playboy Entertainment Group, Inc., 529 U.S. 803, 826 (2000).

[140]*Id.* at 818.

[141]Ashcroft II, 124 S. Ct. at 2801 (Breyer, J., dissenting).

[142]*Id.* at 2798 (emphasis in original).

[143]*Id.* at 2799.

[144]*Id.* at 2800.

Justice O'Connor, who joined in Justice Breyer's dissent, wrote in *Reno* that "discussions about prison rape or nude art ... do not necessarily have any such [redeeming] value for minors."[145] Justice Breyer's conclusion runs contrary to experience as well, since an art gallery was prosecuted in the past for the display of Mapplethorpe photographs and other controversies have arisen with respect to controversial art.[146] The tenuous nature of this analysis is compounded by the fact that he appears to equate terms such as "commercial pornography" with "obscenity" and asserts incorrectly that material appealing to a "prurient interest" is that which "seeks a sexual response."[147] Contrary to this characterization, the Court defines "prurient interest" as relating to a shameful or morbid interest in sex.[148] Material that evokes a "normal" or "healthy" interest in sex, even among adolescents, is not considered "harmful to minors."[149] As a result, Justice Breyer's conclusion that COPA would impose only modest burdens on a narrow category of speech is dubious.

## V. Conclusion

On remand, the continuing litigation over COPA will not be confined to the narrow question of whether filtering software is effective in light of technological advances. When it reaches the merits of this constitutional challenge, the district court will be called upon to resolve the full range of First Amendment issues that were raised

---

[145]Reno v. ACLU, 521 U.S. 844, 896 (1997) (O'Connor, J., dissenting in part).

[146]See Cincinnati v. Contemporary Arts Center, 566 N.E.2d 214 (Ohio Mun. 1990). See also Brooklyn Institute of Arts & Sciences v. New York, 64 F. Supp. 2d 184 (E.D.N.Y 1999).

[147]Ashcroft II, 124 S. Ct. at 2799–2800 (Breyer, J., dissenting).

[148]Miller v. California, 413 U.S. 15, 24 (1973).

[149]E.g., American Booksellers Association, Inc. v. McAuliffe, 533 F. Supp. 50 (N.D. Ga. 1981) (statute prohibiting sale or display to minors of material containing nude figures held overbroad); Allied Artists Pictures Corporation v. Alford, 410 F. Supp. 1348 (W.D. Tenn. 1976) (ordinance prohibiting exposing juveniles to offensive language held invalid); American Booksellers Association. v. Superior Court, 129 Cal. App. 3d 197 (Cal. Ct. App. 1982) (photographs with a primary purpose of causing sexual arousal held not to be harmful to minors); Calderon v. Buffalo, 402 N.Y.S.2d 685 (N.Y. App. Div. 1978) (ordinance restricting sales to juveniles held to be overbroad); Oregon v. Frink, 653 P.2d 553 (Ore. 1982) (statute prohibiting dissemination of nudity to minors is overly broad).

when the case was first filed, including how to define community standards in the online context. Although the basic First Amendment principles upon which the case was remanded have been endorsed by a solid majority of justices, the margin of support is slim. And the differences between those in the current majority and minority camps go to the central meaning of the First Amendment. The eventual decision may have a significant effect on how the First Amendment applies to the internet, how strict scrutiny is applied, and how the obscenity and "harmful to minors" doctrines are defined. In short, the significance of this case to First Amendment law has only increased in the six years it has been in litigation. Much can happen as the case makes its way through the lower courts, including a potential change in the composition of the Supreme Court.

# Function Follows Form: *Locke v. Davey's* Unnecessary Parsing

*Susanna Dokupil*

## I. Introduction

As parents and legislators struggle to implement school choice programs around the country, they wage war on two key battle-grounds: in the court of public opinion and in real courts. In the court of public opinion, school choice is a political winner: Clear majorities of educational consumers oppose heavy-handed bureaucratic control of the educational system. In judicial courts, school choice has also won several key victories, even at the Supreme Court level, but some laws and court decisions still pose obstacles to school choice's implementation.

As the fight continues, private parochial schools remain at the center of the debate. Choice supporters argue that when the government awards public vouchers to students on the basis of need and merit, those students and their parents should have the right to use that scholarship at a religious institution. Opponents of school choice argue that the Establishment Clause of the Constitution, and the principle of church/state separation that it secures, bars those students from using taxpayer dollars to study at religiously affiliated institutions. Given government's domination of education, the argument all too often masks a naked political agenda: the perpetuation of state power over the educational marketplace.

*Locke v. Davey*[1] is a case at the heart of that debate. In the fall of 1999, Joshua Davey, a Washington State resident, enrolled at Northwest College in Kirkland, Washington, eager to train for the ministry. Thanks to his good grades in high school, and because his family met certain income requirements, he had earned a Promise Scholarship from the state of Washington. The state, however, forced

[1]124 S. Ct. 1307 (2004).

327

Davey to forego his award simply because he decided to study theology. In the state of Washington's view, using public funds to pay for theology studies violates the freedom of conscience of its taxpayers.

Washington's articulated position made little sense as the state applied it. In practice, the state excluded from its scholarship program only those students who openly declared their intent to major in a program defined by the college or university as theology. Scholarship recipients could take theology classes, redeem their awards at a college where every class is taught from a Christian perspective, or study comparative religion without any threat to their funding. Scholarship recipients just could not major in theology taught from the perspective of religious truth

Despite the disconnect between theory and practice, Washington believed its constitution required it to exclude theology majors from the Promise Scholarship. The state pointed to Article I, section 11 of its constitution, which provides, in relevant part:

> No public money or property shall be appropriated for or applied to any religious worship, exercise or instruction, or the support of any religious establishment . . .[2]

That provision, said the state, mandated Davey's exclusion from the scholarship program.

Article I, section 11 of the Washington constitution is similar to provisions found in thirty-six other state constitutions. Interpreted broadly, such provisions permit—indeed, require—states to single out religious instruction from otherwise available public benefits. In other words, they specifically disadvantage religious education options for scholarship recipients, a power in deep conflict with a core principle of nondiscrimination established by the federal Constitution. Consider the Free Exercise,[3] Establishment,[4] and Free Speech Clauses[5] of the First Amendment. The Supreme Court has held that the Free Exercise Clause prohibits the government from intentionally

---

[2] Wash. Const. art. I, § 11.
[3] U.S. Const. amend. I, cl. 1.
[4] U.S. Const. amend. I, cl. 2.
[5] U.S. Const. amend. I, cl. 3.

singling out religion for disfavor.[6] The Establishment Clause provides that government regulations may "neither advance[] nor *inhibit*[] religion."[7] In interpreting the Free Speech Clause, the Court has held that where the state funds a wide variety of speakers, it may not exclude religious speakers.[8] Together, those precedents reflect a strong "neutrality principle," which bars discriminatory efforts by states to single out, and penalize, persons who otherwise freely choose to pursue educational ends dictated by their religious beliefs.

Washington administered the Promise Scholarship in a way that discriminated against Davey because of his intent to study theology. As such, the state's scholarship program violates the First Amendment's neutrality principle. Davey's suit gave the Court an opportunity to affirm the neutrality principle it has consistently articulated over the last decade. Sadly, the Supreme Court missed that opportunity and upheld Washington's exclusion of theology majors from its scholarship program. Worse still, the Court's opinion gave short shrift to many key issues in the case, obscuring the contours of the neutrality principle. As a result, the threat of state discrimination against individual religion-based choices looms over the educational marketplace.

Part II, below, briefly discusses the facts of the *Locke* case. Part III outlines how the Washington constitution violates the federal Constitution's principle of religious neutrality. Part IV engages in a critical examination of the Court's opinion in *Locke*. Part V explains that despite the flaws in the opinion, it can be held to its facts to minimize damage to the neutrality principle.

## II. The Background of *Locke v. Davey*

### A. *The Promise Scholarship Program*

On first impression, one would think that Washington's Promise Scholarship program respects students' freedom of educational choice. After all, the program is a classic example of aid awarded on neutral criteria—a feature that typically satisfies the Establishment Clause of the federal Constitution. To be eligible, a student must

---

[6]See Church of the Lukumi Babalu Aye, Inc. v. Hialeah, 508 U.S. 520, 542–43 (1993).

[7]Lemon v. Kurtzman, 403 U.S. 602, 612 (1971) (emphasis added).

[8]Rosenberger v. Rector & Visitors of the University of Virginia, 515 U.S. 819, 829–30, 837 (1995).

- graduate in the top 15 percent of a Washington state high school graduating class;
- have a family income of no more than 135 percent of the state's median income;
- and enroll at least half time at an accredited postsecondary institution within the state.[9]

Students who meet those criteria are at liberty to use their scholarships at any accredited college or university in the state.[10]

The Promise Scholarship has one caveat: Students who pursue a degree in "theology" (as defined by the individual school) cannot receive the award.[11] This provision disqualified Joshua Davey from the program. Davey had met the academic and income requirements for the Promise Scholarship and enrolled at Northwest College, a private religious institution. He intended to enter the ministry, so he declared a double major in Pastoral Ministries and Business Management. Because Northwest College's system of course classifications considers Pastoral Ministries a major in "theology," however, Davey could not receive his scholarship.[12]

Technically, Davey could have taken advantage of some loopholes in the program that might have preserved his award while allowing him to study for the ministry. He could have enrolled half time at Northwest College to study Pastoral Ministries and then enrolled half time at another accredited college where he might have used his scholarship to study Business Management.[13] Or, he could have declared only the Business Management major at Northwest College and taken the same theology courses as electives. Still, even though he could have found a way around the restriction, the fact remains that the Promise Scholarship program placed an extra burden on him solely because of his desire to train for the ministry. Indeed,

[9]Wash. Admin. Code § 250-80-020(12) (2004).

[10]See Wash. Admin. Code § 250-80-020(13) (2004).

[11]See Wash. Admin. Code § 250-80-020(12)(g) (2004) ("'(12) 'Eligible student' means a person who: . . . (g) is not pursuing a degree in theology."). A separate statute also holds that "[n]o aid shall be awarded to any student who is pursuing a degree in theology." See Wash. Rev. Code Ann. § 28B.10.814 (West 2004).

[12]See Wash. Admin. Code § 250-80-020(12)(g) (2004).

[13]The statute allows a student to receive a Promise Scholarship if he "[e]nrolls at least half time in an eligible postsecondary institution in the state of Washington." Wash. Admin. Code § 250-80-020(12)(f) (2004).

given that the Promise Scholarship program permits students in qualifying majors to keep their scholarships while taking the exact same theology classes as electives, the program seems arbitrary: It unfairly penalizes *only* those students brash enough to announce a belief in the subject matter they study.[14]

## B. *The Blaine Amendments and the Washington Constitution*

Washington argued that the statutory provision excluding theology majors like Davey from the scholarship program was rooted in Article I, section 11 of the state's constitution:

> Religious Freedom. Absolute freedom of conscience in all matters of religious sentiment, belief, and worship, shall be guaranteed to every individual, and no one shall be molested or disturbed in person or property on account of religion; but the liberty of conscience hereby secured shall not be so construed as to excuse acts of licentiousness or justify practices inconsistent with the peace and safety of the state. No public money or property shall be appropriated for or applied to any religious worship, exercise or instruction, or the support of any religious establishment.[15]

Article I, section 11 and its kin have a dubious lineage. The provision was enacted in the late nineteenth century when an anti-immigrant movement swept the country in reaction to substantial immigration from Central, Eastern, and Southern Europe. That sentiment found political expression in the Know-Nothing Party, which supported efforts to suppress funding for the Catholic schools attended by many of these immigrant children.[16] Simultaneously, the publicly

---

[14]*Supra* note 13.

[15]Wash. Const. art. I, § 11.

[16]See generally Philip Hamburger, Separation of Church and State (2002). See also Joseph P. Viteritti, Choosing Equality: School Choice, the Constitution, and Civil Society 153 (1999) (noting that Blaine and others like him "employ[ed] constitutional language, invok[ed] patriotic images, [and] appeal[ed] to claims of individual rights. All these ploys would serve to disguise the real business that was at hand: undermining the viability of schools run by religious minorities to prop up and perpetuate a publicly supported monopoly of government-run schools.").

funded "common schools" actively promoted Protestant values,[17] and marginalized immigrant children who did not conform to a "mainstream" Protestant ethic.[18]

The atmosphere of hostility to Catholic immigrants led to the proposal of a federal constitutional amendment designed to codify the nativist's attempt to suppress Catholicism. A leading nativist, Maine Senator James Blaine, introduced the amendment in 1875. The so-called Blaine Amendment provided:

> [n]o State shall make any law respecting an establishment of religion, or prohibiting the free exercise thereof; and no money raised by taxation in any State for the support of public schools, or derived from any public fund therefor, nor any public lands devoted thereto, shall ever be under the control of any religious sect; nor shall any money so raised or lands so devoted be divided between religious sects or denominations.[19]

The amendment failed, but perhaps as many as thirty-three different territories added similar language to their state constitutions in the wake of that amendment.[20] In fact, support for the Blaine Amendment was so strong that the federal government required many territories, including Washington, to include these provisions in their state constitutions as a prerequisite for admission to the Union. The federal Enabling Act of 1889, which authorized the Washington Territory to draft a state constitution as a step toward statehood, required the Washington territorial legislature to insert a provision in its proposed constitution for maintaining—per the "Blaine

---

[17]R. Freeman Butts, The American Tradition in Religion and Education 118 (1950). Horace Mann, the founder of the common school movement, believed that religion—Protestant religion—was essential to teaching moral values. See Horace Mann, Life and Works: Annual Reports of the Secretary of the Board of Education of Massachusetts for the Years 1845–1848, at 292 (1891) ("But it will be said that this grand result in practical morals is a consummation of blessedness that can never be attained without religion, and that no community will ever be religious without a religious education.").

[18]See Eric Treene, The Grand Finale Is Just the Beginning: School Choice and the Coming Battle over Blaine Amendments 6–7 (2002), available at http://www.blaineamendments.org/scholarship/FedSocBlaineWP.html.pdf.

[19] Lloyd Jorgenson, The State and the Non-Public School, 1825–1925, at 138–39 (1987).

[20]See Treene, *supra* note 18, at 3.

Amendment"—public schools free from "sectarian" control.[21] Article I, section 11 of the Washington constitution seems to follow this model.[22]

The Supreme Court has recognized that the nativism underlying state Blaine Amendments is due a hard second look. As the plurality opinion of *Mitchell v. Helms*[23] put it,

> [H]ostility to aid to pervasively sectarian schools has a shameful pedigree that we do not hesitate to disavow . . . . Consideration of the[se] amendment[s] arose at a time of pervasive hostility to the Catholic Church and to Catholics in general, and it was an open secret that "sectarian" was code for "Catholic" . . . . This doctrine, born of bigotry, should be buried now.[24]

## C. Summary of the Locke v. Davey Litigation

Faced with the loss of his scholarship, Davey sued state officials to recover the amount of his award, plus damages, alleging that Washington had impermissibly discriminated against him in his freedom to make educational choices. He challenged the Promise Scholarship program's statutory exclusion of "theology" majors

---

[21]Enabling Act, ch. 180, § 4, 25 Stat. 676–77 (1889).

[22]Article IX, section 4 of the Washington constitution is perhaps the most direct result of this mandate, although it is not at issue in this case. It reads: "All schools maintained or supported wholly or in part by the public funds shall be forever free from sectarian control or influence." Wash. Const. art. IX, § 4.

Article I, section 11, however, follows the same tradition. To be sure, the link between the Blaine Amendment movement and Article I, section 11 of the Washington constitution (the provision at issue in *Locke*) is somewhat conjectural. Article I, section 11 does not use the code word "sectarian" and hence does not have a firm textual link to the language of the original Blaine Amendment. Nonetheless, the Washington Supreme Court has consistently interpreted Article I, section 11 to have the *effect* that a Blaine Amendment would—depriving students of aid because those students attend religious schools. See, e.g., Visser v. Nooksack Valley School Dist., 207 P.2d 198 (Wash. 1949); Witters v. Commission for the Blind, 771 P.2d 1119 (Wash.), cert. denied, 493 U.S. 850 (1989). Although the legislative history of Article I, section 11 does not conclusively prove that these provisions were adopted in response to the Blaine Amendment-inspired requirements of the 1889 Enabling Act, see Br. Amicus Curiae of Legal Historians and Law Scholars on Behalf of Petitioners Gary Locke, et al., Locke v. Davey, 124 S. Ct. 1307 (2004) (No. 02-1315), available at 2002 U.S. Briefs LEXIS 1315, at *28 (July 17, 2003); it is just as difficult to disprove the connection, given the scanty evidence available.

[23]530 U.S. 793 (2000).

[24]*Id.* at 828–29.

from participation. His challenge rested on four provisions of the U.S. Constitution: the Establishment, Free Exercise, and Free Speech Clauses of the First Amendment,[25] and the Equal Protection Clause of the Fourteenth Amendment.[26] As described in greater detail below, Davey argued that each of those provisions prevents Washington from discriminating against scholarship recipients (Article I, section 11 notwithstanding).

The district court granted summary judgment for the state of Washington. On appeal, the Ninth Circuit found for Davey, holding that the state had unconstitutionally excluded religion from an otherwise neutral program and therefore had impermissibly singled out Davey's religiously motivated educational choices for discriminatory treatment.[27] The Supreme Court reversed, Chief Justice William Rehnquist holding for all but Justices Antonin Scalia and Clarence Thomas that Washington had a permissible interest in preventing tax funds from being used to support "the ministry."[28] As described in greater detail below, Rehnquist constructed an opinion that upheld the Promise Scholarship program on the narrowest possible grounds, effectively confining *Locke* to its facts.

## III. Fundamental Principles

Davey should have prevailed easily in his suit. Washington's Promise Scholarship program plainly conflicted with the principles of religious neutrality and nondiscrimination toward religious choice that undergird the First Amendment. Part A examines the religious neutrality principle in general. Part B explains how the exclusion of theology majors from the Promise Scholarship program

---

[25]The First Amendment reads, in relevant part, "Congress shall make no law respecting an establishment of religion, or prohibiting the free exercise thereof; or abridging the freedom of speech . . . . " U.S. Const. amend. I.

[26]The Fourteenth Amendment reads, in relevant part, "All persons born or naturalized in the United States, and subject to the jurisdiction thereof, are citizens of the United States and of the State wherein they reside. No State shall make or enforce any law which shall abridge the privileges or immunities of citizens of the United States; nor shall any State deprive any person of life, liberty, or property, without due process of law; nor deny to any person within its jurisdiction the equal protection of the laws." U.S. Const. amend. XIV, § 1.

[27]See Davey v. Locke, 299 F.3d 748 (9th Cir. 2002).

[28]Locke v. Davey, 124 S. Ct. 1307, 1315 (2004).

offends the Free Exercise, Establishment, and Free Speech Clauses of the First Amendment.

*A. Neutrality Theory and Individual Choice: An Overview*

Over the past two decades, in a series of school choice and school voucher cases, the Supreme Court has enunciated a constitutional theory of religious tolerance: the neutrality principle. The Court has held that the state may award educational aid to students based on religion-neutral criteria even when those students use that aid at religious schools. Neutrality theory dates all the way back to 1947, when the Supreme Court decided the first case in which the Establishment Clause applied to the states.[29] In that case, *Everson v. Board of Education,*[30] the Court upheld a government program that reimbursed parents for the cost of transporting their children to school, whether public or parochial, because the aid went to parents and children, not to the schools.[31] This holding, and others following this reasoning, facilitate the parents' ability to exercise their Constitutional right to direct the education of their children.[32]

In the last twenty years, the Court has expanded on *Everson* to uphold a number of government-sponsored educational programs involving private educational choice.[33] *Mueller v. Allen*[34] began the recent trend by upholding a tax deduction for parents of schoolchildren for textbook expenses. Even though a majority of deductions went to parents of sectarian school students, the Court found the program constitutional because sectarian schools only received tax dollars as a result of parents' independent choices to send their children to those schools.[35]

---

[29]See Everson v. Board of Education of Ewing Township, 330 U.S. 1 (1947).

[30]*Supra* note 29.

[31]See 330 U.S. at 18.

[32]See Pierce v. Society of Sisters, 268 U.S. 510, 534–35 (1925).

[33]See, e.g., Zelman v. Simmons-Harris, 536 U.S. 639 (2002); Mitchell v. Helms, 530 U.S. 793 (2000); Agostini v. Felton, 521 U.S. 203 (1997); Rosenberger v. Rector & Visitors of the University of Virginia, 515 U.S. 819 (1995); Zobrest v. Catalina Foothills School Dist., 509 U.S. 1 (1993); Witters v. Washington Department of Services for the Blind, 474 U.S. 481 (1986); Mueller v. Allen, 463 U.S. 388 (1983).

[34]463 U.S. 388 (1983).

[35]*Id.* at 399 ("It is also true, however, that under Minnesota's arrangement public funds become available only as a result of numerous private choices of individual parents of school-age children.").

Similarly, in *Witters v. Washington Department of Services for the Blind*[36] (the case most relevant to *Locke*), the Court considered a program instituted by the state of Washington that sponsored vocational training for the visually handicapped. The petitioner, Witters, would have been eligible for aid under the terms of the program, but the state commission denied him the aid because he would have used it to study to become a minister at a Christian college.[37] The Supreme Court upheld Witters' freedom to choose under the federal Constitution because (1) the state made aid generally available, regardless of the vocational institution's status as public, private, secular, or religious; (2) the program did not surreptitiously try to fund "religion"; (3) the program offered no incentive to study at sectarian institutions; and, crucially, (4) the decision to support religion through a student's vocational training choice resulted from the choice of the student, not the state.[38] Accordingly, the Court held that Witters had a right to use his award for theological study.

In *Zobrest v. Catalina Foothills School District*,[39] the Court upheld a deaf student's right to use an interpreter provided to him under the Individuals with Disabilities Education Act at a Roman Catholic high school.[40] *Zobrest* recited the *Mueller-Witters* principle: The Constitution allows students and parents to use state aid at religious institutions when the state has awarded that aid to individual children based on neutral criteria. Similarly, *Agostini v. Felton*[41] concluded that state-funded teachers could help disadvantaged children with remedial studies at religious schools. The Court held the aid was constitutional because it "does not result in governmental indoctrination; define its recipients by reference to religion; or create an excessive entanglement [with religion]."[42] In *Mitchell v. Helms*,[43] the Court upheld a program providing state-funded computers and instructional materials to students at religious schools. The plurality

---

[36] 474 U.S. 481 (1986).
[37] *Id.* at 483–84.
[38] *Id.* at 487–88.
[39] 509 U.S. 1 (1993).
[40] *Id.* at 3.
[41] 521 U.S. 203 (1997).
[42] *Id.* at 234.
[43] 530 U.S. 793 (2000).

found the program constitutional because government aid did not result in government indoctrination and did not create any special incentive for religious education.[44] Justice O'Connor concurred, but on narrower grounds.[45]

This "neutrality principle"—the notion that individual aid recipients can use neutrally awarded aid at the school of their choice—culminated in *Zelman v. Simmons-Harris.*[46] The fruition of years of effort, *Zelman* struck a firm blow for the neutrality principle. Even though the decision was 5–4, the majority employed broad language (though narrower than the plurality's in *Mitchell*[47]) to uphold the state's funding program. Chief Justice Rehnquist, writing for the Court, stated that "where a government aid program is neutral with respect to religion, and provides assistance to a broad class of citizens who, in turn, direct government aid to religious schools wholly as a result of their own genuine and independent private choice, the program is not readily subject to challenge."[48]

Together, those cases have established that the federal Constitution does not require an otherwise neutral public benefit program to discriminate against educational choice. Yet, Article I, section 11 of the Washington constitution directs otherwise. As interpreted by the Washington Supreme Court, that provision distorts school choice programs that award aid on neutral criteria—such as household income, achievement, or need for a particular type of assistance—by preventing otherwise qualified recipients from using those awards to pursue a course of study of their choice. For example, in *Witters v. Washington Department of Services for the Blind,*[49] the United States Supreme Court unanimously held that allowing a blind man to use state vocational training aid (awarded on the basis of his disability) to attend a seminary did not violate the federal Establishment

[44]*Id.* at 809–14.
[45]*Id.* at 837–38 (O'Connor, J., concurring).
[46]536 U.S. 639 (2002).
[47]See Clint Bolick, School Choice: Sunshine Replaces the Cloud, 2001–2002 Cato Sup. Ct. Rev. 149, 160–61 (2002).
[48]Zelman, 536 U.S. at 652.
[49]474 U.S. 481 (1986).

Clause.[50] But on remand, the Washington Supreme Court held that Article I, section 11 forbids that very use.[51]

*Locke*, following *Zelman*, takes the next logical step. Although the Establishment Clause plainly allows neutrally awarded funding to go to religious institutions and courses of study as a result of the private choices of the recipients, *Locke* questions whether the Free Exercise Clause requires the state to include those choices in its funding scheme. If so, then the Free Exercise Clause would trump the contrary provisions of the Washington State constitution.[52]

Supporters of Blaine Amendments, however, argue that even though federal law allows states to provide aid to students who choose to study at religious institutions, states retain the option to forbid it. Yet, that proposition contrasts sharply with the Supreme Court's interpretation of the Free Exercise, Establishment, and Free Speech Clauses, which combine to argue that the neutrality principle is a federal constitutional *mandate*.[53]

## B. The Neutrality Principle and the Religion Clauses

The First Amendment has two clauses protecting religious freedom: the Free Exercise Clause and the Establishment Clause. The Free Exercise Clause forbids laws "prohibiting the free exercise" of religion.[54] It operates in conjunction with the Establishment Clause,

---

[50]*Id.* at 489–90.

[51]Witters v. Commission for the Blind, 771 P.2d 1119, 1120 (Wash. 1989) ("[O]ur state constitution prohibits the taxpayers from being put in the position of paying for the religious instruction of aspirants to the clergy with whose religious views they may disagree.").

[52]See U.S. Const. art. VI ("This Constitution . . . shall be the supreme Law of the Land; . . . any Thing in the Constitution or Laws of any State to the Contrary notwithstanding.").

[53]The Equal Protection Clause similarly commands neutrality toward religion. See Niemotko v. Maryland, 340 U.S. 268, 284 (1951) (Frankfurter, J., concurring) ("To allow expression of religious views by some and deny the same privilege to others merely because they or their views are unpopular, even deeply so, is a denial of equal protection of law forbidden by the Fourteenth Amendment."); Kiryas Joel Village School Dist. v. Grumet, 512 U.S. 687, 715 (1994) (O'Connor, J., concurring in part and concurring in the judgment) ("The Religion Clauses . . . and the Equal Protection Clause as applied to religion all speak with one voice on this point: Absent the most unusual circumstances, one's religion ought not to affect one's legal rights or duties or benefits.").

[54]U.S. Const. amend. I, cl. 2.

which prohibits government from making laws "respecting an establishment of religion."[55] The Court, rightly, has interpreted both provisions to ban state efforts to single out religious choice or the exercise of religious conscience for special burdens, disabilities, or exclusions.

### 1. The Free Exercise Clause

Justice Scalia's opinion for the majority in *Employment Division, Department of Human Resources of Oregon v. Smith*[56] sets forth the modern rule for evaluating claims under the Free Exercise Clause: Where a law is facially neutral and generally applicable, and that law incidentally burdens religious exercise, the state need not show a compelling interest and narrowly tailored means to justify it.[57] This principle allows the government broad latitude to enact laws that may, as a secondary or tertiary effect, burden religious exercise.

But, the principle has limits. The Supreme Court has held that if a government policy singles out a religion or a religious practice for disfavor, it violates the Free Exercise Clause. In *Church of Lukumi Babalu Aye, Inc. v. Hialeah*,[58] for example, the Court struck down a municipal ordinance that generally permitted the slaughter of animals, but placed a special prohibition on the slaughter of animals in religious rituals.[59] The Court held that the statute was designed to discriminate against the Santeria religion in which animal sacrifice plays an important ritual role.[60] Thus, the Court subjected the statute to "strict scrutiny"[61] under the Free Exercise Clause: The statute had to serve a "compelling state interest" and be "narrowly tailored" to that interest, burdening religion as little as possible.

The *Lukumi* Court focused on the fact that the ordinance, without mentioning Santeria by name, allowed all animal slaughter *except* ritual slaughter.[62] In other words, the Court looked past the plain

---

[55]U.S. Const. amend. I, cl. 1.

[56]494 U.S. 872 (1990).

[57]*Id.* at 878–79.

[58]508 U.S. 520 (1993).

[59]See *id.* at 527–28, 547.

[60]*Id.* at 531–32.

[61]*Id.* at 531–33. "A law burdening religious practice that is not neutral or not of general application must undergo the most rigorous of scrutiny." *Id.* at 546.

[62]*Id.* at 536. The ordinance made an exception for kosher slaughter. *Id.*

language of the statute to its operation to determine that it discriminated against the Santeria religion. The statute in *Locke*, by contrast,
was not even facially neutral—the discrimination against "theology"
students is written into the statute governing the program.[63] Moreover, the state interpreted the theology exclusion to cover only those
degree programs that taught religion from a perspective of ultimate
truth. Comparative religion studies, for example, qualified for state
aid. Thus, Washington first singled out "theology," then interpreted
that word even more narrowly to single out that subset of theology
majors who actually believe the material.

The most significant differences between the two cases are (1) that
in *Lukumi*, the law in question targeted one particular religion—
Santeria—while here, Washington has targeted religion generally;
and (2) in *Lukumi*, the law in question made a particular religious
exercise illegal, while here, Washington merely excluded theology
from a funding program, leaving Davey and other theology majors
free to believe or worship however they wished. But those distinctions should not compel a different result: As the *Lukumi* Court said,
"At a minimum, the protections of the Free Exercise Clause pertain
if the law at issue discriminates against some or all religious beliefs or
regulates or prohibits conduct because it is undertaken for religious
reasons . . . ."[64]

*Lukumi* stands for the proposition that the Free Exercise Clause
bars discriminatory prohibitions on religious practice. But in *McDaniel v. Paty*[65] the Court went further. The *McDaniel* Court condemned
the exclusion of clergy from generally available public benefits.[66] In
that case, the Court struck a Tennessee statute disqualifying ministers or priests from serving as delegates to the state's constitutional
convention.[67] Although the law did not prevent McDaniel from holding any religious belief or performing any religious practice per se,
the Court found that Tennessee had conditioned holding office on
the relinquishment of a right (being a minister) in violation of the

---

[63]Wash. Rev. Code Ann. § 28B.119.010(8).

[64]508 U.S. at 532 n.86.

[65]435 U.S 618 (1978).

[66]*Id.*

[67]Although thirteen of the states had adopted this English practice in the early days
of the nation's history, most of them later abandoned it. See *id.* at 622–25.

Free Exercise Clause.[68] McDaniel could not simultaneously be a minister and hold office—just as Davey could not simultaneously train for the ministry and receive his scholarship. The Supreme Court has plainly stated that such a forced trade violates the Free Exercise Clause. Together, *McDaniel* and *Lukumi* underscore that the state may not single out religion for disfavor, either by directly prohibiting a religious practice or by denying an otherwise available benefit.

### 2. The Establishment Clause

The Establishment Clause also mandates neutrality toward religion. The second prong of the classic tripartite test, articulated in *Lemon v. Kurtzman*,[69] for evaluating Establishment Clause claims requires that a law's "principal or primary effect must be one that neither advances *nor inhibits* religion. . . ."[70] Thus, discrimination in either direction violates the neutrality principle.

Washington's Promise Scholarship program improperly "inhibits" religion by placing theology studies at a disadvantage relative to secular courses of study. Consider *Witters* and *Mitchell*: In those cases, the Court upheld aid against an Establishment Clause challenge because the aid created no *incentive* to pursue religious instruction and therefore did not "advance" religion. In *Locke*, the Promise Scholarship creates a strong *dis*incentive for recipients to pursue majors the state views as insufficiently secular. Indeed, Joshua Davey himself reported that several of his classmates opted to change their majors once they discovered the state would not fund the one of their choosing.[71] If creating an *incentive* that favors religion improperly "advances" religion under the Establishment Clause, then a program that creates a *dis*incentive for certain religious choices should also unconstitutionally "inhibit" religion.

The state of Washington, by contrast, argues that Article I, section 11 merely protects "taxpayers' consciences"—that is, the hypothetical interest of some taxpayers to avoid paying for religious instruction—by preventing tax dollars from "supporting" religion.

[68]*Id.* at 626.

[69]403 U.S. 602 (1971).

[70]*Id.* at 612. Similarly, the endorsement test bars government from expressing endorsement or disapproval of religion. See, e.g., Capitol Square Review & Advisory Board v. Pinette, 515 U.S. 753, 778 (1995) (O'Connor, J., concurring).

[71]Author's telephone interview with Joshua Davey (May 21, 2004).

Whether the state should fund any student's education is an open question, but once the taxpayers choose to establish a program of general support, that program cannot exclude theology majors. Washington's argument fails for two reasons. First, the Supreme Court has held that when the state awards aid on neutral criteria, as the Promise Scholarship does, that neutrality alone is enough to protect the taxpayer conscience.[72] Second, the taxpayers' conscience is hardly at issue here. The money for the Promise Scholarship goes to *students*, not to schools or institutions. Once the state funds become a part of the student's personal funds, on the understanding that the student is free to choose his course of study, the taxpayers' interests end. The general preferences of a transitory majority should not permit the state to discriminate against some students' choices. Thus, Washington cannot reasonably argue that Article I, section 11 furthers the goals of the Establishment Clause by requiring discrimination against religion.

## C. The Free Speech Clause

Washington's Promise Scholarship program is also suspect under the Free Speech Clause of the First Amendment. The program plainly implicates speech. The Free Speech Clause addresses expressive conduct, and declaring a major is precisely that. As the Ninth Circuit explained, "Expressive conduct, creative inquiry, and the free exchange of ideas are what the educational enterprise is all about. So is pursuing a course of study of one's own choice."[73] Because choosing a major is expressive conduct, the guarantees of the Free Speech Clause apply to the Promise Scholarship program.

In addition, the way the Promise Scholarship is structured also should trigger First Amendment protection for scholarship recipients. The Supreme Court first unfurled the applicable test, "forum analysis," in *Widmar v. Vincent*.[74] In that case, the Court held that a public university's provision of facilities for student group meetings creates a "forum"—a government-sponsored enclave for speech in which the government may not disfavor any speaker's viewpoint.

---

[72]See Board of Regents v. Southworth, 529 U.S. 217, 233 (2000) (holding that neutrality toward private speech sufficed to protect the consciences of those who object to the activities funded).

[73]Davey v. Locke, 299 F.3d 748, 755 (9th Cir. 2002).

[74]454 U.S. 263 (1981).

In *Widmar*, the University of Missouri barred a religious student group from using facilities otherwise available to students, triggering a free speech challenge.[75] The Court held that the exclusion discriminated against the religious group based on the content of its speech. Thus, the restriction failed First Amendment "strict scrutiny."[76] *Widmar*'s bearing on *Locke* is clear: Assuming that the Promise Scholarship qualifies as a "forum," *Widmar* implies that Washington cannot justify discrimination against theology majors.[77]

Fourteen years after *Widmar*, the Court expanded on this forum analysis in *Rosenberger v. Rectors and Visitors of the University of Virginia.*[78] *Rosenberger* held that when a public university awards funds based on neutral criteria to a wide variety of speakers, the government creates a neutral conduit for private speech, and it cannot then selectively deny funding for certain viewpoints simply because the government does not endorse their content.[79]

Critical to the forum analysis, however, is whether the state of Washington has funded its own speech or whether it has created a forum. When the state is the speaker, it has discretion to make content-based choices, and "when the Government appropriates public funds to establish a program it is entitled to define the limits of that program."[80]

Moreover, a broad funding scheme alone does not necessarily create a forum. In *United States v. American Library Association* (hereinafter *ALA*),[81] the Supreme Court considered whether Congress could, as a condition of receiving federal funds, mandate that libraries install filters to prevent minors from viewing pornography.[82] The Court upheld the mandate. A plurality of the Court reasoned that

---

[75]*Id.* at 264.

[76]*Id.* at 269–70.

[77]Significantly, the Court also found that Missouri had no Establishment Clause interest in excluding the religious group. *Id.* at 276. By analogy, then, if choosing a major is expressive conduct protected by the First Amendment in a forum created by the state of Washington, the state also has no Establishment Clause interest in excluding theology majors.

[78]515 U.S. 819 (1995).

[79]*Id.* at 833–34.

[80]Rust v. Sullivan, 500 U.S. 173, 194 (1991).

[81]539 U.S. 194 (2003).

[82]*Id.* at 199.

internet access in public libraries is not a "forum" because the library sought to make available to the public only information it considered valuable.[83] Put simply, the public libraries in *ALA* were not a "forum" because they exercised editorial control over the materials in the library and did not intend to facilitate the speech of publishers generally. *ALA* suggests that a forum exists only where the funding is used to facilitate speech *generally*. By contrast, where the funded program exhibits a certain degree of editorial control over sponsored speech, no forum exists, and the government may pick and choose among the content of the speech it sponsors.

*Widmar, Rosenberger*, and *ALA* suggest the following rule for *Locke*: If the state of Washington provides scholarships based on neutral criteria to students enrolled in programs in which the government or an intermediary that disburses the scholarships retains no editorial control, then Washington may not selectively discriminate against some of those students because of the views they espouse.[84] Put another way, the key question is whether Washington State funded a program that facilitated a diverse set of private viewpoints, or whether the state funded a program in which the sponsorship of a particular speech—e.g., the declaration of a major—was subject to the state's discretion.

In *Locke*, the state of Washington provided scholarships to *all* graduating seniors in the state who met certain achievement and income criteria. By providing those scholarships for any course of study (except one), the state has facilitated expressive conduct. Unlike the state-funded librarians in *ALA*, who must constantly exercise judgment over the material in the public libraries, Washington retains no editorial control over the instruction that Promise Scholarship recipients receive. Nor, for that matter, does the funding program anticipate that other intermediaries who receive and disburse the funding will exercise editorial control. To the contrary, the Promise Scholarship presumes that individuals who qualify will use the funding to pursue their own diverse academic interests. The exclusion of funding for the "theology" choice is the exception that

---

[83]*Id.* at 206–07.

[84]Rosenberger v. Rector & Visitors of the University of Virginia, 515 U.S. 819, 833–34 (1995).

proves the rule. Thus, under *Rosenberger*, the Court should view this exclusion with suspicion.[85]

## IV. The Supreme Court Departs from Principle

The majority in *Locke* departed from the neutrality principle established by the Court's prior holdings. Part A summarizes the key points of the Supreme Court's argument. Part B discusses the argument's weaknesses.

### A. Summary of the Majority Opinion in Locke v. Davey

Chief Justice Rehnquist, writing for the majority, upheld the Promise Scholarship program in an opinion notably short on discussion of previous holdings but long on "historical" analysis. The Court did not deny that the program discriminated against Davey based on religion. Rather, it held that because states since the founding had prohibited the use of taxes to support clergy, Washington State could exclude theology majors from the Promise Scholarship program. "Since the founding of our country," wrote Rehnquist, "there have been popular uprisings against procuring taxpayer funds to support church leaders."[86] Moreover, the Court added, the "burden" on Davey imposed by the funding exclusion is "relatively minor"[87] and "mild[]."[88] Those reasons led the Court to reject Davey's challenges under the Free Exercise Clause.

---

[85]When the government funds its own speech, the Supreme Court has held that the government may discriminate on the basis of content without violating the First Amendment. See, e.g., Rust v. Sullivan, 500 U.S. 173, 194 (1991) (noting that "when the Government appropriates public funds to establish a program it is entitled to define the limits of that program"). That rationale, however, is not applicable to the Promise Scholarship because that program funds a broad array of expression based on neutral criteria, then creates a content-based exception. Moreover, even if one views the Promise Scholarship from the government-as-speaker rubric, the government may not create subsidies with a "coercive effect," engage in "invidious viewpoint discrimination," or infringe on other constitutional rights. See National Endowment for the Arts v. Finley, 524 U.S. 569, 587–88 (1998). Even through the government-speaker lens, the Promise Scholarship still should be unconstitutional because it coercively creates a disincentive to study theology and singles out religion for disfavor.

[86]Locke v. Davey, 124 S. Ct. 1307, 1313 (2004).

[87]*Id.* at 1315.

[88]*Id.* at 1312.

In reaching its conclusion, the Court made a number of suspect analytical choices. First, in applying the Court's previous Free Exercise Clause jurisprudence, the Court failed to address the *degree* of scrutiny that must be applied to the state's departure from the neutrality principle. Second, and closely related, the Court appears to have abandoned the "least restrictive means" test—a test that prohibits discrimination when other *non*discriminatory options are available to the state to achieve the same goal. Third, the Court selectively quotes from the historical record in a way that distorts the import of that record. Fourth, the Court fails to address in any meaningful way the free speech arguments advanced by Davey. Together, these failures combine to make for a particularly weak, at times incoherent, and unconvincing majority opinion.

## B. The Weakness of the Majority's Analysis

### 1. Level of Scrutiny and the Least Restrictive Means Test

The Court's first failure lies with the level of scrutiny applied to the state's funding classification. In *Lukumi*, the majority held that "[a] law burdening religious practice that is not neutral must undergo the most rigorous of scrutiny."[89] Because the Promise Scholarship provides that students receiving the award cannot pursue a degree in theology, the statute is not even facially neutral. Thus, one would expect the Court to apply "strict scrutiny." Yet the Court punts. It never squarely identifies the appropriate level of scrutiny for Davey's free exercise claims, much less applies the strict scrutiny mandated by *Lukumi*.

Given that the facial discrimination written into the Promise Scholarship program is impossible to ignore, the lapse is hard to explain. As Justice Scalia rightly notes in dissent, the state has exacted a penalty *solely* because of a student's chosen course of study.[90] One senses that the Court deemed the strict scrutiny test inconvenient: If the Court had applied strict scrutiny, as *Lukumi* requires, the state would have had to supply a "compelling" interest for its discrimination and would have had to prove that the state had employed the least restrictive means toward that compelling goal. As the Supreme Court has stated elsewhere, "Requiring a State to demonstrate a

[89]*Id.* at 1315–16 (Scalia, J., dissenting).
[90]*Id.* at 1316.

compelling interest and show that it has adopted the least restrictive means of achieving that interest is the most demanding test known to constitutional law."[91] The state would not have been able to meet that demand. As Scalia noted, the state's interest is "a pure philosophical preference" that "has no logical limit and can justify the singling out of religion for exclusion from public programs in virtually any context."[92]

To be sure, the majority observed in a footnote that the state's only interest was avoiding funding of the clergy, and the state would not have unlimited ability to exercise such preferences.[93] But the majority's rule has no logical end. Could Washington State exclude pastors from having library cards to ensure that public money does not sponsor sermon preparation? Could it prohibit pastors from using public highways, or redraw bus routes to avoid churches?

By dispensing with strict scrutiny, the *Locke* majority immunizes its opinion from a key objection: that less restrictive alternatives *are* available to the state to fulfill its interest in zealous protection of taxpayer conscience. Under *Lukumi's* strict scrutiny standard, the Court is supposed to employ the "least restrictive means" test, which requires the state to show that there are no means of pursuing the state goal that would not entail discrimination against religious conscience or religious choice.[94]

The Court gestured toward the least restrictive means test by arguing that the burden "imposed by the restriction on scholarships was not materially significant" and, indeed, was far "milder" than the one considered in *Lukumi* or *McDaniel*. But no one can deny that the state's discrimination created a burden in fact. As Justice Scalia notes in dissent, "[w]hen the State makes a public benefit generally available, that benefit becomes part of the baseline against which burdens on religion are measured; and when the State withholds that benefit . . . it [burdens religion] no less than if it had imposed a special tax."[95] In other words, withdrawing the scholarship is a meaningful form of discrimination.

---

[91]See, e.g., Boerne v. Flores, 521 U.S. 507, 534 (1997).

[92]Locke, 124 S. Ct. at 1318.

[93]*Id.* at 1314 n.5.

[94]See, e.g., Church of the Lukumi Babalu Aye, Inc. v. Hialeah, 508 U.S. 520, 542–43 (1993).

[95]Locke, 124 S. Ct. at 1316 (Scalia, J., dissenting).

Moreover, the burden of the discrimination *is* significant. To be sure, footnote four of the majority opinion commends the state's suggestion that Promise Scholars, to avoid being inconvenienced, may pursue secular and devotional theology degrees at two separate universities.[96] But even if this "alternative" were hypothetically possible, adding an extra university to the undergraduate experience certainly imposes an extra burden on the devotional theology student not borne by any secular student. Davey did not explore whether it actually would be possible to enroll at two schools simultaneously, but the institution nearest Northwest College, the University of Washington, was a good half-hour away.[97] Enrolling in and traveling between two colleges would certainly have had a significant and negative impact on his undergraduate experience. Moreover, some four-year colleges will not award a degree unless the last two years are spent in residency at that college. The Court's conclusion that this burden is "relatively minor" is remarkably unconvincing.[98]

But even so, the Court's speculation about the degree of burden imposed on Davey is beside the point. The strict scrutiny test does not turn on the Court's assessment of the *degree* of discrimination, but on whether *any* discrimination is permitted. Fidelity to that principle requires the Court to consider not whether the discrimination is "burdensome" but whether there are less restrictive means other than discrimination that can promote the same goal. Here the goal advanced in support of the Promise Scholarship is, ostensibly, to zealously avoid giving any state support to religion. Yet the state could have pursued that end through means that did not discriminate against Davey's religiously motivated choices, a point Justice Scalia underscored in dissent:

[96]*Id.* at 1313 n.4.

[97]Author's telephone interview with Joshua Davey (May 21, 2004).

[98]This forced choice underscores the close relationship between Davey's scholarship and *McDaniel*, discussed above. *McDaniel* stands for the proposition that the state cannot deny a minister qua minister an otherwise available benefit; the state cannot force a person to choose between a government benefit and his religious beliefs. Alarmingly, the Court—in order to evade this clear precedent—baldly asserts that the Promise Scholarship "does not require students to choose between their religious beliefs and receiving a government benefit." Locke, 124 S. Ct. at 1312–13. That statement cannot possibly be true, as scholarship recipients like Davey who feel a religious calling to major in theology must choose between that calling and their $3,000.

There are any number of ways [Washington State] could respect both its unusually sensitive concern for the conscience of the taxpayers *and* the Federal Free Exercise Clause. It could make the scholarships redeemable only at public universities (where it sets the curriculum) [and, presumably, can decline to offer degrees in devotional theology], or only for select courses of study [such as, presumably, math or science] . . . . [99]

Either option would allow the state to create a scholarship program that does not facially discriminate against religion while remaining true to its zealous respect for the taxpayers' conscience. But once the government decides to enact a broad program to facilitate educational choice, discrimination against particular students' choices is not an option.

### 2. "Play in the Joints"

Chief Justice Rehnquist, writing for the majority, begins the analysis by citing the principle that "there is room for play in the joints" between the Establishment Clause and the Free Exercise Clause.[100] Generally speaking, the Establishment Clause limits the *benefits* government can confer on religion, and the Free Exercise Clause limits the *burdens* government can place on religion. The Constitution does not limit the state to accommodating religion only as the Free Exercise Clause requires.[101] Conversely, states need not provide as much aid to religious schools or students as the Establishment Clause would permit.

Rehnquist is certainly correct that, in principle, not everything allowed by the Establishment Clause is required by the Free Exercise Clause and vice versa. But, that principle must be interpreted consistently with the parallel principle of nondiscrimination, as established by *Lukumi*, *McDaniel*, and progeny. To be sure, these cases are in tension with some early cases in the equal protection context.[102] But *Lukumi* and *McDaniel* postdate those authorities and in any event get the principle right: that if the state "neutrality" required by the

[99]Locke, 124 S. Ct. at 1317 (Scalia, J., dissenting).

[100]*Id.* at 1311 (quoting Walz v. Tax Commission, 397 U.S. 664, 669 (1970)).

[101]See, e.g., Michael W. McConnell, Religious Participation in Public Programs: Religious Freedom at a Crossroads, 59 U. Chi. L. Rev. 115, 182 (1992).

[102]See, e.g., Norwood v. Harrison, 413 U.S. 455 (1973).

Free Exercise and Establishment Clauses is to mean anything, it must mean that states cannot discriminate on the basis of religion. The state, in order to remain zealously "neutral" with respect to educational choices, may choose not to award any scholarships, award scholarships for specific disciplines (such as math or science), or award scholarships only for study at state universities. It may not, however, award scholarships on need- and merit-based criteria, then exclude an otherwise eligible student for choosing to pursue religious studies. *Locke* stands in tension with that principle. "Play in the joints" does not mean that states have flexibility to *discriminate* against students' religiously motivated educational choices.

Justice Scalia, in dissent, rightly argues as much: "A municipality hiring public contractors may not discriminate *against* blacks or *in favor of* them; it cannot discriminate a little bit each way and then plead 'play in the joints' when haled into court."[103] Here, the state could have established a program that comports with its view of separation of church and state without infringing on the rights of ministry students. What it could not do is discriminate against a religiously motivated choice in a general state aid program. The "play in the joints" principle is a poor substitute for strict scrutiny, and a weak cover for the Court's refusal to consider Washington's less restrictive alternatives. That refusal is a serious departure from the constitutional principle of nondiscrimination.

### 3. Historical Tradition

Turning from the abstract to the concrete, the Court argues that citizens have opposed taxpayer support of religion—particularly support of ministers—since the nation's founding, and the Washington constitution merely expresses that sentiment.[104] Yet the Court misunderstands the history it cites. Even though many founding-era state constitutions contain language similar to that of Article I, section 11, those provisions did not intend to authorize discrimination against ministers, much less discrimination against students' educational choices in a school choice program.

To be sure, Thomas Jefferson and James Madison believed compelled-taxpayer support for religion was an infringement on conscience. In *A Bill for Establishing Religious Freedom*, Jefferson wrote,

---

[103]*Locke*, 124 S. Ct. at 1317 (Scalia, J., dissenting).
[104]*Id.* at 1313–14.

*Function Follows Form:* Locke v. Davey's *Unnecessary Parsing*

That to compel a man to furnish contributions of money for the propagation of opinions which he disbelieves and abhors, is sinful and tyrannical; that even the forcing him to support this or that teacher of his own religious persuasion, is depriving him of the comfortable liberty of giving his contributions to the particular pastor whose morals he would make his pattern.[105]

And Madison famously stated in his *Memorial and Remonstrance Against Religious Assessments:*

Who does not see . . . that the same authority which can force a citizen to contribute three pence only of his property for the support of any one establishment, may force him to conform to any other establishment in all cases whatsoever.[106]

A number of scholars consider those statements to reflect a belief among the Founders that no taxpayer dollars should ever support religion, even as part of an otherwise neutral funding scheme. But as Douglas Laycock has noted, Jefferson's and Madison's writings decried a proposal before the Virginia legislature to single out Christian churches for a subsidy.[107] They do not entail the more extreme position—that government may discriminate against "religious" persons when making public funds available generally for citizens to use according to their own designs.

The Court cites the fact that in the late eighteenth century many states had formal provisions against using tax funds to support the ministry. Tracing the history of such prohibitions, the Court notes eight states with formal exclusions in their constitutions near the time of the founding.[108] To be sure, many of the Founders opposed affirmative state subsidies for religious training. But their opposition

---

[105]Thomas Jefferson, A Bill for Establishing Religious Freedom, 12 June 1779, in 5 The Founders' Constitution 77 (Philip B. Kurland & Ralph Lerner eds., 1987).

[106]James Madison, Memorial and Remonstrance Against Religious Assessments, 20 June 1785, in 5 The Founders' Constitution, *supra* note 105, at 82.

[107]See Douglas Laycock, The Origins of the Religion Clauses of the Constitution: "Nonpreferential" Aid to Religion: A False Claim about Original Intent, 27 Wm. & Mary L. Rev. 875, 895–99 (1986) (explaining that Jefferson, Madison, and the eighteenth-century voters supported no aid to religion over proposals for "nonpreferential" aid to all Christian churches).

[108]Locke, 124 S. Ct. at 1313–14.

did not extend to the exclusion of ministers from a broader public-aid program. Rather, they were opposed simply to special subsidies for the clergy. Unlike with the established churches of yore, the aid program in *Locke* created a broad-based scholarship awarded on neutral criteria. As Scalia observed, the majority identified no examples of states singling out ministers for exclusion from public benefits.[109] Thus, the majority builds an argument on an illusory historical foundation, devoid of a single on-point example.

### 4. Free Speech

The Court's analysis of free speech is particularly weak. Footnote three summarily addresses, in a span of two paragraphs, the arguments against the Promise Scholarship program's religious classification under the Free Speech and Equal Protection Clauses.[110] Citing *American Library Association*, the Court finds that "the Promise Scholarship Program is not a forum for speech. The purpose of the Promise Scholarship Program is to assist students from low- and middle-income families with the cost of postsecondary education, not to 'encourage a diversity of views from private speakers.'"[111] The Court offered no additional discussion as to why the Promise Scholarship was or was not a funding forum.

Without more, the reader can but speculate whether *Locke* portends a narrower interpretation of a limited public forum, or amounts simply to the refusal to find a forum in the context of college scholarships. Certainly, the effect of the Promise Scholarship is to promote a diversity of views by funding a wide variety of individuals pursuing their own personal, and therefore diverse, educational choices. Does the Court believe that in establishing the funding scheme the state must *intend* to facilitate "diverse" speech before First Amendment protections apply? Does the Court believe that the University of Virginia in *Rosenberger* had that intent? Why did the Court believe that Washington State did not have that intent as well as the desire to bring more low-income persons into higher

---

[109]*Id.* at 1317 n.1.

[110]*Id.* at 1312 n.3.

[111]*Id.* at 1312 n.2 (quoting United States v. American Library Association, 539 U.S. 194, 206 (2003)).

education? The Court's failure to distinguish funding education generally and speech specifically further obscures the definition of protected speech in a funding context.

### 5. Anti-Catholic Bigotry and Blaine Amendments

In footnote seven the Court dismisses the argument that anti-Catholic bigotry influenced the drafting of Washington's constitution.[112] Because the Court believes that Article I, section 11 does not have a clear textual connection with the original Blaine Amendment, it concludes that the Blaine Amendment question "is simply not before us."[113] *Locke,* then, does not touch the Blaine Amendments and the impact of anti-Catholic animus on their constitutionality.

At one level, the Court's observation misses the point. Even if there is no perfectly clear historical evidence that Article I, section 11 qualifies as a "Blaine" Amendment, the provision has the effect of one. The history of the Blaine Amendments—both their origins and subsequent applications by many state courts—underscores that Blaine-*like* provisions are troublesome and may well provide a cover for religious intolerance and bigotry. That reason alone suggests these provisions should be considered suspect.

Nonetheless, *Locke's* minimalist analysis has a redeeming virtue. Given the paucity of records surrounding the drafting of Washington's constitution and the inconclusive textual evidence, Article I, section 11 arguably did not present the strongest case for a challenge to state-level Blaine Amendments. A better case for such a challenge would have involved documented legislative history linking the drafting and insertion of the relevant provision to known anti-Catholic forces and a pattern of subsequent discriminatory interpretation. Such evidence could exist in a state with a well-established history of conflict between Protestants and Catholics in the late nineteenth century. The Court, by ducking the question entirely, has saved the battle over the Blaine Amendments for another day when both sides can martial better proof.

### V. A Narrow Decision, a Lost Opportunity

The majority opinion treads carefully, going no further than absolutely necessary to reach its conclusion. The Court decided the case

[112]Locke, 124 S. Ct. at 1314 n.7.
[113]*Id.*

almost entirely on the ministry-funding theory and gave no indication of a willingness to extend its holding to other categories of discrimination. By declining to find a forum within the scope of *Rosenberger*, the Court stemmed the potential for erosion of the neutrality theory. Without a forum, the Court's reasoning cannot weaken the First Amendment protections of *Rosenberger* in other factually dissimilar cases. By avoiding strict scrutiny, the Court circumnavigated the implication that a state can create a "compelling" interest that would warrant violation of the federal Constitution simply by constitutionalizing that interest under its own constitution. By dismissing the Blaine Amendment question, the Court saved that issue, too, for another day. Limiting the holding to the funding of ministerial training at the postsecondary level also steers clear of issues related to school choice at the primary and secondary levels.

Despite the Court's careful machinations, the potential for damage to future school choice cases remains. Although the Court focused on ministerial funding, it basically approved a state's power to enforce constitutional provisions that broadly restrict the flow of state dollars to "religious" persons, even when those dollars only incidentally benefit religion as a result of individual choices. Scalia's dissent perfectly highlights the flaws in the majority's reasoning. Although the opinion was narrowly drawn, the Court still tore a small, carefully edged hole in the neutrality fabric woven by years of precedents. As Scalia presciently concludes, "[h]aving accepted the justification in this case, the Court is less well equipped to fend it off in the future."[114] The damage is certainly greatest to programs like Washington's that promote choice in higher education, but school choice opponents will no doubt attempt to extend the holding to the primary and secondary levels.

Still, the narrowness of the holding offers some comfort to those who want to restrict government's power to discriminate. First, Washington's program singled out only theology majors. Viewed through one lens, that presents perhaps the clearest case of discrimination short of singling out Buddhists or asking scholarship recipients to refrain from church attendance. A broader exclusion, seemingly, would have even less chance of success. The Court, however, relied fairly heavily on the fact that Washington allowed recipients

[114]*Id.* at 1320.

to attend religious colleges and take religious classes in finding a lack of discrimination. From that vantage point, the Court might not look so favorably on using a state Blaine Amendment to exclude all religious schools or certain schools that are "too religious" from a voucher plan serving students at nonpublic schools.

Second, the Court's reliance on historical tradition offers another means of narrowing *Locke's* scope. Here, the Court identified a long history of avoiding the funding of ministers dating back to the founding. Yet no similar tradition exists of avoiding the funding of religious education of primary and secondary school students. To the contrary, America's public schools inculcated Protestant religious values for decades. Thus, based on history, *Locke's* holding should remain confined to ministerial education.

Third, the real showdown over Blaine Amendments still looms in the distance. In the meantime, school choice advocates should argue for a narrow interpretation of state constitutional provisions posing barriers to school choice. More important, they should encourage state legislatures to eliminate those barriers entirely.

The narrowness of the opinion aside, Scalia plainly has the better of the argument. Excluding would-be ministers from a broad-based scholarship program simply because they choose to pursue a religious calling burdens educational choice and liberty of religious conscience. Of the five Promise Scholarship students in *Davey's* entering class who wanted to study theology at Northwest College, at least three, and perhaps four, opted to change their major rather than forego the money.[115] Davey was the fifth. In fact, Davey ultimately changed his major to Religion and Philosophy (also considered a theology major) and went to law school instead of the seminary. Although faith remains an integral part of Davey's life and career, he may never become a church pastor.[116] Against what has the state actually protected the taxpayers? Moreover, to the person of faith, any career can be a type of religious calling, and any life path can and should involve ministry to others. Further, ministry students may not necessarily major in theology. The formulaic exclusion of theology majors does not functionally protect the taxpayer's conscience in the manner the state intended.

---

[115]Author's telephone interview with Joshua Davey (May 21, 2004).
[116]*Id.*

In reality, a strong neutrality principle *advances* the goals the state of Washington sought to promote. The current law enmeshes the state in often close calls about which programs do and do not constitute "theology." Even though the state has delegated the lion's share of that responsibility to the colleges themselves, it still must act as the final arbiter of the meaning of "theology," a term Justice Thomas rightly points out is ambiguous. With the help of individual colleges, the state must decide when reading Saint Augustine is philosophy and when it is theology. That is surely not the role the Founders had in mind for the state.

Plainly, Joshua Davey had the Promise that the state of Washington sought to promote. He has just completed his first year at the Harvard Law School, is active on one of its leading journals, and, not surprisingly, is interested in religious liberty issues.[117] Sadly, by green-lighting discrimination against Davey, the Court has given states a freer hand in enacting measures that may burden all citizens' freedom of religious choice. Fortunately, the Court has not (yet) mandated state discrimination against religiously motivated educational choices. In the wake of *Locke*, the best protection against that threat now is the vigilance—and action—of each state's citizens.

[117]*Id.*

# A Bird Called Hiibel: The Criminalization of Silence

## M. Christine Klein

"You can know the name of [a] bird in all the languages of
the world, but when you're finished, you'll know absolutely
nothing whatever about the bird . . . . So let's look at the bird
and see what it's *doing*—that's what counts."[1]

## I. Introduction

What's in a name? In *Hiibel v. Sixth Judicial District Court of Nevada*,[2]
the Supreme Court decided that there is a great deal in one, and at
the same time nothing at all. The Court held that, under the Fourth
Amendment, a person can be incarcerated for refusing to give his
name when asked for it by a police officer. The Court based its
decision on the evidentiary value of a name: If police officers don't
have access to names, reasoned the Court, they will not be able to
identify suspects and prevent crime. But that rationale is plainly in
tension with the Court's Fifth Amendment analysis in the case.
There, the Court held that disclosure of a name does not "tend to"
incriminate a person and therefore is not protected by the amendment's Self-Incrimination Clause. The two rationales contradict one
another and illustrate the incoherence of the Court's decision—a
decision that serves to dilute Fourth and Fifth Amendment protections[3] and swap clarity for complexity in the law governing search
and seizure.

---

[1]Richard P. Feynman, What Do You Care What Other People Think?, 14 (1988).

[2]124 S. Ct. 2451 (2004).

[3]First Amendment concerns arise as well, although they will not be discussed here.
Citizens engaging in legitimate political protest, door-to-door pamphleteering, and
other anonymous, constitutionally protected speech may find themselves the targets
of *Terry* stops; and if they are subjected to compulsory identification laws as well,
the chilling effect could be substantial.

## II. Factual Background

It all began on May 21, 2000, a bright, clear evening in Winnemucca, Nevada. Dudley Hiibel stood by the right-hand side of his pick-up truck, parked on a wide dirt shoulder adjoining a field on Grass Valley Road.[4] Patrol Deputy Lee Dove of the Humboldt County Sheriff's Office approached, parking behind Hiibel's truck. Unbeknownst to Hiibel, the sheriff's office had received a report that a man had been seen assaulting a woman in a GMC pick-up truck. Deputy Dove was dispatched to investigate, whereupon a witness pointed him to Hiibel's parked truck.

Exiting his vehicle, Dove informed Hiibel that he had received a report of a fight. Hiibel denied knowledge of any fight. Dove asked Hiibel if he had "any identification on [him]." Hiibel said he did not. The female occupant of the truck—Hiibel's teenage daughter—remained inside. A colloquy followed during which Dove explained that he was conducting an investigation and reiterated no fewer than eleven times his demand to "see some identification."[5] At one point, Dove indicated that it "could be a searchable situation." For his part, Hiibel steadfastly refused to produce identification, telling Dove that if there was reason to arrest him, Dove ought to just take him to jail. That led Dove to ask, "Why would I take you to jail if you haven't done anything?" Indeed, when Hiibel asked with what crime he was being charged, Dove responded, "You're not being charged with anything. I'm conducting an investigation."

Finally, after about two-and-a-half minutes, Dove threatened: "You're facing arrest here if I don't get some identification." With Hiibel still refusing to identify himself, Dove handcuffed him and placed him in the back of his patrol car. Soon thereafter, Dove pulled Hiibel's daughter—the alleged victim—from the truck. Two officers forced her to the ground and handcuffed her.

This was *not* a traffic stop. Hiibel was not operating a motor vehicle at the time of his arrest, nor was he charged with any moving violation. Moreover, although trial testimony indicated that Deputy

---

[4]This factual summary is based on the videotape of Hiibel's arrest, which can be viewed at http://papersplease.org/hiibel/video.html.

[5]Of no small relevance to the Court's decision, Deputy Dove never directly asked Hiibel his name. Rather, he demanded, and expected to be shown, a tangible form of identification.

Dove thought Hiibel might have been intoxicated, he was not arrested, charged, or tried for any alcohol-related offense. Finally, although the written citation issued to Hiibel indicated that the police had charged him initially with a domestic battery offense, Nevada dropped that charge prior to trial.[6]

Thus, the *only* conduct for which Hiibel was tried was declining to identify himself. A Humboldt County justice of the peace held in a written opinion that Hiibel's "failure to provide identification obstructed and delayed Dove as a public officer."[7] He fined Hiibel $250. Three years later, Hiibel found himself before the U.S. Supreme Court.

### III. "Stop-and-Identify" Statutes

To understand how Hiibel's arrest and conviction transpired, one must begin with Nevada's "stop-and-identify statute," which provides in relevant part:

1. Any peace officer may detain any person whom the officer encounters under circumstances which reasonably indicate that the person has committed, is committing or is about to commit a crime.

. . .

3. The officer may detain the person pursuant to this section only to ascertain his identity and the suspicious circumstances surrounding his presence abroad. *Any person so detained shall identify himself, but may not be compelled to answer any other inquiry of any peace officer.*[8]

---

[6]In addition, during trial, Deputy Dove admitted that when he arrived at the scene, he did not have probable cause to make an arrest for domestic battery. Transcript of Trial at 19, County of Humboldt v. Hiibel, In the Justice Court of Union Township in and for the County of Humbolt (No. xx-69056) (Feb. 13, 2001). The transcripts of the proceedings are available upon request from the author.

[7]Findings of Fact, Conclusions of Law at 3, County of Humboldt v. Hiibel, In the Justice Court of Union Township in and for the County of Humboldt, State of Nevada (No. xx-69056) (Gene Wambolt, Justice of the Peace). A copy is available from the author upon request.

[8]Nev. Rev. Stat. § 171.123 (2003) (emphasis added). The statute also provides that a citizen may not be detained for more than sixty minutes, and that absent arrest, the detention may not extend beyond the immediate vicinity where it was first effected. The Nevada Supreme Court has described this statute as the "Nevada codification of *Terry*." State v. Lisenbee, 13 P.3d 947, 950 (Nev. 2000) (referring to Terry v. Ohio, 392 U.S. 1 (1968)). *Terry* and its progeny are discussed *infra* Section IV.

No consequences for a detainee's failure to identify himself are set forth in the stop-and-identify statute. However, in Nevada, it is a misdemeanor to "willfully resist[], delay[] or obstruct[] a public officer in discharging or attempting to discharge any legal duty of his office . . . ."[9] Nevada accused Hiibel of "delaying" Deputy Dove, within the meaning of the misdemeanor statute, because in declining to identify himself, Hiibel ran afoul of the "stop-and-identify" statute.

The question *Hiibel* presented to the Supreme Court was whether the Nevada misdemeanor statute, by forcing a person to identify himself to a police officer under penalty of arrest, violates the Fourth and Fifth Amendments. Since many other states criminalize silence, that question has implications beyond Nevada. Moreover, many of those statutes go well beyond Nevada's, compelling the disclosure of significantly more information.[10] Illinois[11] and New York,[12] for example, allow police officers to "demand" a detainee's address and an explanation of his conduct, while Delaware[13] and Rhode Island[14] authorize police to demand a detainee's destination. Moreover, unlike the Nevada statute, most other stop-and-identify statutes do not make clear what information a detainee must provide to avoid arrest on obstruction charges. In New Hampshire, for example, the *loitering* statute provides that a police officer may request a suspect to "identify himself and give an account for his presence and conduct"—but cautions that "[f]ailure to identify or account for oneself, absent other circumstances, . . . shall not be grounds for

---

[9]Nev. Rev. Stat. § 199.280 (2003).

[10]An exception is found in the territory of Guam, where a police officer is permitted to conduct a *Terry* stop to "ascertain[] the identity of the person detained and the circumstances surrounding his presence abroad . . . ." However, "such person shall not be compelled to answer *any* inquiry of the peace officer." 8 Guam Code Ann. §§ 30.10, 30.20 (2003) (emphasis added). For an in-depth discussion of the stop-and-identify statutes of various states and localities, see M. Christine Klein & Timothy Lynch, The Tale of the Anonymous Cowboy: And What He Has to Do with Your State's *Terry* Stop Legislation, ALEC Policy Forum: A Journal for State and National Policymakers 34 (Spring 2004). See also Hiibel v. Sixth Judicial Dist. Court of Nevada, 124 S. Ct. 2451, 2456 (2004) (listing various stop-and-identify statutes).

[11]725 Ill. Comp. Stat. 5/107–14 (2004).

[12]N.Y. Crim Proc. Law § 140.50(1) (McKinney 2004).

[13]Del. Code Ann. tit. 11, § 1902 (2003).

[14]R.I. Gen. Laws § 12-7-1 (2003).

arrest."[15] Yet New Hampshire's stop-and-identify statute—which allows an officer to "demand" a detainee's "name, address, business abroad, and where he is going"—does not provide similar protections.[16] Other statutes, however, do make clear the consequences of a detainee's decision to remain silent: by prescribing arrest. In Massachusetts, for example, police officers "may examine all persons abroad whom they have reason to suspect of unlawful design, and may demand of them their business abroad and whither they are going."[17] The statute warns that "[p]ersons so suspected who do not give a satisfactory account of themselves . . . may be arrested by the police . . . ."[18]

Thus, the concern coming from *Hiibel* goes well beyond the statute before the Court. It is that the decision will be read as authorizing police officers to demand far more than a person's name. Indeed, at oral argument in *Hiibel*, counsel for the United States, arguing as amicus curiae on behalf of the Sixth Judicial District, was asked "[W]hy do you stop at the name?" He responded: "I'm not sure that there's a limitation related to answers to questions."[19] In all likelihood, therefore, it is only a matter of time before one of the many state statutes that provide broader authority for police to compel responses winds its way to the Supreme Court.

## IV. Fourth Amendment Background

The Fourth Amendment provides: "The right of the people to be secure in their persons, houses, papers, and effects, against unreasonable searches and seizures, shall not be violated, and no Warrants shall issue, but upon probable cause . . . ."[20] In the landmark case of *Terry v. Ohio*,[21] the Supreme Court recognized that "[t]his inestimable right of personal security belongs as much to the citizen on the

[15]N.H. Rev. Stat. Ann. § 644:6 (2003).
[16]N.H. Rev. Stat. Ann. § 594:2 (2003).
[17]Mass Gen. Laws ch. 41, § 98 (2003).
[18]*Id.*
[19]Transcript of Oral Argument, Hiibel v. Sixth Judicial Dist. Court of Nevada, 124 S. Ct. 2451 (2004) (No. 03-5554) (argument of Sri Srinivasan), available at 2004 WL 720099, at *55.
[20]U.S. Const. amend. IV. The Fourth Amendment is applicable to the states through the Fourteenth Amendment. Mapp v. Ohio, 367 U.S. 643 (1961).
[21]392 U.S. 1 (1968).

streets of our cities as to the homeowner closeted in his study . . . ."[22] Indeed, "whenever a police officer accosts an individual and restrains his freedom to walk away, he has 'seized' that person."[23]

*A. The "Terry Stop": Terry's Limited Exception to "Probable Cause"*

Until 1968, courts had ruled that it was necessary, absolutely, that police have probable cause before seizing a person.[24] As the Court explained in *Dunaway v. New York*,[25] "The standard of probable cause . . . represented the accumulated wisdom of precedent and experience as to the minimum justification necessary to make the kind of intrusion involved in an arrest 'reasonable' under the Fourth Amendment."[26] But in *Terry*, the Supreme Court "for the first time recognized an exception to the requirement that Fourth Amendment seizures of persons must be based on probable cause."[27] In doing so, the Court carved out a lesser standard for investigative seizures that amount to less than a formal arrest: It held that a police officer who has "reasonable suspicion" that criminal activity "may be afoot" may briefly detain the suspect.[28] *Terry* was a watershed moment in constitutional law. Indeed, the Court would later acknowledge that "[h]ostility to seizures based on mere suspicion was a prime motivation for the adoption of the Fourth Amendment . . . ."[29]

---

[22]*Id.* at 8–9.

[23]*Id.* at 16. See also Davis v. Mississippi, 394 U.S. 721, 726–27 (1969) ("Nothing is more clear than that the Fourth Amendment was meant to prevent wholesale intrusions upon the personal security of our citizenry, whether these intrusions be termed 'arrests' or 'investigatory detentions.'").

[24]Dunaway v. New York, 442 U.S. 200, 208 (1979).

[25]See *supra* note 24.

[26]442 U.S. at 208. See also Kolender v. Lawson, 461 U.S. 352, 363 (1983) (Brennan, J., concurring) ("It has long been settled that the Fourth Amendment prohibits the seizure and detention or search of an individual's person unless there is probable cause to believe that he has committed a crime, except under certain conditions strictly defined by the legitimate requirements of law enforcement and by the limited extent of the resulting intrusion on individual liberty and privacy."); Terry v. Ohio, 392 U.S. 1, 38 (1968) (Douglas, J., dissenting) (arguing that "infringement on personal liberty of any 'seizure' of a person can only be 'reasonable' under the Fourth Amendment if we require the police to possess 'probable cause' before they seize him").

[27]Dunaway, 442 U.S. at 208–09.

[28]Terry, 392 U.S. at 30.

[29]Dunaway, 442 U.S. at 213.

The *Terry* Court authorized stops based on "reasonable suspicion" in order to further a state interest in "effective crime prevention and detection."[30] As it explained, that interest "underlies the recognition that a police officer may in appropriate circumstances and in an appropriate manner approach a person for purposes of investigating possibly criminal behavior even though there is no probable cause to make an arrest."[31] The Court emphasized that it did "not retreat from [its] holdings that the police must, whenever practicable, obtain advance judicial approval of searches and seizures through the warrant procedure."[32] But the Court also recognized that it was "deal[-ing] [with] necessarily swift action predicated upon the on-the-spot observations of the officer on the beat—which historically has not been, and as a practical matter could not be, subjected to the warrant procedure."[33]

Because *Terry* created an exception to the long-standing general rule of probable cause, the Court has been "careful to maintain" its "narrow scope."[34] The central inquiry, when evaluating the constitutionality of a *Terry* stop, is "whether the officer's action was justified at its inception, and whether it was reasonably related in scope to the circumstances which justified the interference in the first place."[35] The Court subsequently has explained that "the investigative methods employed should be the least intrusive means reasonably available to verify or dispel the officer's suspicion in a short period of time."[36]

---

[30]Terry, 392 U.S. at 22.

[31]*Id.*

[32]*Id.* at 20.

[33]*Id.* Justice Douglas vehemently criticized this conclusion, arguing that "[t]o give power to the police to seize a person on some grounds different from or less than 'probable cause' would be handing them more authority than could be exercised by a magistrate in issuing a warrant to seize a person," thus "tak[ing] a long step down the totalitarian path." *Id.* at 36 n.3, 38 (Douglas, J., dissenting). Although rejected by the other eight members of the *Terry* Court, Justice Douglas's analysis is helpful to understanding the significance of the inroads made by *Terry* on the Fourth Amendment's historic protections.

[34]Ybarra v. Illinois, 444 U.S. 85, 93 (1979).

[35]Terry, 392 U.S. at 20.

[36]Florida v. Royer, 460 U.S. 491, 500 (1983).

## B. Scope of a Terry Stop: The Weapons Frisk

When Deputy Dove approached Hiibel, he was effecting what is known as a "*Terry* stop"—that is, Dove stopped Hiibel based on a "reasonable suspicion" that Hiibel was up to no good. Hiibel conceded that Dove's initial approach to investigate was appropriate and did not itself violate the Fourth Amendment. But the Fourth Amendment "proceeds as much by limitations upon the scope of governmental action as by imposing preconditions upon its initiation."[37] It was to the "scope" of Deputy Dove's investigation that Hiibel objected.

The main focus in *Terry* (as in *Hiibel*) is not on "whether the officer's action was justified at its inception,"[38] but rather on the limits that must be imposed on a valid seizure conducted under "reasonable suspicion." The officer in *Terry* had conducted a "pat-down" frisk for weapons during the course of his investigation; the question the Court faced, therefore, was whether it was constitutionally permissible for him to do so. In holding that the pat-down was permitted, the Court explained that it was concerned with "*more* than the governmental interest in investigating crime": It was concerned also with the "immediate interest of the police officer in taking steps to assure himself that the person with whom he is dealing is not armed with a weapon that could unexpectedly and fatally be used against him."[39] Accordingly, the Court held that "[t]here must be a *narrowly drawn* authority to permit a reasonable search for weapons for the protection of the police officer, where he has *reason to believe that he is dealing with an armed and dangerous individual*,"[40] regardless of whether he has probable cause to arrest the individual for a crime. The Court added, "[t]he officer need not be absolutely certain that the individual is armed; the issue is whether a reasonably prudent man in the circumstances would be warranted in the belief that his safety or that of others was in danger."[41]

But the Court placed limits on the power to frisk. It cautioned that a "search for weapons in the absence of probable cause to

---

[37]*Terry*, 392 U.S. at 28–29.

[38]*Id.* at 20.

[39]*Id.* at 23.

[40]*Id.* at 27 (emphasis added).

[41]*Id.*

arrest . . . must, like any other search, be *strictly circumscribed* by the exigencies which justify its initiation," and must therefore be "limited to that which is necessary for the discovery of weapons which might be used to harm the officer or others nearby. . . ."[42] Moreover, said the Court, "[t]he *sole* justification of the search . . . is the protection of the police officer and others nearby, and it must therefore be confined in scope to an intrusion reasonably designed to discover guns, knives, clubs, or other hidden instruments for the assault of the police officer."[43] In determining that the specific search at issue in *Terry* was constitutionally valid, the Court observed that the police officer "confined his search strictly to what was minimally necessary to learn whether the men were armed and to disarm them once he discovered the weapons. He *did not conduct a general exploratory search* for whatever evidence of criminal activity he might find."[44]

The Court has emphasized subsequently that "[n]othing in *Terry* can be understood to allow a generalized 'cursory search for weapons' or, indeed, any search whatever for anything but weapons."[45] And the Court "invariably" has recognized that "a reasonable belief that [a suspect is] armed and presently dangerous" is a "predicate to a patdown of a person for weapons."[46] Thus, not every person subjected to a *Terry* stop will also be subjected to a *Terry* frisk.

Those limits, placed by the Court on a *Terry* stop, are absent from the Nevada scheme Hiibel challenged. In Nevada, every person subjected to a *Terry* stop *will* be compelled, under threat of arrest, to produce identification; and the officer need not have any "reason to believe that he is dealing with [a] . . . dangerous individual."[47] Thus, in authorizing police to search for identification even in the absence of a safety concern, the Nevada stop-and-search scheme departs from the principle, articulated in the *Terry* line of cases, that a person must be considered armed and dangerous before he may be subject to a search during a *Terry* stop. That departure indicates

---

[42]*Id.* at 25–26 (emphasis added).
[43]*Id.* at 29 (emphasis added).
[44]*Id.* at 30 (emphasis added).
[45]Ybarra v. Illinois, 444 U.S. 85, 93–94 (1979).
[46]*Id.* at 92–93.
[47]Terry, 392 U.S. at 27.

the flaw in the analogy between a *Terry* frisk and a *Hiibel* identification demand—drawn, for example, by the Nevada Supreme Court, which reasoned that "[r]equiring identification is far less intrusive than conducting a pat-down search of one's physical person."[48] The issue is not whether compelling an individual to identify himself is more or less intrusive than a weapons frisk; rather, it is whether there is a *justification* for the demand, as there was for the frisk. Just as a weapons frisk must be justified by "more than the governmental interest in investigating crime,"[49] so must a demand for identification. The exigencies that justify a weapons search simply do not arise in the case of compelled identification.

Moreover, the scope of a request for identification is actually greater than the scope of a *Terry* weapons search. While the frisk is a physical intrusion, it is brief in time and limited in scope. Although a demand for identification may be limited in time, it is far more extensive in scope, for at least two reasons.

First, as the dissenting justices of the Nevada Supreme Court noted, during a *Terry* stop, "an officer's authority to search is limited to a pat-down to detect weapons"; an officer "may not detect a wallet and remove it for search."[50] But when identification is compelled, this limitation is circumvented—"the officer can now, figuratively, reach in, grab the wallet and pull out the detainee's identification."[51] The detainee either must himself furnish identification or, if he refuses to do so, must submit to an arrest under the stop-and-identify and obstruction statutes, pursuant to which the police will conduct a search and acquire his identification.[52]

Second, unlike a frisk, which is limited in duration and simply informs the officer whether or not the suspect is armed, obtaining a person's identity is the tip of the iceberg concerning what an officer

---

[48]Hiibel v. Sixth Judicial Dist. Court of Nevada, 59 P.3d 1201, 1206 (Nev. 2002).

[49]Terry, 392 U.S. at 23.

[50]Hiibel, 59 P.3d at 1209 (Agosti, J., dissenting).

[51]*Id.*

[52]Moreover, as one commentator has noted: "If arresting officers are permitted to 'bootstrap' themselves into probable cause, then the intrusion necessitated by a compelled response to a request for identification arguably would be intolerably greater than the intrusion of a brief frisk allowed" by *Terry*. See Alan D. Hallock, Note: Stop-and-Identify Statutes After Kolender v. Lawson: Exploring the Fourth and Fifth Amendment Issues, 69 Iowa L. Rev. 1057, 1072 (1984).

can then discover. Over thirty years ago, Justice Harlan recognized the "dynamic growth of techniques for gathering and using information culled from individuals by force of criminal sanctions."[53] A decade later, a court of appeals explained that the identification of a "suspicious" individual "grants the police unfettered discretion to initiate or continue investigation of the person long after the detention has ended."[54] In this age of multiple, cross-linked, computerized databases, disclosure of one's name is guaranteed to unleash a torrent of additional information.[55] In his dissent in *Hiibel*, Justice Stevens made this very point, observing that a name "can provide the key to a broad array of information about the person, particularly in the hands of a police officer with access to a range of law enforcement databases. And that information, in turn, can be tremendously useful in a criminal prosecution."[56]

## C. Post-Terry *Analysis of Demands for Identification*

Prior to *Hiibel*, the Court had not directly ruled whether identification can be compelled during a *Terry* stop. But the Court had provided enough signals such that the only other federal court to review the Nevada stop-and-identify statute held that the right not to identify oneself is "so clearly established" that the Nevada stop-and-identify and obstruction statutes did not furnish a reasonable basis for an arrest.[57]

The first signal is found in *Terry* itself, where Justice White wrote a separate concurring opinion to address a matter "put[] . . . aside"

[53]California v. Byers, 402 U.S. 424, 453–54 (1971) (Harlan, J., concurring).

[54]Lawson v. Kolender, 658 F.2d 1362, 1368 (9th Cir. 1981), aff'd, 461 U.S. 352 (1983).

[55]For an extensive discussion of the constitutional implications of readily accessible public and private databases, see Brief of Amici Curiae Electronic Privacy Information Center (EPIC) and Legal Scholars and Technical Experts, Hiibel v. Sixth Judicial Dist. Court of Nevada, 124 S. Ct. 2451 (2004) (No. 03-5554), available at 2004 WL 22970604 and http://www.abditum.com/hiibel/pdf/epic_amicus.pdf.

[56]Hiibel v. Sixth Judicial Dist. Court of Nevada, 124 S. Ct. 2451, 2464 (2004) (Stevens, J., dissenting).

[57]Carey v. Nevada Gaming Control Board, 279 F.3d 873, 881 (9th Cir. 2002) (Section 1983 case). Although no other federal court had reviewed the Nevada statute specifically, an inter-circuit split existed as to the constitutionality of stop-and-identify statutes generally. See, e.g., Oliver v. Woods, 209 F.3d 1179 (10th Cir. 2000) (holding that a similar Utah statute was constitutionally sound).

by the majority, the "matter of interrogation during an investigative stop."[58] He explained:

> There is nothing in the Constitution which prevents a policeman from addressing questions to anyone on the streets. Absent special circumstances, the person approached may not be detained or frisked but may refuse to cooperate and go on his way. However, given the proper circumstances, such as those in this case, it seems to me the person may be briefly detained against his will while pertinent questions are directed to him. *Of course, the person stopped is not obliged to answer, answers may not be compelled, and refusal to answer furnishes no basis for an arrest,* although it may alert the officer to the need for continued observation.[59]

Less than a year after deciding *Terry*, the Court decided *Davis v. Mississippi*,[60] a Fourth Amendment case involving a teenager taken into custody on less than probable cause and forced to undergo fingerprinting. In *Davis*, the Court referred to "the settled principle that while the police have the right to request citizens to answer voluntarily questions concerning unsolved crimes they have no right to compel them to answer."[61] Similarly, in *Dunaway v. New York*, decided a decade later, the Court emphasized the "narrow scope" of *Terry*, quoting favorably Justice White's *Terry* concurrence that a detainee on reasonable suspicion cannot be compelled to answer questions.[62]

The Court had its first opportunity to decide whether a person could be convicted for refusing to identify himself in *Brown v. Texas*.[63] In *Brown*, as in *Hiibel*, police arrested, charged, and convicted a detainee based on nothing more than the detainee's refusal to identify himself upon demand. The Court, however, avoided reaching the question whether refusal to identify oneself is a ground for arrest.

---

[58]392 U.S. at 34 (White, J., concurring).

[59]*Id.* (White, J., concurring) (emphasis added).

[60]394 U.S. 721 (1969).

[61]*Id.* at 726 n.6.

[62]Dunaway v. New York, 442 U.S. 200, 210 & n.12 (1979).

[63]443 U.S. 47 (1979).

Instead, it reversed the conviction because the seizure was effected on less than "reasonable suspicion."[64]

On the same day *Brown* was decided, the Court decided *Michigan v. DeFillippo*.[65] Police stopped Gary DeFillippo pursuant to a city ordinance similar to the one at issue in *Hiibel*; the ordinance authorized police to execute *Terry* stops and made it "unlawful" for a detainee to "refuse to identify himself, and to produce verifiable documents or other evidence of such identification."[66] A search incident to DeFillippo's arrest revealed that he was carrying illegal drugs. He was then charged with a drug offense, but not for violation of the stop-and-identify statute.[67]

The state appellate court found that the city ordinance violated the Fourth Amendment and therefore ruled that the arrest and the subsequent search were invalid.[68] The Supreme Court reversed, on the ground that the "invalidity of the Detroit ordinance . . . does not undermine the validity of the arrest made for violation of that ordinance . . . ."[69] The Court, however, avoided ruling on the constitutionality of the ordinance itself. The Court merely "[a]ssum[ed], *arguendo*, that a person may not constitutionally be required to answer questions put by an officer in some circumstances."[70] But the Court did suggest that the ordinance was not "so grossly and flagrantly unconstitutional that any person of reasonable prudence would be bound to see its flaws."[71]

Justice Brennan, joined by Justices Marshall and Stevens, vigorously dissented, directly addressing the issue of constitutionality that the majority had avoided. Although writing in dissent, Justice Brennan did not contradict the majority on this point but rather elaborated on the assumption the majority had made. Relying in part on Justice White's *Terry* concurrence as well as *Davis v. Mississippi*, Justice Brennan explained that the "Court's assumption that

[64]*Id.* at 53.
[65]443 U.S. 31 (1979).
[66]*Id.* at 33 & n.1.
[67]*Id.* at 34.
[68]*Id.* at 34–35; see also People v. DeFillippo, 262 N.W.2d 921 (Mich. Ct. App. 1977).
[69]DeFillippo, 443 U.S. at 40.
[70]*Id.* at 37.
[71]*Id.* at 38.

the Detroit ordinance is unconstitutional is well founded; the ordinance is indeed unconstitutional and patently so," and reasoned that "[i]n the context of criminal investigation, the privacy interest in remaining silent simply cannot be overcome at the whim of any suspicious police officer."[72]

He noted that the ordinance,

> by means of a transparent expedient—making the constitutionally protected refusal to answer itself a substantive offense—sanctions circumvention by the police of *the Court's holding* that refusal to answer police inquiries during a *Terry* stop furnishes no basis for a full-scale search and seizure. Clearly, this is a sheer piece of legislative legerdemain not to be countenanced.[73]

Noting the intersection between the Fourth and Fifth Amendments, Justice Brennan further observed:

> [I]ndividuals who chose to remain silent would be forced to relinquish their right not to be searched ... while those who chose not to be searched would be forced to forgo their constitutional right to remain silent. This Hobson's choice can be avoided only by invalidating such police intrusions whether or not authorized by ordinance and *holding fast to the rule of Terry and its progeny: that police acting on less than probable cause may not search, compel answers, or search those who refuse to answer their questions.*[74]

Clearly, it was the perception of three justices that the issue had already been decided.

The matter was addressed a few years later in *Florida v. Royer*,[75] where the Court observed:

> [L]aw enforcement officers do not violate the Fourth Amendment by merely ... asking [a person on the street] if he is willing to answer some questions .... The person approached, however, need not answer any question put to him; indeed, he may decline to listen to the questions at

---

[72]*Id.* at 43 (Brennan, J., dissenting).

[73]*Id.* at 45 (Brennan, J., dissenting) (emphasis added).

[74]*Id.* at 46 (Brennan, J., dissenting) (emphasis added).

[75]460 U.S. 491 (1983).

all and may go on his way. He may not be detained even momentarily without reasonable, objective grounds for doing so; and *his refusal to listen or answer does not, without more, furnish those grounds.*[76]

The same year, the issue of compelled identification arose more directly in *Kolender v. Lawson.*[77] A California statute required "persons who loiter or wander on the streets to provide a 'credible and reliable' identification and to account for their presence when requested by a peace officer" pursuant to a valid *Terry* stop.[78] The Court declined to address Fourth and Fifth Amendment issues,[79] instead holding that the statute was "unconstitutionally vague within the meaning of the Due Process Clause of the Fourteenth Amendment" because it "fail[ed] to clarify what is contemplated by the requirement that a suspect provide a 'credible and reliable' identification."[80]

Although the majority declined to reach Fourth Amendment concerns, Justice Brennan did so at some length in his concurrence. He explained that

> probable cause, and nothing less, represents the point at which the interests of law enforcement justify subjecting an individual to any significant intrusion beyond that sanctioned in *Terry*, including either arrest *or the need to answer questions that the individual does not want to answer* in order to avoid arrest or end a detention.[81]

Accordingly, he reasoned that "[m]erely to facilitate the general law enforcement objectives of investigating and preventing unspecified crimes, States may not authorize the arrest and criminal prosecution of an individual for failing to produce identification or further information on demand by a police officer."[82] He added that because the "scope of seizures of the person on less than probable cause that *Terry* permits is strictly circumscribed," the suspect "must be free

---

[76]*Id.* at 497–98 (citations omitted) (emphasis added).

[77]461 U.S. 352 (1983).

[78]*Id.* at 353.

[79]*Id.* at 361 n.10.

[80]*Id.* at 353–54.

[81]*Id.* at 369 n.7 (Brennan, J., concurring) (emphasis added).

[82]*Id.* at 362 (Brennan, J., concurring).

to leave after a short time and to decline to answer the questions put to him."[83] Justice Brennan further noted that police officers "may ask their questions in a way calculated to obtain an answer. But they may not *compel* an answer . . . ."[84]

A year later, *Berkemer v. McCarty*[85] addressed the application of *Miranda*[86] protections to a traffic stop. The Court held that roadside questioning of a motorist detained pursuant to a routine traffic stop does not constitute "custodial interrogation" for purposes of *Miranda*.[87] In reaching this conclusion, the Court observed that "the usual traffic stop is more analogous to a so-called 'Terry stop' than to a formal arrest."[88] It went on to discuss *Terry* stops, observing that

> [an] officer may ask the detainee a moderate number of questions to determine his identity and to try to obtain information confirming or dispelling the officer's suspicions. *But the detainee is not obliged to respond.* And, unless the detainee's answers provide the officer with probable cause to arrest him, he must then be released.[89]

The Court did not address this topic again for twenty years, when it decided *Hiibel*. In *Hiibel*, the Court made an about-face and rejected its "lengthy history" of "concurring opinions, of references, and of clear explicit statements."[90]

## V. Fifth Amendment Background

The Fifth Amendment's Self-Incrimination Clause provides that "[n]o person . . . shall be compelled in any criminal case to be a witness against himself . . . ."[91] The privilege against self-incrimination is founded on (1) an "unwillingness to subject those suspected

[83]*Id.* at 364–65 (Brennan, J., concurring).

[84]*Id.* at 366.

[85]468 U.S. 420 (1984).

[86]Miranda v. Arizona, 384 U.S. 436 (1966).

[87]468 U.S. at 442.

[88]*Id.* at 439 (citation omitted).

[89]*Id.* at 439–40 (emphasis added) (footnotes omitted).

[90]Hiibel v. Sixth Judicial Dist. Court of Nevada, 124 S. Ct. 2451, 2465 (2004) (Breyer, J., dissenting). The Court's opinion in *Hiibel* is analyzed *infra* Section VI.

[91]U.S. Const. amend. V. The Fifth Amendment privilege against self-incrimination is applicable to the states through the Fourteen Amendment. Malloy v. Hogan, 378 U.S. 1 (1964).

of crime to the cruel trilemma of self-accusation, perjury or contempt," and on (2) "respect for the inviolability of the human personality and of the right of each individual 'to a private enclave where he may lead a private life.'"[92] The Court has directed that the Self-Incrimination Clause "must be accorded liberal construction in favor of the right it was intended to secure."[93]

The Fifth Amendment privilege protects a suspect from "being compelled to . . . provide the State with evidence of a testimonial or communicative nature."[94] A communication is "testimonial" when it "explicitly or implicitly, relate[s] a factual assertion or disclose[s] information."[95] The Court has recognized that "[t]here are very few instances in which a verbal statement . . . will not convey information or assert facts. The vast majority of verbal statements thus will be testimonial and, to that extent at least, fall within the privilege."[96] On the other hand, certain acts—such as furnishing an incriminating blood sample[97] or handwriting exemplar[98]—may be compelled because they are not "testimonial."[99]

Testimonial statements fall within the scope of the Self-Incrimination Clause when those statements are likely to be used in a prosecution, or lead to evidence that may be used in a prosecution.[100] The privilege "not only extends to answers that would in themselves support a conviction under a . . . criminal statute but likewise embraces those which would furnish a link in the chain of evidence

---

[92]Doe v. United States, 487 U.S. 201, 212 (1988) (quoting Murphy v. Waterfront Commission of New York Harbor, 378 U.S. 52 (1964)).

[93]Hoffman v. United States, 341 U.S. 479, 486 (1951).

[94]Pennsylvania v. Muniz, 496 U.S. 582, 589 (1990) (quoting Schmerber v. California, 384 U.S. 757, 761 (1966)).

[95]496 U.S. at 589 (quoting Doe, 487 U.S. at 210).

[96]Doe, 487 U.S. at 213–14. In that case, the Court held that a suspect could be compelled to sign a consent form waiving a privacy interest in foreign bank accounts that might exist, although he was not required to state whether such accounts actually existed. The Court determined that the suspect was making a "nonfactual statement." *Id.* at 213 n.11.

[97]Schmerber v. California, 384 U.S. 757 (1966).

[98]Gilbert v. California, 388 U.S. 263 (1967).

[99]A rule of thumb for deciding whether a communication is testimonial is to ask whether a lie could be told. George Fisher, Evidence 800 (2002). A suspect can lie about his name, but a fingerprint cannot lie.

[100]Kastigar v. United States, 406 U.S. 441, 445 (1972).

needed to prosecute . . . ."[101] Accordingly, the Fifth Amendment's protection applies whenever compelled statements "lead to the discovery of incriminating evidence even though the statements themselves are not incriminating and are not introduced into evidence."[102] A name is plainly testimonial in this sense. A name "discloses information or asserts facts." A name is a key to discovery of information that could lead to incriminating information or information that may be used in a prosecution. On the basis of these concerns, five out of nine justices concluded in *California v. Byers*[103] that stating one's name can be incriminatory.[104] Similarly, in *DeFillippo*, Justice Brennan, joined by Justices Marshall and Stevens, concluded that in a *Terry*-stop scenario, detainees "have . . . a right to remain silent, and, as a corollary, a right not to be searched if they choose to remain silent."[105] And in *Kolender v. Lawson*,[106] analyzing a hypothetical situation in which a jogger not carrying identification might be required to answer questions concerning the route that he followed to arrive at the place he was detained, the Court made this observation:

> To the extent that [the California statute] criminalizes a suspect's failure to answer such questions put to him by police officers, Fifth Amendment concerns are implicated. It is a "settled principle that while police have the right to request citizens to answer voluntarily questions concerning unsolved crimes they have no right to compel them to answer."[107]

Protecting the "right to remain silent" in cases in which police demand identification is not only consistent with precedent but consistent also with our legal traditions. The right is entrenched in

---

[101]Hoffman v. United States, 341 U.S. 479, 486 (1931).

[102]United States v. Hubbell, 530 U.S. 27, 37 (2000).

[103]402 U.S. 424 (1971).

[104]*Id.* at 448 (Harlan, J., concurring); *id.* at 460 (Black, J., joined by Douglas and Brennan, JJ., dissenting); *id.* at 464 (Brennan, J., joined by Douglas and Marshall, JJ., dissenting). Chief Justice Burger, joined by Justices Stewart, White, and Blackmun, concluded that "[d]isclosure of name and address is an essentially neutral act," at least in the context of a non-criminal regulatory scheme. *Id.* at 432 (plurality opinion).

[105]Michigan v. DeFillippo, 443 U.S. 31, 45 (1979) (Brennan, J., joined by Marshall and Stevens, JJ., dissenting).

[106]461 U.S. 352 (1983).

[107]*Id.* at 360 n.9 (quoting Davis v. Mississippi, 394 U.S. 721, 727 n.6 (1969)).

American law and culture[108] and is easily understood by police and citizens alike. It is incorporated in the *"Miranda* rights" that must be read to a person arrested with probable cause. Indeed, when Dudley Hiibel was arrested under Nevada's obstruction statute, he was informed of his "right to remain silent"—*even though he had just been arrested for exercising that very right.*

## VI. The Opinions in *Hiibel*

### A. Analysis of the Nevada Supreme Court Opinion

After losing before the Justice Court and the Sixth Judicial District Court, Hiibel took his case to the Nevada Supreme Court on a petition for writ of certiorari, arguing that he had a constitutional right to refuse to identify himself. The Nevada Supreme Court disagreed in a contentious 4–3 decision that addressed Hiibel's Fourth Amendment claim only.[109]

The majority began by recognizing that the "ability to wander freely and anonymously, if we so choose, without being compelled to divulge information to the government about who we are or what we are doing" is "[f]undamental to a democratic society."[110] This "'right to be let alone'—to simply live in privacy—is a right protected by the Fourth Amendment and undoubtedly sacred to us all."[111]

This, however, was but lip service. The court quickly put aside that concern and analyzed Hiibel's right to anonymity under a balancing test that proved highly deferential to the government. It explained that "[r]easonable people do not expect their identities— their names—to be withheld from officers"[112]—even though it is the reasonableness of government action, not citizen action, that matters under the Fourth Amendment. Furthermore, the majority observed

---

[108]The Supreme Court has recognized this fact. See, e.g., Brogan v. United States, 522 U.S. 398, 405 (1998) ("And as for the possibility that the person under investigation may be unaware of his right to remain silent: In the modern age of frequently dramatized 'Miranda' warnings, that is implausible.").

[109]Hiibel v. Sixth Judicial Dist. Court of Nevada, 59 P.3d 1201 (Nev. 2002). Hiibel petitioned for rehearing seeking explicit resolution of his Fifth Amendment challenge, but that petition was denied without opinion.

[110]*Id.* at 1204.

[111]*Id.* (footnotes omitted).

[112]*Id.* at 1206.

that "we reveal our names in a variety of situations every day without much consideration"[113]—even though such quotidian disclosures are voluntary, not made under threat of jail time. The majority concluded that "any intrusion on privacy . . . is outweighed by the benefits to officers and community safety" and added that the "public interest in requiring individuals to identify themselves to officers when a reasonable suspicion exists is overwhelming."[114] In the course of applying this balancing test, the Nevada Supreme Court gave an enormous degree of deference to the government. The court offered myriad "worst case" scenarios involving sex offenders lurking outside day care centers and the need to enforce restraining orders, explaining: "In these situations, it is the observable conduct that creates a reasonable suspicion, but it is the requirement to produce identification that enables an officer to determine whether the suspect is breaking the law."[115]

The majority then embarked on a rather remarkable tangent, asserting: "*Most importantly*, we are at war against enemies who operate with concealed identities and the dangers we face as a nation are unparalleled."[116] The court specifically invoked the September 11, 2001, terrorist attack, the Columbine school massacre, the anthrax scare, the subsequent (and unrelated) sniper murders in the D.C. area, and concerns about terrorism generally—none of which had anything to do with Dudley Hiibel. After reviewing this parade of horribles, the majority concluded that "[t]he point of requiring a suspect to provide identification during a lawful investigatory stop has been reached."[117] So overwrought was the majority's reasoning that a concurring justice wrote separately to preemptively refute criticisms that the majority "somehow overreacted to the dangers presented by the war against domestic and international terrorism."[118] The majority concluded by saying that

[113]*Id.* at 1206.

[114]*Id.* at 1205.

[115]*Id.* at 1205–06. That this raises Fifth Amendment concerns is readily apparent, illustrating the dangers of analyzing Fourth Amendment claims in a vacuum.

[116]*Id.* at 1206 (emphasis added).

[117]*Id.* The majority appears to be suggesting that prior to this "point," a suspect could *not* have been compelled to provide identification, but that because of current events, the Fourth Amendment now allows what it once prohibited. This is a peculiar approach to constitutional interpretation indeed.

[118]*Id.* at 1207 (Maupin, J., concurring).

[t]o deny officers the ability to request identification from suspicious persons creates a situation where an officer could approach a wanted terrorist or sniper but be unable to identify him or her if the person's behavior does not rise to the level of probable cause necessary for an arrest.[119]

The majority's reasoning boiled down to this: Civil liberties can impede effective police work. Police could be even more effective if they were allowed to approach whomever they wished, reasonable suspicion or not, and demand answers to all sorts of questions, including and beyond mere identity. But the Fourth Amendment is not properly viewed as a mere impediment to making an arrest.

Three of seven Nevada Supreme Court justices filed a vigorous dissent:

As the majority aptly states, the right to wander freely and anonymously, if we so choose, is a fundamental right of privacy in a democratic society. However, the majority promptly abandons this fundamental right by requiring "suspicious" citizens to identify themselves to law enforcement officers upon request, or face the prospect of arrest.[120]

### B. The U.S. Supreme Court's Opinion: Fourth Amendment

Justice Kennedy wrote the U.S. Supreme Court's majority opinion and was joined by Justices Rehnquist, O'Connor, Scalia, and Thomas. The Court construed its grant of jurisdiction to reach only the question whether Nevada could compel oral identification through the threat of arrest.[121]

---

[119]*Id.* at 1206.

[120]*Id.* at 1207 (Agosti, J., dissenting).

[121]In its rendition of the underlying facts of the case, the majority explained that it understood Deputy Dove's request for identification "as a request to produce a driver's license or some other form of *written* identification." Hiibel v. Sixth Judicial Dist. Court of Nevada, 124 S. Ct. 2451, 2455 (2004). If that interpretation is correct—and the videotape of the arrest shows that it is—then Hiibel was arrested, *not* for refusing to state his name but for failing to produce it in written form. Yet the Court understood the Nevada Supreme Court as interpreting the stop-and-identify statute "to require only that a suspect disclose his name" and therefore construed its appellate jurisdiction to reach only that question. *Id.* at 2457. The majority left open the question whether a statute requiring written identification would be constitutional, as long as it is not unduly vague under *Kolender*. This is a question with urgent real-world significance in light of, for example, the 9/11 Commission Report's recommendation that the federal government "set standards for the issuance of birth certificates and sources of identification, such as drivers licenses." Report of the National Commission on Terrorist Attacks Upon the United States ("9/11 Commission"), released July 22, 2004, at 390, available at http://www.9–11commission.gov/report/911Report.pdf.

## 1. A Red Herring

The Court quickly established that it meant to work on a blank slate and disregard prior Fourth Amendment precedents. It said first that "the Fourth Amendment does not impose obligations on the citizen but instead provides rights against the government."[122] As a result, "the Fourth Amendment itself cannot require a suspect to answer questions."[123] But, said the Court, "This case concerns a different issue . . . Here, the source of the legal obligations arises from Nevada state law, not the Fourth Amendment. Further, the statutory obligation does not go beyond answering an officer's request to disclose a name.[124]

It is instructive to parse this curious bit of legal "reasoning." The observation that the Fourth Amendment "does not impose obligations on the citizen but instead provides rights against the government" is a truism. But the inference the Court then draws, that "[a]s a result, the Fourth Amendment itself cannot require a suspect to answer questions" is a striking non sequitur. Of course "the Fourth Amendment itself" cannot require a suspect to answer questions. To the contrary, as the Court has just noted in the preceding sentence, the Fourth Amendment "does not impose obligations on the citizen"—at all. Indeed, any obligation to answer questions would not only *not* stem from the Fourth Amendment but would arise as an exception or limitation to the protections offered by the Fourth (and Fifth) Amendment.

The majority's suggestion that this case is "different" because "the source of the legal obligation arises from Nevada state law, not the Fourth Amendment" is equally curious.[125] Different from what? This is a garden variety case involving the question of whether the Nevada statute, which imposes an obligation on the individual, is consistent with the protections recognized by the Fourth Amendment. Justice Brennan confronted a similar question in his *DeFillippo*

---

[122]Hiibel, 124 S. Ct. at 2459.

[123]*Id.*

[124]*Id.*

[125]It is not clear what this means. The "issue" just raised by the majority—that is, that "the Fourth Amendment itself cannot require a suspect to answer questions"— is not an issue at all; it is a truism. It is akin to saying that "the Fifth Amendment itself cannot require a person in any criminal case to be a witness against himself." Neither statement raises any discernible "issue."

dissent where he explained that the question cannot simply be whether a seizure and search are authorized by state law but whether they are reasonable under the Fourth Amendment.[126] He concluded that the stop-and-identify ordinance at issue in *DeFillippo* "commands that which the Constitution denies the State power to command and makes 'a crime out of what under the Constitution cannot be a crime.'"[127] Those exact concerns were at issue in *Hiibel*. The Nevada statute requires a *Terry* detainee to state his name. Is that requirement prohibited by the Fourth Amendment, or is it not?

*2. Privacy in the Balance: The Government's Interest Trumps*

The majority determined that requiring a detainee to state his name, subject to arrest, is not prohibited by the Fourth Amendment. It did so by "balancing [the Nevada statute's] intrusion on the individual's Fourth Amendment interests against [the statute's] promotion of legitimate government interests."[128] The majority explained that "[t]he request for identity has an immediate relation to the purpose, rationale, and practical demands of a *Terry* stop,"[129] and that "questions concerning a suspect's identity are a routine and accepted part of many *Terry* stops."[130] The Court added that obtaining a name serves "important government interests," including the officer's interest in assessing "the threat to [his] own safety," the "possible danger to the potential victim," and whether the suspect "is wanted for another offense, or has a record of violence or mental disorder."[131]

This rationale is not convincing. At the outset, the concern that law enforcement officers are often killed or wounded in the line of duty by armed criminals was a concern recognized in *Terry*[132] and

---

[126]Michigan v. DeFillippo, 443 U.S. 31, 43 (1979) (Brennan, J., dissenting). As discussed *supra*, Section IV(C), Justice Brennan's dissent on this issue fleshed out an assumption made by the majority; it did not directly conflict with the majority opinion.

[127]*Id.* at 45 (Brennan, J., dissenting) (quoting Coates v. Cincinnati, 402 U.S. 611, 616 (1971)).

[128]Hiibel, 124 S. Ct. at 1259 (quoting Delaware v. Prouse, 440 U.S. 648, 654 (1979)).

[129]Hiibel, 124 S. Ct. at 1289.

[130]*Id.* at 2458. Of course, the problem is not whether the questions are routine—they undoubtedly are; it is whether answers to those questions can be compelled under threat of arrest.

[131]*Id.*

[132]392 U.S. 1, 23–24 (1968).

addressed by the Court's authorization of a limited frisk for weapons. Moreover, as the Nevada Supreme Court dissent and Justice Breyer's dissent here both explained, there is no "evidence that an officer, by knowing a person's identity, is better protected from potential violence."[133] A criminal history simply does not present the same sort of imminent threat as does a gun. Indeed, in *Hiibel*, there was nothing in the record to indicate that if Hiibel had told Deputy Dove his name, the officer would have, from the name alone, been better able to "assess" the situation.[134]

Furthermore, even assuming a detainee's name will be generally helpful to the state's criminal investigation, that is not enough to overcome the Fourth Amendment's default protections. As Justice Brennan explained in his concurring opinion in *Kolender*:

> Where probable cause is lacking, we have expressly declined to allow significantly more intrusive detentions or searches [beyond weapons frisks] on the *Terry* rationale, *despite the assertion of compelling law enforcement interests.* "For all but those narrowly defined intrusions, the requisite 'balancing' has been performed in centuries of precedent and is embodied in the principle that seizures are 'reasonable' only if supported by probable cause."[135]

To be sure, in some unusual circumstances—perhaps in a very small town, or where the suspect is famous (or infamous) enough that his name will be instantly known—an officer might immediately know from a mere name whether the suspect is "wanted for another offense," or be able immediately to assess "the threat to [his] own safety." As a general rule, however, such information will not be available absent running the detainee's name through one or more databases. But doing so takes time and deliberation and so hardly serves the same protective purpose as a weapons frisk, which will inform the officer of imminent danger of bodily harm. As the Nevada Supreme Court dissent noted, "[I]t is the observable conduct, not

---

[133]Hiibel v. Sixth Judicial Dist. Court of Nevada, 59 P.3d 1201, 1209 (Nev. 2002) (Agosti, J., dissenting).

[134]Moreover, Deputy Dove did not conduct a *Terry* frisk on Hiibel, and there is no indication from the videotape of the arrest that he was concerned about any imminent physical threat.

[135]Kolender v. Lawson, 461 U.S. 352, 363 (1983) (quoting Dunaway v. New York, 442 U.S. 200, 214 (1979) (other citations omitted) (emphasis added)).

the identity, of a person, upon which an officer must legally rely when investigating crimes and enforcing the law."[136]

In this sense, *Hiibel* differs significantly from *United States v. Hensley*,[137] a precedent invoked by Nevada in favor of its stop-and-search regime. In *Hensley*, the police were searching for the alleged driver of a get-away car after an armed robbery; they knew his identity as Thomas Hensley and had distributed a wanted flyer.[138] The Court held that "where police have been unable to locate a person suspected of involvement in a past crime, the ability to briefly stop that person, ask questions, or check identification in the absence of probable cause promotes the strong government interest in solving crimes and bringing offenders to justice."[139] By contrast, the government interest in obtaining information in Hiibel is more speculative: In *Hiibel*, Deputy Dove was not looking for "Dudley Hiibel." Thus, unlike in *Hensley*, the name would not have assisted his investigation in any way nor have protected his safety.

Finally, the majority asserts that "[t]he threat of criminal sanction helps ensure that the request for identity does not become a legal nullity."[140] That hardly addresses the constitutional question. The threat of criminal sanction might help ensure any number of otherwise discretionary acts. After all, the police can make any number of requests beyond mere identity that a suspect need not answer. Faced with a silent suspect, those requests will also be "legal nullities." Justice Brennan addressed this concern in his *Kolender* concurrence:

> We have never claimed that expansion of the power of police officers to act on reasonable suspicion alone, or even less, would further no law enforcement interests. But the balance struck by the Fourth Amendment between the public interest in effective law enforcement and the equally public interest in safeguarding individual freedom and privacy from arbitrary governmental interference forbids such expansion.[141]

---

[136]Hiibel, 59 P.3d at 1209 (Agosti, J., dissenting).

[137]469 U.S. 221 (1985).

[138]*Id.* at 223.

[139]*Id.* at 229.

[140]Hiibel v. Sixth Judicial Dist. Court of Nevada, 124 S. Ct. 2451, 2459 (2004).

[141]461 U.S. 352, 365 (1983) (Brennan, J., concurring) (citation omitted).

Against the government's interest, the *Hiibel* majority weighed the intrusiveness of the search. The Court suggested the intrusiveness is negligible, explaining that the "Nevada statute does not alter the nature of the stop itself" because it does not change its "duration" or its "location."[142] Although the statute does not alter the location, it could well alter the duration, because once the officer has the suspect's name, he must then take the next step of running it through a database to gather the very information the majority indicates "serves important government interests."[143] Moreover, the statute most certainly does alter the "nature" of the stop. A detainee who chooses not to speak, or who does not wish to give his name, will be arrested, tried, convicted, and burdened with a criminal record. A detainee who decides to provide his name will provide the state with the key to an enormous amount of information through a series of computerized, cross-linked databases. Either way, the result is a *de facto* "suspicious persons registry." This is not an insignificant shift in the law of *Terry* stops.

### 3. The Reasonableness Requirement

With its balancing test, the majority has determined that a *Terry* suspect must provide his name when asked. Or has it? Although such a rule, however incompatible with the Constitution, would have the advantage of setting a "bright-line," the majority quickly moved to blur any such clarity.

The majority recognized Hiibel's concerns that the Nevada statute might effectively "circumvent[] the probable cause requirement" by "allowing an officer to arrest a person for being suspicious," thus "creat[ing] a risk of arbitrary police conduct" that is not constitutionally permissible.[144] According to the majority, however, those concerns are misplaced:

> Petitioner's concerns are met by the requirement that a *Terry* stop must be justified at its inception and "reasonably related" in scope to the circumstances which justified the initial stop. Under these principles, an officer may not arrest a suspect for failure to identify himself if the request for

---

[142]Hiibel, 124 S. Ct. at 2459.

[143]*Id.* at 2458.

[144]*Id.* at 2459.

identification is not reasonably related to the circumstances justifying the stop.[145]

Thus, the rule is not simply that a *Terry* suspect must provide his name when asked. The rule is that a *Terry* suspect must provide his name when asked if and only if the request for identification is "reasonably related to the circumstances justifying the stop." Given the majority's reasoning, when might the request for identification *not* be "reasonably related to the circumstances justifying the stop"? The majority does not say. It is left for police officers and suspects to decide for themselves, on the spot.

The majority provides two possible interpretations of the "reasonableness" requirement, but they are of little use, especially when viewed in conjunction:

First, the majority offers up *Hayes v. Florida*.[146] In *Hayes*, police transported a suspect to the police station for fingerprinting, without probable cause, and then arrested him when his fingerprints matched those found at a crime scene.[147] The state court analogized the situation to a *Terry* stop and held that the officers' "reasonable suspicion" made their actions appropriate.[148] The Supreme Court reversed because "transportation to and investigative detention at the station house without probable cause or judicial authorization together violate the Fourth Amendment."[149] The Court went on, in dicta, to address a hypothetical situation involving a "brief detention in the field for the purpose of fingerprinting, where there is only reasonable suspicion not amounting to probable cause."[150] The Court suggested that such a detention was not "necessarily impermissible under the Fourth Amendment,"[151] explaining:

> There is thus support in our cases for the view that the Fourth Amendment would permit seizures for the purpose of fingerprinting, if there is reasonable suspicion that the suspect has committed a criminal act, *if there is a reasonable*

[145]*Id.*
[146]470 U.S. 811 (1985).
[147]*Id.* at 812–13.
[148]*Id.* at 813.
[149]*Id.* at 815.
[150]*Id.* at 816.
[151]*Id.*

> basis for believing that fingerprinting will establish or negate the
> suspect's connection with that crime, and if the procedure is
> carried out with dispatch.[152]

According to the *Hiibel* majority, this dicta from *Hayes* suggests
that *"Terry* may permit an officer to determine a suspect's identity
by compelling the suspect to submit to fingerprinting *only if* there
is a 'reasonable basis for believing that fingerprinting will establish
or negate the suspect's connection with that crime.'"[153] Is this to be
the standard? That is, may a police officer force a suspect to reveal
his name under penalty of arrest only if there is a "reasonable basis
for believing that disclosure of the name will establish or negate the
suspect's connection with that crime"? This standard seems quite
favorable to suspects, and was almost certainly *not* met in Dudley
Hiibel's situation.

But, the majority suggested a second interpretation of the "reasonableness" requirement, one that is not quite so lenient. The majority
asserted that "[i]t is clear in this case that the request for identification
was 'reasonably related in scope to the circumstances which justified'
the stop."[154] Why is it clear? Was there a "reasonable basis" for
Deputy Dove to believe that the words "Dudley Hiibel" would
"establish or negate" Hiibel's connection with the alleged crime of
domestic assault? No—it is clear, said the majority, because "[t]he
officer's request was a commonsense inquiry, not an effort to obtain
an arrest for failure to identify after a *Terry* stop yielded insufficient
evidence."[155]

Then is *this* to be the standard: that the request be a "common-
sense" inquiry? In what circumstances, if any, would it not be "common sense" for an officer to ask a *Terry* suspect for his identity? It
is difficult to imagine any such circumstances. If those circumstances
do not exist, then a detainee's failure to identify himself can result
in an arrest at any time, despite the majority's caveat that the request
for identification must be "reasonably related to the circumstances
justifying the stop," and despite the majority's invocation of *Hayes*.

---

[152]*Id.* at 817 (emphasis added).

[153]Hiibel v. Sixth Judicial Dist. Court of Nevada, 124 S. Ct. 2451, 2460 (2004) (quoting
Hayes v. Florida, 470 U.S. 811, 817 (1985)) (emphasis added).

[154]*Id.*

[155]*Id.*

*Hiibel* represents a shift in post-*Terry* jurisprudence. The balancing test established by *Terry* was not meant to be anything other than a narrow exception to the default rule of probable cause. As the Court has acknowledged, "the protections intended by the Framers could all too easily disappear in the consideration and balancing of the multifarious circumstances presented by different cases . . . ."[156] The Court in the past has understood that a "single, familiar standard is essential to guide police officers," and that its "reluctance to depart from the proved protections afforded by the general rule [probable cause], are reflected in the narrow limitations emphasized in the cases employing the balancing test."[157] Yet the Court now eschews a "single, familiar standard," and instead has created a veritable waterfall of exceptions to the historic probable cause standard that will be all but impossible for an officer on the beat to apply consistently and correctly.

## C. *The U.S. Supreme Court's Opinion: Fifth Amendment*

As recognized by the majority, to qualify for the Fifth Amendment privilege, "a communication must be testimonial, incriminating, and compelled."[158] The majority assumed, without deciding, that stating one's name is testimonial and thus within the Fifth Amendment's scope.[159] But it was careful to hedge its bets, explaining that "[s]tating one's name *may* qualify as an assertion of fact relating to identity," and that "[p]roduction of identity documents *might* meet the definition as well."[160] The majority decided against Hiibel solely on the basis that "disclosure of his name presented no reasonable danger of incrimination."[161] This saves for another day the question of whether a *Terry* detainee, the disclosure of whose identity clearly presents a "reasonable danger of incrimination," may nonetheless be forced to provide it because it is not "testimonial." The public would have been well-served had the Court simply decided that it is, or at least decided the question one way or another. In his dissent,

---

[156]Dunaway v. New York, 442 U.S. 200, 213 (1979).

[157]*Id.* at 213–14.

[158]Hiibel, 124 S. Ct. at 2460 (citing United States v. Hubbell, 530 U.S. 27, 34–38 (2000)).

[159]Hiibel, 124 S. Ct. at 2460.

[160]*Id.* (emphasis added).

[161]*Id.*

Justice Stevens addressed the issue the majority avoided, determining that a "testimonial communication" was indeed involved.[162] He found of particular significance that "the communications must be made in response to a question posed by a police officer," reasoning that "[s]urely police questioning during a *Terry* stop qualifies as an interrogation, and it follows that responses to such questions are testimonial in nature."[163]

Bypassing the "testimonial" question, the majority instead reasoned that Hiibel's "refusal to disclose his name was not based on any articulated real and appreciable fear that his name would be used to incriminate him, or that it 'would furnish a link in the chain of evidence needed to prosecute him.'"[164] Instead, the majority decided that Hiibel "refused to identify himself only because he thought his name was none of the officer's business," not because his name "could have been used against him in a criminal case."[165]

According to the majority's reasoning, then, the less guilty one is, the fewer constitutional protections one has. An innocent person subjected to a *Terry* stop can never show that his name might be used to incriminate him, or that it would furnish a link in the chain of evidence needed to prosecute him, because he has done nothing incriminating. In other words, under the majority's decision, the question is not whether a *Terry* detainee's name has the potential to be incriminating in general under the Nevada statute, but whether a particular *Terry* detainee's name might be incriminating. The innocent thus have no constitutional protections at all and can be forced to speak under penalty of arrest and criminal conviction. Ted Bundy has a constitutional right to remain silent when asked for his identity during a *Terry* stop; Justice Kennedy does not. This is a perverse result.

The majority did attempt, however, to generalize the incriminating nature of identity, falling back on what it described as the "narrow scope" of the disclosure requirement.[166] The majority reasoned:

---

[162]*Id.* at 2463 (Stevens, J., dissenting).
[163]*Id.* (Stevens, J., dissenting).
[164]*Id.* at 2461.
[165]*Id.*
[166]*Id.*

One's identity is, by definition, unique; yet it is, in another sense, a universal characteristic. Answering a request to disclose a name is likely to be so insignificant in the scheme of things as to be incriminating only in unusual circumstances.[167]

The majority observed that "[i]n every criminal case, it is known and must be known who has been arrested and who is being tried," and that "[e]ven witnesses who plan to invoke the Fifth Amendment privilege answer when their names are called to take the stand."[168] But at that point, there has been an arrest warrant supported by probable cause, and an indictment supporting trial, in the case of a criminal suspect, or a lawfully-issued subpoena, in the case of a witness. The names of the suspect or witness are already known. Those situations present a far cry from the person stopped on the street, without probable cause, and forced to speak or face arrest; forced to forfeit his anonymity and privacy, or face a criminal record.

Despite brushing off legitimate Fifth Amendment concerns, the majority conceded that "a case may arise where there is a substantial allegation that furnishing identity at the time of a stop would have given the police a link in the chain of evidence needed to convict the individual of a separate offense."[169] It reserved until another day its consideration, in such a case, of "whether the privilege applies, and, if the Fifth Amendment has been violated, what remedy must follow."[170] Of course, such a test case will arise only as to a person who is guilty. An innocent person, approached by the police without probable cause, simply has no Fifth Amendment right to remain silent.

### D. The Conflict in the Majority's View Between the Fourth and Fifth Amendments

Well over a century ago, the Court stated:

We have already noticed the intimate relation between the two amendments. They throw great light on each other. For the "unreasonable searches and seizures" condemned in the

---

[167]*Id.*

[168]*Id.*

[169]*Id.*

[170]*Id.*

> fourth amendment are almost always made for the purpose of compelling a man to give evidence against himself, which in criminal cases is condemned in the fifth amendment; and compelling a man "in a criminal case to be a witness against himself," which is condemned in the fifth amendment, throws light on the question as to what is an "unreasonable search and seizure" within the meaning of the fourth amendment.[171]

Justice Brennan also alluded to the intersection between the Fourth and Fifth Amendments in his *DeFillippo* dissent, noting that the police officer "commanded respondent to relinquish his constitutional right to remain silent and then arrested and searched him when he refused to do so."[172] He added that *Terry* detainees should not be forced to "choose between forgoing their right to remain silent and forgoing their right not to be searched if they choose to remain silent."[173]

In its Fourth Amendment analysis, the *Hiibel* majority, referring to *Hayes*, suggested its belief that a police officer may force a suspect to reveal his name under penalty of arrest if there is a "reasonable basis for believing that [disclosure of the name] will establish or negate the suspect's connection with that crime."[174] But in that scenario, what is permissible under the Fourth Amendment would be prohibited under the Fifth.

On the other hand, if under the Fifth Amendment a detainee's name is of no moment in either incriminating him or furnishing a link in the chain of evidence needed to prosecute him, what legitimate government interest could there be, consistent with the Fourth Amendment, in obtaining it?

The majority's opinion creates tension between its Fourth and Fifth Amendment analyses: It indicated both that knowing a detainee's name is crucial to the effectiveness and safety of standard police

---

[171]Boyd v. United States, 116 U.S. 616, 633 (1886). See also Brown v. Illinois, 422 U.S. 590, 592, 601 (1975) (noting, in cases lying "at the crossroads of the Fourth and the Fifth Amendments, that "[f]requently ... rights under the two Amendments may appear to coalesce ....").

[172]Michigan v. DeFillippo, 443 U.S. 31, 46 (1979) (Brennan, J., dissenting).

[173]*Id.*

[174]124 S. Ct. at 2460.

work, and at the same time, that knowing a suspect's name will be of use only rarely, in "unusual circumstances."

## E. Dissenting Opinions

Justice Breyer, joined by Justices Souter and Ginsburg, dissented, first addressing the majority's Fourth Amendment analysis. Preferring a bright-line, easily administered rule—and one in line with precedent—Justice Breyer explained:

> [T]his Court's Fourth Amendment precedents make clear that police may conduct a *Terry* stop only within circumscribed limits. And one of those limits invalidates laws that compel responses to police questioning.[175]

Reviewing the "lengthy history" of concurring opinions, references, "clear explicit statements," and "strong dicta" indicating that there is a right not to answer questions posed during a *Terry* stop, Justice Breyer admonished: "There is no good reason now to reject this generation-old statement of the law."[176] To the contrary, "[t]here are sound reasons rooted in Fifth Amendment considerations for adhering to this Fourth Amendment legal condition circumscribing police authority to stop an individual against his will."[177]

Moving on to those Fifth Amendment concerns, Justice Breyer pointed out some of the more obvious "[a]dministrative concerns"—concerns that, considering the pervasiveness and variety of stop-and-identify statutes, are not merely academic:

> Can a State, in addition to requiring a stopped individual to answer "What's your name?" also require an answer to "What's your license number?" or "Where do you live?" Can a police officer, who must know how to make a *Terry* stop, keep track of the constitutional answers? After all, answers to any of these questions may, or may not, incriminate, depending upon the circumstances.[178]

Noting the majority's acknowledgement of "unusual circumstances" wherein the Fifth Amendment might be violated, Justice

---

[175]*Id.* at 2464 (Breyer, J., dissenting).
[176]*Id.* at 2465 (Breyer, J., dissenting).
[177]*Id.* (Breyer, J., dissenting).
[178]*Id.* at 2465–66 (Breyer, J., dissenting).

Stevens wondered: "How then is a police officer in the midst of a *Terry* stop to distinguish between the majority's ordinary case and this special case where the majority reserves judgment?"[179]

Justice Breyer rebuked the majority:

> The majority presents no evidence that the rule enunciated by Justice White and then by the *Berkemer* Court, which for nearly a generation has set forth a settled *Terry* stop condition, has significantly interfered with law enforcement. Nor has the majority presented any other convincing justification for change. I would not begin to erode a clear rule with special exceptions.[180]

Justice Stevens made a similar point in his separate dissent observing: "Given our statements to the effect that citizens are not required to respond to police officers' questions during a *Terry* stop, it is no surprise that [Hiibel] assumed, as have we, that he had a right not to disclose his identity."[181]

Justice Stevens addressed only the Fifth Amendment issue. Alluding to the *Byers* analysis, he first noted that the Nevada law imposes a duty to speak upon a narrow class of individuals who are "'inherently suspect of criminal activities.'"[182] Recognizing that the Nevada statute compels a suspect only to identify himself, Justice Stevens observed that "[p]resumably the statute does not require the detainee to answer any other question because the Nevada Legislature realized that the Fifth Amendment prohibits compelling the target of a criminal investigation to make any other statement."[183] As discussed above,[184] numerous other states and localities have made no such distinction, and it remains an open question whether Justice Stevens' presumption will prove accurate.

Justice Stevens concluded that "the broad constitutional right to remain silent . . . is not as circumscribed as the Court suggests, and does not admit even of the narrow exception defined by the Nevada

---

[179]*Id.* at 2466 (Breyer, J., dissenting).

[180]*Id.* (Breyer, J., dissenting).

[181]*Id.* at 2462–63 (Stevens, J., dissenting).

[182]*Id.* at 2461 (Stevens, J., dissenting) (quoting Albertson v. Subversive Activities Control Board, 382 U.S. 70, 79 (1965)).

[183]Hiibel, 124 S. Ct. at 2462 (Stevens, J., dissenting).

[184]See Section III *supra*.

statute."[185] He observed that the Fifth Amendment privilege is widely available "outside of criminal court proceedings" and is meant to protect persons "in all settings in which their freedom of action is curtailed in any significant way from being compelled to incriminate themselves."[186] Those protected include, inter alia, an indicted defendant at trial, the unindicted target of a grand jury investigation, and an arrested subject during custodial interrogation in a police station.[187] Justice Stevens thus reasoned that "[t]here is no reason why the subject of police interrogation based on mere suspicion, rather than probable cause, should have any lesser protection," and that indeed, the "Fifth Amendment's protections apply with equal force in the context of *Terry* stops."[188] Justice Stevens then took issue with the majority's definition of "incriminating," noting that "our cases have afforded Fifth Amendment protection to statements that are 'incriminating' in a much broader sense than the Court suggests."[189] He explained:

> The Court reasons that we should not assume that the disclosure of [Hiibel's] name would be used to incriminate him or that it would furnish a link in a chain of evidence needed to prosecute him. But why else would an officer ask for it? And why else would the Nevada Legislature require its disclosure only when circumstances "reasonably indicate that the person has committed, is committing or is about to commit a crime"? If the Court is correct, then [Hiibel's] refusal to cooperate did not impede the police investigation. Indeed, if we accept the predicate for the Court's holding, the statute requires nothing more than a useless invasion of privacy.[190]

## VII. Implications of the *Hiibel* Decision

After *Hiibel*, any citizen approached by police with a demand for identification cannot be certain whether declining to respond is a constitutionally respected right, or a crime. If the approach is not

---

[185]Hiibel, 124 S. Ct. at 2462 (Stevens, J., dissenting).

[186]*Id.* (Stevens, J., dissenting) (quoting Miranda v. Arizona, 384 U.S. 436, 467 (1966)).

[187]Hiibel, 124 S. Ct. at 2462 (Stevens, J., dissenting).

[188]*Id.* (Stevens, J., dissenting).

[189]*Id.* (Stevens, J., dissenting).

[190]*Id.* at 2464 (Stevens, J., dissenting).

based on "reasonable suspicion," or if the demand for identification is not "reasonably related" to the officer's reasonable suspicion (under either the strict *Hayes* "establish or negate" standard, or the lenient "commonsense inquiry" standard, whichever is ultimately found to apply), then failure to respond *is* a right. If revealing one's identity would lead to a substantial risk of self-incrimination, then failure to respond *might* be a right. Otherwise, failure to respond is a crime.[191] The onus is on the citizen to decide which scenario applies.

The dilemma in which a *Terry* detainee will now find himself was long ago recognized by Justice Brennan, in his *Kolender* concurrence:

> [A]rrest and the threat of a criminal sanction have a substantial impact on interests protected by the Fourth Amendment, far more severe than we have ever permitted on less than probable cause. . . . [T]he validity of such arrests will be open to challenge only after the fact, in individual prosecutions for failure to produce identification. Such case-by-case scrutiny cannot vindicate the Fourth Amendment rights of persons . . . , many of whom will not even be prosecuted after they are arrested . . . . A pedestrian approached by police officers has no way of knowing whether the officers have "reasonable suspicion"—without which they may not demand identification . . . .—because that condition depends solely on the objective facts known to the officers and evaluated in light of their experience . . . . The pedestrian will know that to assert his rights may subject him to arrest and all that goes with it: . . . [including] the expense of defending against a possible prosecution. The only response to be expected is compliance with the officers' requests, whether or not they are based on reasonable suspicion, and without regard to the possibility of later vindication in court. *Mere reasonable suspicion does not justify subjecting the innocent to such a dilemma.*[192]

---

[191]That is, it is certainly a crime in those states with stop-and-identify statutes. But it is not at all clear that *Hiibel* applies *only* to states with stop-and-identify statutes. Because those statutes are generally considered codifications of *Terry*, a court could find that a suspect who does not identify himself is delaying or obstructing a police officer in discharging his common law legal duty, as authorized by *Terry*, *Hiibel*, and state court cases adopting their reasoning, to investigate suspicious circumstances.

[192]Kolender v. Lawson, 461 U.S. 352, 367–69 (1983) (Brennan, J., concurring) (emphasis added) (citations and footnotes omitted).

The *Hiibel* decision also raises interesting federalism issues. The question of a "national ID card" remains one of substantial import and debate in recent years. States that wish to provide greater civil liberties protections to their citizens may nevertheless find themselves faced with federal law officers stopping those citizens to demand identification.

## VIII. Conclusion

The Court has strayed far from the bright-line rules of probable cause and the "right to remain silent." It has replaced clarity with an array of exceptions and exceptions-to-exceptions so internally inconsistent and difficult to apply that the net result is a discernible erosion of constitutional liberties. Now that the Court has rejected a simple rule allowing a person to refuse to answer *any* questions during a *Terry* stop, it is only a matter of time before it has the opportunity to decide, first, whether its rollback of Fourth Amendment protections will be limited to a search for mere identity, or whether the state will be empowered to arrest its citizens for rebuffing a wide variety of intrusive inquiries; and second, whether the Fifth Amendment even matters during a *Terry* stop. One can only hope that, in the line of cases that will inevitably follow *Hiibel*, the Court adheres more closely to constitutional first principles.

# The *Pringle* Case's New Notion of Probable Cause: An Assault on *Di Re* and the Fourth Amendment

*Tracey Maclin**

## I. Introduction

Among Americans, guilt by association has never been a popular method of categorizing individuals. Particularly when it comes to criminal charges, Americans have rightly believed that an individual should not be judged solely on the basis of the company that he keeps. Fourth Amendment law has embraced a similar norm. Generally speaking, a full search or seizure of a person "must be supported by probable cause *particularized* with respect to that person."[1] In the arrest context, this means probable cause to arrest exists when police have reliable information or evidence that singles out a person or persons for arrest.[2] The requirement of particularized or individualized probable cause targeting a person "cannot be undercut or avoided by simply pointing to the fact that coincidentally there exists probable cause to search or seize another or to search the premises

---

*For their very helpful comments on an earlier version of this article, I want to thank Yale Kamisar and Wayne LaFave. I also want to thank Meredith Scull for her work as my research assistant. In the interest of full disclosure, the reader may want to know that I was counsel of record and author of an amicus brief filed on behalf of the American Civil Liberties Union and the National Association of Criminal Defense Lawyers in the *Pringle* case.

[1] Ybarra v. Illinois, 444 U.S. 85, 91 (1979) (emphasis added).

[2] When I say evidence that "singles out" a person or persons for arrest, I agree with Professor Silas Wasserstrom's analysis that this means that before an officer can arrest a person, he needs enough proof to support the belief that the "suspect arrested *did commit* the offense." Silas J. Wasserstrom, The Incredible Shrinking Fourth Amendment, 21 Am. Crim. L. Rev. 257, 337 (1984). "Such a belief would clearly not be warranted if the facts available to the officer made it as likely as not that he was wrong." *Id.* at 307 (footnote omitted).

where the person may happen to be."[3] Put simply, guilt by association is not a permissible ground for arrest.[4]

It might be argued that mere proximity to others suspected of
crime is insufficient proof of probable cause because every individual
is "clothed with [their own] constitutional protection."[5] After all, it
is just as likely that a person's association with others suspected of
criminality has an innocent explanation. Under this view, "the
phrase 'probable cause' suggests a quantum of evidence at least
sufficient to establish more than a fifty percent probability—at least
some sort of more-likely-than-not or preponderance of the evidence
standard."[6] The problem with this argument is that the modern
Court has expressly denied that probable cause mandates such proof.
In *Illinois v. Gates*,[7] the Court explained that probable cause does not
require a more-likely-than-not showing of guilt.[8] In fact, the *Gates*
opinion, written by then-Justice Rehnquist, asserted that "probable
cause requires only a probability or *substantial chance* of criminal
activity, not an actual showing of such activity."[9]

---

[3] Ybarra, 444 U.S. at 91. In this article, I will sometimes use the terminology "particularized" or "individualized" suspicion. When I use these terms, I am referring to
the degree or quantum of evidence needed to establish probable cause under the
Fourth Amendment. See, e.g., Wyoming v. Houghton, 526 U.S. 295, 302 (1999)
(acknowledging the creation of an exception to the "individualized probable cause"
rule); *id.* at 311–13 (Stevens, J., dissenting) (using the terminology "individualized
probable cause" and "individualized suspicion" interchangeably). The current
Supreme Court does not dispute that probable cause requires a "belief of guilt [that]
must be particularized with respect to the person to be searched or seized." Maryland
v. Pringle, 124 S. Ct. 795, 801 (2003) (citing Ybarra, 444 U.S. at 91). My use of this
terminology should not be confused with the reasonable suspicion or individualized
suspicion that is required under *Terry v. Ohio*, 392 U.S. 1 (1968) and its progeny. The
individualized suspicion required under the *Terry* cases is a lesser standard of proof
than the probable cause standard.

[4] See Sibron v. New York, 392 U.S. 40, 62 (1968) ("The inference that persons who
talk to narcotics addicts [over a period of eight hours] are engaged in the criminal
traffic in narcotics is simply not the sort of reasonable inference required to support
an intrusion by the police upon an individual's personal security.").

[5] Ybarra, 444 U.S. at 91.

[6] Wasserstrom, *supra* note 2, at 306 (footnote omitted).

[7] 462 U.S. 213 (1983)

[8] *Id.* at 235 (observing that a preponderance of the evidence standard is not the
equivalent of probable cause, and that "it is clear that 'only the probability, and not
a prima facie showing, of criminal activity is the standard of probable cause'")
(citations omitted).

[9] *Id.* at 243 n.13 (emphasis added).

In *Maryland v. Pringle*,[10] the Court confronted the tension between an individualized conception of probable cause (and the related rule that "mere proximity" does not provide probable cause) and the modern Court's view that probable cause does not require a more-likely-than-not showing of guilt. In *Pringle*, police stopped a car occupied by three men for a traffic violation. A consensual search of the car revealed a large amount of cash in the glove compartment and five glassine baggies of cocaine hidden in the backseat armrest. After the men refused to provide any information about the money or narcotics, all three were arrested. A unanimous Court explained that the arrest of all three men was permissible because it is "an entirely reasonable inference from these facts that any or all three of the occupants had knowledge of, and exercised dominion and control over, the cocaine."[11] In reaching this result, the Court insisted that its holding was consistent with the principle of particularized probable cause and was not an endorsement of guilt by association.[12]

This article contends that the Court's actions speak louder than its words, and demonstrate that the Court's fidelity to individualized probable cause is more apparent than real. Prior to *Pringle*, a person's mere presence with others independently suspected of criminality did not, by itself, provide probable cause for a search or arrest.[13] In a post-*Pringle* world, however, police have significantly more authority to arrest a person based on his mere association with others suspected of a crime.

---

[10] 124 S. Ct. 795 (2003).

[11] *Id.* at 800.

[12] *Id.* at 800–01.

[13] See, e.g., United States v. Di Re, 332 U.S. 581 (1948) and Ybarra, discussed *infra* notes 40–56 and accompanying text. The result in *Ker v. California*, 374 U.S. 23 (1963), is not to the contrary. In *Ker*, the Court found there was probable cause to arrest a suspect's wife, Diane Ker, who was present when police entered George Ker's home to arrest him. After a warrantless entry to arrest George Ker, police encountered Diane Ker as she exited her kitchen. Inside the kitchen, officers observed a brick-shaped package of marijuana in plain view. The *Ker* Court observed: "Even assuming that [Diane Ker's] presence in a small room with the contraband in a prominent position on the kitchen sink would not alone establish a reasonable ground for the officers' belief that she was in joint possession with her husband, that fact was accompanied by the officers' information that [George] Ker had been using his apartment as a base of operations for his narcotics activities." *Id.* at 36–37. Thus the facts in *Ker* involved an arrestee with something more than mere spatial association with another suspected of criminality.

## II. The Context of *Pringle* as It Arrives at the Court

The facts in *Pringle* are undisputed. On August 7, 1999, at 3:16 a.m., Officer Jeffrey Snyder of the Baltimore County Police Department stopped a car for speeding and for the driver's failure to wear a seatbelt. Inside the car were three men: Donte Partlow, the driver and owner of the vehicle; Joseph Pringle, the passenger in the front seat; and Otis Smith, the backseat passenger. When Partlow opened the glove compartment to obtain his registration, Officer Snyder noticed a large roll of cash. After determining that there were no outstanding warrants for Partlow, the officer issued Partlow a verbal warning.

After a second officer arrived on the scene, Officer Snyder asked Partlow if he had any weapons or narcotics in the car. Partlow said no, and gave Snyder permission to search the car. The search disclosed $763 from the glove compartment and five glassine plastic baggies containing cocaine concealed from view in the backseat armrest. Officer Snyder questioned the men separately about the drugs and told them that unless someone told him who possessed the drugs, "you are all going to get arrested."[14] None of the men provided any information about the drugs or money, and Officer Snyder proceeded to arrest all three suspects. Two hours later at the police station, Pringle waived his *Miranda* rights[15] and confessed to owning the cocaine. Pringle also told the police that Partlow and Smith did not know or have anything to do with the money or drugs. The police then released Partlow and Smith.

Pringle was charged with possession of cocaine and with possession with intent to distribute cocaine. The trial court found there was probable cause to arrest Pringle, and denied Pringle's suppression motion. Pringle was later convicted of possession of cocaine and possession of cocaine with intent to distribute. The Maryland Court of Special Appeals affirmed the trial court's holding. The Maryland Court of Appeals, the state's highest court, reversed the appellate court and held there was no probable cause to arrest Pringle.

The state high court explained that the facts did not show that Pringle had knowledge and dominion or control over the drugs,

---

[14]Joint Appendix at 47, Maryland v. Pringle, 124 S. Ct. 795 (2003) (No. 02-809) (hereinafter "Joint Appendix").

[15]See Miranda v. Arizona, 384 U.S. 436 (1966).

which were elements of the crime of possession under Maryland law. Accordingly, the court held that "a police officer's discovery of money in a closed glove compartment and cocaine concealed behind the rear armrest of a car is insufficient to establish probable cause for an arrest of a front seat passenger, who is not the owner or person in control of the vehicle, for possession of cocaine."[16] Three judges dissented. Writing for the dissenters, Judge Battaglia contended there was probable cause to arrest all three men. He argued that the majority had erroneously conflated "the probable cause standard for an arrest and the sufficiency of evidence standard for a conviction."[17]

When *Pringle* arrived at the U.S. Supreme Court, several factors made it an attractive case for full review. For starters, the prosecution had lost below.[18] Second, Judge Battaglia's dissent undoubtedly had been noticed by some members of the Court. For "law-and-order" conservatives, Judge Battaglia made a plausible (and perhaps appealing) claim that the majority had improperly grafted onto the probable cause standard a requirement that police officers have probable cause for each element of the crime *before* undertaking an arrest.[19]

Third, the state's certiorari petition claimed that tension existed between two categories of probable cause cases. The State of Maryland interpreted *United States v. Di Re* [20] and *Ybarra v. Illinois*[21] "to stand for the proposition that probable cause must be examined on an individualized basis, and not by a person's mere proximity to someone else suspected of criminal activity."[22] The state prosecutor

---

[16] Pringle v. Maryland, 805 A.2d 1016, 1028 (Md. 2002).

[17] *Id.* at 1034 (Battaglia, J., dissenting).

[18] See, e.g., California v. Carney, 471 U.S. 386, 396–401 (1985) (Stevens, J., dissenting) (criticizing the Court's tendency to review search and seizure cases where a state supreme court has upheld a citizen's assertion of a constitutional right).

[19] See Pringle, 805 A.2d at 1035 ("What more would the majority require to justify an arrest? From the emphasis in its opinion, the majority would seemingly require police officers to consider whether the evidence gathered would be legally sufficient for a possession conviction *prior* to making the arrest.").

[20] 332 U.S. 581 (1948).

[21] 444 U.S. 85 (1979).

[22] Petition for Certiorari at 8, Maryland v. Pringle, 124 S. Ct. 795 (2003) (No. 02-809) (hereinafter "Pet. Cert.").

argued, however, that *Wyoming v. Houghton*[23] cast doubt on the continuing validity of the proposition established by *Di Re* and *Ybarra* "in the context of a car search during which both a driver and passengers were present."[24] *Houghton* had stated that a car passenger "will often be engaged in a common enterprise with the driver, and have the same interest in concealing the fruits or evidence of their wrongdoing."[25] The state prosecutor maintained that *Houghton's* "common enterprise" approach departed from the individualized suspicion model of probable cause adopted in *Di Re* and *Ybarra*.

Finally, the facts in *Pringle* gave the Court an opportunity to resolve a "probable cause" issue that had bedeviled the lower courts for a long time. That issue, as Professor LaFave explained in his treatise, often surfaces "when the police are investigating a known crime and obtain information concerning the offender which does not point exclusively to one particular individual, in which case the question is whether they may nonetheless arrest a person or perhaps two or more persons from the suspect class."[26]

The Supreme Court granted certiorari to decide the following question: Where drugs and a roll of cash are found in the passenger compartment of a car with multiple occupants, and all deny ownership of those items, is there probable cause to arrest all occupants of the car?

## III. The Court's Probable Cause Precedents

To understand and appreciate Pringle's argument, one has to grapple with the Court's previous probable cause cases. Before police can make a warrantless arrest, they must have probable cause that the arrestee has committed or is about to commit a crime. For decades, the Court has adopted the formal position that police have probable cause to arrest where "the facts and circumstances within their knowledge and of which they had reasonably trustworthy

---

[23] 526 U.S. 295 (1999).

[24] Pet. Cert. at 8.

[25] Houghton, 526 U.S. at 304–05.

[26] 2 Wayne R. LaFave, Search and Seizure § 3.2(e), at 60 (3d ed. 1996). See also Wayne R. LaFave, Arrest: The Decision To Take a Suspect into Custody 259 (1965) ("The basic question is when, if ever, it is permissible to arrest a group of suspects, or one suspect from a group of suspects, when it reasonably appears that the actual offender is within the group.").

information were sufficient to warrant a prudent man in believing that [a particular person] had committed or was committing an offense."[27]

This straightforward description of probable cause masks the difficulty in explaining how probable cause functions in the legal world. This difficulty is a long-standing problem. As one historian has observed, while courts, for centuries, have used the terms "probable cause" and "reasonable cause" to summarize or supplement the causes of suspicion that may trigger a lawful arrest, the terminology had been utilized "without much concern for the precise meaning of probable or reasonable."[28]

Recently, the Supreme Court abandoned the task of trying to explain what probable cause means under the Fourth Amendment. "Articulating precisely what 'reasonable suspicion' and 'probable cause' mean is not possible."[29] The Court has stated that probable cause and its counterpart reasonable suspicion should not be viewed as legal technicalities, but rather as "common-sense, nontechnical conceptions that deal with 'the factual and practical considerations of everyday life on which reasonable and prudent men, not legal technicians, act.'"[30] Thus, the Court has eschewed "[r]igid legal rules"[31] and embraced a totality-of-the-circumstances model for determining whether probable cause exists in a particular case.

Generally speaking, the Court has accepted the notion that under the Fourth Amendment, probable cause represents "the best compromise" between safeguarding citizens from "unfounded charges of crime" and giving "fair leeway" for law enforcement to provide the community with adequate "protection."[32] As part of that compromise, the Court has interpreted probable cause to require an individualized or particularized basis for an intrusion. The Court's early (and seminal) probable cause cases involved fact patterns where

---

[27] Beck v. Ohio, 379 U.S. 89, 91 (1964).

[28] Barbara J. Shapiro, "Beyond Reasonable Doubt" and "Probable Cause": Historical Perspectives on the Anglo-American Law of Evidence 141 (1991).

[29] Ornelas v. United States, 517 U.S. 690, 695 (1996).

[30] *Id.* at 695 (citations omitted).

[31] Illinois v. Gates, 462 U.S. 213, 232 (1983).

[32] Brinegar v. United States, 338 U.S. 160, 176 (1949).

police had sufficient information to justify singling out or targeting a specific person or persons for search or seizure.

For example, in *Carroll v. United States*,[33] a prohibition era case, federal law enforcement officers had particular reason to focus on "the Carroll boys" because they had offered to sell liquor to the officers on a previous occasion and because shortly after that proposed sale, the officers had observed the suspects heading to Detroit, which the Court assumed to be "one of the most active centers for introducing illegally into this country spirituous liquors for distribution into the interior."[34] The probable cause determination in *Carroll* turned on whether the officers had probable cause to search the suspects' vehicle when, "[t]wo months later these officers suddenly met the same men on their way westward presumably from Detroit."[35] The *Carroll* Court concluded there was probable cause to stop and search the vehicle for illegal liquor.

Similarly, in *Brinegar v. United States*,[36] a federal prohibition agent had reason to target Brinegar because the agent "had arrested [Brinegar] about five months earlier for illegally transporting liquor; had seen [Brinegar] loading liquor into a car or truck in Joplin, Missouri, on at least two occasions during the preceding six months, and knew [Brinegar] to have a reputation for hauling liquor."[37] In *Brinegar*, the probable cause issue focused on whether the prohibition agent had sufficient evidence to search Brinegar's car when he saw the vehicle heading for the Oklahoma border and it "appeared to be 'heavily loaded' and 'weighted with something.'"[38] The Court ruled there was probable cause to search Brinegar's vehicle.

Finally, in *Illinois v. Gates*,[39] police had particularized suspicion focusing on the Gateses because of an anonymous letter that accused them of drug trafficking and specified in detail their *modus operandi*. The existence of probable cause in *Gates* turned on whether the police corroboration of the letter's predictions was sufficient to prove

---

[33] 267 U.S. 132 (1925).
[34] *Id.* at 160.
[35] *Id.*
[36] *Supra* note 32.
[37] 338 U.S. at 162.
[38] *Id.* at 163.
[39] 462 U.S. 213 (1983).

the reliability of and basis of knowledge supporting the informant's allegations. Departing from the so-called *Aguilar-Spinelli* two-pronged standard for determining probable cause,[40] *Gates* held that probable cause is to be determined from a totality-of-the-circumstances approach, and ruled that probable cause had been established under the facts.

*Carroll, Brinegar,* and *Gates*—which involved scenarios where the police had reason to believe that particular persons were engaged in *unknown* crime—represent one strand of probable cause precedent. In these cases, the question is whether there is probable cause that a crime has been committed. But there is no uncertainty about who the offenders were *if* it was sufficiently probable that there was an offense in the first place. There is, however, another strand of probable cause precedent, exemplified by *United States v. Di Re.*[41] In *Di Re,* the police, during the course of investigating a *known* crime, encountered a person who, but for his presence with others suspected of criminality, could not have been arrested. *Di Re* presented the Court, for the first time, with an opportunity to address in detail whether association or access to others involved with crime constitutes probable cause to arrest or search.

In *Di Re,* an informant, Reed, told a federal investigator that he planned to purchase counterfeit gasoline coupons from Buttitta. Accompanied by a Buffalo police detective, the investigator followed Buttitta's car to the place where Reed said the purchase would occur. The officers approached the car and observed Reed in the backseat holding the counterfeit coupons. Reed told the officers that Buttitta had given him the coupons. Buttitta was driving the car, and Di Re sat next to Buttitta. All three men were arrested. A search of Di Re's person at the police station disclosed one hundred coupons in an envelope concealed between his shirt and underwear.

The government defended the search in *Di Re* on two grounds. First, the government asserted the search was reasonable because there was probable cause to search the car itself. The government asked the Court "to extend the assumed right of car search

[40] See Aguilar v. Texas, 378 U.S. 108 (1964); Spinelli v. United States, 393 U.S. 410 (1969). Under the two-pronged test, a police affidavit based on an informant's tip had to show both a sufficient "basis of knowledge" for the tip and provide sufficient facts establishing the "reliability" or "veracity" of the informant.

[41] 332 U.S. 581 (1948).

[announced in *Carroll*] to include the person of occupants because 'common sense demands that such right exist in a case such as this where the contraband sought is a small article which could easily be concealed on the person.'"[42] The *Di Re* Court rejected this argument, explaining that Di Re's mere presence in a vehicle suspected of holding contraband did not provide probable cause to justify a search of *his* person. The Court was "not convinced that a person, by mere presence in a suspected car, loses immunities from search of his person to which he would otherwise be entitled."[43]

Alternatively, the government argued that the search of Di Re was justified as incident to a lawful arrest. The government defended the arrest on the theory that Di Re's presence in the car gave the officers probable cause to believe that Di Re was involved in a conspiracy to possess counterfeit coupons. The Court rejected this contention, and explained that:

> The argument that one who "accompanies a criminal to a crime rendezvous" cannot be assumed to be a bystander, forceful enough in some circumstances, is farfetched when the meeting is not secretive or in a suspicious hide-out but in broad daylight, in plain-sight of passers-by, in a public street of a large city, and where the alleged substantive crime is one which does not necessarily involve any act visibly criminal.[44]

The Court cautioned against inferring "[p]resumptions of guilt" from mere proximity with others involved with crime.[45] Finally, the *Di Re* Court noted that "whatever suspicion" might attach to Di Re's "mere presence seems diminished, if not destroyed," when the informant, Reed, failed to implicate Di Re, as he did Buttitta, as part of the "conspiracy" and "[a]ny inference that everyone on the scene of a crime is a party to it must disappear if the Government informer singles out the guilty person."[46]

*Di Re* is one of two cases upon which Pringle's challenge to the legality of his arrest heavily relied. The other case was *Ybarra v.*

[42] *Id.* at 586.
[43] *Id.* at 587.
[44] *Id.* at 593.
[45] *Id.*
[46] *Id.* at 594.

*Illinois*.[47] *Ybarra* involved a valid search warrant of a tavern and a bartender for narcotics. It was argued, *inter alia*, that the existence of a valid warrant eliminated the requirement that police have individualized suspicion with respect to each person subject to search.[48] The *Ybarra* Court rejected that argument. The Court reiterated that particularized suspicion is an essential component of probable cause, and thirty years after *Di Re* was decided, endorsed the principle announced in that case that police may not search or arrest everyone found at the scene of a crime, even when the intrusion may serve a legitimate investigative function of the police.

Ybarra was a patron of a tavern when the police arrived to execute a search warrant. A search of Ybarra revealed narcotics. The Court addressed two issues that were pertinent in *Pringle*. First, the Court rejected the claim that the police had probable cause to search Ybarra. Concededly, the warrant permitted a search of the premises and Ybarra was on the premises at the time of the search. The Court, however, held that this connection was not enough to support a search. A person's "mere propinquity to others independently suspected of criminal activity does not, without more, give rise to probable cause to search that person."[49]

*Ybarra* explained that the probable cause standard requires a suspicion that is "particularized with respect to" the target of the search or seizure.[50] The requirement of individualized or particularized suspicion "cannot be undercut or avoided by simply pointing to the fact that coincidentally there exists probable cause to search or seize another or to search the premises where the person may happen to be."[51] The Court explained that each patron of the tavern was "clothed with constitutional protection," and that "individualized protection was separate and distinct" from the protection possessed by the owner of the tavern and the bartender.[52] Thus, the warrant to search the premises and the bartender provided "no authority

---

[47] 444 U.S. 85 (1979).

[48] *Id.* at 107 (Rehnquist, J., dissenting) ("[I]n place of the requirement of 'individualized suspicion' as a guard against arbitrary exercise of authority, we have here the determination of a neutral and detached magistrate that a search was necessary.").

[49] *Id.* at 91 (citing Sibron v. New York, 392 U.S. 40, 62–63 (1968)).

[50] 444 U.S. at 91.

[51] *Id.*

[52] *Id.* at 91–92.

whatever to invade the constitutional protections possessed individually by the tavern's customers."[53]

The other issue addressed in *Ybarra* concerned the state's claim that the reasonable suspicion standard of *Terry v. Ohio*[54] should be extended to promote the evidence-gathering function of a search warrant. In an argument that would resemble the position Maryland proposed in *Pringle*, the state of Illinois urged the *Ybarra* Court "to permit evidence searches of persons who, at the commencement of the search, are on 'compact' premises subject to a search warrant, at least where the police have a 'reasonable belief' that such persons 'are connected with' drug trafficking and 'may be concealing or carrying away the contraband.'"[55] The Court's response was clear: "Over 30 years ago, [we] rejected a similar argument in *United States v. Di Re.*"[56]

There were obvious differences between *Di Re* and *Ybarra*. For example, the officers in *Di Re* lacked a search warrant, whereas the police in *Ybarra* had one. *Di Re* involved a vehicle and *Ybarra* involved a public tavern. Also, the state of Illinois did not concede, as the United States did in *Di Re*, that a valid search warrant for a building would not authorize the search of all persons found on the premises. Despite these differences, the *Ybarra* Court concluded that "the governing principle in both cases is basically the same," namely probable cause requires adequate information—particularized suspicion—that justifies singling out the target of a police intrusion.[57]

## IV. The *Pringle* Decision

In *Pringle*, Chief Justice Rehnquist wrote a compact and cryptic opinion for a unanimous Court. After describing the facts and procedural history of the case, the chief justice offered a cursory statement of the black-letter law of probable cause: that probable cause "is incapable of precise definition or quantification into percentages because it deals with probabilities and depends on the totality of

---

[53] *Id.* at 92.
[54] 392 U.S. 1 (1968).
[55] Ybarra, 444 U.S. at 94.
[56] *Id.*
[57] *Id.* at 95.

the circumstances."[58] And he acknowledged that the crux of probable cause depends both upon a reasonable ground for belief of guilt, and a finding that "the belief of guilt must be particularized with respect to the person to be searched or seized."[59]

The chief justice began his analysis with the statement that it is a "reasonable inference from these facts that any or all three of the occupants had knowledge of, and exercised dominion and control over, the cocaine."[60] Thus, according to the chief justice, "a reasonable officer could conclude that there was probable cause to believe that Pringle committed the crime of possession of cocaine, either solely or jointly."[61]

The chief justice peremptorily dismissed Pringle's reliance on *Di Re* and *Ybarra*. First, he distinguished *Ybarra* because Pringle and his companions were in a relatively small car, not a public tavern. Pringle's location in a vehicle was significant because the Court, three years earlier, had stated in *Wyoming v. Houghton* that ' "a car passenger—unlike the unwitting tavern patron in *Ybarra*—will often be engaged in a common enterprise with the driver, and have the same interest in concealing the fruits or the evidence of their wrongdoing.' "[62] Therefore, the Court found it reasonable for Officer Snyder to "infer a common enterprise" among Pringle and his companions because "[t]he quantity of drugs and cash in the car indicated the likelihood of drug dealing, an enterprise to which a dealer would be unlikely to admit an innocent person with the potential to furnish evidence against him."[63] The chief justice then summarily rejected Pringle's reliance on *Di Re*. He explained that—unlike in *Di Re* where the informant had singled out the driver as part of a criminal conspiracy, but had not singled out Di Re—"[n]o such singling out occurred in this case; none of the three men provided information with respect to the ownership of the cocaine or money."[64]

---

[58] Maryland v. Pringle, 124 S. Ct. 795, 800 (2003).

[59] *Id.* (citing Ybarra v. Illinois, 444 U.S. 85, 91 (1979)).

[60] Pringle, 124 S. Ct. at 800.

[61] *Id.*

[62] *Id.* at 801 (quoting Wyoming v. Houghton, 526 U.S. 295, 304–05 (1999)).

[63] Pringle, 124 S. Ct. at 801.

[64] *Id.*

## V. Troublesome Aspects of *Pringle*

The length, tone and unanimity of the chief justice's opinion suggest that the Court viewed *Pringle* as a rather trivial case. Although unanimous or lopsided majority decisions occasionally mask deep divisions within the Court on a particular issue,[65] *Pringle* seems to reflect the views of most, if not all, of the current justices regarding the meaning of probable cause in the twenty-first century: namely, the view that probable cause, like its counterpart reasonable suspicion, should not be seen as a rigid or fixed legal concept. To the modern Court, probable cause is better understood as a common-sense, elastic measure of guilt—geared for laypersons, not legal minds. In short, probable cause is the equivalent of reasonableness. Did the police, based on the facts available, act reasonably in arresting the suspect? In the real world, this understanding of probable cause authorizes broad police discretion.[66] Viewed from this perspective, *Pringle* becomes an easy case.

[65] See Donald A. Dripps, Constitutional Theory for Criminal Procedure: Dickerson, Miranda and the Continuing Quest for Broad-But-Shallow, 43 Wm. & Mary L. Rev. 1, 3 (2001) (explaining the fact that "Chief Justice Rehnquist, for decades an implacable critic of *Miranda*, wrote the majority opinion [in *Dickerson v. United States* is] . . . a sure sign of a compromise opinion, intentionally written to say less rather than more, for the sake of achieving a strong majority on the narrow question of *Miranda's* continued validity.").

[66] See Illinois v. Gates, 462 U.S. 213, 235 (1983) (asserting that "the term probable cause, according to its usual acceptation, means less than evidence which would justify condemnation. . . . It imports a seizure made under circumstances which *warrant suspicion.*") (citation and internal quotations omitted) (emphasis added); *id.* at 238 (stating that the task of the magistrate when issuing a search warrant "is simply to make a practical, common-sense" decision whether, based on the totality of the facts, "there is a *fair probability* that contraband or evidence of a crime will be found in a particular place") (emphasis added). As Professor Wasserstrom has pointed out, the former passage in *Gates* "effectively define[s] probable cause as reasonable suspicion." Wasserstrom, *supra* note 2, at 336. The latter passage's use of the words "fair probability" instead of the words "probable cause" is objectionable because

> " 'Fair probability[]' . . . is a vague concept; it possibly could mean a twenty percent chance, a ten percent chance, or even a five percent chance that the evidence will be found. Fair probability can only mean 'some possibility,' which, in turn, translates to 'reason to suspect.' "

*Id.* at 338. See also United States v. Arvizu, 534 U.S. 266, 277 (2002) (stating that "[a] determination that reasonable suspicion exists, however, need not rule out the possibility of innocent conduct"); see also Illinois v. Wardlow, 528 U.S. 119, 126 (2000) (conceding that Fourth Amendment doctrine accepts the risk that "persons arrested and detained on probable cause to believe they have committed a crime may turn out to be innocent").

Normally, one should pause before undertaking a harsh critique of a unanimous opinion of the Court. In this case, however, I feel fortified because Professor LaFave, the nation's foremost expert on the Fourth Amendment,[67] agrees with me that *Pringle* is a poorly reasoned decision.[68] Indeed, *Pringle* is a much more significant, and disturbing, case than the opinion of the Court would lead one to believe. Three things are particularly striking about the chief justice's opinion. First, while the chief justice does not deny that individualized suspicion is an element of probable cause, he never explains why that element is satisfied under the facts. Second, *Pringle* claims to follow the "totality-of-the-circumstances" standard for measuring whether probable cause exists in a particular case. But a closer look at the inferences that the chief justice accepts indicates that the Court effectively creates a *per se* rule that police discovery of contraband or evidence of criminality provides probable cause to arrest multiple suspects on the scene. Finally, the chief justice's opinion would have the reader believe that the result in *Pringle* is consistent with the Court's probable cause precedents. The chief justice's opinion, however, provides no serious analysis of *Di Re* and *Ybarra*, which may suggest that the two rulings no longer command the full respect of the Court. I examine each feature of the opinion in greater detail below.

## A. Individualized Suspicion as an Element of Probable Cause

Although the Court has been reluctant to define the concept of probable cause with any precision or quantification, the Court's precedents have recognized that particularized or individualized suspicion is an essential element of probable cause. Chief Justice Rehnquist's opinion in *Pringle* readily concedes the point when he notes that probable cause requires "that the belief of guilt must be particularized with respect to the person to be searched or seized."[69]

---

[67] The justices of the Rehnquist Court have cited to Professor LaFave's Fourth Amendment scholarship at least twenty-one times since the start of the 1986–1987 Term. Search of Westlaw SCT database (July 17, 2004) (searching for United States Supreme Court citations to Professor LaFave on Fourth Amendment issues from January 1, 1986, to the present).

[68] See 3 Wayne R. LaFave, Search and Seizure § 7.1(c) (4th ed. forthcoming 2004) (on file with author).

[69] Maryland v. Pringle, 124 S. Ct. 795, 800 (2003) (citing Ybarra v. Illinois, 444 U.S. 85, 91 (1979)).

The chief justice's unqualified endorsement of the individualized suspicion component is somewhat surprising, particularly because the solicitor general's brief had questioned the continuing validity of *Di Re*'s reasoning.[70] But while the chief justice pays lip service to individualized suspicion, he never explains why that element is satisfied in *Pringle*.

The requirement of particularized probable cause to validate a search or seizure did not have its origin in the Warren Court's revolution in criminal procedure. On the contrary, the requirement predates the adoption of the Fourth Amendment. As Professor Thomas Davies recently explained, "'probable cause' *alone* was not the common-law standard for criminal warrants; . . . common law required that arrest or search warrants had to be based on an allegation of an offense or theft 'in fact' as well as 'probable cause of suspicion' as to a particular person to be arrested or place to be searched."[71]

The American colonists and the Framers of the Constitution also recognized that searches and arrests were unreasonable if conducted without particularized or individualized suspicion. Prior to the 1780s, the colonists focused their wrath on writs of assistance and general warrants. These law enforcement tools granted customs officials and law enforcement officers unchecked discretion to intrude into the homes and businesses of the colonists. Although writs of assistance and general warrants were universally damned by the colonists, by the 1780s, colonial protests against British search and seizure practices also extended to general excise searches and search warrants, which were often issued groundlessly.[72] The colonists widely denounced these intrusions for a lack of particularized suspicion. As Justice O'Connor has noted, these protests demonstrated

---

[70] Brief of United States as Amicus Curiae Supporting Petitioner at 7, Maryland v. Pringle, 124 S. Ct. 795 (2003) (No. 02-809) (stating that "the continuing validity of *Di Re* is uncertain in light of later decisions clarifying that a car's passengers normally may be assumed to be engaged in a joint enterprise with each other").

[71] Thomas Y. Davies, Recovering the Original Fourth Amendment, 98 Mich. L. Rev. 547, 703 (1999) (footnote omitted).

[72] William Cuddihy, The Fourth Amendment: Origins and Original Meaning, 602–1791, 1402 (unpublished Ph.D. Dissertation, Claremont Graduate School 1990).

that "the individualized suspicion requirement has a legal pedigree as old as the Fourth Amendment itself."[73]

It is a fair summary of the history of the Fourth Amendment to say that the provision reflected the Framers' desire to control the discretion of ordinary law enforcement officers and to eliminate governmental intrusions lacking particularized suspicion.[74] The intrusions that motivated the Framers' thinking and protests were broad, suspicionless *searches*.[75] On the other hand, the Framers found *arrest* authority less troubling because common-law rules established strict limits on an officer's power to arrest. "Except for the vicarious concerns over the use of general warrants for arrests in connection with the English Wilkesite cases, which involved both arrests and searches of houses and papers, the prerevolutionary controversies were devoid of any consideration of arrest authority."[76] The absence of protest regarding a constable's arrest authority is not surprising because "the Framers understood that justifications for warrantless arrests and accompanying searches were quite limited," and they "did *not* perceive the peace officer as possessing any significant *ex officio* discretionary arrest or search authority."[77] And despite many statements to the contrary in the Court's Fourth Amendment jurisprudence and academic articles, "framing-era common law never permitted a warrantless officer to justify an arrest or search according to any standard as loose or flexible as 'reasonableness.'"[78]

---

[73] Vernonia School Dist. 47J v. Acton, 515 U.S. 646, 678 (1995) (O'Connor, J., dissenting).

[74] See, e.g., Davies, *supra* note 71, at 556, 590 (the "larger purpose for which the Framers adopted the [amendment . . . was] to curb the exercise of discretionary authority by officers"; the Framers "were concerned that legislation might make general warrants legal in the future, and thus undermine the right of security in person and house. Thus, the Framers adopted constitutional search and seizure provisions with the precise aim of ensuring protection of person and house by prohibiting legislative approval of general warrants.").

[75] *Id.* at 590, 601.

[76] *Id.* at 601 (referring to the British legal cases starting in 1763 sparked by John Wilkes's publication of a seditious journal against the British Crown; Wilkes and his colleagues challenged the Crown's authority to search and arrest any person connected with the seditious publication).

[77] *Id.* at 640 (emphasis added); see also *id.* at 641 ("The bottom line is that the Framers perceived warrant authority as the salient mode of arrest and search authority.").

[78] *Id.* at 578 (footnote omitted).

The common law treated particularized suspicion as an intrinsic prerequisite for a warrantless arrest. As Professor Davies explains, the "felony in fact" rule was the "operative common-law justification for a warrantless arrest" in American law in 1789.[79] Under this rule, an officer could justify a warrantless arrest "only upon proof that a 'felony in fact' had actually been committed by someone and that there was 'probable cause of suspicion' to think the arrestee was that person."[80] The "felony in fact" rule imposed substantial limitations on a constable's arrest authority. Arrests based solely on probable cause were impermissible.[81] Not only did the officer have to know that a "felony in fact" had been committed, but he also needed probable cause of suspicion to think that a particular person—the arrestee—committed the crime.

It is not surprising that Chief Justice Rehnquist omits any reference to the "legal pedigree" of the individualized suspicion requirement in *Pringle*. Three years ago the Court announced—in an opinion written by Justice Scalia, and joined by the chief justice—that a historical inquiry is the starting point for *every* Fourth Amendment case. Since then, the Rehnquist Court's consideration of history in search and seizure cases has neither been predictable, nor consistent.[82] In this case, however, the chief justice's omission of historical concerns is readily explained: *Pringle* recognizes that individualized suspicion is an element of probable cause.

What is less readily explained is *why* the chief justice believed that element had been satisfied. As Professor LaFave notes, the chief justice "never offers a single word by way of specific explanation"[83] that would justify a finding of individualized suspicion. Instead, the chief justice suggests, in conclusory fashion, that it is "an entirely

---

[79] *Id.* at 632.

[80] *Id.*

[81] The authority to arrest on probable cause alone was established in England in 1827, long after the Fourth Amendment had been ratified. See Beckwith v. Philby, 108 Eng. Rep. 585 (1827). The "first American reported decisions to endorse the [stand-alone] probable cause standard for warrantless arrests by officers were the 1844 Pennsylvania decision *Russell v. Shuster*, [8 Watts & Serg. 308 (Pa. 1844)] and the 1850 Massachusetts decision *Rohan v. Swain*, [59 Mass. (5 Cush.) 281 (1850)]." Davies, *supra* note 71, at 636–37 (footnotes omitted).

[82] See generally, Tracey Maclin, Let Sleeping Dogs Lie: Why the Supreme Court Should Leave Fourth Amendment History Unabridged, 82 B.U. L. Rev. 895 (2002).

[83] 3 LaFave, *supra* note 68, § 7.1(c).

reasonable inference . . . that any or all three of the occupants had knowledge of, and exercised dominion and control over, the cocaine" found hidden in the backseat armrest.[84] Therefore, "a reasonable officer could conclude that there was probable cause to believe Pringle committed the crime of possession of cocaine, either *solely* or jointly."[85]

That inference, however, is baseless. Professor LaFave already has noted that "it is not easy to see what logic would support" the chief justice's inference that Pringle alone was in possession of cocaine.[86] "[I]f an inference of sole possession was to be drawn, it would most logically be drawn as to Partlow, who was both the driver and the owner of the vehicle."[87] The fact that Partlow granted the officer consent to search the car hardly points to Pringle's guilt as the sole possessor of the cocaine. And it is not obvious why Pringle's guilt should be inferred from the fact that there was a large roll of cash in the glove compartment "directly in front of Pringle."[88] As Professor LaFave points out, "there is no fact in the case suggesting it was more likely that Pringle put the money in the glove compartment during the journey than that Partlow had put the money there beforehand, nor is there even an indication that the contents of the glove compartment had been visible to Pringle prior to the time that Partlow opened the compartment to get his registration upon the request of the police."[89]

Although it may not always please the justices and their critics, Fourth Amendment cases often turn on factual details that seem innocuous at first reading. For better or for worse, the Court's Fourth

---

[84] Maryland v. Pringle, 124 S. Ct. 795, 800 (2003).

[85] *Id.* (emphasis added).

[86] 3 LaFave, *supra* note 68, § 7.1(c).

[87] *Id.*

[88] Pringle, 124 S. Ct. at 800.

[89] 3 LaFave, *supra* note 68, § 7.1(c). Professor LaFave also notes that none of the facts make "Partlow a more likely sole participant than the rear-seat passenger Smith, who was the closest to the hidden cocaine which, considering its hiding place, might well have been quickly concealed as the vehicle was being pulled over. Though the Court contends that the hidden cocaine was 'accessible to all three men,' it would have taken a contortionist to hide the drugs there from a front-seat position during the stopping of the vehicle." *Id.*

Amendment jurisprudence is replete with "hair-splitting distinctions" that decide cases.[90] What is striking about *Pringle* is that the logic upholding one of the chief justice's explanations of the case—that Pringle was in sole possession of the cocaine—is not supported by the facts.

Equally troublesome is the conflict between the chief justice's legal conclusion and the individualized probable cause rule established in *Di Re* and *Ybarra*. Chief Justice Rehnquist makes no serious effort to reconcile the result in *Pringle* with *Di Re*. Recall that the *Di Re* Court began its analysis by rejecting the government's claim that Di Re's presence in a car containing contraband provided probable cause to search Di Re himself. "We are not convinced that a person, by mere presence in a suspected car, loses immunities from search of his person to which he would otherwise be entitled."[91] If Di Re's presence in a vehicle containing contraband in *plain view* did not provide probable cause to search Di Re, why does Pringle's presence in a car containing *hidden* contraband provide probable cause to arrest Pringle? Chief Justice Rehnquist never explains this discrepancy.

The *Di Re* Court also rejected the government's alternative argument that there was probable cause to arrest Di Re. Although the government conceded in *Di Re* that the only person who committed an offense in the "open presence" of the police was the informant, Reed, the government insisted that Di Re could also be arrested on conspiracy and possession charges.[92] The *Di Re* Court disagreed as to both counts. On the possession charge, the Court concluded that Di Re's presence in the vehicle did not provide probable cause for an arrest, and explained that "[i]t is admitted that at the time of arrest the officers had no information implicating Di Re and no information pointing to possession of any coupons, unless his presence in the car warranted that inference."[93]

If there was no probable cause to arrest Di Re on possession charges, notwithstanding his presence in a vehicle with someone who openly possessed contraband, then why was there probable

---

[90] Quarles v. New York, 467 U.S. 649, 664 (1984) (O'Connor, J., op.).

[91] United States v. Di Re, 332 U.S. 581, 587 (1948).

[92] *Id.* at 592.

[93] *Id.*

cause to arrest Pringle when the only contraband involved was hidden from view? Again, the chief justice provides no explanation for this inconsistency. The fact that the contraband was "accessible to" Pringle does not distinguish his case from that of Di Re, because Di Re had just as much access to contraband.

The chief justice's opinion further conflicts with the Court's holding in *Ybarra*. Like the defendant in *Ybarra*, Pringle "made no gestures indicative of criminal conduct, made no movements that might suggest an attempt to conceal contraband, and said nothing of a suspicious nature to the police officer[]."[94] Furthermore, as in *Ybarra*, Officer Snyder "knew nothing in particular"[95] about Pringle, except that he was present, along with two other occupants, in an automobile that contained illegal drugs. But *Ybarra* (and *Di Re*) had already established that a person's mere presence or association with others suspected of criminality does not constitute probable cause to search or arrest that individual.

*Ybarra* held that the standard of probable cause requires particularized suspicion of the person searched or seized. The particularized suspicion requirement "cannot be undercut or avoided by simply pointing to the fact that coincidentally there exists probable cause to search or seize another or to search the premises where the person may happen to be."[96] The chief justice cites this principle, but offers no explanation as to why the facts demonstrate individualized probable cause that Pringle solely possessed the cocaine.

In short, *Pringle*—while paying lip service to individualized suspicion—effectively appears to have denuded probable cause of any such requirement.

B. *"Common Enterprise" as Probable Cause*

The second striking aspect of *Pringle* is the expansive nature of the "common enterprise" inference drawn by Chief Justice Rehnquist. Although the chief justice insists that his reasoning is consistent with prior precedent and the totality-of-the-circumstances test for measuring probable cause, a closer look at *Pringle* indicates that there is reason to doubt the chief justice on both points.

---

[94] Ybarra v. Illinois, 444 U.S. 85, 91 (1979).

[95] *Id.*

[96] *Id.*

As noted above, the chief justice first concludes that an inference that Pringle solely possessed the drugs is reasonable under the facts. He also supports his holding on the alternative inference that *"any or all three* of the occupants had knowledge of, and exercised dominion and control over, the cocaine" discovered hidden in the backseat armrest.[97] A few paragraphs later, the chief justice reiterates that "it was reasonable for the officer to infer a *common enterprise* among the three men."[98] He then explains that the "quantity of drugs and cash in the car indicated the likelihood of drug dealing, an enterprise to which a dealer would be unlikely to admit an innocent person with the potential to furnish evidence against him."[99]

The chief justice's conclusion that it was reasonable to infer a drug conspiracy from these facts mirrors the arguments presented by the prosecutors. Maryland had argued that "when multiple occupants are present in a car containing illegal drugs, a commonsense inference can be drawn that *any or all* of the occupants have knowledge of the drugs found in the car."[100] Likewise, the amicus brief of the solicitor general had stated that "the presence of drugs—without more—immediately reveals criminal activity. . . . [T]he discovery of an amount of narcotics suitable for distribution in the passenger compartment supports an inference that *all* of the car's occupants were aware of, and hence involved with, the drugs."[101]

There are several problems with the chief justice's "common enterprise" theory: First, the inference flies in the face of the *Di Re* Court's refusal to draw the same inference from facts that were even more incriminating than the facts in *Pringle*; second, the chief justice makes no effort to tie his inference with the common experience of drivers and passengers; and finally, as a practical matter, the inference drawn by the chief justice translates into a rule that allows police to arrest everyone on the scene anytime they discover contraband in compact spaces. Simply stated, the chief justice's inference is unlikely to be confined to "car" cases.

---

[97] Maryland v. Pringle, 124 S. Ct. 795, 800 (2003) (emphasis added).

[98] *Id.* at 801 (emphasis added).

[99] *Id.*

[100] Brief of Petitioner at 17, Maryland v. Pringle, 124 S. Ct. 795 (2003) (No. 02-809) (emphasis added).

[101] Brief for the United States as Amicus Curiae Supporting Petitioner at 15, Maryland v. Pringle, 124 S. Ct. 795 (2003) (No. 02-809) (emphasis added).

*1. Is* Pringle's *"Common Enterprise" Theory Consistent With*
Di Re?

The inference that Pringle and his companions were involved
in a drug trafficking conspiracy cannot be reconciled with *Di Re's*
holding. As described earlier, in *Di Re* the government argued that
Di Re's presence in a vehicle with others who openly possessed
contraband provided probable cause to believe Di Re was involved
in a conspiracy. The *Di Re* Court, however, concluded that "[a]n
inference of participation in conspiracy does not seem to be sustained
by the facts peculiar to this case."[102] The Court explained that "[t]here
is no evidence that it is a fact or that the officers had any information
indicating that Di Re was in the car when Reed obtained ration
coupons from Buttitta, and none that he heard or took part in any
conversation on the subject."[103] Yet, the record in *Pringle* is also
devoid of any facts or evidence that Officer Snyder "had any information indicating that [Pringle] was in the car when [the cocaine
was hidden inside the armrest], and none that [Pringle] heard or
took part in any conversation on the subject."[104]

The *Di Re* Court was also unwilling to infer a conspiracy where
"the alleged substantive crime is one which does not necessarily
involve any act *visibly* criminal."[105] In *Pringle,* "the alleged substantive crime" did not involve conduct visible to the occupants of the
car or to Officer Snyder. Indeed, a comparison of *Di Re* and *Pringle*
indicates that Chief Justice Rehnquist was "too generous in finding
an inference of 'common enterprise' where the evidence of criminality was at all times concealed from view and where there was absolutely no indication as to whether the 'enterprise' of drug dealing
would be activated in minutes, hours, days or weeks, while the
Court in *Di Re* refused to draw inferences which were much more
compelling."[106] Unless a reader of *Pringle* was well-versed on the
facts and holding in *Di Re,* he would never know from Chief Justice
Rehnquist's opinion that the *Di Re* Court, faced with facts *more*

---

[102]United States v. Di Re, 332 U.S. 581, 593 (1948).

[103]*Id.*

[104]*Id.*

[105]*Id.* (emphasis added).

[106]3 LaFave, *supra* note 68, § 7.1(c).

417

suggestive of a criminal conspiracy, refused to draw the same inference of criminality that the chief justice draws in *Pringle*.

Chief Justice Rehnquist distinguishes *Di Re* by noting that the informant in *Di Re* had singled out the driver, but not Di Re, as the person who provided the contraband coupons. He then quotes the *Di Re* Court's statement that " '[a]ny inference that everyone on the scene of a crime is a party to [the conspiracy] must disappear if the Government informer singles out the guilty person.' "[107] By contrast, said the chief justice in *Pringle*, "no such singling out occurred [in the *Pringle* case]; none of the three men provided information with respect to the ownership of the cocaine and money."[108]

This is a rather curious, and misleading, way to distinguish *Di Re*. First, as noted, the facts in *Di Re* are just as incriminating as the facts in *Pringle*, given that the counterfeit coupons were in plain view and "accessible to all three men."[109] As Professor LaFave points out, Di Re's involvement in the conspiracy hardly is negated by the fact that the driver in *Di Re* "was the one doing the handing over" of the coupons.[110] An inference that all three men in *Di Re* were involved in the conspiracy is supported by the "fact [that Di Re] was transported to the scene of the prearranged sale of the counterfeit coupons, which was (to use the language of the Court in *Pringle*) 'an enterprise to which a dealer would be unlikely to admit an innocent person with the potential to furnish evidence against him.' "[111]

Second, it is true that the *Di Re* Court stated that "[a]ny inference that everyone on the scene of a crime is a party to it must disappear if the Government informer singles out the guilty party."[112] But what the chief justice does not directly acknowledge is that *prior* to making this statement, the *Di Re* Court had already concluded that Di Re's

---

[107]Maryland v. Pringle, 124 S. Ct. 795, 801 (2003) (quoting United States v. Di Re, 332 U.S. 581, 594 (1948)).

[108]124 S. Ct. at 801.

[109]*Id.* at 800.

[110]3 LaFave, *supra* note 68, § 7.1(c).

[111]*Id.*

[112]Di Re, 332 U.S. at 594. The *Di Re* Court's characterization of the permissible inferences to be drawn from the facts is somewhat curious because the informant merely said that he had obtained the coupons from Buttita, the driver, which says nothing one way or the other about Di Re's possible involvement.

mere presence in the vehicle did not support an inference of participation in a conspiracy. This is what the *Di Re* Court said prior to
the quotation cited by Chief Justice Rehnquist:

> The argument that one who "accompanies a criminal to a
> crime rendezvous" cannot be assumed to be a bystander,
> forceful enough in some circumstances, is farfetched when
> the meeting is not secretive or in a suspicious hide-out but
> in broad daylight, in plain-sight of passers-by, in a public
> street of a large city, and where the alleged substantive crime
> is one which does not necessarily involve any act visibly
> criminal . . . . Presumptions of guilt are not lightly to be
> indulged from mere meetings.

> Moreover, *whatever suspicion* might result from Di Re's mere
> presence seems diminished, if not destroyed, when Reed,
> present as the informer, pointed out Buttitta, and Buttitta
> only, as the guilty party. No reason appears to doubt that
> Reed willingly would involve Di Re if the nature of the
> transaction permitted. Yet he did not incriminate Di Re.[113]

Of course, it might be argued that Di Re's *presence* in the vehicle
supported an inference of Di Re's participation in a conspiracy, but
Reed's failure to single out Di Re to the police negated that inference.
This interpretation of *Di Re*, however, is contrary to the language
of the first paragraph quoted above, which plainly concludes that
mere presence, under the circumstances, is not enough to infer a
suspect's participation in a conspiracy. Furthermore, the use of the
term "[m]oreover" in the second paragraph suggests that the "singling out" factor—which Chief Justice Rehnquist says was decisive—was not necessary to the result in *Di Re*. The chief justice's
interpretation of *Di Re* is disingenuous. If the "singling out" incident
was the crucial fact, one would expect the *Di Re* Court to zero in
on that point early in its opinion, rather than wait until the end of
the opinion to draw attention to this detail.

Third, even if Chief Justice Rehnquist's interpretation of the "singling out" factor is correct, his reliance on the additional factor that
"none of the three men [in *Pringle*] provided information with respect
to the ownership of the cocaine or money" is inconsistent with what
*Di Re* said about an analogous argument the government had made

[113] *Id.* at 593–94 (emphasis added).

in that case. In *Di Re*, the government argued "that the officers could infer probable cause from the fact that Di Re did not protest his arrest, did not at once assert his innocence, and silently accepted the command to go along to the police station."[114] The Court's full reply to this argument merits repeating:

> [C]ourts will hardly penalize failure to display a spirit of resistance or to hold futile debates on legal issues in the public highway with an officer of the law. A layman may not find it expedient to hazard resistance on his own judgment of the law at a time when he cannot know what information, correct or incorrect, the officers may be acting upon. It is likely to end in fruitless and unseemly controversy in a public street, if not in an additional charge of resisting an officer. If the officers believed they had probable cause for his arrest on a felony charge, it is not to be supposed that they would have been dissuaded by his profession of innocence.
>
> It is the right of one placed under arrest to submit to custody and to reserve his defenses for the tribunals erected by the law for the purpose of judging his case. *An inference of probable cause from a failure to engage in discussion of the merits of the charge with arresting officers is unwarranted.* Probable cause cannot be found from submissiveness, and the presumption of innocence is not lost or impaired by neglect to argue with a policeman. It is the officer's responsibility to know what he is arresting for, and why, and one in the unhappy plight of being taken into custody is not required to test the legality of the arrest before the officer who is making it.[115]

Apparently, the chief justice believes that Pringle or the others could have negated the inference that all three were involved in a conspiracy by offering an explanation to Officer Snyder as to who owned the cocaine. The failure to provide an explanation, presumably, confirmed the officer's suspicion that the men were part of a drug trafficking conspiracy. This conclusion is mistaken for several reasons.

First, Pringle was under no obligation to bring forth "any information" to establish a lack of probable cause for his arrest. If courts

---

[114] *Id.* at 594.

[115] *Id.* at 594–95 (emphasis added).

cannot "penalize [a] failure to display a spirit of resistance or to hold futile debates on legal issues in the public highway" with police officers, why does it matter that Pringle did not provide any information to the police regarding the cocaine or money? Isn't Pringle being "penalize[d]" by the Court when the probable cause analysis permits a negative inference to be drawn from the fact that he did not provide information or otherwise cooperate with the police?

Moreover, if it is an "unwarranted" application of Fourth Amendment principles to draw "[a]n inference of probable cause from a failure to engage in discussion of the merits of the charge with arresting officers," why, when determining whether probable cause exists, is it permissible to consider Pringle's failure to deny ownership of the cocaine or otherwise implicate his companions? If "[p]robable cause cannot be found from submissiveness," it is not self-evident why it can be found from silence.

Second, there are legitimate reasons why a person questioned by the police would not acknowledge or deny ownership of illegal narcotics under these circumstances. Inferences of guilt should not be easily drawn whenever a person relies on "the broad constitutional right to remain silent."[116] The Fifth Amendment's Self-Incrimination Clause protects drivers and passengers from incriminating themselves, and it is a crime to make a false statement to a federal or state law enforcement officer.[117] If Pringle had been allowed to call an attorney during his confrontation with Officer Snyder, "[a]ny lawyer worth his salt w[ould] tell [him] in no uncertain terms to make no statement to police under any circumstances."[118]

Professor LaFave and others, however, have argued that a court, when making the probable cause determination, may validly consider the responses that suspects give to police officers' questions.[119]

---

[116] Hiibel v. Sixth Judicial Dist. Court of Nevada, 124 S. Ct. 2451, 2462 (2004) (Stevens, J., dissenting).

[117] See, e.g., 18 U.S.C. § 1001(2) (2002); Md. Code Ann. § 9-501 (2002).

[118] Watts v. Indiana, 338 U.S. 49, 59 (1949) (Jackson, J., op.).

[119] 2 LaFave, *supra* note 26, § 3.6(f), at 330. In United States v. Ortiz, 422 U.S. 891, 897 (1975), the Court, in dicta, acknowledged that a suspect's responses to police questioning "properly may be taken into account in deciding whether there is probable cause to search a particular vehicle."

Prior to *Pringle*, the Court had repeatedly stated, in contexts involving consensual encounters and investigative detentions, that a suspect's refusal to answer police questions cannot be grounds for detaining or arresting the suspect.[120] According to Professor LaFave, however, "it does not necessarily follow that the suspect's refusal must be ignored completely by the officer."[121]

Professor LaFave contends that "the better view is that refusal to answer is one factor which an officer may consider, together with the evidence that gave rise to his prior suspicion, in determining whether there are grounds for an arrest."[122] Professor LaFave notes that this conclusion is based on the "commonsense" view that, as a general matter, innocent persons normally respond to police questioning.[123] Thus, the probable cause calculus can properly include a suspect's failure to respond to police questioning because that decision "is concerned with 'the factual and practical considerations of everyday life on which reasonable and prudent men, not legal technicians act.'"[124]

I disagree with Professor LaFave's conclusion because I am not sure how an "innocent" person would react in these circumstances.

---

[120] See, e.g., Florida v. Bostick, 501 U.S. 429, 437 (1991) (in the context involving a consensual encounter, explaining that "[w]e have consistently held that a refusal to cooperate, without more, does not furnish the minimal level of objective justification needed for a detention or seizure"); Berkemer v. McCarty, 468 U.S. 420, 439 (1984) (in the context involving a traffic stop, explaining that an "officer may ask the detainee a moderate number of questions to determine his identity and to try to obtain information confirming or dispelling the officer's suspicions. But the detainee is not obliged to respond."). The result in Hiibel v. Sixth Judicial Dist. Court of Nevada, 124 S. Ct. 2451 (2004), does not affect this norm. *Hiibel* upheld the conviction of a person who had refused to identify himself to a police officer during a lawful *Terry* stop. *Hiibel* did not involve a suspect's refusal to answer police inquires or questions about *criminal evidence* the police had found during a lawful investigative stop. In fact, the Court expressly observed "a case may arise where there is a substantial allegation that furnishing identity at the time of a stop would have given the police a link in the chain of evidence needed to convict the individual of a separate offense." *Id.* at 2454. In a post-*Hiibel* world, someone in Pringle's shoes may not have the right to refuse to identify himself without negative consequence, but *Hiibel* does not support the proposition that a refusal to answer police questions about criminal evidence can be grounds for arrest.

[121] 2 LaFave, *supra* note 26, § 3.6(f), at 330.

[122] *Id.* at 330–31.

[123] *Id.* at 331.

[124] *Id.* (quoting Brinegar v. United States, 338 U.S. 160, 175 (1949)).

Perhaps, Professor LaFave is correct that, as a general matter, "common sense" or common experience suggests that innocent persons generally respond to police interrogations. But such reactions may be dictated by a fear of police authority, stem from a previous unpleasant experience with police who reacted negatively to the assertion of one's constitutional rights, or derive from ignorance of one's constitutional rights.

On the other hand, a well-informed, innocent person may choose to exercise his Fifth Amendment rights and not risk the fact that his explanation may be perceived as a false statement. The chief justice's observation that a negative inference can be drawn from a person's failure to provide any information regarding criminal evidence penalizes those who may simply, and correctly, believe they are not competent to deal with a police officer. Whatever the case, neither police officers nor the judiciary honor the spirit of the Self-Incrimination Clause if negative inferences can be drawn for Fourth Amendment purposes whenever a suspect—as in *Pringle*—refuses to respond to police questioning.[125]

Finally, another kind of "common sense" may explain why a saavy person in Pringle's shoes would remain silent in the face of police questioning. Providing an explanation for the cocaine or money, particularly one that the officer does not believe, again, to quote *Di Re*, is "likely to end in fruitless and unseemly controversy in a public street," if not in an "additional charge" of providing a false statement to a law enforcement officer.[126] Remaining silent was the best thing Pringle could do for himself.

Moreover, as a practical matter, there is no reason to believe that an explanation would have prompted the immediate release of any of the men. Even if Pringle (or one of his companions) had given a good faith explanation that described his innocence, or if the backseat passenger had confessed to the crime, there is no hint or suggestion

---

[125] *Cf.* Rachel Karen Laser, Unreasonable Suspicion: Relying on Refusals to Support Terry Stops, 62 U. Chi. L. Rev. 1161, 1178–79 (1995) (noting that the right to refuse a consensual search is undermined "if the exercise of that right can be used against a person . . . . The nature of a right is that its exercise is protected from harmful legal consequences. Such harmful legal consequences are present whether the refusal to consent is used against an individual as the sole factor or as one of many factors contributing to a *Terry* stop or search.") (footnote omitted).

[126] United States v. Di Re, 332 U.S. 581, 594 (1948).

in the chief justice's opinion (or any other precedent of the Court) that Officer Snyder was required to release the other men.

For example, if Smith, the backseat passenger, had claimed that he was a hitchhiker picked up shortly before the traffic stop, there is no search and seizure precedent of the Court (including *Pringle*) that requires the officer to accept that declaration and immediately release Smith.[127] Similarly, if Smith had confessed to owning the cocaine and money, and Pringle and Partlow claimed their innocence, under the government's theory of the case, the officer still could have arrested all three.[128]

Again, there is nothing in *Pringle* that disputes or suggests disagreement with the government's argument on this point. In fact, because the Court holds that the officer had probable cause to believe that Pringle committed the crime of possession of cocaine, "either solely or *jointly*,"[129] the chief justice seems to endorse the government's position that police are not required to credit a person's

---

[127]This hypothetical was discussed during the oral argument in *Pringle*:
QUESTION: The hitchhiker—the hitchhiker example poses a question for the arresting officer, because does he have to accept the declaration of someone that I'm just a hitchhiker here?
MR. BAIR (COUNSEL FOR MARYLAND): No, and—and that, of course, goes back to whether it's undisputed in some way, I don't know quite how it would be undisputed. You've always got the—the officer who on the scene is making a reasonable judgment [sic] from all the facts and circumstances, and one of those is, I don't have to believe the criminal or criminals in this car. I know there are drugs in the car, we have a known crime here being committed in the presence of the officer, possession or possession with intent to distribute drugs.
Transcript of Oral Argument at 18, Maryland v. Pringle, 124 S. Ct. 795 (2004) (hereinafter "Oral Argument Transcript").

[128]QUESTION: You'd think if the—if the backseat person or whoever it was that confessed had confessed while the officer was arresting him, there would have remained the probable cause as to the other two? Could he have said, I don't believe you, I'll take all three of you in anyway?
MR. SRINIVASAN (ASSISTANT TO THE SOLICITOR GENERAL): There might well have been, Justice Stevens, because an officer's not required to believe the version of events that's given to him by people on the scene. It might well be the case that they have a coordinated plan in advance to pin the blame on a particular person as opposed to the other two, and an officer can take into account the totality of circumstances in making that type of assessment.
Oral Argument Transcript at 23–24. Cf. Di Re, 332 U.S. at 594 ("If the officers believed they had probable cause for [Di Re's] arrest on a felony charge, it is not to be supposed that they would have been dissuaded by this profession of innocence.").

[129]Maryland v. Pringle, 124 S. Ct. 795, 801 (2003) (emphasis added).

innocent explanation. Put simply, the "failure-to-offer-any-information" factor constitutes a win-win situation for the police. A failure to provide information counts against the suspect. But if the suspect does provide an explanation, the police are not required to credit the explanation and can still arrest everyone on the scene.

### 2. *The "Evidentiary" Basis of* Pringle's *"Common Enterprise" Inference*

As Professor LaFave explains in the newest edition of his treatise, the facts of *Pringle* do not provide strong evidence for the chief justice's "common enterprise" theory. Professor LaFave agrees that the quantity of drugs and money indicate a likelihood of drug dealing, but he points to other contingencies that undermine the inference that *all three* men were involved in a drug conspiracy: "Nothing at all was known about where the vehicle was headed or what the purpose of the journey was, and nothing at all was known about the association of the three individuals except that they happened to be together at the moment the vehicle was stopped by the police officer."[130] According to LaFave, this lack of information, when combined with the fact that there is no evidence in the record that either the money or drugs were in open view during the trip, demonstrate that "the Court has made a good many leaps in logic in concluding there was probable cause that the occupants of the vehicle consisted not only of a 'dealer' of drugs but also others who had been 'admit[-ted] to the 'enterprise' of drug dealing.'"[131]

To bolster his conclusion that there was probable cause of a drug conspiracy, the chief justice notes that "'a car passenger—unlike the unwitting tavern patron in *Ybarra*—will often be engaged in a common enterprise with the driver, and have the same interest in concealing the fruits or the evidence of their wrongdoing.'"[132] I share Professor LaFave's view that the claim that car passengers typically act in concert with the driver "is grounded in nothing more than the Court's earlier dubious assumption, put forward without any empirical support in *Wyoming v. Houghton*."[133]

---

[130] 3 LaFave, *supra* note 68, § 7.1(c).

[131] *Id.* (citations omitted).

[132] Pringle, 124 S. Ct. at 801 (quoting Wyoming v. Houghton, 526 U.S. 295, 304–05 (1999)).

[133] 3 LaFave, *supra* note 68, § 7.1(c).

It is not surprising that the chief justice's "common enterprise" inference rests on a premise lacking empirical support. The chief justice has recently explained that the probable cause and reasonable suspicion standards need not be based on "empirical studies dealing with inferences drawn from suspicious behavior," and that the Court will not "demand scientific certainty from judges or law enforcement officers where none exists."[134] Rather than rely on empirical data, the chief justice has instructed that "commonsense judgments and inferences about human behavior" must control determinations of probable cause and reasonable suspicion.[135] But neither common-sense nor common experience, dictate the logic employed in *Pringle*.

The chief justice's inference rests on the premise that a car passenger will often be aware of the contents of accessible parts of an automobile, even if those contents are hidden from view. The accuracy of this premise is not obvious. The innocent graduate student who is offered a ride home by a friend or classmate after a late-night party will not search underneath the seat, open the backseat armrest, or examine the glove compartment before accepting the ride home. Likewise, the office worker who offers to drive two colleagues to a weekend beach house late on a Friday night will not demand the right to search the bags of his invitees before starting the trip. As Justice Powell noted,

> [T]here are countless situations in which individuals are invited as guests into vehicles the contents of which they know nothing about, much less have control over. Similarly, those who invite others into their automobile do not generally search them to determine what they may have on their person; nor do they insist that any handguns [or drugs] be identified and placed within reach of the occupants of the automobile. Indeed, handguns [and drugs] are particularly susceptible to concealment and therefore are less likely than are other objects to be observed by those in an automobile.[136]

---

[134] Illinois v. Wardlow, 528 U.S. 119, 125 (2000). See also United States v. Arvizu, 534 U.S. 266, 277 (2002) (emphasizing that under a totality test, "due weight" must be accorded the factual inferences drawn by law enforcement officers in determining whether reasonable suspicion exists).

[135] Wardlow, 528 U.S. at 125.

[136] County Court of Ulster County v. Allen, 442 U.S. 140, 174 (1979) (Powell, J., dissenting).

None of this matters, however, to the chief justice. He makes no effort to ground his "common enterprise" theory on empirical data or any other daily experience of motorists. As two commentators have expressed, here, as elsewhere, the chief justice eschews "[r]eliance on evidence about the real world," which, in turn, permits the Court to avoid disclosing the "normative judgments" and "interpretative choices"[137] that explain the inferences and legal conclusions established in *Pringle*.

### 3. Has Pringle *Created a New Rule That Will Extend Beyond Car Cases?*

As Justice Powell's observations suggest, the "common enterprise" inference approved in *Pringle* was not dictated by a "common sense" approach for determining probable cause. But does it follow that *Pringle* translates into a new *per se* rule that permits the arrest of multiple suspects whenever police discover contraband in compact spaces? There is reason to think so. The basis for that concern is twofold: one, *Pringle* adopts the logic of *Wyoming v. Houghton*, which itself creates a per se rule for probable cause cases involving automobiles; and two, there is no principled justification for limiting *Pringle's* logic to cases involving vehicles.

### a. The Parallels Between Pringle and Houghton

To see how *Pringle* may translate into a new per se rule, a closer look at *Houghton* is warranted. *Houghton* held that "police officers with probable cause to search a car may inspect passengers' belongings found in the car that are capable of concealing the object of the search."[138] Writing for the majority, Justice Scalia's opinion in *Houghton* conceded that the search of Houghton's purse was not based on individualized probable cause that it contained drugs.[139] Justice Scalia also conceded that his assertion that a car passenger "will often be engaged in a common enterprise with the driver, and have the same interest in concealing the fruits or the evidence of their wrongdoing," will "not always be present" in every case involving

---

[137] Tracey L. Meares & Bernard E. Harcourt, Foreword: Transparent Adjudication and Social Science Research in Constitutional Criminal Procedure, 90 J. Crim. L. & Criminology 733, 746, 735, 793 (2000).

[138] Wyoming v. Houghton, 526 U.S. 295, 307 (1999).

[139] *Id.* at 302.

multiple occupants of a vehicle.[140] Nevertheless, *Houghton* announced a bright-line rule that a passenger's belongings can always be searched because "the balancing of interests must be conducted with an eye to the generality of cases."[141] The upshot of *Houghton* is that a car passenger's companionship and access to another person suspected of criminal behavior is *always* sufficient to establish probable cause to search the belongings of the passenger left in the car, even where there is no individualized probable cause to justify the search.

*Houghton* undoubtedly changed the rules for *searches* of a car passenger's belongings left in the car. But there was nothing in Justice Scalia's opinion to suggest that *Houghton*'s *per se* rule also governed the *arrest* of a passenger. In fact, Justice Scalia was careful to draw a distinction between a search of property left in a car and a search of the person.[142] Justice Scalia's distinction between searches of property and searches of persons makes good sense, as well as good constitutional law. The reduced expectation of privacy associated with property found in cars derives from the fact that vehicles rarely serve as

---

[140] *Id.* at 304–05.

[141] *Id.* at 305. Justice Breyer's concurring opinion also acknowledged that Houghton created a bright-line rule that authorizes searches of passengers' belongings. *Id.* at 307–08. (Breyer, J., concurring).

[142] Acknowledging the authority of *Di Re* and *Ybarra*, which invalidated personal searches of individuals who were in close proximity to others suspected of crime, *Houghton* specifically distinguishes a search of a passenger's property from a search of the passenger's person. Justice Scalia explains that a search of a passenger's property is reasonable because of the "reduced expectation of privacy" associated with property found in a vehicle. Houghton, 526 U.S. at 303. It is unreasonable, however, to search a passenger's person absent individualized probable cause. That is because "the degree of intrusiveness upon personal privacy and indeed even personal dignity," makes the search of the person "differ substantially from the package search at issue" in *Houghton. Id.* at 303. If, to use the language of Justice Scalia, the Fourth Amendment affords "significantly heightened protection [ ] against searches of one's person," and the "traumatic consequences" associated with a personal search are not to be visited upon a passenger due to his presence in a car containing contraband, *id.* at 303, it is difficult to understand why the far more traumatic consequences inherent in an arrest may be visited upon a passenger due to his presence in a vehicle containing contraband. In other words, if the analysis employed in *Houghton* would not authorize a search of Pringle's person, certainly permitting Pringle's arrest flies in the face of *Houghton*'s reasoning. Cf. 3 Wayne R. LaFave, Search and Seizure, § 7.2, at 124 (3d ed. 1996) (Pocket Part 2003) (observing that "*Houghton* actually reaffirms *Di Re*").

the repository of personal effects; are subject to pervasive governmental regulation; and are exposed to traffic accidents that "render all their contents open to public scrutiny."[143] None of these justifications for searching property translate into an equivalent lesser expectation of freedom for passengers inside the vehicle. Thus, *Houghton* said nothing to vitiate *Di Re's* holding that "companionship with an offender at the very time of the latter's criminal conduct is not inevitably sufficient to establish probable cause for arrest of the companion."[144]

*Houghton's per se* rule that permits searching a passenger's property based solely upon accessibility to others was intended only to apply to the *search* context.[145] Prior to *Pringle*, lower courts have tended to conduct a more nuanced analysis of police power to *arrest* multiple occupants of a vehicle when drugs or contraband were found hidden inside the vehicle. Relying on the analysis of *Di Re*, some lower courts reasoned that the visibility of contraband or other evidence of criminality to third persons is an important factor. When contraband was not in plain view, the lower courts required something more than companionship or access to establish probable cause for arrest. "When the suspected criminal activity [is] such that its existence [is] not evident to others in the vicinity, it is then necessary to give careful consideration to those aspects of the extent and nature of the association which may indicate that the associate is also an accomplice."[146] These cases supported *Pringle*, because in his case, the criminal conduct at issue—cocaine possession—also was not evident to others on the scene. Officer Snyder was unaware of the drugs until he searched the car. And Pringle made no furtive gestures or other suspicious movements. In short, the facts in *Pringle* did not involve any telltale signs of suspicious behavior often observed by the police to support the inference that Pringle was an accomplice in criminal behavior.[147]

---

[143] Houghton, 526 U.S. at 303 (citations omitted).

[144] 2 LaFave, *supra* note 26, § 3.6(c), at 310.

[145] *Cf.* Houghton, 526 U.S. at 308 (Breyer, J., concurring) ("Obviously, the [bright-line] rule applies only to automobile searches .... And it does not extend to the search of a person found in that automobile").

[146] 2 LaFave, *supra* note 26, § 3.6(c), at 311 (footnote omitted).

[147] *Id.* at 312 n.108 (listing cases in which suspicious conduct of a person supported an inference that he was involved with the criminality of his traveling companions).

In *Pringle*, however, the chief justice abandoned the nuanced analysis of *Di Re*, and embraced the broad, *per se* reasoning of *Houghton*. For the chief justice, it is inconsequential that the cocaine discovered in *Pringle* was hidden from view. For the chief justice, the fact that the cocaine was "accessible to all three men" was more important.[148] This "accessibility" factor, however—much like *Houghton*'s bright-line rule—is simultaneously over-inclusive and under-inclusive. Purses and briefcases located in the passenger compartment are also accessible to other passengers. If the cocaine was found in a knapsack owned by Smith, the rear seat passenger, would it be reasonable for the police to infer that all three men were engaged in a drug conspiracy because Smith's knapsack "was accessible to all three men"? On the other hand, accessibility proves very little because *Di Re* already established that a passenger's presence and accessibility to another involved with crime does not automatically justify the arrest of the passenger. This is especially so, as Professor LaFave has noted, "when, as in *Di Re*, it is very possible for the criminal conduct to be occurring without the knowledge of the companion."[149]

Ultimately, the logic and inferences approved in *Pringle* track the reasoning of *Houghton*. *Houghton* permitted a search based on nothing more than companionship and accessibility to someone who was suspected of criminality. *Pringle* permits an arrest based on the same criteria. Just as *Houghton* eviscerated the individualized probable cause requirement in the search context, so *Pringle* goes a long way toward crippling *Di Re*'s individualized probable cause requirement in the arrest context. As Professor LaFave explains, *Pringle* permits an inference of "probable cause of a joint enterprise without the critical 'something extra' that lower courts have typically required in cases of this genre—that the passenger in question had been a co-traveler for a longer time, had fled from the police, or in response to police questioning had been untruthful, evasive or very nervous."[150]

### b. Problems of Containment

Finally, there is no principled basis for confining *Pringle*'s reasoning to car cases. The "common enterprise" inference is equally

---

[148] Maryland v. Pringle, 124 S. Ct. 795, 800 (2003).

[149] 2 LaFave, *supra* note 26, § 3.6 (c), at 310.

[150] 3 LaFave, *supra* note 68, § 7.1(c) (footnote omitted).

appropriate in contexts not involving automobiles. Consider, for example, the following hypothetical: Assume Baltimore police come to A's studio apartment at 3:00 a.m. in response to a noise complaint. A is having a party with two or three of his closest friends. After telling A to lower the music, the police obtain A's consent to search the premises for weapons or drugs. An officer lifts a pillow on the couch and discovers a large amount of money and several baggies of cocaine. After A and his friends refuse to talk about the money or drugs, the police arrest everyone on the premises.

Why shouldn't *Pringle's* logic validate all of the arrests? In the hypothetical case, no less than in *Pringle*, A and his friends were found in a relatively small private apartment, not a public place. The money and drugs were accessible to everyone in the room. "The quantity of drugs and cash [found in the couch] indicated the likelihood of drug dealing, an enterprise to which a dealer would be unlikely to admit an innocent person with the potential to furnish evidence against him."[151] After being questioned, A and his friends "failed to offer any information with respect to the ownership of the cocaine or the money."[152] And there was no "singling out" as to who owned the drugs or money.

Put simply, where drugs and money are discovered in a confined spatial context, there is a sufficient personal nexus between the individuals in that space, and none of the persons provide an explanation or information regarding the ownership of the drugs or money, the logic of *Pringle* provides probable cause to arrest everyone on the scene.

Is there a neutral principle that cabins *Pringle's* holding to cases involving "a relatively small automobile"?[153] I would say no. Although one could plausibly interpret *Pringle* only to apply in contexts involving small vehicles,[154] it is not obvious why *Pringle's*

---

[151] Pringle, 124 S. Ct. at 801.

[152] *Id.* at 800.

[153] *Id.* at 801.

[154] See 3 LaFave, *supra* note 68, § 7.1(c). Professor LaFave appropriately observes that "it is important to note [*Pringle*] did not merely distinguish cars from premises. The Court tells us *Pringle* is not merely a vehicle case, but rather a 'relatively small automobile' case, which suggests that the *Pringle* inference would not apply in the case of a larger vehicle, where it could not as readily be asserted that the place where the drugs were found was 'accessible to all three men.'"

logic should be restricted to cars. "[I]f one accepts the result in *Pringle* then it cannot be said the inference drawn in that case would *never* be appropriate when several people are present in private premises, especially if the premises are small or at least the drugs are found in a particular location where, once again, all those present had ready access."[155]

All of these considerations suggest that the Court has established a precedent that will extend beyond "automobile" cases. Concededly, the Court has adopted a very narrow view of the protection provided by the Fourth Amendment regarding vehicle *searches* supported by probable cause.[156] The diminished constitutional protection afforded cars and containers found inside cars stems from the unique history of automobile searches.[157] *Pringle*, however, is not a car *search* case; it is a probable cause *arrest* case. If a factual scenario comparable to *Pringle* arose in a hotel room or back street alley, then there is no principled basis for not applying *Pringle's* "common enterprise" inference to justify the arrest of multiple persons on the scene.

### V. Final Thoughts: No Alternative to "Investigative" Arrests?

This article has attempted to demonstrate that the logic and result in *Pringle* not only conflicts with some of the Court's probable cause cases, particularly *Di Re* and *Ybarra*, but also—more basically— goes a long way toward weakening the concept of individualized probable cause. On the other hand, a unanimous Court disagrees with my thesis. *Pringle* both acknowledges that probable cause requires a belief of guilt that is "particularized with respect to the person to be searched or seized,"[158] and insists that its holding is consistent with the Court's earlier probable cause precedents.

I suspect, however, that a few of the justices joined the chief justice's opinion not because they believed that his analysis was

---

[155] *Id.*

[156] See generally David A. Harris, Car Wars: The Fourth Amendment's Death on the Highway, 66 Geo. Wash. L. Rev. 556, 556-57 (1998) (observing that "it is no exaggeration to say that in cases involving cars, the Fourth Amendment is all but dead . . . . Put simply, the Court has conferred upon the police nearly complete control over almost every car on the road and the people in it.").

[157] See generally Wyoming v. Houghton, 526 U.S. 295, 300–01 (1999).

[158] Maryland v. Pringle, 124 S. Ct. 795, 800 (2003) (citation omitted).

consistent with precedent or the individualized probable cause requirement. The unanimity behind *Pringle* may be explained by other factors. Perhaps, all of the justices joined the chief justice's opinion because they "could discern no other, workable rule"[159] or because they all agree that the probable cause standard is sufficiently elastic to allow for "investigative" arrests.[160]

On the first point, the thrust of Pringle's argument was that his arrest was not supported by individualized probable cause. That meant that the officer should have done one of two things: only arrest the driver or arrest none of the men. Obviously, the latter option was not going to garner any votes. But the justices were also unimpressed with Pringle's argument that law enforcement interests were adequately served by arresting the driver only. That argument was raised in Pringle's brief and surfaced once during the oral argument,[161] but it did not attract the support of any of the justices as a viable alternative to arresting all of the men.

A "driver only" arrest rule certainly has its disadvantages from a law enforcement perspective. First, the driver may not be the guilty party, which means that if the passengers are not simultaneously arrested with the driver, it may be difficult to find them if the police subsequently obtain evidence proving the driver's innocence. Second, assuming that the driver and passengers are engaged in a drug conspiracy, a "driver only" arrest rule may undermine law enforcement interests because the driver may, even after sufficient inducements are offered by the police or prosecutor, be unwilling to implicate his conspirators.

---

[159]Maryland v. Wilson, 519 U.S. 408, 423 (1997) (Kennedy, J., dissenting).

[160]Professor LaFave has suggested a third explanation for the result in *Pringle*. That is, collectively the justices may have believed that there was probable cause to arrest *Pringle* "simply because there was a nearly-100% probability that one of the three occupants of the car was the guilty party and the subsequent investigation had not produced any basis for picking one over the others." E-mail message from Professor Wayne R. LaFave, David C. Baum Professor of Law Emeritus, University of Illinois College of Law, to Tracey Maclin, Professor, Boston University School of Law (July 13, 2004) (on file with author). Although this way of looking at *Pringle* was implicit in several of the questions asked during oral argument, as Professor LaFave recognizes, "not one word on this point appears in the Court's opinion." *Id.*

[161]Brief of Respondent at 37–38, Maryland v. Pringle, 124 S. Ct. 795 (2003) (No. 02-809); Oral Argument Transcript at 37–38.

For similar reasons, permitting the police to conduct a *Terry*-type investigation without arrest is equally unattractive from a law enforcement perspective.[162] Officer Snyder initially pursued that option without success; detaining and interrogating all three men did not identify the owner of the drugs and money. When that strategy failed, the officer decided to arrest everyone. On the other hand, a "driver only" arrest rule does have one advantage under the facts in *Pringle*. "One would think that if an inference of sole possession was to be drawn, it would most logically be drawn as to [the driver], who was both the driver and owner of the vehicle."[163]

The second factor working against Pringle was that the justices apparently see no tension between investigative arrests and the probable cause standard. The "dead body" hypothetical will help to clarify my point. If Pringle's arrest was illegal due to a lack of individualized suspicion when drugs were discovered hidden in the back seat armrest, then his arrest would also be illegal if a dead body were found in the trunk. True, a dead body in the trunk, like drugs in the trunk, is not accessible to the passengers. Few criminal defense lawyers, however, want to argue that police cannot arrest a passenger traveling in a car that contains a dead body. That's why the prosecutor for Maryland was quick to raise the hypothetical during oral argument.[164] Nonetheless, the "dead body" hypothetical

---

[162] See 2 LaFave, *supra* note 26, § 3.2(e), at 67 (discussing the pros and cons of a rule that does not permit the arrest of multiple suspects when the police cannot satisfy a more-probable-than-not standard for arresting anyone).

[163] 3 LaFave, *supra* note 68, § 7.1(c), citing Leavell v. Commonwealth, 737 S.W.2d 695, 697 (Ky. 1987) (explaining that the "person who owns or exercises dominion and control over a motor vehicle in which contraband is concealed, is deemed to possess the contraband").

[164] QUESTION: How about the trunk?
MR. BAIR: I think the trunk changes things a little bit, but of course you have to look at the totality of the circumstances, Justice Ginsburg.
QUESTION: Why a little bit? I thought this whole case was predicated—your whole case was predicated on those drugs between the armrest and the backseat were accessible to all three people in that car.
MR. BAIR: That's—
QUESTION: Now, if you have something in a locked trunk, it truly is not accessible to the passengers.
MR. BAIR: It certainly is not as accessible, and of course it's not as immediately accessible, but, for instance, if there had been a large quantity of drugs in the trunk or if there had been a dead body in the trunk, I think then there is a—the calculus changes in terms of totality of the circumstances, and I think if it were that situation, even though that particular evidence was in the trunk, I think there's still a—*strong inference that could be drawn that everyone in the car knew about it, because who would*

should be irrelevant to the analysis, if we are to take seriously the Court's unwillingness to modify probable cause based on the seriousness of the crime.[165] While the "dead body" scenario certainly challenges the justices' willingness to adhere to the particularized probable cause rule, the result in *Pringle* demonstrates that it did not require a provocative fact pattern for the Court to give short shrift to the concept of individualized probable cause. Indeed, if there had been five or six men in the car, I suspect a majority of the Court would have still upheld arresting everyone, even though arresting such a large number of persons would transform the probable cause test into a meaningless measure of suspicion.[166]

*Pringle* indicates that the justices view the probable cause test as being sufficiently flexible to serve multiple purposes. Probable cause serves the traditional function of setting the standard for identifying which persons should be arrested in order to initiate the process of prosecution. In this sense, probable cause is the standard used to apprehend the guilty and those who should be charged with an offense. *Pringle* did not involve this traditional function of probable cause. Rather, *Pringle* involved a different aspect of probable cause. *Pringle* demonstrates that the justices also view probable cause as a standard, sufficiently elastic, to allow police to arrest and interrogate in order to decide which persons to charge. Yet, on this view,

---

*take the chance in terms of taking along innocent passengers—*
QUESTION: Well, let's stick to the five—these five bags that were stuck in a Ziploc bag. The Ziploc bag is in the trunk, not a dead body.
MR. BAIR: I understand. I think in that case there would be a much closer case, it would be a much more difficult case vis-à-vis all three occupants of the car.
Oral Argument Transcript at 8–9 (emphasis added).

[165] See 2 LaFave, *supra* note 26, §3.2(a), at 28–29.

[166] As noted above, in recent years the Court has emphasized that the probable cause test does not require a more-likely-than-not demonstration of guilt, and can neither be quantified nor precisely defined. See Illinois v. Gates, 462 U.S. 213, 235 (1983); Ornelas v. United States, 517 U.S. 690, 695 (1996). However, if under the *Pringle* facts, only one person was guilty of the offense, arresting five or six persons to facilitate the identification of that person means that probable cause tolerates a twenty or seventeen percent chance, respectively, of apprehending the correct person. Similarly, where five or six persons are found in a car that contains hidden narcotics and money, resting an inference of conspiracy on the accessibility of the drugs seems a rather thin reed to support the arrest of such a larger number of persons.

probable cause is broad enough to tolerate arrests that serve an investigative function.[167]

Although it is not surprising that the Rehnquist Court would perceive the probable cause standard as a tool to *facilitate*, rather than hinder, police apprehension of multiple persons for purposes of interrogation, *Pringle* illustrates just how far the Rehnquist Court has separated itself from its predecessors on this point. In *Mallory v. United States*,[168] the Court took a very different view. In that case, police suspected that one of three men had committed a rape. All three were arrested and interrogated at the police station. Mallory eventually confessed to the crime and was convicted. The Supreme Court reversed the conviction because Mallory had not been promptly taken to a federal magistrate for arraignment between the time of his arrest and confession. According to the *Mallory* Court, the failure to promptly arraign Mallory was not excused by the fact two other men were suspected by the police. Speaking for a unanimous Court, Justice Frankfurter observed: "Presumably, whomever the police arrest they must arrest on 'probable cause.' It is not the function of the police to arrest, as it were, at large and to use an interrogating process at police headquarters in order to determine whom they should charge before a committing magistrate on 'probable cause.'"[169]

---

[167] This, essentially, was the argument made by the prosecutors in *Pringle*. See Brief of Petitioner at 25, Maryland v. Pringle, 124 S. Ct. 795 (2003) (No. 02-809) ("By arresting all three, the officer more precisely could determine criminal culpability. Pringle confessed, and the other two were set free."); Brief of the United States as Amicus Curiae Supporting Petitioner at 30, Maryland v. Pringle, 124 S. Ct. 795 (2003) (No. 02-809) (conceding that innocent persons may be arrested, but insisting that arresting all the vehicle's occupants "will facilitate *further investigation* that enables the officer to conclude in short order that a particular person should be released") (emphasis added). Cf. 3 LaFave, *supra* note 68, § 7.1(c) (recognizing the validity of the position that "views the probable cause test as something less than more-probable-than-not and views arrests as sometimes serving an investigative function").

[168] 354 U.S. 449 (1957).

[169] *Id.* at 456.

Although *Mallory's* dicta on probable cause was not greeted with universal approval,[170] some viewed *Mallory* as requiring "evidence sufficient to charge one and only one person prior to arrest."[171] Whatever the precedential weight of *Mallory's* dicta, *Di Re* and *Ybarra*

[170] Shortly after *Mallory* was decided, Judge Alexander Holtzoff disagreed with the Court's conclusion on probable cause. "In [*Mallory*] there were three suspects. There was reasonable ground to arrest every one of them. After an interrogation of each of the three, two were cleared within a few hours and the third was held." Statement of the Honorable Alexander Holtzoff, U.S. District Judge for the District of Columbia, in Hearings on Confessions and Police Detention before the Subcommittee on Constitutional Rights of the Senate Committee on the Judiciary, 85th Cong., 2d Sess. 4–5 (1958), quoted in LaFave, Arrest, *supra* note 26, at 261 n.73.

Modern commentators continue to question *Mallory's* implication that probable cause does not permit multiple arrests to facilitate a police investigation where only one person is suspected as the perpetrator. See, e.g., Joseph D. Grano, Probable Cause and Common Sense: A Reply to the Critics of Illinois v. Gates, 17 U. Mich. J.L. Ref. 465, 479 (1984) (arguing that under the common law "an arrest prompted further investigation; it did not reflect an already formed decision to charge the person with a crime"). The Model Code of Pre-Arraignment Procedure permits arrests without proof that satisfies a more-probable-than-not standard. See Model Code of Pre-Arraignment Procedure 14 (1975). Other commentators have relied on the famous hypothetical from the Restatement (Second) of Torts § 119, comment I (1965) that says there is probable cause to arrest two persons found bending over a dead body, where each accuses the other of the crime, both to question the wisdom of a more-probable-than-not standard for probable cause and to justify investigative arrests. See, e.g., 2 LaFave, *supra* note 26, § 3.2(e), at 64–65 ("If the function of arrest were merely to produce persons in court for purposes of their prosecution, then a more-probable-than-not test would have considerable appeal. But there is also an investigative function which is served by the making of arrests.") (footnote omitted). Finally, the prosecutor in *Pringle* proffered the hypothetical of four persons sitting at a card table with a "smoking gun" in the middle of table and one of the persons slumped over the table (apparently dead or shot) as an illustration of the havoc that would be wrought if multiple arrests were not permitted under the facts in *Pringle*. Brief of Petitioner at 28, Maryland v. Pringle, 124 S. Ct. 795 (2003) (No. 02-809).

The prosecution's hypothetical is not comparable to the facts in *Pringle*. The contraband discovered in *Pringle* was *not* in plain view of the occupants or the police. In the prosecutor's hypothetical, the gun and dead body are obviously in plain sight of the other persons sitting at the table. The other arguments against the more-probable-than-not standard of probable cause and in favor of investigative arrests are not so easily rebutted. To be sure, under a more-probable-than-not standard of probable cause, police will have less authority to make arrests. But that concession does not prove (or disprove) that investigative arrests are valid under the Fourth Amendment. *Cf.* Henry v. United States, 361 U.S. 98, 104 (1959) ("Under our system suspicion is not enough for an officer to lay hands on a citizen. It is better, so the Fourth Amendment teaches, that the guilty sometimes go free than that citizens be subject to easy arrest."). The problem with the way that the Rehnquist Court defines probable cause—that is, as a "fluid concept . . . not readily, or even usefully, reduced clearly established the constitutional norm of individualized probable cause for most searches and seizures, and forbade arrests based on the arrestee's mere proximity to others suspected of criminality. *Pringle* pays lip service to the principle of individualized probable cause, but that constitutional rule cannot coexist very long with a view of probable cause that allows the arrest of multiple persons to facilitate the government's ability to identify which particular individual to charge as an offender.

---

to a neat set of legal rules," Illinois v. Gates, 462 U.S. 213, 232 (1983), which requires only a "fair probability" or "substantial chance" of criminality, *id*. at 238, 243 n.13— is that it provides too much discretion to the police. Put simply, the definition of probable cause embraced in *Gates* (and *Pringle*) is the equivalent of a general reasonableness test. See Wasserstrom, *supra* note 2, at 340 (noting that under *Gates*, "the probable cause requirement is effectively subsumed under a test of general reasonableness"). I share Professor Wasserstrom's view that under this definition of probable cause, the chance that a suspect is innocent of the charge is only one "factor [ ] in assessing the reasonableness of the officer's actions. The officer is only required to have *some reason* to think that the . . . suspect committed the crime." *Id*. (emphasis added). This is certainly not the Framers' view of probable cause, see Davies, *supra* note 71, at 578, nor is it consistent with the Framers' understanding of an officer's authority to make warrantless arrests. See id. at 627–34. For better or worse, I tend to favor the more-probable-than-not test for measuring an officer's arrest authority. (Whether a more-probable-than-not test is appropriate for *searches* is a different question. "Clearly, the more-likely-than not interpretation of probable cause has certain problems when applied to searches, which do not arise when applied to arrests." *Id*. at 306 n.240.) While a more-probable-than-not test may have the drawback of a fixed standard, the advantage of this standard is that it informs the officer that "unless he thinks that the suspect *has*, not *might have*, committed the offense, he must investigate further before he can" arrest. *Id*. at 307.

[171] LaFave, Arrest, *supra* note 26, at 261 n.71. *Cf.* 2 LaFave, *supra* note 26, § 3.2(d), at 61 (listing *Mallory* as one of three Supreme Court cases that "suggests that probable cause to arrest does not exist unless the information at hand singles out one individual").

# The Confrontation Clause Re-Rooted and Transformed

*Richard D. Friedman**

## I. Introduction

For several centuries, prosecution witnesses in criminal cases have given their testimony under oath, face to face with the accused, and subject to cross-examination at trial. The Confrontation Clause of the Sixth Amendment to the U.S. Constitution guarantees the procedure, providing that "[i]n all criminal prosecutions, the accused shall enjoy the right . . . to be confronted with the witness against him." In recent decades, however, judicial protection of the right has been lax, because the U.S. Supreme Court has tolerated admission of out-of-court statements against the accused, without cross-examination, if the statements are deemed "reliable" or "trustworthy." This year, in *Crawford v. Washington*,[1] the Supreme Court did a sharp about-face, holding that a testimonial statement cannot be admitted against an accused, no matter how reliable a court may deem it to be, unless the accused has had an adequate opportunity to cross-examine the witness who made the statement.

*Crawford* is not only a vindication of the rights of the accused but a victory for fidelity to constitutional text and intent. And yet the decision leaves many open questions, and all lawyers involved in the criminal justice process will have to adjust to the new regime that it creates.

The transformation achieved by *Crawford* is crystallized by considering the facts of the case itself.[2] Michael Crawford, upset by a report that Kenneth Lee had made advances on his wife Sylvia, went with Sylvia to Lee's apartment. A violent fight followed, during the course

*Portions of this article have been previously published in *Criminal Justice*, a journal published by the American Bar Association, and in the *International Journal of Evidence & Proof*.

[1] 124 S. Ct. 1354 (2004).

[2] See *id.* at 1356–59 (reciting facts of the case).

of which Crawford was cut badly on the hand and stabbed Lee in the stomach, seriously injuring him. That night, Sylvia and Michael Crawford both made tape-recorded statements to the police at the station-house. The statements were similar in many respects, but Sylvia's tended to damage Michael's contention of self-defense. Michael eventually was tried on charges stemming from the incident. Sylvia was unwilling to testify at trial against her husband, and was deemed by all parties to be unavailable as a witness. Accordingly, the prosecution offered Sylvia's station-house statement.

The case therefore fits the mold of what I have called "station-house testimony"—a statement by a witness of an alleged crime, made knowingly and privately to investigating officers, with the clear anticipation on the part of all that the statement may be used as prosecution evidence at trial. A lay observer as well as a lawyer may have a strong intuitive sense that such a statement ought not be used to help convict an accused. And yet, until this year, prevailing doctrine failed to give a sufficiently clear signal that this was so. Sylvia's statement was admitted into evidence over Michael's objection, he was convicted, and the Washington Supreme Court eventually upheld the conviction, holding that the "interlock" of Sylvia's and Michael's statements rendered Sylvia's sufficiently trustworthy for Confrontation Clause purposes.[3]

The U.S. Supreme Court then reviewed the case. What is notable is not that the Court reversed Crawford's conviction, nor even that it did so unanimously. Rather, as I explain more fully below, what makes *Crawford* a landmark is that the Court discarded the flabby doctrine that it had used to apply the Confrontation Clause and instead adopted an approach that better fits the meaning and intent of the Clause.

Part II of this article explores the values underlying the Confrontation Clause and its historical background. Part III shows how the principle driving the Clause became obscured by a hopelessly flawed body of doctrine. Part IV lays out the elements of the testimonial framework adopted by *Crawford*. Part V examines, the areas of criminal procedure left unchanged by *Crawford*, and the open questions that future courts will have to settle in the wake of this watershed decision.

---

[3] *Id.* at 1358.

## II. Values, History, and Text

A cornerstone of the Anglo-American legal system has long been that a witness may not testify against an accused unless the witness confronts the accused with the testimony. The requirement that prosecution testimony be given this way—rather than, say, in writing or behind closed doors, as have been the methods in some systems—serves a range of purposes:

- *Openness.* Confrontation guarantees openness of procedure, which among other benefits ensures that the witness's testimony is not the product of torture or of milder forms of coercion or intimidation. This is particularly important given the contrast to early Continental systems, in which coercion of witnesses examined privately was very common.
- *Adversarial Procedure.* Confrontation provides a chance for the defendant, personally or through counsel, to dispute and explore the weaknesses in the witness's testimony. In an earlier day, that chance came in the form of a wide-open altercation in court. Today it comes in the form of cross-examination, usually through counsel. The U.S. Supreme Court has repeatedly endorsed John Henry Wigmore's characterization of cross-examination as "beyond any doubt the greatest legal engine ever invented for the discovery of truth."[4] Of course, as Wigmore recognized, cross-examination may sometimes lead the trier of fact away from the truth rather than toward it. But the constitutionally required "beyond a reasonable doubt" standard of persuasion in a criminal case reflects the extreme disutility of a false conviction.[5] The same consideration demands that

---

[4] 5 John H. Wigmore, Evidence § 1367, at 32 (James Chadbourn rev. 1974) (quoted in part in Lilly v. Virginia, 527 U.S. 116, 123 (1999) (plurality opinion)). See also White v. Illinois, 502 U.S. 346, 356 (1992); Maryland v. Craig, 497 U.S. 836, 844 (1990); Perry v. Leeke, 488 U.S. 272, 283 n.7 (1989); Kentucky v. Stincer, 482 U.S. 730, 736 (1987); California v. Green, 399 U.S. 149, 158 (1970); Ford v. Wainwright, 477 U.S. 399, 415 (1986); Lee v. Illinois, 476 U.S. 530, 540 (1986); Watkins v. Sowders, 449 U.S. 341, 348 n.4 (1981); Roberts v. Ohio, 448 U.S. 56, 63 n.6 (1980); cf. United States v. Salerno, 505 U.S. 317, 328 (1992) (Stevens, J., dissenting) ("Even if one does not completely agree with Wigmore's assertion . . . one must admit that in the Anglo-American legal system cross-examination is the principal means of undermining the credibility of a witness whose testimony is false or inaccurate.").

[5] See In re Winship, 397 U.S. 358, 361–64 (1970).

the accused be able to cross-examine adverse witnesses even if sometimes that requirement prevents the conviction of a guilty person.

- *Discouragement of Falsehood.* Confrontation discourages falsehood as well as assists in its detection. The prospect of testifying under oath, subject to cross-examination, in the presence of the accused makes false accusation much more difficult than it would be otherwise, or so at least is the well-settled belief.[6]
- *Demeanor as Evidence.* If, as is usually the case, the confrontation occurs at trial or (in modern times) in a videotaped proceeding, the trier of fact has an opportunity to assess the demeanor of the witness.[7]
- *Elimination of Intermediaries.* Confrontation eliminates the need for intermediaries, and along with it any doubt about what the witness's testimony is.
- *Symbolic Purposes.* Beyond these instrumental purposes, confrontation of prosecution witnesses serves a "strong symbolic purpose" that repeatedly has been recognized by the Supreme Court.[8] Even if confrontation had no impact on the quality of the prosecution's evidence, it would be important to protect because, as the Court said in *Coy v. Iowa*[9] and repeated in *Maryland v. Craig,*[10] "there is something deep in human nature that regards face-to-face confrontation between accused and accuser

---

[6]Maryland v. Craig, 497 U.S. 836, 846 (1990); Coy v. Iowa, 487 U.S. 1012, 1019–20 (1988) ("It is always more difficult to tell a lie about a person 'to his face' than 'behind his back.'"). See also Richard A. Posner, An Economic Approach to the Law of Evidence, 51 Stan. L. Rev. 1477, 1490 (1999) ("The witness whose credibility would be destroyed by cross-examination will not be called at all or will try to pull the sting of the cross-examiner by acknowledging on direct examination the facts that a cross-examiner could be expected to harp on."). Of course, the same prospect may deter the giving of truthful testimony. But, again, the tradeoff accords with the fundamental value underlying the "beyond a reasonable doubt" standard. See Craig, 497 U.S. at 846–47; Coy, 487 U.S. at 1020.

[7]Craig, 497 U.S. at 844; Mattox v. United States, 156 U.S. 237, 242–43 (1895) (confrontation gives the accused the opportunity "of compelling [the witness] to stand face to face with the jury in order that they may look at him, and judge by his demeanor upon the stand and the manner in which he gives his testimony whether he is worthy of belief").

[8]Craig, 497 U.S. at 846; Lee v. Illinois, 476 U.S. 530, 540 (1986).

[9]*Supra* note 6.

[10]*Supra* note 6.

as 'essential to a fair trial in a criminal prosecution.'"[11] It is not only fairness to the accused that is at stake, but also the moral responsibility of witnesses and of society at large, for "requiring confrontation is a way of reminding ourselves that we are, or at least want to see ourselves as, the kind of people who decline to countenance or abet what we see as the cowardly and ignoble practice of hidden accusation."[12]

• *The Weight of History.* The symbolic value of confrontation is enhanced by the history of the right, which I will now review.[13] Indeed, the very fact that for many centuries accused persons have had the right to confront the witnesses against them makes it especially important to continue to honor that right.

If an adjudicative system is rational, then it must rely in large part on the testimony of witnesses and prescribe the conditions under which they may testify. For many systems, one such condition is that testimony must be given under oath. Another common condition, characteristic of the common law system but not limited to it, is that testimony of a prosecution witness must be given in the presence of the accused, subject to questioning by him or on his behalf. The ancient Hebrews required confrontation,[14] as did the Romans. A Roman governor, Festus, pronounced: "It is not the manner of the Romans to die before the accused has met his accusers face to face, and has been given a chance to defend himself against the charges."[15] Once the irrational methods of medieval adjudication, such as trial by ordeal and by battle, withered away, Western legal systems developed different approaches to testimony. Continental systems tended to take testimony on written questions—behind closed doors and out of the presence of the parties—for fear that the witnesses

---

[11] Craig, 497 U.S. at 847, quoting Coy, 487 U.S. at 1017, quoting in part Pointer v. Texas, 380 U.S. 400, 404 (1965).

[12] See generally Sherman J. Clark, An Accuser-Obligation Approach to the Confrontation Clause, 81 Neb. L. Rev. 1258 (2003).

[13] A more extensive historical discussion, with fuller citations, may be found in Richard D. Friedman and Bridget McCormack, Dial-In Testimony, 150 U. Pa. L. Rev. 1171, 1202–09 (2002).

[14] Deut. 19:15–18.

[15] Acts 25:16.

would be coached or intimidated. By contrast, beginning in the fifteenth century and continuing for centuries afterward, numerous English judges and commentators—John Fortescue, Thomas Smith, Matthew Hale, and William Blackstone among them—praised the open and confrontational style of the English criminal trial. In a celebrated sixteenth century description, for example, Smith spoke approvingly of an "altercation" between accuser and accused. Nearly two centuries later, Sollom Emlyn proclaimed, "In other Countries, the Witnesses are examin'd in private, and in the Prisoner's Absence; with us, they are produced face to face, and deliver their Evidence in open Court, the Prisoner himself being present, and at liberty to cross-examine them." And later in the eighteenth century Blackstone spoke of "the confronting of adverse witnesses" as being among the advantages of "the English way of giving testimony, *ore tenus"*—that is, by word of mouth, or orally.[16]

To be sure, the norm of confrontation was not always respected. First, a set of courts in England followed Continental procedures rather than those of the common law. Precisely for that reason, they were politically controversial. Most of them (notably the Court of Star Chamber) were viewed as arms of an unlimited royal power and did not survive the upheavals of the seventeenth century. Second, from the reign of Queen Mary, justices of the peace were required by statutes to examine felony witnesses, and these examinations were admissible at trial, even though the witness had not been cross-examined, if the examination was taken under oath and the witness was then unavailable. This treatment—which almost certainly numbered among the chief abuses at which the Confrontation Clause was aimed—was a continuing source of controversy, and in 1696, in the celebrated case of *Rex v. Paine*,[17] the court refused to extend it to misdemeanor cases; eventually, the practice was abolished by statutes for felony cases as well. Finally, and perhaps most significant, the Crown, when trying to control its political adversaries through treason prosecutions and other uses of the criminal law, sometimes used testimony taken out of the presence of the accused.

---

[16] For full citations, see Friedman & McCormack, *supra* note 13, at 1203–04.

[17] 87 Eng. Rep. 584 (K.B. 1696); 90 Eng. Rep. 527 (K.B. 1696); 90 Eng. Rep. 1062 (K.B. 1696); 91 Eng. Rep. 246 (K.B. 1696); 91 Eng. Rep. 1387 (K.B. 1696).

The battle for confrontation was most clearly fought in the treason cases of Tudor and Stuart England. Even early in the sixteenth century, treason defendants demanded that witnesses be brought before them; often they used the term "face to face." The notorious case of Walter Raleigh was one of many in which Crown prosecutors used confessions made by alleged accomplices of the accused, even though the confessions were not made under oath or before the accused. The self-accusing nature of such statements was said to be an adequate substitute for the usual requirements of testimony. But in 1662, the judges of the King's Bench ruled unanimously and definitively in *Tong's Case*[18] that a pretrial confession "cannot be made use of as evidence against any others" than the confessor himself.[19]

The confrontation right naturally found its way to America. There, the right to counsel developed far more quickly than in England, and with it an adversarial spirit that made confrontation especially crucial. The right became a particular focus of American concerns in the 1760s, when the Stamp Acts and other parliamentary regulations of the colonies provided for the examination of witnesses upon interrogatories in certain circumstances. Not surprisingly, the early state constitutions guaranteed the confrontation right. Some used the time-honored "face to face" formula; as early as 1776, others, following Hale and Blackstone, adopted language strikingly similar to that later used in the Sixth Amendment's Confrontation Clause.[20]

The Confrontation Clause states simply:

> In all criminal prosecutions, the accused shall enjoy the right
> . . . to be confronted with the witnesses against him.[21]

Note that nothing in the history of the Clause, or in its text, suggests that the confrontation right was considered contingent, inapplicable upon a judicial determination that the particular testimony was reliable. Rather, the Clause established as a categorical rule a basic procedural norm that a witness may not be heard for the prosecution unless the accused has an opportunity to be confronted by her—

---

[18] Case of Thomas Tong, 84 Eng. Rep. 1061 (K.B. 1662).

[19] *Id.* at 1062 (cited in Lilly v. Virginia, 527 U.S. 116, 141 (1999) (Breyer, J., concurring)).

[20] Friedman & McCormack, *supra* note 13, at 1207–08.

[21] U.S. Const. amend. VI, cl. 3.

that is, the witness must speak in the presence of the accused, and subject to cross-examination. Like Festus, we can say that it is not our way to allow an accused to be convicted of a crime unless the witnesses against him testify to his face.

## III. *Roberts* and the Obscuring of the Confrontation Principle

I have presented a view of a relatively uncluttered confrontation principle written into the Constitution by the Sixth Amendment. But later the picture got badly muddied. Here is a brief speculative account, which I have developed in greater detail elsewhere.[22]

### A. The Rise of the Roberts Framework

The law against hearsay has not played a role in the historical account underlying the Confrontation Clause, just as it does not enter into the text of the Clause. Hearsay law, like evidence law more generally, was not well developed at the time the constitutions of the states of the United States, or the U.S. Constitution, articulated the confrontation right, much less during previous centuries. In the eighteenth century, the term hearsay closely conformed to the lay sense of the word: Hearsay was what a witness contended she heard another person say.

Around the beginning of the nineteenth century, the conception of hearsay expanded.[23] The reason for this expansion appears to have been the growing role of criminal defense lawyers, who emphasized, with respect to nontestimonial statements as well as testimonial

---

[22] Friedman & McCormack, *supra* note 13, at 1209-27

[23] See Thomas Peake, A Compendium of the Law of Evidence 10 (1801). Peake said, in the course of his discussion of hearsay, that certain written memoranda made in the ordinary course of business are admissible as "not within the exception as to hearsay evidence." He used "exception" in the same sense that today we would use "objection." The statement, therefore, is that these memoranda are not excluded by the hearsay rule; implicit may be the inchoate idea that other writings would be. About a decade later, S.M. Phillipps made the principle clear: The exclusionary rule "is applicable to statements in writing, no less than to words spoken," the only difference being that there is greater facility of proof in the case of writings than of oral statements. 1 S.M. Phillipps, A Treatise on the Law of Evidence 173 (1st Amer. ed. from the 2d London ed. 1816). The point did not gain instant universality. Francis Buller, An Introduction to the Law Relative to Trials at Nisi Prius 294b n. (Richard Whalley Bridgman ed., 7th ed. 1817), follows Peake's treatment, virtually to the point of plagiarism. 3 Jeremy Bentham, Rationale of Judicial Evidence 447–48 (1827), treats written evidence as distinct from hearsay, but claims that the same rules apply to both.

ones, the lack of an opportunity for cross-examination. This emphasis led to sharper recognition that evidence is not ideal when the value of the evidence depends on the credibility of a person not testifying in court.[24] This recognition in turn led to, or at least was associated with, articulation of the modern definition of hearsay as an out-of-court statement offered to prove the truth of what it asserts.[25]

As the law of hearsay expanded, exceptions to the hearsay rule multiplied. Since the early nineteenth century, the trend has been to expand those exceptions and to admit more statements into evidence. The articulated basis for the law largely has been shaped by Wigmore's emphasis on "trustworthiness," but I suspect the actual bounds of the hearsay doctrine were also shaped by an unarticulated adherence to the confrontation principle. Inevitably, over time, the confrontation principle was diluted and obscured: Treating non-testimonial statements on a par with testimonial ones meant that an opportunity for cross-examination could not be regarded as an absolute precondition for admission, but only as a desirable, and sometimes dispensable, condition.[26]

So long as the Confrontation Clause was a limitation only on the federal judicial system, its bounds, and its relationship to hearsay doctrine, did not matter very much; pretty much any result the Supreme Court would reach by applying the Confrontation Clause it could also reach by applying nonconstitutional doctrine as well.[27]

---

[24] In a contemplative discussion, Thomas Starkie noted that the exclusionary rule does not apply "where declarations . . . possess an intrinsic credit beyond the mere naked unauthorized assertions of a stranger." 1 Thomas Starkie, A Practical Treatise on the Law of Evidence 46 (1st American ed. 1826).

[25] Note the following passage from 1 S.M. Phillipps, A Treatise on the Law of Evidence 229 (7th ed. 1829), not found in earlier editions (including the 6th edition of 1824): "Hearsay is not admitted in our courts of justice, as proof of the fact which is stated by a third person."

[26] Lost was the recognition of a critical difference between statements made "for the express purpose of being given in evidence" and "the natural effusions of a party . . . who speaks upon an occasion, when his mind stands in an even position, without any temptation to exceed or fall short of the truth." Phillipps, *supra* note 23, at 175, quoting in part Eldon, L.C., in Whitlocke v. Baker, 13 Ves. Jr. 510, 514 (1807), and citing Berkeley Peerage Case, 4 Camp. 402, 171 E.R. 128 (1811), in which some of the judges drew the distinction.

[27] Note, for example, the celebrated case of Shepard v. United States, 290 U.S. 96, 98 (1933), in which the Court held the statement, "Dr. Shepard has poisoned me," which it characterized as an "accusation," inadmissible on hearsay grounds, without mentioning the Confrontation Clause.

But in 1965 the Court held that the Fourteenth Amendment incorporates the Confrontation Clause against the states.[28] What the Clause prevents then became critical. The trouble was that by this time the Court had nearly lost sight of the purpose behind the Clause. And so in *Ohio v. Roberts*,[29] after fifteen years of deciding cases without an overall theory of the Clause, the Court concocted a doctrine that virtually conformed the meaning of the Clause to ordinary hearsay law.

The essential elements of the *Roberts* doctrine were as follows: First, *Roberts* held that any hearsay statement made by a person who did not testify in court and offered against a criminal defendant posed a confrontation issue. Second, hearsay could be admitted without an opportunity for cross-examination if the statement satisfied certain conditions. The primary condition to be satisfied was that the statement be "reliable." A statement would be deemed reliable if it either fit within a "firmly rooted hearsay exception" or was supported by "particularized guarantees of trustworthiness." Third, in some set of circumstances, the scope of which was never clear, another condition for admissibility was that the person had to be unavailable at trial.[30]

All of these elements proved to be troublesome. First, the scope of the *Roberts* doctrine was too broad. The Confrontation Clause says nothing about hearsay, and many statements that fit within the basic definition of hearsay—that is, out-of-court statements offered to prove the truth of what they assert—do not plausibly threaten to violate the right of a defendant "to be confronted with the witnesses against him."

Second, reliability is a poor criterion, inappropriate for the Confrontation Clause. Trials are not supposed to be limited to reliable evidence. Much of the evidence that is admitted—including, often, testimony that has been subjected to cross-examination—is highly *un*reliable. The function of the trial is to give the fact-finder an opportunity to make its best assessment of the facts after considering all the evidence properly presented, reliable and unreliable. Moreover, the hearsay exceptions do not all do a good job of sorting out

---

[28] Pointer v. Texas, 380 U.S. 400 (1965).

[29] 448 U.S. 56 (1980).

[30] See *id.* at 65–66.

reliable from unreliable evidence. A great deal of mundane hearsay raises no strong grounds for doubt, and yet does not fit within an exception. Conversely, much hearsay is plainly of dubious trustworthiness, even though it fits within a well-established exception. For example, there is a long-standing exception for certain "dying declarations." The traditional justification for this exception is that no one about to meet her Maker would do so with a lie upon her lips. In today's world, this idea is nearly laughable—and it is not made less so by the Supreme Court's pious assertion in 1990 that the rationale for the exception is so powerful that cross-examination would be of "marginal utility."[31]

If a statement was not deemed to fit within a firmly rooted hearsay exception, it could yet satisfy the reliability requirement of *Roberts* by meeting the "particularized guarantees of trustworthiness" test. That test was notoriously amorphous and manipulable. The Court tried to put some order on this case-by-case inquiry by insisting that corroborating evidence could not satisfy it; only "circumstances . . . that surround the making of the statement and that render the declarant particularly worthy of belief" could be used.[32] This limitation perplexed the lower courts, which strained mightily against it.

Finally, the unavailability requirement proved equally difficult. The Court never applied the requirement beyond the context in which it was first articulated (i.e., where the statement at issue fit within the hearsay exception for former testimony.) At times, it appeared that this was the only context in which the Court *would* apply the exception, at times it appeared that the Court might apply the requirement to statements fitting within certain other exceptions,

---

[31] Idaho v. Wright, 497 U.S. 805, 820 (1990). Further, though a statement might appear to fit within a firmly rooted exception, at least in the view of the forum state, admission could yet be intolerable. Consider Lee v. Illinois, 476 U.S. 530 (1986). There, the statement at issue was a confession by one Thomas, according to which both he and Lee played central roles in a gruesome double murder. Thomas was deemed unavailable at Lee's trial, by reason of privilege, and so the state offered the confession, contending reasonably that it was a declaration against interest. The Court's response, that such a categorization defines too large a class for meaningful Confrontation Clause analysis, *id.* at 544 n.5, was buried in a footnote, perhaps because the Court could not easily reconcile that response with its attempt in *Roberts* to make dispositive the broad categorizations of hearsay law.

[32] Wright, 497 U.S. at 819.

but the matter remained unresolved. Even knowledgeable observers expressed confusion.

## B. The Testimonial Framework

In the end, the Roberts framework—clunky, confusing, and manipulable—did not provide meaningful protection against the giving of testimony behind closed doors. In recent years, there were glimmers of hope that the Court might change course. Concurring opinions by Justice Thomas, joined by Justice Scalia, in White v. Illinois,[33] and by Justices Breyer and Scalia in Lilly v. Virginia,[34] suggested the possibility of a radical transformation. Finally, in Crawford, seven justices converted the suggestion to reality, adopting a new organizing principle that treats the Confrontation Clause as a guarantee that testimony offered against an accused must be given in the manner prescribed for centuries, in the presence of the accused and subject to cross-examination.

Recall that in Crawford the Washington Supreme Court held that Sylvia Crawford's statement, made in the station house to investigating officers, was admissible against Crawford, even though Sylvia was considered unavailable to testify at trial, because the statement was deemed sufficiently reliable to satisfy Roberts. The U.S. Supreme Court reversed unanimously. The chief justice and Justice O'Connor would simply have held that Sylvia's statement did not satisfy Roberts. The other seven justices, in an opinion by Justice Scalia, agreed that various factors—including the fact that Sylvia said her eyes were closed during part of the incident!—pointed to the unreliability of her statement. But this majority declined to rest the decision on Roberts. Rather, the majority pointed to these factors, and the fact that the Washington courts had concluded the statement was admissible, as a stark indication of the failure of Roberts. Accepting the proposal made by Crawford, and supported by amici curiae (friends-of-the-court), the Court discarded the Roberts doctrine and adopted instead a "testimonial" approach to the Confrontation Clause.

The essence of the testimonial approach may be grasped by considering Crawford's treatment of the three elements of the Roberts doctrine outlined above.

---

[33] 502 U.S. 346, 358 (1992) (Thomas, J., concurring).

[34] 527 U.S. 116, 141 (1999) (Breyer, J., concurring); id. at 143 (Scalia, J., concurring).

First, *Crawford* makes clear that the principal—and perhaps only—focus of the Confrontation Clause is *testimonial* statements. Justice Scalia, for example, called "testimonial" statements the "principal object" of the Sixth Amendment.[35] This proposition is in accord with the text of the Confrontation Clause; as noted above, the Clause speaks of "witnesses," the most natural meaning of which is those who give testimony.[36] The historical account given in Part II demonstrates that a focus on testimonial statements is also in accord with the basic idea that motivated adoption of the Clause, one that is still crucial to the Anglo-American system—that, in contrast to the procedures of some systems of medieval Europe, witnesses against an accused should give their testimony in the presence of the accused and subject to oral cross-examination. Just what statements are to be considered testimonial is an important question, one that is discussed below and that undoubtedly will be the subject of many cases in coming years. The Court declined to furnish a comprehensive definition.

Second, the Court ruled that if a statement is "testimonial" and is offered to prove the truth of what it asserts, that statement cannot be admitted against an accused unless he has an opportunity to cross-examine the maker of the statement. As Justice Scalia emphasized, "Where testimonial statements are at issue, the *only* indicium of reliability sufficient to satisfy constitutional demands is the one the Constitution actually prescribes: confrontation."[37] In other words, reliability cannot substitute for cross-examination.

Third, in contrast to *Roberts*, under which unavailability had an uncertain role that was difficult to defend,[38] the *Crawford* Court emphasized that the testimonial approach makes the role of unavailability quite clear and logical. As Justice Scalia explained, testimonial

---

[35] Crawford v. Washington, 124 S. Ct. 1354, 1365 (2004).

[36] The Latin for "witness" is "testis." That word shares a root with "testimonium," the core meaning of which is "the testimony of a witness." And that, of course, is the source of the English word "testimony." The derivation appears to be through the Old French; thus, in the modern French witness is "témoin" and testimony is "témoinage." See, e.g., Adolf Berger, Encyclopedic Dictionary of Roman Law, 43(2) Trans. Am. Phil. Soc. 335, 735 (1953); 17 Oxford English Dictionary 833 (2d ed. 1989).

[37] Crawford, 124 S. Ct. at 1374 (emphasis added).

[38] See, e.g., *id.* at 1369.

statements may be admitted "only where the declarant is unavailable, and only where the defendant has had a prior opportunity to cross-examine."[39] Ordinarily, the opportunity for cross-examination should occur at trial. But if the witness—that is, the maker of the testimonial statement—is unavailable to testify at trial, then cross-examination at an earlier proceeding will be acceptable as a second-best substitute.

## IV. Matters That Remain Unchanged

*Crawford* reflects a paradigm shift in the doctrine of the Confrontation Clause. Nonetheless, Crawford and amici went to some pains to assure the Supreme Court that adoption of the testimonial approach would alter the results in few, if any, of the Court's own precedents. A considerable number of decisions in the lower courts, however, would come out differently under *Crawford*. To set the groundwork for understanding how *Crawford* alters the doctrinal landscape and the important issues that are likely to arise, it will first help to examine several respects in which *Crawford* does *not* change the law.

First, under *Crawford*, as before, a statement does not raise a confrontation issue unless it is offered to prove the truth of a matter that it asserts. This is the rule of *Tennessee v. Street*,[40] which *Crawford* explicitly reaffirms.[41] In *Street* itself, for example, the defendant contended that the police coerced him to make a statement similar to that of an accomplice's confession. The Court ruled unanimously that the prosecution therefore could introduce the accomplice's confession to demonstrate not that it was true but that it was substantially different from the defendant's. That result would be unchanged under *Crawford*. There may be questions as to how far a prosecutor may take this "not for the truth" argument. For example, if the prosecutor argues that the statement is being offered as support for the opinion of an expert witness, in some cases that might be considered too thin a veneer. Nonetheless, the basic doctrine remains in place.

Second, many statements that were admissible under *Roberts* will still be admissible under *Crawford*, though the grounds of decision

[39] *Id.*
[40] 471 U.S. 409, 414 (1985).
[41] Crawford, 124 S. Ct. at 1369 n.9.

will be different. The question is not, as some analysts have posed it, whether *Crawford* preserves given hearsay exceptions. The rule against hearsay and the Confrontation Clause are separate sources of law—and *Crawford* stops the tendency to meld them. The question for Confrontation Clause purposes in each case is whether the given statement is testimonial. The fact that a statement fits within a hearsay exception does not alter its status with respect to that question. But one can say that *most* statements that fit within certain hearsay exceptions are not testimonial. For example, under *Roberts*, business records and conspirator statements were deemed reliable because they fell within "firmly rooted" hearsay exemptions. Under *Crawford*, almost all such statements will be considered non-testimonial, and therefore the Confrontation Clause will impose little, if any, obstacle to their admissibility.

Third, the rule of *California v. Green*[42] also is preserved. As the *Crawford* Court summarized the rule, "[W]hen the declarant appears for cross-examination at trial, the Confrontation Clause places no constraints at all on the use of his prior testimonial statements."[43] In my view, the rule is a dubious one. It fails to take into account the serious impairment of the ability to cross-examine that arises when a witness's prior statement is admitted and the witness does not re-assert its substance, effectively walking away from it.[44] But the Court has shown no inclination to modify the rule. Indeed, it was reinforced by Justice Scalia himself in *United States v. Owens*,[45] a case involving a witness whose severe head injuries destroyed much of his memory—and it now becomes more important than ever for prosecutors. If a witness makes a statement favorable to a prosecutor, but the prosecutor is afraid that the witness will not stand by the statement at trial, the prosecutor should not argue that the statement is "reliable." Rather, the prosecutor should bring the witness to trial, or otherwise ensure that the defendant has had an adequate opportunity for cross. If the witness reaffirms the substance of the prior statement, all is well and good for the prosecutor. If

---

[42] 399 U.S. 149 (1970).

[43] 124 S. Ct. at 1369 n.9.

[44] See Richard D. Friedman, Prior Statements of a Witness: A Nettlesome Corner of the Hearsay Thicket, 1995 Sup. Ct. Rev. 277.

[45] 484 U.S. 554 (1988).

she testifies at variance from the statement, then the Confrontation Clause does not bar admissibility of the statement.

Fourth, in applying *Roberts*, the Court developed a body of case law concerning what constitutes proof of unavailability (assuming the given statement can be introduced only if the declarant is unavailable), and that case law—including part of *Roberts* itself—is left untouched, for better or worse. At argument in *Crawford*, the chief justice asked what impact the testimonial approach would have on *Mancusi v. Stubbs*,[46] a key case in this line and one in which he wrote the majority opinion.[47] The proper answer is simple: None at all.

Fifth, *Crawford* explicitly preserves the principle that the accused should be deemed to have forfeited the confrontation right if the accused's own misconduct prevented him from having an adequate opportunity to cross-examine the witness.[48] The right may be forfeited, for example, if the accused murdered or intimidated the witness. The forfeiture principle may take on greater importance under *Crawford*, as explained below.

Sixth, the rule of *Maryland v. Craig*[49] is unchanged, at least for now. In that case, the Court held that, upon a particularized showing that a child witness would be traumatized by testifying in the presence of the accused, the child may testify in another room, with the judge and counsel present but the jury and the accused connected electronically. *Crawford* addresses the question of *when* confrontation is required; *Craig* addresses the question of *what* procedures confrontation requires. The two cases can coexist peacefully, and nothing in *Crawford* suggests that *Craig* is placed in doubt. And yet, Justice Scalia dissented bitterly in *Craig*. The categorical nature of his opinion in *Crawford* squares better with his *Craig* dissent than with Justice O'Connor's looser majority opinion in *Craig*, and presumably he would welcome the opportunity to overrule *Craig*. Whether he would have the votes is an open question.

---

[46] 408 U.S. 204 (1972).

[47] Transcript of Oral Argument, Crawford v. Washington, 124 S. Ct. 1354 (2004) (No. 02-9410), available at 2003 WL 22705281.

[48] 124 S. Ct. at 1370.

[49] 497 U.S. 836 (1990).

Finally, *Crawford* leaves intact the final succor of prosecutors, the rule that a violation of the confrontation right may be harmless and therefore not require reversal.[50]

## V. Changes and Open Questions

That *Crawford* leaves much of the *status quo ante* unchanged does not gainsay that it changes a great deal, and not just the conceptual framework of the Confrontation Clause. Here I will address respects in which *Crawford does* change the law, questions that it leaves open, and adjustments to existing law that might be adopted in its wake.

*A. The Basic Change*

Most fundamentally, of course, *Crawford* ends the prosecutorial use of testimonial statements made to police in circumstances where the accused cannot confront his accuser. That means that when a prosecutor attempts to introduce a testimonial statement made by a person who is not a witness at trial, the prosecutor will not be able to argue that the statement should be admitted because it is reliable. Unless the accused either has had the opportunity to cross-examine the declarant, or has forfeited the right to confront her, the statement cannot be admitted.

Thus, to take an obvious example, some courts have been willing to admit grand jury testimony given by a witness who is not available at trial, persuading themselves that various factors—including the fact that the testimony was given under oath—are in the aggregate sufficiently strong "particularized guarantees of trustworthiness" to excuse the absence of an opportunity for cross-examination. *Crawford* means that this practice must stop. Similarly, station-house statements, of the type involved in *Crawford* itself, and statements made in plea hearings may not be introduced by the prosecution unless either the witness testifies at trial or she is unavailable and the accused has had an opportunity to cross-examine her.

Courts have already begun to apply cases consistently with these principles. In one Detroit murder case pending on appeal when *Crawford* was decided, the prosecutor has since confessed error, because the conviction depended in part on statements made to a polygraph examiner by a friend of the accused. Consider also *United*

---

[50] Delaware v. Van Arsdall, 475 U.S. 673 (1986). See also, e.g., Moody v. State, 594 S.E.2d 350 (Ga. 2004).

*States v. Saner*,[51] a post-*Crawford* decision in which the accused, a bookstore manager, objected to admission of a statement by a competitor, made to a Justice Department lawyer and paralegal, that the two managers had fixed prices. The court held, properly, that because the accused had not had a chance to cross-examine the competitor, who asserted the Fifth Amendment privilege at trial, *Crawford* precluded admissibility of the competitor's statement.[52]

## B. The Meaning of "Testimonial"

The most significant question that arises, of course, is how far the category of "testimonial" statements extends.

### 1. Standards

The *Crawford* Court did not have difficulty in concluding that Sylvia's statement was testimonial: "Statements taken by police officers in the course of interrogations," as Sylvia's was, are "testimonial under even a narrow standard."[53] As the Court elaborated:

> Whatever else the term covers, it applies at a minimum to prior testimony at a preliminary hearing, before a grand jury, or at a former trial; and to police interrogations. These are the modern practices with closest kinship to the abuses at which the Confrontation Clause was directed.[54]

So much for the core. The boundaries of the category will have to be marked out by future cases. The Court quoted three standards without choosing among them:

- "*ex parte* in-court testimony or its functional equivalent—that is, material such as affidavits, custodial examinations, prior testimony that the defendant was unable to cross-examine, or similar pretrial statements that declarants would reasonably expect to be used prosecutorially";
- "extrajudicial statements . . . contained in formalized testimonial materials, such as affidavits, depositions, prior testimony, or confessions"; and

---

[51] 313 F. Supp. 2d 896 (S.D. Ind. 2004).

[52] *Id.* at 902–03.

[53] *Crawford v. Washington*, 124 S. Ct. 1354, 1364 (2004).

[54] *Id.* The Court noted that "[s]tatements taken by police officers in the course of interrogations are . . . testimonial under even a narrow standard." *Id.*

- "statements that were made under circumstances which would lead an objective witness reasonably to believe that the statement would be available for use at a later trial."[55]

I believe the third of these is the most useful and accurate. It captures the animating idea behind the Confrontation Clause—the prevention of a system in which witnesses can offer their testimony in private without cross-examination. In some cases, under this view, a statement should be considered testimonial even though it was not made to a government official.[56]

It is by no means certain that this standard will ultimately prevail. Some language in *Crawford* emphasizes the role of government officers in creating testimony. For example, having used the term "interrogation," the Court takes care to note that Sylvia's statement, "knowingly given in response to structured police questioning, qualifies under any conceivable definition";[57] at another point, it noted that "[i]nvolvement of government officers in the production of testimony with an eye toward trial presents unique potential for prosecutorial abuse."[58] This emphasis on government involvement might suggest that the Court will stick closely to a minimalist definition of testimonial statements.

That would be a mistake, however. I do not believe that participation by government officials in creation of the statement—either receipt of it as its initial audience or active procurement of it through interrogation—is the essence of what makes a statement testimonial.

---

[55] *Id.* (citations omitted).

[56] Most obvious, a government investigator may use a private intermediary to procure testimony, (but see People v. Geno, LC No. 01-046631-FC, 2004 WL 893947 (Mich. Ct. App. Apr. 27, 2004)), or a witness might use an intermediary as her agent for transmitting testimony to court. Thus, a declaration by a dying person identifying her killer should be considered testimonial even though the only person who hears it is a private individual; the purpose of the communication is presumably not merely to edify the listener but to pass on to the authorities the victim's identification of the killer, and the understanding of both parties to the communication is that the listener will play his role. Similarly, a complainant should not be able to avoid confrontation by passing on her information to a private intermediary who effectively runs a testimony-transmission operation—"Make this videotape and I'll pass it on to the proper authorities. You don't even have to take an oath, and after the tape is done you can even leave the state if you want."

[57] 124 S. Ct. at 1365 n.4.

[58] *Id.* at 1367 n.7.

The confrontation right was recognized in older systems in which there was no public prosecutor, and victims or their families prosecuted crimes themselves. The idea behind the confrontation right is that the judicial system cannot try an accused with the aid of testimony by a witness whom the accused has not had a chance to confront. The prosecutor plays no essential role in the violation. Thus, if just before trial a person shoved a written statement under the courthouse door, asserting that the accused did in fact commit the crime, that would plainly be testimonial even though no government official played a role in preparing the statement.[59] One ground for hope in this respect is that *Crawford* itself noted that one of the statements involved in the notorious *Raleigh* case was a letter.[60]

In some cases a problem that nearly is the reverse arises—an investigative official may be seeking to procure evidence, but the declarant may not understand this. I believe that in the usual case the investigator's anticipation should not alter characterization of the statement. If the declarant does not recognize she is creating evidence that may be used in a criminal proceeding, then the nature of what she is doing in making the statement is not testimonial. Thus, a conversation between criminal confederates, with no anticipation of a leak to the authorities, is not ordinarily testimonial, and if in fact the authorities are surreptitiously recording the conversation, that should not change the result.[61] On the other hand, investigators probably should not be allowed to disguise their intent gratuitously—that is, for the purpose of defeating the confrontation right. Accordingly, even apart from a standard like the third one quoted above, perhaps a statement should be considered testimonial in what might be called an "invited statement" context in which the statement fits a description such as this:

---

[59] Indeed, the *prosecutor* cannot violate the confrontation right; there is nothing wrong with a prosecutor interviewing a witness out of the presence of the accused, and it is only when the *court* admits the witness's statement into evidence that the right is violated. It is thus the court's conduct that is state action for constitutional purposes.

[60] 124 S. Ct. at 1360.

[61] See People v. Torres, No. CRF01-84916, 2004 WL 575205 (Cal. Ct. App. Mar. 24, 2004; as modified on denial of rehearing, Apr. 13, 2004) (unpublished op.).

Before the statement is made, (1) a recipient of the statement anticipates evidentiary use of the statement, but does not inform the declarant of this anticipation, and (2) the prosecution does not demonstrate that disclosure of anticipation of evidentiary use would have substantially diminished the probability that the declarant would have made the statement.

The idea behind the second prong of such a test would be that if disclosing the recipient's investigatory activity would not inhibit the declarant from making the statement, then the disclosure probably ought to be made; on the other hand, if the disclosure would likely prevent the statement from being made, then the investigator has sufficient reason for declining to make a disclosure. This rule seems to me to have some merit, but it may be too complicated to be applied satisfactorily.

### 2. Special Cases

Many cases will arise, in a wide variety of circumstances, in which it is a close question whether a statement should be deemed testimonial. I will address here two of the most important recurring types of cases.

#### a. When Are 911 Calls Testimonial?

Consider first the example of statements made in calls to 911 operators. In recent years, courts have often admitted these statements—most characteristically, by complainants in domestic violence cases—even though the caller has not testified in court. Under *Crawford*, this practice would not be allowed *if* the statement is deemed "testimonial." The extent to which these calls are "testimonial," however, is an open question.

The court in one post-*Crawford* case, in justifying its decision that statements in 911 calls should not be deemed testimonial, declared:

> Typically, a woman who calls 911 for help because she has just been stabbed or shot is not contemplating being a "witness" in future legal proceedings; she is usually trying simply to save her own life.[62]

---

[62] People v. Moscat, 777 N.Y.S.2d 875 (N.Y. Crim. Ct. 2004).

This generalization fits some cases, but not all. In some cases, the caller does not perceive that she is any longer in immediate danger, and the primary purpose of the call is simply to initiate investigative and prosecutorial machinery. Indeed, often the call occurs a considerable time after the particular episode has closed, and often the caller gives a good deal of information that is not necessary for immediate intervention. In a broader set of cases, the caller's motives are mixed but she is fully aware that what she says has potential evidentiary value.

Consider, for example, *State v. Davis*,[63] now on review in the Washington Supreme Court (the same court from which *Crawford* came). The complainant called 911 and, in response to questions by the operator, disclosed that the defendant had beaten her with his fists and then run out the door, further disclosed that she had a protection order against him, and explained the reasons why he had been in her house. The complainant did not testify at trial, and the 911 tape was played to the jury. In closing argument, the prosecutor said,

> [A]lthough she is not here today to talk to you[,] she left something better. She left you her *testimony* on the day that this happened . . . . [T]his shows that the defendant, Adrian Davis, was at her home and assaulted her.[64]

Then the prosecutor played the 911 tape again.[65] Here, the statement has strong claim to be considered testimonial.

*Davis* and cases like it suggest that the 911-call scenario should not be dismissed by broad generalizations about the "typical" case. Rather, a case-by-case assessment is necessary. Indeed, even if a 911 call is nothing but an urgent plea for protection, the court should closely scrutinize it. I will repeat here the analysis that Bridget McCormack and I have given:

> To the extent the call itself is part of the incident being tried, the fact of the call presumably should be admitted so the prosecution can present a coherent story about the incident. But even in that situation, the need to present a coherent

[63] 64 P.3d 661 (Wash. Ct. App. 2003).

[64] State v. Davis, Kings Cty. Super. Ct., King Co. No. 01102794-4 (KNT), Report of Proceedings, May 5, 2001, at 55, conviction affirmed, 64 P.3d 661, review granted, 75 P.3d 969 (Wash. Sept. 5, 2003).

[65] *Id.*

story does not necessarily justify admitting the contents of
the call. And even if the circumstances do warrant allowing
the prosecution to prove the contents of the call, those contents generally should not be admitted to prove the *truth* of
what they assert . . . . To the extent that the contents of the
call are significant only as the caller's report of *what has
happened,* such a report usually should be considered
testimonial.[66]

### b. When Are Statements by Children "Testimonial"?

Another type of case that frequently will test the limits of the term
"testimonial" involves statements by children, typically alleging
some kind of abuse. Suppose, for example, a young child tells a
police officer that an adult has physically or sexually abused her. If
an adult made such a statement, it would clearly be testimonial. But
can a different result occur in the case of a very young child?

At some point, the statement of a very young child may perhaps
be considered more like the bark of a bloodhound than like the
testimony of an adult human; that is, the child may be reacting
to and communicating about what occurred, with no sense of the
consequences that her communication may have. Arguably, fidelity
to the text and policies of the Confrontation Clause suggests that
some degree of understanding of the consequences of the statement
is necessary before a declarant may be considered a "witness." *If*
that is true, the better rule would probably be that a person is not
a witness unless she understands that the statement, if accepted, is
likely to lead to adverse consequences for the person accused. Under
this view, a child could be a witness even if she had no real understanding of the legal system; it would be enough to know that telling
a police officer about a bad thing that a person did would likely
cause that person to be punished.

In deciding whether a child is capable of acting as a "witness,"
the moral as well as cognitive development of the child may well
be material. My colleague Sherman Clark has argued that part of
what drives the confrontation right is not simply the formal categorization of a person as a "witness," but also the moral sense of the
obligation of an accuser to confront the accused.[67] If he is right—

---

[66] Friedman & McCormack, *supra* note 13, at 1243 (emphasis added).
[67] Clark, *supra* note 12, at 1282.

461

and I believe there is a good deal of force to the argument—then the important question is not only whether the child understands the punitive consequences of the statement, but also "the level of obligation and responsibility we are willing to put on the shoulders of children."[68]

Even assuming a given child is capable of making a testimonial statement, the fact that the declarant is a child can complicate the question of whether the particular statement should be deemed testimonial. As I suggested earlier, when an adult makes a statement accusing a person of a crime, the statement should be considered testimonial, even though the statement is made to a private individual, if the declarant understands that the listener will pass the information on to the authorities. But consider children's statements to intermediaries—for instance, a child's statement to his mother. This situation may be materially different from that of the adult witness, because even a child sufficiently mature to be capable of being considered a witness may have no understanding that the third party will pass the statement on to the authorities.

There are different ways to approach this problem. One view is that the statement is not testimonial if a child in the position of the declarant would not understand that the information would reach the authorities. A second view is that if the child, without understanding the particulars, expects the mother to visit adverse consequences upon the assailant, then the child should be deemed to be testifying within his or her ability to do so. And a third view is that differentiating by maturity is simply inappropriate and unadministrable, so the perspective of a reasonable adult should govern determination of whether a statement is deemed testimonial.[69]

Furthermore, the supplemental standard I have suggested as a possibility in "invited statement" contexts may be appropriate in certain cases involving statements by children. Under that standard,

---

[68] Id.

[69] See People v. Sisavath, 118 Cal. App. 4th 1396 (Cal. 2004) (applying to a four-year-old child's statement standard of reasonable expectation of an "objective observer," and rejecting the view that this should be applied by considering "an objective witness in the same category of persons as the actual witness"); State v. Courtney, Nos. A03-790, A03-791, 2004 WL 1488539 (Minn. Ct. App. July 6, 2004) (six-year-old child's interview with child protective services worker is testimonial; no suggestion that declarant's age is relevant).

the statement should be deemed testimonial (1) if the investigative nature of the conversation is withheld from the child but (2) it does not appear that the nondisclosure was necessary to procure the statement. Again, the idea is that the investigator should not be allowed to withhold the purposes of her inquiries gratuitously in an effort to defeat the confrontation right—but the complexity of this inquiry gives me some qualms whether this standard should be applied.

Plainly, this is an extraordinarily complex and difficult area, and pending further guidance from the Court it will remain very uncertain.[70]

### 3. What Constitutes an "Opportunity for Cross-Examination"?

Under *Crawford*, the confrontation right presumptively is violated if a statement is considered "testimonial" but the witness does not testify at trial. By contrast, the confrontation right is not violated where the witness is unavailable and the accused has had a prior opportunity for cross-examination. In the wake of *Crawford*, a wise prosecutor, aware of the possibility that a key witness may be unavailable, will often take the witness's deposition early in the investigation. *Crawford* therefore raises an important question about what constitutes an adequate "prior opportunity for cross-examination."

For example, suppose a laboratory report is a critical piece of evidence. In most circumstances, the lab report should be considered testimonial, because the report is prepared in anticipation of its introduction at trial. Therefore, the lab technician who made the report should testify at trial if she is available to do so. If she becomes unavailable through no fault of the accused (by accidental death, for example), and the accused has not had an opportunity to cross-examine her, then the report should not be considered admissible. But if the prosecution takes her deposition—that is, a pretrial examination, subject to oath and cross-examination—and the technician later becomes unavailable, the prosecutor may use the deposition *if* the deposition presented an adequate opportunity for cross-examination.

---

[70] Compare, e.g., People v. Geno, LC No. 01-046631-FC, 2004 WL 893947 (Mich. Ct. App. Apr. 27, 2004), with Snowden v. State, 846 A.2d 36 (Md. Ct. Spec. App. 2004).

Because *Crawford* increases the prosecutor's incentive to take a deposition, we can expect pressure to amend the rules of criminal procedure in jurisdictions, including at the federal level, in which depositions are not now readily available, and perhaps even to allow depositions before charges have been brought. If a deposition is taken very early, obviously there will often be a question whether it gave the accused an adequate opportunity to cross-examine. Did counsel have enough time to prepare? Did counsel know what issues to press, and have the information at hand that would enable her to do so effectively? The better approach would *not* be to assume that early opportunities are inadequate per se; in many cases, counsel will have little difficulty, even with limited preparation and even before matters have proceeded very far, determining what questions to ask. Rather, if the defendant had an opportunity to cross-examine the witness at deposition but the witness is unavailable at trial, the confrontation right should not require exclusion unless the defense shows some particular reason to believe the opportunity was inadequate.

One more change in prosecutorial practice may well follow from *Crawford*. Suppose a prosecutor announces an intention to use a witness's statement and invites the defense to demand a deposition of the witness if it wants to be assured of cross-examining the witness. If the defendant does not make the demand, the witness is unavailable at trial, and the prosecution offers the statement, would this procedure suffice to protect adequately the "opportunity for confrontation"? Perhaps, by not making the demand though being warned of the possible consequences, the defendant would be deemed to have waived the confrontation right. Or perhaps the procedure would be considered a violation of the accused's passive right to do nothing and "be confronted with" the witnesses against him. We may never know for sure unless the procedure is tried.

### 4. What Constitutes "Forfeiture"?

The idea that the accused cannot claim the confrontation right if the accused's own misconduct prevents the witness from testifying at trial is a very old one. *Crawford* explicitly reaffirms it,[71] and justifiably so.

[71] Crawford v. Washington, 124 S. Ct. 1354, 1370 (2004).

Forfeiture often raises difficult issues. If a witness is murdered shortly before she was scheduled to testify against the accused, what showing of the accused's involvement does the prosecution have to make? Is it enough that the accused acquiesced in the wrongdoing? And how is participation or acquiescence to be determined; is the mere fact that the accused benefited from the murder enough to raise a presumption that the accused acquiesced in it?

One issue on which *Crawford* gives little or no guidance may be expected to become particularly pressing now. Suppose the wrongful act that allegedly rendered the witness unavailable is the *same* act with which he is charged. May the act nevertheless cause a forfeiture of the confrontation right? For example, suppose the accusation is of child sexual abuse and the prosecution argues that the abuse itself has intimidated the child from testifying in court (though she previously made a statement describing it). Or suppose the accusation is of murder, the prosecution contending that the accused struck a fatal blow and that the victim made a statement identifying the accused and then died?

The first reaction of many observers is that in such situations forfeiture would be bizarre. And yet, for reasons I will summarize briefly, I believe that in some circumstances it is appropriate.[72] In post-*Crawford* cases, two state supreme courts have agreed.[73]

The objection most frequently made to applying forfeiture doctrine in situations of this sort is that it is bootstrapping: The accused is held to have forfeited the confrontation right on the ground that he or she committed the very act on which the trial centers—an act that he or she is accused of committing, but denies committing and is presumed not to have committed. On closer analysis, I do not believe the objection carries weight. The situation is analogous to the one that often arises when a defendant is accused of conspiracy and the prosecution argues that the hearsay rule poses no bar to admission of a statement made by a conspirator in support of the conspiracy. In each of these cases, the same factual issue—the defendant's participation in the conspiracy in the one case, and his commission of the wrongful act that rendered the witness unavailable

---

[72]See Richard D. Friedman, Confrontation and the Definition of Chutzpa, 31 Isr. L. Rev. 506 (1997).

[73]People v. Moore, No. 01CA1760, 2004 WL 1690247 (Col. July 29, 2004); State v. Meeks, 88 P.3d 789 (Kan. 2004).

in the other—may arise as a threshold matter for evidentiary purposes and when determining guilt, but so what? The issue will likely be decided for the two different purposes by different fact-finders—the judge deciding threshold evidentiary matters and the jury determining guilt—and on different factual bases.[74]

Another objection is that presumably the crime was not committed *for the purpose* of rendering the witness unavailable. But again I respond with a shrug. The point of forfeiture doctrine is that the accused has acted wrongfully in a way that is incompatible with maintenance of the right. Suppose that an informer makes a statement to the police describing a drug kingpin's illegal activities. But the informer stays undercover and, before the kingpin knows anything about the statement, the two get into a fight over a card game. The kingpin goes to a closet, pulls out a gun, and murders the informer. If the kingpin is tried on drug charges and the prosecution wants to introduce the informer's statement, the kingpin should not succeed in arguing, "But I haven't had a chance to cross-examine him." The appropriate response is, "And whose fault is that? You murdered him."

As interpreted in this way, forfeiture doctrine can solve one of the puzzles of the confrontation right. The *Crawford* Court accurately noted that the "dying declaration" exception is the only exception commonly applicable to testimonial statements that had been well-established at the time of the Sixth Amendment's adoption in 1791.[75] The Court then said, with apparently studied ambiguity, "If this exception must be accepted on historical grounds, it is sui generis."[76] It seems highly unlikely that the Court would generally exclude statements that fit within the dying declaration exception, thus achieving a remarkably unappealing evidentiary result that courts have avoided for several hundred years.

On the other hand, admitting these statements on the ground suggested by the Court raises problems of its own. It obscures the clarity of the principle adopted by *Crawford*, that if a statement is testimonial it cannot be introduced against the accused unless he had an opportunity to cross-examine the witness. And it does so on

---

[74]See generally Bourjaily v. United States, 483 U.S. 171 (1987); Fed. R. Evid. 104(a).
[75]Crawford v. Washington, 124 S. Ct. 1354, 1367 n.6 (2004).
[76]*Id.*

very weak grounds, for (as noted above) the rationale generally cited for the dying declaration exception is absurd. A far better resolution would be to recognize that, however the admissibility of dying declarations usually has been defended, it really is best understood as a reflection of the principle that a defendant who renders a witness unavailable by wrongful means cannot complain about her absence at trial. That principle also explains, incidentally, why (1) the hearsay exception for dying declarations is limited to those that describe the *cause* of death, and (2) the declaration will not be admitted unless death appeared *imminent* at the time the declaration was made.

**C.** Crawford's *Impact on Non-Testimonial Statements*

If a statement is deemed not to be testimonial, what is the impact of the Confrontation Clause? *Crawford* does not resolve the matter. The theory of the opinion suggests, and the Court explicitly preserves the possibility of, "an approach that exempted such statements from Confrontation Clause scrutiny altogether."[77] But, in an apparent compromise, the Court also indicated that *Roberts*, or some standard even more flexible, might also be applied in this context.[78]

Numerous post-*Crawford* courts, having determined the statements at issue were not testimonial, have gone through the *Roberts* analysis and—not surprisingly—determined that the statements were admissible.[79] It is easy enough to see why a court disposed to admit a statement would follow this approach: If instead the court held that the Confrontation Clause did not apply at all to non-testimonial statements, it might leave itself vulnerable to reversal if a higher court held that *Roberts* continues to apply to such a statement. So it is prudent to run through the *Roberts* analysis, which a court can always find is satisfied if it wants to (that being one of the problems with *Roberts*.) No terrible harm is done, perhaps, but the process is wasteful, because courts will continue to run through it with predictable results.[80] Until a prosecutor is brave enough to press the

[77] *Id.* at 1374.

[78] *Id.*

[79] See, e.g., State v. Rivera, 844 A.2d 191 (Conn. 2004); People v. Coker, Nos. 238738, 238739, 2004 WL 626855 (Mich. Ct. App. Mar. 30, 2004).

[80] In State v. Blackstock, No. COA03-732, 2004 WL 1485849 (N.C. Ct. App. July 6, 2004), the court, having determined that certain statements were not testimonial, appears to have concluded they were not admissible under *Roberts*—but it also clearly concluded that the state statements were rendered inadmissible by the hearsay rule. Thus, *Roberts* had no effect on the outcome. I know of no post-*Crawford* case in which

point, it is doubtful that there will be a clear test in the Supreme Court on the proposition that outside the context of testimonial statements, the Confrontation Clause has no force.

## VI. Conclusion

Plainly, *Crawford* leaves open many very important questions. In particular, the impact of the opinion may be very different depending on whether the Supreme Court adopts a broad or narrow understanding of the term "testimonial." But what is most important is that the jurisprudence of the Confrontation Clause, after a long detour, has been set on the proper course. This means that the discourse can be rational and candid. Rather than manipulating unanswerable questions as to whether a given statement is sufficiently "reliable" to warrant admission, the courts will be asking whether admission violates the time-honored and constitutionally protected right of a criminal defendant to insist witnesses against him testify subject to cross-examination.

Even in the pages of this journal, I am willing to confess that I am not a strict originalist in constitutional interpretation. I believe that there are some questions of constitutional law that cannot be answered most usefully by asking what the public meaning was of the constitutional text at the time it was adopted, or what the intention of the Framers was. But in this context, all indications are in alignment. The historical background shows that the meaning of the text and the intention of the Framers are quite clear, and the unequivocal procedural rule on which they insisted continues to resonate today as one of the central aspects of our system of criminal procedure. The *Crawford* Court properly said, "By replacing categorical constitutional guarantees with open-ended balancing tests, we do violence to their design."[81] The Constitution does not always speak in terms of categorical guarantees, but when it does, as in the case of the Confrontation Clause, it should be heeded. Give credit to the Court for disenthralling itself from a doctrine that had grown familiar but had no basis in the Constitution and was utterly unsatisfactory, and for recognizing the essence of the confrontation right.

---

a court has decided that a statement was (1) not excluded by the hearsay rule, (2) not testimonial for purposes of the Confrontation Clause, and yet (3) rendered inadmissible by *Roberts*.

[81] *Crawford v. Washington*, 124 S. Ct. 1354, 1373 (2004).

# A Fistful of Denial: The Supreme Court Takes a Pass on Commerce Clause Challenges to Environmental Laws

*John C. Eastman*[1]

## I. Introduction

Ever since the Supreme Court's landmark decision in *United States v. Lopez*[2] invalidating the Gun-Free School Zones Act[3] as beyond the scope of Congress's Commerce Clause power, scholarly commentators from both sides of the ideological spectrum have wondered whether the Court would apply the reasoning of that case in the context of federal environmental laws. Many agreed that, if faithfully applied, *Lopez* sounded a death knell for a slew of environmental legislation that had at best only a tenuous connection with interstate commerce.[4] For some, that was even more reason to deride the *Lopez*

---

[1] Professor Eastman was counsel of record in *Rancho Viejo, LLC v. Norton*, 323 F.3d 1062 (D.C. Cir. 2003), cert. denied, 124 S. Ct. 1506 (2004), and filed amicus curiae briefs on behalf of The Claremont Institute Center for Constitutional Jurisprudence in United States v. Morrison, 529 U.S. 598 (2000), and Solid Waste Agency v. United States Army Corps of Engineers, 531 U.S. 159 (2001), all of which are addressed in this article.

[2] 514 U.S. 549 (1995).

[3] 18 U.S.C. § 922(q)(1)(A) (1990).

[4] See, e.g., Eric Brignac, The Commerce Clause Justification of Federal Endangered Species Protection: Gibbs v. Babbitt, 79 N.C. L. Rev. 873(2001); Alan T. Dickey, United States v. Lopez: The Supreme Court Reasserts the Commerce Clause as a Limit on the Powers of Congress, 70 Tul. L. Rev. 1207 (1996); John P. Frantz, The Reemergence of the Commerce Clause as a Limit on Federal Power: United States v. Lopez, 19 Harv. J.L. & Pub. Pol'y 161 (1995); William Funk, The Court, the Clean Water Act, and the Constitution: SWANCC and Beyond, 31 Envtl. L. Rep. (Envtl. L. Inst.) 10,741 (2001); Christine A. Klein, The Environmental Commerce Clause, 27 Harv. Envtl L. Rev. 1, 1 (2003); Bradford C. Mank, Protecting Intrastate Threatened Species: Does the Endangered Species Act Encroach on Traditional State Authority and Exceed the Outer Limits of the Commerce Clause?, 36 Ga. L. Rev. 723, 770-80 (2002); Donald H. Regan, How to Think About the Federal Commerce Power and Incidentally Rewrite United States v. Lopez, 94 Mich. L. Rev. 554 (1995); John H. Turner, Lopez Lives: Can an Expansive View of Federal Wetlands Regulation Survive? An Overview of

decision, but for originalists, it was a welcome prospect. Not only would the Court be enforcing the Constitution's limits on Congressional power "to regulate Commerce . . . among the . . . States,"[5] as it ought, but it would be resurrecting the sound theoretical foundation on which those limits were built, returning decisionmaking authority to a level of government close enough to the people to ensure that both the benefits *and costs* of environmental policy were fully considered by those who would suffer any adverse consequences of a wrong decision.

A fistful of five environmental cases pressing the Commerce Clause challenge were presented to the Court this past term by way of petitions for writs of certiorari. The first four petitions were summarily denied, and the fifth will not be considered until the Court returns to work in October. This article addresses the significance of those cases and places them in the larger context of the general recalcitrance of the lower courts to apply *Lopez* in the environmental law arena.

## II. The *Lopez* Revolution: Revival of Constitutional Limits or Mere Anomaly?

Between the New Deal jurisprudential "revolution" and the Court's decision in *Lopez*, it appeared that the Court viewed Congress's commerce power over local environmental policy as virtually unbounded. Leading constitutional law scholars regarded limits inherent in the Constitution's structure or in the Commerce Clause itself as essentially unenforceable. By 1978, for example, Harvard Law Professor Lawrence Tribe would write, "The Supreme Court has . . . largely abandoned any effort to articulate and enforce *internal* limits on congressional power—limits inherent in the grants of power themselves."[6] Professor Gerald Gunther would write in the tenth edition of his Constitutional Law textbook shortly thereafter, "After nearly 200 years of government under the Constitution, there

---

Decisions Regarding the "Proactive" Reach of the Commerce Clause, in Wetlands Law and Regulation (ALI-ABA Course of Study), May 31, 2000, WL SE88 ALI-ABA 197, at 199-201; Jeffrey H. Wood, Recalibrating the Federal Government's Authority to Regulate Intrastate Endangered Species After SWANCC, 19 J. Land Use & Envtl. L. 91 (2003).

[5]U.S. Const. art. I, § 8, cl. 3.

[6]Lawrence Tribe, American Constitutional Law 224 (1978).

are very few judicially enforced checks on the congressional commerce power."[7]

Moreover, the virtually unfettered discretion Congress gave to the regulatory agencies ensured that the boundless power was fully exploited. The U.S. Army Corps of Engineers, for example, acting pursuant to a statute designed to protect the flow of commerce through the navigable waterways of the United States, successfully prosecuted the owner of a truck repair shop for removing some old tires from and adding fill dirt to his own land so that he could expand his garage.[8] The land became soggy during Pennsylvania's rainy season due to runoff from a nearby manmade overpass; it was deemed a "wetland," therefore, which according to the Corps qualified it as a "navigable water" of the United States, necessitating a Clean Water Act permit before fill dirt—a "pollutant" under the Act—could be added.[9] Reached prior to *Lopez*, that decision was allowed to stand.

Given that near sixty-year history of judicial deference to the expansion of federal regulatory power, *Lopez* came as something of a shock. For the first time since the New Deal, the Supreme Court said "no." Yet for five years thereafter, lower courts routinely rebuffed *Lopez*-like challenges to a host of federal laws having little or no connection to interstate commerce. Although petitions for certiorari were filed in many of these cases, the Supreme Court routinely denied certiorari in them, leading many commentators to believe that *Lopez* had quickly become merely an anomaly[10]: the Court had resurrected limits on Congress's power that it apparently had no stomach to enforce, particularly in controversial arenas such as environmental law.

Many legal scholars were surprised, therefore, when five years after *Lopez* the Court chose a challenge to the Violence Against Women Act[11] to reiterate its commitment to *Lopez* and its principled

---

[7]Gerald Gunther, Constitutional Law 113 (10th ed. 1980).

[8]United States v. Pozsgai, 999 F.2d 719, 721-23 (3d Cir. 1993), cert. denied, 510 U.S. 1110 (1994).

[9]*Id.* at 721–24.

[10]See, e.g., Glenn H. Reynolds & Brannon P. Denning, Lower Court Readings of Lopez, or What if the Supreme Court Held a Constitutional Revolution and Nobody Came?, 2000 Wisc. L. Rev. 369 (2000) (citing cases).

[11]42 U.S.C. § 1371 et seq.

adherence to the doctrine that ours is a limited government of specifically enumerated powers. *United States v. Morrison*[12] was what is known as a "bad facts" case, involving an alleged gang rape of a young college student by two members of a university football team.[13] Surely the Court—surely Justice O'Connor, widely believed to be the key swing vote on the Court—would not deprive co-ed Christy Brzonkala of the federal remedy that Congress had provided over something as technical as the alleged rapists' claim that the Commerce Clause did not provide constitutional authority for the law. Yet even in this controversial arena, the Court adhered to its *Lopez* precedent and the original understanding of the Constitution's limits that it had begun to revive.[14] Without a connection to interstate commerce, criminal conduct such as Christy Brzonkala had alleged was a matter for state, not federal law.[15]

## III. *Lopez* in the Environmental Law Context, and Lower Court Recalcitrance

With the lower courts suitably chastised for having ignored the high Court's *Lopez* decision, the stage was set for new challenges to federal environmental laws having no connection to interstate commerce. Yet the lower courts again proved reticent to apply the principles of *Lopez*, and now *Morrison*, in the environmental context. The Fourth Circuit, for example, widely regarded as one of the circuit courts most consistently committed to the original understanding of the Constitution, refused to apply (or rather artificially distinguished) *Lopez* and *Morrison* in a Commerce Clause challenge to the federal Endangered Species Act.[16] In that case, *Gibbs v. Babbitt*,[17] farmers challenged the constitutionality of the act as a defense against criminal prosecution for having shot federally protected red wolves that were threatening their crops and livestock.[18] (Shooting

---

[12]529 U.S. 598 (2000).

[13]*Id.* at 602.

[14]*Id.* at 607–18.

[15]*Id.* at 611–13.

[16]16 U.S.C. § 1631 et seq.

[17]214 F.3d 483 (4th Cir. 2000).

[18]*Id.* at 489.

a red wolf would have been permissible if the farmers' children were threatened, but only if the risk to them was imminent!)

The panel decision in *Gibbs* was held pending the Supreme Court's decision in *Morrison*. When rendered, *Morrison* all but compelled the conclusion that Congress had no authority under its commerce power to criminalize the taking of red wolves on private property. Red wolves had not been articles of commerce for more than a century![19] Nevertheless, the Fourth Circuit opinion by then-Chief Judge J. Harvey Wilkinson, over a vigorous dissent from Judge J. Michael Luttig, held that the fact that the red wolf was not an article of commerce was no barrier to congressional power. A nexus with interstate commerce was established, the panel's majority said, by tourists traveling to red wolf "howling" events in North Carolina,[20] by a few scientists traveling to the state to study the red wolf,[21] and by farmers seeking to protect crops destined for commerce.[22] Under such reasoning, *Morrison* would have been decided differently—at least if Congress could reasonably have believed the old adage that "women love to shop."[23] Yet the Court denied a petition for certiorari in the case, letting Judge Wilkinson's controversial decision stand.[24]

In short order, however, the Supreme Court accepted another opportunity to address the challenge presented by the Fourth Circuit and repeatedly pressed by the Department of Justice that *Lopez* simply did not apply to environmental laws. In *Solid Waste Agency of Northern Cook County v. United States Army Corps of Engineers*[25] (hereinafter *SWANCC*), the Department of Justice contended that the U.S. Army Corps of Engineers had the power, pursuant to the Commerce Clause, to regulate a proposed local landfill because migratory birds sometimes stopped to bathe in the puddles that developed after a rain in the gravel pit that was to be the site of the

---

[19]*Id.* at 495; see also *id.* at 507 (Luttig, J., dissenting).

[20]*Id.* at 493.

[21]*Id.* at 494.

[22]*Id.* at 495.

[23]Sonya Hamlin, The Communication Challenges of the New Jury: Chapter Excerpt from What Makes Juries Listen Today (American Law Institute 14), June 6–7, 2002, quoting William Dunn, The Baby Bust: A Generation Comes of Age 40 (1993) (referring to the hobby-like fondness for shopping of "twenty-something women").

[24]Gibbs v. Norton, 531 U.S. 1145 (2001).

[25]531 U.S. 159 (2001).

landfill.[26] *Lopez* and *Morrison* were limited to criminal law matters, according to Justice Department lawyers, because such were traditional state functions.[27] Although the Supreme Court rejected the government's position on statutory construction grounds, it left no doubt that the *Lopez* analysis was not limited to criminal law but applied in the environmental law context as well.[28]

## IV. The October 2003 Term: *Cert. Denied*

Thus, the path was again cleared for Commerce Clause challenges to federal environmental laws having nothing to do with interstate commerce. And again the lower courts skirted the clear import of *Lopez* and *Morrison*, and the equally clear dicta from *SWANCC*, to avoid enforcing the Constitution's limits on congressional power in the environmental arena. In *United States v. Rapanos*,[29] for example, the Sixth Circuit—*after a specific remand from the Supreme Court for further consideration in light of SWANCC*[30]—upheld the criminal convictions of John and Judith Rapanos for adding fill dirt to their own property, accepting the government's contention that the property contained "wetlands" that fell within the "navigable waters" jurisdiction of the U.S. Army Corps of Engineers under the Clean Water Act, even though the property was some twenty miles from the nearest navigable stream.[31] The Corps' claim of jurisdiction was premised on the regulatory definition of "navigable waters" as including "wetlands adjacent to traditional navigable waters," and on the fact that a 100-year-old manmade drainpipe connected the Rapanos' marsh to Hoppler Creek, which in turn was connected to the Kawkawlin River and ultimately to Saginaw Bay and Lake Huron.[32] The opinion was written by then-Chief Judge Boyce Martin, and joined by Circuit Judges Alan Norris and John Rogers. The

[26]*Id.* at 167.

[27]Brief of Respondent, SWANCC v. U.S. Army Corps of Engineers, 531 U.S. 159 (2001) (No. 99-1178), available at 2000 WL 1369439, at *38–39.

[28]SWANCC, 531 U.S. at 173–74.

[29]339 F.3d 447 (6th Cir. 2003), cert. denied, 124 S. Ct. 1875 (2004), petition for reh'g denied, 124 S. Ct. 2407 (2004).

[30]Rapanos v. United States, 533 U.S. 913 (2001).

[31]Rapanos, 339 F.3d at 449, 452–54.

[32]*Id.* at 449.

Supreme Court summarily denied the Rapanos' petition for certiorari on April 5, 2004, and their petition for rehearing on May 24, 2004.[33] The Court likewise denied certiorari this past term in two other *SWANCC*-like cases despite a clear and expressly acknowledged split among the federal courts of appeals on the import of *SWANCC* to federal claims of jurisdiction over waters that are not adjacent to "navigable-in-fact" waters of the United States. It denied certiorari in a Fourth Circuit case, *United States v. Deaton*,[34] on the same day that it denied certiorari in the *Rapanos* case, and it denied certiorari earlier in the term in *United States v. Rueth Development Company*,[35] a case arising out of the Seventh Circuit.

*Deaton* involved a civil enforcement action against a Maryland property owner who dug a ditch across his own twelve-acre parcel of land to help drain some standing water that was causing unhealthful conditions on his property. Once drained, the standing water ran into a "roadside ditch," then (at least when enough rain had fallen) through a culvert to another roadside ditch on the other side of the road, also known as the "John Adkins Prong of Perdue Creek" (amazingly, a point of contention in the litigation). From there, it flowed into Perdue Creek proper, which in turn flowed into Beaverdam Creek, "a natural watercourse with several dams and ponds"[36]—the dams no doubt erected by the natural creatures after whom the creek was named. None of those waters was navigable, of course—not the standing water on Deaton's property, not the "roadside ditch," not the culvert under the road, not the Adkins Prong, not even Beaverdam Creek.[37] More than eight miles from Deaton's property, however, Beaverdam Creek does flow into the Wicomico River, which is navigable in parts, and twenty-five miles further on the Wicomico River flows into the Chesapeake Bay.[38] The

---

[33]See note 29 *supra*.

[34]332 F.3d 698 (4th Cir. 2003), cert. denied, 124 S. Ct. 1874 (2004) (hereinafter "Deaton II").

[35]335 F.3d 598 (7th Cir. 2003), cert. denied, 124 S. Ct. 835 (2003).

[36]Deaton II, 332 F.3d at 702.

[37]Id. at 708 (noting appellant's argument that "water flowing from the ditch must pass through several other nonnavigable watercourses before reaching the navigable Wicomico River").

[38]Id. at 702.

Corps of Engineers asserted jurisdiction, therefore, not because some of Deaton's standing water made it to the Chesapeake Bay in a polluted condition (it did not), but because the dirt he had piled alongside the ditch he dug on his own property was considered a "pollutant" that he had "deposited" into a "wetland" without a permit—the "wetland" being the same area from which the dirt had been taken moments before it was "deposited" alongside the newly dug ditch.[39] Before the Fourth Circuit, the Corps prevailed in its claim that it had jurisdiction over Deaton's ditch, based on the contention that it was a "navigable water" of the United States, or at least adjacent to one, and that this was somehow properly within Congress's power to regulate commerce among the states.[40]

The land at issue in the Seventh Circuit's *Rueth Development* case[41] had a similarly attenuated connection to "navigable waters" of the United States. Rueth Development put some fill dirt on its property in Dyer, Indiana. The trial court found that the fill dirt was "placed in wetlands 'adjacent to an unnamed tributary to Dyer Ditch, which flows north to Hart Ditch, which flows north to the Little Calumet River, which is a navigable water of the United States.'"[42] The Seventh Circuit, in an opinion by Judge Joel Flaum that was joined by Judges Richard Posner and Michael Kanne, upheld the Corps' claim that it had jurisdiction because Rueth Development's wetlands were "adjacent" to a navigable water, despite the fact that by the court's own description, the wetlands were five steps removed from the navigable Little Calumet River.[43]

Both the Fourth and Seventh Circuits, like the Sixth Circuit in *Rapanos* and the Ninth Circuit in another similarly attenuated case, *Headwaters, Inc. v. Talent Irrigation District*,[44] read *SWANCC* narrowly as applying only to the Corps' "migratory bird" claim of jurisdiction, and not to the broader constitutional principle also articulated in

---

[39]See, e.g., United States v. Deaton, 209 F.3d 331, 333–34 (4th Cir. 2000) (summarizing litigation history) (hereinafter "Deaton I").

[40]Deaton II, 332 F.3d at 702.

[41]United States v. Rueth Development Co., 333 F.3d 598 (7th Cir. 2003).

[42]*Id.* at 600.

[43]*Id.*

[44]243 F.3d 526 (9th Cir. 2001).

the decision.[45] In contrast, in an opinion by Judge Edith Jones, joined by Judges Thomas Reavley and Grady Jolly, the Fifth Circuit in *In re Needham*[46] rejected such a narrow reading of *SWANCC* (and the broad reading of the scope of the federal government's jurisdiction proffered by the Department of Justice), but nevertheless rendered judgment for the government because of a factual stipulation that an oil spill at issue in the case occurred in a waterway that was actually adjacent to navigable waters.[47] The case is currently on remand to the bankruptcy court for initial consideration of the bankrupt's other defenses, so it is not yet ripe for a petition for certiorari. Perhaps, after the case works its way back up through the courts after remand, the Supreme Court will give renewed consideration to this circuit split and to the stretched jurisdictional claims being made by the Corps of Engineers under the supposed authority of regulating commerce among the states.

On a parallel track to the Supreme Court this term were two challenges to listings, under the federal Endangered Species Act, of wholly intrastate, noncommercial species as "endangered." In an opinion by Judge Merrick Garland, joined by Chief Judge Douglas Ginsberg and Judge Harry Edwards, the D.C. Circuit had held in *Rancho Viejo, LLC v. Norton*[48] that the extension of the Endangered Species Act to the Southwestern Arroyo Toad, which resides only in southern California and has never been an article of commerce, was permissible because the regulation affected home building and other economic activities.[49] The Fifth Circuit, in an opinion by Judge Rhesa Hawkins Barksdale, joined by Judges Eugene Davis and James Dennis, upheld the extension of the Endangered Species Act to several species of Texas cave bugs that, because of their isolation from other species, could not even be said to support a biological life chain that included commercial species.[50] Although both circuits upheld the extension of the Endangered Species Act to the species

---

[45]See notes 29 to 43 and accompanying text. See also Headwaters, 243 F.3d at 533.

[46]354 F.3d 340 (5th Cir. 2003).

[47]*Id.* at 346.

[48]323 F.3d 1062 (D.C. Cir. 2003), reh'g en banc denied, 334 F.3d 1158 (D.C. Cir. 2003).

[49]323 F.3d at 1065–69.

[50]GDF Realty Investments, Ltd. v. Norton, 326 F.3d 622, 622 (5th Cir. 2003), reh'g en banc denied, 362 F.3d 286 (5th Cir. 2004).

at issue, they did so on mutually exclusive rationales, each rejecting the ground of decision on which its sister circuit had rested.

The extent of the conflict in reasoning between the two circuits was made clear by the two D.C. Circuit judges who dissented from the denial of a petition for rehearing that was filed in the *Rancho Viejo* case. Judge David Sentelle noted that the reasoning upon which the D.C. Circuit grounded its ruling was "conspicuously in conflict" with the reasoning of the Fifth Circuit in the *GDF Realty* case.[51] And newly-appointed Judge John Roberts noted in addition that the decision was also "inconsistent" with the Supreme Court's decisions in *Lopez* and *Morrison*.[52]

Judges Sentelle and Roberts actually raised several points of disagreement between the two circuit courts. First, and perhaps most fundamental, was whether the prohibition on the "take" of wholly-intrastate, noncommercial species could be viewed as aimed at economic activity simply because the particular litigant was an economic actor. The D.C. Circuit viewed Rancho Viejo's status as a home builder as dispositive.[53] The Fifth Circuit rejected that contention, noting,

> Neither the plain language of the Commerce Clause, nor judicial decisions construing it, suggest that . . . Congress may regulate activity (here, Cave Species takes) solely because non-regulated conduct (here, commercial development) by the actor engaged in the regulated activity will have some connection to interstate commerce . . . . To accept [such an] analysis would allow application of otherwise unconstitutional statutes to commercial actors, but not to non-commercial actors. There would be no limit to Congress' authority to regulate intrastate activities, so long as those subjected to the regulation were entities which had an otherwise substantial connection to interstate commerce.[54]

The Fifth Circuit found its analysis consistent with *SWANCC*, in which the Supreme Court, albeit in *dictum*, noted that aggregation

---

[51]Rancho Viejo, LLC v. Norton, 334 F.3d 1158, 1159 (D.C. Cir. 2003) (Sentelle, J., dissenting from denial of petition for reh'g en banc).

[52]*Id.* at 1160 (Roberts, J., dissenting from denial of petition for reh'g en banc).

[53]Rancho Viejo, 323 F.3d at 1068–69.

[54]GDF Realty, 326 F.3d at 634–35.

based on the nature of the actor, rather than on the activity that was the object of the regulation, would "raise significant constitutional questions."[55] Following the high Court's admonition in *SWANCC* that it is necessary "to evaluate the precise object or activity that, in the aggregate, substantially affects interstate commerce," and its focus on the activity "to which the statute *by its terms* extends," the Fifth Circuit looked only to the specific regulated activity— "takes"—and not the commercial nature of the actor undertaking that activity.[56] The D.C. Circuit, in contrast, relying on the very same passage from *SWANCC*, held that the "precise activity" to be considered was Rancho Viejo's planned commercial development, not the "take" of species actually prohibited by the Endangered Species Act.[57]

The second point of disagreement between the two courts was a fairly technical but extremely important one, namely, whether the Supreme Court's pre-*Lopez* decision in *United States v. Salerno*[58] prevented a facial challenge on Commerce Clause grounds to any statute that reaches some commercial activity. As Judge Roberts noted in his dissent from the denial of the petition for rehearing en banc in *Rancho Viejo*, "the approach [regarding *Salerno*] of the panel in [*Rancho Viejo*] ... conflicts with the opinion of a sister circuit ...."[59] The D.C. Circuit relied on the older decision in *Salerno* despite the obvious inconsistency between *Salerno* and *Lopez*—Alfonso Lopez had brought his gun to school in order to sell it, a commercial transaction that, under *Salerno*, would have prevented the facial challenge accepted by the Supreme Court in *Lopez*. The Fifth Circuit, in contrast, rejected the applicability of *Salerno* in the post-*Lopez* Commerce Clause context. "[L]ooking primarily beyond the regulated activity [i.e., beyond the "take" of endangered species, to commercial development that is only indirectly regulated by the Endangered Species Act] in such a manner would 'effectually obliterate' the limiting

[55]*Id.* at 634 (citing SWANCC, 531 U.S. at 173).

[56]326 F.3d at 634.

[57]Rancho Viejo, 323 F.3d at 1072.

[58]481 U.S. 739 (1987).

[59]Rancho Viejo, LLC v. Norton, 334 F.3d 1158, 1160 (D.C. Cir. 2003) (Roberts, J., dissenting from denial of petition for reh'g en banc).

purpose of the Commerce Clause," the Fifth Circuit held.[60] More fundamentally, the Fifth Circuit recognized that, if *Salerno* were carried over to the Commerce Clause context, "the facial challenges in *Lopez* and *Morrison* would have failed."[61] "[R]egulation of gun possession near schools, at issue in *Lopez*, would arguably pass constitutional muster as applied to a possessor who was a significant gun salesman," noted the Fifth Circuit, so the Gun Free Schools Zone Act "could not have been facially unconstitutional."[62] The Fifth Circuit also noted that "the Violence Against Women Act, at issue in *Morrison*, would arguably have been a constitutional exercise of congressional power if it were used to prosecute a person who committed violence against women and then sold a substantial number of videotapes of the encounter in interstate markets."[63] That would have been enough for the Violence Against Women Act to withstand a facial challenge, but such a result is contrary to the actual holding of *Morrison*.

In holding that GDF Realty's own nature as a commercial developer was not sufficient for the Commerce Clause analysis, the Fifth Circuit apparently found dispositive from *Lopez* the fact that Alfonso Lopez brought his gun to school for sale.[64] The D.C. Circuit, in contrast, dismissed that fact, contending that because it was not mentioned in the Supreme Court's own *Lopez* opinion, "the Supreme Court attached no significance to it."[65] The D.C. Circuit seems to have missed the point of the Supreme Court's refusal to attach any significance to this uncontested evidence. While hugely significant under the D.C. Circuit's *Salerno* analysis, the fact that Alfonso Lopez brought his gun to school *to sell*—an obvious commercial motivation on the part of the actor—had no significance for the Supreme Court in *Lopez* or the Fifth Circuit in *GDF Realty* precisely because "neither the purposes nor the design *of the statute* ha[d] an evident commercial

[60]GDF Realty, 326 F.3d at 634 (citing National Labor Relations Board v. Jones & Laughlin Steel Corp., 301 U.S. 1, 37 (1937)).

[61]GDF Realty, 326 F.3d at 635.

[62]*Id.* at 634 (citing Salerno, 481 U.S. at 745).

[63]326 F.3d at 635.

[64]*Id.*; see also United States v. Lopez, 2 F.3d 1342, 1345 (5th Cir. 1993), aff'd, 514 U.S. 549 (1995).

[65]Rancho Viejo, LLC v. Norton, 323 F.3d 1062, 1072 (D.C. Cir. 2003).

nexus."[66] A recent decision of the Ninth Circuit reached the same conclusion (albeit with respect to a different statute): "[T]he regulation [banning possession of machine guns] does not have an economic purpose . . . . More likely, [it] was intended to keep machineguns out of the hands of criminals—an admirable goal, but not a commercial one."[67]

Third, the Fifth and D.C. Circuits disagreed on whether *Lopez* and *Morrison* permitted aggregation of non-economic as well as economic activity for purposes of demonstrating a substantial effect on interstate commerce—another important issue, for if aggregation is permitted, even trivial effects on the national economy would justify Congress's regulatory power. While the D.C. Circuit held that non-economic activity could be aggregated to determine whether there was a substantial enough effect on interstate commerce to authorize federal action,[68] the Fifth Circuit held that "[i]n the light of *Lopez* and *Morrison*, the key question for purposes of aggregation is whether the nature of the regulated activity is economic."[69] This was important, according to the Fifth Circuit, lest the Commerce Clause be stripped of all limits. "[A]ny imaginable activity of mankind can affect the alertness, energy, and mood of human beings," noted the Fifth Circuit, "which in turn can affect their productivity in the workplace, which when aggregated together could reduce national economic productivity. Such reasoning would eliminate any judicially enforceable limit on the Commerce Clause, *thereby turning that clause into what it most certainly is not, a general police power.*"[70]

The Fifth Circuit recognized that the Supreme Court in "*Morrison* noted, for aggregation purposes, the importance of the economic nature of the regulated activity" when it specifically acknowledged that it had heretofore aggregated intrastate activity "*only* where that activity *is economic in nature.*"[71] To allow aggregation of "noneconomic and noncommercial activity" "so long as, if aggregated,"

---

[66]United States v. Morrison, 529 U.S. 598, 611 (2000) (quoting Lopez, 514 U.S. at 580 (Kennedy, J., concurring)) (emphasis added); GDF Realty, 326 F.3d at 634—35.

[67]United States v. Stewart, 348 F.3d 1132, 1137 (9th Cir. 2003).

[68]Rancho Viejo, 323 F.3d at 1072.

[69]GDF Realty, 326 F.3d at 630.

[70]*Id.* at 629 (quoting United States v. Ho, 311 F.3d 589, 599 (5th Cir. 2002)).

[71]326 F.3d at 630 (quoting Morrison, 529 U.S. at 613 (emphasis added)).

there would be "a substantial effect" on commerce, held the Fifth Circuit, "would vitiate *Lopez* and *Morrison*'s seeming requirement that the intrastate instance of activity be commercial."[72] "*Lopez* and *Morrison* stand against such a proposition."[73]

By contrast, the D.C. Circuit, relying on the identical passage from *Morrison*, implied that the Supreme Court had rejected a categorical rule, thus permitting the aggregation of noneconomic activity in order to demonstrate a substantial effect on commerce.[74]

The Fifth Circuit's position is not only a better reading of *Morrison*, but it is in accord with decisions of the First, Second, Third, Fourth, Ninth, and Eleventh Circuits as well.[75]

Although the Supreme Court denied certiorari in *Rancho Viejo* on March 1, 2004, the conflict in reasoning between the circuits was highlighted even more by six judges on the Fifth Circuit Court of Appeals whose own opinions dissenting from that court's denial of the petition for rehearing en banc in the *GDF Realty* case were released on February 27, 2004—the very day that the Supreme Court considered the D.C. Circuit's *Rancho Viejo* case at conference.

Particularly significant is the lengthy opinion by Circuit Judge Edith Jones—joined by Circuit Judges Grady Jolly, Jerry Smith, Harold DeMoss, Edith Brown Clement, and Charles Pickering—dissenting from the denial of the petition for rehearing en banc.[76] In her opinion, Judge Jones referenced explicitly the circuit split that has developed between the Fifth Circuit in *GDF Realty* and the D.C.

---

[72]326 F.3d at 638.

[73]*Id.*

[74]Rancho Viejo, LLC v. Norton, 323 F.3d 1062, 1072 (D.C. Cir. 2003); see also United States v. Rodia, 194 F.3d 465, 481 (3d Cir. 1999) ("'the specific activity that Congress is regulating need not itself be objectively commercial, as long as it has a substantial effect on commerce"); cf. United States v. Bongiorno, 106 F.3d 1027, 1031 (1st Cir. 1997) (noting that the Court consistently has interpreted the Commerce Clause "to include transactions that might strike a lay person as 'noncommercial'").

[75]See United States v. Zorrilla, 93 F.3d 7, 8 (1st Cir. 1996); United States v. Holston, 343 F.3d 83, 88 (2d Cir. 2003); Freier v. Westinghouse Electric Corp., 303 F.3d 176, 200-03 (2d Cir. 2002), cert. denied, 538 U.S. 998 (2003); United States v. Whited, 311 F.3d 259, 271 (3d Cir. 2002), cert. denied, 538 U.S. 1065 (2003); Gibbs v. Babbitt, 214 F.3d 483, 491 (4th Cir. 2000); United States v. McCoy, 323 F.3d 1114, 1119–20 (9th Cir. 2003); United States v. Cortes, 299 F.3d 1030, 1035 (9th Cir. 2002); United States v. Ballinger, 312 F.3d 1264, 1270 (11th Cir. 2002).

[76]GDF Realty Investments, Ltd. v. Norton, 362 F.3d 286, 287–93 (5th Cir. 2004) (Jones, J., dissenting from denial of petition for reh'g en banc).

Circuit in *Rancho Viejo*. She stated that in *GDF Realty*, the Fifth Circuit "panel correctly determined, *unlike other courts,* that the 'regulated activity' under the ESA is Cave Species *takes,* not the appellants' planned commercial development of the land."[77] The mention of "other courts" that had reached the opposite conclusion refers expressly to the *Rancho Viejo* case, which found, as noted by Judge Jones, "that the regulated activity was not the ESA take but rather the 'construction of a commercial housing development.' "[78]

Judge Jones' opinion also highlighted how the decisions in both *GDF Realty* and *Rancho Viejo,* despite their contradictory reasoning, are fundamentally at odds with the Supreme Court's decisions in *Lopez, Morrison,* and *SWANCC.* The Fifth Circuit "panel's 'interdependent web' analysis of the Endangered Species Act," she wrote, "gives . . . subterranean bugs federal protection that was denied the school children in *Lopez* and the rape victim in *Morrison.*"[79] Jones properly concluded that "the panel's commerce clause analysis [was] in error," and that the panel's broad interpretation of the aggregation principle "would not only sustain every conceivable application of the ESA, but entirely undercuts *Lopez* and *Morrison.*"[80]

Nevertheless, as noted, the Supreme Court denied certiorari in *Rancho Viejo* on March 1, 2004, and denied a petition for rehearing in that case on April 19, 2004. A petition for a writ of certiorari was filed in *GDF Realty* on May 27, 2004—too late to be considered in the Court's 2003 term. The government's opposition was filed in early September, however, so we should soon know whether the Court will take up the issues presented by *GDF Realty* and *Rancho Viejo* in the October 2004 term.

## V. Why This Matters

With the Court granting certiorari in roughly eighty cases out of approximately 8,000 petitions filed each term, denials of petitions are certainly the norm, not the exception, and a denial in most cases is hardly newsworthy. Why the attention to these cases, then?

---

[77]*Id.* at 288 (emphasis added).
[78]*Id.* at 288–89 (citing Rancho Viejo, 323 F.3d at 1062).
[79]362 F.3d at 288–89.
[80]*Id.* at 289.

There are several reasons why this fistful of certiorari denials is both noteworthy and significant. Regarding the three Clean Water Act cases (*Rapanos, Deaton,* and *Rueth Development*), the Court has already acknowledged the certiorari-worthy nature of the issues presented. Two terms ago, in *Borden Ranch Partnership v. United States Army Corps of Engineers,*[81] the Court considered a similar Commerce Clause challenge to Clean Water Act regulations by a farmer who was fined (massively) for plowing his central California fields using a "deep-ripping" method designed to allow rainwater to actually reach the roots of his crops.[82] The Ninth Circuit upheld the fines,[83] but after granting the certiorari petition the Supreme Court was unable to reach a decision. With Justice Kennedy recusing himself because he knew the farmer in the case, the Court affirmed the judgment of the Ninth Circuit when it divided 4–4.[84] An affirmance under such circumstances does not have precedential value, so the issue remains unresolved at the Supreme Court level. The Court's refusal to grant certiorari in any of the three Clean Water Act cases presented to it this term, raising nearly identical issues, is therefore noteworthy.

The Court's denials are significant from a long-term jurisprudential perspective as well. While the Court will often wait, sometimes for years, to resolve splits among the lower courts, it typically moves much more quickly when fundamental rights are involved, and when the lower courts seem to be challenging very recent precedent from the Supreme Court itself. Both are at stake in these cases.

Unlike many of the rights that the Court seems to be recognizing or creating with increasing frequency,[85] the property rights at issue in the cases discussed above are expressly protected in the federal Constitution, protections that the Founders believed to be one of the core purposes of just and consensual government. As the publisher of this *Review* recently stated the matter,

---

[81]261 F.3d 810 (9th Cir. 2001), aff'd by an equally divided Court, 537 U.S. 99 (2002).

[82]261 F.3d at 812.

[83]*Id.* at 818.

[84]Borden Ranch Partnership v. United States Army Corps of Engineers, 537 U.S. 99 (2002).

[85]See, e.g., Lawrence v. Texas, 539 U.S. 558 (2003); Romer v. Evans, 517 U.S. 620 (1996); Roe v. Wade, 410 U.S. 959 (1973); Goldberg v. Kelly, 397 U.S. 254 (1970); Griswold v. Connecticut, 381 U.S. 479 (1965).

America's Founders understood clearly that private property is the foundation not only of prosperity but of freedom itself. Thus, through the common law and the Constitution, they protected property rights—the rights of people to freely acquire and use property. With the growth of the modern regulatory state, however, governments at all levels today are eliminating those rights through so-called regulatory takings—regulatory restraints that take property rights, reducing the value of the property, but leave title with the owner. And courts are doing little to protect such owners because the Supreme Court has yet to develop a principled, much less comprehensive, theory of property rights.[86]

In contrast with the Court's quick grants of certiorari in unenumerated rights cases, often without the benefit of circuit splits among the lower courts, the slow percolation the Court often allows in cases involving property rights lends credence to the view that there is a hierarchy of rights and that property rights are near the bottom of the hierarchy.

Equally fundamental is the continued vitality of *Lopez* itself, and the vision of a limited Constitution the case revived, particularly with respect to the scope of the Commerce Clause. To understand the significance of *Lopez* it is important to appreciate what the Founders understood they had delegated to the national government—and what they had not delegated.

When the Framers met in Philadelphia in 1787, it was widely acknowledged that a stronger national government was necessary if the United States was to survive and thrive. The Continental Congress could not honor its commitments under the Treaty of Paris; it could not meet its financial obligations; and it could not ensure the limbs and property of its citizens, especially those living on the western frontier. Perhaps of greatest concern, however, was the inability of the central government to counteract the crippling trade barriers that were being enacted by the several states against each other, for the Framers rightly perceived that the disputes over commerce threatened the national unity that was critically important to

---

[86]Roger Pilon, Property Rights and Regulatory Takings, Cato Handbook for Congress, 108th Congress, at 145 (2002).

the survival of the new nation.[87] Indeed, the first convention called to address problems with the Articles of Confederation, held at Annapolis in 1786, was specifically devoted to concerns about interstate commerce and navigation.[88] There was thus general agreement about the need to give the national government more power over interstate commerce.

But the Framers were equally cognizant of the fact that the deficiencies of the Articles of Confederation existed by design, due to a genuine and almost universal fear of a strong centralized government.[89] Our forebears had not successfully prosecuted the war against the King's tyranny merely to erect another form of tyranny in its place.

The central problem faced by the convention delegates, therefore, was to create a government strong enough to meet the threats to the safety and happiness of the people, yet not so strong as to itself become a threat to the people's liberty.[90] The Framers drew on the best political theorists of human history to craft a government that was most conducive to that end. The idea of separation of powers, for example, evident in the very structure of the Constitution, was drawn from Montesquieu, out of recognition that the "accumulation of all powers, legislative, executive, and judiciary, in the same hands . . . may justly be pronounced the very definition of tyranny."[91]

---

[87]See, e.g., Letter from Tench Coxe to the Virginia Commissioners at Annapolis (Sept. 13, 1786), reprinted in 3 The Founders' Constitution 473–74 (P. Kurland & R. Lerner eds., 1987) (noting that duties imposed by the states upon each other were "as great in many instances as those imposed on foreign Articles"); The Federalist No. 22, at 144–45 (Alexander Hamilton) (C. Rossiter & C. Kesler eds., 1999) (referring to "[t]he interfering and unneighborly regulations of some States," which were "serious sources of animosity and discord" between the states); New York v. United States, 505 U.S. 144, 158 (1992) ("The defect of power in the existing Confederacy to regulate the commerce between its several members [has] been clearly pointed out by experience") (quoting The Federalist No. 42, at 267 (C. Rossiter ed., 1961)).

[88]See generally, Report of the Annapolis Convention of 1786, reprinted in 3 The Annals of America 68 (1968).

[89]See, e.g., Bartkus v. Illinois, 359 U.S. 121, 137 (1959) ("the men who wrote the Constitution as well as the citizens of the member States of the Confederation were fearful of the power of centralized government and sought to limit its power"); Garcia v. San Antonio Metropolitan Transit Authority, 469 U.S. 528, 568–69 (1985) (Powell, J., dissenting, joined by Burger, C.J., Rehnquist, J., and O'Connor, J.).

[90]See The Federalist No. 51, at 322 (James Madison) (C. Rossiter ed., 1961).

[91]The Federalist No. 47, *supra* note 90, at 301 (James Madison).

But the Framers added their own contribution to the science of politics. In what can only be described as a radical break with past practice, they rejected the idea that the government was sovereign and indivisible. Instead, they contended that the people themselves were the ultimate sovereign;[92] they could delegate all or part of their sovereign powers to a single government or to multiple governments as, in their view, was "most likely to effect their Safety and Happiness."[93] As a result, it became and remains one of the most fundamental tenets of our constitutional system of government that the sovereign people delegated to the national government only certain, enumerated powers, leaving the residuum of power to be exercised by the state governments or by the people themselves.[94]

This division of sovereign powers between the two great levels of government was not simply a constitutional add-on, by way of the Tenth Amendment.[95] Rather, it is inherent in the doctrine of enumerated powers that is embodied in the Constitution itself. Article I of the Constitution provides, for example, that "All legislative Powers *herein granted* shall be vested in a Congress of the United States."[96] And the specific enumeration of powers, found principally in Article I, section 8, was likewise limited.

[92]See, e.g., James Wilson, Speech at the Pennsylvania Ratifying Convention (Nov. 26, 1787), reprinted in 2 J. Wilson, The Works of James Wilson 770 (R. McCloskey ed., 1967).

[93]The Declaration of Independence para. 2 (U.S. 1776).

[94]See, e.g., The Federalist No. 39, *supra* note 90, at 256 (James Madison) (noting that the jurisdiction of the federal government "extends to certain enumerated objects only, and leaves to the several States a residuary and inviolable sovereignty over all other objects"); The Federalist No. 45, *supra* note 90, at 292–93 (James Madison) ("The powers delegated by the proposed Constitution to the federal government are few and defined. Those which are to remain in the State governments are numerous and indefinite."); McCulloch v. Maryland, 17 U.S. (4 Wheat.) 316, 421 (1819) (Marshall, C.J.) ("We admit, as all must admit, that the powers of the government are limited, and that its limits are not to be transcended."); Gregory v. Ashcroft, 501 U.S. 452, 457 (1991) ("The Constitution created a Federal Government of limited powers.").

[95]See U.S. Const. amend. X ("The powers not delegated to the United States by the Constitution, nor prohibited by it to the States, are reserved to the States respectively, or to the people.").

[96]U.S. Const. art. I, § 1 (emphasis added); see also U.S. Const. art. I, § 8 (enumerating powers so granted); McCulloch, 17 U.S. (4 Wheat.) at 405 ("This government is acknowledged by all, to be one of enumerated powers. The principle, that it can exercise only the powers granted to it, . . . is now universally admitted."); United States v. Lopez, 514 U.S. 549, 552 (1995) ("We start with first principles. The Constitution creates a Federal Government of enumerated powers.").

Perhaps foremost among the powers granted to the national government was the power to regulate commerce among the states, but for the Founders, "commerce" was trade, or commercial intercourse between nations and states, not business activity generally.[97] Indeed, in *Gibbons v. Ogden*,[98] the first major case arising under the Commerce Clause to reach the Supreme Court, it was contested whether the commerce power even extended as far as to include "navigation." Chief Justice Marshall, for the Court, held that it did, but even under his definition, "commerce" was limited to "intercourse between nations, and parts of nations, in all its branches."[99]

This is a far cry from the expansive reading of Marshall's opinion in *Gibbons* that prevailed after *Wickard v. Filburn*[100] and the other New Deal-era Commerce Clause cases. Rather, the *Gibbons* Court specifically rejected the notion "that [commerce among the states] comprehend[s] that commerce, which is completely internal, which is carried on between man and man in a State, or between different parts of the same State, and which does not extend to or affect other States."[101] In other words, for Chief Justice Marshall and his colleagues, the Commerce Clause did not even extend to trade carried on between different parts of a state. The notion that the power to regulate commerce among the states included the power to regulate all other kinds of business activity was completely foreign to the Marshall Court.

That understanding of the Commerce Clause, the original understanding, continued for nearly a century and a half. Manufacturing

---

[97]See, e.g., Corfield v. Coryell, 6 F. Cas. 546, 550 (C.C.E.D.Pa. 1823) (Washington, J., on circuit) ("Commerce with foreign nations, and among the several states, can mean nothing more than intercourse with those nations, and among those states, for purposes of trade, be the object of the trade what it may."); Lopez, 514 U.S. at 585 (Thomas, J., concurring) ("At the time the original Constitution was ratified, 'commerce' consisted of selling, buying, and bartering, as well as transporting for these purposes.").

[98]22 U.S. (9 Wheat.) 1 (1824).

[99]*Id.* at 190; see also Corfield, 6 F. Cas. at 550 ("Commerce . . . among the several states . . . must include all the means by which it can be carried on, [including] . . . passage over land through the states, where such passage becomes necessary to the commercial intercourse between the states.").

[100]317 U.S. 111 (1942).

[101]Gibbons, 22 U.S. (9 Wheat.) at 194 (quoted in United States v. Morrison, 529 U.S. 598, 616 (2000)).

was not included in the definition of commerce, held the Court in *United States v. E.C. Knight Co.*,[102] because "Commerce succeeds to manufacture, and is not a part of it."[103] "The fact that an article is manufactured for export to another State does not of itself make it an article of interstate commerce . . . ."[104] Neither were retail sales included in the definition of "commerce."[105] For the Founders and the Courts that decided these cases, regulation of such activities as retail sales, manufacturing, and agriculture was part of the police power reserved to the states, not part of the power over commerce delegated to Congress.[106] And, as the Court noted in *E.C. Knight*, it was essential to the preservation of the states and therefore to liberty that the line between the two powers be retained:

> It is vital that the independence of the commercial power and of the police power, and the delimitation between them, however sometimes perplexing, should always be recognized and observed, for, while the one furnishes the strongest bond of union, the other is essential to the preservation of the autonomy of the States as required by our dual form of government . . . .[107]

[102]156 U.S. 1 (1895).

[103]*Id.* at 12.

[104]*Id.* at 13; see also Kidd v. Pearson, 128 U.S. 1, 20 (1888) (upholding a state ban on the manufacture of liquor, even though much of the liquor so banned was destined for interstate commerce).

[105]See The License Cases, 46 U.S. (5 How.) 504 (1847) (upholding state ban on retail sales of liquor, as not subject to Congress's power to regulate interstate commerce); see also A.L.A. Schecter Poultry Corp. v. United States, 295 U.S. 495, 542, 547 (1935) (invalidating federal law regulating in-state retail sales of poultry that originated out-of-state and fixing the hours and wages of the intrastate employees because the activity related only indirectly to commerce).

[106]See, e.g., E.C. Knight, 156 U.S. at 12 ("That which belongs to commerce is within the jurisdiction of the United States, but that which does not belong to commerce is within the jurisdiction of the police power of the State.") (citing Gibbons, 22 U.S. (9 Wheat.) at 210; Brown v. Maryland, 25 U.S. (12 Wheat.) 419, 448 (1827); The License Cases, 46 U.S. (5 How.) at 599; County of Mobile v. Kimball, 102 U.S. 691 (1880); Bowman v. Chicago & Northwestern Railway Co., 125 U.S. 465 (1888); Leisy v. Hardin, 135 U.S. 100 (1890); In re Rahrer, 140 U.S. 545, 555 (1891)).

[107]E.C. Knight, 156 U.S. at 13; see also Carter v. Carter Coal Co., 298 U.S. 238, 301 (1936) (quoting *E.C. Knight*); Garcia v. San Antonio Metropolitan Transit Authority, 469 U.S. 528, 572 (1985) (Powell, J., dissenting, joined by Burger, C.J., and Rehnquist and O'Connor, JJ.) ("federal overreaching under the Commerce Clause undermines the constitutionally mandated balance of power between the States and the Federal Government, a balance designed to protect our fundamental liberties").

Thus, much more than constitutional purity was at stake when the Supreme Court decided *Lopez*, and much more remains at stake as the principles of *Lopez* are applied in parallel contexts. The Founders believed that centralized government would tend to become tyrannical, but they also thought it would become unaccountable and inefficient. As with the notoriously erroneous five-year plans of Stalin's Soviet Union, command-and-control bureaucracies are simply not very good at balancing costs and benefits, or getting right the incentives necessary for good policymaking. Indeed, in many instances, they may be legally disabled from even considering the economic costs of their regulatory policies.

Two news items of 2003 highlight the nature of the problem. Because of the absolutist nature of the Endangered Species Act, extraordinary efforts have been demanded by the U.S. Fish and Wildlife Service to protect the silvery minnow in Colorado, including the refusal to release water to downstream users from the reservoirs that serve as the minnow's habitat. The Service's demands exacerbated the drought conditions in northern New Mexico, leaving an insufficient supply of water for the region's piñon trees. Without enough water, the trees were unable to produce sap, their primary defense against insects. The result was a bark beetle infestation that, by latest estimates, will destroy between 80 and 85 percent of the region's piñon trees, and has already destroyed 96 percent of the trees in some higher elevation areas.[108]

Even more troubling were the October 2003 California wildfires. The Endangered Species Act was again the culprit. Required by law to protect species habitat to the exclusion of all else, the U.S. Fish and Wildlife Service prevented California officials from utilizing prudent forestry management tools because of a putative threat to the southwestern arroyo toad habitat—the same critter at issue in the *Rancho Viejo* case discussed above—leaving southern California's forests a tinderbox of excessive growth and dead brush.[109] The tragic

---

[108]See Rio Grande Silvery Minnow v. Keys, 333 F.3d 1109 (10th Cir. 2003); Tom Sharpe, Colder Weather Has Not Stopped Beetles, The Santa Fe New Mexican, Nov. 11, 2003, at A-1.

[109]See, e.g., Jia-Rui Chong, Federal Agency Faulted in Fires; San Bernadino Officials Say the Fish and Wildlife Service Held Up Crucial Controlled Burns, Los Angeles Times, Dec. 15, 2003, at B1.

irony: In addition to the loss of human life and property, much of the sacrosanct species habitat was itself destroyed by the fires.[110]

The lower courts' reticence to apply the principles of *Lopez* in the environmental context, and the Supreme Court's denials of certiorari in the face of that reticence, is therefore not only a threat to constitutional principle but to sound environmental policy as well.

This fall, the Court will have the opportunity to end its silence with respect to the Endangered Species Act when it considers the still-pending petition for certiorari in the *GDF Realty* case. Within a year or two it may well have the opportunity to speak again on the permissible scope of federal regulation under the Clean Water Act, should the *Needham* case work its way to the Court. The Court demonstrated in *Lopez, Morrison,* and *SWANCC* that it was up to the task. The next round of decisions on petitions for certiorari may well demonstrate whether it remains so.

---

[110]See, e.g., Ben Goad and Jennifer Bowles, Fire Official Faults Agency, The Riverside Press-Enterprise, Dec. 16, 2003, at A1.

# The Upcoming 2004–2005 Term

*Thomas C. Goldstein*

## I. Introduction

As of the publication of this volume, the Supreme Court has selected roughly half of the cases it will decide in the 2004–2005 term. The justices now consistently hear around eighty cases a term, and they have accepted forty to date.[1] Those cases will fill the monthly argument calendars for October, November, and December 2004, leaving a handful left over for January 2005. Assuming recent practice holds, the remainder will be selected between late September (when the justices return from their summer recess) and late January—the latest date by which cases can be briefed in time for the final argument sitting in April.

None of the pending cases will have the timeless significance of this year's executive detention rulings, or of the affirmative action rulings described by Roger Pilon in last year's *Cato Supreme Court Review*. But that is an almost impossibly high bar to meet, and the docket is of course not yet full. There are several interesting, high profile petitions for certiorari now pending or on their way to the Court and, for several years, the most notable cases have coincidentally been selected and argued late in the term.

This article describes the leading cases of the 2004–2005 term, both the cases already selected for review and the most interesting candidates for certiorari. The article focuses on the cases that directly implicate Madisonian principles—that is, the cases that test the extent to which the Supreme Court is committed to the principle that ours is a government of limited, enumerated powers.

---

[1] See Richard Cordray, The Calendar of the Justices: How the Supreme Court's Timing Affects its Decisionmaking, 36 Ariz. St. L.J. 183 n.110 and accompanying text (2004) (showing that since the mid-90s the Court's docket has now stabilized at approximately eighty cases per term).

## II. The 2004–2005 Term's Leading Cases

Six cases to be decided in the 2004–2005 term are particularly noteworthy, and three have already attracted a great deal of attention. Each of these three asks the Court to resolve unresolved questions about constitutional limits on government's regulatory power: whether the First Amendment allows the government to compel farmers to finance advertising for their products, whether the Twenty-First Amendment permits a state to prohibit the importation of wine from another state, and whether the Commerce Clause permits the federal government to prohibit the intrastate growing and distribution of marijuana for medicinal use.

*Veneman v. Livestock Marketing Association*[2] involves the constitutionality of a compelled advertising program enacted by Congress in the Beef Promotion and Research Act. The statute requires beef producers and importers to pay an assessment on each head of cattle to fund generic advertising of beef.[3] In *United States v. United Foods, Inc.*,[4] the Supreme Court held that a similar program for the promotion of mushrooms violated the First Amendment by compelling producers to fund speech with which they disagreed.[5] The Eighth Circuit held in *Livestock Marketing Association v. U.S. Department of Agriculture*[6] that the same result followed under the beef program.[7]

The government contends that the beef program should be sustained on two theories that the Supreme Court did not address in *United Foods*. Principally, it argues that the advertisements are immune from First Amendment scrutiny because they are "government speech."[8] The board that selects and purchases the advertisements, the government notes, is selected and overseen by the Secretary of Agriculture.[9] The court of appeals rejected this argument

[2] Livestock Marketing Association v. U.S. Department of Agriculture, 335 F.3d 711 (8th Cir. 2003), cert. granted sub nom. Veneman v. Livestock Marketing Association, 124 S. Ct. 2389 (May, 24, 2004) (No. 03-1164).

[3] 7 U.S.C. § 2904 (2004).

[4] 533 U.S. 405 (2001).

[5] *Id.* at 410–11. The author was counsel to the producer in *United Foods* and is counsel to the producer in *Livestock Marketing Association*.

[6] Livestock Marketing Association v. U.S. Department of Agriculture, 335 F.3d 711 (8th Cir. 2003).

[7] *Id.* at 725–26.

[8] Reply Brief for the Petitioners at 1, Veneman v. Livestock Marketing Association., 124 S. Ct. 2389 (2004) (No. 03-1164), available at 2004 WL 1081115.

[9] 7 U.S.C. § 2904 (2004).

principally on the ground that "the government speech doctrine clearly does not provide immunity for all types of First Amendment claims."[10] The court emphasized that the producers' objection is to the *assessment* rather than the *advertisements*.[11] They do not contend that the government cannot itself promote beef; rather, they argue (and the court of appeals held) that the First Amendment prevents the government from requiring particular individuals to engage in speech or associate together for the purpose of promoting speech through the assessments.

Alternatively, the government contends that the assessment is constitutional under the intermediate scrutiny reserved for regulation of commercial speech.[12] The court of appeals concluded that the Beef Act does not sufficiently advance an important government interest to be sustained.[13] "'[S]urely the interest in making one entrepreneur finance advertising for the benefit of his [or her] competitors, including some who are not required to contribute, is insufficient.'"[14] Here too, the government's argument seems directed at justifying the Beef Board's advertising, as opposed to answering the objectors' argument that *they* cannot be compelled to fund that advertising and be associated with it.

The *Livestock Marketing Association* case presents the Court with the opportunity to bring further clarity to the unresolved status of "commercial speech" under the First Amendment. The case also arises in a context that calls on the justices to account for both the First Amendment right against compelled speech and association (as reaffirmed in *United Foods*), and also the government's ability to adopt user fees that place the burden of government programs on those who benefit the most. Those competing concerns each evoke important interests. On the one hand, the government's argument suggests the possibility of a system of targeted fees that theoretically would have the benefit of reducing tax burdens on the general citizenry. But compelled advertising programs, at bottom, represent

---

[10] Livestock Marketing Association, 335 F.3d at 720.

[11] *Id.* at 721.

[12] Reply Brief for the Petitioners at 12, Veneman v. Livestock Marketing Association., No. 03-1164 (U.S. May 24, 2004).

[13] Livestock Marketing Association, 335 F.3d at 722.

[14] *Id.* at 725 (quoting United States v. United Foods, Inc., 533 U.S. 405, 418 (Stevens, J., concurring)).

a troubling intrusion into free markets, including the vital free market of ideas.

*Granholm v. Heald*[15] (which is consolidated with another case, *Swedenburg v. Kelly*[16]) involves the constitutionality of state statutes that permit in-state, but not out-of-state, wineries to ship directly to in-state consumers. Approximately half the states now have such laws. In the internet era, "[s]tate bans on interstate direct shipping represent the single largest regulatory barrier to expanded e-commerce in wine."[17] The statutes impede the interstate transportation of wine, which leads wineries to contend that they are invalid under the so-called "dormant Commerce Clause." According to that doctrine, the congressional power to "regulate Commerce . . . among the several States" forbids states from discriminating against interstate commerce.[18]

The states, by contrast, contend that the statutes are authorized by the Twenty-First Amendment, which authorizes states to regulate the "transportation or importation . . . of intoxicating liquors."[19] They specifically defend the statutes as reasonable measures to ensure that out-of-state wineries (which are not subject to direct regulation by the recipient state) do not ship their products to minors.[20] Also, the statutes are defended on the ground that, by requiring out-of-state wineries to use in-state distributors, they ensure that states receive the applicable taxes from wineries.[21]

*Granholm* presents another test of the Supreme Court's commitment to freedom of interstate commerce, albeit in the difficult context of the Constitution's seeming commitment to the states of a broad power to regulate the importation of a particular type of product. The statutes are, at bottom, protectionist measures intended to benefit in-state wineries. These categorical bans on direct importation might

---

[15] 342 F.3d 517 (6th Cir. 2003), cert. granted, 124 S. Ct. 2389 (May 24, 2004) (No. 03-1116).

[16] 358 F.3d 223 (2d Cir. 2003), cert. granted, 124 S. Ct. 2391 (May 24, 2004) (No. 03-1274).

[17] Federal Trade Commission, Possible Anticompetitive Barriers to E-Commerce: Wine 3, 14 (2003), available at http://www.ftc.gov/os/2003/07/winereport2.pdf.

[18] U.S. Const. art. I, § 8, cl. 3.

[19] U.S. Const. amend. XXI, § 2.

[20] Petition for Certiorari at 3–4, Granholm v. Heald, No. 03-1116 (U.S. May 24, 2004), available at 2004 WL 226297.

[21] *Id.*

not survive a Commerce Clause challenge given that states could satisfy their legitimate objectives through more limited licensing requirements. On the other hand, it does not seem possible to say that the statutes further *no* legitimate interest relating to the states' regulation of alcohol consumption. It is true that *Bacchus Imports v. Diaz*,[22] invalidated Hawaii's tax exemptions for locally produced liquor, but it did so only on the ground that the exemptions were "mere economic protectionism" not intended "to carry out any other purpose of the Twenty-First Amendment."[23] Under that precedent, among others, it seems likely that the states will prevail unless the justices are willing to give greater weight to the fact that these statutes are a direct affront to the national interests that the Commerce Clause was intended to further.

*Ashcroft v. Raich*[24] also involves the distribution of power between the state and federal governments to regulate commerce. The federal Controlled Substances Act (CSA) makes it illegal to "manufacture, distribute, or dispense, or possess with intent to manufacture, distribute, or dispense" any controlled substance, subject to certain exceptions.[25] So-called "Schedule 1" narcotics, including marijuana, may not be dispensed for medical uses under the CSA.[26] California law, by contrast, permits the medicinal use of marijuana. California residents brought this suit, alleging that the application of the CSA to the purely intrastate growing and noncommercial distribution of marijuana for medicinal purposes exceeds Congress's power under the Commerce Clause. The Ninth Circuit held that the plaintiffs were entitled to a preliminary injunction because they had a strong likelihood of success on their Commerce Clause claim.[27]

The Supreme Court seems almost certain to reverse. The merits of the nation's war on drugs have been hotly debated.[28] Also, the view that federal drug laws are unwarranted could draw support

---

[22]468 U.S. 263 (1984).

[23]*Id.* at 276.

[24]352 F.3d 1222 (9th Cir. 2003), cert. granted, 124 S. Ct. 2909 (June 28, 2004) (No. 03-1454).

[25]21 U.S.C. § 841(a) (2004).

[26]United States v. Oakland Cannabis Buyers' Co-op., 532 U.S. 483, 490 (2001).

[27]Raich v. Ashcroft, 352 F.3d 1222,1227 (9th Cir. 2003).

[28]See, e.g., Gene Healy and Robert A. Levy, The War on Drugs, in Cato Handbook for Congress, 108th Congress, 171–91 (2002).

in this case from those that favor a shift in the balance of regulatory power from the federal government to the states. But the modern Supreme Court does not embrace either of those views. Instead, the justices have held firmly to the view that Congress's commerce power is extensive. Under current doctrine, it seems implausible to say that the effect of medicinal marijuana production and use on interstate commerce is so small as to forbid federal regulation.

Three other leading cases of the 2004–2005 term, which have received somewhat less attention, are nonetheless equally important. First, in October the Court will consider two cases (*United States v. Booker*[29] and *United States v. Fanfan*[30]) that ask whether and to what extent the Federal Sentencing Guidelines are consistent with the Fifth and Sixth Amendments.[31] *Apprendi v. New Jersey*[32] held that the right to a jury trial on proof beyond a reasonable doubt (along with the right to a grand jury indictment in federal courts) requires that "[o]ther than the fact of a prior conviction, any fact that increases the penalty for a crime beyond the prescribed statutory maximum must be submitted to a jury."[33] This past term, in *Blakely v. Washington*,[34] the same majority held that *Apprendi* invalidated a sentencing scheme in which a judicial "finding . . . neither admitted by [the defendant] nor found by a jury" resulted in a heightened sentence.[35]

The *Blakely* dissenters predicted that the Court's holding would essentially invalidate the Federal Sentencing Guidelines, which rely heavily on judicial fact-finding.[36] The Guidelines (together with Federal Rule of Criminal Procedure 32(i)) regularly require judges to find facts that determine each of the core elements of a defendant's sentence: the base offense level, any sentencing enhancement, and

---

[29] 375 F.3d 508, (7th Cir. 2004), cert. granted, 2004 WL 1713654 (U.S. Aug. 2, 2004) (No. 04-104).

[30] 2004 WL 1723114 (D. Me.), cert. granted, 2004 WL 1713655 (U.S. Aug. 2, 2004) (No. 04-105).

[31] The author is counsel to the National Association of Criminal Defense Lawyers and National Association of Federal Defenders in these cases.

[32] 530 U.S. 466 (2000).

[33] *Id.* at 490.

[34] 124 S. Ct. 2531 (2004).

[35] *Id.* at 2537.

[36] See, e.g., *id.* at 2543 (O'Connor, J., joined by Breyer, J., and Rehnquist, C.J., dissenting); *id.* at 2550 (Kennedy, J., jointed by Breyer, J., dissenting).

any upward departure. As Justice O'Connor noted in dissent, "If the Washington scheme does not comport with the Constitution, it is hard to imagine a guidelines scheme that would."[37]

Blakely immediately generated an enormous amount of litigation over the constitutionality of the Sentencing Guidelines. The Supreme Court subsequently stepped in, agreeing to hear Booker and Fanfan on an expedited basis to decide two questions: whether Apprendi bars increases in a defendant's sentence under the Guidelines pursuant to judicial fact-finding, and the extent to which the Guidelines are consistent with the Fifth and Sixth Amendments.[38] Both cases will be argued in October.

The great majority of lower courts that have considered the Guidelines in light of Blakely have concluded that the Guidelines are subject to the rule of Apprendi, and the Supreme Court is likely to agree. As Justice O'Connor's dissent makes clear, the justices were well aware of Blakely's implications for the Guidelines.

But it is much harder to predict exactly what the Court will hold regarding the ongoing role of the Guidelines. The lower courts have adopted a variety of inconsistent approaches, from use of juries to determine the facts that control a defendant's sentence under the Guidelines to invalidation of the Guidelines under Apprendi.[39] For its part, the government argues that in cases that require judicial fact-finding, if "the Guidelines as a whole cannot be implemented as intended, [then] the [district] court should therefore sentence the defendant in its discretion within the maximum and minimum provided by statute for the offense of conviction."[40] In the government's view, however, the Guidelines would be unaffected in cases that do not call for judicial fact-finding. Of note, the Court faces the

---

[37] Id. at 2550 (O'Connor, J., dissenting).

[38] See Petition for a Writ of Certiorari at 2, United States v. Booker, No. 04-104 (U.S. Aug. 2, 2004); Petition for a Writ of Certiorari at 2, United States v. Fanfan, No. 04-105 (U.S. Aug. 2, 2004).

[39] Compare United States v. Landgarten, No. 04-CR-70 (JBW), 2004 U.S. Dist. LEXIS 13172, at *1–*2 (E.D.N.Y. July 15, 2004) (ordering a sentencing jury trial to determine "whether the enhancement factors are proved beyond a reasonable doubt"), with United States v. Jaamar, No. 6:04-cr-35-Orl-31KRS, 2004 U.S. Dist. LEXIS 13496, at *22 (M.D. Fla. July 19, 2004) (finding that "the determinate scheme set up by the Guidelines violates the Constitution and can no longer be used in any case").

[40] Petition for Certiorari at 16, United States v. Booker, No. 04-104 (U.S. Aug. 2, 2004), available at http://www.usdoj.gov/osg/briefs/2004/2pet/7pet/2004-0104.pet.aa.pdf.

dilemma that it may not be able to muster a majority for any particular result if the four justices who dissented in *Apprendi* and *Blakely* adhere to their view that those cases were wrongly decided and that the Sentencing Guidelines are completely consistent with the Fifth and Sixth Amendments.

In October, the Court will also hear argument in *Roper v. Simmons*,[41] which presents the question whether the Eighth Amendment permits the execution of persons for crimes they committed between the ages of sixteen and eighteen. The Court previously held in *Thompson v. Oklahoma*[42] that the Constitution forbids capital punishment for crimes committed by persons younger than sixteen. The Missouri Supreme Court in this case extended that rule to all minors.

The question presented by *Roper* is significant given the ongoing national debate over the death penalty. The case is also noteworthy because it involves two other controversial, and related, areas of the Court's recent jurisprudence. First, current Eighth Amendment doctrine determines whether a punishment is "cruel and unusual" by reference to "evolving standards of decency."[43] That standard is heavily criticized by those who embrace an originalist understanding of the Constitution's meaning.[44] Second, in identifying relevant standards of decency, a majority of the Court has looked increasingly to international norms, not merely domestic conceptions. For example, in *Atkins v. Virginia*,[45] the Court overruled its prior precedent to hold that the Eighth Amendment prohibits the execution of the mentally retarded. The six-justice majority explained its rejection of precedent by reasoning that such executions "ha[ve] become truly unusual, and it is fair to say that a national consensus has developed against [them]."[46] Further, the Court noted that "within the world community, the imposition of the death penalty for crimes committed by mentally retarded offenders is overwhelmingly disapproved."[47]

---

[41] 112 S.W.3d 397 (Mo. 2003), cert. granted, 124 S. Ct. 1171 (Jan. 26, 2004) (No. 03-633).

[42] 487 U.S. 815 (1988).

[43] Trop v. Dulles, 356 U.S. 86, 101 (1958).

[44] See, e.g., Antonin Scalia, A Matter of Interpretation 40–49 (1998).

[45] 536 U.S. 304 (2002).

[46] *Id.* at 316.

[47] *Id.* at 316 n.21.

A final major case of the 2004–2005 term will be *Tenet v. Doe*,[48] which presents the question whether individuals who claim that the CIA had employed them at one time may bring a suit alleging that the government broke a promise to provide them with financial assistance. In *Totten v. United States*,[49] the Supreme Court held that the president could not be sued under a contract for the provision of confidential intelligence. The Ninth Circuit in *Tenet v. Doe* held, however, that "*Totten* does not require immediate dismissal as to the [plaintiffs'] case because their claims . . . do not arise out of an implied or express contract."[50] The Supreme Court granted the government's petition for certiorari, which alleges that the court of appeals' decision is precluded by *Totten*.[51] Although the Supreme Court has hesitated to find implied repeals of rights to sue, it is likely that the justices will find that this suit represents too great a risk of exposing classified information to be allowed to go forward. Still more interesting will be how the justices resolve the government's attempt to extend the political question doctrine to preclude any suit that "arises out of, and depends upon, a classified fact."[52]

## III. Other Important Cases of the 2004–2005 Term

Several other cases in the upcoming term have a lower profile, but nonetheless raise particularly important questions or present the Court with the opportunity to bring clarity to important areas of the law.

*Johnson v. California*[53] involves a Fourteenth Amendment challenge to racial discrimination. The State of California initially houses newly arrived prison inmates in two-person cells principally according to race. According to the state, "the chances of an inmate being assigned a cell mate of another race [are] 'pretty close' to zero percent."[54] A district court dismissed an African American prisoner's civil rights

---

[48] 329 F.3d 1135 (9th Cir. 2003), cert. granted, 124 S. Ct. 2908 (June 28, 2004) (No. 03-1395).

[49] 92 U.S. 105 (1875).

[50] 319 F.3d 1135, 1146 (9th Cir. 2003).

[51] Petition for Writ of Certiorari at 11–12, Tenet v. Doe, No. 03-1395 (U.S. June 28, 2004).

[52] See *id.* at 11, 13.

[53] 321 F.3d 791 (9th Cir. 2003), cert. granted, 124 S. Ct. 1505 (Mar. 1, 2004) (No. 03-636).

[54] Johnson v. California, 321 F.3d 791 (9th Cir. 2003).

suit challenging the policy as unconstitutional, and the Ninth Circuit affirmed. The court of appeals held that the racial segregation was subject not to strict scrutiny but instead to the deferential standard of review applicable to the government's decisions regarding prison administration. Because the plaintiff was unable to rebut the state's claim that the policy reduced the risks of prison violence, the court of appeals deemed it constitutional.[55]

The Supreme Court is likely to reverse. Although the Court's recent decisions in the affirmative action cases demonstrate that the justices have sharply different conceptions of the anti-discrimination principle of the Fourteenth Amendment, there is common ground that racial distinctions generally should be avoided.[56] The Ninth Circuit applied lower constitutional scrutiny on the ground that the case arose in the prison context. But the Supreme Court is unlikely to hold that the deference usually afforded prison officials extends to permitting routine racial segregation given the importance of the constitutional right at stake. Instead, if the state can demonstrate that a particular racial classification is truly necessary to advance a compelling interest, it will be sustained under the strict scrutiny standard. Of note, the federal government, which operates the nation's most extensive prison system, has filed a brief arguing that the court of appeals should have applied a more rigorous constitutional standard and invalidated the program.

In *Ballard v. Commissioner of Internal Revenue*[57] (consolidated with *Estate of Kanter v. Commissioner of Internal Revenue*[58]), the Court will consider the legality of a novel system used by the Tax Court for deciding certain cases. So-called "special trial judges" conduct extensive proceedings and produce nonpublic opinions for tax court judges. Although the point is disputed, it appears that the Tax Court gives the special trial judges deference as finders of fact. Through this process, the Tax Court found that two individuals owed very considerable unpaid taxes. They appealed on the ground that the use

---

[55] *Id.* at 794.

[56] See Gratz v. Bollinger, 539 U.S. 244 (2003); Grutter v. Bollinger, 539 U.S. 306 (2003).

[57] 321 F.3d 1037 (11th Cir. 2003), cert. granted, 124 S. Ct. 2065 (Apr. 26, 2004) (No. 03-184).

[58] 337 F.3d 833 (7th Cir. 2003), cert. granted, 124 S. Ct. 2066 (Apr. 26, 2004) (No. 03-1034).

of a secret opinion was unlawful and violated their Fifth Amendment rights to due process of law.[59] The Seventh and Eleventh Circuits rejected their argument,[60] and the Supreme Court subsequently granted certiorari and consolidated the two cases.

The fact that the Supreme Court has agreed to hear the cases despite the absence of any circuit conflict is a strong signal that the justices intend to reverse. The petitioners have a substantial argument that it is impossible for a litigant to assess (and challenge if necessary) the Tax Court's ruling without access to the secret opinion of the special trial judge on which it is based. And the very fact that the system is so unusual—it apparently is not employed in any other U.S. court system—is an indication that it does not comport with due process. As Judge Cudahy explained, dissenting in the Seventh Circuit case: "Transparency is the universal practice of agencies and courts employing these decisional practices. The question then becomes, if there are policy reasons that dictate transparency for everyone else, why do these reasons not apply to the Tax Court?"[61]

The Court also has before it in the 2004–2005 term two interesting employment discrimination cases—one involving age discrimination, the other sex discrimination—that touch on the power of federal regulatory agencies. In *Smith v. City of Jackson*,[62] the Court will decide whether "disparate impact claims"—those that rely on an employment policy's adverse effect on a protected group, not an assertion of personal discrimination—are cognizable under the Age Discrimination in Employment Act (ADEA).[63] The plaintiffs in this case challenge a police department pay plan that gave larger raises to younger workers. They contend that the statute reaches disparate impact claims, although the employer will prevail so long as it can establish that the challenged policy pursues some reasonable objective.

The case is too close to call. A majority of the Court is openly hostile to disparate impact claims, regarding it as unreasonable to

---

[59] See, e.g., *Kanter*, 337 F.3d at 840; *Ballard*, 321 F.3d at 1038.

[60] *Kanter*, 337 F.3d at 841; *Ballard*, 321 F.3d at 1043.

[61] *Kanter*, 337 F.3d at 874 (Cudahy, J., dissenting).

[62] 351 F.3d 183 (5th Cir. 2003), cert. granted, 124 S. Ct. 1724 (Mar. 29, 2004) (No. 03-1160). The author is counsel to the petitioners in *Smith*.

[63] Age Discrimination in Employment Act, 29 U.S.C. §§ 621–634 (2004).

hold employers liable for innocent policies that have unintended negative effects on employees. But in 1971, the Court held that disparate impact claims are cognizable under Title VII of the Civil Rights Act of 1964,[64] which uses identical language to that in the ADEA.[65] And the Equal Employment Opportunity Commission, which has the authority to implement the ADEA, has provided by regulation that the statute reaches disparate impact claims[66]; there is a strong argument that the Court is obliged to defer to that administrative interpretation.

*Jackson v. Birmingham Board of Education*[67] involves the scope of Title IX of the Education Amendments of 1972. The statute provides that "[n]o person in the United States shall, on the basis of sex, be excluded from participation in, be denied the benefits of, or be subjected to discrimination under any education program or activity receiving Federal financial assistance."[68] The case arises from the claim of a girls' basketball coach that the Birmingham Board of Education retaliated against him for complaining that the team was receiving unequal funding. The Eleventh Circuit held that Title IX does not create an implied private right of action to remedy retaliation.[69]

As with *Smith*, it is very difficult to predict how the Supreme Court will rule in *Jackson*. In recent years, a five-justice majority of the Court has repeatedly rejected claims that various federal statutes create implied rights of action, avowedly rejecting prior precedent that more liberally recognized such claims. The Court has also specifically provided that federal agencies do not have the power to authorize implied rights of action not otherwise provided for by statute.[70] On the other hand, the Court has already held that Title IX does create a private right of action.[71] The court of appeals simply declined

---

[64] 42 U.S.C. § 2000(e) (2000).

[65] Griggs v. Duke Power Co., 401 U.S. 424, 430–32 (1971).

[66] See 46 Fed. Reg. 47,274, 47,275 (Sept. 29, 1981) (amending 29 C.F.R. § 1625.7(d)).

[67] 309 F.3d 1333 (11th Cir. 2002), cert. granted, 124 S. Ct. 2834 (June 14, 2004) (No. 02-1672)

[68] 20 U.S.C. § 1681(a).

[69] Jackson v. Birmingham Bd. of Education, 309 F.3d 1333, 1347 (11th Cir. 2002).

[70] Alexander v. Sandoval, 532 U.S. 275 (2001).

[71] Cannon v. University of Chicago, 441 U.S. 677, 683 (1979).

to apply that ruling to a claim for retaliation. And the relevant federal agency—the Department of Education—has adopted a regulation indicating that retaliation claims are cognizable.[72]

The Court also has before it three important search and seizure cases with a single unifying theme. In each, the Court will address a circumstance in which an individual was initially detained for one reason, but was subjected to a further search or detention that arguably violates the Fourth Amendment. And in each, the Court seems likely to rule in favor of the government.

*Illinois v. Caballes*[73] will address the extent to which the Fourth Amendment applies do drug-sniffing dog searches, which are an increasingly prevalent police practice. The specific question presented is whether officers conducting a legitimate traffic stop may, without probable cause, bring a drug detection dog to the car to see if it alerts the police.[74] In this case, Illinois police stopped a car for a minor speeding violation and, while writing a ticket, walked a dog around the car, where it detected marijuana in the trunk. The Illinois Supreme Court (divided four-to-three) ordered the marijuana suppressed as the fruits of an unconstitutional search.[75]

The U.S. Supreme Court granted the state's petition for certiorari and is likely to reverse. The justices have held that the Fourth Amendment prohibits the use of high technology devices (such as a thermal sensor) to search within a dwelling without probable cause.[76] But a dog that detects scent is a far more common and accepted investigatory tool, and one that is unlikely to be deemed an unreasonable search given the lessened Fourth Amendment protections that are associated with automobiles.

*Devenpeck v. Alford*[77] will address the extent to which the police may justify a detention based on reasons they did not express at the time. The police in this case suspected that Jerome Alford had been impersonating a police officer and pulled over his car. During

---

[72] 34 C.F.R. §§ 100.7(e), 106.71.

[73] 802 N.E.2d 202 (Ill. 2003), cert. granted, 124 S. Ct. 1875 (Apr. 5, 2004) (No. 03-923).

[74] Brief for the Petitioner at (i), Illinois v. Caballes, No. 03-923 (U.S. Apr. 5, 2004).

[75] People v. Caballes, 802 N.E.2d 202, 205 (Ill. 2003).

[76] Kyllo v. United States, 533 U.S. 27 (2001).

[77] 333 F.3d 972 (9th Cir. 2003), cert. granted, 124 S. Ct. 2014 (Apr. 19, 2004) (No. 03-710).

questioning, the officers discovered that Alford had recorded their conversation and arrested him for making an illegal recording in violation of the Washington Privacy Act.[78] A state court judge threw out the charge.[79]

Alford then filed a civil rights suit. In response, the officers argued that, even if Alford had not violated the Privacy Act, they had probable cause to arrest him for impersonating an officer. The Ninth Circuit held that the alternative justification for the arrest was irrelevant because it was not "closely related" to the basis for the arrest articulated by the officers at the time.[80] The court of appeals also held that the officers were not entitled to qualified immunity, reasoning that it was well established at the time that Alford's conduct could not be deemed a violation of the Privacy Act.[81] The Supreme Court seems likely to reverse based on the principle that the authority to seize or arrest an individual is measured by an objective standard, not the officer's subjective intent. Assuming that the police did have probable cause to arrest Alford for impersonating an officer, that will probably be sufficient to defeat his suit.

Finally, *Muehler v. Mena*[82] presents the question whether the police may question an individual about criminal activity for which he was not lawfully detained, and whether the police may continue to detain the occupant of a dwelling during a lawful search of the premises. In this case, police entered a suspected gang safe house with a warrant to search it in the course of an investigation of a suspected gang shooting. Once in the house, they detained Iris Mena for two to three hours in handcuffs and questioned her about her immigration status without probable cause either that she was involved in gang activity or was an illegal immigrant. The Ninth Circuit held that the questioning and continued detention both violated the Fourth Amendment.[83] Rehearing en banc was denied over the dissent of seven judges.[84]

[78] Washington Rev. Code Ann. § 9.73.010 (2004).

[79] See, e.g., Alford v. Haner, 335 F.3d 972, 975 (9th Cir. 2003).

[80] *Id.* at 976.

[81] *Id.* at 977.

[82] 332 F.3d 1255 (9th Cir. 2003), cert. granted, 124 S. Ct. 2842 (June 14, 2004) (No. 03-1423).

[83] Mena v. Simi Valley, 332 F.3d 1255, 1263–64 (9th Cir. 2003), reh'g denied, 354 F.3d 1015 (9th Cir. 2004).

[84] *Id.*

The Supreme Court seems likely to reverse, at least in part. The Ninth Circuit's holding that the questioning of Mena constitutes a search is, even if correct, an extension of existing law that would defeat qualified immunity. Nor is it likely that the Court will conclude that the facts of the physical detention—the period of two to three hours in particular—were so extreme as to be clearly unreasonable.

## IV. Noteworthy Petitions for Certiorari

When the justices return from their summer recess, they will consider more than 1,500 pending petitions for certiorari. Petitions presenting three issues are particularly noteworthy.

*Bass v. Madison*[85] and *Cutter v. Wilkinson*[86] involve the constitutionality under the Establishment Clause of Section 3 of the Religious Land Use and Institutionalized Persons Act of 2000.[87] The statute, in relevant part, forbids federal, state, and local governments from "impos[ing] a substantial burden on the religious exercise of a person residing in or confined to an institute," except as the "least restrictive means" of furthering "a compelling government interest."[88] The Sixth Circuit held in *Cutter* that the statute violates the Establishment Clause, a holding that conflicts with the ruling of the Fourth Circuit in *Bass*, as well as other rulings of the Seventh and Ninth Circuits. According to the Sixth Circuit, the statute impermissibly seeks "to advance religion generally by giving religious prisoners rights superior to those of nonreligious prisoners" and has the "inevitable effect" of "induc[ing] nonreligious inmates to adopt a religion."[89] The Court is almost certain to grant review to decide the Establishment Clause issue in one or both cases. State officials have also sought certiorari on the question whether Congress had the constitutional authority to enact the statute in the first instance, but because there is no circuit conflict on that question, the justices are less likely to agree to decide it.

---

[85] Madison v. Riter, 355 F.3d 310 (4th Cir. 2003), petition for cert. filed, 2004 WL 763796 (U.S. Apr. 6, 2004) (No. 03-1404).

[86] 349 F.3d 257 (6th Cir. 2003), petition for cert. filed, Apr. 19, 2004 (No. 03-9877).

[87] 42 U.S.C. §§ 2000cc—2000cc-5.

[88] 42 U.S.C. § 2000cc-1(a) (2004).

[89] Cutter v. Wilkinson, 349 F.3d 257, 266 (6th Cir. 2003).

No fewer that four pending petitions for certiorari ask the Court to decide in what circumstances the government may display a monument of the Ten Commandments.[90] As the number of petitions suggests, there has been a torrent of litigation on the issue. But each case tends to reflect the unique factual circumstance of the particular monument at issue—in particular, its historical and physical context. Until a clear circuit conflict emerges on a question of law, the justices will likely avoid stepping into such a controversial issue.

Finally, the justices will have the opportunity to decide an important and recurring property rights question: whether a state may use its eminent domain authority to seize property for development by another private party. In *Kelo v. New London*,[91] the Connecticut Supreme Court held that a municipality may condemn private homes to be redeveloped as part of a broad municipal development plan. The homeowners have sought certiorari, asserting that state supreme courts have adopted a variety of conflicting standards for determining when eminent domain can be used to further private redevelopment. Given the necessarily fact-bound nature of such takings challenges, the petition is far from sure to be granted, but the case is sufficiently important that it merits close attention.

---

[90] Van Orden v. Perry, 351 F.3d 173 (5th Cir. 2003), petition for cert. filed, 2004 WL 972724 (U.S. Mar. 31, 2004) (No. 03-1500); Baker v. Adams County/Ohio Valley School Bd., 86 Fed. Appx. 104 (6th Cir. Jan. 12, 2004), available at 2004 WL 68523, petition for cert. filed sub nom. Johnson v. Baker, 2004 WL 1378658 (U.S. June 14, 2004) (No. 03-1661); American Civil Liberties Union of Kentucky v. McCreary County, Kentucky, 354 F.3d 438 (6ᵗʰ Cir. 2003), petition for cert. filed, 2004 WL 1427470 (U.S. June 21, 2004) (No. 03-1963).

[91] 843 A.2d 500 (Conn. 2004), petition for cert. filed, 2004 WL 1659558 (U.S. July 19, 2004) (No. 04-108).

# Contributors

**Vikram David Amar** is a professor of law at the University of California, Hastings College of the Law. He is a 1988 graduate of the Yale Law School, where he served as an articles editor for the Yale Law Journal. Upon graduating from law school in 1988, Professor Amar clerked for William A. Norris of the U.S. Court of Appeals for the Ninth Circuit, and then for Justice Harry A. Blackmun of the U.S. Supreme Court. Professor Amar writes, teaches and consults in the public law fields, especially constitutional law, civil procedure, and remedies. He is a co-author (along with William Cohen and Jonathan Varat) of *Constitutional Law: Cases and Materials* (Foundation Press, 12th ed. 2005), and is a co-author on a number of volumes of the *Wright & Miller Federal Practice and Procedure Treatise* (West Publishing Co.). Professor Amar has published scholarly articles in a variety of the nation's leading law journals, and authors a bi-weekly column on constitutional matters for Findlaw.com (the most frequently visited website devoted to legal issues.) He is a frequent commentator on local and national radio and TV, and has written dozens of op-ed pieces for newspapers and magazines. Prior to teaching, he spent a few years at Gibson, Dunn & Crutcher LLP.

**Robert Corn-Revere** is a partner in the Washington, D.C., office of Davis Wright Tremaine LLP, specializing in First Amendment, internet, and communications law. He successfully argued *United States v. Playboy Entertainment Group, Inc.*, in which the U.S. Supreme Court struck down section 505 of the Telecommunications Act of 1996 as a violation of the First Amendment. He also served as lead counsel in *Motion Picture Association v. FCC*, in which the U.S. Court of Appeals for the D.C. Circuit vacated video description rules imposed on networks by the Federal Communications Commission (FCC). Corn-Revere also has served as counsel in First Amendment litigation involving the Communications Decency Act, the Child Online Protection Act, internet content filtering in public libraries, public broadcasting regulations and export controls on encryption software. In 1999, Corn-Revere was listed on a 30th Anniversary Roll of Honor by the American Library Association Office of Intellectual Freedom and Freedom to Read Foundation for his role as lead counsel in *Mainstream Loudon v. Board of Trustees of the Loudoun County Library*. Prior to joining Davis Wright Tremaine LLP, Corn-Revere served as chief counsel to interim chairman James H. Quello of the FCC. He has written extensively on First Amendment, internet, and communications-related issues and is a frequent speaker at professional conferences. He is also an adjunct scholar to the Cato Institute in Washington, D.C.

**Walter Dellinger** is head of the Appellate Practice at O'Melveny & Myers in Washington, D.C., and the Douglas B. Maggs Professor of Law at Duke University. A graduate of the University of North Carolina and Yale Law School, Professor Dellinger served as law clerk to Justice Hugo L. Black. He has published articles on constitutional law for scholarly journals including the *Harvard Law Review*, the *Yale Law Journal*, and the *Duke Law Journal* and has written articles for the *New York Times*, *Washington Post*, *Newsweek*, *New Republic* and the *London Times*. He spent 1988-89 as a Fellow at the National Humanities Center and has lectured in several countries. In 1993, he was nominated by the president to be assistant attorney general for the Justice Department's Office of Legal Counsel and was confirmed by the Senate. He served as head of OLC from 1993 until he became acting solicitor general for the 1996-97 term of the Supreme Court. His arguments before the United States Supreme Court have included cases involving the Physician Assisted Suicide laws, the Brady Act, the Line Item Veto, the Cable Television Act, the Religious Freedom Restoration Act, *Clinton v. Jones*, aid to parochial schools, the Americans with Disabilities Act, the Census Act, redistricting, federal jurisdiction and other matters.

**Susanna Dokupil** is of counsel at Alexander Dubose Jones & Townsend LLP. She received her J.D. from Harvard Law School, where she was editor-in-chief of the *Harvard Journal of Law & Public Policy* and line editor for the *Harvard International Law Journal*. She clerked for the Honorable Jerry E. Smith of the U.S. Court of Appeals for the Fifth Circuit, then joined the trial section of Baker Botts LLP.

Before law school, Ms. Dokupil received her B.A., *magna cum laude,* in the University Scholars program and her M.A. in Church-State Studies from Baylor University. Ms. Dokupil's work has appeared in the *Texas Review of Law & Politics, West Virginia Law Review, Journal of Church & State, American Enterprise, National Review Online, Washington Times, Houston Chronicle, Los Angeles Daily Journal,* and on numerous websites; she writes regularly for *The American Enterprise Online* (www.taemag.com). She and her husband Michael reside in Houston, Texas, with their twin boys, David and Benjamin.

**John C. Eastman** is a professor of law at Chapman University School of Law and the Director of the Center for Constitutional Jurisprudence, a public interest law firm affiliated with the Claremont Institute for the Study of Statesmanship and Political Philosophy. He has a Ph.D. in Government from the Claremont Graduate School and a J.D. from the University of Chicago Law School. Prior to joining the Chapman law faculty, Dr. Eastman served as a law clerk to Justice Clarence Thomas, and to Judge J. Michael Luttig of the U.S. Court of Appeals for the Fourth Circuit. He practiced law with Kirkland & Ellis LLP, representing corporate clients in complex commercial contract litigation and in consumer litigation. Professor Eastman has also represented various pro bono clients or appeared as amicus curiae in matters involving property rights, economic opportunity, and first amendment freedom of speech, freedom of association, and freedom of religion issues, including *Boy Scouts of America v. Dale, United States v. Morrison, Solid Waste Agency of Northern Cook County v. U.S. Army Corps of Engineers, Zelman v. Simmons-Harris* (the Ohio school voucher case), and *Grutter v. Bollinger* (the Michigan affirmative action case). Professor Eastman is a frequent commentator on television and radio, including C-SPAN, Fox News, and NPR; has a weekly segment on the nationally-syndicated Hugh Hewitt show debating current legal issues with Professor Erwin Chemerinsky; and has published op-eds in newspapers around the country, including the *Washington Post,* the *Wall Street Journal,* and the *Orange County Register.*

**Richard D. Friedman** is the Ralph W. Aigler Professor of Law at the University of Michigan Law School. He earned a B.A. and a J.D. from Harvard, where he was the editor of the *Harvard Law Review,* and a D.Phil. in modern history from Oxford University. Professor Friedman has written extensively on the confrontation right, and he authored an amicus brief, which was joined by several other law professors, in *Crawford v. Washington*; he also sat at the counsel's table during oral argument in that case. He has testified before the Advisory Committee on the Federal Rules of Criminal Procedure; is the general editor of *The New Wigmore*, a multi-volume treatise on evidence; and has been designated to write the volume on the Hughes Court in the *Oliver Wendell Holmes Devise History of the United States Supreme Court*. In addition, he has published an evidence textbook, *The Elements of Evidence*, as well as a number of articles and essays in the nation's leading law journals. Professor Friedman clerked for Judge Irving R. Kaufman of the U.S. Court of Appeals for the Second Circuit, and was then an associate for the law firm of Paul, Weiss, Rifkind, Wharton & Garrison in New York City. He joined the University of Michigan Law School faculty in 1988 from Cardozo Law School.

**Thomas C. Goldstein** is the founder and partner of the Washington, D.C., law firm of Goldstein & Howe, P.C. The firm specializes in litigation before the Supreme Court of the United States and almost all of its cases are in that forum. Mr. Goldstein also teaches Supreme Court litigation at Stanford Law School. Since founding the firm in 1990, he has briefed dozens of cases at the Court, arguing eleven, spanning the gamut of federal law issues, including the First Amendment, ERISA, federal preemption, administrative law, and civil procedure. He will argue his twelfth case this fall. Mr. Goldstein has also taken a central role in numerous other leading Supreme Court matters, including serving as second chair to David Boies in *Bush v. Gore*, and serving as second chair to Laurence Tribe in *Nike v. Kasky* and *New York Times Co. v. Tasini*. Mr. Goldstein was recently named one of the top forty-five lawyers under the age of forty-five by *American Lawyer* magazine, which also profiled him as one of the nation's half-dozen leading Supreme Court advocates. *Legal Times* recently named him one of the leading appellate attorneys in Washington. Before founding Goldstein & Howe, he was an attorney with Boies & Schiller, LLP (now Boies, Schiller & Flexner, LLP ). His practice focused on Supreme Court litigation as well as commercial litigation and arbitration. Previously, he was an attorney in the appellate section of Jones, Day, Reavis and Pogue and a law clerk to the Honorable Patricia M. Wald of the U.S. Court of Appeals for the D.C. Circuit.

**Erik S. Jaffe** is a solo appellate attorney in Washington, D.C., whose practice emphasizes First Amendment and other constitutional issues. He is a 1986 graduate of Dartmouth College, and a 1990 graduate of Columbia Law School. Following law school he clerked for Judge Douglas H. Ginsburg on the U.S. Court of Appeals for the D.C. Circuit, practiced for five years at Williams & Connolly in Washington, D.C., clerked for Justice Clarence Thomas on the U.S. Supreme Court during the October 1996 term, and then began his solo appellate practice in 1997. Since 1999 Mr. Jaffe has been involved in eighteen cases at the merits stage before the U.S. Supreme Court. He represented one of the successful respondents in the First Amendment case of *Bartnicki v. Vopper*, and authored Cato's amicus brief in *McConnell v. FEC*. Jaffe also has authored amicus briefs in cases such as *Republican Party of Minnesota v. Kelly* (judicial speech); *Zelman v. Simmons-Harris* (vouchers); *Watchtower Bible and Tract Society v. Village of Stratton* (anonymous speech); *United States v. United Foods, Inc.* (compelled advertising); *Boy Scouts of America v. Dale* (freedom of expressive association); and *United States v. Morrison* (Commerce Clause).

**Neal K. Katyal** is the John Carroll Research Professor of Law at the Georgetown University Law Center. Prior to coming to Georgetown, he was law clerk to Justice Stephen G. Breyer of the U.S. Supreme Court and to Judge Guido Calabresi of the U.S. Court of Appeals for the Second Circuit. During 1998-99, Professor Katyal served as national security adviser to the deputy attorney general, U.S. Department of Justice. He served as chief counsel to the military defense lawyers in *Rasul v. Bush*; and is counsel to JAG officer Lt. Commander Charles Swift in *Swift v. Rumsfeld*, an action challenging the constitutionality of the Guantanamo military commissions. Professor Katyal served as co-counsel to Vice President Al Gore in the United States Supreme Court case of *Bush v. Palm Beach Canvassing Board* in 2000, and was a visiting professor at Yale Law School in 2001-02 and Harvard Law School in 2002. Professor Katyal's publications have appeared in a number of leading academic journals and his primary academic interests include constitutional law (primarily separation of powers, constitutional legitimacy, presidential power, slavery and affirmative action), criminal law (particularly cyber-crime, conspiracy, architectural solutions to crime and the role of deterrence), and education law.

**M. Christine Klein** is a litigation attorney practicing with Hunton & Williams LLP in Richmond, Virginia. While emphasizing appellate matters, the substance of her practice has ranged from franchising and distribution disputes to defense of mass toxic tort lawsuits. In addition, she spent four years with the Cato Institute. Ms. Klein received her B.A. with High Distinction from the University of Virginia in 1991, and her J.D. from the University of Virginia School of Law, where she was a member of the Virginia Law Review, in 1994. She then served as a law clerk for the Hon. Andrew J. Kleinfeld, United States Court of Appeals for the Ninth Circuit, in Fairbanks, Alaska. She is licensed to practice law in both Virginia and Alaska. Ms. Klein was co-author of the Cato Institute's amicus brief in *Hiibel v. Sixth Judicial District Court of Nevada.*

**Gary Lawson** is a professor of law at Boston University School of Law, where he teaches courses in administrative law, advanced administrative law, and property. In the early part of his career, Professor Lawson twice clerked for U.S. Supreme Court Justice Antonin Scalia, first at the U.S. Court of Appeals for the D.C. Circuit, and then again at the Supreme Court. Professor Lawson authored Cato's amicus brief in *Sabri v. United States.* He is widely published in a number of leading law journals and is the author of a casebook on federal administrative law. Recent articles include "Delegation and Original Meaning" for the *Virginia Law Review,* "Controlling Precedent: Congressional Regulation of Judicial Decisionmaking" for *Constitutional Commentary,* and "When Did the Constitution Become Law?"(co-authored with Guy Seidman) for the *Notre Dame Law Review.* Professor Lawson is a founding member of the Federalist Society.

**Robert A. Levy** is senior fellow in constitutional studies at the Cato Institute, which he joined in 1997 after twenty-five years in business. He is also an adjunct professor at the Georgetown University Law

Center, a director of the Institute for Justice, and a member of the board of visitors of the Federalist Society. Levy received his Ph.D. in business from American University in 1966. That year he founded CDA Investment Technologies, a major provider of financial information and software. Levy was chief executive officer of CDA until 1991. He then earned his J.D. in 1994 from George Mason University, where he was chief articles editor of the law review. The next two years he clerked for Judge Royce C. Lamberth on the U.S. District Court for the District of Columbia, and for Judge Douglas H. Ginsburg on the U.S. Court of Appeals for the D.C. Circuit. Levy has written numerous articles on investments, law, and public policy. His writing has appeared in the *New York Times, Wall Street Journal, USA Today, Washington Post, National Review, Weekly Standard, Journal of the American Medical Association* and many other publications. He has also discussed public policy on national radio and TV programs, including ABC's *Nightline*, CNN's *Crossfire*, Fox's *The O'Reilly Factor*, MSNBC's *Hardball*, and NBC's *Today Show*. Levy's latest book, *Shakedown: How Corporations, Government, and Trial Lawyers Abuse the Judicial Process*, will be published in 2004.

**Timothy Lynch** is director of the Cato Institute's Project on Criminal Justice and associate director of Cato's Center for Constitutional Studies. Mr. Lynch is an outspoken critic of police misconduct, the drug war, gun control, and the militarization of police tactics. Since September 11, Lynch has decried several antiterrorism initiatives for their impact on civil liberties. Mr. Lynch has published articles in the *New York Times, Washington Post, Wall Street Journal, Los Angeles Times, ABA Journal*, and *National Law Journal*. He has appeared on such television programs as the "Lehrer Newshour," "NBC Nightly News," "ABC World New Tonight," Fox News Channel's "The O'Reilly Factor," and C-SPAN's "Washington Journal." Mr. Lynch has also filed several amicus briefs in the U.S. Supreme Court in pending cases involving constitutional rights, including the landmark "enemy combatant" case, *Hamdi v. Rumsfeld*. He is the editor of the book *After Prohibition: An Adult Approach to Drug Policies in the 21ˢᵗ Century*. Mr. Lynch is a 1990 graduate of the Marquette University School of Law and is a member of the Wisconsin and District of Columbia bars.

**Tracey Maclin** is a professor of law at Boston University School of Law. Named in 1996 by the *National Law Journal* as one of the nation's "Rising Stars in Law," Professor Maclin is also a recipient of Boston University's highest teaching award. He has served as counsel of record for the ACLU and the National Association of Criminal Defense Lawyers in a number of U.S. Supreme Court cases, and, this past term, authored the ACLU's amicus brief in *Maryland v. Pringle*. Prior to teaching, Professor Maclin served as law clerk to Judge Boyce F. Martin, Jr., of the U.S. Court of Appeals for the Sixth Circuit. He was then an associate at the New York law firm of Cahill, Gordon & Reindel, and taught at the University of Kentucky College of Law. He has held visiting professorships at Harvard Law School and Cornell Law School. Professor Maclin writes extensively on criminal procedure and the Fourth Amendment in a number of leading academic law journals and for the popular press.

**Mark K. Moller** is the editor-in-chief of the *Cato Supreme Court Review*. Prior to joining Cato in March 2004, Mr. Moller was an appellate attorney at the Washington, D.C., office of Gibson, Dunn & Crutcher LLP. While in private practice, Mr. Moller specialized in civil litigation involving federal preemption and other constitutional choice-of-law questions, multidistrict class action procedure, RICO, ERISA and consumer fraud. He was part of the team that successfully litigated *Bush v. Gore* before the Supreme Court; wrote many of the key briefs in the high profile multidistrict class-actions against the managed care industry; and served as an advisor to Miguel A. Estrada, a nominee to the U.S. Court of Appeals for the D.C. Circuit, during his Senate confirmation hearings. Mr. Moller is a 1999 graduate of the University of Chicago Law School, where he served on the law review, and received a Master of Laws in legal history from the University of Cambridge in 2000, where he studied with noted English legal historian J.H. Baker. He has discussed the Supreme Court on radio and television, including the Kojo Nnamdi Show, Voice of America, the Armstrong Williams Show, and the Sam Donaldson Show.

**Roger Pilon** is vice president for legal affairs at the Cato Institute. He holds Cato's B. Kenneth Simon Chair in Constitutional Studies and is the founder and director of Cato's Center for Constitutional

Studies. Established in 1989 to encourage limited constitutional government at home and abroad, the Center has become an important force in the national debate over constitutional interpretation and judicial philosophy. Mr. Pilon's work has appeared in the *New York Times, Washington Post, Wall Street Journal, Los Angeles Times, Legal Times, National Law Journal, Harvard Journal of Law & Public Policy, Notre Dame Law Review, Stanford Law & Policy Review, Texas Review of Law & Politics,* and elsewhere. He lectures and debates at universities and law schools across the country and testifies often before Congress. Before joining Cato, Pilon held five senior posts in the Reagan administration, including at State and Justice. He has taught philosophy and law and was a national fellow at Stanford's Hoover Institution. Mr. Pilon holds a B.A. from Columbia University, an M.A. and Ph.D. from the University of Chicago, and a J.D. from the George Washington University School of Law. In 1989 the Bicentennial Commission presented him with the Benjamin Franklin Award for excellence in writing on the U.S. Constitution. In 2001 Columbia University's School of General Studies awarded him its Alumni Medal of Distinction.

**Jonathan Turley** is the J.B. and Maurice Shapiro Professor of Public Interest Law at the George Washington University Law School. Professor Turley has written extensively in areas including constitutional law, national security law, tort law, legal theory, and legal history, and has published in a variety of leading law journals. He has served as counsel in a number of well-known constitutional, criminal, and national security cases, including espionage cases like the Nicholson and King spy cases, as well as representation of four former U.S. attorneys general opposing the so-called Secret Service privilege during the Clinton impeachment litigation. In addition, he is a frequent witness before the House and Senate on constitutional and statutory issues, has served as a consultant on homeland security issues for members of Congress and state legislators, and is a nationally known legal commentator. In a recent study by Judge Richard Posner, Professor Turley was ranked thirty-eight in the top 100 most-cited "public intellectuals," the second most-cited law professor in the county. He has worked as the on-air legal analyst for NBC/MSNBC news and CBS news during the impeachment and election controversies.

## ABOUT THE CATO INSTITUTE

The Cato Institute is a public policy research foundation dedicated to the principles of limited government, individual liberty, free markets, and private property. It takes its name from *Cato's Letters*, popular libertarian pamphlets that helped to lay the philosophical foundation for the American Revolution.

Despite the Founders' libertarian values, today virtually no aspect of life is free from government encroachment. A pervasive intolerance for individual rights is shown by government's arbitrary intrusions into private economic transactions and its disregard for civil liberties.

To counter that trend, the Cato Institute undertakes an extensive publications program that addresses the complete spectrum of policy issues. It holds major conferences throughout the year, from which papers are published thrice yearly in the *Cato Journal*, and also publishes the quarterly magazine *Regulation*.

The Cato Institute accepts no government funding. It relies instead on contributions from foundations, corporations, and individuals and revenue generated from the sale of publications. The Institute is a nonprofit, tax-exempt educational foundation under Section 501(c)(3) of the Internal Revenue Code.

## ABOUT THE CENTER FOR CONSTITUTIONAL STUDIES

Cato's Center for Constitutional Studies and its scholars take their inspiration from the struggle of America's founding generation to secure liberty through limited government and the rule of law. Under the direction of Roger Pilon, the center was established in 1989 to help revive the idea that the Constitution authorizes a government of delegated, enumerated, and thus limited powers, the exercise of which must be further restrained by our rights, both enumerated and unenumerated. Through books, monographs, conferences, forums, op-eds, speeches, congressional testimony, and TV and radio appearances, the center's scholars address a wide range of constitutional and legal issues—from judicial review to federalism, economic liberty, property rights, civil rights, criminal law and procedure, asset forfeiture, tort law, and term limits, to name just a few. The center is especially concerned to encourage the judiciary to be "the bulwark of our liberties," as James Madison put it, neither making nor ignoring the law but interpreting and applying it through the natural rights tradition we inherited from the founding generation.

CATO INSTITUTE
1000 Massachusetts Ave., N.W.
Washington, D.C. 20001